THE LAW OF SUCCESSION

PARRY & KERRIDGE

THE LAW OF SUCCESSION

THIRTEENTH EDITION

BY

ROGER KERRIDGE
Emeritus Professor of Law; University of Bristol
Solicitor

assisted by

A.H.R. BRIERLEY
Solicitor, Shrewsbury

SWEET & MAXWELL

First Edition 1937
Second Edition 1947
Third Edition 1953
Fourth Edition 1961
Fifth Edition 1966
Sixth Edition 1972
Seventh Edition 1977
Eighth Edition 1983
Ninth Edition 1988
Tenth Edition 1996
Second Impression. .... .1997
Eleventh Edition 2002
Second Impression. .... .2006
Twelfth Edition 2009
Second Impression 2010
Thirteenth Edition 2016

Published in 2016 by Thomson Reuters (Professional) UK Limited, trading as Sweet & Maxwell, Friars House, 160 Blackfriars Road, London, SE1 8EZ (Registered in England & Wales, Company No.1679046. Registered Office and address for service: 2nd floor, 1 Mark Square, Leonard Street, London, EC2A 4EG).

**For further information on our products and services, visit www.sweetandmaxwell.co.uk*

Typeset by Servis Filmsetting Ltd, Stockport, Cheshire
Printed and bound by CPI Group (UK) Ltd, Croydon, CR0 4YY

No natural forests were destroyed to make this product; only farmed timber was used and re-planted.

A CIP catalogue record for this book is available from the British Library.

ISBN 978-0-414-03358-0

PREFACE

For the past hundred years or so, the law of Succession has, in England, been a neglected subject. It was not thus in England in the nineteenth century, and is not so elsewhere at the present time. Few universities appear to offer full courses in Succession, and most lawyers seem to have only a vague understanding of the subject. One welcome recent development has been the reporting of many more Succession cases than had been the tradition. This has been due both to the publication of the Wills and Trusts Law Reports and to reporting by neutral citation. But what these reported cases then demonstrate is a mixture of the fascinating and the absurd; too many lawyers seem prepared to involve themselves in this field with only a limited grasp of what it involves. Those who advise would-be testators, those who draft wills, those who challenge wills and those who sit as judges in Succession cases, all need a reasonable degree of expertise, but far too many seem to lack it. Will drafting should not be considered as something to be undertaken by a non-specialist. No part of property law should be more important to a client than that his will is correctly prepared: and, if it has not been correctly prepared, it should be competently challenged; and those responsible for its incorrect preparation should be held to account. Will-drafting should be a reserved legal activity, but it is in part the fault of the legal profession that it is not, in that the profession has failed to take seriously the whole topic of will-preparation and of the protection of would-be testators. On the front cover of this edition is a photograph of someone who held lawyers in general, and Succession lawyers in particular, in thinly disguised contempt—Colonel Wintle (see Chapter 5). Given the way the legal profession treated him, at least at the start of his campaign, he had a point. The law of Succession is like Thackeray's novel, *Vanity Fair*—it has no hero. But Colonel Wintle was as close as one gets: he was brave, clever, reasonably honest, and jolly good fun. He died 50 years ago this year, but what he set out to achieve has been achieved only in small part. The way in which beneficiaries remain able to involve themselves in the making of wills in England is little short of a scandal.

On the bright side, it may be noted that the Law Commission have just commenced a project reviewing the law of Wills and that they intend to focus on (i) will-making and testamentary capacity; (ii) what makes a will valid (this will cover formalities); (iii) rectification; and (iv) mutual wills. How worthwhile this project will be must, to some extent, depend on how wide the net is thrown. Will they look at "suspicious wills" in the context of capacity? They certainly should. Will they look again at some aspects of interpretation in the context of rectification? Which comes first, rectification or construction? The problem here is that Succession has been so neglected for so long that a bit of dabbling at the edges might serve only to disguise the depth of the malaise. The changes made to the intestacy rules, and to family provision, since the appearance of the last edition, were not at all radical, but whether that was or was not a good thing must remain a matter of opinion. The question as to whether the interests of children should be trumped by their step-parents, and/or by their parents' cohabitants, is probably more divisive than some policy makers would have us believe.

The text of this edition is believed to be up-to-date to the feast day of St Gildas, 29 January 2016. Since then, leave has been given for an appeal to the Supreme Court in *Ilott v Mitson* (see Chapter 8) and this appeal is likely to be heard early next year. This will be the first family provision case to be heard by the Supreme Court and should assist in clarifying the position of adult children involved in family provision disputes. Alternatively, it could re-open the question whether English law might not benefit from some form of forced heirship. The tax changes made by the March 2016 Budget came too late to be included in Chapter 16, but they are relatively minor, and there will, doubtless, be many more changes to the tax rules during the life of this volume.

The chapters in this edition follow, by and large, the pattern in the previous, 12th, edition. The order of topics always causes some difficulty, but the only significant change has been to move rectification from Chapter 5 (where it was linked with Capacity) to Chapter 10 (where it comes under Interpretation). The first sixteen chapters have all, to a greater or lesser (generally a greater) extent, been expanded, but this has meant that, to prevent the book from becoming unwieldy, there has been some pruning of the material in Chapter 17 onwards. Some of what has gone was of largely historical interest and it is to be hoped that what has been deleted will not be too much missed.

The editor would like to thank his former colleague, Nigel Furey, for his assistance with the passages relating to insolvency and to pay tribute to officials in the Law Commission and in the Ministry of Justice who have, when asked, supplied information on proposed developments and changes in the law. He would like to offer particular thanks to the staff at Sweet and Maxwell for their kindness and for the way in which they pretended to believe his not-always convincing excuses for delays in producing promised text.

The Feast Day of St.Padarn
16 April 2016

Roger Kerridge
Bristol

A H R Brierley
Shrewsbury

CONTENTS

TABLE OF CASES

TABLE OF STATUTES

TABLE OF STATUTORY INSTRUMENTS

CHAPTER 1

INTRODUCTION
THE TRANSFER OF PROPERTY ON DEATH

The law of succession is concerned with the transfer or devolution of property on death. It can be divided into two principal topics: the law of intestate succession and the law of wills. But not all transfers on death are covered by the law of intestate succession or the law of wills. There are a number of ways in which property which belongs to, or which may appear to belong to, an individual during his[1] lifetime may pass on his death *other* than by his will or in accordance with the intestacy rules. **1–01**

I. JOINTLY OWNED PROPERTY

English law provides for two forms of concurrent ownership of both real and personal property. Where there is a beneficial tenancy in common, each owner has a separate interest and, on his death, his share passes under his will or under the rules applicable to his intestacy. But where there is a beneficial joint tenancy, there is a single interest and a right of survivorship, the *jus accrescendi*. As each joint owner dies, his rights are extinguished and vest in the surviving joint owner or owners. Beneficial joint ownership of real and personal property may be severed with the result that the joint tenancy is converted into a tenancy in common.[2] The creation of joint ownership, and the failure to sever a joint tenancy, are **1–02**

[1] "His" in this context is, of course, shorthand for "his or hers". The old-fashioned convention of assuming that the masculine includes the feminine is adopted for the sake of brevity. Whenever there is a reference in this book to someone who may be male or female (a testator, a beneficiary, a witness, etc.) he or she is referred to as "he". Some may think this old-fashioned, but the alternatives all seem to be inelegant and/or ungrammatical.

[2] Megarry & Wade, *The Law of Real Property*, Charles Harpum et al (eds) 8th edn (London: Sweet & Maxwell, 2012) para.13–036. For severance by a "course of dealing" see *Williams v Hensman* (1861) 1 John & H. 546; *Szabo v Boros* [2002] W.T.L.R. 1389; *Re Woolnough* [2002] W.T.L.R. 595; *Carr v Isard* [2007] W.T.L.R. 409. In *Quigley v Masterson* [2012] 1 All E.R. 1224, a woman was held to have effected a severance by notice shortly before her cohabitant's death and so to have lost her right of survivorship. The judge referred to the "policy that the court should lean in favour of severance where it properly can". A *beneficial* joint tenancy may be severed, but not a *legal* joint tenancy: Megarry & Wade, para.13–050.

both acts or omissions which are part of the law of succession in the wider sense,[3] and a will draftsman who fails to give adequate advice to a testator as to the severance of a joint tenancy may be held liable in negligence to an intended beneficiary under a will whose gift is rendered ineffective by such failure.[4]

II. PROPERTY HELD IN TRUST

1–03 If an individual holds the legal, but not the beneficial, title to property then, on his death, although the legal title will pass under his will or under the intestacy rules applicable to his estate, the beneficial title will remain vested in the person who has beneficial title. This is obvious in the case of an express trust, but it is true also in the case of a resulting or a constructive trust. Suppose that the legal title to property is vested in X and X dies; if, during his lifetime, X had been a constructive trustee holding the property for the benefit of Y, or for himself and Y as beneficial tenants in common, Y's interest would *not* pass under X's will, or under the intestacy rules applicable to X's estate, although X's interest (if any) would, of course, pass.[5]

III. NOMINATIONS

A. PENSION SCHEME NOMINATIONS[6]

1–04 An insurance policy on a person's life may belong to him and the proceeds of the policy will then, on his death, fall into his estate and be disposed of by his will; but the policy may not be his and in that case it will not be so disposed of. So, for example, a policy effected under the Married Women's Property Act 1882[7] (MWPA 1882) is not the deceased's policy but is held on trust.[8] The same principle will apply if an express trust has been created over the policy. But apart from cases of MWPA policies and policies held

[3] See Chadwick LJ in *Carr-Glynn v Frearsons* [1998] All E.R. 326 at 336. "On a proper analysis, the service of a notice of severance was part of the will-making process."
[4] See Chap.15.
[5] Constructive trusts are most likely to arise in this context where X and Y are co-habiting, see *Stack v Dowden* [2007] 2 A.C. 432 and *Jones v Kernott* [2012] 1 A.C. 776. For a more detailed discussion of constructive trusts, see Hanbury and Martin, *Modern Equity*, 20th edn (London: Sweet & Maxwell, 2015), Chaps 12 and 13.
[6] See A. Braun, "Pension Death Benefits: Opportunities and Pitfalls", Chap.10 in B. Häcker and C. Mitchell (eds), *Current Issues in Succession Law* (Oxford: Hart Publishing, 2016).
[7] Married Women's Property Act 1882 45 & 46 Vict. c.75.
[8] A policy of insurance effected under s.11 of the MWPA 1882 by a spouse on his life for the benefit of the other spouse, or the children, is held upon trust for them; it does not form part of the deceased's estate and (provided there was no intent to defraud his creditors) it is not subject to his debts.

under express trusts, it is necessary to consider lump sum payments—which may be of substantial value—linked with pension schemes.

Contributory pension schemes often provide that if an employee, who would have received a pension on retirement, dies before reaching retirement age, the pension fund's trustees will make a lump sum payment,[9] a form of insurance. The pension scheme's rules will indicate to whom the payment is to be made. There is usually provision in the scheme's rules for the employee to nominate the person or persons to whom he would like the payment to be made. The question then arises as to whether, when there is such a nomination, it is a testamentary disposition. The answer seems to be that it depends in each case on the provisions of the individual pension scheme.[10] In the Canadian case of *Re MacInnes*[11] an employee's contributions to a contributory savings fund were held in such a way that during the employee's lifetime he had an absolute beneficial interest in his share of the fund. He was, therefore, in effect, the owner of his share and it could pass only under a document which complied with the formality rules applicable to testamentary dispositions.[12] **1–05**

MacInnes can be contrasted with two decisions where, in the light of the rules applicable to the pension schemes in question, it was held that nominations were not testamentary dispositions: *Re Danish Bacon Co Ltd Staff Pension Fund Trusts*,[13] and *Baird v Baird*.[14] The reasoning in these cases may be faultless[15] but the result, particularly in the *Baird* case, could be thought to be unfortunate. "Non-statutory nominations are odd creatures"[16] and these two cases decided that the deceased employees, under the applicable rules, did *not* have beneficial interests in the pension funds but powers, under the funds' rules, to nominate beneficiaries to receive benefits payable on their deaths.[17] This meant that in neither case

[9] Often called a "death in service payment".

[10] *Baird v Baird* [1990] 2 A.C. 548 at 561.

[11] *Re Maclinnes* [1935] 1 D.L.R. 401.

[12] For formalities see below, para.4–01.

[13] *Danish Bacon Co Ltd Staff Pension Fund Trusts* [1971] 1 W.L.R. 248 (Megarry J).

[14] *Baird v Baird* [1990] 2 A.C. 548 PC.

[15] Though Megarry J's decision in the *Danish Bacon Pension Fund* case was criticised by Chappenden in 1972 J.B.L. 20. In *Baird* the deceased's interest was non-assignable and the trustees had to approve the making, and revocation, of a nomination; it is not easy, therefore, to see how, on these facts, the court could have decided the case any other way.

[16] Megarry J in *Danish Bacon Co Ltd Staff Pension Fund Trusts* [1971] 1 W.L.R. 248, at 256.

[17] The pension fund rules may be influenced by tax considerations. Arranging things in such a way that the deceased does not have a beneficial interest will probably mean that the benefits are not subject to inheritance tax as part of his estate. See Chap.16. But the cases can be confusing. In *Gold v Hill* [1999] 1 F.L.R. 54 the deceased's "life insurance and accident benefit plan" appears to have provided that the benefit ($350,000) "would be paid" to his nominated beneficiary. So, it might well have been possible to argue that the position was the same as in *MacInnes*. The employer in *Gold v Hill* was probably not an English company (the deceased was a deep-sea diver) and the scheme was probably not drafted with English law, or English tax rules, in mind. In *Kempe v IRC* [2007] W.T.L.R. 955 the scheme was American and the position seems to have been exactly as it was in *MacInnes*, but the litigation in *Kempe* related only to the tax position and nobody appears to have raised the formalities issue.

was a nomination a testamentary disposition. So, in the *Danish Bacon* case, the nomination was not subject to the Wills Act formality rules and in *Baird* the testator's marriage did not revoke it. By contrast, a will is revoked by marriage[18] and so are *statutory* nominations.[19] A well-drawn pension scheme should make provision for what will happen if the nominator marries after making a nomination or, at the very least, the nominator should be warned that his nomination may be treated differently from a testamentary disposition.

B. STATUTORY NOMINATIONS

1–06 Several statutes permit a person entitled to certain funds or investments to dispose of them by a written nomination operating at his death. Instances include a sum payable by a Friendly Society,[20] Industrial and Provident Society,[21] and Trade Union[22]: in each case the sum nominated cannot exceed £5,000.[23]

National Savings Certificates[24] and savings in the National Savings Bank[25] also pass under a nomination if it was made before 1 May 1981: in these cases no monetary limit applies.

1. Comparison with a gift by will

1–07 A statutory nomination, like a will, has no effect until the nominator dies and is, therefore, ambulatory during the nominator's lifetime.[26] It follows that the nominee takes no interest in the nominated funds or investments so long as the nominator is still alive; during his lifetime the nominator remains free to deal with the nominated funds or investments as he pleases. Again, if the nominee predeceases the nominator, the nomination fails.[27] Similarly, a gift by will normally fails by lapse if the beneficiary predeceases the testator.[28]

[18] This is the general rule—for further details see below, paras 7–02—7–14.

[19] For statutory nominations, see below, paras 1–06—1–09. For an example of the revocation of a statutory nomination by marriage, see Friendly Societies Act 1974 s.66(7).

[20] Friendly Societies Act 1974 ss.66—67.

[21] Industrial and Provident Societies Act 1965 ss.23—24.

[22] Trade Union and Labour Relations (Consolidation) Act 1992 s.17, Trade Union (Nominations) Regulations 1977 (SI 1977/789) and Trade Union (Nominations) (Amendment) Regulations 1984 (SI 1984/1290).

[23] Administration of Estates (Small Payments) Act 1965 ss.2 and 6; Administration of Estates (Small Payments) (Increase of Limit) Order 1984 (SI 1984/539).

[24] National Debt Act 1972 s.11; Savings Certificates Regulations 1991 (SI 1991/1031) reg.37 and Sch.2.

[25] National Savings Bank Act 1971 ss.2 and 8(2); National Savings Bank Regulations 1972 (SI 1972/764) regs 33 and 38.

[26] See below, para.3–02.

[27] *Re Barnes* [1940] Ch.267; see also Savings Certificates Regulations 1991 Sch.2 para.4(1)(a); National Savings Bank Regulations 1972 reg.35(1); Trade Union (Nominations) Regulations 1977 reg.3(1).

[28] For lapse, and the exceptions to lapse, see below, paras 14–11—14–27.

In several other respects, however, a statutory nomination differs from a will: **1–08**

(i) A person who has attained 16 years of age can make a statutory nomination but normally a person must attain 18 years before he can make a valid will[29];

(ii) The formal requirements are different. In the case of money payable by a Friendly Society, for instance, a statutory nomination must be by writing under the nominator's hand, delivered at, or sent to, the registered office of the society or branch, or made in a book kept at that office.[30] In the case of National Savings Certificates and savings in the National Savings Bank, signature by the nominator in the presence of an attesting witness was[31] also required.[32] The formal requirements as to signature and witnesses are different for a will, and a testator is not required to deposit his will anywhere but may retain possession of it during his lifetime;[33]

(iii) Although the marriage of the nominator or testator automatically revokes both a statutory nomination[34] and a will,[35] the other rules governing revocation are different. A statutory nomination may be revoked by a notice complying with the same formal requirements as a statutory nomination but (unlike a will) cannot be revoked by a will or codicil.[36]

A person can, and often does, dispose of such funds or investments by will instead of employing a statutory nomination. Indeed, if a person contemplates making a will, it is usually better for him to dispose of all his assets by the will and not to employ a statutory nomination. He can then, if he wishes, revoke or vary any of its provisions by a subsequent will or codicil.

The Law Commission, in their 2009 Consultation Paper *Intestacy and Family Provision Claims on Death*,[37] provisionally proposed that the **1–09**

[29] Exceptionally, an infant who is a privileged testator can make a valid will: see below, para.4–36.

[30] Friendly Societies Act 1974 s.66(1).

[31] "*was*" because no further nominations are possible under these provisions.

[32] Savings Certificates Regulations 1991 Sch.2; National Savings Bank Regulations 1972 reg.33(2).

[33] Section 126 of the Senior Courts Act 1981 makes provision for the *voluntary* deposit of a will in the Court's custody by a testator during his lifetime: very few wills are so deposited. Sections 23–25 of the Administration of Justice Act 1982 (which are not yet in force) make provision for voluntary deposit in the custody of the Principal Registry of the Family Division, which is to register any will so deposited, and is to function as the national body for the purposes of the Council of Europe Convention on the Establishment of a Scheme of Registration of Wills, Cmnd.5073 (1972).

[34] See, e.g. Friendly Societies Act 1974 s.66(7).

[35] For the two exceptions to the general rule that a will is revoked by the marriage of the testator see below, paras 7–05—7–13.

[36] *Bennett v Slater* [1899] 1 Q.B. 45. For the effect of divorce on a gift by will to the former spouse see below, paras 14–28—14–34.

[37] CP No.191.

£5,000 limit[38] which applies to statutory nominations should be reviewed with a view to its being raised. The consultation revealed considerable dissatisfaction with the current law, but disagreement as to any potential reform. Many of those who were consulted suggested that the requirement of a grant of representation reduced the risk of fraud, and so they were not enthusiastic about a simple revision of the £5,000 limit. In their 2011 Report,[39] the Law Commission recommended that the Government should commission a review of the small payments regime, considering, among other things, the £5,000 limit, the range of assets covered, the protection afforded to asset holders and the formalities to be followed when applying for assets to be released.

[38] The £5,000 limit was set in 1984, and would have to be more than doubled, if it were to compensate for inflation.

[39] Law Com. No.331, and also called *Intestacy and Family Provision Claims on Death.*

CHAPTER 2

INTESTACY[1]

Intestacy is either total or partial.[2] There is a total intestacy where the deceased does not effectively dispose of any beneficial interest in any of his property by will.[3] There is a partial intestacy where the deceased effectively disposes of some, but not all, of the beneficial interest in his property by will.[4] **2–01**

The main rules relating to intestacy are contained in Pt IV of the Administration of Estates Act 1925 which has been amended by the Intestates' Estates Act 1952, the Family Provision Act 1966, the Family Law Reform Act 1969, the Administration of Justice Act 1977, the Family Law Reform Act 1987, the Law Reform (Succession) Act 1995, the Trusts of Land and Appointment of Trustees Act 1996, the Civil Partnership Act 2004 and the Inheritance and Trustees' Powers Act 2014. All references in this chapter to the Act, or to the 1925 Act, are to the Administration of Estates Act 1925 as thus amended, and all references in this chapter to the 2014 Act are to the Inheritance and Trustees' Powers Act 2014.

I. TOTAL INTESTACY

A. ADMINISTRATION OF ASSETS

Part III of the 1925 Act deals with the administration of assets before distribution. **2–02**

[1] For a fuller account of the law relating to intestacy, see Sherrin and Bonehill, *The Law and Practice of Intestate Succession*, 3rd edn (London: Sweet & Maxwell, 2004). For Comparative Succession Law, see K. Reid, M. de Waal and R. Zimmermann (eds), *Comparative Succession Law, Vol.2: Intestate Succession* (Oxford: Oxford University Press, 2015).

[2] For the rules of private international law governing intestate succession, see Dicey, Morris & Collins, *The Conflict of Laws*, 15th edn (London: Sweet & Maxwell, 2012), paras 27–010 et seq.; *Theobald on Wills*, 17th edn, (London: Sweet & Maxwell, 2010), paras 2–002 et seq.; *Re Collens* [1986] Ch.505.

[3] *Re Skeats* [1936] Ch.683 (total intestacy where will appointed an executrix but made no disposition of property).

[4] See below, para.2–49.

1. Power of sale

2–03 Section 33(1) of the 1925 Act provides that "on the death of a person intestate as to any real[5] or personal estate, that estate shall be held in trust by his personal representatives with the power to sell it."[6]

2. Payment of debts and expenses

2–04 The personal representatives must pay the intestate's funeral, testamentary and administration expenses, debts and other liabilities out of the deceased's ready money and out of any net money arising from disposing of any other part of his estate.[7] They have power during the minority of any beneficiary, or the subsistence of any life interest, to invest any money held by them.[8]

3. Residuary estate defined

2–05 The "residuary estate of the intestate," which is distributable among the persons beneficially entitled on intestacy under Pt IV of the Act, means (i) the residue of the deceased's ready money and of any net money arising from disposing of any other part of his estate, together with any investments for the time being representing such money, and (ii) any part of the intestate's estate remaining unsold and not required for administration purposes.[9]

B. THE SURVIVING SPOUSE OR CIVIL PARTNER

1. Civil partners

2–06 The Civil Partnership Act 2004, which came into force on 5 December 2005, gives same-sex couples who register their partnerships the same succession rights as married couples. All references in this chapter to spouses include civil partners.[10]

[5] The rules of inheritance applicable to realty under the general law in force before 1926 still apply (i) to an unbarred entail (Law of Property Act 1925 s.130(4); Administration of Estates Act 1925 ss.45(2) and 51(4)); and (ii) on the death of a person who was a lunatic of full age at the end of 1925 and who dies without recovering testamentary capacity, as regards realty as to which he died intestate (Administration of Estates Act 1925 s.51(2) and see *Re Bradshaw* [1950] Ch.582 and *Re Sirett* [1969] 1 W.L.R. 60). For these rules of inheritance, see the 5th edn of Megarry & Wade, *The Law of Real Property* (1984), pp.539 et seq.; the rules are not discussed in the latest, 8th edn, 2012.

[6] This subsection is as substituted by the Trusts of Land and Appointment of Trustees Act 1996 Sch.2, para.5(1). The original subsection provided for a trust for sale, with a power to postpone sale: the effect was, in substance, the same.

[7] Administration of Estates Act 1925 s.33(2).

[8] Administration of Estates Act 1925 s.33(3).

[9] Administration of Estates Act 1925 s.33(4).

[10] The Marriage (Same Sex Couples) Act 2013 makes marriage of same sex couples lawful in England and Wales, but does not otherwise amend any of the intestacy legislation.

2. How long the intestate's spouse must survive him, to take a beneficial interest

How long the intestate's spouse[11] must survive the intestate, in order to take any beneficial interest on his intestacy, depends upon when the intestate died. **2–07**

(a) *Intestate died on or before 31 December 1995*

If the intestate died on or before 31 December 1995, it did not matter that the spouse survived the intestate only for a very short time: provided the spouse survived the intestate, he took a beneficial interest. **2–08**

Where the intestate and his spouse died on or after 1 January 1953 and on or before 31 December 1995, in circumstances rendering it uncertain which of them survived the other, the general presumption in s.184 of the Law of Property Act 1925[12]—that the younger survives the elder—did not apply. Instead, the younger spouse was presumed not to have survived the elder intestate.[13] It follows that, if a husband aged 60 and his wife aged 59 both died intestate, in November 1995, in circumstances rendering it uncertain which of them survived the other, neither took on the other's intestacy. If their child also died and it was uncertain whether he survived them, the child, being younger, was presumed to have survived each of them.[14]

(b) *Intestate dies on or after 1 January 1996*

If the intestate dies on or after 1 January 1996, then, in order to take any beneficial interest on his intestacy,[15] his spouse must survive him by 28 days.[16] This reform followed one of the recommendations in the Law Commission's 2009 Report *Distribution on Intestacy*.[17] **2–09**

[11] See *Re Seaford* [1968] P. 53 (no divorce after death). A person remains a spouse until the decree absolute of divorce (as opposed to the decree nisi) has been pronounced. In *Official Solicitor v Yemoh* [2011] 4 All E.R. 200, a man domiciled in Ghana had contracted six polygamous marriages under Ghanaian customary law and the six widows were, together, held to be his "spouse" for the purposes of s.46 of the Administration of Estates Act 1925.

[12] See below, paras 14–17 et seq.

[13] Administration of Estates Act 1925 s.46(3), added by the Intestates' Estates Act 1952 s.1(4).

[14] The child would then take on the statutory trusts—see below, para.2–37.

[15] Where spouses hold property as beneficial joint tenants, the spouse who takes by right of survivorship, the *jus accrescendi*, does not, of course, take on intestacy. He does not need to survive 28 days and s.184 of the Law of Property Act 1925 (see para.2–08 above) applies.

[16] Administration of Estates Act 1925 s.46(2A), inserted by the Law Reform (Succession) Act 1995 ss.1(1) and (3).

[17] Law Com. No.187. The Law Commission originally recommended a 14 day survivorship period (para.57 of the Report), but the 14 days was extended to 28 days by an amendment tabled by Lord Mishcon, a practicing solicitor, when the Bill was at committee stage in the House of Lords (Hansard, 27 February 1995).

3. Effect of judicial separation

2–10 If either spouse dies intestate while a decree of judicial separation is in force and the separation is continuing, the surviving spouse is treated as already dead and takes no beneficial interest on intestacy.[18]

4. Beneficial interest taken by spouse

2–11 The beneficial interest of a surviving spouse in the residuary estate varies in extent according to the state of the intestate's family at or after his death and according to whether the deceased died before, or on or after, 1 October 2014, the date when the Inheritance and Trustees' Powers Act 2014 came into force.

(a) *Where the intestate died before October 2014 leaving both a spouse and issue*

2–12 Where the intestate died before 1 October 2014 leaving issue (i.e. children, grandchildren or remoter lineal descendants) who attained the age of 18 years or married under that age,[19] a surviving spouse took the following three interests:

2–13 **(i) The "personal chattels" absolutely.** The definition of this expression in s.55(1)(x) of the 1925 Act, before it was amended by the 2014 Act, read as follows:

> "'Personal chattels' mean carriages, horses, stable furniture and effects (not used for business purposes), motor cars and accessories (not used for business purposes), garden effects, domestic animals, plate, plated articles, linen, china, glass, books, pictures, prints, furniture, jewellery, articles of household or personal use or ornament, musical and scientific instruments and apparatus, wines, liquors and consumable stores, but do not include any chattels used at the death of the intestate for business purposes nor money or securities for money."

Broadly, this definition included all articles of personal use or ornament and all the contents of the home, but excluded money, securities for money, and chattels used at the death of the intestate for business purposes. A motor car used for both business and private purposes by, for instance, a doctor or solicitor appeared to fall outside the definition of personal chattels.

2–14 **(ii) The fixed net sum with interest.** Between 1966 and 2009, the fixed net sum was adjusted every few years by statutory instrument.[20] If the intestate died on or after 1 February 2009, it was £250,000.[21] It was payable

[18] Family Law Act 1996 s.21. The surviving spouse may nevertheless apply to the court for reasonable financial provision under the Inheritance (Provision for Family and Dependants) Act 1975, see Chap.8.

[19] Administration of Estates Act 1925 ss.46(1)(i) and (4) and ss.47(1)(i) and (2)(c).

[20] Family Provision Act 1966 s.1.

[21] Family Provision (Intestate Succession) Order 2009 (SI 2009/135). It has remained £250,000

free of death duties[22] and costs, with interest at the specified rate (which was 6 per cent per annum from October 1983 to September 2014) from the date of death until it was paid.

(iii) A life interest in one-half of the balance of the residuary estate: i.e. the balance after withdrawing the personal chattels and providing for the fixed net sum with interest.[23] 2–15

A surviving spouse who was entitled to such a life interest in half the residuary estate might elect to have it redeemed and to receive its capital value from the personal representatives.[24]

The extent of the beneficial interest of a surviving spouse might have depended on events after the intestate's death. If the intestate left at his death an only child aged six years, and the child died unmarried under the age of 18 years, the surviving spouse took the entire estate absolutely, and not merely the personal chattels, the statutory legacy and a life interest in half the residue. 2–16

(b) *Where the intestate dies on or after1 October 2014 leaving both a spouse and issue*

Where the intestate dies on or after 1 October 2014 leaving issue[25] who attain the age of 18 years or marry under that age,[26] a surviving spouse takes the following three interests: 2–17

(i) The "personal chattels" absolutely. The definition of this expression in s.55(1)(x) of the 1925 Act, as amended by the 2014 Act, now reads as follows: 2–18

> "'Personal chattels' means tangible movable property, other than any such property which –
> consists of money or securities for money, or
> was used at the death of the intestate solely or mainly for business purposes, or
> was held at the death of the intestate solely as an investment:"

The revised section, instead of attempting to list what *are* personal chattels, includes all tangible movable property *other than* money, securities for money, and chattels used solely or mainly for business purposes, or solely

since the 2014 Act came into force, though it would have been logical to update it when the 2014 Act came into force.

[22] The term "death duties" is used in Administration of Estates Act s.46(1)(2) and now means inheritance tax; it previously covered other taxes. Property passing from one spouse to another, whether inter vivos or on death, is, in any event, exempt from inheritance tax, see Chap.16.

[23] Subject to the beneficial interest of the surviving spouse, the residuary estate was held on the statutory trusts for the issue of the intestate. For an explanation of "the statutory trusts" see below, para.2–37.

[24] For further details of the rules applicable to this redemption, see para.2–15 of the 12th edn of this book.

[25] For the meaning of "issue" see paras 2–36 et seq.

[26] Administration of Estates Act 1925 ss.46(1)(i) and (4) and ss.47(1)(i) and (2)(c).

as an investment. There are few reported cases on the original section, and this probably indicates that it worked satisfactorily, but the new section is slightly clearer and certainly wider, in that it gives to the spouse property which is used for business purposes but which is *not mainly* so used.

2–19 **(ii) The fixed net sum with interest.** If the intestate dies on or after 1 February 2009 the fixed net sum is £250,000.[27] Under Sch.1A to the 1925 Act as inserted by the 2014 Act,[28] the statutory legacy will now be reviewed whenever the consumer prices index has risen by more than 15 per cent since the previous review and it must, in any case, be reviewed every five years. Unless the Lord Chancellor otherwise determines, it will then be increased by reference to the increase in the consumer prices index. It remains payable free of death duties[29] and costs, but with simple interest at the Bank of England rate effective at the end of the day on which the intestate died. The payment of both the fixed net sum and the interest is charged on the residuary estate but the interest is primarily payable out of the income of the residuary estate. The fixed net sum is generally referred to as the *statutory legacy*: it bears a close resemblance to a general pecuniary legacy given to a surviving spouse by will, with a direction in the will that it is to be paid immediately after the testator's death.

2–20 **(iii) An absolute interest in one-half of the balance of the residuary estate.** Where the intestate died before October 2014, leaving a spouse and issue, the spouse took a life interest in one half of the balance of the residuary estate. Since October 2014, it has become an absolute interest in one half.

2–21 In most cases, whether before or after 1 October 2014, the statutory legacy will exhaust the residuary estate of the intestate and in consequence the surviving spouse alone benefits on intestacy, even though there are issue.[30] This will be particularly common where the intestate and

27 Family Provision (Intestate Succession) Order 2009 (SI 2009/135). It has remained £250,000 *since* the 2014 Act came into force. Given that the 2014 Act says that the statutory legacy must be reviewed every five years, it would have been logical to revise it in 2014, which was five years after the last revision. The failure to revise it in 2014 may have been an oversight.

28 Schedule 1A was inserted into the Administration of Estates Act 1925 by s.2 of, and Sch.1 to, the 2014 Act. The introduction of five yearly reviews was a change, but not a major one. The addition of a review where the consumer prices index rises by 15% was a late amendment to the Schedule, inserted as the 2014 Bill was being debated in the House of Lords. Between 1966 and 2014, the Lord Chancellor had the power to fix the statutory legacy from time to time by statutory instrument under s.1 of the Family Provision Act 1966. He was not obliged to exercise this power according to any particular time scale, but there was, during those years, only one period when there was a gap of more than six years between revisions. The statutory legacy, where there were issue, was £1,000 from 1925 to 1952; £5,000 from 1953 to 1966; £8,750 from 1967 to 1972; £15,000 from 1972 to 1977; £25,000 from 1977 to 1981; £40,000 from 1981 to 1987; £75,000 from 1987 to 1993; £125,000 from 1993 to 2009 and has been £250,000 since 2009.

29 For the term "death duties" see fn.22.

30 When the Inheritance and Trustees' Powers Bill was being discussed in Commons Committee on 3 March 2014, the Minister of State stated that fewer than 10% of those who died intestate left property worth more than £250,000 (the amount of the statutory legacy).

his spouse owned the matrimonial home as beneficial joint tenants, with the result that the home will pass to the survivor by operation of law and not on intestacy.

(c) *Where the intestate died before October 2014 leaving a spouse, leaving no issue, but leaving a specified relative*

This head applied if the intestate left no issue who attained the age of 18 years or married under that age, but left, in addition to the spouse, one or more of the following specified relatives: a parent, or a brother or sister of the whole blood, or issue of a brother or sister of the whole blood who (in the case of the brother or sister or issue) attained the age of 18 years or married under that age.[31] Under this head a surviving spouse took the following interests: **2–22**

(i) The personal chattels absolutely. The surviving spouse had the same entitlement to the personal chattels, whether or not there were issue. **2–23**

(ii) The fixed net sum with interest. In this case, if the intestate died on or after 1 February 2009[32] and before 1 October 2014, the fixed net sum was £450,000. **2–24**

(iii) One-half of the balance absolutely. The surviving spouse was entitled to the *capital* of one-half of the balance.[33] **2–25**

The specified relatives took the other half of the balance in the order set out in paras 2–43–2–44 below. **2–26**

(d) *Where the intestate died before October 2014 leaving a spouse, but leaving no issue and no specified relative*

Even before October 2014, if the intestate left no issue who attained the age of 18 years or married under that age and no specified relative (as described above), the surviving spouse took *the entire residuary estate absolutely*.[34] **2–27**

(e) *Where the intestate dies on or after 1 October 2014 leaving a spouse, but leaving no issue*

If the intestate dies on or after 1 October 2014, the spouse takes the entire estate. It does not matter which other relatives survive. **2–28**

[31] Administration of Estates Act 1925 s.47(1)(i).
[32] It would have been £1,000 if he had died before 1953; £20,000 between 1953 and 1966; £30,000 between 1967 and 1972; £40,000 between 1972 and 1977; £55,000 between 1977 and 1981; £85,000 between 1981 and 1987; £125,000 between 1987 and 1993 and £200,000 between 1993 and 2009.
[33] In this case, pre-October 2014, the spouse was entitled to one-half of the *capital* at a time when, had there been issue, he or she would have been entitled only to a *life interest* in half the balance.
[34] Administration of Estates Act 1925 ss.46(1)(i), 47(2)(b) and (4).

5. Acquisition by surviving spouse of the matrimonial home

2–29 Even in the unusual cases where the surviving spouse does not inherit the entire estate,[35] the Second Schedule to the Intestates' Estates Act 1952 contains three different provisions which make it easier for her or him to acquire "the matrimonial home."[36] The Act uses this expression in an unusually wide sense. All three provisions apply to the intestate's interest in a dwelling-house in which the surviving spouse was resident at the intestate's death, without any requirement as to residence by the intestate.

(a) *Power of appropriation enlarged*

2–30 Personal representatives have a statutory power to appropriate any asset of a deceased's estate in or towards satisfaction of any interest in his estate.[37] This statutory power cannot, however, be used if the value of the asset to be appropriated exceeds the beneficiary's interest in the estate. The Second Schedule creates a limited exception by permitting the appropriation of an interest in a dwelling-house in which the surviving spouse was resident at the intestate's death, partly in satisfaction of an interest of the surviving spouse in the intestate's estate, and partly in return for the payment of "equality money" by the surviving spouse to the personal representatives.[38]

(b) *Right to appropriation of matrimonial home*

2–31 Normally a beneficiary who wishes to take a particular asset of the estate cannot require the personal representatives to exercise the statutory power of appropriation in his favour. The Second Schedule gives the surviving spouse a special right to *require* the personal representatives to appropriate the intestate's interest in a dwelling-house in which the surviving spouse was resident at the intestate's death: the appropriation is to be made in or towards satisfaction of any absolute interest of the surviving spouse in the intestate's estate, or partly in satisfaction of that interest and partly in return for the payment of equality money by the surviving spouse.[39]

2–32 **(i) Interest in dwelling-house.** The intestate's interest in the dwelling-house may be freehold or leasehold. This special right does not apply, however, to a tenancy which would expire, or be determinable by the landlord by notice, within two years from the intestate's death unless the surviving spouse would be entitled to acquire the freehold or an extended lease under the Leasehold Reform Act 1967.[40]

[35] i.e where there are issues and the estate exceeds the statutory legacy, or where the intestate died before 1 October 2014 leaving specified relatives and the estate exceeded it.
[36] Intestates' Estates Act 1952 s.5.
[37] Administration of Estates Act 1925 s.41: see below, paras 23–21 et seq.
[38] Sch.2 para.5(2).
[39] *Re Phelps* [1980] Ch.275.
[40] Sch.2 para.1(2); Leasehold Reform Act 1967 s.7(8): the enfranchisement rights under the 1967 Act have been extended by the Leasehold Reform, Housing and Urban Development

Normally the consent of the court to the exercise of this special right is not required.[41]

(ii) Time limit and mode of exercise. This special right must be exercised within 12 months from the first general grant of representation to the intestate's estate (unless the court extends this time limit)[42] by giving written notice to the personal representatives.[43] It cannot be exercised after the death of the surviving spouse.[44] During this period of 12 months the personal representatives must not, without the written consent of the surviving spouse, sell or otherwise dispose of the intestate's interest in the dwelling-house, unless this is necessary for the purposes of administration owing to want of other assets.[45] **2–33**

(iii) Valuation. Before deciding whether to exercise this special right, the surviving spouse may require the personal representatives to have the intestate's interest in the dwelling-house valued, and to inform the surviving spouse of the result of the valuation.[46] The intestate's interest in the dwelling-house is to be appropriated at its value at the time of appropriation, and not at the time of the intestate's death.[47] **2–34**

(c) *Purchase of matrimonial home*

Normally a purchase of an asset from the estate by a personal representative is voidable at the instance of any beneficiary.[48] The Second Schedule creates a limited exception by providing that this rule shall not prevent a surviving spouse, who is one of two or more personal representatives, from purchasing from the estate an interest in a dwelling-house in which the surviving spouse was resident at the intestate's death.[49] The exception does not apply if the surviving spouse is the sole personal representative.[50] **2–35**

Act 1993 ss.63–68. The personal representatives *may* appropriate a short tenancy to which this special right does not apply, but cannot be required to do so.

41 In four cases the surviving spouse may not exercise the special right without an order of the court, which must be satisfied that its exercise is not likely to diminish the value of the other assets in the residuary estate or make them more difficult to dispose of. The four cases are where the dwelling-house (i) forms part of a building the whole of which is comprised in the residuary estate; (ii) is held with agricultural land which is so comprised; (iii) as to the whole or part was at the intestate's death used as a hotel or lodging house, or (iv) as to part was at the intestate's death used for non-domestic purposes; Sch.2, paras 2 and 4(2).

42 Sch.2 para.3(1)(a), (3).

43 Sch.2 para.3(1)(c). If the surviving spouse is one of the personal representatives, notice must be given to the other personal representative(s): if the surviving spouse is the sole personal representative no notice is required.

44 Sch.2 para.3(1)(b).

45 Sch.2, para.4(1), (3) and (5). The restriction on sale does not apply if the surviving spouse is a personal representative.

46 Sch.2 para.3(2): see also Administration of Estates Act 1925 s.41(3).

47 *Re Collins* [1975] 1 W.L.R. 309 (value of house was £4,200 at intestate's death in 1971 and £8,000 at hearing of case in 1974).

48 See Hanbury and Martin, *Modern Equity*, 20th edn (London: Sweet & Maxwell, 2015), paras 22–008 et seq.

49 Sch.2 para.5(1).

50 Where the exception is not applicable, the surviving spouse needs the leave of the court

C. THE ISSUE

2–36 Subject to the beneficial interests of the surviving spouse (if any), the residuary estate is held on the "statutory trusts" for the intestate's issue.[51] "Issue"[52] is an old-fashioned term for lineal descendants; i.e. children, grandchildren and remoter descendants.[53]

1. The statutory trusts

2–37 Under the statutory trusts such of the children of the intestate as are living[54] at the intestate's death are beneficially entitled, if more than one in equal shares, subject to two qualifications:

(i) subject to representation, i.e. subject to the rule that such of the issue of a deceased child as are living[55] at the intestate's death take that child's share, if more than one in equal shares, *per stirpes*[56]; and
(ii) subject to the rule that no child or other issue is entitled to a vested interest until he or she attains the age of 18 years or marries under that age.

Consider an example:

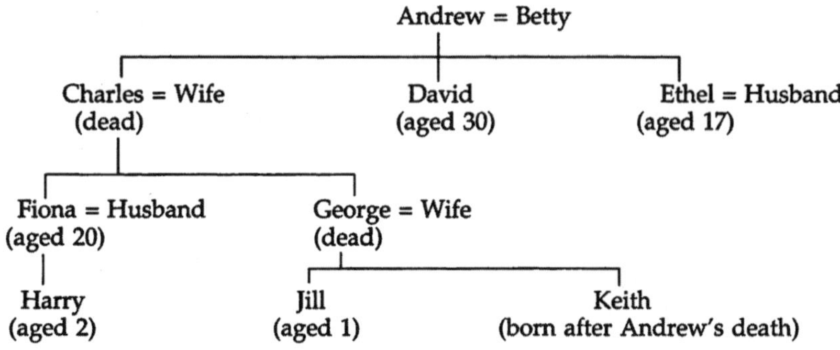

for the purchase: alternatively the surviving spouse may purchase the interests of the other beneficiaries from them if they are sui juris.

[51] ss.46(1) and 47(1).

[52] The term is both singular and plural.

[53] The Law Commission, in their 2011 Report, *Intestacy and Family Provision Claims on Death*, Law Com. No.331, preferred to use the word "descendants": but "issue" remains the word used in the Administration of Estates Act 1925, even as amended in 2014.

[54] References to a child (or issue) living at the intestate's death include a child (or issue) *en ventre sa mère* at the death, s.55(2).

[55] See fn.54, above.

[56] *Per stirpes* means through each stock of descent. No issue can take whose parent is living at the intestate's death and so capable of taking, s.47(1)(i).

Andrew died intestate on 1 March 2016, leaving a widow Betty, an adult son David and a daughter Ethel. Andrew's other son Charles and Andrew's grandson George had predeceased him, but he was survived by Charles's adult daughter Fiona and George's minor daughter Jill. George's son Keith was *en ventre sa mère* at Andrew's death and is accordingly treated as then living.[57] Under the intestacy rules Andrew's residuary estate is distributed or held in trust as follows:

(i) His surviving spouse Betty takes the personal chattels absolutely, £250,000 with interest, and one-half of the balance of the residuary estate.
(ii) The other half of the balance of the residuary estate is held on the statutory trusts for Andrew's issue. Under the statutory trusts David (having attained 18 years) and Ethel (having married) each take vested one-third shares. Fiona, Jill and Keith take Charles's one-third share *per stirpes*,[58] with the result that Fiona takes a vested one-sixth share, and Jill and Keith (taking in place of George) will each take a vested one-twelfth share if each attains the age of 18 years or marries under that age.[59] If Jill and Keith both die unmarried under that age, Fiona will take the whole of Charles's one-third share. Harry takes nothing because his mother Fiona is living at Andrew's death and so is herself capable of taking.[60]

2. Adopted children

Under the Adoption and Children Act 2002 an adopted child is treated **2–38** for purposes of intestacy as the child of the couple who adopted him (or, in any other case, as the child of his adopter), and not as the child of his natural parents.[61] A child adopted by a couple is therefore treated as the brother or sister of the whole blood of any other child, or adopted child, of

[57] See fn.54, above.
[58] For what happens where a child of the intestate survives the intestate but cannot take because he has murdered the intestate, but where he has a child of his own who could take in his place, see Chap.14 at paras 14–82 et seq.
[59] The income and half the capital of the respective shares of Jill and Keith may be applied during infancy for their respective benefit under the statutory powers of maintenance and advancement: s.47(1)(ii); Trustee Act 1925 ss.31 and 32: for these powers see Hanbury and Martin, *Modern Equity*, 20th edn (London: Sweet & Maxwell, 2015) paras 21–022 et seq.
[60] See fn.56, above.
[61] ss.67 and 144(4). In *S v TI* [2006] W.T.L.R. 1461 a five year old child would, on adoption, have lost his entitlement to his deceased natural father's estate because such interest would have vested only when he attained 18 (see para.2–37 above). To avoid this result, an order was made under the Variation of Trusts Act 1958 vesting most of the estate in him before adoption. Section 69 of the Adoption and Children Act 2002 has now been amended by s.4 of the 2014 Act, so that, if immediately before adoption a child has a contingent interest in the estate of its parent, that interest shall not be affected by the adoption. This amendment applies only in relation to adoptions effected on or after 1 October 2014, but covers both intestate and testate succession. As to adoption by one of the child's natural parents see s.67(4), and as to protection of personal representatives see s.72. In the case of a death intestate before 1 January 1976, the Adoption Act 1958 ss.16 and 17 and provisions containing references to those sections continue to apply, Adoption and Children Act 2002 Sch.4 para.17.

the couple. In any other case, the adopted child is treated as the brother or sister of the half blood of any other child, or adopted child, of the adopter. The Act applies to an adoption order made by a court in any part of the UK, the Isle of Man or the Channel Islands,[62] and to certain overseas adoptions.[63]

3. Legitimated children

2–39 Under the Legitimacy Act 1976 a legitimated person[64] (and any other person) is entitled to take any interest on intestacy as if the legitimated person had been born legitimate.[65]

4. Illegitimate children

2–40 An illegitimate child has always taken on the intestacy of his spouse or legitimate issue and similarly his spouse and legitimate issue have always taken on his intestacy. But, at common law, as regards ancestors and collaterals, an illegitimate child was not put on the same footing on intestacy as a legitimate child.[66]

Then, under s.14 of the Family Law Reform Act 1969, on a death intestate after 1969:

(i) An illegitimate child (or his legitimate issue if he was dead) took on the intestacy of each of his parents as if he had been born legitimate. For this purpose he was put on an equal footing with the legitimate issue of each of his parents.

(ii) Each of his parents took on the intestacy of the illegitimate child as if he had been born legitimate.

Both these rights of intestate succession depended solely on proof of parentage[67] and it was, for instance, immaterial that the father never supported or recognised the illegitimate child as his before either of them died. These rights of intestate succession under s.14 were limited in their scope. An illegitimate child did not take on the intestacy of his brothers or sisters, grandparents, or uncles or aunts, and none of them took on his intestacy: if an illegitimate child died intestate without leaving a

[62] The Adoption Act 1958 ss.16 and 17 only applied to an adoption order made in the Isle of Man or Channel Islands on a death intestate after 15 July 1964.

[63] s.66: for the relevant rules of private international law see Dicey, Morris & Collins, *The Conflict of Laws*, 14th edn (London: Sweet & Maxwell, 2006), paras 20–092 et seq.

[64] A legitimated person is one whose parents were married to one another after he was born.

[65] Legitimacy Act 1976 ss.5(1)–(4), 10(1): as to posthumous legitimation see s.5(6) and as to protection of personal representatives see s.7. In the case of a death intestate before 1 January 1976, the Legitimacy Act 1926 ss.3–5 continues to have effect, Legitimacy Act 1976 Sch.1, para.2(1). For the relevant rules of private international law see Dicey, Morris & Collins, *The Conflict of Laws*, 15th edn (London: Sweet & Maxwell, 2012), paras 20–041 et seq.

[66] Legitimacy Act 1926 s.9 (now repealed) gave *limited* rights of intestate succession between a mother and her illegitimate child on deaths before 1970.

[67] Family Law Reform Act 1969 s.14(4) raises a presumption that an illegitimate child is not survived by his father unless the father proves the contrary.

surviving spouse, issue or parent, his estate passed as bona vacantia to the Crown.[68]

Section 18 of the Family Law Reform Act 1987 then reversed the common law rule if the intestate dies after 3 April 1988. Under s.18, references to any relationship between two persons are to be construed without regard to whether the father and mother of either of them (or of any person through whom the relationship is deduced) were married to each other at any time. Thus, on a death after 3 April 1988, an illegitimate child is entitled to take on the intestacy of his brothers or sisters, grandparents, and uncles or aunts, and likewise they are entitled to take on the intestacy of the illegitimate child.[69]

5. Artificial insemination[70]

Section 27 of the Family Law Reform Act 1987 provides that where a child is born to a married woman as the result of artificial insemination, the child will be treated as the child of the woman and her husband *unless* it is proved that the woman's husband did not consent to the insemination. **2–41**

The Human Fertilisation and Embryology Act 1990 covers the case where an embryo, or a sperm and eggs, are placed in a woman who then gives birth to the child. Section 27 of this Act states that the woman who carries the child is to be treated as the child's mother and s.28 says that her husband will be treated as the child's father unless it is shown that he did not consent to the placing.[71]

D. THE OTHER RELATIVES

If the intestate leaves no spouse who survives him by 28 days and no issue of the intestate attains a vested interest, then the residuary estate of the intestate is held in trust for the relatives of the intestate in the order set out below.[72] Any person who takes a vested interest under a particular paragraph excludes any person falling within a subsequent paragraph. **2–42**

1. Parents

Surviving parents take in equal shares absolutely; if only one survives the intestate, that parent takes absolutely. **2–43**

[68] See below, para.2–48.

[69] Family Law Reform Act 1987 s.18(2) raises a presumption that an illegitimate child is not survived by his father, or by any person related to the child only through his father, unless the contrary is shown.

[70] See article by R. Atherton in (1999) 19 LS 139.

[71] If the sperm is that of the woman's husband, he will *be* the child's father—this is covered by s.28(2)(b).

[72] The Human Fertilisation and Embryology Act 1990 s.46(1).

2. Brothers and sisters of the whole blood of the intestate, on the statutory trusts

2–44 The statutory trusts applicable under this paragraph (and also under paras 3, 5 and 6 below) are the same as those for the intestate's issue.[73] The result under this paragraph is (i) that such of the issue of a deceased brother or sister as are living at the intestate's death take the deceased brother's or sister's share, if more than one in equal shares, *per stirpes*, and (ii) that no brother or sister, or issue of a deceased brother or sister, is entitled to a vested interest until he or she attains the age of 18 years or marries under that age.

If the intestate died before October 2014, the specified relatives,[74] those within paras 1 and 2, could take even though the intestate left a surviving spouse,[75] but relatives within any of the later paragraphs could take nothing if the intestate left a surviving spouse, even if he died before the provisions of the 2014 Act came into force

3. Brothers and sisters of the half blood[76] of the intestate, on the statutory trusts

4. Grandparents

2–45 Surviving grandparents take in equal shares absolutely; if only one survives the intestate, that grandparent takes absolutely.

5. Uncles and aunts of the whole blood, on the statutory trusts

2–46 Such an uncle or aunt must be a brother or sister of the whole blood of a parent of the intestate: thus an uncle's, or aunt's, spouse is excluded, although usually called aunt or uncle.

6. Uncles and aunts of the half blood, on the statutory trusts

2–47 Such an uncle or aunt must be a brother or sister of the half blood of a parent of the intestate.

E. BONA VACANTIA[77]

2–48 If the intestate leaves no surviving spouse, and no issue or other relative of the intestate attains a vested interest under the rules set out

[73] The Human Fertilisation and Embryology Act 1990 s.47(3); see above, para.2–37.
[74] See above, para.2–16.
[75] If the intestate left a surviving spouse, the other half of the balance of the residuary estate (para.2–26, above) was held in trust for relatives within paras 1 or 2 in that order.
[76] Brothers and sisters of the *whole* blood have the same father *and* mother; brothers and sisters of the *half* blood have the same father *or* mother, i.e. they have one parent in common.
[77] See generally, N. D. Ing, *Bona Vacantia* (1971).

above,[78] the Crown[79] takes the residuary estate of the intestate as *bona vacantia*.[80] The Crown in its discretion may provide out of the estate for dependants of the intestate, whether or not related to him, and for other persons for whom the intestate might reasonably have been expected to make provision.[81]

II. PARTIAL INTESTACY

A partial intestacy arises where the deceased effectively disposes of some, but not all, of the beneficial interest in his property by will.[82] When this happens, the intestacy rules take effect subject to the provisions contained in the will. Thus the will prevails over the intestacy rules. **2–49**

1. Rules as to administration on a partial intestacy

The power of sale in s.33(1) of the Administration of Estates Act 1925 and the direction to the personal representatives to pay funeral, testamentary and administration expenses, debts and other liabilities in s.33(2) both apply on a partial intestacy. Section 33(2) also provides that the personal representatives (having paid the funeral, testamentary and administration expenses, debts and liabilities) shall set aside a fund sufficient to provide for any pecuniary legacies bequeathed by the will.[83] Section 33(7) provides that s.33 "has effect subject to the provisions contained in the will". **2–50**

Section 33(1) will not apply to an asset held upon an express trust for sale imposed by the will[84]: the express trust for sale will exclude the power of sale.

2. Rules as to distribution on a partial intestacy

Where there is a partial intestacy, s.49(1) makes Pt IV of the Act applicable to any of the deceased's property (or interest in that property)[85] not effectively disposed of by his will, subject to the provisions contained in the **2–51**

[78] For steps to be taken by a solicitor who has acted for the intestate and who believes that he will be able to locate the next-of-kin, see S. Rigden (2001) 151 N.L.J. 928.

[79] Or Duchy of Lancaster, or Duchy of Cornwall.

[80] The Human Fertilisation and Embryology Act 1990 s.46(1)(vi).

[81] The Human Fertilisation and Embryology Act 1990 s.46(1)(vi).

[82] This will usually occur where the will included a residuary gift which has failed—possibly because the residuary beneficiary has pre-deceased the testator (a case of failure by lapse). For this, and other causes of failure, see Chap.14.

[83] As to expenses, debts and liabilities see paras 21–01 et seq.; and, as to legacies, see paras 21–88 et seq.

[84] Before the enactment of the Trusts of Land and Appointment of Trustees Act 1996, trusts for sale were routinely included in wills to avoid the accidental creation of strict settlements. They are no longer *de rigueur*, but express trusts for sale may still be created; see P.H. Pettit (1997) 113 L.Q.R. 207. For arguments for and against the inclusion of express trusts for sale in wills, see R. Mitchell [1999] Conv. 84.

[85] "Property" in s.49(1) includes any interest in real or personal property, s.55(1)(xvii): see *Re McKee* [1931] 2 Ch.145 at 161 and 163.

will.[86] Part IV, of course, includes ss.46 and 47,[87] which specify the persons beneficially entitled on a total or partial intestacy. The personal representative of the deceased, subject to his rights and powers for the purposes of administration, is a trustee of such undisposed of property for the persons beneficially entitled on intestacy.[88]

Section 49(1) operates as if the legislature had inserted at the end of every deceased's will an ultimate gift of any undisposed of property (or interest in property) in favour of the persons beneficially entitled on intestacy.[89] Section 49(1) is always applicable on a partial intestacy, whether the deceased dies wholly intestate as to a particular asset or intestate as to some beneficial interest in that asset.

3. Subject to the provisions contained in the will

2–52 Both s.33 and s.49(1) take effect "subject to the provisions contained in the will". This qualification refers to effective provisions and not to provisions which become inoperative for any reason.[90]

(a) *Inoperative provision*

2–53 A provision in a will does not take effect if the gift in the will to which it is ancillary fails. In *Re Thornber*[91] the deceased by his will directed his trustees to pay an annuity to his wife out of the income of his residuary estate, and to accumulate any surplus income for 21 years from his death or until his wife's earlier death, and at the expiration of the accumulation period to hold his residuary estate and the accumulations upon trust for his children. The deceased died childless in 1933. The Court of Appeal held that the direction to accumulate surplus income was inoperative because the trust of the accumulations for the children had failed. Under s.49(1) the surplus income passed to the persons beneficially entitled on intestacy free from the inoperative provision for accumulation.

A provision may also become inoperative by disclaimer. In *Re Sullivan*[92] the deceased's will gave his widow a life interest in his residuary estate, with remainder to their children. The will provided that copyright royalties[93] were to be treated not as income but as capital, which meant that, under the will, the royalties would not be paid to the widow. The deceased died childless. The widow then disclaimed her life interest and the effect of her disclaimer was that the provision in the will relating to the royalties became inoperative. The effect was that the royalties were

[86] See para.2–52.
[87] The reference to "intestate" in ss.46 and 47 includes a person who leaves a will but dies intestate as to some beneficial interest in his real or personal estate, s.55(1)(vi).
[88] Administration of Estates Act 1925 s.49(1)(b), which adds the qualification "unless it appears by the will that the personal representative is intended to take such part beneficially". The word "expressly" in s.49(1)(b) may be a misprint for "effectively".
[89] *Re McKee*, [1931] 2 Ch.145 above, at 161.
[90] *Re Thornber* [1937] Ch.29.
[91] *Re Thornber* [1937] Ch.29.
[92] *Re Sullivan* [1930] 1 Ch.84.
[93] The deceased owned valuable copyrights.

treated as income and became payable to the widow under the intestacy rules then in force.

(b) *Provision intended to operate on intestacy*

A deceased may insert in his will a provision intended to operate on his intestacy. Romer LJ suggested a suitable clause in *Re Thornber*,[94] "In the event of any of my property being undisposed of by this my will and the provisions of section 49 taking effect I direct that any such property shall be dealt with [in a particular way]". In *Re Sullivan* the deceased could have inserted such a clause in his will. Had he done this, the provision that the copyright royalties should be treated as capital would have applied on his intestacy. **2–54**

III. REFORM OF THE INTESTACY RULES[95]

A. THE 1925 LEGISLATION

The rules which govern intestacy were radically reformed in 1925 and were then modified in 1952.[96] Before 1926, the rules which governed the devolution of *real property*, properly termed rules of *inheritance*, were completely different from the rules which governed the devolution of *personalty*. Real property passed to the heir, the eldest son if there was one.[97] A married man's personalty passed to his personal representatives and was divided between his widow and children; a married woman's personalty passed to her husband. The effect of the 1925 property legislation was to abolish the distinctions which related to the devolution of real property and personalty and to cease to differentiate between males and females. Widows gained, eldest sons lost. **2–55**

B. THE LAW COMMISSION'S 1989 REPORT AND THE ABOLITION OF HOTCHPOT

In 1989, the Law Commission produced a Report, *Family Law Distribution on Intestacy*,[98] which discussed both whether spouses should be granted **2–56**

[94] *Re Thornber* [1937] Ch.29 at 36–37.
[95] See R. Kerridge, "Intestacy Reform in 2014—Unfinished Business", Chap.1 in B. Häcker and C. Mitchell (eds), *Current Issues in Succession Law* (Oxford: Hart Publishing, 2016).
[96] The 1952 changes followed a Report by the Morton Committee—*Report of the Committee on Intestate Succession* (1951) Cmd.8310. For an account of the 1952 reforms, see S. M. Cretney [1994] Denning LJ 35. The major change in 1952 was a huge increase in the size of the statutory legacy.
[97] If there was no son, the intestate's daughters, if any, inherited as coparceners; i.e. they held in undivided shares but without any right of survivorship.
[98] Report on *Family Law Distribution on Intestacy* (Law Com. No.187 (1989)).

more generous provision and whether cohabitants should be entitled to inherit on intestacy. The main problem area when considering reform during the past quarter of a century has been the spouse's entitlement. The 1925 legislation had been a victory for widows over first-born sons. Ever since 1925, "progress" seems to have dictated that spouses should get more. They gained in 1952,[99] and subsequent changes to the size of the statutory legacy had also worked in their favour.[100]

The 1989 Law Commission Report,[101] made three recommendations for reform of the intestacy rules, together with a further set of proposals to provide for cohabitants.[102]

The three recommendations for reform of the intestacy rules were:

(i) that (subject to (iii) below) a surviving spouse should in all cases take the intestate's whole estate;
(ii) that the statutory hotchpot rules[103] should be repealed; and
(iii) that a spouse should inherit under the intestacy rules only if he or she survived the intestate for 14 days.[104]

The first of these three recommendations was, of course, the most important.

1. The surviving spouse's entitlement—proposed reforms 1989 to 1995

2–57 The Law Commission's principal recommendation in its 1989 Report was that a surviving spouse should in all cases take the intestate's whole estate. This recommendation met with opposition and was not enacted. Although in most cases of intestacy since 1926, a surviving spouse has inherited the whole estate, the operation of the rules has been arbitrary. Between 1952 and 2009, the amount of the statutory legacy was increased periodically, but often with steep increases.[105] And the surviving spouse takes the statutory legacy irrespective of whether any property passes to him as a surviving joint tenant.[106] These problems would be cured by giving the surviving spouse the entire estate, but this simple solution is also arbitrary.

2–58 If a rule is introduced to the effect that a spouse will, in all cases, inherit the entire estate, and if the spouse is not the parent of the deceased's children, then, when two people who each have children by earlier unions marry, and they each die intestate a few months apart, the property of

[99] In 1952, there were huge increases to the statutory legacy—which was increased from £1,000 to £5,000 where there were issue, and from £1,000 to £20,000 where there were no issue.

[100] See fnn.28 and 32.

[101] Which had been preceded, a year earlier, by a Working Paper, Law Com. WP No. 108, *Distribution on Instestacy*, and by a survey of public opinion.

[102] The proposals relating to cohabitants are discussed in Chap.8 at paras 8–82 et seq.

[103] For an explanation of the hotchpot rules, see paras 2–59 et seq.

[104] The original proposal was 14 days—it was amended, to 28 days in the Lords, see fn.17 above.

[105] See fnn.28 and 32.

[106] For an explanation of property passing to a surviving joint tenant, see Chap.1, para.1–02.

both of them will end up in the hands of the survivor's children. This can operate like a lottery. It is true that the survivor could make a will leaving the property she[107] received from her deceased spouse to the deceased spouse's children, but it is not likely that she will go to the trouble of making a will the purpose of which would be to take property away from her own descendants. It was on this basis, and to avoid the lottery, that, soon after the 1989 Report was published, the present editor suggested that where a married person died leaving a spouse and issue, none of whom were the spouse's issue, such a spouse should take not the entire estate absolutely, as suggested by the Law Commission, but only a life interest, with remainder to the deceased's descendants.[108] As it was, neither this suggestion, nor the Law Commission's recommendation, was accepted. The major change suggested by the Law Commission was shelved, though, as consolation prize to those who had wanted to give the spouse everything, the statutory legacy was increased significantly.[109]

2. Second recommendation[110]—repeal of the hotchpot[111] rules

Where someone died totally or partially intestate, on or before 31 December 1995, three hotchpot rules might have applied. The principle behind hotchpot was that beneficiaries should not benefit more than once. The first of the three rules was ancient and its inclusion in the Administration of Estates Act confirmed it. The second was added in 1925 and the third in 1952. **2–59**

(a) *Hotchpot on total or partial intestacy—lifetime advancements to children*

The first and main hotchpot rule—which applied on total or partial intestacy—was based on the maxim that "equality is equity" and that children should not take the same benefit twice. The rule had a long history and went back to the time before the enactment of the Statute of Distribution 1670.[112] It was given statutory form as s.3 of the 1670 Statute, and when the 1670 Statute was repealed, with effect from 1 January 1926, it was re-enacted as s.47(1)(iii) of the Administration of Estates Act 1925. It required "any money or property which, by way of advancement or on the marriage of a child of the intestate, ha[d] been paid to such child by the intestate" to be brought into account on the division of his residuary estate into shares under the statutory trusts. For example, if during his lifetime an intestate gave £100,000 to his elder child on marriage, and **2–60**

107 "She" in this context means "he or she", but that is clumsy and the survivor is statistically more likely to be a woman.

108 Roger Kerridge, "Distribution on Intestacy: The Law Commisson's Report (1989)" [1990] 54 *Conv.* 358.

109 It was raised, in 1993, from £75,000 to £125,000 where the deceased had issue, and from £125,000 to £200,000 where he did not have issue.

110 In the Report, this appeared as though it was two separate recommendations: one to cover intestacy, and the other to cover partial intestacy; but it is really one recommendation.

111 The word "hotchpot" derives from the French *hochepot*, a dish shaken up.

112 The Statute of Distribution 1670 was the statute which dealt with intestate succession to personalty and remained in force from 1670 to 1925.

then died a widower, leaving a residuary estate worth £400,000 which was divisible between his two adult children, the elder child would receive a further £150,000 and the younger child £250,000. Each child would then have received the same total amount.

This rule applied only to gifts to *children*, not to remoter descendants, nor to other members of the family; and it applied only where the gift was *by way of advancement or on the marriage of the child*. A gift by way "of advancement" implied a gift for the purpose of establishing the child in life, or of making a permanent provision for him. Payments made for education, or maintenance, or by way of temporary assistance were not advancements.[113] The onus of proving that a payment or transfer was "by way of advancement" lay on the party who asserted it.[114]

(b) *Hotchpot on partial intestacy—benefits given by the will to the issue*

2–61 Section 49(1)(a)[115] required beneficial interests acquired by any *issue* of the deceased *under his will* to be brought into hotchpot on a partial intestacy. The sub-section, inserted in 1925, was badly drafted[116] and was not easy to construe. There was a particular problem[117] where the intestate had bequeathed property to one of his grandchildren under his will and that grandchild had a brother or sister who had not benefited under the will.[118]

(c) *Hotchpot on partial intestacy—benefits given by the will to the surviving spouse*

2–62 Section 49(1)(aa) of the Administration of Estates Act 1925 (inserted in 1952)[119] enacted that a surviving spouse who acquired any beneficial interests under the deceased's will (other than personal chattels specifically bequeathed) was not entitled to the full amount of the statutory legacy under the intestacy rules. Instead, the surviving spouse took the statutory legacy *less* the value at the deceased's death of such beneficial interests. This hotchpot rule reduced the amount of the statutory legacy, but not the other beneficial interests of a surviving spouse under the intestacy rules.

113 *Taylor v Taylor* (1875) L.R. 20 Eq. 155 (payment of fee to special pleader for intending barrister to read in chambers, payments made to curate to assist him in his living expenses, and payment of army officer's debts held not advancements). But see also the more recent case of *Hardy v Shaw* [1976] Ch.82, where gifts of shares in a family company by a mother to two of her adult children were advancements.

114 *Hardy v Shaw* above at 87.

115 As amended by the Intestates' Estates Act 1952.

116 "As bad a piece of draftmanship as one could conceive, in many respects," per Danckwerts J in *Re Morton* [1956] Ch.644 at 647: "great difficulties of language," per Pennycuick J in *Re Grover's W.T.* [1971] Ch.168, 174.

117 It was much discussed in class—to the dismay of generations of Succession students.

118 This was because of the way in which s.49 referred across to s.47. The two sections were not entirely compatible. This is discussed more fully in the 10th edition of this book at pp.52 and 53.

119 It was inserted into the 1925 Act by s.3(2) of the Intestates Estates Act 1952. It was inserted in order to compensate for a huge increase in the statutory legacy, which took effect at the same time.

(d) *Contrary intention*

The application of the hotchpot rules was excluded by a contrary intention on the part of the deceased, "expressed or appearing from the circumstances of the case".[120] **2–63**

(e) *Abolition of the hotchpot rules*

The 1989 Law Commission Report recommended that all three hotchpot rules should be repealed. This recommendation was carried into effect by s,1(2) of the Law Reform (Succession) Act 1995 which applies to all intestates dying on or after 1 January 1996. No hotchpot rule applies on the death of any intestate dying on or after 1 January 1996. **2–64**

(f) *Should the hotchpot rules have been abolished?*

Generally, the hotchpot rules appear, during the latter part of the twentieth century, to have been regarded as complicated, and largely irrelevant, remnants from an earlier age. But their reputation may have done them an injustice. There were three separate rules, and, insofar as there were proposals for modification or repeal, it is suggested that the three rules should have been considered separately. The main hotchpot rule—which applied on total or partial intestacy where there were lifetime advancements to children—was a sensible rule based on the intestate's presumed intention and on the maxim that "equality is equity". It is true that it would apply only where there were significant lifetime gifts (or gifts on marriage) followed by the donor's intestacy, and that donors who make significant lifetime gifts are not the kind of people who usually die intestate; but in the sorts of situation where it did apply, it was fair. It was suspected in some circles that, at the time when it applied, many practitioners overlooked it. The least good reason for abolishing the rule was that practitioners dealing with intestacies could not be bothered to make the relevant enquiries. Insofar as the estates of those who died intestate on or before 31 December 1995 are still in the process of being wound up,[121] it is essential that the proper enquiries are made. **2–65**

And there is an oddity in relation to the abolition of the main hotchpot rule. The rule has been abolished for intestacies, but its sister rule, the rule which applies to wills, has not been abolished. The sister rule which applies to wills is not *called* "hotchpot", but forms part of the "equitable presumption of satisfaction"—the "presumption against double portions" and the "presumption that legacies are satisfied by portions".[122] These are, essentially, different forms of the same rule, all based on the maxim "equality is equity". Suppose that a father, a widower, makes a will leaving his **2–66**

[120] s.47(1)(iii).

[121] The estates of some intestates are not dealt with for many years after their deaths.

[122] See *Hawkins on the Construction of Wills*, 5th edn (London: Sweet & Maxwell, 2000), pp. 429–431. See also *Re Cameron* [1999] Ch.386; *Re Clapham, Barraclough v Mell* [2005] W.T.L.R. 1289; *Evans v HSBC Trust Co* [2005] W.T.L.R. 1289; and see Chap.13.

entire estate to his two children in equal shares and then makes a substantial lifetime gift to one of them; prima facie, the equitable presumption of satisfaction applies and the value of the gift is taken into account on the father's death. The same would have happened if the father had died intestate on or before 31 December 1995. But if the father dies *intestate* on or after 1 January 1996 the hotchpot rule will not apply—so there is an arbitrary distinction between the case of the testate and the intestate parent. It is submitted that the main hotchpot rule was not as "old fashioned" or arbitrary as it was sometimes portrayed. It may have been a rule which did not apply very often, but when it did apply it was fair and just.

2–67 The second hotchpot rule—the one which covered benefits given by the will to issue—was badly drafted; but the cure for bad draftsmanship is redrafting, not abolition.

2–68 As to the third hotchpot rule—the one which dealt with benefits given by the will to the surviving spouse—the Law Commission recommended abolition; but this recommendation was based on the supposition that the Commission's main recommendation (that the surviving spouse should inherit the whole of the intestate's estate) would be accepted and put into effect. If the main recommendation had been put into effect, this third hotchpot rule would have become redundant. But as the main recommendation was not enacted, it is arguable that, far from being repealed, the third hotchpot rule should have been extended (or a fourth rule added), to cover not only property passing to the spouse under the will, but also the value of any property which vests in the surviving spouse as a surviving joint tenant under the *jus accrescendi*, the right of survivorship.

2–69 There was, and remains, a strong argument for reintroducing the three hotchpot rules in place between 1953 and 1995, and then extending the third rule (or adding a fourth rule), to cover property passing to the spouse under the *jus accrescendi*. This would be both simple and fair. Again, it would be of some assistance in cases where the issue are not the issue of a surviving spouse on intestacy. The better solution in this kind of case would be to give the spouse only a life interest,[123] but, if this were not adopted, and if the married couple held property as beneficial joint tenants, the hotchpot solution would, at least, bring some limited relief to the issue.[124] As things stand, this reform has little hope of being introduced. But it may well be that the ungenerous treatment meted out to the children who are not the surviving spouse's children will be of more concern in the future and so this suggestion should be kept on the table for further discussion at a later date.

Although the abolition of the three hotchpot rules may make life easier for succession practitioners, it was not of obvious long term benefit to the system, and it does create an arbitrary distinction between cases where persons who have made substantial gifts to their children die testate or intestate.

[123] See para.2–58.

[124] Where a couple are married and have children by earlier unions, they should not, if properly advised, hold property as beneficial joint tenants. But they are not always properly advised.

C. THE 2005 CONSULTATION PAPER

In June 2005 the Ministry of Justice[125] produced a Consultation Paper entitled *Administration of Estates—Review of the Statutory Legacy*. This Consultation Paper appeared to be a thinly disguised re-attempt to enact the first of the Law Commission's 1989 proposals—that the surviving spouse should receive the whole estate. **2–70**

1. The suggested increase in the statutory legacy

At the heart of the 2005 Consultation Paper was an account of the potential problems faced by surviving spouses who risked being evicted from their houses by the deceased's children. In order to overcome the supposed problem, it was suggested that the statutory legacy should be more than doubled, in real terms, so that the statutory legacy where the deceased had issue would be raised from £125,000 to £350,000. The authors of the Consultation Paper justified their suggestion that the statutory legacy needed to undergo such a huge revision by pointing to the rise in house prices; and visions were conjured up of aged widows and widowers being ejected from their houses by their granite-hearted offspring. What was particularly interesting about this Consultation Paper was that (i) it contained erroneous statistics, and (ii) almost nobody noticed. **2–71**

When attempting to calculate the statistical probability that the statutory legacy will, or will not, be sufficient to permit a surviving spouse to remain in what was the matrimonial home, it will be important to calculate what percentage of cases involve deceased married intestates who were the sole owners of the houses in which they lived, because these are the cases where the survivor is likely to find that the statutory legacy will be insufficient to cover the value of the house. The Consultation Paper stated, correctly, that the price of housing had, since 1993, risen by much more than the general rate of inflation. But the problem with this argument in favour of the rise in the statutory legacy was that it pre-supposed that the deceased, and he alone, owned the matrimonial home. The Consultation Paper made it seem as though approximately 35 per cent of married persons who died intestate in England and Wales were the sole owners of the houses in which they lived. But this was wrong; the correct figure was approximately 6 per cent. The analysis of the calculations which demonstrated this error were set out in an article written shortly after the Consultation Paper appeared[126] and the Ministry of Justice, when publishing their Response to the 2005 Consultation,[127] had to admit **2–72**

125 In 2005, the body which began the consultation process was called The Department for Constitutional Affairs. It had been created in 2003 to replace the Lord Chancellor's Department and then, in 2007, it was enlarged and was renamed The Ministry of Justice. It avoids confusion if it is referred to from the start as the Ministry of Justice.

126 Roger Kerridge, "Reform of the Law of Succession: the Need for Change, Not Piecemeal Tinkering" [2007] 71 *Conv*. 47.

127 There is a three page Annex B to the Response to the Consultation Paper in which the

the mistake. The corrected figures showed that the vast majority, i.e. 80 per cent, of those who die intestate are, in fact, beneficial joint tenants.[128]

2. Intestates holding as beneficial joint tenants

2–73 As explained above,[129] if a married couple are beneficial joint tenants of the house in which they live at the time when the first of them dies intestate, the survivor will take the house before any calculation needs to be made as to his or her entitlement to the statutory legacy. The statutory legacy will, in the vast majority of cases like this, considerably exceed the value of the part of the deceased's estate which passes under the intestacy rules, because this will not include the jointly owned property. So, where did the figures lead? The Consultation Paper set out to demonstrate that the intestacy rules did not treat surviving spouses generously enough. In fact, a careful examination of the figures produced for the Paper showed the opposite. There is a way of compensating for this over-generosity, and it was discussed briefly earlier in this chapter,[130] but the official line seems always to be to ignore anything which could have the effect of not favouring the spouse. The 2005 Consultation Paper had been designed to prepare the way for a huge increase in the statutory legacy. Those who drafted it wanted to increase it from £125,000 to £350,000 where there were issue. After the demonstration of the errors in the maths, the statutory legacy was raised, in February 2009,[131] from £125,000 to £250,000 where there were issue.

2–74 In percentage terms, the 2009 rises in the statutory legacy were about half what the Ministry of Justice had originally suggested. But this led on to the next round of suggested reforms. The Ministry of Justice then asked the Law Commission to consider a project to review the law of intestacy and family provision. A Law Commission Consultation Paper was published in October 2009 and this was followed in December 2011 by a Report, *Intestacy and Family Provision Claims on Death*.[132]

Ministry of Justice acknowledged that their figures had been seriously misleading. How the errors came to be made was never properly explained. Lawyers in England are notoriously bad at sums, but it is surprising: (i) that such serious errors were made in the first place and (ii) that they almost escaped notice. The figures in the Consultation Paper were complicated, but whoever compiled them should have seen what was wrong.

[128] The corrected figures, agreed in a three page Annex B to the Ministry of Justice Response to the 2005 Consultation (itself undated, but published in 2008), showed that approximately 80% of those who died married and intestate were beneficial joint tenants of the houses in which they lived, only 6% were sole owners, another 6% were tenants (non-owners), 5% were beneficial tenants in common and 3% were sole owners who survived.

[129] See Chap.1, para.1–02.

[130] If the surviving spouse were to benefit as a surviving beneficial joint tenant under the *jus accrescendi*, such benefit could be accounted for by way of hotchpot—a new extended hotchpot rule; see para.2–69 above.

[131] By the Family Provision (Intestate Succession) Order 2009 (SI 2009/135).

[132] Law Com. No.331.

D. THE LAW COMMISSION'S 2011 REPORT

1. The surviving spouse's entitlement

As in 1989, the principal focus of the Law Commission's 2011 Report was on the spouse's entitlement. In 1989, the Commission had recommended that the spouse should, in all cases, inherit the entire estate. That recommendation had not been adopted. This time, as well as making recommendations in relation to cohabitants[133] and as well as suggesting a number of minor reforms,[134] the Law Commission took a different approach. Where there were no issue, the spouse should take the entire estate. In other words, the spouse would no longer share with the deceased's parents, or brothers or sisters. But where there were issue (whom the Law Commission, using more up-to-date English, preferred to call "descendants"), it suggested that the existing system should continue, except that the spouse should take his or her half of the balance of the estate absolutely, rather than for life. **2–75**

2. The problem where the issue are not the issue of the surviving spouse

The real problem area remains, as it has always been, the case where the issue are not the issue of the surviving spouse. If Mr Smith dies intestate and all his property passes to his wife, who is also the mother of his children, and she dies intestate without remarrying, the property, or what is left of it, will end up by going to the children as, presumably, Mr Smith would have wished and expected. But, if Mrs Smith remarries, makes no will, and predeceases her new husband, his children (or his other next of kin) will end up benefitting.[135] The 2011 proposals for reform did nothing to help this kind of situation, but made things slightly worse. Twenty years ago, the editor of this book suggested that, where someone died intestate leaving a spouse and issue, but the issue were not the issue of the spouse, the spouse should take only a life interest. The objection to this approach is that it is said to be complicated, but second or subsequent marriages, where there are issue from earlier unions, always lead to complications. And the Law Commission, in attempting to avoid them, had to disregard the findings of a survey of public opinion it had itself commissioned. Prompted by the wish of the Commission to have up-to-date information on public attitudes to intestacy and inheritance, the Nuffield Foundation funded a programme of research and this involved seeking the views of over 1,500 respondents to a series of questions about what should happen to someone's property if he or she died intestate. On the question of competition between second spouses and children of earlier unions, the **2–76**

[133] See Chap.8 at paras 8–82 et seq.

[134] These included redefining "personal chattels", see paras 2–13 and 2–18 above, and indexing and recalculating interest on the statutory legacy, see paras 2–14 and 2–19 above.

[135] A relatively extreme example of this kind of thing is *Re Callaghan* [1985] Fam. 1, where the first husband's property ended up, passing not to his son, but to the second husband's sisters.

research showed that less than 15 per cent of respondents favoured giving everything to the spouse; and well under half of the respondents would give the second spouse priority over the children of a prior union.[136] The Law Commission's recommendation gives, of course, significant priority to the second spouse,[137] so much so that in the vast majority of cases he or she will take everything.[138]

3. The problem where the deceased intestate lacked mental capacity at the time of his marriage

2–77 Quite apart from the problem which arises where someone dies intestate leaving a spouse and children from an earlier union, there is another type of case where a married person dies intestate and which raises particular difficulties. This type of case was not referred to at all by the Law Commission, either in 1989 or in 2011. This is where it is alleged that the deceased (who will probably have been very old and/or in poor health), lacked mental capacity at the time of his marriage ceremony. Since the enactment of the Nullity of Marriage Act 1971, the effect of absence of consent on a marriage has been to make it voidable not void,[139] and a *voidable* marriage *does* revoke any will already made by either party. This is so whether the voidable marriage is subsequently annulled or not.[140] The position where a marriage is

[136] The respondents' answers varied according to the age(s) of the children and the ages of the respondents themselves. The respondents who were most pro-second spouse were the middle aged, those who were older or younger tended to be more biased towards the children. See *Inheritance and the family: attitudes to will-making and intestacy*, Report by National Centre for Social Research, published in August 2010, Executive Summary and Tables 4.7 and 7.3. And it is not only the views of respondents to surveys which demonstrate that second marriages cause particular problems. There have been two recent mutual wills cases where the courts have gone out of their way to find mutual wills, almost certainly to protect the interests of the issue of an earlier union: *Fry v Densham-Smith* [2010] EWCA Civ 1410; [2011] W.T.L.R. 387 and *Shovelar v Lane* [2011] EWCA Civ 802, [2012] 1 W.L.R. 637 For a further discussion of *Densham-Smith* see para.15–38. The courts, like the respondents to the survey, appear to understand that the interests of the issue of an earlier marriage should not be entirely subordinated to those of a later spouse.

[137] The Law Commission seemed to give greater emphasis to the findings of what it called the "Nuffield survey" in relation to the entitlement of cohabitants than in relation to the entitlement of children of earlier unions.

[138] There is another way (apart from the suggestion of the life interest) of treating the spouse who is not the parent of the deceased's children less generously than one who is. It is to give such a spouse a smaller statutory legacy. A version of this is to be found in the United States' Uniform Probate Code. A number of American states have now adopted rules which give a smaller share of an intestate's estate to a spouse who is not the parent of his children than to one who is, and the principle has been adopted in Australia (with New South Wales taking the lead), by the Nordic countries (particularly Sweden), by France and by the Netherlands. This method of dealing with the problem could, of course, be combined with an amended hotchpot rule. Disappointingly, the Law Commission did not examine the rules adopted in other jurisdictions. See R. Kerridge, "Intestacy Reform in 2014—Unfinished Business", Chap.1 in B. Häcker and C. Mitchell (eds), *Current Issues in Succession Law* (Oxford: Hart Publishing, 2016).

[139] The Civil Partnership Act 2004 s.50 states the grounds on which a civil partnership is voidable; these include lack of valid consent and mental disorder.

[140] This is the position since 1 August 1971. Before the enactment of the Nullity of Marriage Act 1971, the effect of a decree of annulment on a voidable marriage was to deem it never to have existed. The 1971 Act did *two* things. It reclassified marriages where there was absence

voidable on the ground of absence of consent is now hugely unsatisfactory. Since 1971, it has been possible for someone who lacks testamentary capacity to contract a voidable marriage which will revoke a will he made when he had capacity.[141] It is impossible to tell how many cases there may have been, since 1971, where marriages have come to light after the death of one of the parties in circumstances where there was a serious likelihood that he or she lacked capacity at the time of the marriage. If he is dead, no challenge can lie, so there is no point in considering what might have been done had the marriage come to light earlier.[142]

As long ago as 1980, the Law Reform Committee in their twenty-second Report[143] considered various suggestions for dealing with this problem and concluded that their preferred solution would be that, where a deceased person had entered into a marriage while incapable through mental disorder of managing and administering his property and affairs, the court should have a discretion under the family provision legislation[144] to make provision for persons who would have benefited under any will which was revoked by the marriage. This topic is discussed in more detail, in Chapter 7.[145] The Law Reform Committee's proposal has not been implemented, but, surprisingly, both of the Law Commission Reports, that of 1989 and that of 2011, ignored the problem altogether. There are various criticisms which could be levelled at the Law Reform Committee's proposed solution, but to ignore the problem, when looking at reform of intestacy, is hard to explain. **2–78**

In spite of problems over children of earlier unions and in spite of problems over voidable marriages, the Law Commission's 2011 Report recommended giving the surviving spouse a larger share of the intestate's estate. He or she would get the whole estate in all cases where there were no issue and would get the personal chattels, plus the statutory legacy, plus half the balance of the estate absolutely, where there were issue. There were to be no special rules to deal with the situation where the issue are not the surviving spouse's issue.[146] In March 2013 the Government announced acceptance of **2–79**

of consent as voidable rather than void *and* it enacted that a voidable marriage which was annulled should henceforth be treated as having existed during the period between the ceremony and the decree absolute of nullity.

[141] *Re Roberts* [1978] 1 W.L.R. 653.

[142] *Morley-Clarke v Brooks* [2011] W.T.L.R. 297 is a case where a man who had had a stroke and who was suffering from dementia married his "carer". His sons attempted to annul the "marriage" but were too late; he died before the annulment was granted and there was then nothing they could do.

[143] *The Making and Revocation of Wills*—Cmnd.7902 (1980) 16–18.

[144] Legislation which gives the court a discretion to provide for those who are not properly provided for by a will, or by the intestacy rules, see Chap.8.

[145] See paras 7–04 et seq.

[146] The Law Commission's Report made no attempt to look at the law in other jurisdictions, common law, civil law or mixed. In fact, it is not at all unusual for legal systems to apply different intestacy rules where a surviving spouse is the parent of surviving children, from those which it will apply where she is not. The following systems apply different intestacy rules to surviving spouses who are not the parents of surviving children from those applicable to those who are: the United States, Australia (NSW taking the lead), the Nordic countries (particularly Sweden), France, the Netherlands, and Brazil. Spain draws a minor distinction. When the size of the jurisdictions, and the relative modernity of the changes are factored in,

the recommendations concerning intestacy[147] contained in the 2011 Report and the Inheritance and Trustees' Powers Act 2014, an act which implemented the reforms suggested by the Law Commission's 2011 Report, other than those relating to cohabitants, came into force on 1 October 2014. Those who are cynical about the recommendations, and who consider them too spouse-centered, may wonder to what extent there is a subconscious desire by government to ensure that property remains in, or is put into, the possession of the older generation.[148] The advantage of this, to government, is linked to the funding of pensions and care for the aged.[149]

4. Cohabitants

2–80 The Law Commission's 2011 Report recommended that qualifying cohabitants should be entitled to benefit from the estate of a deceased partner under the intestacy rules. This recommendation has not been enacted. It will be discussed further in Chapter 8, the chapter dealing with family provision. The recommendation does, of course, relate to intestacy, but it is simpler to deal with it after considering family provision, because it involves an examination of what it means to be "living as a person's spouse or civil partner",[150] and that is covered in the family provision context. To discuss the topic in this present chapter would involve unnecessary repetition.

the strength of the case for drawing the distinction, or at least giving it proper consideration, increases.

[147] Though not those concerning cohabitants.

[148] For an English law reform project, this was high speed. When perpetuities were being reformed, it took eleven years for the recommendations of the relevant Law Commission Report (Law Com. No.251), published in 1998, to be enacted. This is probably not the place to speculate on the politics behind the two Law Commission Reports of 1989 and 2011, nor on the manner in which the Reports were dealt with by the governments of the day, but it is worth noting that the 2011 Report had attached to it *two* draft bills, one covering its recommendations concerning intestacy, other than those covering cohabitants, and the other covering cohabitants. The inference is that those who drafted the 2011 Report expected that the two sets of recommendations would meet with different responses. It was always probable that the recommendations concerning cohabitants would prove controversial and would not be greeted with undiluted enthusiasm by a coalition government. But it could also be suggested that inserting the recommendations concerning cohabitants into the Report had the effect, intended or otherwise, of drawing attention away from the (arguably unsatisfactory) manner in which the Report failed to deal with the problem which arises when someone dies intestate leaving a spouse and issue who are not the spouse's issue. The Report, in concentrating on provision for the spouse, has, arguably, failed to look to a future in which there are likely to be more and more cases where the surviving spouse is not the parent of the surviving issue. Such consolation as there is, for those who regard the present round of reforms with misgiving, consists in remembering that (i) matters would be worse still if cohabitants were included as beneficiaries on intestacy (and could, therefore, trump issue) and (ii) the vast majority of those who might be affected by these proposed changes will not, in any case, die intestate.

[149] Fiona R Burns, "Surviving spouses, surviving children and the reform of total intestacy law in England and Scotland: past, present and future" (2013) 33 *Legal Studies* 85 at 117: "While governments and law commissions may acknowledge the importance of family relationships, they will be concerned about how to fund pensions and aged care." More property in the hands of the aged also means higher revenue from taxes on death.

[150] See paras 8–52 and 8–82 et seq.

CHAPTER 3

THE NATURE OF WILLS

I. A WILL IS INTENDED TO TAKE EFFECT ONLY AT DEATH

A will is the expression by a person of wishes which he intends to take effect only at his death. In order to make a valid will, a testator must have a testamentary intention (or *animus testandi*), i.e. he must intend the wishes to which he gives deliberate expression *to take effect only at his death.* It is not, however, necessary that the testator should intend to make, or be aware that he is making, a will.[1] **3–01**

1. A will is ambulatory

A will has no effect until the testator dies.[2] This is the basic characteristic of a will and it is usually expressed by saying that a will is, by its very nature, ambulatory until the testator's death. Thus a will cannot confer benefits whilst the testator is still alive. If a testator makes a will giving his house to his nephew, the nephew takes no interest in the house until the testator's death. A will does not limit the testator's rights of ownership and accordingly he remains free to sell, give away, or otherwise dispose of,[3] his house during the rest of his lifetime. Furthermore, the nephew cannot disclaim any interest under the will until the testator has died; for, until the death, the nephew has no proprietary interest which can be disclaimed.[4] **3–02**

2. A document intended to take effect only at death is a will

A document intended by a person to be his will is usually worded so as to describe itself as his "will." If the document is intended to be **3–03**

[1] *Milnes v Foden* (1890) 15 P.D. 105; *Re Stable* [1919] P.7 (soldier's privileged will): see below, paras 4–29—4–38.

[2] But revocation of a previous will by another will or codicil takes effect when the latter is executed if the testator's intention to revoke is absolute; see below, paras 7–27—7–38.

[3] He may want to mortgage Blackacre, or to create a lease over it—in these cases, he may be disposing of part of his interest in it; the fact that he has given the house to his nephew in his will, in no way restricts his freedom of action in relation to these transactions. For the Rule in *Lawes v Bennett* (the rule that specific gifts are adeemed by the exercise of options) see paras 14–46 et seq.

[4] *Re Smith* [2001] 1 W.L.R. 1937: see below Chap.14, paras 14–70 et seq.

supplementary to a will, it is usually worded so as to describe itself as a "codicil." Indeed, a professional draftsman invariably inserts words describing the document as a will or a codicil at the beginning, in order to make the nature of the document clear immediately.[5] But it is not necessary for a document which is intended to operate as a will or codicil to describe itself as such. Whatever form it takes, any document can be proved[6] as a will or codicil if (i) the person executing it intended it to take effect only at his death and (ii) it was duly executed. To be duly executed, normally a document must have been signed and witnessed in accordance with the formalities required by the Wills Act 1837.[7] As Lord Penzance put it in *Cock v Cooke*,[8]

> "It is undoubted law that whatever may be the form of a duly executed instrument, if the person executing it intends that it shall not take effect until after his death, and it is dependent upon his death for its vigour and effect, it is testamentary."

Thus a document duly executed by a person who intended it to take effect only at his death can be admitted to probate as a will or codicil even though in form it appears to be instructions for a will,[9] an outline will provision,[10] a cheque,[11] a letter,[12] a deed,[13] or a statutory nomination.[14]

3. Ascertaining intention

3–04 In deciding whether a document can be proved as a will or codicil, the court ascertains the intention of the person who executed it, both from the language of the document and from extrinsic evidence.

If the document appears on its face to be testamentary, a rebuttable presumption arises that the deceased intended it to take effect only at his death. Clearly, this presumption arises if a document describes itself as a will or codicil. It has been suggested that the presumption arises if the document, whatever its form, has been signed and witnessed in accordance

[5] Two alternative forms of commencement of a will in common use are: "This is the last Will and Testament of me John Smith of (address and description)." *or* "I John Smith of (address and description) hereby revoke all former wills and testamentary dispositions made by me and declare this to be my last Will."

[6] See below, paras 18–01 et seq.

[7] See below, para.4–02. Exceptionally, a privileged testator may make an informal will without any formalities; see below, para.4–27.

[8] *Cock v Cooke* (1866) L.R. 1 P. & D. 241, 243: see *Robertson v Smith* (1870) L.R. 2 P. & D. 43; *In the Goods of Coles* (1871) L.R. 2 P. & D.362.

[9] *Torre v Castle* (1836) 1 Curt. 303; *Godman v Godman* [1920] P. 261, 281 et seq., (reviewing the authorities); *Re Meynell* [1949] W.N. 273 (where the testator's instructions to his solicitor for his will were duly executed with the required formalities because the testator's physical condition made him liable to die suddenly).

[10] *Re Chapman* [1999] C.L.Y. 4647.

[11] *Bartholomew v Henley* (1820) 3 Phill. 317.

[12] *In the Goods of Mundy* (1860) 2 Sw. & Tr. 119.

[13] *In the Goods of Morgan* (1866) L.R. 1 P. & D. 214.

[14] *In the Goods of Baxter* [1903] P. 12: see above, paras 1–06—1–07.

with the formalities required by the Wills Act 1837.[15] An unusual example of the application of the presumption was in *Re Berger*,[16] where a Hebrew manuscript, a "zavah", which had been duly executed in accordance with the Wills Act, was admitted to probate. The presumption may be rebutted by cogent extrinsic evidence proving that the document was not intended to take effect at death. Thus the court refused probate of a will on proof that the deceased made it in jest as a specimen of a will made in as few words as possible.[17]

Conversely, if a document does not appear to be testamentary on its face, the burden of proving that the maker of the document intended it to take effect only at his death lies on those seeking probate of it.[18] This burden can be discharged by extrinsic evidence. Thus in *Jones v Nicolay*,[19] where an order on a banker to pay £4,000 to X at 12 days' sight was signed by its maker T and attested by two witnesses, extrinsic evidence was admissible to prove that this was done when T knew he was dangerously ill and that he intended the order to be a codicil to his will.

4. Comparison with an inter vivos disposition by deed

Unlike a will, an inter vivos disposition of property by deed takes effect forthwith; or, if the deed is executed by the grantor conditionally on the occurrence of some event other than his own death, it takes effect on the occurrence of that event. If, however, the condition is that the deed shall take effect only at the death of the grantor, it cannot take effect as a disposition inter vivos[20] but operates as a will or codicil if it was duly executed. In *In the Goods of Morgan*[21] the deceased, during his lifetime, executed three deeds of gift conveying property to trustees for the benefit of his children: each deed of gift contained a clause directing that it was not to take effect until after his death. The court held that the three deeds of gift together contained the will of the deceased and granted probate of them, as they had been signed and witnessed in accordance with the appropriate formalities. In the absence of such a clause in each deed of gift showing the deceased's intention, the result would have been the same if extrinsic evidence had proved that the deceased intended these deeds to take effect only at his death.[22] On the other hand, if these deeds had not been signed and witnessed in accordance with the formalities required by the Wills Act 1837, they would not have constituted a valid will unless the deceased was privileged and so entitled to make a will without any formalities.[23] **3–05**

15 per Barnard J in *Re Meynell* [1949] W.N. 273.

16 *Re Berger* [1990] Ch. 118; Court of Appeal, affirming the decision of Warner J.

17 *Nichols v Nichols* (1814) 2 Phill. 180 ("I leave my property between my children; I hope they will be virtuous and independent; that they will worship God, and not black coats"); see *Lister v Smith* (1865) 3 Sw. & Tr. 282 (sham codicil).

18 *King's Proctor v Daines* (1830) 2 Hagg.Ecc. 218.

19 *Jones v Nicolay* (1850) 2 Rob. Ecc. 288.

20 *Governors and Guardians of the Foundling Hospital v Crane* [1911] 2 K.B. 367.

21 *In the Goods of Morgan* (1866) L.R. 1 P. & D. 214.

22 *In the Goods of Slinn* (1890) 15 P.D. 156. Contrast *Corbett v Newey* [1998] Ch.57, discussed below at para.3–09.

23 See below, paras 4–29 et seq.

A settlement of property does not become a will merely because it postpones the possession of property by, or even the vesting of property in, a beneficiary until the death of the settlor. For instance, a settlor may execute a settlement by deed of his house on the settlor for life, with remainder to X in fee simple if X survives the settlor. Under this settlement, X's interest only vests in him in possession if he survives the settlor. Nevertheless, provided that the settlor intended the settlement to take effect forthwith, or on the occurrence of some event other than his own death, the settlement constitutes an inter vivos disposition.[24]

II. A WILL IS REVOCABLE UNTIL DEATH

3–06 Another important characteristic is that a will, by its very nature, is revocable by the testator until his death. A testator cannot make his will irrevocable during his lifetime. Thus a declaration by a testator in his will that it is irrevocable does not prevent him from subsequently revoking it.[25]

1. Joint wills

3–07 If two or more persons duly execute the same document as the will of both of them—which would be most unusual—it constitutes a joint will and is treated as the separate will of each of them.[26] Each is therefore free to revoke or vary the joint will so far as it applies to him at any time, whether or not the other person is still alive.[27] If one dies leaving the joint will unrevoked, probate will be granted of the joint will as the will of the deceased testator.[28] If the other dies leaving the joint will unrevoked, probate will be granted of the joint will as the will of the other deceased testator. The sole merit of a joint will is that it can effectively exercise a power[29] given to two persons jointly to appoint by will,[30] but the cases where such a power is given are extremely rare.

[24] It would be odd for a settlor to execute such a settlement in view of the inheritance tax rules which now apply to life interests; see F.A. 2006 s.156 and Sch.20.

[25] *Vynior's Case* (1609) 8 Co. Rep. 81b; *In the Estate of Heys* [1914] P.192, 197. For contracts to leave property by will, see below, Chap.6, paras 6–01 et seq.

[26] *Re Duddell* [1932] 1 Ch.585.

[27] *Hobson v Blackburn and Blackburn* (1822) 1 Add. 274. Contrast this with the position where there are mutual wills, which are discussed in Chap.6 at paras 6–33 et seq.

[28] The practice, adopted in *In the Goods of Piazzi-Smyth* [1898] P. 7, of proving only that part of the joint will which becomes operative upon the death of the first to die, is not now followed. The Principal Registry maintains an index of joint wills which have been proved in respect of one of the testators.

[29] For an explanation of powers, see Hanbury and Martin, *Modern Equity*, 20th edn (London: Sweet & Maxwell, 2015), Chap.7.

[30] *Re Duddell* [1932] 1 Ch.585.

III. A TESTATOR CAN LEAVE ONLY ONE WILL

A testator may leave more than one expression of his testamentary intentions: he may, for instance, leave several documents worded so as to describe themselves as his will or as codicils to his will. But as the Privy Council pointed out in *Douglas-Menzies v Umphelby*,[31] however many testamentary documents a testator may leave: **3–08**

> "It is the aggregate or the net result that constitutes his will, or, in other words, the expression of his testamentary wishes. The law, on a man's death, fi nds out what are the instruments which express his last will. If some extant writing be revoked, or is inconsistent with a later testamentary writing, it is discarded. But all that survive this scrutiny form part of the ultimate will or effective expression of his wishes about his estate. In this sense it is inaccurate to speak of a man leaving two wills; he does leave, and can leave, but one will."[32]

Sometimes the word "will" is used in a different sense, to denote a particular expression by a testator of his testamentary intentions—e.g. "the deceased made a formal will in England and later made an informal privileged will whilst serving as a soldier in Northern Ireland."

IV. CONDITIONAL WILLS

A testator may state in his will that he intends it to take effect only if some specified condition is satisfied: for example, "If I survive my wife and inherit under her will"[33]; or "in case anything should happen to me during the remainder of the voyage."[34] If the specified condition is not satisfied, the will does not take effect. **3–09**

In *Corbett v Newey*[35] a testatrix executed a will subject to a condition which was *not* expressed on its face. She intended that the will should not take effect immediately but only after she had made certain inter vivos gifts. The Court of Appeal held that, while it is possible to have a will which is *on its face* conditional, it is not possible to call extrinsic evidence[36] to show that a will which appears on its face to be unconditional is, in fact,

[31] *Douglas-Menzies v Umphelby* [1908] A.C. 224, 233. This case concerned two testamentary documents, one disposing of the testator's estate in Great Britain and the other disposing of his estate in Australia. Accordingly, the Privy Council did not advert to the possibility of an oral expression of testamentary intentions by a privileged testator. To take account of this possibility, it may be better to say that a testator can leave only one will which is the net result of every valid expression of his testamentary intentions during his lifetime. This is the strict meaning of the word "will".

[32] Quoted and applied by Sir Denys Buckley in *Re Berger* [1990] Ch.118.

[33] *In the Estate of Thomas* [1939] 2 All E.R. 567.

[34] *In the Goods of Robinson* (1870) L.R. 2 P. & D. 171.

[35] *Corbett v Newey* [1998] Ch.57.

[36] Evidence from outside the will.

subject to a condition. It was, therefore, held that the testatrix lacked the necessary *animus testandi* and the will was invalid.[37]

A distinction also needs to be drawn between a case where the will contains a condition, and a case where a testator refers in his will to a possible future event merely in order to show his reason for making his will. An instance is *In the Goods of Dobson*[38] where the will began with the words, "In case of any fatal accident happening to me, being about to travel by railway, I hereby leave" The testator survived his railway journey; and on his death Lord Penzance held that the will was not conditional, saying "the testator's meaning seems to me to have been this: 'My mind is drawn to the consideration that all railway travelling is attended with danger, and therefore I think that I had better make my will'."[39]

3–10 It is a question of construction whether words used (i) show that the testator intended the will to take effect only if a specified condition is satisfied (a conditional will), or (ii) refer to a possible future event in order to show the testator's reason for making his will (an unconditional will). When deciding this question, the court considers the provisions of the will, read as a whole in the light of the surrounding circumstances in which it was made.[40] In *In the Goods of Cawthorn*[41] a testator wrote out but did not execute his will, which began with the words, "In the prospect of a long journey, should God not permit me to return to my home, I make this my last will." Some months after returning home from this journey he executed his will in the presence of two witnesses. Extrinsic evidence proved that he was not then contemplating any journey and the court held that the will was unconditional and therefore admissible to probate.

If a conditional will contains a clause revoking a previous will but the specified condition is not satisfied, the conditional will is entirely inoperative and the previous will remains unrevoked.[42] However, a conditional codicil which referred to a previous will was admitted to probate, even though the specified condition was not satisfied, on the ground that it would have the effect of confirming the earlier will, or of making the earlier will valid if it had not been duly executed.[43]

[37] By the time that the testatrix had died, the "condition" had been fulfilled. There had been, before this case, no clear authority on this point and there appeared to be disagreement between the editors of the standard textbooks on what the law was. It may also be suggested that the decision in the case does not tie in logically with the doctrine of conditional revocation (the "condition" in a case of conditional revocation does not need to appear in any testamentary document), see below, paras 7–39 et seq.

[38] *In the Goods of Dobson* (1866) L.R. 1 P.& D. 88: see *Burton v Collingwood* (1832) 4 Hagg. 176 ("lest I should die before the next sun").

[39] *In the Goods of Dobson* (1866) L.R. 1 P.& D. 88, 89.

[40] *In the Goods of Spratt* [1897] P. 28 (where many of the cases are considered); *Folds v Abrahart* [2004] W.T.L.R 327 ("if we [testator and wife] should die together"). For admissible extrinsic evidence see below, paras 10–43 et seq.

[41] *In the Goods of Cawthorn* (1863) 3 Sw. & Tr. 417 (the journey was from Bideford to Shrewsbury).

[42] *In the Goods of Hugo* (1877) 2 P.D. 73; *In the Estate of O'Connor* [1942] 1 All E.R. 546.

[43] *In the Goods of Mendes da Silva* (1861) 2 Sw. & Tr. 315; *In the Goods of Colley* (1879) 3 L.R.Ir. 243: but see *Parsons v Lanoe* (1748) 1 Ves.Sen. 189, 190. For confirmation (or "republication") of a will, see paras 7–65 et seq.

A conditional will must be distinguished from a conditional gift in a will. For instance, a gift by will of "£1,000 to X if he swims the English Channel" is a conditional gift: if X does not satisfy the specified condition, the gift to him fails; but the will as a whole still takes effect. **3–11**

A condition to the effect that a beneficiary who challenges a will loses the benefits given to him by the will is, in principle, valid, at least where there is a gift over[44]; and, in *Nathan v Leonard*,[45] John Martin QC[46] held that such a condition would be valid even if gifts to persons other than the challenger would be divested by it. Nevertheless, on the facts, the condition before him, in a non-professionally drawn codicil, was too uncertain to be enforced.

V. PROVISIONS IN A WILL[47]

The main function of most wills is to dispose of the testator's property after his death. By his will the testator may make gifts, either directly to a person beneficially or to trustees upon trust. Another important function of wills is to appoint one or more executors to administer the testator's estate after his death.[48] Sometimes wills deal with various other matters in addition to disposing of the testator's property and appointing executors. They may give instructions as to the disposal of the testator's body, they may appoint testamentary guardians for his minor children, and they may exercise testamentary powers of appointment.[49] These matters are dealt with in more detail in Chapter 9, where a specimen will is set out and discussed. **3–12**

[44] *Cooke v Turner* (1846) 15 M & W 727.
[45] *Nathan v Leonard* [2003] 1 W.L.R. 827.
[46] Sitting as a deputy judge of the High Court.
[47] See also Chap.9.
[48] See below, paras 17–01 et seq.
[49] For an explanation of powers, see Hanbury & Martin, *Modern Equity*, 20th edn (London: Sweet & Maxwell, 2015), Chap.7; see also below, para.9–26.

Chapter 4

FORMALITIES[1]

I. FORMAL WILLS

A. INTRODUCTION

The formalities prescribed for making a will provide some sort of safeguard not only against forgery and undue influence[2] but also against hasty or ill-considered dispositions[3]: the formalities emphasise the importance of the act of making a will and serve as a check against imprudent action. In general, formalities can be justified by the need to provide reliable evidence of a person's testamentary intentions, which may have been expressed many years before his death.[4] **4–01**

Before the coming into force of Section 9 of the Wills Act 1837, there were different formalities for wills relating to different sorts of property. For example, the formalities required for a will intended to devise freeholds were different from the formalities required for a will intended to bequeath leaseholds. There "were ten different laws for regulating the execution of wills under different circumstances".[5]

It was, therefore, quite possible that a pre–1838 will would be held invalid in relation to one type of property while it was valid in relation to other property. The idea behind the enactment of s.9 was that all wills

[1] For a comparative account, see K. Reid, M. de Waal and R. Zimmermann (eds), *Comparative Succession Law, Vol.1: Testamentary Formalities* (Oxford: Oxford University Press, 2011).

[2] They provide "some sort of" safeguard, but it is not always adequate—see Chap.5 for a discussion of the position of vulnerable testators.

[3] Law Reform Committee's 22nd Report, *The Making and Revocation of Wills*, Cmnd.7902 (1980), p.3.

[4] Prof J. H. Langbein suggested in an article in the Harvard Law Review, (1975) 88 Harv. L. R. 489, that the formalities rules have four functions; (i) the evidentiary function, to provide reliable evidence of testamentary intention and the terms of the will; (ii) the channeling function, to standardise the processes whereby the estate passes to the beneficiaries; (iii) the cautionary function, to impress upon the testator the seriousness of what he is involved in and; (iv) the protective function, to protect him against imposition. See also G. Miller, *The Machinery of Succession*, 2nd edn (Aldershot: Dartmouth Publishing Group, 1996), pp.12 and 13.

[5] See the Fourth Report of the Real Property Commissioners (1833) p.12 and W. Holdsworth et al. (eds) *A History of English Law*, 7th edn (London: Sweet & Maxwell, 1965) Vol.15, p.172.

should be executed according to one form which could be easily and generally understood.[6]

4–02 The original s.9, first enacted in 1837,[7] was amended by the Wills Act Amendment Act 1852.[8] Section 17 of the Administration of Justice Act 1982 then substituted a new s.9. But the change from the original s. 9 to the substituted section was more a change of form than of substance. The similarities of substance (between the original section and the substituted section) are much more marked than the differences.

If a testator dies on or after 1 January 1983, the substituted s.9 provides that:

> "No will[9] shall be valid unless—
> (a) it is in writing, and signed by the testator, or by some other person in his presence and by his direction; and
> (b) it appears that the testator intended by his signature to give effect to the will; and
> (c) the signature is made or acknowledged by the testator in the presence of two or more witnesses present at the same time; and
> (d) each witness either—
> (i) attests and signs the will; or
> (ii) acknowledges his signature,
> in the presence of the testator (but not necessarily in the presence of any other witness), but no form of attestation shall be necessary."

Section 9 applies to all wills required to be executed in accordance with English internal law,[10] except wills of privileged testators and "statutory" wills of mentally disordered patients.[11]

[6] The recommendations contained in the Fourth Report of the Real Property Commissioners (1833) led to the enactment of s.9 of the Wills Act 1837, which came into force on 1 January 1838.

[7] As originally enacted, s.9 of the Wills Act read:
"And be it further enacted, That no will shall be valid unless it shall be in Writing and executed in manner herein-after mentioned; (that is to say,) it shall be signed at the Foot or End thereof by the Testator, or by some other Person in his Presence and by his Direction; and such Signature shall be made or acknowledged by the Testator in the Presence of Two or more Witnesses present at the same Time, and such Witnesses shall attest and shall subscribe the Will in the presence of the Testator, but no Form of Attestation shall be necessary."

[8] Otherwise known as Lord St. Leonards' Act. The original s.9, as amended in 1852, applies to any testator who died before 1 January 1983.

[9] "Will" includes a testament, a codicil, an appointment by will or by writing in the nature of a will in exercise of a power, and any other testamentary disposition; Wills Act 1837 s.1. A nomination under a pension scheme is not a testamentary disposition, *Re Danish Bacon Co. Staff Pension Fund Trusts*, see above, para.1–05.

[10] For the rules of private international law governing the formal validity of wills see Dicey, Morris & Collins, *The Conflict of Laws*, 15th edn (London: Sweet & Maxwell, 2012), paras 27–030 et seq.; *Theobald on Wills*, 17th edn (London: Sweet & Maxwell, 2010), Chap.2.) For the Convention on International Wills see ss.27, 28 and 76(5) and (6) of the Administration of Justice Act 1982—ss.27 and 28 are *not* yet in force.

[11] For privileged testators see below, paras 4–29 et seq. For "statutory" wills see below, paras 5–10 et seq.

The court has no power to admit to probate an authentic will which is invalid under s.9.[12]

B. REQUIREMENTS OF SECTION 9

Section 9 has five requirements:

1. The will must be in writing

Under s.9 a will must be in writing but there are no restrictions as to the materials[13] on which, or by which, it may be written, or as to what language[14] may be used. It may be handwritten or typed, or a printed form[15] may be used; many "home-made" wills are made by filling up the spaces on printed will forms in the testator's handwriting. No particular form of words needs to be used: "all for mother" has been held to be a valid will.[16] **4–03**

A will may be made in pencil or in ink, or in a combination of the two, but there is a presumption that the pencil writing in such a combination was only deliberative and it will be excluded from probate unless the court decides that it represented the testator's definite intention.[17]

2. The will must be signed

(a) *Methods of signature by the testator*

Instead of signing his name,[18] the testator may sign by marking the will in some way intended by him as his signature. Thus initials,[19] a stamped signature,[20] or a mark such as a cross, or an inked thumb mark,[21] or a mark of any shape,[22] are all sufficient if intended by him as his signature. A mark suffices even though the testator's hand was guided by another person[23] and it is immaterial whether the testator could write or not. A mark is a useful method of signature for illiterates and those suffering **4–04**

[12] See Law Reform Committee's 22nd Report, *The Making and Revocation of Wills*, Cmnd.7902 (1980), pp.3–4: for reform see below, paras 4–23 et seq.

[13] *Hodson v Barnes* (1926) 43 T.L.R. 71 (writing on empty egg shell).

[14] *Whiting v Turner* (1903) 89 L.T. 71 (will written in French language); *Kell v Charmer* (1856) 23 Beav. 195 (sums bequeathed represented in letters using jeweller's private code).

[15] Interpretation Act 1978 s.5 and Sch.1.

[16] *Thorn v Dickens* [1906] W.N. 54 ("probably the shortest will ever known").

[17] *In the Goods of Adams* (1872) L.R. 2 P. & D. 367.

[18] Signing in an assumed name suffices: *In the Goods of Redding* (1850) 2 Rob.Ecc. 339.

[19] *In the Goods of Savory* (1851) 15 Jur. 1042.

[20] *In the Goods of Jenkins* (1863) 3 Sw. & Tr. 93.

[21] *In the Estate of Finn* (1935) 105 L.J.P. 36 ("merely a blot" as his thumb slipped and the mark smudged). See also *Re Parsons* [2002] W.T.L.R. 237, where a thumb print sufficed.

[22] *In the Estate of Holtam* (1913) 108 L.T 732 ("a sort of broken line"); *In the Goods of Kieran* [1933] I.R. 222. A seal intended as his signature probably suffices, *In the Estate of Bulloch* [1968] N.I. 96, 99.

[23] *Wilson v Beddard* (1841) 12 Sim. 28.

from severe physical disability, although it is desirable for the attestation clause to state that the testator signed with his mark.[24]

In *In the Goods of Chalcraft*[25] the testatrix was dying and signed a codicil "E. Chal" but was unable to complete her signature: this was held to be a sufficient signature on the ground that what she wrote was intended by her to be the best that she could do by way of writing her name. In another case[26] the will began "I, Emma Cook" and the testatrix wrote the words "Your loving mother" at the end: the court admitted the will to probate, being satisfied that the testatrix meant the words "Your loving mother" to represent her name.

(b) *Signature on the testator's behalf*

4–05 The will may be signed by some other person in the testator's presence and by his direction. The person signing may be one of the attesting witnesses[27] and he may sign his own name instead of that of the testator.[28] In *Kayll v Rawlinson*[29] the first witness was present when the testator signed his will, but the second was not. The first witness sought out the second witness and then told her that both the testator and he had signed. The testator was present when this statement was made by the first witness to the second, but did not himself say or do anything, either to confirm, or to contradict, what had been said. It was held that this was a sufficient acknowledgement by the testator of his signature. It is suggested that the decision is correct. Silence by the testator, when someone else makes a statement in his presence to the effect that he has signed his will, and when the person to whom the statement is made can see his signature on the will, does, in the absence of special circumstances leading to a cause for concern, indicate an acknowledgement by the testator of what it has been said that he has done. To insist, in addition, that he nods his head, or murmurs some kind of additional confirmation, would lead only to an investigation into the finer details of an event which may well, in any case, be poorly recollected some years later, after the testator has died.[30]

(c) *Connection of signature with pages of will*

4–06 If a will is written on more than one page, of which only the last is duly executed, all the pages ought to be attached in some way at the time of execution so as to constitute a single testamentary document. In order to reduce the risk of fraud or accidental loss, it is desirable that the pages

[24] To make it clear that the mark is intended by the testator to be his signature.

[25] *In the Goods of Chalcraft* [1948] P. 222; cf. *Re Colling* [1972] 1 W.L.R. 1440.

[26] *In the Estate of Cook* [1960] 1 W.L.R. 353.

[27] *Smith v Harris* (1845) 1 Rob.Ecc. 262.

[28] *In the Goods of Clark* (1839) 2 Curt. 329. If someone signs on the testator's behalf, the attestation clause should record this.

[29] *Kayll v Rawlinson* [2010] EWHC 1269 (Ch); [2010] W.T.L.R. 1443.

[30] Contrast this case with *Barrett v Bem*, paras 4–19 and 5–41, below, where the Court of Appeal held that when someone other than the testator signs a will on his behalf, there needs to be a "positive and discernible communication". It is suggested that there are obvious differences between the two cases, but they do not relate to the testator's "discernible communication", as such.

should be securely attached. It suffices, however, if at the time of execution the pages are held together by the testator's finger and thumb[31] or pressed together on a table by the testator with his hand.[32] Moreover, the Irish courts have even suggested that it suffices if at the time of execution the pages, though not touching, are all in the same room and under the control of the testator.[33]

(d) *Position of signature*

The original s.9 required that the testator's signature had to be "at the foot or end" of the will. The courts interpreted this strictly.[34] The Wills Act Amendment Act 1852 attempted to undo the effects of this strict interpretation by setting out an exhaustive—if verbose—definition of the meaning of "at the foot or end". Essentially, the 1852 Act provided that it did not matter if there was a blank space between the end of the will and the signature; and it did not matter that the signature was placed on a page on which no part of the will was written: but the signature could never operate to give effect to any part of the will which was underneath it or which followed it. The provisions of the 1852 Act were applied with reasonable leniency—although the attitude of the courts seemed sometimes to vary.[35] **4–07**

The significant change made by the Administration of Justice Act 1982 related to the position of the signature. The substituted s.9 (applicable to a death on or after 1 January 1983) does not require the signature to be at the foot or end of the will. The change is illustrated by *Wood v Smith*[36] where the testator made a holograph will[37] which began with the words "My will by Percy Winterbone" but did not sign the will anywhere else. The Court of Appeal, upholding the trial judge,[38] held that when the testator wrote his name at the head of the document, this was his signature; once this was established, there could be no problem about its position.[39]

(e) *Signing the wrong documents—switched wills*

In *Marley v Rawlings*[40] a solicitor prepared mirror wills for a husband and wife, but the wills were accidentally switched at the time of execution, so **4–08**

[31] *Lewis v Lewis* [1908] P. 1.
[32] *In the Estate of Little* [1960] 1 W.L.R. 495.
[33] *Sterling v Bruce* [1973] N.I. 225; *In the Goods of Tiernan* [1942] I.R. 572.
[34] e.g. *Smee v Bryer* (1848) 1 Rob.Ecc. 616 (will held invalid because the signature of the testatrix was not placed in the eight-tenths of an inch left blank at the bottom of a page but on the next page).
[35] It was probably not possible to reconcile all the cases, but this is now of largely historical interest. For further details of the pre-1983 position, see the 9th (1988) edition of this book pp.32 and 33.
[36] *Wood v Smith* [1993] Ch.90.
[37] A holograph will is one which is in the testator's handwriting.
[38] Mr David Gilliland QC (sitting as a deputy judge of the High Court).
[39] See also *Weatherhill v Pearce* [1995] 1 W.L.R. 592. *Quaere* whether the result in *Wood v Smith* would have been the same if the testator's name at the start of the will had been in block capitals.
[40] *Marley v Rawlings* [2015] A.C. 129.

that each executed the will prepared for the other. The error did not come to light on his wife's death, but was discovered after Mr Rawlings died, three years later. The question was whether the will which Mr Rawlings had executed could be rectified under s.20 of the Administration of Justice Act 1982, thereby undoing the effect of the mistake. Rectification, in this context, consists of altering the words in a will to right a "clerical error" and it will be discussed further in Chapter 10. But the point which is of concern here is the relationship between s.9 of the 1837 Act, the section covering execution, and s.20 of the 1982 Act, the section covering rectification. Both at first instance and in the Court of Appeal, it was held that rectification could not apply, because Mr Rawlings had not executed "his will"—there had been a failure of due execution. The Supreme Court disagreed. In effect, it held that s.20 trumped s.9. As Lord Neuberger put it:

> ". . .it appears to me that the reference to a will in section 20 means any document which is on its face intended to be a will, and is not limited to a will which complies with the formalities."[41]

It is suggested that, insofar as the Supreme Court held that s.20 of the 1982 Act takes precedence over s.9 of the 1837 Act, this must, in the context of rectification, be correct and is to be welcomed. There is a more detailed discussion of this case in Chapter 10.[42]

3. The testator must intend by his signature to give effect to the will

4–09 Under the substituted s.9, a will is invalid unless "it appears that the testator intended by his signature to give effect to the will".

The original s.9[43] did not expressly state that the signature had to have been written with the intention of giving effect to the will; but the requirement was implied.[44]

The substituted s.9 states that it must *appear* that the testator intended by his signature to give effect to the will; but it does not *require* the intention to appear *from the will*. It often appears presumptively from an attestation clause that a testator intended by his signature to give effect to the will, but such a clause is neither necessary nor conclusive.

Before 1983, it was possible to call extrinsic evidence[45] as to the words and actions of the testator in order to ascertain what he intended by his signature. It is still possible to call such evidence in relation to post-1982 deaths and this is also illustrated by *Wood v Smith*.[46] Once it was established that the words "Percy Winterbone" *were* a signature, there could be

[41] *Marley v Rawlings* [2015] A.C. 129 at para.65.

[42] The reference to a "document" in the context of rectification, may create problems, see discussion in Chap.10 at para.10–08 fn.24.

[43] As amended by Lord St Leonards' Act, see above, fn.8.

[44] *In the Estate of Bean* [1944] P. 83: see also *Re Beadle* [1974] 1 W.L.R. 417: but contrast *In the Goods of Mann* [1942] P. 146.

[45] Extrinsic evidence is evidence not contained in the will itself.

[46] *Wood v Smith* [1993] Ch.90, see above, para.4–07.

no problem about the signature's position. But two questions remained. Could the signature give effect to the words of the will (the dispositive contents) which were written after it in time? And could extrinsic evidence be admitted as to whether the testator had intended by his signature to give effect to the will? The trial judge admitted evidence from the witnesses[47] that the testator had told them that by writing his name he intended to give testamentary effect to the document he was writing. On the basis of this evidence, the Court of Appeal held that the testator's signature could give effect to dispositive provisions written after it, provided that the signing and the writing of the will were "all one operation."[48]

The test of "all one operation" was derived from *Re White*[49] where the testator made a will in 1981 and altered it in 1984. He did not sign or initial the alterations, but they were initialled by witnesses. It was suggested on behalf of those who would benefit from the 1984 alterations that the testator's 1981 signature could give effect to the 1984 alterations, as though the altered (1984) will was a newly executed will. This was not accepted: the signature and the writing of the alterations were clearly not all one operation.[50]

4. The testator's signature must be made or acknowledged in the presence of witnesses

The signature of the testator must be either made or acknowledged by the testator in the presence of two witnesses present at the same time. This requirement has not changed since 1837. **4–10**

(a) *Signature made in their presence*

The witnesses need not know that the document is a will.[51] It is sufficient that the witnesses see the testator in the act of writing his signature, although they never see the signature and do not know what he is writing.[52] But the requirement is not satisfied if a witness, although present in the same room, is not aware that the testator is writing.[53] Furthermore, if a witness leaves before the testator completes his intended signature, the requirement is not satisfied.[54] **4–11**

[47] This was, of course, extrinsic evidence; it was not contained in the will itself.
[48] There was no problem as to the admissibility of the extrinsic evidence. The Court of Appeal overruled the trial judge in deciding that the testator's signature *did* give effect to words which were written after it. The idea of "all one operation" appears to come originally from Andrew Park Q.C.'s judgment in *Re White*, below, and it may well cause problems in the future. In fact, probate of the will in *Wood v Smith* was ultimately refused (and the trial judge affirmed) because the testator lacked capacity; see below, para.5–04.
[49] *Re White* [1991] Ch 1, Andrew Park QC (sitting as a deputy judge of the High Court).
[50] See also below, para.7–50. *Wood v Smith* and *Re White* are easily reconciled, though the Court of Appeal in *Wood v Smith* expressed reservations about obiter dicta in *Re White*.
[51] *In the Estate of Benjamin* (1934) 150 L.T. 417.
[52] *Smith v Smith* (1866) L.R. 1 P. & D. 143.
[53] *Brown v Skirrow* [1902] P. 3.
[54] *Re Colling* [1972] 1 W.L.R. 1440 (see below, para.4–17).

(b) *Signature acknowledged in their presence*

4–12 If the signature on the will was not made in the simultaneous presence of two witnesses, the signature must subsequently be acknowledged by the testator in their simultaneous[55] presence. There are three requisites for a valid acknowledgment:

(i) The will must already have been signed before acknowledgment.
(ii) At the time of acknowledgment the witnesses must see the signature or have the opportunity of seeing it. If, at that time, the signature is covered by the folding of the will,[56] or with blotting paper,[57] there can be no valid acknowledgment: it does not suffice that the testator would have uncovered the signature and allowed the witnesses to see it had he been asked.[58]
(iii) The testator must acknowledge the signature by his words or conduct.

An express acknowledgment by the testator is desirable[59] but not essential; no particular form of words is required. The testator may acknowledge his signature by gestures.[60] Indeed it is sufficient that he (or someone in his presence and on his behalf) simply requests the witnesses to sign the document which is before them, without telling them that it is his will.[61] As Cotton LJ summed up the position in *Daintree v Butcher*,[62]

> "When the paper bearing the signature of the testatrix was put before two persons who were asked by her or in her presence to sign as witnesses, that was an acknowledgment of the signature by her. The signature being so placed that they could see it, whether they actually did see it or not, she was in fact asking them to attest that signature as hers."

(c) *Who can be witnesses*

4–13 A blind person is incapable of being a witness to a will because it cannot be signed in his "presence" and he cannot be a "witness" to a visible act such as signing for the purposes of s.9.[63] Moreover the requirement that the signature shall be made or acknowledged in the "presence" of

[55] See discussion of *Re Groffman* [1969] 1 W.L.R. 733, below, at para.4–27.
[56] *Hudson v Parker* (1844) 1 Rob.Ecc. 14.
[57] *In the Goods of Gunstan* (1882) 7 P.D. 102.
[58] *Re Groffman* [1969] 1 W.L.R. 733, (see below, para.4–27).
[59] By saying "this is my signature" or words to that effect.
[60] *In the Goods of Davies* (1850) 2 Rob.Ecc. 337.
[61] *Daintree v Butcher* (1888) 13 P.D. 102: see also *Gaze v Gaze* (1843) 3 Curt. 451. But if the testator is acknowledging a signature made by another person on his behalf, it appears not to be sufficient for someone in his presence and at his request to ask witnesses to sign whilst the testator remains passive, *In the Goods of Summers* (1850) 2 Rob.Ecc. 295.
[62] *Dainbnee v Butcher* (1888) 13 P.D. 102, 103.
[63] *In the Estate of Gibson* [1949] P. 434; however at pp.437 and 440 Pearce J left open the possibility that "in peculiar circumstances" a blind man can be a witness to a will: perhaps a

two witnesses needs their mental as well as their bodily presence. As Dr. Lushington put it in *Hudson v Parker*,[64] "What could possibly be the object of the Legislature, except that the witnesses should see and be conscious of the act done, and be able to prove it by their own evidence: if the witnesses are not to be mentally, as well as bodily, present, they might be asleep, or intoxicated, or of unsound mind."

Obviously it is desirable[65] to choose literate witnesses of sound mental capacity and of fixed residence, in case they may later be required to give evidence as to the validity of the will.

The Wills Act 1837 contains other provisions which are relevant to who can be witnesses. Section 15 deprives a witness and his or her spouse of any benefit under the will[66] but allows such a witness to give evidence as to whether or not the will is valid. Thus a beneficiary under a will, or the spouse of a beneficiary, is technically a good attesting witness. Similarly, s.16 allows a creditor (whose debt is charged on any property by the will) or his or her spouse to be a witness; and s.17 specifically states that the executor of a will is competent to witness its execution.

5. The witnesses must sign or acknowledge

(a) *Presence of the testator*

The witnesses need not sign in one another's presence.[67] But each witness must sign (or acknowledge his signature, if the testator dies after 1982) "in the presence of the testator". The testator must be mentally, as well as physically, present: if the testator becomes insensible before both witnesses have signed, the will is invalid.[68] If a witness signs, the testator must either see the witness sign, or have the opportunity of doing so if he had chosen to look[69] or had not been blind.[70] **4–14**

blind person can witness a will written and signed in braille if the testator acknowledges his signature, see (1949) 23 A.L.J. 360.

64 *Hudson v Parker* (1844) 1 Rob.Ecc. 14, 24.

65 It is clearly desirable, provided the will *has* been properly executed, and on the supposition that there was no problem as to the testator's mental capacity. Those who are involved in attempting to arrange the execution of "suspicious" wills may well prefer to choose witnesses who will *not* be available to give evidence; and such persons may deliberately choose witnesses who will be difficult to trace, or who are not expected to survive the testator. The presumption that a will *has* been duly executed (see below, para.4–21) can sometimes act as a shield which protects those who have bullied or defrauded testators. This is discussed further in Chap.5, see paras 5–32 et seq.

66 See below, paras 14–03 et seq.

67 This has been the rule since 1837; it is *not* a 1982 change. Nevertheless, a commonly used attestation clause states that the will was signed by the testator in the presence of two witnesses and then signed by them in his presence *and* in each other's.

68 *Right v Price* (1779) 1 Doug. 241; *In the Goods of Chalcraft* [1948] P. 222.

69 *Casson v Dade* (1781) 1 Bro.C.C. 99 (testatrix in her carriage able to see witnesses signing in attorney's office through the windows); *Tribe v Tribe* (1849) 1 Rob.Ecc. 775 (testatrix unable to turn herself in bed to see witnesses sign; will held invalid); *Newton v Clarke* (1839) 2 Curt. 320.

70 *In the Goods of Piercy* (1845) 1 Rob.Ecc. 278. A blind testator's "presence" is different from a blind witness's "presence," see *In the Estate of Gibson* [1949] P. 434, see above, para.4–13.

(b) *Methods of signature by witnesses*

4–15 Instead of signing his name, a witness may sign by marking the will in some way intended by him as his signature.[71] The words "Servant to Mr. Sperling" have been held a sufficient signature by a witness, being intended as an identification of himself as the person attesting.[72] The witness must himself sign,[73] although his hand may be guided by another witness or a third person.

(c) *Position of signatures of witnesses*

4–16 The position upon the will of the signatures of the witnesses is immaterial provided they intend by their signatures to attest[74] the testator's operative signature.[75] But their signatures, if not on the same sheet of paper as the will, must be on a sheet of paper physically connected with it.[76] If the testator signs the will and the witnesses sign a duplicate, the will is invalid.[77]

(d) *Attestation and subscription (death before 1983)*

4–17 The original s.9 required the witnesses to *attest*, i.e. bear witness that the signature had been made or acknowledged by the testator in their simultaneous presence,[78] and to *subscribe* the will, i.e. sign it at the foot or end. Thus the witnesses had to intend by their signatures to attest the due execution of the will by the testator. If a person signed without any intention to attest, his signature was excluded from probate.[79] The witnesses had to attest the testator's operative signature. If the testator signed his will both at the top and at the bottom, and the witnesses saw the top signature but not the bottom signature which was covered by blotting paper, the will was invalid.[80]

The original s.9 specified the required order of events. Before either witness signed, the testator had first to make or acknowledge his signature in their simultaneous presence. If that was not done, the will was invalid.[81]

[71] *In the Goods of Ashmore* (1843) 3 Curt. 756; *In the Estate of Bulloch* [1968] N.I. 96 (rubber stamp). A seal is insufficient unless intended as his signature, *In the Estate of Bulloch*, see above.
[72] *In the Goods of Sperling* (1863) 3 Sw. & Tr. 272.
[73] *In the Estate of Bulloch*, see above.
[74] For the meaning of "attest" see below, paras 4–17 et seq.
[75] *In the Goods of Braddock* (1876) 1 P.D. 433; *In the Goods of Streatley* [1891] P. 172; *In the Estate of Denning* [1958] 1 W.L.R. 562 (see below, para.19–24). A witness who acknowledges his signature under the substituted s.9 is not required to attest.
[76] *In the Goods of Braddock*, above (witnesses to codicil signed on back of will to which codicil was pinned: codicil held valid).
[77] *In the Goods of Hatton* (1881) 6 P.D. 204.
[78] *Hudson v Parker*, (1844) 1 Rob Ecc. 14 at p.26.
[79] *In the Goods of Sharman* (1869) L.R. 1 P. & D. 661 (three signatures, two attesting and the third as residuary legatee: the third was excluded from probate).
[80] *In the Estate of Bercovitz* [1962] 1 W.L.R. 321; *Re Beadle* [1974] 1 W.L.R. 417. Note that in post-1982 cases the operative signature need not be at the foot or end of the will.
[81] *Wyatt v Berry* [1893] P. 5: see also *Hindmarsh v Charlton* (1861) 8 H.L.C. 160; *In the Estate of Davies* [1951] 1 All E.R. 920.

In *Re Colling*[82] the testator, who was in hospital, started to sign his will in the presence of a nurse and of another patient as witnesses. Before he had completed his intended signature, the nurse was called away to attend to another patient. During her absence the testator completed his signature and the other witness signed. When the nurse returned, both the testator and the other witness acknowledged their signatures and the nurse signed the will. The will was held invalid because the testator neither made nor acknowledged his signature in the presence of both witnesses before both signed it. If, after the testator acknowledged his signature in the presence of both of them, the other witness had signed the will again, it would have been valid.

(e) *Attestation and signature, or acknowledgement (death after 1982)*

The substituted s.9 requires each witness *either* (i) to attest and sign the will *or* (ii) to acknowledge[83] his signature. This amendment to s.9 reverses the effect of *Re Colling*. After 1982, one or both witnesses may sign the will. The testator may then make or acknowledge his signature in their simultaneous presence and each witness may then attest and sign the will, or acknowledge his previous signature, in the presence of the testator. The will is then valid. There is still a required order of events under the substituted s.9, but the amendment means that an acknowledgement by a witness of his previous signature has the same effect as his actual signature. It is a relatively minor change and it is unlikely that there will be many cases like *Re Colling* which will be affected by it. **4–18**

In *Barrett v Bem*[84] the question arose, seemingly for the first time, as to whether a *beneficiary* might sign the testator's will on his behalf. The judge at first instance held that such a signature was valid, and granted probate. The Court of Appeal allowed an appeal against this decision on the ground that there had been no "positive and discernible communication" of the testator's instruction to the beneficiary to sign the will. It is suggested that the decision to refuse probate was correct, but the true ground of invalidity should have been, not the form of communication, but the fact that this will had to be regarded as "suspicious" from almost every possible angle.[85] This was a will in the making of which the beneficiary had taken a major part, and even by the relatively indulgent standards usually adopted by lawyers in England to this kind of situation, the treatment meted out to the beneficiary by the trial judge appeared indulgent. Had this case not involved signing by a beneficiary, but by, say, some independent third party who had no personal interest in the execution, the question of the communication of instructions might have been viewed differently. It is worth comparing and contrasting this case with that of *Kayll v Rawlinson*[86] **4–19**

[82] *Re Colling* [1972] 1 W.L.R. 1440.

[83] For the nature of an acknowledgement see above, para.4–12.

[84] *Barrett v Bem* [2012] EWCA Civ 52; [2012] Ch. 573.

[85] A "suspicious" will is one in the making of which a beneficiary has played a part. "Suspicious" wills are discussed in Chap.5. The formality rules should, inter alia, offer protection to testators against those who wish to take advantage of them, but such protection as they do offer seems seriously inadequate.

[86] *Kayll v Rawlinson* [2010] EWHC 1269 (Ch); [2010] W.T.L.R. 1443.

where it was decided, in effect, that an *acknowledgement* by a testator of his signature could be passive. There could, of course, be different rules to cover instructions to sign on the testator's behalf, on the one hand, and acknowledgment of his (or a witness's) signature, on the other, but it is not readily apparent why there should be. What is important is that the court should be satisfied that the testator's indication, whether it be active or passive, and whether it be of an instruction to sign or an acknowledgement of a signature already made, is both clear *and* the result of his own volition.[87]

6. Attestation

4–20 It is not entirely clear what is involved in "attestation", under the substituted section, above and beyond the witness's signature. If he acknowledges his previous signature, he is not, it seems, required to attest, but if he signs and does not acknowledge he is supposed to "attest and sign". In *Sherrington v Sherrington* the trial judge held that there had been a failure to attest, because there had been "no intention to verify or attest the testator's signature"[88] but the Court of Appeal thought that this was "plainly wrong".[89] Once all the other provisions concerned with signatures and timing have been complied with, it does seem hard to see how there is room to find fault with the execution of a will solely on the ground that "attestation" is somehow lacking.

7. Presumption of due execution

4–21 Where a will appears to have been duly executed, but there is no proof of due execution, it may be inferred. To quote Lindley LJ in *Harris v Knight*:[90]

> "The maxim, '*omnia praesumuntur rite esse acta*,' is an expression, in a short form, of a reasonable probability, and of the propriety in point of law of acting on such probability. The maxim expresses an inference which may reasonably be drawn when an intention to do some formal act is established; when the evidence is consistent with that intention having been carried into effect in a proper way; but where the actual observance of all due formalities can only be inferred as a matter of probability."

The maxim applies with more or less force according to the circumstances of each case. It is particularly important where, for example, witnesses are dead or cannot be traced; and it is not applicable if observance of the formalities is disproved by the evidence.[91] In *Channon v Perkins*[92] the two wit-

[87] See para.5–41 below.
[88] *Sherrington v Sherrington* [2004] W.T.L.R. 895, 909.
[89] *Sherrington v Sherrington* [2005] 3 F.C.R. 538, 559.
[90] *Harris v Knight* (1890) 15 P.D. 170, 179.
[91] *In the Estate of Bercovitz* [1961] 1 W.L.R. 892, [1962] 1 W.L.R. 321.
[92] *Channon v Perkins* [2006] W.T.L.R. 425. See also *Sherrington v Sherrington* [2005] 3 F.C.R. 538; *Re Morgan* [2008] W.T.L.R. 73.

nesses whose signatures appeared on the will accepted that the signatures were theirs, but denied having any recollection of attesting it. The Court of Appeal, reversing the trial judge, considered that the fact that someone could not remember witnessing a document some years before did not indicate that the event had not taken place. There was no positive evidence to rebut the presumption of due execution and so probate was granted.[93]

A borderline, and unsatisfactory, case is *Couwenbergh v Valkova*. The testatrix was alleged to have made two wills in favour of someone who lodged in her house and there was prolonged litigation involving a number of different challenges to each of the wills, one set of challenges relating to due execution. Blackburne J, in arriving at the final decision, after a series of hearings and appeals, included the following passage in his judgment[94]

> "On the question of due execution I have not been persuaded that the two wills were not duly executed. I make it clear, however, that this is a conclusion which I have reached with considerable hesitation."

He then proceeded to refuse probate to each of the two wills on the basis that the testatrix lacked capacity. The wills were "suspicious" (i.e. they had been prepared by the beneficiary—who had herself given instructions to solicitors) and should never have been made. The case may be regarded as an illustration of the lack of protection afforded to a vulnerable testatrix by the formality rules. It should have been much easier than it was to conclude that these wills were invalid.[95]

8. Attestation clause

Section 9 provides that no form of attestation is necessary. Nevertheless, **4–22**
an attestation clause[96] is highly desirable because it facilitates the grant of probate.

(i) In the absence of an attestation clause, a district judge or registrar must, before granting probate in common form, require the due execution of the will to be established by affidavit evidence.[97]

(ii) An attestation clause raises a stronger presumption that the will was duly executed[98] than if no such clause is present. Moreover the presumption of due execution applies with more force in the case of a formal than an informal attestation clause.[99]

[93] See also *Kentfield v Wright* [2010] EWHC 1607 (Ch).

[94] At [2008] EWHC 2451(Ch) para.298.

[95] The case is discussed further in Chap.5, see para.5–41, and mentioned briefly in Chap.15, see para.15–08.

[96] An example reads, "Signed by the said X in our joint presence and then by us in his." Other forms of attestation clause are available for illiterate or blind testators and for wills signed by an amanuensis for the testator, see below, para.5–26, fnn.110 and 111.

[97] N.C.Prob. Rules 1987, r.12: r.12 does not apply to wills of privileged testators (r.17): for probate in common form see below, para.18–10 and for an affidavit of due execution see below, para.19–23.

[98] See above, para.4–21 and below, para.19–24.

[99] *Vinnicombe v Butler* (1864) 3 Sw. & Tr. 580.

C. REFORM OF THE FORMALITIES RULES[100]

4–23 Unfortunately, some authentic wills, which unquestionably represent the true intention of the testator, fail for non-compliance with the prescribed formalities. The number of wills which are submitted to probate and rejected for non-compliance with these formalities is relatively small; most of them are home-made wills.[101] However, as a result of legal advice, most defectively executed wills are never submitted to probate; so there are no reliable statistics to indicate the true extent of the problem.[102]

The Law Reform Committee, in their 22nd Report,[103] considered two proposals for legislative reform:

(a) *Confer dispensing power on court*

4–24 The first proposal was to confer on the court a dispensing power to admit a will to probate if the court were satisfied that, notwithstanding its defective execution, it was genuine. The Law Reform Committee rejected this proposal on the ground that such a power might create more problems than it would solve. The Committee considered that, by making it less certain whether a defectively executed will was capable of being admitted to probate, such a power could lead to litigation, expense and delay and this burden would tend to fall on small estates disposed of by home–made wills.[104]

(b) *Relax formalities rules*

4–25 The second proposal was to relax the formalities prescribed by s.9.

This was the proposal favoured by the Law Reform Committee which recommended the two changes which were, in substance, enacted by the Administration of Justice Act 1982. The Committee recommended that:

(i) A will should be admitted to probate if it was apparent "on its face" that the testator intended his signature to validate it, regardless of where on the will the signature was placed.[105] The amendment made in 1982 (by substituting the new version of s,9) differs very slightly from the Law Reform Committee's recommendation, in that it does not require the testator's intention to appear on the face of the will.

[100] See generally: Langbein (1975) 88 Harv.L.R. 489 and (1987) 87 Columbia L.R. 1; Miller (1987) I.C.L.Q. 559; and Davey [1980] Conv. 64 and 101.

[101] In a three-month survey by the Family Division Principal Registry in 1978, 40,664 wills were admitted to proof and 97 wills were rejected, 93 of them for non-compliance with the s.9 formalities; of the 97 rejected wills, 91 were home-made and six professionally drawn, see Law Reform Committee's 22nd Report, p.31.

[102] See memorandum submitted to Law Reform Committee in May 1978 on behalf of the Law Society, p.5.

[103] Law Reform Committee's 22nd Report, *The Making and Revocation of Wills*, Cmnd.7902 (1980).

[104] Law Reform Committee's 22nd Report at pp.3–4.

[105] Law Reform Committee's 22nd Report, pp.4–5 and 27.

(ii) An acknowledgment of his signature by an attesting witness should have the same effect as his actual signature.[106]

The two amendments made to s.9 amounted to little more than minor tinkering. In an article[107] written before publication of the Law Reform Committee's 22nd Report, Professor J.H. Langbein favoured the introduction of a rule which would grant probate to any will which complied substantially with the required formalities. This suggestion was then enacted in Queensland,[108] but, having seen it in operation there, and noting that a will had to be "near perfect" to pass the "substantial compliance test", Professor Langbein changed his mind and opted[109] to support a dispensing power, a version of which had been introduced slightly earlier in South Australia where a judge needs to be satisfied "that there can be no reasonable doubt that the deceased intended the document to constitute his will".[110] This requirement imposes a high standard of proof, but the minimum formality in South Australia for the exercise by the court of its dispensing power is simply an unsigned document.[111] It is such a dispensing power that the English Law Reform Committee thought too radical, but there is much to be said in its favour and Professor Langbein regarded the South Australian experiment as '"a triumph of law reform". The introduction of such a power might lead to litigation, but at least such litigation would ensure that an authentic will did not fail for non-compliance with the prescribed formalities. **4–26**

An example of a case where a will would certainly have been saved, had there been a dispensing power, is that of *Re Groffman*[112] to which the Law Reform Committee chose to make no reference. In *Re Groffman*, the testator had been married twice and had adult children by his first marriage. He wanted to make a will, the purpose of which was to ensure that some of his property passed to his children by his first marriage and that it did not all pass to his second wife. The testator went to a solicitor and arranged for his will to be drafted and engrossed. The solicitor then sent the will to the testator with instructions as to how it was to be executed. The testator knew that he had to sign or acknowledge the will in the presence of two independent witnesses; so one evening he took the will, which he had already signed, to a social function where he knew that he would find two suitable people. If he had then acknowledged his signature in the presence of the two witnesses who signed the will in his presence, there would have been no problem. But that did not happen. Having arrived at the function, the testator chose two friends as witnesses and indicated to them that he had his will with him and that **4–27**

[106] Ibid at pp.5–6 and 27.
[107] (1975) 88 Harv.L.R. 489.
[108] Queensland Succession Act 1981 s.9: see Miller (1987) I.C.L.Q. 559 at pp.566–567.
[109] (1987) 87 Columbia L.R. 1. In this latter article, Prof Langbein described the Queensland attempt at reform as "a flop".
[110] Wills Act Amendment Act (No. 2) 1975 s.9 inserting a new s.12 in the Wills Act 1936–1975 (S.A.).
[111] *In the Estate of Williams* (1984) 36 S.A.S.R. 423: see Miller (1987) I.C.L.Q. 559 at pp.567–573.
[112] *Re Groffman* [1969] 1.W.L.R. 733.

he wanted them to witness his signature. At this point, the will was still in his pocket. He then went with one of the witnesses into an adjoining room, took his will from his pocket, acknowledged his signature in the presence of this witness —who then signed—and the witness then left the room just as the second witness entered it. The testator then acknowledged his signature in the presence of the second witness who then signed. It was held by Simon P. that the will had not been properly executed. As he said[113] "I have been satisfied that the document does represent the testamentary intentions of the deceased, I would very gladly find in its favour; but I am bound to apply the Statute, which has been enacted by Parliament." The amendments made in 1982 have no effect in relation to a case like *Re Groffman*. Having said this, *Weatherhill v Pearce*[114] indicates a more liberal approach to the formalities requirements. Judge Kolbert, relying on the presumption of due execution, upheld the validity of a will in a case where there was considerable doubt as to whether the two witnesses had both been present together when the testatrix acknowledged her signature. He made it clear that his approach was "to give effect to clear testamentary wishes if it is possible and proper to do so and that as the law leans against intestacy the court should not be astute to undermine a will".[115] It is submitted that this approach should be welcomed and followed, though it will be of no assistance in cases where it can be demonstrated, as a fact, that the witnesses were not present together. This occurred in the 2011 case of *Ahluwalia v Singh*[116] where a will was set aside despite its being accepted that this "frustrated the testator's intentions".[117]

Will draftsmen need to be careful to ensure that they explain clearly to testators how their wills are to be executed if they do not supervise the execution themselves.[118] In addition, they must check that the wills have (so far as they can tell) been properly executed before they lodge them for safekeeping.[119]

4-28 In July 2014, the Law Commission published their Twelfth Programme of Law Reform. One of their projects was to review the law of wills and it was announced that they would focus "on four key areas that have been identified as potentially needing reform". One of these four was formalities.[120] It had been planned that the project would be commenced early in 2015, but it has now been postponed and will not be begun until the Commission have published a scoping paper on marriage, when a revised timetable on the wills project will be outlined. The wills project, when it is begun, is expected to take "around three years".

113 At p.737.

114 *Weatherhill v Pearce* [1995] 1 W.L.R. 592.

115 *Weatherhill v Pearce* [1995] 1 W.L.R. 592, 598. Two other cases where the judges took a reasonably liberal approach are *Couser v Couser* [1996] 1 W.L.R. 1301 (Judge Colyer QC) and *Re Chapman* [1999] C.L.Y. para.4647 (Laddie J).

116 *Ahluwalia v Singh* [2011] EWHC 2907 (Ch); [2012] W.T.L.R. 1.

117 *Ahluwalia v Singh* [2011] EWHC 2907 (Ch) at para.127.

118 *Esterhuizen v Allied Dunbar* [1998] 2 F.L.R. 668.

119 *Humblestone v Martin Tolhurst Partnership* [2004] P.N.L.R. 26. And see Chap.15.

120 The other three are capacity, rectification and mutual wills.

II. PRIVILEGED WILLS

4–29 Roman law gave a privilege to legionaries by exempting them from the ordinary formality rules applicable to the execution of wills. Originally, this privilege lasted throughout military service, but Justinian limited it to the time when the legionary was *in expeditione*, i.e. when he was in actual service with the colours.[121] English law followed suit and the Statute of Frauds[122] enabled soldiers and sailors to make informal wills disposing of their personalty. Section 11 of the Wills Act 1837 took its wording from the Statute of Frauds and provides "that any soldier being in actual military service, or any mariner or seaman being at sea, may dispose of his personal estate" without any formalities whatever. The Wills (Soldiers and Sailors) Act 1918 extended this privilege to realty[123] (as well as to personalty) if the testator dies after 5 February 1918, and widened the scope of the privilege in other respects.

1. Privileged testators

4–30 There are three categories of privileged testators:

(a) *A soldier in actual military service*

4–31 In this context "soldier" includes a member of the Air Force,[124] a female army nurse,[125] and a member of the W.A.A.F[126] In the leading case of *Re Wingham*[127] Denning LJ said that it "includes not only the fighting men but also those who serve in the Forces, doctors, nurses, chaplains, W.R.N.S., A.T.S., and so forth."

To be privileged, a soldier is required by s.11 to be "in actual military service" when he makes his will. In *Re Wingham* the Court of Appeal held that a member of the Royal Air Force undergoing training as a pilot in Canada in 1943 was privileged and therefore entitled to make an informal will, because he was liable at any time to be ordered to proceed to some area in order to take part in active warfare. The test adopted by the Court of Appeal is that a soldier is in actual military service if he is actually serving with the armed forces "in connection with military operations which are or have been taking place or are believed to be imminent."[128] A soldier employed in internal security operations against

121 See W. W. Buckland, *A Text-Book of Roman Law*, 3rd edn (Cambridge: Cambridge University Press, 1963), by P. G. Stein, p.361.

122 The Statute of Frauds 1677 s.23.

123 The Wills (Soldiers and Sailors) Act 1918 s.3: this section embraces the privileged testator's realty and realty over which he has a general or special power of appointment exercisable by will, obiter in *Re Earl of Chichester's W.T.* [1946] Ch.289.

124 Wills (Soldiers and Sailors) Act 1918 s.5(2).

125 *In the Estate of Stanley* [1916] P. 192.

126 *In the Estate of Rowson* [1944] 2 All E.R. 36.

127 *Re Wingham* [1949] P. 187, 196.

128 *Re Wingham* [1949] P. 187, 196 and see p.192; at p.196 Denning LJ said, "Doubtful cases may arise in peacetime when a soldier is in, or is about to be sent to, a disturbed area or an

terrorists in Northern Ireland in 1978 was held in *Re Jones*[129] to be in actual military service. On the other hand, a soldier serving in England or abroad in peacetime when military operations are not imminent is not privileged.[130]

A soldier is in actual military service from the time he receives orders in connection with a war believed to be imminent.[131] Long after fighting has ceased a soldier may still be in actual military service as a member of an army of occupation.[132]

To be privileged, a soldier need not be so circumstanced that he would have been privileged as a legionary who was *in expeditione* under Roman law,[133] or be in danger from enemy action, or be cut off from skilled advice. The privilege was borrowed from Roman law and these factors explain the reasons for its existence; but they do not determine its limits, which depend on the construction of s.11 of the Wills Act 1837 and the Wills (Soldiers and Sailors) Act 1918.[134]

(b) *A mariner or seaman being at sea*

4–32 Mariner or seaman includes all ranks of Her Majesty's naval or marine forces[135] and of the merchant service, and has even been held to extend to a woman typist employed aboard a liner.[136]

The words "being at sea" in s.11 have been liberally construed. The privilege has been held applicable to a seaman who made his will while serving in a ship permanently stationed in Portsmouth harbour.[137] Moreover, a seaman is regarded as constructively "at sea" if he makes his will on land in the course of a voyage[138] or whilst under orders to join a ship. In *Re Servoz-Gavin, Ayling v Summers*[139] a ship's radio officer who

isolated post, where he may be involved in military operations. As to these cases, all I say is that, in case of doubt, the serving soldier should be given the benefit of privilege": see also *Re Jones* [1981] Fam. 7, 10.

[129] *Re Jones* [1981] Fam. 7 (soldier shot on patrol said, "If I don't make it, make sure Anne gets all my stuff"; held valid will).

[130] *In the Estate of Grey* [1922] P. 140.

[131] *Gattward v Knee* [1902] P. 99; *Re Rippon* [1943] P. 61 (territorial officer under orders to join unit).

[132] *In the Estate of Colman* [1958] 1 W.L.R. 457 (soldier on leave in England in 1954 from British Army of the Rhine held privileged): see also *Re Limond* [1915] 2 Ch.240.

[133] See above, para.4–29.

[134] *Re Wingham* [1949] P. 187: see also *Re Booth* [1926] P. 118 and *In the Goods of Hiscock* [1901] P. 78, 80.

[135] Wills (Soldiers and Sailors) Act 1918 s.2.

[136] *In the Goods of Hale* [1915] 2 I.R. 362 (typist on the Lusitania). See *In the Estate of Knibbs* [1962] 1 W.L.R. 852 (barman on liner); *Re Rapley* [1983] 1 W.L.R. 1069, 1073 (nature of service must be sea service but immaterial in what capacity).

[137] *In the Goods of M'Murdo* (1868) L.R. 1 P. & D. 540. See also *In the Goods of Austen* (1853) 2 Rob.Ecc. 611 (admiral on board ship in Rangoon river on a naval expedition privileged) and *In the Goods of Patterson* (1898) 79 L.T. 123 (master on board ship lying in the Thames before starting ocean voyage held privileged).

[138] *In the Goods of Lay* (1840) 2 Curt. 375 (shore leave).

[139] *Re Servoz-Gavin, Ayling v Summers* [2011] Ch 162; this case follows *In the Goods of Newland* [1952] P. 71: see also *In the Goods of Wilson* [1952] P. 92; cf. *Re Rapley*, above, (apprentice seaman on leave and not under orders to join another ship not privileged). *Re Servoz-Gavin*

made his will in England during his leave ashore, whilst under orders to join a ship a few days later, was held privileged.

(c) *Any member of her majesty's naval or marine forces so circumstanced that if he were a soldier he would be in actual military service*[140]

Such a person is privileged even though not at sea.[141] **4–33**

2. Extent of the privilege

A testator who falls within one of the above three categories at the time of making his will is privileged in certain respects. **4–34**

(a) *Informal will*

The testator can make a will without any formalities whatever. It may be written, whether signed or witnessed or not, or it may be nuncupative, i.e. oral.[142] **4–35**

The testator must, however, intend deliberately to give expression to his wishes in the event of his death, although he need not know that he is making a will: in this respect there is no difference between a formal will and an informal will.[143] In *In the Estate of Beech*[144] the testator executed a formal will in 1917, disposing in detail of his property. Later, whilst on active service in France in 1918, he wrote two letters to his son referring to dispositions which he had already made by his will. The Court of Appeal held that the letters were not admissible to probate as an informal will, because the testator did not intend what he wrote to be remembered as an expression of his wishes in the event of his death: he was merely giving his son a summary of his existing will. Again, in *In the Estate of Knibbs*[145] a barman on a liner (whilst privileged as a mariner at sea) said to the head barman, in the course of a conversation about their families' affairs, "If anything ever happens to me, Iris will get anything I have got." The court held that this statement did not constitute an informal will in favour of his sister Iris because it was merely imparted as a matter of interest in an exchange of family gossip.

holds that the privilege applies to a seaman who is serving on, or is under orders to join, a foreign registered ship, provided the seaman is himself domiciled in England and Wales.

140 Wills (Soldiers and Sailors) Act 1918 s.2.

141 See *In the Estate of Anderson* [1916] P. 49, 52; *In the Estate of Yates* [1919] P. 93 (s.2 applied to a sailor who made his will before, but died after, the 1918 Act came into operation).

142 *Re Stable* [1919] P. 7 (oral statement, "If I stop a bullet everything of mine will be yours," by soldier to fiancée; held a valid will): see also *In the Estate of Yates* above, (farewell words by Navy officer to son at railway station); *Re Jones* [1981] Fam. 7.

143 *Re Stable* above; *In the Goods of Spicer* [1949] P. 441.

144 *In the Estate of Beech* [1923] P. 46: see also *In the Estate of MacGillivray* [1946] 2 All E.R. 301 and *In the Estate of Donner* (1917) 34 T.L.R. 138 (deceased stated he was content not to make a will owing to his (incorrect) belief that all his estate would pass to his mother on intestacy).

145 *In the Estate of Knibbs* [1962] 1 W.L.R. 852.

An informal will made when the testator was privileged remains valid until revoked, notwithstanding that the testator ceases to be privileged.[146]

(b) *Infant*

4–36 A person under the age of 18 years can make a will whilst privileged,[147] and, if he does so, can subsequently revoke it whether or not he is still privileged and able to make a will.[148]

3. Should the privilege be retained?

4–37 It is easy to understand why it was thought reasonable to grant privileges to soldiers in the seventeenth century when "servicemen were likely to be engaged in long campaigns abroad and thus cut off from the facilities for making a will"[149] but it is not easy to justify the need for, or the scope of, the privilege as it exists more than three hundred years later. The Latey Committee on the Age of Majority, reporting in 1967, thought that the distinction between what was and was not "actual military service" had become "blurred to the point of extinction by long-range weapons and informal hostilities"[150] and it recommended that the privilege should be extended to all members of the armed forces of any age whether or not in actual military service. Nothing has been done about this recommendation. The Law Reform Committee noted in their Twenty-Second Report that the evidence submitted on the question of retention of the privilege was divided. They appeared to be swayed by the fact that the Ministry of Defence was strongly in favour of the retention of the privilege and so recommended that it should be retained in its present form.[151]

The arguments for retention do not appear to be strong. Serving members of the armed forces are *more*, rather than less, likely than

[146] *Re Booth* [1926] P. 118 (informal will made on actual military service in 1882 admitted to probate after testator's death in 1924). For revocation or alteration by a privileged testator see below, paras 7–34 and 7–51.

[147] Wills (Soldiers and Sailors) Act 1918 s.1 (as amended by Family Law Reform Act 1969 s.3(1)(b)) which overrode the decision in *Re Wernher* [1918] 1 Ch.339.

[148] Family Law Reform Act 1969 s.3(3); *semble* an infant who is no longer privileged cannot revoke by an informal instrument. The Wills (Soldiers and Sailors) Act 1918 enacted that an infant, whilst privileged, could make a will disposing not only of his personalty but also of his realty. But s.51(3) of the Administration of Estates Act 1925 then provided that where an infant, who died after 1925 without having been married, was at his death equitably entitled under a settlement to a fee simple estate in land, he was deemed to have had an entailed interest. This provision was amended by the Trusts of Land and Appointment of Trustees Act 1996, so that an infant who dies after 1996 without having been married and without issue is deemed to have had a life interest. The reason for the change in 1997 is that it is no longer possible to create new entails—the change is more one of form than of substance. The effect of the provision, both in its pre-1997 and in its post-1996 forms, is to make the land revert to the donor. For further discussion, see Megarry & Wade, *The Law of Real Property*, 8th edn (London: Sweet & Maxwell, 2012), paras 36–015—36–018.

[149] Law Reform Committee's 22nd Report, *The Making and Revocation of Wills* Cmnd.7902 (1980) at p.9.

[150] Report of the Committee on the Age of Majority (1967) Cmnd.3342, para.417.

[151] Law Reform Committee's 22nd Report, *The Making and Revocation of Wills* Cmnd.7902 (1980) p.9: cf. Davey [1980] Conv. 70–72; Cole [1982] Conv. 185; Critchley (1999) 58 C.L.J. 49.

average members of the public to be able to obtain legal advice and so be able to make valid formal wills. All the arguments in favour of the need for formalities—those which relate to providing reliable evidence of the testator's wishes, to hasty or ill-considered dispositions and to the protection of the testator—apply as strongly to members of the armed forces as they do to anyone else. The privilege is not directly linked to the imminence of death. It has been applied to some people who have never been at high risk; furthermore, a privileged will remains valid after the person who made it has ceased to be privileged.[152] It seems odd that someone who made a privileged will while he was a serving soldier, during the Second World War, in 1944, may die more than seventy years later and that such a privileged will may then be granted probate. Contrast this with the accident victim who is not a serviceman but who wants to make an informal will just before he dies. He is accorded no privilege. It is not easy to see why the soldier should be treated differently from the accident victim.

There have not been many reported cases during the last fifty years **4–38** which have involved privileged wills, but the recent case of *Re Servoz-Gavin*[153] provides a demonstration of the problems they can raise. Here, evidence was given that a ship's radio officer who had died in 2005 had, in 1985, and again in 1990, made privileged oral wills in favour of his aunt. The case involved a point of law, seemingly not discussed in any earlier case, as to whether the privilege of making an informal will extended to a sailor who was domiciled in England, but who served on ships which were not British registered. There was also a doubt as to whether the testator, who had been on shore leave, between voyages, when the wills were made, had been "at sea". Both these questions were decided in favour of the propounder of the wills and it is suggested that they should have been so decided. But the real problem in this case relates to the evidence called to prove the making of the oral wills. The wills were in favour of the testator's aunt, his mother's unmarried sister, but she, a 98-year-old at the time of the trial, gave evidence that she had herself made a will in favour of E, who was her great-niece, and it was E's mother who gave evidence establishing the authenticity of the 1990 will. In accepting this evidence, the court, in effect, granted probate of an oral will on the evidence of the mother of the ultimate beneficiary. The lenient treatment meted out by English law to those who attempt to obtain probate of "suspicious wills" is a topic discussed in the next chapter.[154] Those who are uneasy about the way in which persons are permitted to take part in the preparation of wills under which they will benefit may also evince a degree of anxiety when the evidence which supports an oral will comes from someone very closely linked with, or related to, a beneficiary.

[152] In Roman Law, a privileged will remained valid for a maximum of one year after discharge from military service. Buckland, *A Text-Book of Roman Law*, 3rd edn (Cambridge: Cambridge University Press, 1963), p.361.
[153] *Re Servoz-Gavin* [2011] Ch.162.
[154] See paras 5–40 et seq.

III. INCORPORATION OF DOCUMENTS

4–39 A testator may incorporate in his will a document which has not been duly executed by him and so make that document part of his will.

1. Requirements for incorporation

4–40 This doctrine of incorporation by reference applies if the following three requirements are satisfied. However, a document referred to in a will is not incorporated if the testator directs in his will that it is not to form part of the will.[155]

(a) *Document already in existence*

4–41 The document must already be in existence when the will is executed.[156] The onus of proving this lies on the person seeking to rely on the doctrine. If the document comes into existence after the will is executed, but before the execution of a codicil confirming the will, this first requirement is satisfied because the will is treated as having been re-executed at the date of execution of the codicil.[157]

(b) *Referred to in the will as already in existence*

4–42 The will must refer to the document as being already in existence when the will is executed. If the will refers to "a memorandum *already* written by me" this requirement is satisfied. On the other hand, a reference in a will to such articles "as may be described in a paper in my own handwriting,"[158] or to friends "to be named in a letter addressed to X,"[159] does not satisfy this requirement. If a will refers to an already existing document "or any substitution therefor or modification thereof," again this requirement is not satisfied and there is no incorporation even of the existing document.[160]

If the will is confirmed by a codicil and the document comes into existence between the execution of the will and the codicil, this second

[155] *Re Louis* (1916) 32 T.L.R. 313.

[156] *Singleton v Tomlinson* (1878) 3 App.Cas. 404. The rules relating to incorporation by reference have no direct link with the rules relating to secret trusts (see Chap.6), though some secret trusts cases appear to demonstrate a degree of confusion. The rule (if it is a rule) that a half secret trust must be communicated to the trustee before the execution of the will (see below para.6–24) *may* be a sub-conscious translation of the rule that incorporation by reference must be of a document which is already in existence.

[157] *In the Goods of Lady Truro* (1866) L.R. 1 P. & D. 201: for confirmation, or "republication", see below paras 7–65 et seq. and for revival, which has the same effect, see below, paras 7–56 et seq.

[158] *In the Goods of Sutherland* (1866) L.R. 1 P. & D. 198.

[159] *In the Goods of Reid* (1868) 38 L.J.P. & M. 1; *University College of North Wales v Taylor* [1908] P. 140.

[160] *Re Jones* [1942] Ch.328, but see p.331. If an existing settlement is incorporated in a will, a power to vary conferred on the testator by the settlement is invalid when incorporated, *Re Edwards' W.T.* [1948] Ch.440; *Re Schintz's W.T.* [1951] Ch.870.

requirement is satisfied only if the will refers to the document as being already in existence. In *In the Goods of Smart*[161] the testatrix by her will directed her trustees to give specified articles "to such of my friends as I *may* designate in a book or memorandum that will be found with this will." Three years later she made the memorandum and afterwards she executed a codicil to her will. The court held that the will (though speaking from the date of execution of the codicil) still referred to a future document and did not refer to the memorandum as being already in existence at the date of execution of the codicil, when the will must be treated as having been re-executed. If, instead, the will had read "as I *have* designated," this second requirement would have been satisfied.[162]

(c) *Identified in the will*

The document must be sufficiently described in the will to enable it to be identified.[163] If the description in the will is so vague as to be incapable of being applied to any document in particular, it does not suffice.[164] This third requirement applies even though both the will and the document are written on the same piece of paper: the document is not incorporated if the will contains no reference to it.[165] **4–43**

2. Effects of incorporation

(a) *Admissible to probate*

A document incorporated in a duly executed will is admissible to probate as part of the will.[166] The incorporated document is then open to inspection by the public. If a testator wishes to avoid this he can employ a secret trust.[167] **4–44**

(b) *Testamentary effect*

The incorporated document operates as part of the will and is subject to the ordinary rules—such as lapse[168] and ademption[169]—applicable to wills.[170] **4–45**

[161] *In the Goods of Smart* [1902] P. 238: see also *Durham v Northen* [1895] P. 66.
[162] *In the Goods of Lady Truro* (1866) L.R. 1 P. & D. 201.
[163] *In the Goods of Garnett* [1894] P. 90: *In the Estate of Mardon* [1944] P. 109.
[164] *Allen v Maddock* (1858) 11 Moo.P.C. 427, 454. It is submitted that *In the Estate of Saxton* [1939] 2 All E.R. 418 was wrongly decided (will, "I give and bequeath among the following persons": lists found with will held to be incorporated despite absence of any other means of identification in the will).
[165] *In the Goods of Tovey* (1878) 47 L.J.P. 63; *In the Estate of Bercovitz* [1962] 1 W.L.R. 321.
[166] In special circumstances the incorporated document (or an examined copy) will not be required to be filed in the registry, *In the Goods of Balme* [1897] P. 261 (lengthy library catalogue incorporated, but filing not required); *In the Goods of Sibthorp* (1866) L.R. 1 P. & D. 106 (third party in possession of incorporated document: filing not required).
[167] See Chap.6.
[168] See below, paras 14–11 et seq.
[169] See below, paras 14–35 et seq.
[170] *Bizzey v Flight* (1876) 3 Ch.269.

(c) *Incorporation of invalid will in duly executed codicil*

4–46 If the requirements for incorporation are satisfied, a testator may incorporate an invalidly executed will or codicil in a subsequent duly executed codicil.[171] For instance, in *In the Goods of Heathcote*[172] a testatrix made an invalid will and later duly executed a codicil describing itself as "a codicil to the last will and testament of me". On proof that she had made no other will, the court held that the invalid will was sufficiently described in the codicil to enable it to be identified and it could be admitted to probate as incorporated in the codicil. In *In the Goods of Almosnino*[173] a woman drew up a paper in her own handwriting, signed it and put it in an envelope which she sealed; on the envelope she wrote "I confirm the contents written in the inclosed document"; she then signed the envelope and her signature was witnessed in accordance with s.9 of the Wills Act. The court held that the paper was incorporated in the memorandum and both were admissible to probate.[174]

3. Statutory Will Forms 1925[175]

4–47 Section 179 of the Law of Property Act 1925 authorises the Lord Chancellor to publish these forms which a testator may incorporate in his will in any manner indicating an intention to do so. By incorporating one or more of these forms in his will a testator may reduce the length of his will. The forms are, however, seldom used in practice, owing to. the inconvenience of having to refer to the relevant forms in order to understand the will.

171 *Allen v Maddock* (1858) 11 Moo. P.C. 427.
172 *In the Goods of Heathcote* (1881) 6 P.D. 30.
173 *In the Goods of Almosnino* (1859) 29 L.J.P. 46.
174 See also *Re Nicholls* [1921] 2 Ch.11.
175 S.R. & O. 1925, No. 780; see Hallett's *Conveyancing Precedents* (London: Sweet & Maxwell, 1965), pp.994 et seq.

CHAPTER 5

THE MAKING OF WILLS: CAPACITY—THE MIND OF THE TESTATOR

I. INTRODUCTION

In the past, aliens, traitors, felons, and married women were all subject to special rules restricting their right to make wills. All of them are now able to make valid wills.[1] The only class of people now generally unable to make wills are minors. **5–01**

Until 1837, a minor could make a valid will of personal estate at fourteen if a boy, or at twelve if a girl. The Wills Act 1837 s.7, enacted that no will should be valid if made by a person under twenty-one—reduced to eighteen for wills made on or after 1 January 1970[2]—and s.11 of the Wills Act[3] qualifies s.7 by excepting wills made by minor soldiers in actual military service or by minor seamen at sea.

1. Testator must have testamentary intention—*animus testandi*

It is sometimes said that a testator must intend to make a will. Strictly this is inaccurate, though it is a convenient way of stating the basic requirement that a testator must have a testamentary intention (or *animus testandi*), i.e. must intend the wishes he expresses *to take effect only at his death*. If a person intends a duly executed[4] document to take effect only at his death, it can be admitted to probate as his will whether or not he intended to make, or was aware that he was making, a will.[5] Similarly, a privileged testator[6] must give deliberate expression to his wishes in the event of his death but he need not know that he is making a will.[7] **5–02**

[1] For the history of the position of married women and criminals—see *Theobald on Wills*, 13th edn (London: Sweet & Maxwell, 1971), paras 103–105. As to aliens, see *Theobald on Wills*, 14th edn (London: Sweet & Maxwell, 1982), p.29, fn.6.

[2] Family Law Reform Act 1969 s.3(1)(a).

[3] As explained and extended by the Wills (Soldiers and Sailors) Act 1918—and see above, Chap.4.

[4] For an explanation of "duly executed" see above, Chap.4.

[5] *Milnes v Foden* (1890) 15 P.D.105.

[6] Privileged testators are those who may make informal wills—see above, Chap.4.

[7] *Re Stable* [1919] P.7.

The Court of Appeal in *Corbett v Newey*[8] held that a testatrix who executed a will subject to a condition which was not expressed on the face of the will—that the will was not to take effect at the date of execution, but only when the conveyances of two forms had taken place—lacked the necessary *animus testandi* and the will was invalid.[9]

A case where *animus testandi* was not discussed, but where it should have been, was *Sherrington v Sherrington*.[10] The facts in that case, which also involved other issues, are set out later in this chapter[11] and the point will be dealt with there.

2. Capacity, undue influence and fraud

5–03 As well as testamentary intention, there are four other requirements for the making of a valid will:

(a) The testator must be mentally capable of making a will;
(b) He must not make it as a result of the undue influence of another person;
(c) He must not make it as a result of the fraud of another person;
(d) He must know and approve of the contents of his will.

II. THE TESTATOR'S UNDERSTANDING

A. TESTAMENTARY CAPACITY

1. The *Banks v Goodfellow* test of testamentary capacity[12]

5–04 The testator must be mentally capable of making a will. A classic statement of the test to be applied is contained in the judgment of Cockburn CJ in *Banks v Goodfellow*[13]:

> "It is essential that a testator shall understand the nature of the act and its effects; shall understand the extent of the property of which he is

[8] *Corbett v Newey* [1998] Ch.57.

[9] The Court of Appeal further held that it would be contrary to the Wills Act 1837 to allow extrinsic evidence of the testatrix's intentions to be used to write a condition into the will which was not there. See above, Chap.3, para.3–09. Quaere whether there is a problem reconciling the decision in *Corbett v Newey* with the doctrine of conditional revocation discussed below in Chap.7 at paras 7–39 et seq. The condition, in the case of conditional revocation, does *not* have to be expressed on the face of the will.

[10] *Sherrington v Sherrington* [2004] W.T.L.R. 895.

[11] At para.5–44.

[12] For capacity to make a gift inter vivos see *Re Beaney* [1978] 1 W.L.R. 770, and to consent to a marriage see *In the Estate of Park* [1954] P. 112, 120–122, 131–133 and 135–136.

[13] *Banks v Goodfellow* (1870) L.R. 5 Q.B. 549, 565. Testamentary capacity was established in *Re Parsons* [2002] W.T.L.R. 237 and *Hoff v Atherton* [2005] W.T.L.R. 99, but not in *Brown v Deacy* [2002] W.T.L.R. 781 or *Tchilingirian v Ouzounian* [2003] W.T.L.R. 709.

> disposing; shall be able to comprehend and appreciate the claims to which he ought to give effect; and, with a view to the latter object, that no disorder of the mind shall poison his affections, pervert his sense of right, or prevent the exercise of his natural faculties—that no insane delusion shall influence his will in disposing of his property and bring about a disposal of it which, if the mind had been sound, would not have been made."

This test has four elements. It requires that the testator should:

(i) understand the effect of his wishes being carried out at his death, although he need not understand their precise legal effect[14];
(ii) understand the extent of the property of which he is disposing, although he is not required to carry in his mind a detailed inventory of it[15];
(iii) recall those who have claims upon him and understand the nature of those claims; and
(iv) suffer from no disorder of the mind such as to poison his affections or pervert his sense of right, and no insane delusions which might influence his will or poison his mind.[16]

In *Wood v Smith*[17] the testator told someone—at the time he was making his will—that he had investments worth £17,000, whereas the actual value of his investments was in excess of £105,000. This showed that he was "seriously confused as to the extent of his assets",[18] and the trial judge decided that this was consistent with such confusion of mind as to indicate that the deceased lacked testamentary capacity.[19]

The testator must have "a memory to recall the several persons who may be fitting objects of the testator's bounty, and an understanding to comprehend their relationship to himself and their claims upon him."[20] In *Harwood v Baker*[21] a will executed by a testator on his death-bed, giving all his property to his wife, was held invalid because, owing to his illness,

[14] *Banks v Goodfellow*, (1870) L.R. 5 Q.B. 549 at p.567.

[15] *Waters v Waters* (1848) 2 De G. & Sm. 591,621 ("*generally* the state of his property and what it consists of"): see *Re Beaney* [1978] 1 W.L.R. 770, 773.

[16] It has been suggested that (iv) is simply a restatement of (iii), but this was not accepted in *Kostic v Chaplin* [2008] W.T.L.R. 655 where Henderson J referred to the Court of Appeal decision in *Sharp v Adam* [2006] W.T.L.R. 1059. See also *Re Loxston* [2006] W.T.L.R. 1567 at 1627, where Nicholas Strauss QC suggested that the testator must (1) be able to understand the nature of the act of making a will; (2) know which persons he should consider as possible beneficiaries; (3) be able to understand the extent of the property of which he is disposing; (4) not be subject to any disorder of the mind as shall "poison his affections, pervert his sense of right, or prevent the exercise of his natural faculties"; and (5) have the mental capacity to make decisions which take into account the relevant property, persons and circumstances and arrive at a "rational, fair and just" testament.

[17] *Wood v Smith* [1993] Ch.90.

[18] *Wood v Smith* [1993] Ch.90, 114.

[19] The Court of Appeal upheld the trial judge's decision that the onus of establishing testamentary capacity had not been discharged.

[20] per Sir James Hannen in *Boughton v Knight* (1873) L.R. 3 P. & D. 64, 65–66.

[21] *Harwood v Baker* (1840) 3 Moo.P.C. 282: see *Battan Singh v Amirchand* [1948] A.C. 161.

the testator was unable to comprehend and weigh the claims upon him of his relatives. It did not suffice that the testator knew that he was giving all his property to his wife and excluding all his relatives: he must also have been "capable of recollecting who those relatives were, of understanding their respective claims upon his regard and bounty, and of deliberately forming an intelligent purpose of excluding them from any share of his property."[22]

A will is not invalid merely because, in making it, the testator is moved by capricious, frivolous, mean or even bad motives. If he satisfies this test of testamentary capacity he "may disinherit his children, and leave his property to strangers to gratify his spite, or to charities to gratify his pride."[23]

The same test applies whether the testator has been mentally impaired from birth or has suffered impairment of the mind during his lifetime, whether through injury, physical or mental illness, senility or addiction.[24]

2. The Mental Capacity Act 2005

5–05 The Mental Capacity Act 2005[25] came into force on 1 October 2007.[26] It does not have retrospective effect, but there is some doubt as to whether the Act's provisions apply even in a case where a testator made his will after it took effect and such a will is subsequently challenged. Should the Act's provisions be taken into account in contentious probate proceedings where they relate to a will which was made after it came into force?[27] If in such a case, there is a distinction between the *Banks v Goodfellow* test and the tests applicable under the Act, which prevail? The distinctions between the tests are subtle, but in some cases they could be crucial. Under the 2005 Act, there is a presumption that a person has capacity, unless it is established that he lacks it.[28] This is not so at common law, where the initial onus is on the propounder of a will to prove capacity. Having said this, s.3(1) of the Act then seems to operate as a counterbalance by requiring a person to be able to understand all the information relevant to the making of a decision. And what may be more significant is that s.3(4) of the Act requires the testator to be able to understand, use or weigh information as to the reasonably foreseeable consequences of the choices open to him. This seems to go further than anything required by *Banks v Goodfellow*.

22 *Harwood v Baker* above, at p.290.
23 per Sir James Hannen in *Boughton v Knight* above, at p.66. The will is not invalid, but it may be open to someone to make a claim for family provision—see below, Chap.8.
24 See *Richards v Allan* [2001] W.T.L.R. 1033, (testatrix diabetic, taking drugs, and having possibly suffered stroke). This case is discussed below, at para.5–40. See also *Chana v Chana* [2001] W.T.L.R. 205.
25 The Act had its origins in the Law Commission's Report on *Mental Incapacity* (Law Com. No. 231, 1995). The draft legislation was further considered in a Report *Making Decisions* issued by the Department for Constitutional Affairs in October 1999 (Cm. 4465).
26 (S.I. 2007/1897).
27 See P. Reed, "Capacity and Want of Knowledge and Approval", in B. Häcker and C. Mitchell (eds), *Current Issues in Succession Law* (Oxford: Hart Publishing, 2016), Chap.7.
28 2005 Act s.1(2).

So, does the Act apply where a will has been made since it came into force? The question did not have to be answered in *Simon v Byford*[29] where the will was made in 2005, or in *Scammell v Farmer*[30] where the will had been made in 2003. In *Scammell*, the trial judge did discuss, obiter, whether the Act would have applied, if the will had been executed after it came into force and he thought that it would not, because it is not within the purposes of the Act to ascertain whether a particular testator had capacity to make a will, when such will is challenged after his death. In *Re Walker*[31] Nicholas Strauss QC,[32] in a carefully reasoned judgment, took the same view, holding that the Act did not apply to the retrospective assessment of capacity in contentious probate proceedings, it applied only to decisions taken by the Court of Protection on behalf of those who lacked capacity during their lifetimes.[33]

The judgment in *Walker* must be contrasted with the approach taken in two other first instance cases, *Fischer v Diffley*[34] and *Bray v Pearce*[35] in each of which it was held that the 2005 Act is the starting point for the modern approach to the assessment of capacity. The approach taken in *Walker* was based on careful reading of the 2005 Act and of the Code of Practice which accompanied it, but applying different tests when the Court of Protection has to decide during someone's lifetime whether he has capacity to make a will, and when the Court of Chancery has to decide after his death whether he had capacity to make one, does appear illogical. The conflicting decisions referred to above are all at first instance and, at some stage, this problem will have to be brought before the Court of Appeal.[36]

3. Effect of delusions

A delusion in the mind of a testator deprives him of testamentary capacity if the delusion influences, or is capable of influencing, the provisions of his will.[37] A testator suffers from a delusion if he holds a belief on any subject **5–06**

[29] *Simon v Byford* [2014] W.T.L.R. 1097.

[30] *Scammell v Farmer* [2008] W.T.L.R. 1261.

[31] *Re Walker* [2015] W.T.L.R. 493.

[32] Sitting as a deputy judge of the High Court.

[33] The Court of Protection has jurisdiction over the property, financial affairs and personal welfare of persons who lack the mental capacity to make decisions for themselves. Section 45 of the Mental Capacity Act 2005 established it as a superior court of record. Before that section came into force in 2007, it was an office of the Supreme Court and had originally been known as the Office of the Commissioners in Lunacy, then as the Office of the Master in Lunacy. In 1947, it became known as the Court of Protection. For an account of its history, see *Re L (WJG)* [1966] Ch.135 and see also *Re B (a patient)* [2006] 1 W.L.R. 278, 281. The jurisdiction of the Court of Protection in relation to the making of statutory wills is discussed below in paras 5–10—5–14.

[34] *Fischer v Diffley* [2014] W.T.L.R. 757.

[35] Unreported case dated 6 March 2013, Mr Murray Rosen QC sitting as a deputy judge of the High Court.

[36] In July 2014, the Law Commission published their Twelfth Programme of Law Reform. One of their projects was to review the law of wills and it was announced that they would focus "on four key areas that have been identified as potentially needing reform". One of these four was capacity. The project has now been postponed.

[37] *Dew v Clark* (1826) 3 Add. 79, 5 Russ. 163 (father's insane aversion to only daughter); *Battan Singh v Amirchand* [1948] A.C. 161 (*delusion T had no relatives*); *Re Bellis* (1929) 141 L.T. 245 (*delusion T had already benefited one daughter far more than the other*).

which no rational person could hold, and which cannot be permanently eradicated from his mind by reasoning with him.[38] In *Boughton v Knight*, Sir James Hannen told a jury to put to themselves

> "this question, and answer it; can I understand how any man in possession of his senses could have believed such and such a thing? And if the answer you give is, I cannot understand it, then it is of the necessity of the case that you should say the man is not sane."[39]

In practice, it may be difficult to distinguish between grave misjudgement and delusion, particularly in relation to a testator's assessment of the character of a possible beneficiary under his will.[40] Certainly a parent is not incapacitated from making a will because he has formed an unduly harsh view of his child's character. But if the parent's misjudgment really stems from an irrational aversion towards his child, amounting to a delusion, then the parent lacks testamentary capacity.[41] In *Re Ritchie* [42] a woman's will in favour of charity was prepared for her by a solicitor and its execution was witnessed by a doctor, but her children succeeded in having it set aside on the ground that she suffered from paranoia and had delusions. The case contains a useful discussion[43] of the rules to be applied when a parent disinherits a child.

A delusion in the mind of a testator does not deprive him of testamentary capacity if it cannot have had any influence upon him in making his will. In *Banks v Goodfellow*[44] the testator suffered from the delusion that he was pursued and molested by a certain man, who was already dead and who was in no way connected with the testator, and by devils or evil spirits whom the testator believed to be visibly present. Nevertheless the court held that the testator had testamentary capacity because the delusions were not capable of having had any influence on the provisions of his will.

4. Time for satisfying the test

5–07 The testator must have testamentary capacity at the time when he executes the will. Alternatively, it suffices if the testator has testamentary capacity at the time when he gives instructions for the preparation of the will provided (i) the will is prepared in accordance with his instructions; and (ii) at the time of execution he is capable of understanding, and does understand, that he is executing a will for which he has given instructions. This alternative

[38] *Dew v Clark* (1826) 3 Add. 79, 90.
[39] *Boughton v Knight* (1873) L.R. 3 P. & D. 64, 68.
[40] *Sharp v Adam* [2006] W.T.L.R. 1059 (stud farm owner suffering from M.S. disinherited both daughters and left farm to employees, held irrational, will refused probate). Contrast this case with *Blackman v Man* [2008] W.T.L.R (will prepared by bank for woman who suffered from mild dementia, estate left to Chinese couple with whom testatrix was friendly, nephews and nieces disinherited, will upheld).
[41] *Dew v Clark* above; *Boughton v Knight*, (1873) L.R. 3 P. & D.64; *Kostic v Chaplin* [2007] EWHC 2298 (Ch).
[42] *Re Ritchie, Ritchie v Nat Osteoporosis Soc* [2009] EWHC 709 (Ch).
[43] *Re Ritchie, Ritchie v Nat Osteoporosis Soc* [2009] EWHC 709 (Ch) at paras 165–170.
[44] *Banks v Goodfellow* (1870) L.R. 5 Q.B. 549.

is useful in cases where a testator's capacity deteriorates after giving instructions. This happened to the testatrix in *Parker v Felgate*[45] but her will was upheld because, on being roused from a partial coma at the time of execution, she was capable of understanding, and did understand, that she was executing a will for which she had given instructions. It was immaterial that, at the time of execution, she was incapable of remembering her instructions, or even of understanding each clause of the will if it had been put to her.

In *Parker v Felgate* the testatrix had given her instructions directly to her solicitor. In *Battan Singh v Amirchand*[46] the Privy Council said that the principle enunciated in *Parker v Felgate* should be applied with the greatest caution where the testator gives instructions to a lay intermediary who repeats them to the solicitor:

> "The opportunities for error in transmission and of misunderstanding and of deception in such a situation are obvious, and the court ought to be strictly satisfied that there is no ground for suspicion, and that the instructions given to the intermediary were unambiguous and clearly understood, faithfully reported by him and rightly apprehended by the solicitor."[47]

The warning given in *Amirchand* seems not to have been heeded in the **5–08** recent case of *Re Perrins*[48] where not only did the beneficiary act as a go-between between the testator and the solicitors who prepared the will, but, there was also a delay of more than a year between the giving of instructions and the execution (in *Parker v Felgate* itself the delay had been two weeks). Surprisingly, given these facts, Lewison J applied the rule in *Parker v Felgate* and granted probate, and his decision was upheld by the Court of Appeal[49] which then refused leave for a further appeal to the Supreme Court. It is suggested that there were "grounds for suspicion" in this case[50] and that, although the rule in *Parker v Felgate* should be retained, it should be applied only in the most exceptional circumstances—not on facts such as these.[51]

5. Consequences of incapacity

A will or codicil is wholly invalid if executed at a time when the testator **5–09** lacked testamentary capacity, but there may be a limited exception to this

[45] *Parker v Felgate* (1883) 8 P.D. 171: see also *Perera v Perera* [1901] A.C. 354, 361–362 , *Clancy v Clancy* [2003] W.T.L.R. 1097 and *Otuka v Alozie* [2005] All E.R (D) 265.

[46] *Batton Singh v Amirchand* [1948] A.C. 161.

[47] ibid at p.169.

[48] *Re Perrins, Perrins v Holland* [2011] Ch 270.

[49] *Re Perrins, Perrins v Holland* [2011] Ch 270.

[50] For a discussion of "suspicious wills" see Pt V of this chapter, paras 5–32 et seq.

[51] There was particular sympathy for the beneficiary under the will in *Parker v Felgate*, it was The Great Ormond St Hospital for Sick Children. And, had the will failed, the property would have passed to the creditors of the testatrix's father and brother, who had both been adjudicated bankrupt. The reason for not allowing a further appeal in *Perrins* may have been that the costs were getting out of hand. See also P. Reed, "Capacity and Want of Knowledge and Approval", Chap.7 in B. Häcker and C. Mitchell (eds), *Current Issues in Succession Law* (Oxford: Hart Publishing, 2016)

rule where only part of a will is affected by a delusion. In *In the Estate of Bohrmann*,[52] a testator made a will which included gifts to English charities. He later developed an insane delusion to the effect that the London County Council was persecuting him. He then executed a codicil to his will, one clause of which substituted United States charities for the equivalent English charities. Langton J decided that the relevant clause in the codicil was affected by the delusion and he upheld the validity of the original will and the codicil *with the exception of the clause in the codicil which substituted the US charities for the English charities*. This appears to be the only reported case in which a court has treated a testator as having testamentary capacity to make part, but not the whole, of a will or codicil. In taking this approach, Langton J relied by way of analogy on the court's practice of deleting from testamentary instruments anything not brought to the knowledge and approval of the testator.[53] The scope of this exception to the general rule remains unsettled but it is probably narrow. In fact there are doubts about both the exception itself and the analogy.[54]

B. STATUTORY WILLS

5–10 Since 1970[55] it has been possible for the Court of Protection[56] to order the execution of a will for an adult patient whom the Court has reason to believe is incapable of making a valid will for himself. This power is now contained in s.18 of the Mental Capacity Act 2005.[57] Such wills are commonly referred to as "statutory" wills[58] and may make any provision which the person lacking capacity could have made if he had not been suffering from "an impairment of, or a disturbance in the functioning of, the mind or brain".[59]

1. Formalities for a statutory will

5–11 A statutory will must be executed with the formalities specified in para.3 of Sch.2 to the Mental Capacity Act 2005, which requires a statutory will to:

(a) state that it is signed by P (the person lacking capacity) acting by the person authorised by the court (such person will usually be P's deputy)[60];

[52] *In the Estate of Bohrmann* [1938] 1 All E.R. 271.
[53] See below, paras 5–28 et seq.
[54] See C. A. Wright (1938) 16 Can.Bar Rev. 405, 410–411; R. F. Cross (1950) 24 A.L.J. 12.
[55] Before the 2005 Act came into force, the provisions covering "statutory wills" were contained in the Mental Health Act 1983. Statutory wills were originally introduced by the Administration of Justice Act 1969 s.17.
[56] For the history, and an explanation, of the Court of Protection see fn.33.
[57] This section is supplemented by Sch.2.
[58] C.H. Sherrin in (1983) 13 Fam. Law 135 suggests that it would be better to call them "judicial" wills, but the term "statutory" wills is now in general use.
[59] Mental Capacity Act 2005 s.2.
[60] P's deputy is the person appointed under s.16 of the Mental Capacity Act 2005. Deputies

(b) be signed by the authorised person with P's name and with his own name, in the presence of two or more witnesses present at the same time;
(c) be attested and subscribed by those witnesses in the presence of the authorised person[61]; and
(d) sealed with the official seal[62] of the court.

2. Contents of a statutory will

Before the 2005 Act came into force, the Court would, broadly speaking, attempt to make for the patient the will it supposed he would, had he not been incapable, have made for himself. This was the "substituted judgment" approach. In *Re D(J)*[63] Megarry VC said that there were various factors to be considered. The Court had to assume that the patient was having a brief lucid interval during which he had a full knowledge of the past and a realisation that he would relapse into incapacity as soon as the will was executed.[64] Under the 2005 Act, the emphasis is no longer on what the patient might be expected to have done, but it on what is in his best interests—the "balance sheet" approach, a structured decision making process. In *Re P*[65] Lewison J said that the person drafting the statutory will now had to take into account "all relevant circumstances", forming a value judgement giving effect to the patient's best interests, and that it was relevant to these interests how the patient would be remembered after his death. *Re P* appears, for the moment, to be the leading authority on the approach to be taken under the 2005 Act, but what is missing from the report of the case is a clear indication as to how the statutory will here would have differed from one which had been drafted on the basis of the old rules—the details of the will as drafted in *Re P* are not reported. The overall impression is that the "best interests" approach probably leads to a greater degree of generosity to charities than the "substituted judgment" approach would have done, but this is not certain.[66] **5–12**

were formerly known as receivers. The deputy may be empowered to take decisions concerning P's personal welfare and/or his property and affairs.

[61] The formalities for statutory wills may be compared and contrasted with the formalities applicable under s.9 of the Wills Act; see Chap.4, paras 4–03 et seq.

[62] The sealing of a statutory will is *evidential*, a purely ministerial act, the draft will having been approved by the Court of Protection before the will is signed. It is, therefore, possible for the sealing to take place after death, *Re Hughes*, *The Times*, 8 January 1999.

[63] *Re D(J)* [1982] Ch.237.

[64] An illustration of the operation of the "substituted judgment" approach is *Re C* [1991] 3 All E.R. 866.

[65] *Re P* [2010] Ch 33.

[66] In *Re JC, D v JC* [2012] W.T.L.R. 1211 Denzil Lush (the Senior Judge of the Court of Protection) expressed reservations about the new approach, and implied that it might sometimes be harder to apply than the old one. On the particular facts of the case, there were problems because the patient was someone who had never, in his whole life, done "the right thing"; and so working out what was in his "best interests" was almost impossible.

3. Using statutory wills to protect vulnerable testators from those who have attempted to take advantage of them

5–13 An unusual case, illustrating the use to which the statutory will procedure can be put, is *Re Davey*.[67] This case pre-dates the 2005 Act, but the changes effected by the Act are not relevant to it. At the age of ninety-two, O, an unmarried woman, went to live in a nursing home and shortly afterwards, in September 1979, she made an apparently rational will leaving her property to various members of her family. During the course of October and November she was examined by two consultant psychiatrists who thought that she was suffering from mental deterioration and that she was, by then, incapable of managing her affairs. There was a brief delay while her family and her solicitors discussed who should be appointed her receiver, to look after her affairs.[68] Papers were filed with the Court of Protection in support of an application for the appointment of a receiver but no receiver had been appointed when, on 17 December the Court of Protection received a letter informing the Court that, unbeknown to O's family or solicitors, O had, at the end of October, gone through a Register Office ceremony of marriage with D, a male nurse from the nursing home where she lived. As her marriage would revoke any previous will,[69] this meant that if O were now to die she would die intestate and a substantial part of her estate would pass to the man to whom she had been married for less than two months.[70] On 18 December, the Court made an order appointing the Official Solicitor as O's receiver and on 20 December, the newly appointed receiver applied to the deputy master of the Court of Protection for the execution of a statutory will. No notice of this application was given to D or to any member of O's family. The statutory will which the receiver applied for was in the same terms as the September will. The deputy master ordered the execution of the will and execution took place on 21 December. O died six days later. D appealed against the order and sought to have the will set aside. Fox J dismissed his appeal. The course taken by the deputy master had given the best prospect of a just result because, had O lived longer, D could have applied for a further statutory will, and now that she had not survived, D could make an application under the family provision legislation.[71]

5–14 *Re Davey* was a case where the statutory will procedure was used to protect O from those who were minded to take advantage of her, and there

[67] *Re Davey* [1981] 1 W.L.R. 164. See also *Re F* [2004] W.T.L.R. 657.

[68] Receivers are now known as deputies, see above, fn.60.

[69] See below, Chap.7.

[70] For the applicable intestacy rules, see above, Chap.2. Her marriage may have been voidable, but once she was dead it would be too late to obtain a decree of annulment; see above paras 2–77 et seq. and below, para.7–04. The fact that it has, since 1971, been too late to obtain a decree of nullity after the death of someone who lacked capacity at the time of his marriage is, of course, a serious fault in the system and one which should have been put right some time ago.

[71] See below, Chap.8. There is a link between the cases of *Re Davey* and *Re Stott*, see below para.5–37, fn.156. O was a resident (or should one say "victim") in the same nursing home as Lady Stott.

have been two other such cases. In *Re M*[72] Munby J ordered the making of a statutory will for a childless widow, the effect of which was to revoke a "suspicious will",[73] and to reinstate an earlier will which benefitted a friend of the testatrix and a number of charities. *Re D*[74] was essentially similar in that the effect of the statutory will was to revoke a home-made "suspicious will" which benefitted two of the testatrix's children at the expense of the third. In neither of these two cases should the "suspicious wills" have been made in the first place, but revoking them in this way was almost certainly simpler and cheaper than waiting until the testatrices had died, and then challenging the "suspicious wills" in contentious probate proceedings,

III. UNDUE INFLUENCE, FRAUD AND FORGERY

A will must not be made as a result of either the undue influence or the fraud of another person. **5–15**

1. Undue influence

In a court of probate undue influence means coercion, i.e. the testator is coerced into making a will (or part of a will) which he does not want to make. Undue influence may take many forms. **5–16**

> "Persuasion, appeals to the affections or ties of kindred, to a sentiment of gratitude for past services, or pity for future destitution, or the like, —these are all legitimate, and may be fairly pressed on a testator. On the other hand, pressure of whatever character, whether acting on the fears or the hopes, if so exerted as to overpower the volition without convincing the judgment, is a species of restraint under which no valid will can be made. In a word, a testator may be led but not driven; and his will must be the offspring of his own volition, and not the record of someone else's."[75]

The problem with undue influence is to decide what degree of influence is *undue*? When does persuasion become coercion? Sir J P Wilde said in *Hall v Hall* that a testator might be "led but not driven"[76] but this is not particularly helpful. The nineteenth-century cases as a whole seem to show that considerable pressure must be exerted before there is any chance of a finding of undue influence.[77]

[72] *Re M (Statutory Will)* [2011] 1 W.L.R. 344.
[73] A "suspicious will" is one in the making of which a beneficiary has played a part. It will be suggested below that it is too easy, in England, for beneficiaries to obtain probate of such wills. See below paras 5–32 et seq.
[74] *Re D (Statutory Will)* [2012] Ch.57.
[75] per Sir J.P. Wild (later Lord Penzance) in *Hall v Hall*, (1868) L.R. 1 P. & D. 481, 482.
[76] *Hall v Hall* (1868) L.R. 1 P. & D. 481, 482.
[77] In *Hall v Hall* itself the testator's will was pronounced against on the basis that he had

An immoral influence exercised over the testator by another person does not constitute undue influence in the absence of coercion. To quote Sir James Hannen in his charge to the jury in *Wingrove v Wingrove*,[78]

> "[A] young man may be caught in the toils of a harlot, who makes use of her influence to induce him to make a will in her favour, to the exclusion of his relatives. . .; yet the law does not attempt to guard against those contingencies. . .It is only when. . .a testator is coerced into doing that which he or she does not desire to do, that it is undue influence."[79]

2. Fraud

5–17 Some cases state, or imply, that undue influence and fraud are the same thing.[80] This is incorrect. Undue influence consists of coercing the testator. Fraud, by contrast, consists of deceiving him.[81] For example, it would be fraud to tell a testator that a potential beneficiary had done something or had said something of which the testator would disapprove, when he had not. Undue influence and fraud were correctly distinguished by Sir Cresswell Cresswell[82] in *White v White & Cato*[83] and by Butt J in *Riding v Hawkins*.[84]

3. Forgery

5–18 It is sometimes alleged that a testator's signature to his will has been forged.[85] If the testator's signature to a purported will has been forged, then the will has not been executed, and it could also be suggested that

been subjected to violence, threats and intimidation by his wife. The case is unusual. See also *Baker v Batt* (1838) 2 Moo. P.C. 317; *Barry v Butlin* (1838) 2 Moo. P.C. 480; *Boyse v Rossborough* (1857) 6 H.L.C. 2. Recent wills cases where there have been findings of undue influence are *Killick v Pountney* [2000] W.T.L.R. 41, *Re Edwards* [2007] W.T.L.R. 1387, *Schrader v Schrader* [2013] W.T.L.R. 701 and *Schomberg v Taylor* [2013] W.T.L.R. 1413.

[78] *Wingrove v Wingrove* (1885) 11 P.D. 81, 82.

[79] It is interesting to contrast this passage with Chadwick LJ's misunderstanding of Lord Hatherley's reference to "the righteousness of the transaction" in *Fulton v Andrew* (see below, para.5–43). Some Victorian judges were judgmental in a way not encountered today, but they did *not* permit their moral code to interfere with their decisions in the way implied in *Fuller v Strum* (see again, para.5–43).

[80] See *Barry v Butlin* (1838) 2 Moo. P.C. 480; *Boyse v Rossborough* (1857) 6 H.L.C. 2; *Lowe v Guthrie* [1909] A.C. 278.

[81] *Killick v Pountney* [2000] W.T.L.R. 41 and *Re Edwards* [2007] W.T.L.R. 1387 are both recent cases where the wills were set aside on the ground of undue influence, but the judgments appear to confuse undue influence with fraud. In fact, it is probable that in each of the two cases, there was *both* undue influence *and* fraud. The deceased were coerced *and* deceived. The two grounds are separate, but it will be suggested below that, in the case of a "suspicious will" the onus should be on the propounder to demonstrate that neither is involved. See below paras 5–58 et seq.

[82] The first Judge Ordinary of the Court of Probate (which had been established in 1858).

[83] *White v White & Cato* (1862) 2 Sw. & Tr. 504.

[84] *Riding v Hawkins* (1889) 14 P.D. 56.

[85] In theory, it might be alleged that a whole will has been forged, but the allegation almost always concerns the testator's *signature* to a typed document or to a paper written out in someone else's handwriting.

this is a form of fraud[86]; but forgery should be specifically pleaded. There was doubt, until recently, as to the standard of proof when forgery was alleged: was it something akin to the criminal standard of "beyond all reasonable doubt" or was it the civil standard of "on a balance of probabilities"? It was held in *Vaccianna v Herod*[87] that the standard is the civil standard—though the more serious the allegation, the more convincing the proof required. The will in *Vaccianna* was set aside for forgery, as were the wills in *Supple v Pender*[88]; *Treasury Solicitor v Doveton*[89]; *Lim v Thompson*[90]; *Gudavadze v Kay*[91]; and *Haider v Syed*.[92] Allegations of forgery in *Re Rowinska* and in *Fuller v Strum* were dismissed.[93]

Randall v Randall[94] may well have been a case of forgery, but no challenge lay because the person who wished to challenge the will was held to have had no "interest" in the estate. This case is referred to in Chapter 18.[95]

IV. POWER OF COURT TO ALTER WORDS IN A WILL

There are three limited powers to alter the words in a will: **5–19**

(a) A court of probate can *omit* from the will words of which the testator did not know and approve.
(b) A court of equity can order *rectification* of the will, if the testator dies on or after 1 January 1983.
(c) A court of construction can *construe* the will as if certain words had been inserted, omitted or changed, if it is clear from the will itself both that an error has been made in the wording and what the substance of the intended wording was.

[86] See Williams Mortimer and Sunnucks, *Executors, Administrators and Probate*, 20th edn (London: Sweet & Maxwell, 2013), para.13–65. It is not fraud in the usual sense in which the term occurs in probate. Probate fraud is fraud on the testator, this, if it is fraud, is on potential beneficiaries.

[87] *Vaccianna v Herod* [2006] W.T.L.R. 367, Blackburne J.

[88] *Supple v Pender* [2007] W.T.L.R. 1461.

[89] *Treasury Solicitor v Doveton* [2008] EWHC 2812.

[90] *Lim v Thompson* [2010] W.T.L.R. 661.

[91] *Gudavadze v Kay* [2012] W.T.L.R. 1753.

[92] *Haider v Syed* [2014] W.T.L.R. 387.

[93] *Re Rowinska* is discussed below in para.5–40 and *Fuller v Strum* is discussed in para.5–43. *Vaccianna v Herod* and *Supple v Pender* seem to be the first cases for a generation in which allegations of forgery have been upheld. This all ties in with the reluctance of judges in probate cases to come to decisions which imply misbehaviour by anyone, see below paras 5–40 et seq. It would not have been difficult for the judges at first instance in *Strum* and *Rowinska* to have found forgery, but each found against the will on another ground. In *Strum*, an appeal by the propounder of the will was then allowed and he obtained probate, see below para.5–43. The fact that there have been more cases recently in which there have been findings of forgery is to be welcomed, but there have also been cases such as *Smith v Springford* [2009] W.T.L.R. 705 and *Watts v Watts* [2014] EWHC 668 where the judges seem to have been reluctant to state, straightforwardly, that there has been forgery. In the latter case, there was a finding that the testatrix's signature had been "inserted by the beneficiary", but it was not said that it was "forged".

[94] *Randall v Randall* [2015] W.T.L.R. 99.

[95] See para.18–11, fn.31.

A. OMISSION OF WORDS FROM PROBATE

5–20 If a testator died before 1983, the court had no power, when admitting the will to probate, to *add* to it words intended by the testator.[96] In this respect the court was "enslaved" by the formalities required for a will by the Wills Act 1837.[97] A probate court had power only to *omit* from the will words of which the testator did not know and approve, leaving a blank space in the probate copy. This will be discussed further in paras 5–29—5–31 below.

B. RECTIFICATION

5–21 If the testator dies on or after 1 January 1983, and if a problem with the wording of his will arises as a result of a clerical error, or of a failure by the draftsman to understand his instructions, s.20 of the Administration of Justice Act 1982 empowers the court to order that the will shall be rectified so as to carry out his intentions.[98] Rectification is discussed in Chapter 10.[99]

C. SUPPLYING, OMITTING OR CHANGING WORDS BY CONSTRUCTION

5–22 It has traditionally been held that a court of construction[100] can *construe* the will as if certain words had been inserted, omitted or changed, if it is clear from reading the will as a whole *both* that an error has been made in the wording *and* what the substance of the intended wording should have been. The court of construction exercises great caution over reading words into a will and has done so very rarely. It seems probable that, now that it is possible to obtain rectification under s.20 of the Administration of Justice Act, and now that the rules which apply to the interpretation of the words which are in the will have been modified by s.21 of the same Act,[101] the occasions when the court will insert words into a will by construction will be very few and far between.[102]

[96] *Harter v Harter* (1873) 3 P. & D. 11, 19; *Morrell v Morrell* (1882) 7 P.D. 68; *In the Goods of Schott* (1901) P.

[97] *Re Reynette-James* [1976] 1 W.L.R. 161.

[98] Administration of Justice Act 1982 ss.73(6) and 76(11); see N.C.Prob. Rules 1987, r.55; C.P.R. 1998, Pt 57.12. In the High Court, rectification is assigned to the Chancery Division, Senior Courts Act 1981 s.61(1) and Sch.I.

[99] See paras 10–04 et seq.

[100] As contrasted with a court of probate.

[101] See below, Chap.10 paras 10–04 et seq.

[102] An example of the exercise of this power is *Re Whitrick* [1957] 1 W.L.R. 884. Were the facts of this case to recur nowadays it may well be that the will would *either* be rectified *or* an intentionalist construction would make it unnecessary to resort to this power—see Chap.10 for the construction of wills.

V. LACK OF KNOWLEDGE AND APPROVAL CASES OF MISTAKE

1. Two types of cases where lack of knowledge and approval may be raised or alleged

Cases where it is alleged that the testator lacked knowledge and approval of the contents of his will tend to fall into two broad groups, although there is some overlap between them. On the one hand, there are cases where the alleged lack of knowledge and approval results from inadvertence or mistake, without there being any suggestion that the testator lacked mental capacity, or that he was subject to undue influence or fraud. On the other, there are cases where the alleged lack of knowledge and approval is linked with problems about the testator's mental capacity and/or with allegations of undue influence or fraud. **5–23**

2. Knowledge and approval

A testator must know and approve of the contents of his will. If he says to another person, "I will execute any will you draw up for me," and a will is drawn up and the testator executes it in ignorance of its contents, the will is invalid.[103] A valid will must be the result of a testator's own intelligence and volition, although the contents of the will need not originate from the testator provided he understands and approves them.[104] **5–24**

3. Time of knowledge and approval

The normal rule is that the testator must know and approve of the contents of his will at the time when he executes it.[105] But in *In the Estate of Wallace*[106] Devlin J held valid a will which the testator executed on the day before his death, even though the testator did not know or approve its contents at the time of execution.[107] The will was held valid on the basis that the testator understood that he was executing a will which had been prepared in accordance with instructions which he had given earlier to his solicitor. This case follows the principle laid down in relation to testamentary capacity in *Parker v Felgate*.[108] **5–25**

[103] *Hastilow v Stobie* (1865) L.R. 1 P. & D. 64. And see L Smith, "What is Left of the Non-Delegation Principle?" Chap.9 in B. Häcker and C. Mitchell (eds), *Current Issues in Succession Law* (Oxford: Hart Publishing, 2016).
[104] *Constable v Tufnell* (1833) 4 Hagg.Ecc. 465, 477. A testator does not, of course, need to know or approve of the contents of a "statutory" will.
[105] *Hastilow v Stobie* (1865) L.R. 1 P. & D. 64; *Guardhouse v Blackburn* (1866) L.R. 1 P.D. 109, 116.
[106] *In the Estate of Wallace* [1952] 2 T.L.R. 925; see also *Re Flynn* [1982] 1 W.L.R. 310, 319–320.
[107] Because, at the time of execution, the testator had not read the will or had it read to him.
[108] See above, para.5–07. But note that there are misgivings about cases where the principle in *Parker v Felgate* is extended, particularly if intermediaries are involved; see above, paras 5–07 and 5–08.

4. Presumption where testator is dumb, blind or illiterate

5–26 If the testator could not speak or read and write and if he gave instructions for his will by signs, the court requires evidence as to the signs used, establishing that the testator understood and approved of the contents of his will.[109] Similarly, the knowledge and approval of a blind or illiterate testator must be proved, e.g. by evidence that the will was read over to him before execution.[110] The same rule applies if the will was signed by some person on the testator's behalf.[111]

5. Inadvertence or mistake

5–27 A testator's lack of knowledge and approval of the whole, or part, of the contents of a will which he executes may be due to his inadvertence; or to a mistake on his part, or to a mistake on the part of the draftsman employed by him.

If a mistake results either from a clerical error, or from a failure to understand the testator's instructions, it has, if the testator died on or after 1 January 1983, been possible to cure it by means of rectification.[112] Rectification is discussed in Chapter 10.[113] In *Marley v Rawlings*[114] the Supreme Court took a liberal view as to what constituted a "clerical error". As a result, many cases where wills would previously have been refused probate on the ground that the testator lacked knowledge and approval, will no longer be refused it. Such wills will be rectified and then obtain probate.

6. Mistake as to the whole will

5–28 In *In the Goods of Hunt*[115] a woman, who resided with her sister, prepared two wills for their respective execution and by mistake she executed the will prepared for her sister. The court refused probate because the deceased did not know and approve of any part of the contents of the will

[109] *In the Goods of Geale* (1864) 3 Sw.& Tr.431 (testator deaf and dumb and illiterate: detailed evidence as to signs by which testator communicated); *In the Goods of Owston* (1862) 2 Sw. & Tr. 461 (testator deaf and dumb and illiterate); *In the Estate of Holtam* (1913) 108 L.T. 732 (testatrix unable to speak or write due to stroke); *Buckenham v Dickinson* [2000] W.T.L.R. 1083.

[110] *Fincham v Edwards* (1842) 3 Curt. 63, 4 Moo.P.C.198 (proof by other evidence than reading over suffices): see N.C.Prob.Rules 1987 r.13. The attestation clause for the witnesses in the will of a blind or illiterate testator should include a statement that the testator signed the will "after the same had first been read over to him in our presence and had appeared to be perfectly understood and approved by him in the presence of us both."

[111] See N.C.Prob. Rules 1987 r.13. The attestation clause in a will signed by some other person on behalf of the testator should include a statement similar to that appropriate to the will of a blind or illiterate testator.

[112] See Admin of Justice Act 1982 ss.20, 73(6) and 76.

[113] See paras 10–04 et seq.

[114] *Marley v Rawlings* [2015] A.C. 129, see paras 10–08 et seq.

[115] *In the Goods of Hunt* (1875) LR 3 P. & D. 250: see also *In the Estate of Meyer* [1908] P.353 (woman executed codicil meant for her sister: probate refused). The Commonwealth courts take a different view, see Hardingham, *The Law of Wills* (Law Book Company, 1977), p.64.

which she had executed—"if she had known of the contents she would not have signed it."[116]

This is an example of a case where, if the mistake were to occur since the decision in *Marley v Rawlings*,[117] it would almost certainly[118] be cured by rectification.

7. Mistake by testator as to part of will

5–29 If a testator died before 1983, the court had no power, when admitting the will to probate, to *add* to it words intended by the testator.[119] In this respect the court was "enslaved" by the formalities required for a will by the Wills Act 1837.[120] A probate court had power only to *omit* from the will words of which the testator did not know and approve, leaving a blank space in the probate copy.

No problem was caused by omitting words of which the testator did not know and approve, provided their omission did not alter the sense of the rest of the will.[121] Thus the court would order the omission of a "self-contained" part of the will, such as a revocation clause[122] or the residuary gift in a will.[123] The court also omitted the word "forty" from a bequest of "the forty shares in John Morrell & Co. Limited," so that all the testator's 400 shares passed under the bequest as he intended.[124] It was, however, held that, where the testator died before 1983, the court would not order the omission of words, of which the testator did not know and approve, if this would alter the sense of the rest of the will.[125]

If the testator has made a mistake as to the words in his will, this will usually be because he or someone else has made a clerical error or because someone has failed to understand his instructions. In any of these circumstances, if the testator has died since 1983, the will can be rectified. Where rectification is not possible, the pre-1983 rules still operate and the probate court still has the power to omit from the will words of which the testator did not know and approve, leaving a blank space in the probate copy.

8. Mistake by draftsman as to part of will

5–30 If a testator died before 1983 and if by a slip or a clerical error the draftsman had inserted in his will words contrary to the testator's instructions,

[116] *In the Goods of Hunt* (1875) LR 3 P. & D. 250, 252. But the error in this type of case may now be cured by rectification. See *Marley v Rawlings* [2015] A.C. 157 discussed below in paras 10–08 et seq.

[117] See fn.116, above.

[118] "almost certailnly", because it might be necessary to find out exactly how the mistake occurred.

[119] *Harter v Harter* (1873) 3 P. & D. 11, 19; *Morrell v Morrell* (1882) 7 P.D. 68; *In the Goods of Schott* (1901) P.

[120] *Re Reynette-James*, [1976] 1 W.L.R. 161.

[121] *Rhodes v Rhodes* (1882) 7 App.Cas. 192.

[122] *Re Phelan* [1972] Fam. 33. the revocation clause formed part of a printed will form.

[123] *In the Goods of Duane* (1862) 2 Sw. & Tr. 590.

[124] *Morrell v Morrell* (1882) 7 P.D. 68.

[125] *Re Horrocks* [1939] P. 198.

the testator would not have known and approved of those words unless the discrepancy came to his notice.[126] In such cases, the incorrectly inserted words could be omitted from the probate copy, leaving a blank space. Where, in this type of case, the testator has died since 1983, rectification will now be possible.

9. Mistake as to the words used, not as to their legal effect

5–31 Whoever makes the mistake, whether it is the testator or the draftsman employed by him, it must relate to the words used in the will and not to their legal effect. If the testator knows and approves of the words used in his will, it does not matter that he or his draftsman is mistaken as to their legal effect; the words must be admitted to probate.[127] In *Collins v Elstone*[128] the testatrix executed a will on a printed will form which a friend had obtained for her. The printed will form contained a clause which revoked all previous wills. The testatrix read this and asked her friend what it meant; she was assured (incorrectly) that the effect of the clause would not be to revoke a previous will she had made. It was held that, given that she had executed the will knowing that the clause was in it, she was bound by the clause even though she misunderstood its effect.

This type of error cannot be cured by omitting the words from the probate copy of the will, because the testator did know of them and approve them. Nor can the error be cured by rectification, because it is not a "clerical error" (it is a drafting error) and it does not result from a failure to understand the testator's instructions. It *might*, depending on the circumstances, be possible, where the testator has died since 1983, to cure mistakes of this kind by adopting a liberal approach to the construction (i.e. interpretation) of the relevant will. Construction is discussed in Chapter 10.

VI. SUSPICIOUS WILLS: WILLS MADE BY VULNERABLE TESTATORS

1. The problem

5–32 A will may be challenged on the ground that it was not duly executed,[129] or that the testator lacked *animus testandi*, or that he lacked capacity, or that he had been subjected to fraud or undue influence, or that he had

[126] *In the Goods of Oswald* (1874) L.R. 3 P. & D. 162 (revocation clause included *per incuriam* without instructions); *Morrell v Morrell* (1882) 7 P.D. 68 (T intended to give all his shares; counsel wrote "40" by mistake); *Smith v Thompson* (1931) 47 T.L.R. 603; *In the Goods of Walkeley* (1893) 69 L.T. 419 (error in house number in engrossing will from draft); *Re Morris* [1971] P. 62 (mistake in codicil as to numbering of clause in will); *In the Goods of Boehm* [1891] P. 247 (T intended to give legacies to Georgiana and Florence; counsel wrote Georgiana twice and omitted Florence).

[127] *In the Estate of Beech* [1923] P. 46, 53.

[128] *Collins v Elstone* [1893] P.1.

[129] See above, Chap.4.

not known and approved of its contents. But how—in practice—should someone set about attacking a suspicious will?

Suppose that an aged relative—from whom members of the family were expecting to inherit property—dies leaving a will which does not make the kind of provision which the family expected. Suppose, further, that the will was prepared by someone who benefits under it, or is related to someone who benefits. Section 9 of the Wills Act 1837[130] does not provide much protection in this kind of case: it does not require that a will be prepared by a solicitor, or that the witnesses are acquainted with the testator,[131] or that the witnesses are independent of the beneficiaries[132]; and there is nothing to prevent a beneficiary from being present when a will is executed. There is said to be a "golden rule" that when a solicitor is drawing up a will for an aged testator, or for a testator who has been seriously ill, the will should be witnessed or approved by a medical practitioner who ought to record his examination and his findings. The rule has been applied in at least five first instance cases during the last forty years to invalidate wills,[133] but these cases have all been reasonably extreme. *Wood v Smith*[134] is a good example of a case where a solicitor who originally interviewed the testator formed an incorrect impression of his mental state. The solicitor noted that the testator "could clearly remember what his assets were" whereas, unbeknown to the solicitor, the statement made by the testator to the solicitor indicated that the testator had no idea of the size of his estate.

2. The position in the nineteenth-century

During the course of the nineteenth-century, there was a considerable amount of litigation over what may broadly be called "suspicious wills". In most cases, those challenging the wills did so on the grounds that there had been undue influence or fraud. The challenges were not generally successful. It seems that no attack on a will on the ground of fraud has ever succeeded. Challenges on the ground of undue influence were occasionally successful, but the vast majority of such challenges failed too.[135] **5–33**

Shortly after the Court of Probate was established in 1857, there were enacted the Contentious Probate Rules 1862.[136] Rule 40a of these rules was designed to restrict the way in which suspicious wills could be challenged. Some fanciful pleas had been attempted in the early years of the

[130] See Chap.4.

[131] To verify his mental state.

[132] Beneficiaries cannot take if they themselves, or their spouses, have witnessed the will, Wills Act 1837 s.15, see below, Chap.14, but witnesses may be parents, children or friends of beneficiaries.

[133] See *Kenward v Adams, The Times*, 29 November 1975; *Re Simpson* (1977) 121 S.J. 224; *Buckenham v Dickinson* [2000] W.T.L.R. 1083; *Re Key* [2010] 1 W.L.R. 2020; *Walters v Smee* [2009] W.T.L.R. 521.

[134] *Wood v Smith* [1992] 3 All E.R. 556.

[135] See Vol.59 (2000) C.L.J. 310–334. There have been two recent cases where undue influence has been found, *Killick v Pountney* [2000] W.T.L.R. 41 and *Re Edwards* [2007] W.T.L.R. 1387, but such cases are unusual.

[136] They were amended in 1865.

nineteenth-century and Rule 40a was an attempt to introduce some order into an area of confusion.[137]

Rule 40a made it clear that there were only four pleas which might be entered if a party wished to question the testator's mental state and/or free will: (i) lack of capacity, (ii) undue influence,[138] (iii) fraud and (iv) lack of knowledge and approval. Furthermore r.40a made it clear that a plea of lack of knowledge and approval could not be used as a cloak for a plea of undue influence or fraud. If someone wanted to challenge a will on the ground that there had been undue influence or fraud, he had to do so openly.[139]

The combination of r.40a and the case law meant that it was particularly difficult to challenge a "suspicious will".

3. *Wintle v Nye*

5–34 Kitty Wells left a will which had been prepared for her by her solicitor, Nye, which had been witnessed by his clerks and which left most of her property to him. The case was not, on the face of it, particularly unusual. There had been many cases in the previous hundred years or so where solicitors had prepared wills under which they had benefited, and almost all of these wills had been upheld. The odd thing in *Wintle v Nye* was that a member of Miss Wells's family, Alfred Daniel Wintle, a retired cavalry colonel, was determined to challenge this will.[140] Colonel Wintle was advised by his lawyers to challenge the will on the ground that Miss Wells lacked knowledge and approval. The advice to challenge the will on this ground ran counter to r.40a.[141] In effect, Wintle's lawyers were using the plea of lack of knowledge and approval as a cloak for what was, in substance, a plea of fraud. Given that there was no suggestion that Miss Wells lacked capacity, and given that she had made a will in favour of her solicitor, Nye, any suggestion that she did not know that the will was in his favour must have amounted to an implied suggestion that he had misled her, i.e. that he had been fraudulent.

[137] The confusion began when, before 1858, judges in the Prerogative Court referred to "presumptions" and "suspicions" without making it clear what was presumed and/or what was suspected. See, e.g. *Ingram v Wyatt* (1828) 1 Hagg. Ecc. 384.

[138] Sometimes referred to as "duress" or "imposition", *Constable v Tufnell* (1833) 4 Hagg. Ecc. 465.

[139] The introduction of the plea of lack of knowledge and approval was problematic. Sir Cresswell Cresswell, the first Judge Ordinary of the Court of Probate, had, in *Middlehurst v Johnson* (1861) 30 LJ (P.M.A.) 14 and in *Cunliffe v Cross* (1863) 3 Sw. & Tr. 37 refused to allow it. Sir Cresswell was killed in an accident shortly after *Cunliffe* and Sir J.P. Wilde, who succeeded him, allowed the plea in *Hastilow v Stobie* (1865) L.R. 1 P. & D. 64. Almost immediately afterwards, he then drafted r.40a, in order to restrict the scope of the plea he had allowed. In subsequent cases it has been suggested that the plea of lack of knowledge and approval can be traced back to *Barry v Butlin* (1838) 1 Curt. Ecc. Rep. 614; 2 Moo.P.C. 480, but this is incorrect. It is true that there were references in the case to knowledge and approval but *not* to a *plea* of *lack* of knowledge and approval. No-one would have understood this better than Sir Cresswell Cresswell, who was counsel for the challenger in the case.

[140] This is a very slightly simplified version of the facts of the case. For further details see Vol.59 (2000) C.L.J. 310–334.

[141] Rule 40a of the 1862 Rules (as amended in 1865) was still in force.

Barnard J gave a direction to the jury[142] in the course of which he quoted a well–known passage from the judgment of Parke B. in *Barry v Butlin*,[143] who had said: **5–35**

"If a party writes or prepares a will, under which he takes a benefit, that is a circumstance that ought generally to excite the suspicion of the Court, and calls upon it to be vigilant and jealous in examining the evidence in support of the instrument, in favour of which it ought not to pronounce unless the suspicion is removed, and it is judicially satisfied that the paper propounded does express the true Will of the deceased."[144]

The jury decided in favour of Nye and Wintle appealed to the Court of Appeal. In order to succeed, Wintle had to show that Barnard J had misdirected the jury. The Court of Appeal, by a majority, found against him. On Wintle's further appeal to the House of Lords, their Lordships decided, unanimously, that there had been a misdirection. Viscount Simonds suggested that Barnard J had been correct to set out the position as it had been expressed by Parke B. in *Barry v Butlin*, but he then went on to say[145]:

"It is not the law that in no circumstances can a solicitor or other person who has prepared a will for a testator take a benefit under it. But that fact creates a suspicion that must be removed by the person propounding the will. In all cases the court must be vigilant and jealous. The degree of suspicion will vary with the circumstances of the case. It may be slight and easily dispelled.[146] It may, on the other hand, be so grave that it can hardly be removed. In the present case the circumstances were such as to impose on the respondent as heavy a burden as can well be imagined. Here was an elderly lady who might be called old, unversed in business, having no one upon whom to rely except the solicitor who had acted for her and her family; a will made by him under which he takes the bulk of her large estate; a will made, it is true, after a number of interviews extending over a considerable time, during which details of her property and of her proposed legacies and annuities were said to have been put before her, but in the end of a complexity which demanded for its comprehension no common understanding: on her part, a wish disclosed in January, 1937, to leave her residuary estate to charity which was by April superseded by a devise of it to him, and, on his part, an explanation of the change which was calculated as much to aggravate as to allay suspicion: the will retained by him and no copy of it given to her: no independent advice received by her, and, even according to his own account, little pressure exercised by him to persuade her to get it:

[142] This was—surprisingly—a jury trial.
[143] *Barry v Butlin* (1838) 2 Moo. P.C. 480.
[144] *Barry v Butlin* (1838) 2 Moo. P.C. 480, 482.
[145] *Re Berrey's W.T.* [1959] 1 W.L.R. 284, 291.
[146] Parke B in *Barry v Butlin* (1838) 2 Moo. P.C. 480 at 485, gave as an example the case of a man of acknowledged business competence with an estate of £100,000, leaving all his property to his family except £50 to his solicitor who prepared the will.

a codicil cutting out reversionary legacies to charities allegedly for the benefit of annuitants but in fact, as was reasonably foreseeable, for the benefit of the residuary beneficiary. All these facts and others that I do not pause to enumerate demanded a vigilant and jealous scrutiny by the judge in his summing-up and by the jury in the consideration of their verdict."

5–36 The problem with this is that there appears to be an inconsistency between the way in which the case had been pleaded and the complaint about the trial judge's summing up. The reference back to *Barry v Butlin* by Barnard J was inappropriate, because *Barry v Butlin* was not a case where the person challenging the will had alleged lack of knowledge and approval.[147] *Barry v Butlin* was a case in which a son had been disinherited by his father in favour of the father's solicitor, doctor and butler, and the son had challenged the will on various grounds including fraud and undue influence. The son had failed. But the reference to "suspicious circumstances" in *Barry v Butlin* was perfectly rational. Anyone looking at the facts of *Barry v Butlin*, and having read the pleadings in that case, had to be suspicious as to whether the beneficiaries under the will had been involved in improper conduct. The problem with *Wintle v Nye* is that no allegation of impropriety was made by Wintle against Nye. And so what would Barnard J have said to the jury if they had asked him what they were supposed to be suspicious of? Surely, the expression "suspicious circumstances" implies a suspicion of wrongdoing by someone, and it is inappropriate to raise "suspicious circumstances" unless the person challenging the will has alleged fraud, or undue influence, or both. Colonel Wintle, on the advice of his legal team, had not done this. It is true that he won the case,[148] but the manner of his victory is questionable.

4. The position after *Wintle v Nye*

5–37 Ten years after *Wintle v Nye* reached the House of Lords, Scarman J said, obiter, in *In the Estate of Fuld (dec'd)*[149]:

"Lord Penzance once said[150] of the issues of testamentary capacity, knowledge and approval, undue influence and fraud, that they very often merged into one another. That position has been made abundantly clear by the decision of the House of Lords in *Wintle v. Nye*. it may well be that positive charges of fraud and undue influence will not feature as largely in the pleadings of probate cases, now that *Wintle v. Nye* has

[147] See above, fn.139.

[148] Strictly speaking, he did not win. The verdict of the House of Lords was that the trial judge had misdirected the jury and that, therefore, there should be a retrial. But, at this stage, Nye surrendered. He surrendered, in part, because the popular press were portraying him as a villain.

[149] *In the Estate of Fuld (dec'd)* [1968] P. 675, 722. Scarman J had been Wintle's counsel and had drafted the pleadings in *Wintle v Nye*. See fn.151.

[150] Scarman J did not say where Lord Penzance had said this, and the writer has not been able to trace the passage.

been decided, as they have done in the past; clearly it would be preferable if they did not."[151]

Scarman J's approach was that it was "preferable" for those challenging wills to do so on the basis of lack of knowledge and approval. But if a will were challenged on this basis, so that a plea of undue influence or fraud was disguised as one of mistake, quite apart from the fact that this ran counter to the express provisions of r.40a, it was hard both for those challenging the will, and for those defending it, to know what they needed to prove and to disprove.

One direct result of *Wintle v Nye* was that the Law Society laid down new standards of professional conduct for solicitors who might take interests under wills which they had prepared.[152] The stringency of these standards was shown in *Re A Solicitor*[153] where the decision of the Disciplinary Committee of the Law Society in striking off the roll two solicitor–beneficiaries—who had failed to advise their clients to obtain independent advice before making wills in the solicitors' favour—was upheld.[154]

Although solicitors are no longer able to make wills in their own favour, there is nothing to prevent other persons from taking advantage of vulnerable testators. The burden of proving that a testator had capacity, and that he knew and approved of the contents of his will, lies on the person propounding the will,[155] but the burden of proving undue influence or

[151] Given that Scarman had been Wintle's counsel, had drafted the pleadings in *Wintle v Nye*, and had then lost the case, it might be thought disingenuous of him to have implied that this was the correct way of proceeding. Col Wintle did win in the House of Lords, but he had, by then, dispensed with his legal team. Wintle, when speaking on the radio (as a guest on "Desert Island Discs", in 1962) put it like this: "Then, having seen the mess that the people who were representing me made of the thing, I decided to chuck the whole lot out and to deal with the situation myself." That was Wintle's polite version for the radio, what he said about his legal team when he was not being recorded was unprintable.

[152] See now *Cordery on Legal Services* and *the Law Society's Wills and Inheritance Protocol.*

[153] *Re A Solicitor* [1975] 1 Q.B. 475. The Law Society now insists that a solicitor must renounce any significant benefit under a will unless the client *has taken* separate advice; it is not sufficient that the solicitor has advised the client to take separate advice.

[154] In fact, Nye was, himself, also struck off, on 7 April 1960, more than a year after he had lost the case in the House of Lords. Had he been struck off before Colonel Wintle began his crusade, everything would have looked different and the trial judge could not possibly have conducted the case as he did. It is hard for the Law Society to explain why Nye was struck off when he was (later, rather than sooner), and the editor of this book had great difficulty in establishing that the striking off had taken place at all. He was informed at one stage, by the Solicitors Regulation Authority, that they had no record and that they could think of no other organizations or individuals who might have one. In due course, and contrary to what the SRA had said, the assistant editor discovered that the Solicitors Disciplinary Tribunal did have a record. There seems to have been a desire, in some circles, to hush the whole thing up. The reality is that the Law Society changed the rules *after* Col Wintle had won his case in the Lords, and then pretended that the rules they were now introducing had always been in place.

[155] *Richards v Allan* [2001] W.T.L.R. 1031. In *Barry v Butlin*, it was said that the propounder must "satisfy the conscience of the Court, that the instrument so propounded is the last will of a free and capable testator." (1838) 2 Moo. P.C. 480, 482. See also *Cleare v Cleare* (1869) L.R. 1 P. & D. 655. On proof that the testator was of testamentary capacity and that he duly

fraud lies on the person challenging the will and the onus of proving misconduct is reasonably heavy. To make matters worse, someone who challenges a will on the ground that there has been fraud or undue influence, and who then loses the case, normally has to pay the costs.[156]

5. Transfer of contentious probate to the Chancery Division

5–38 In 1970, when the Probate Divorce and Admiralty Division of the High Court became the Family Division,[157] contentious probate was transferred to the Chancery Division. At that time, one writer wondered whether the transfer might make a difference to the approach taken.[158] He noted the reluctance of probate judges to presume misconduct and suggested that their Chancery colleagues might be more robust. There is no sign that this has happened.

6. Procedural changes

5–39 The procedural rules relating to contentious probate are now contained in Pt 57 of the Civil Procedure Rules 1998.[159] The rules require that any party who contends that the testator did not know of and approve the contents of his will at the time when he executed it must give particulars of the facts and matters relied on.[160] The rules similarly require any party who contends that the execution of the will was obtained by undue influence or fraud to set out the contention specifically and give particulars of the facts and matters relied on.[161] Although lack of knowledge and approval on the one hand and fraud and undue influence on the other are covered by separate paragraphs in the rules, it will now be easier than it was to raise issues of fraud and undue influence under the cover of a plea of lack of knowledge and approval. So it will be easier to justify the *Wintle v Nye* approach under the current rules than it was under their predecessors.

executed the will, a rebuttable presumption arises, in ordinary circumstances, that he knew and approved of its contents. The evidential burden of proof then shifts to the person opposing the will to rebut this presumption.

156 The court has discretion over the costs, but the normal rule is that the losing party pays—see below para.5–58. In *Re Stott* [1980] 1 All E.R. 259, Lady Stott had made a will in favour of the proprietress of the nursing home in which she was living: the challenge was based on lack of capacity and lack of knowledge and approval, even though the circumstances strongly suggested undue influence and/or fraud. The nursing home was the one in which the ninety two year old woman who married the male nurse in *Re Davey* had been living, see above, para.5–13, fn.71.

157 Under the Administration of Justice Act 1970.

158 P. V. Baker (1970) 86 L.Q.R. 447.

159 The procedural rules which had been introduced in the 1860s were slightly amended in the 1960s and became R.S.C. Order 76, r.9(3). When the Civil Procedure Rules 1998 were brought into force in April 1999, contentious probate proceedings were included in the list of specialist proceedings in r.49(2). There was also a practice direction. By Civil Procedure (Amendment No. 2) Rules 2001 (SI 2001/1388), Pt 57 was added, and this has been in force since 15 October 2001. Pt 57 is in five sections: I Probate Claims (i.e. Contentious Probate); II Rectification; III Substitution and Removal of PRs; IV Family Provision Claims; and V Presumption of Death Proceedings.

160 Pt 57.7(3).

161 Pt 57.7 (4)(c).

This is not a welcome development because it will become more difficult to tell what allegations are really being made.

7. Recent case law

If a will is challenged on the grounds of lack of capacity and lack of knowledge and approval, a judge who decides to refuse probate, but who does not wish to suggest misbehaviour by anyone concerned in the preparation of the will, usually finds that the testator lacked capacity, but that there was no lack of knowledge and approval.[162] To find that there was both lack of capacity and lack of knowledge and approval is to hint at misconduct,[163] while a finding of lack of knowledge and approval by itself generally gives a clearer indication.[164] Having said this, challenges based on lack of knowledge and approval rarely succeed. The difficulties faced by those minded to challenge wills are illustrated by a number of recent cases. In *Ewing v Bennett*[165] a will made by a solicitor for a woman who was very deaf, suffered from dizziness and memory loss, and who was in the early stages of senile dementia with periodic forgetfulness, was upheld by the trial judge: and the Court of Appeal refused to interfere with his decision. In *Re Dabbs*[166] a will prepared on the principal beneficiary's computer for a testator, who died in circumstances which caused the coroner's jury to return a verdict of unlawful death, was also upheld.[167] In *Hubbard v Scott*[168]a lonely, childless, eighty-seven year old widower made a will, less than three weeks before his death, in favour of his Polish cleaner, whom he had probably known for less than three months. The will was prepared by a solicitor to whom the testator had been escorted by the beneficiary, and the beneficiary was present both when instructions for the will were given, and at the time when it was executed. This will obtained probate. In *Re Devillebichot*,[169] less than two weeks before he died of cancer, a man executed a will, which had been prepared for him by his brothers and sisters, in their presence, and with no doctor or lawyer in attendance. The will disinher- **5–40**

[162] *Re Loxston* [2006] W.T.L.R. 1567. See B Sloan, "Reversing Testamentary Dispositions in Favour of Informal Carers", Chap.8 in B. Häcker and C. Mitchell (eds), *Current Issues in Succession Law* (Oxford: Hart Publishing, 2016).

[163] *Re Key* [2010] 1W.L.R. 623.

[164] *D'Eye v Avery* [2001] W.T.L.R. 227; *Re Rowinska* [2006] W.T.L.R. 487; *Devas v Mackay* [2009] EWHC 1951 (Ch); *Re Tociapski* [2013] W.T.L.R. 1821.

[165] *Ewing v Bennett* [2001] W.T.L.R. 249.

[166] *Re Dabbs* [2001] W.T.L.R. 527.

[167] It is true that, strictly speaking, the question whether the testator had been unlawfully killed (i.e. murdered) was a separate question from the question whether his will had been properly executed. It is possible that there was nothing wrong with the execution of the will, but that, after it was executed, the testator was unlawfully killed. If his killer was a beneficiary under the will, the killer would then be deprived of such benefit by the forfeiture rule, see below, Chap.14 paras 14–64 et seq. Having said this, the combination of facts in this case suggests foul play all round. It is understood that there were further proceedings in relation to this death, and to the application to it of the forfeiture rule; these proceedings are believed to have been compromised.

[168] *Hubbard v Scott* [2012] W.T.L.R. 29.

[169] *Re Devillebichot* [2013] W.T.L.R.

ited his only daughter, but was upheld.[170] In *Simon v Byford*[171] a woman suffering from dementia, during the course of a party to celebrate her eighty-eighth birthday, with no solicitor present, but in the presence of those who would benefit, made a will which revoked an earlier professionally drawn will which had favoured one of her sons. He, of course, was not at the party. The decision to grant probate of this will was upheld by the Court of Appeal.

There have, since 2000,[172] been cases where probate has been refused, on the basis of lack of knowledge and approval, but all have been ones where the evidence against the will was overwhelming. In *Buckenham v Dickenson*[173] the testator was "very deaf and partially blind" and the trial judge held that the reading over of a will to him, by a solicitor, was an "idle ceremony". In *d'Eye v Avery*[174] the testator had had a massive stroke, was a patient of the Court of Protection and executed his will in a bank when the principal beneficiary was present. In *Richards v Allan*[175] the testatrix was a diabetic who was taking drugs which could affect her mental state, and her doctor had diagnosed her as possibly having suffered a recent stroke. The will was prepared by a solicitor who was related to the principal beneficiary and was executed in such a way that the testatrix's sister would not find out about the execution.[176] In *Re Rowinska*[177] a Polish woman, who had previously executed a professionally drawn will in favour of members of her family and of Polish charities, was alleged, seven weeks before she died, to have made a new will leaving her entire estate to the man who fixed her television ariel. The will had been prepared on his computer.[178] In *Devas v Mackay*,[179] a will was produced by the testatrix's "carer" which disinherited the testatrix's children and left her estate to the carer's son, whom the testatrix had never met. At the time the will was

[170] This was in spite of the fact that the trial judge made a number of references to "suspicious circumstances" and criticised one of the witnesses, who was a magistrate and who had chosen not to involve a solicitor.

[171] *Simon v Byford* [2014] W.T.L.R. 1097.

[172] The significance of the year 2000 is that, it was then that the Wills and Trusts Law Reports were first published, and it was in the following year that neutral citations were introduced. It has been much easier to find contentious probate cases since 2000/2001 than it was before 2000.

[173] *Buckenham v Dickenson* [2000] W.T.L.R. 1083.

[174] *d'Eye v Avery* [2001] W.T.L.R. 227.

[175] *Richards v Allan* [2001] W.T.L.R. 1031.

[176] This will was declared invalid both on the basis of lack of capacity and lack of knowledge and approval.

[177] *Re Rowinska, Wyniczenko v Plucinska-Surowka* [2006] W.T.L.R. 487.

[178] Of course the testatrix did not know and approve of the contents of this "will". But, on the assumption that her signature was not forged (see above, para.5–18), this must have been a case of fraud. To refuse probate on the ground of lack of knowledge and approval is to make it seem as if no misbehaviour has occurred, but it must have done. And nothing is said in the judgment about costs. A very rare recent case, where dishonest behaviour was uncovered, is *Re Papillon* [2008] W.T.L.R. 269. The beneficiary who prepared the will was caught out because English was not her mother tongue. But cases like *Rowinska* and *Papillon*, where either the testator or the propounder have serious problems with the language, are rare and actually emphasise how easy it can be to obtain probate where there is simply a lack of evidence.

[179] *Devas v Mackay* [2009] EWHC 1951 (Ch).

supposed to have been executed, the testatrix was paralysed and was suffering from dementia; and the witnesses to the will were the carer and the testatrix's secretary. Furthermore, money had been removed by the carer from the testatrix's bank accounts while she was alive; it is always easier to persuade the court to refuse probate where the beneficiary has not only taken part in the preparation of the will but has also taken property from the testator while he or she was still alive. This will was set aside for lack of knowledge and approval, but that was not the end of the story and the case will be referred to further below.[180] Then, in *Turner v Phythian*[181] the beneficiary not only prepared a will whereby a childless widow left her entire estate to him and his wife, but went further and arranged that her sister should also make him a significant bequest.[182] In *Burgess v Hawes*[183] a woman who suffered from high blood pressure, was diabetic, and who had probably[184] suffered a stroke, was taken by one of her daughters to see a solicitor who then prepared a will disinheriting the woman's son and benefitting only her daughters. The solicitor did not enquire about earlier wills and took his instructions from the daughter, who both arranged for the making of this will and also accepted significant "gifts" from the mother before her death. The most surprising thing about this case is that the Court of Appeal seemed hesitant about upholding the trial judge's decision to refuse probate. A more open and shut example of a "suspicious will" it would be hard to imagine.[185]

Apart from the cases mentioned in the preceding paragraph, where wills were refused probate for lack of knowledge and approval, there have also been cases where what have clearly been "suspicious wills" (i.e. wills in the preparation of which beneficiaries have played a part) have been set aside on other grounds. The effect of this is to make it more difficult than it otherwise would be for potential challengers to decide on how to launch their attacks on wills which clearly deserve to be set aside. In *Couwenbergh v Valkowa*[186] there were a whole series of cases, both at first instance and in the Court of Appeal relating to two wills purportedly made by a German refugee who lived in England in favour of someone who lodged in her house. These wills were prepared by solicitors who had not seen the testatrix on the basis of instructions given to the solicitors by the **5–41**

180 See para.5–42. Two further examples of wills set aside for lack of knowledge and approval where money had also been taken by beneficiaries from the testators before their deaths are *Re Tociapski* [2013] W.T.L.R. 1821 and *Pearce v Beverley* [2014] W.T.L.R. 85.

181 *Turner v Phythian* [2013] W.T.L.R. 899.

182 The sister was still alive when the first will was challenged, so when the bequest in the sister's will came to light, there was time for her to revoke it. The beneficiary's greed in attempting to take advantage of both sisters told against him.

183 *Burgess v Hawes* [2013] W.T.L.R. 453.

184 "probably" because the evidence as to the woman's condition had to be pieced together after her death.

185 The Court of Appeal's hesitation, such as it was, was based on the fact that the will had been prepared by someone described by the court as "an experienced and independent lawyer". But no solicitor should have prepared a will in these circumstances. This case is discussed further in Chap.15, see below para.15–08.

186 *Couwenbergh v Valkowa* [2008] EWHC 2451 (Ch). This is actually a reference to the second first instance hearing.

lodger/beneficiary. At one stage the members of the testatrix's family who had challenged the wills were ordered to pay costs to the Legal Services Commission who had provided legal aid for the lodger/beneficiary. The members of the family were resolute and fought on. There was considerable doubt as to whether either will had ever been properly executed, but, in the end, both wills were refused probate on the ground that the testatrix had lacked capacity. The decision does not do justice to the challengers—these wills should never have been made in the first place, and the part played by the solicitors in their production is referred to in Chapter 15.[187] An even worse case was *Barrett v Bem*[188] where it was claimed that a man who died in hospital had, three hours before his death, executed a will in favour of one of his sisters. The will was handwritten by the beneficiary's daughter and it was originally claimed that the testator had signed it himself. After two separate trials, it was clear that the signature which purported to be that of the testator was not his, and that those who had given evidence in favour of the will had told lies. In spite of this, the trial judge granted probate on the basis that the *beneficiary* had signed the will on the testator's behalf. An appeal against this finding was upheld on the ground that there had been insufficient evidence to support the trial judge's finding that the will had been signed *at the testator's direction*. There was no sign of a *positive and discernible communication* from the testator to the beneficiary, instructing her to sign on his behalf. The refusal of probate in this case is, of course, to be welcomed, but the way of getting to the result was almost surreal. The signing of the will by a beneficiary should, even if no lies had been told, have been enough to cause any reasonable court to refuse probate without any further discussion. The way in which the courts in England agonise over the setting aside of wills which should never have seen the light of day is hard to comprehend.

5–42 And while on the subject of wills which have been set aside, but for the wrong reasons, look again at *Devas v Mackay*. The decision in that case was that the will should be refused probate for lack of knowledge and approval. But, after the probate proceedings had been concluded, the police began an investigation and the propounders of the will were *then* charged with forgery. A number of those who had participated in the scheme were convicted and sentenced to terms of imprisonment.[189] What is disturbing about this case is that it was not until *after* the probate proceedings had been concluded that the forgery was discovered. How or why those who challenged the will in the probate proceedings failed to challenge on the ground of forgery is not clear. The burden of proof in criminal proceedings would (or certainly should) have been heavier than in the probate proceedings. And, if forgery was missed by the challengers in this case, it raises questions as to whether this is the only case where this has occurred.[190]

[187] See para.15–08.

[188] *Re Lavin, Barrett v Bem* [2012] Ch 573.

[189] At the Cambridge Crown Court on 18 June 2010.

[190] A careful analysis of the cases where forgery has been alleged, seems to show that it is often very hard to prove. See *Fuller v Strum* in para.5–43 below.

Before finalising this list of cases, cases which demonstrate how hard it is in England nowadays successfully to challenge wills prepared by beneficiaries, there are two more which deserve special mention, *Fuller v Strum*[191] and *Sherrington v Sherrington*.[192] In *Strum*, the will was drawn up by one of the principal beneficiaries. The trial judge had before him a report, by a court appointed handwriting expert, that there was "very strong positive evidence" that the testator's signature on the will had been forged. He did not accept this report, but followed instead the *Wintle v Nye* approach of referring to a "suspicion" having been aroused and held that the testator had not known and approved of almost the entire contents of the will.[193] The Court of Appeal set aside the trial judge's order and pronounced in favour of the will.[194] **5–43**

This is a case where the person challenging the will (the testator's son) had pleaded lack of knowledge and approval, even though the honest plea (in addition to forgery) would have been undue influence or fraud. Just as in *Wintle v Nye*, it is not easy to see what the trial judge was referring to when he talked about a "suspicion". Given the way the case was pleaded and fought, the decision of the Court of Appeal appears to be correct. But the confusion is emphasized by another expression which crops up in the case. The trial judge referred to a phrase used by Lord Hatherley in *Fulton v Andrew*[195] where he described the burden which the law imposes on a person who has been instrumental in procuring a will under which he takes a benefit as "the onus of showing the righteousness of the transaction". Chadwick LJ appeared to think[196] that the trial judge had fallen into the error of believing that he had a licence to refuse probate to a document of which he disapproved. It is suggested that Chadwick LJ was wrong in this respect and the error is significant. Lord Hatherley's phrase is concerned with suspicions of fraud or undue influence surrounding the execution of the document. The matter is discussed further below.[197]

There is a sequel to *Fuller v Strum*. Those who had advised the testator's son failed to notice that the testator had almost certainly died domiciled in Israel, not in England; so the substantive law governing the validity of the "will" should have been Israeli law.[198] The relevant provision of Israeli law is s.35 of the Inheritance Law 5725–1965 which reads as follows:

> **"Will in favour of witnesses, etc.**
> 35. A provision in a will—other than an oral will—in favour of a person who prepared the will or witnessed it or was otherwise concerned in its preparation, or in favour of such a person's spouse, is void."

[191] *Fuller v Strum* [2002] 1 W.L.R. 1097.
[192] *Sherrington v Sherrington* [2005] 3 F.C.R. 538. See also *Franks v Sinclair* [2007] W.T.L.R. 439.
[193] *Wintle v Nye* [2001] W.T.L.R. 677.
[194] *Fuller v Strum* [2002] 1 W.L.R. 1097.
[195] *Fulton v Andrew* (1875) L.R. 7 H.L. 448 at 471.
[196] *Fuller v Strum* [2002] 1 W.L.R. 1097 at 1118–1119.
[197] See below, para.5–53.
[198] *Re Fuld's Estate (No.3), Hartley v Fuld* [1968] P. 675.

In April 2008, on an (unopposed) application by an Israeli lawyer acting for the son,[199] a court in Israel awarded the whole of the testator's estate to the son. As a question of Conflict of Laws, it seems reasonably clear that this case should not have been decided according to English law in the first place, but for the Succession lawyer the main interest lies in comparing and contrasting the approaches of English law and another system—Israeli law in this case—to a suspicious will. There will be some who think that the result so straightforwardly achieved by Israeli law is to be preferred to the result much less straightforwardly achieved by English law.[200]

5–44 *Sherrington*[201] is another unsatisfactory case. Richard Sherrington, a solicitor had been married twice; his relationship with his second wife was found by the trial judge to be "very bad".[202] He executed a will, which had been prepared for him by his non-legally-qualified stepdaughter, in which he left his entire estate to his second wife; he died in a car accident shortly afterwards. The will was challenged, by the adult children of his first marriage, on the grounds of lack of due execution and lack of knowledge and approval. The trial judge found against the will on both grounds,[203] but the Court of Appeal held that he was wrong on both points.[204] The problem in this case is, again, that the plea of lack of knowledge and approval is a dishonest plea. The honest plea in this case would have been undue influence. The will was badly drafted, but it was essentially straightforward. The Court of Appeal took the approach that it was "fanciful" to suggest that the testator did not know that the will he was executing was one which left everything to his wife; and so he knew and approved of its contents. While it is clear that the testator had *knowledge* of the contents of the will, the question the Court of Appeal appeared not to address was whether he also *approved* it. The Court of Appeal, noting that the contents of the will were "surprising", went on to say:

> "Further, at the time he executed the Will the deceased was only 56 and may well have thought that he would have ample time to alter the terms of the Will in due course."

But, if at the time he executed the will, the testator intended, for whatever reason, to alter it before he died, he did not *approve* it as a will, and it should have been refused probate. There is also another point here, raised earlier in this chapter.[205] *If* the testator in this case, when he executed his

[199] The instructions came from the assistant editor, who discovered the domicile point.
[200] For a discussion of possible reform, see below, paras 5–49 et seq.
[201] *Sherrington v Sherrington* [2005] 3 F.C.R. 538.
[202] The trial judge was criticised by the Court of Appeal for admitting evidence as to the state of the marriage, after indicating that he was not interested in hearing it; but, putting to one side the question as to what evidence he should have admitted, the trial judge clearly formed the view that the marriage was unhappy.
[203] *Sherrington v Sherrington* [2004] W.T.L.R. 895.
[204] The question of due execution was discussed in Chap.4 (see above, para.4–20) where it was suggested that the decision of the Court of Appeal was correct. It is less easy to understand the verdict of the Court of Appeal on the question of knowledge and approval.
[205] See above, para.5–02.

will, intended to alter its terms before he died, he seems to have lacked *animus testandi*. This is, in a sense, a further indication of the confusion involved in the plea of lack of knowledge and approval. No-one who lacks *animus testandi* ever *approves* the document he is executing as his will.

One of the reasons for pleading lack of knowledge and approval appears to be connected with costs. Those who unsuccessfully plead lack of knowledge and approval hope to be awarded costs from the estate, or at least not to have a costs order made against them. Colonel Wintle, when he had lost his case at first instance, was denied his costs, but the claimants in *Sherrington* fared even worse. They had to pay the entire costs of the appeal, in addition to all their own costs and half the successful wife's costs at first instance. The Court of Appeal made this order on the basis that the litigation had been "very hostile".[206] **5–45**

8. Summary of the present approach[207]

The present approach (or should it be called "the standard approach"?)[208] **5–46** obscures the issues in contentious probate cases, so that it is not clear what those challenging suspicious wills are alleging. This is the *Wintle v Nye* approach, as explained by Scarman J in *In the Estate of Fuld (dec'd)*[209] and it causes confusion. It consists of pleading lack of knowledge and approval in cases where the logical pleas would be undue influence and/or fraud, and then assuming that the trial judge will mention "a suspicion" or "suspicious circumstances", though without specifying what the suspicion is a suspicion of. The confusion is worsened by a fundamental disagreement between the judges as to the relationship between the plea of lack of knowledge and approval, on the one hand, and the various other pleas, on the other. In *Re Key* Briggs J, having, quite appropriately, criticised a solicitor for taking part in the making of a will in which he should not have taken part, and having held that the testator lacked capacity, then went on to say "a conclusion that a testator lacks capacity necessarily compels a conclusion that he did not know and approve the contents of his will."[210] It is submitted that this is self-evidently correct. No one who lacks capacity,

206 *Sherrington v Sherrington* [2005] EWCA Civ 410. The court expressed the hope that the successful wife would be "merciful" before she sought to enforce any such order as they had made, but, after something so "hostile" it seems odd to make such an order in the hope that it will not be enforced.

207 On the whole, it is easier to challenge lifetime gifts than it is to challenge wills. This is unsurprising: lifetime gifts are optional, whereas property has to devolve on death. The cases on lifetime gifts are not, therefore, a reliable indicator of how successful challenges might be where the disposition has been a disposition on death. For examples of challenges to lifetime gifts see: *Re Craig* [1971] Ch.95; *Re Brocklehurst* [1978] Ch.14; *Re Morris* [2001] W.T.L.R. 1137; *Hammond v Osborn* [2002] W.T.L.R. 1125; *Re Davidge* [2003] W.T.L.R. 959; *Pesticcio v Huet* [2004] W.T.L.R. 699; *Randall v Randall* [2005] W.T.L.R 119; *Goodchild v Bradbury* [2007] W.T.L.R. 463; *Re S, D v R* [2011] W.T.L.R. 449; *Curtis v Pulbrook* [2011] W.T.L.R. 1503; *Hart v Burbidge* [2015] W.T.L.R. 1203; *Kicks v Leigh* [2015] W.T.L.R. 579.

208 It is referred to here as "the present approach" but its origins can be traced back to what went on in the ecclesiastical courts, before the Court of Probate was set up in 1858. See Chap.7 in Vol.5 *Modern Studies in Property Law* (Oxford: Hart Publishing, 2009).

209 *In the Estate of Fuld (dec'd)* [1968] P. 675, 722, see above, para.5–37.

210 *Re Key* [2010] 1 W.L.R. 2020 at para.116.

or who has been unduly influenced, or who has been the object of fraud, can be truly said to have both *known* and *approved* of the contents of a will he has executed. In each of these circumstances, either knowledge, or approval, or possibly both, must be missing. The plea of lack of knowledge and approval overlaps, almost entirely with the other pleas.[211] Having said this, it seems that Briggs J's view, though logically correct, is not universally held. Some judges seem to think that lack of knowledge and approval can only be found if the testator *did* have capacity.[212] This latter approach would make more sense *if* it were clear that a finding of lack of knowledge and approval were a coded way of saying that the testator had been unduly influenced or defrauded, and, in particular, that it would be used to deny probate to wills prepared by beneficiaries, but that is not clear.

5–47 In the recent case of *Gill v Woodall*[213] a mother had disinherited her daughter and left her estate to an animal charity. The judge at first instance set the will aside on the ground of undue influence over the testatrix by her husband. Lord Neuberger MR, giving the judgment of the Court of Appeal, agreed that the will should be refused probate, but on the ground that there had been lack of knowledge and approval, not undue influence. It is submitted that the decision of the Court of Appeal in *Gill* was not one which will assist in making the law any clearer. The will should have been set aside, but it is suggested that the correct ground for this was lack of capacity, and that the problem in the case is that the challengers had failed to plead it. The testatrix "suffered from agoraphobia with panic disorder to a serious degree" while her husband "was a stubborn, self-opinionated, domineering man who was prone to losing his temper quite easily which led to outbursts of fury". This was not a beneficiary made will, and what really seems to have happened here is that the court used the lack of knowledge and approval ground as one to cover up an error in the pleadings.[214] A finding of lack of knowledge and approval usually hints at misbehaviour by a beneficiary in the will-making process.[215] It has been a disguised way of hinting at undue influence and fraud and it has regularly been linked with the "suspicious circumstances rule" (though without clearly explaining who is suspected of what). That has been the position ever since *Wintle v Nye*. The decision in *Gill v Woodall* makes a confused situation even more confused than it was before.

5–48 Furthermore, a challenge based on undue influence, or fraud, may give a different result from a challenge based on lack and knowledge and approval. If there is a finding of fraud —or undue influence—it may be that the court will hold that the property the wrongdoer has inherited will be impressed with a constructive trust.[216] In *Wintle v Nye* the result of the

[211] The sole occasion when the plea of lack of knowledge and approval does not (logically) overlap with any other plea, is when a testator who does not lack capacity makes a mistake which has not been induced by fraud. This is why the introduction of the plea, by Sir J P Wilde, see fn.139 has caused so much of a problem.

[212] *Re Ashlettle* [2013] W.T.L.R. 1331; *Marcou v Goodwin* [2014] W.T.L.R. 605.

[213] *Gill v Woodall* [2011] Ch 380.

[214] See All E.R. Rev 2011 pp.421–423.

[215] See above para.5–40.

[216] There is no clear authority on what happens when fraud is proved (because it never is).

successful challenge based on lack of knowledge and approval was that the will was set aside and the testatrix's property passed to her next-of-kin. This was *not*, in fact, the optimum outcome. Evidence had emerged during the course of the case that she had originally intended to make a will largely in favour of local charities; Nye appears to have talked her out of this. Had the verdict in *Wintle v Nye* been a verdict of fraud, Nye could have been obliged to hold the property on a constructive trust for the charities which the testatrix appears to have wanted to benefit.[217]

VII. REFORMING THE LAW RELATING TO SUSPICIOUS WILLS AND WILLS MADE BY VULNERABLE TESTATORS[218]

1. The present position

Part V of this chapter attempted to set out the law, as it is at present, in relation to "suspicious wills", i.e. wills prepared by beneficiaries, or in the making of which beneficiaries have played a part. The rules are confused. It is too easy for would-be beneficiaries to take advantage of those who are frail in mind or body, and it is too hard for those who are minded to challenge suspicious wills to do so successfully. Many of the wills which have been successfully challenged, have been so challenged only because those who were minded to challenge them were strong willed and/or had deep pockets.[219] It cannot be known how many cases there have been where wills which deserved to be challenged have escaped formal scrutiny.[220] **5–49**

But in *Betts v Doughty* (1879) 5 P.D. 26 those challenging a will were permitted to amend their pleadings so that, if they had succeeded, the estate would have been held on a constructive trust. The parties then came to terms. But it is logical that in all cases of fraud, and in some cases of undue influence (the ones where the testator has been coerced into making a will different from the will he wanted to make) the estate should be held on a constructive trust for those whom the testator wished to benefit.

[217] See *Re Moss* [2000] W.T.L.R. 1033 where there was confusion over the effect of different pleas on who would benefit if a challenge to the will were successful. In *Wintle v Nye*, the fact that a successful challenge to the will would have resulted (and did, eventually, result) in a windfall for the next-of-kin, may explain, in part, why the jury at the original first instance hearing were less sympathetic to the challenger than they might have been expected to be. Col Wintle had taken an assignment of his interest from one of the next-of-kin in order to give himself *locus standi*, but the next-of-kin themselves were almost entirely unknown to Kitty Wells and there was no indication that she ever intended them to benefit from her estate.

[218] In July 2014, the Law Commission published their Twelfth Programme of Law Reform. One of their projects was to review the law of wills and it was announced that they would focus "on four key areas that have been identified as potentially needing reform". One of these four was capacity. The project has now been postponed. It is to be hoped (though with no especial confidence) that when the Law Commission do come to look at "Capacity" they will expand their investigation into the field of "suspicious wills".

[219] The challenger in *Couwenbergh v Valkova*, see above para.5–41 deserves commendation for his unflinching persistence, and the testatrix's daughter in *Burgess v Hawes*, see above para.5–40 may be applauded for offering support to her disinherited brother, when this was against her own financial interest.

[220] It is almost certain that no challenge at all is launched against some thoroughly suspicious

2. The history

5–50 At the heart of Charles Dickens's novel, Bleak House, there is the fictional case of *Jarndyce v Jarndyce*, a case concerning "a will", which meandered on until the whole estate had been absorbed in costs and those who had taken part in the litigation were all ruined, mad, or both. *Jarndyce* was supposed to be based on a case which had actually come before the Court of Chancery, but the case is not named. Dickens does say, in the Preface to Bleak House that "there is [a]. . .well-known suit in Chancery, not yet decided, which was commenced before the close of the last century, and in which more than double the amount of seventy thousand pounds has been swallowed up in costs." This is probably a reference to the *Thellussson* litigation, which began with *Thellusson v Woodford*[221] in 1799 and ended soon after Bleak House was published in 1852–53, but there are a number of other cases of which Dickens may also have been thinking.[222] In one sense, Dickens's account was misleading. Chancery, in the early nineteenth century, may have been slow and wasteful, and the lawyers who practiced in Chancery may have been self-indulgent, but they did *not* deal with probate. Chancery had jurisdiction over the interpretation of wills and it dealt also with trusts in wills. The *Thellusson* litigation began with a case concerning an accumulation trust in a will—it was not the will which was in dispute, but the trust. Disputes as to whether wills should be granted probate (i.e. the kinds of disputes covered in this chapter) were not heard in Chancery in Dickens's day. Before 1858, disputes over the granting of probate to wills of personalty[223] were heard in the ecclesiastical courts, the Church courts, the chief of which was the Prerogative Court which sat at Doctors' Commons in London. The equivalent disputes concerning wills of realty came before the common law courts[224]—Chancery was involved neither in disputes over grants of probate to wills of personalty nor in the equivalent common law litigation relating to wills of realty. In 1858, as an indirect result of the reform of divorce law, jurisdiction over probate was transferred to the newly created Court of Probate, but this was, in reality, a re-constituted version of the Prerogative Court, with very much the same personnel, and the same way of doing things —or, rather, of not doing things. The 1858 change meant that the lawyers who had practiced in the ecclesiastical courts[225] extended their influence so that they had jurisdiction over wills of realty as well as testaments of personalty. In the 1870s,

wills, while there are other cases where the propounders of documents which invite serious investigation enter into compromises with their opponents, who are persuaded not to proceed to litigation.

221 *Thellusson v Woodford* (1799) 4 Ves Jun 227.

222 Holdsworth, in *Charles Dickens as a Legal Historian* Yale UP 1928 does not attempt to identify the case (or cases).

223 Wills of personalty were known as "testaments". "Wills", properly speaking, dealt with realty. That is the origin of the phrase "last Will and Testament".

224 In fact, very few cases of challenges to wills of realty do seem to have come before the common law courts. This was probably because most freehold land was held in strict settlements and could not be devised by will.

225 They were known as "advocates" and had been trained quite separately from the barristers who worked in the common law courts and in Chancery.

the work of the Court of Probate was transferred to the Probate, Divorce and Admiralty Division of the High Court, and it was not until 1971 that Chancery did, at last, obtain jurisdiction over contentious probate. The problem was that, by then, it was too late. Contentious probate operated on the basis of a system crafted by the lawyers of the ecclesiastical courts and its failings are their responsibility. *Wintle v Nye*[226] is a case based on a fundamental confusion, a case where fraud is dressed up as "lack of knowledge and approval". But the lawyers who drafted the pleadings were not Chancery lawyers, they were the lawyers of the Probate, Divorce and Admiralty Division and were the heirs to a tradition which has been much more damaging to those minded to challenge suspicious wills than the Chancery tradition would have been.

In the early nineteenth century, when the abolition of the probate jurisdiction of the ecclesiastical courts was being discussed, it was suggested that the jurisdiction should be given to Chancery. It is to be regretted that this did not happen. By describing the *Jarndyce* litigation as concerning "a will" in Chancery, Dickens may have actually done long term harm. Whatever may have been the faults of Chancery, those of the ecclesiastical courts and their successor courts were, in the context of "suspicious wills" greater, and the confusion sown in these courts is still with us today. **5–51**

3. Three possible reforms

It is submitted that there are three possible ways in which the position might be reformed or improved. The first is to adopt the Roman Law approach, the second is to adopt a version of the rules which Chancery applies when dealing with lifetime gifts (i.e. "equitable undue influence") and the third is to apply the doctrine of the "unrighteous transaction". **5–52**

(a) *Introducing into English law the Roman Law rule for beneficiary-made wills*

The Roman Law approach to beneficiary made-wills was straightforward. A will prepared by a beneficiary (or in the making of which a beneficiary had played a part) was void under the provisions of the *Lex Cornelia de Falsis, and,* lest there might be any misunderstanding, the beneficiary in question was liable to the penalty for forgery under that law. Roman law deemed a beneficiary-made will to have been forged. The penalty varied according to the date and to the defendant's status, but if he were unlucky, it was crucifixion.[227] Roman law took a dim view of beneficiary-made wills. **5–53**

If one were starting with a clean slate, drawing up a set of rules to be applied from scratch in a brand new legal code, there is much to be said for adopting some variation of the Roman Law rule (though possibly omitting the extreme version of the penalty).[228] A form of the Roman Law

[226] See above paras 5–34 et seq.

[227] If he were "lucky", he might be sentenced to a life of slavery in the salt mines. The contrast with the position in England is stark.

[228] The lawyers who practiced in the ecclesiastical courts knew all about the Roman Law rule for beneficiary-made wills, they were trained in Roman Law. But, in this instance, they chose not to follow it. See R. Kerridge, "Draftsmen and Suspicious Wills", Chap.7 in

rule is the rule adopted in Israel and it was applied (straightforwardly) in the *Strum* case.[229]

But we cannot adopt such a rule in England and Wales today, it is too late. There are too many wills in existence where beneficiaries have played a part in their making and where the testators are still living; and, among these wills, there will be some (it will be impossible to guess how many) which should not automatically be refused probate.

(b) *Applying the equitable undue influence rules (which apply to lifetime gifts) to wills*

5–54 At least two writers[230] have, in the recent past, suggested that the rules which Equity applies to lifetime gifts, the rules which come under the heading of "equitable undue influence", could be applied to English wills. These rules make it relatively easy, in some circumstances, to set aside inter vivos gifts. There are, however two problems with the suggestion. First, "undue influence" in equity is not the same as what is termed "undue influence" in the probate context. Undue influence in probate law consists of pressure exerted on the testator,[231] whereas the "influence" which becomes "undue" in equity stems essentially from affection, not pressure. Undue influence in equity consists of taking advantage of someone who holds the donee in high regard or in affection.

And there is another, more significant distinction in that, in some circumstances, equity presumes undue influence. It may do this when there is proof of: (i) a relationship falling within a particular class, or involving a history of undue influence; and (ii) a transaction which excites suspicion or calls for explanation.[232] The problem with attempting to incorporate this approach into the probate context is that it would invalidate wills made in favour of those whom testators held in regard or affection, close members of their families; and this, in the probate context, would be odd, almost absurd. What is needed in probate are rules designed to invalidate wills in the preparation of which beneficiaries have played a part, not wills made in favour of those towards whom the testators felt particular affection. So, a straightforward transposition of the equitable undue influence rules into the probate context would, it is submitted, not work well at all.[233]

M. Dixon (ed.), *Modern Studies in Property Law*, Vol.5 (Oxford: Hart Publishing, 2009) at p.161.

229 See above para.5–43.

230 See P. Ridge, "Equitable Undue Influence and Wills" (2004) 120 L.Q.R. 617 and L. Mason, "Undue Influence and Testamenary Dispositions: an Equitable Jurisdiction in Probate Law" [2011] Conv. 115.

231 What is now called undue influence in probate was originally called "imposition", in some of the earlier case it was called both "imposition" and "undue influence" and in *Barry v Butlin* it was said that probate undue influence was equivalent to "duress". Calling it "undue influence" rather than "imposition" seems to have been part of the tendency in the ecclesiastical courts to tone down any suggestion of misbehavior.

232 *Snell's Equity*, edited by J. McGhee QC, 3rd edn (London: Sweet & Maxwell, 2015), paras 8–014 et seq.

233 See R. Kerridge, "Undue Influence and Testamenary Dispositions: a Response" [2012] Conv. 129.

(c) *The rule, or doctrine, of the "unrighteous transaction"—the Chancery lawyers' approach to wills*

There have only ever been two cases where a challenge to the validity of an English will has reached the House of Lords.[234] One of the two is, of course, *Wintle v Nye*, but the other is *Fulton v Andrew*.[235] In *Fulton* Lord Hatherley said this: **5–55**

> "[I]t is enough in their case [i.e. in that of 'ordinary legatees' who have taken no part in the will-making process] that the will was read over to the testator and that he was of sound mind and memory, and capable of comprehending it. But there is a farther onus upon those who take for their own benefit, after having been instrumental in preparing or obtaining a will. They have thrown upon them the onus of shewing the righteousness of the transaction."

In *Fuller v Strum*,[236] the trial judge referred to what Lord Hatherley had said, and refused to grant probate to most of the will.[237] The case then went to the Court of Appeal, where the trial judge's decision was reversed and where Chadwick LJ included the following passage in his judgment:

> "It is important to appreciate that Lord Hatherley's phrase – redolent of morality as it now seems to be[238] – is not to be taken by the court as a licence to refuse probate to a document of which it disapproves, whether that disapproval stems from the circumstances in which the document was executed as a will or whether it stems from the contents of the document. The question is not whether the court approves of the circumstances in which the document was executed or of its contents. The question is whether the court is satisfied that the contents do truly represent the testator's testamentary intentions."

The approaches of Lord Hatherley and of Chadwick LJ represent two opposed ways of dealing or, rather, in the case of the latter, of not dealing, with beneficiary-made wills.

[234] Before 1833, appeals from the Prerogative Court would have gone to the High Court of Delegates, the history of which was an unhappy mixture of pantomime and scandal. On 1 February 1833, the appeal functions of the High Court of Delegates were transferred to the Privy Council. When the Court of Probate was created in 1858, appeals were redirected to the House of Lords. Since then, the only two English validity cases to reach the Lords have been *Fulton v Andrew* and *Wintle v Nye*. A number of cases on construction have reached the Lords, see Chap.10. *Marley v Rawlings*, see below para.10–08 concerned rectification. But only two English cases on the essential validity of a will got this far. *Lowe v Guthrie* [1909] A.C. 278 was also a case on the validity of a will, it was a Scottish appeal.

[235] *Fulton v Andrew* (1875) L.R. 7 H.L. 448.

[236] *Fuller v Strum* [2002] 1W.L.R. 1097.

[237] It would, of course, have been simpler if he had refused probate to all of it.

[238] The reference, by Chadwick LJ, to "morality" is probably intended to ridicule Hatherley, who was a very sincere churchman and who, for more than forty years, was a Sunday School teacher in his own parish of St Margaret's Westminster. Lord Westbury once described him as "a mere bundle of virtues, without a redeeming vice."

What Lord Hatherley had said was that for a beneficiary to become involved in the will-making process may be an "unrighteous transaction", meaning that it may well involve undue influence and/or fraud; and so the onus should be on the propounder of the will to show that neither undue influence nor fraud was involved.[239] That was Lord Hatherley's onus. Chadwick LJ appeared to suggest that Lord Hatherley had intended to say that it would be an "unrighteous transaction" to disinherit one's son (*Strum* was a case where a son was disinherited) but Lord Hatherley had *not* meant this. It was not the fact of disinheritance which was unrighteous, it was the way in which it was effected. It is not at all clear what Chadwick LJ was suggesting when he appeared to draw a distinction between "the circumstances in which the document was executed" and "the question whether the court is satisfied that the contents truly represent the testator's testamentary intentions". The whole point here is that the circumstances in which the document was executed may cause one not to be satisfied that the contents represented the testator's intentions.

5–56 Lord Hatherley was a Chancery lawyer, as was Lord Cairns, another of the judges in *Fulton*.[240] They both gave robust judgments, making it clear that they thought that any beneficiary who took part in the will-making process should have cast upon him the onus of demonstrating that there had been no misbehaviour—i.e. no undue influence and no fraud. This was the Chancery lawyers' approach to this situation, to the problem raised by beneficiary-made wills. What has gone wrong is that it is not being followed, in spite of the fact that it has the authority of the House of Lords.[241] When contentious probate was transferred from the Probate, Divorce, and Admiralty Division of the High Court, to Chancery, in 1971, P.V. Baker wondered whether the judges would now take a more

[239] Fraud and undue influence are different, see above para.5–17, but the onus should be on the propounder to show that *neither* was involved.

[240] Lord Cairns was, like Lord Hatherely, a devout churchman. He was strict, austere and unpopular, but was regarded as one of the best lawyers of his generation.

[241] Bizarrely, some recent references to Lord Hatherley's speech in *Fulton* make it seem as though the point he was making was almost the exact opposite of what he was actually saying. In *Simon v Byford* [2013] W.T.L.R. 1615 the trial judge quoted Lord Hatherley as having said: "When you are once satisfied that a testator of a competent mind has had his will read over to him, and has thereupon executed it. . .those circumstances afford very grave and strong presumption that the will has been duly and properly executed by the testator." This trial judge was quoting, at second hand, a passage from *Gill v Woodall* [2011] Ch 380 where Lord Neuberger MR had said that Lord Hatherley had spoken these words. Each time the words were repeated, they became more misleading. Lord Hatherley did *not* begin his sentence with the word "When", as the trial judge in *Byford* implied that he had done. His sentence was much longer and, in fact, referred to "*. . . the supposed existence of a rigid rule, by which, when. . .*" (italics added). He was actually saying that, where a beneficiary had been involved in the will-making process, the "*supposed rigid rule*" should *not* be applied. Lord Neuberger in *Woodall* did not begin his quotation with a high case "W" and so did imply that the sentence had been cut, but did not explain how. And in *Woodall* he did refuse probate to the will, though not, it is suggested, for the correct reason. See above para.5–47. But the third hand reference to the quotation in *Byford*, a case where a suspicious will was being granted probate, is totally misleading. The whole point of what Lord Hatherley was saying was that the making of this type of will was an "unrighteous transaction, and he would *not* have granted it probate. So, on the one hand, Lord Hatherley is being taken to task for his "morality" and, on the other, he is being completely misrepresented.

Chancery-based approach to the cases.[242] The misfortune is that they did not. Instead of Chancery lawyers inserting backbone into the existing rules, they seem to have been infected by what might be politely called the "relaxed" approach taken by their brothers in the Court of Probate and their predecessors in the Prerogative Court. That is what seems to have happened to Chadwick LJ. Although he was himself a Chancery lawyer, his was not the approach of Lords Hatherley and Cairns, the Chancery lawyers: it was the confused approach of the probate lawyers who drafted the pleadings in *Wintle v Nye*, who lost the case, and who then left Wintle to fight on, alone and unaided. There is, in this context, nothing wrong with some morality.[243]

4. The "suspicious circumstances" rule, or doctrine—the Probate lawyers' approach to wills

It is worth comparing and contrasting the rule or doctrine of the "unrighteous transaction" (a chancery lawyers' formulation), with the "suspicious circumstances" rule or doctrine (the probate lawyers' formulation). On the face of it, the two rules, or doctrines seem to be slightly different ways of expressing the same thing. Phrasing such a rule in terms of an "unrighteous transaction" is clearer and more straightforward than phrasing it in terms of "suspicious circumstances", but applied sensibly either rule (or doctrine) should lead to the same result. What has gone wrong is that the "suspicious circumstances" rule has not been applied sensibly by the probate lawyers. Expressed as the "suspicious circumstances" rule, it takes its origin from a number of cases in the ecclesiastical courts and, in particular, from Parke B.'s judgment in the Privy Council in the appeal from the Prerogative Court in *Barry v Butlin*, Parke B.'s way of expressing it is regularly reproduced—he put it like this: **5–57**

> "The rules of law, according to which cases of this nature are to be decided. . .are two, the first, that the onus probandi lies in every case upon the party propounding a will; and he must satisfy the conscience of the Court that the instrument so propounded is the last will of a free and capable testator.
>
> The second is that if a party writes or prepares a will under which he takes the benefit, that is a circumstance which ought generally to excite the suspicion of the Court, and calls upon it to be vigilant and jealous in examining the evidence in support of the instrument, in favour of which it ought not to pronounce unless the suspicion is removed, and it is judicially satisfied that the paper propounded does express the true will of the deceased."

The problem with this passage, and possibly the reason why it has become so popular with probate lawyers, is that it contains a fudge. It speaks of a "suspicion", but it does not say what the suspicion is a suspicion

[242] P. V. Baker (1970) 86 L.Q.R. 447.

[243] For the reference to "morality" see above fn. 241.

of. After Sir J.P. Wilde, in *Hastilow v Stobie* in 1865,[244] made the mistake of admitting the plea of lack of knowledge and approval,[245] that fudged plea became combined with what might be called a non-judgmental (or fudged) reading of Parke B.'s reference to "suspicious circumstances". During the course of the nineteenth-century, it had been suggested in various cases[246] that there would be a presumption of fraud or undue influence when someone prepared a will for a testator under which he took a significant benefit, whether directly or indirectly. The judges paid lip-service to this presumption but it seemed to come, in practice, to mean almost nothing.[247] It was almost always counter-balanced by their reluctance to uphold any allegation that anyone had misbehaved[248] and the result was that those who prepared wills in their own favour almost always succeeded in obtaining probate of them. But what *must* the "suspicious circumstances" rule mean? Some probate lawyers appear to think that there can be a suspicion without its being a suspicion of anything in particular – a form of free-standing suspicion of nothing. A "suspicion" must be a suspicion of something. A suspicion of nothing is not a suspicion. "I suspect nothing" means "I do not suspect". And so, logically, the reference to "suspicious circumstances" in the context of a will must be a suspicion of something, and that something must be misbehaviour, i.e. undue influence or fraud. It has to be, because these are the forms of misbehaviour which are relevant in this context. In other words, what the "suspicious circumstances" rule should do, in the probate context, is to create an evidential presumption that there has been fraud or undue influence. It ends up, if applied logically, by having very much the same effect as Lord Hatherley's reference to the "unrighteous transaction". The trial judge in *Strum* was right when he combined the two (by referring to an "unrighteous transaction" and to "suspicious circumstances") as though they were one, and Chadwick LJ was wrong to take him to task for what he had done. If judges were to apply the presumption rigorously, it would make it more difficult for the unscrupulous to take advantage of the old and frail without imposing an unreasonable burden on genuine beneficiaries.[249]

5. A suggestion for the course which ought now to be followed when dealing with beneficiary-made wills

5–58 The correct course now is to apply whatever the rule or doctrine is called—whether it is called "the doctrine of the unrighteous transaction" or the

[244] *Hastilow v Stobie* (1865–69) L.R. 1 P. & D. 64.

[245] His predecessor, Sir Cresswell Cresswell had twice refused to allow it; see above fn.139.

[246] In particular, in *Barry v Butlin* see above.

[247] In *Barry v Butlin* itself the will had been prepared by a solicitor: and the solicitor, the doctor and the butler had benefited under it. The son was disinherited. The son lost the case (and paid the costs). This set a pattern which it was difficult to break.

[248] There are a small number of nineteenth-century cases where the courts do appear to have applied a meaningful presumption of misbehaviour. An example is *Parker v Duncan* (1890) 62 L.T. 642 (Sir James Hannen P).

[249] In practice, the upright beneficiary is likely to insist that the testator draw up his will with the benefit of professional assistance, so that there can be no suspicion of misbehaviour.

"suspicious circumstances rule"—in such a way that whenever a beneficiary has prepared a will in his own favour, or has played any significant part in the preparation of such a will, there is a meaningful presumption both of fraud and of undue influence, so that the onus is on him, the beneficiary, to convince the court that no such misbehavior has occurred, that he has neither misled nor bullied the testator.[250]

And a meaningful presumption in this respect necessarily involves a re-think of the approach to costs. At the present time, the reports of cases often fail to specify the costs orders which are made, but C.P.R. 57.7(5) encourages those challenging wills to do so on the basis of lack of capacity or lack of knowledge and approval. If they do this, they are supposed to stand a reasonable chance of obtaining an order for their costs from the estate, or, at least, not having an order for costs made against them, even when they lose. C.P.R. 57.7(5) can be traced back to a costs rule of the Prerogative Court in the early nineteenth-century. When Colonel Wintle's legal team decided to challenge Kitty Wells's will in favour of her solicitor Nye on the ground that she lacked knowledge and approval, rather than on the straightforward ground of fraud,[251] they may well have expected to lose the case, but they probably expected that their defeated client would be awarded his costs from the estate. They did lose the case (at first instance) but the trial judge did not award the colonel his costs. Paying his legal team almost bankrupted Colonel Wintle. The *Sherrington* case[252] was at least as bad, the challengers (the testator's children) had to pay not only their own costs but part of the other side's costs as well. This also was a case where they had not openly alleged fraud or undue influence, they had pleaded only lack of knowledge and approval.[253] If there is to be a meaningful presumption of misbehavior when a beneficiary is involved in the will making process, it follows that there should be not only a greater readiness to countenance pleas of fraud and undue influence, but also a much greater readiness to award costs against those who had been involved in the "unrighteous transaction" or who—and it amounts to the same thing—had created the "suspicion" (even if the challenge to the will is unsuccessful).[254]

[250] See R. Kerridge, "Wills made in suspicious circumstances: the problem of the vulnerable testator" (2000) 59 C.L.J. 310.

[251] See above para.5–36.

[252] See above para.5–44.

[253] In both *Wintle* and *Sherrington*, the pleas were "lack of knowledge and approval" but it was clear that the challengers believed that there had been misbehaviour. Encouraging clients to adopt this approach may give them the worst of all worlds. The attack is blunted, the case is lost, and the challenger ends up paying for his defeat. Col Wintle won his case in the Lords, in part at least, because the press were overwhelmingly on his side. The case was a *cause célebre*. Things might well have gone differently had he not obtained publicity. That is why his victory has been such small consolation to those who have followed the same path.

[254] The suggestion that someone who has alleged fraud or undue influence and who has then lost the case should be awarded his costs out of the estate is not without precedent. This was the result reached in the case of *Mitchell and Mitchell v Gard and Kingwell* (1863) 3 Sw. & Tr. 275 where the persons challenging a will made in favour of a solicitor *were* awarded their costs in spite of the fact that their challenge was based on undue influence and was unsuccessful. For the normally accepted rules on costs (not, themselves always easy to follow), see below paras 19–36 et seq.

5–59 The effect of creating a meaningful presumption of misbehavior whenever a beneficiary has been involved in the will-making process, would be twofold. On the one hand, many more "suspicious wills" would be set aside. On the other, the cases in the course of which wills were being contested would not drag on. There would be two groups of losers and the latter group would be the members of the legal profession who have, for so long, prolonged litigation when wills are challenged. The purpose of the law is not to make work for lawyers.

5–60 In the early years of the nineteenth century, when wills of personalty were being challenged before the ecclesiastical courts, there is no doubt that cases did drag on and it was strongly suspected that the advocates who practiced in those courts encouraged this state of affairs because it provided them with a reasonable livelihood. It was they who failed to create clear rules for the setting aside of beneficiary-made wills, and that failure still haunts the system today. The statistics concerning what happened when wills were challenged during the early part of the nineteenth century are interesting. Either way, the cases dragged on. If the wills were made by solicitors in their own favour, such wills usually obtained probate. If they were made by other persons in their own favour, they generally did not obtain probate. So, what has changed? The cases still drag on, that has not changed. Solicitors can no longer make wills in their own favour. This is a change which resulted from the publicity surrounding the case of *Wintle v Nye*. After the case was over, the Law Society changed the rules and made it clear that no solicitor could take any significant benefit under a will he had prepared for a client—the penalty was striking off. It was made to seem as though this new approach had always been in place. It had not. Had there been a rule in place before *Wintle v Nye* that a solicitor could take no significant benefit under a will he had prepared for a client, there would have been nothing to litigate. Wintle's victory would have been a walk-over at first instance. He did not win in the House of Lords because of a Law Society rule, he won because the general public had read about the case in their newspapers and were outraged by what had happened. By that stage, the whole legal profession had woken up to the fact that the rules had to change, and they did. But the other change concerns persons who are neither solicitors nor professional will-draftsmen, but who have simply prepared wills themselves in their own favour, or who have taken part in the will-making process as intermediaries between the testators and the draftsmen. Here there has been no improvement—rather the reverse.

6. Should will-writing be regulated?

5–61 The fact that solicitors can no longer make wills in their own favour is a change for the better. But the other change which has taken place is that wills which are not in favour of solicitors, but in the making of which beneficiaries have played a part, appear more, rather than less, likely to obtain probate nowadays than they were two hundred years ago.[255]

[255] For the statistics on the setting aside of pre-1858 wills see See R. Kerridge, "Draftsmen

Earlier in this part of this Chapter, there was a reference to the novel Bleak House and to the fictional case of *Jarndyce v Jarndyce*. The problem that the courts have, today, with contentious probate, is illustrated by passage from Mummery LJ's judgment in the Court of Appeal in *Burgess v Hawes* where he refers to *Jarndyce*. **5–62**

> "The cost of contesting the 2007 Will is a calamity for this family in every way. By the standards of a present day probate case the Deceased's estate is modest, less than £200,000. We were told in general terms that efforts to achieve a family compromise came to nothing . . . The failed negotiations mean that the estate will become, if it has not already become, worthless. A 6 day trial with 26 witnesses does not come cheap. Now there is this appeal. It may be recalled that the foggy family law suit in *Jarndyce v. Jarndyce* dragged on before the Lord Chancellor for generations until nothing was left for the parties to take. The CPR and the efforts of legal advisers have not dissuaded these parties from following a course leading to the dissipation of the whole of the Deceased's estate in costs and legal fees, which has happened faster than under the dilatory procedures of the unreformed Court of Chancery in the *Jarndyce* days."[256]

This makes it sound as though the fault lay with the family, with the litigants. But the point of Bleak House is, surely, that the fault lay with the lawyers. The family, the litigants, were the victims; they ended up ruined, or mad, or both, because of the way in which the lawyers were operating the system.

In *Burgess v Hawes*, a case discussed earlier in this chapter[257] and also in Chapter 15,[258] the will which was refused probate (though only after a lengthy trial at first instance *and* an appeal hearing), had been prepared by a solicitor. Solicitors should *not* prepare wills when they are aware that beneficiaries are involved in their creation. Here the Law Society is at fault for not giving clear guidance to its members. Solicitors are no longer (since *Wintle v Nye*) permitted to make wills in their own favour, but there are no clear sanctions when, in effect, they take instructions from beneficiaries, rather than from their clients. A genuine problem for an upright will draftsman at the present time is that, if he refuses to take instructions in circumstances where he suspects that a testator is being manipulated or pressurized by a beneficiary, he may guess that the testator will probably be taken elsewhere, to another draftsman, who will be less hesitant, and that the only effect of failing to prepare the requested will will be to give the work to a rival who will accept the assignment and suffer no penalty. There will seldom be any record of the fact that a will draftsman has refused to go ahead, and if someone else prepares a will in this kind of case the refusal becomes, in effect, an empty gesture.[259] **5–63**

and Suspicious Wills", Chap.7 in M. Dixon (ed.) *Modern Studies in Property Law*, Vol.5 (Oxford: Hart Publishing, 2009) at p.163.

256 [2013] W.T.L.R. 453 at para.5.

257 See above para.5–40.

258 See below para.15–08.

259 See below para.15–08.

5–64 Will-writing is, at the present time in England and Wales, unregulated. Probate is a reserved legal activity, but will-writing is not.[260] A person needs no qualifications to set himself up as a will-writer and there is nothing to stop him from charging for such services. In February 2013, the Legal Services Board recommended to the Lord Chancellor that will-writing activities should be reserved (i.e. regulated). In May 2013 the Lord Chancellor announced his decision not to accept the Legal Service Board's recommendation. The Law Society were clearly disappointed. It is respectfully suggested that will-writing should be regulated. In fact, it would be possible to go even further and to say that home-made wills should henceforth be banned, that only professionally drawn wills should be admitted to probate.[261] But, the quid pro quo for the introduction of any kind of rule about the regulation of will-writing would need to be that those professionals (and solicitors in particular) should first put their house in order. They need to put an end to the practice of taking part in the preparation of wills in circumstances where they are aware that beneficiaries are involved in the process. Only then can they be entitled to ask for others to be excluded from this kind of work.

[260] Under Sch.2 to the Legal Services Act 2007, there are six reserved legal activities, of which one is probate. This means that only persons with specified qualifications may practice in these six areas. The logic, such as it is, behind making probate a reserved legal activity, while will-writing is not, probably relates to the fact that probate practitioners (like conveyancers) have access to relatively large sums of clients' money. It is true that will-writers do not handle large sums of money, but poor quality will-writing leads to huge problems and expense.

[261] See R. Kerridge, Vol.59 (2000) C.L.J. 310, 332. In *Re Parsons* [2002] W.T.L.R. 237 the judge expressed disquiet that a licenced conveyancer (as opposed to a solicitor) had accepted instructions to draft a will for an incapacitated testator whose health was obviously failing. The judge suggested that, in circumstances like this, it should always be correct practice (in addition to obtaining the report and attendance of a doctor) for the instructions for the will to be taken, and its execution supervised, by a qualified solicitor with experience of wills. Nevertheless, he then granted probate of the will. This is the problem: judges indicate unhappiness, but not to a degree which causes them to declare against the will.

Chapter 6

PROMISES TO LEAVE PROPERTY BY WILL; SECRET TRUSTS; MUTUAL WILLS; DONATIONES MORTIS CAUSA; THE RULE IN STRONG V BIRD

I. PROMISES TO LEAVE PROPERTY BY WILL

A. REMEDY IN CONTRACT

1. Validity of contract

A contract by which T promises P to leave to P by will specific property[1] (such as T's house), a pecuniary legacy,[2] or the whole or a specified share of his residuary estate, is valid. Of course, under general principles of contract law, such a promise must either be supported by valuable consideration[3] or be made by deed[4]; there must be an intention to create legal relations,[5] and the terms of the contract must not be uncertain.[6] Moreover, if the contract relates to land and was made after 26 September 1989 it is void if it is not in writing.[7] If it was made before 27 September 1989 it is not enforceable unless there is a signed memorandum satisfying s.40 of the Law of Property Act 1925,[8] or the equitable doctrine of part performance applies.[9] **6–01**

[1] *Synge v Synge* [1894] 1 Q.B. 466 (to leave P life interest in house); *Parker v Clark* [1960] 1 W.L.R. 286 (to leave house and contents to P, Q and R jointly).

[2] *Hammersley v De Biel* (1845) 12 Cl. & F. 45; *Graham v Wickham* (1863) 1 De G.J. & Sm. 474.

[3] *Soulsbury v Soulsbury* [2007] W.T.L.R. 1841 (promise by ex-wife not to enforce order for periodical payments was consideration).

[4] At common law, deeds had to be executed under seal, but this requirement was abolished by the Law of Property (Miscellaneous Provisions) Act 1989 s.1(2).

[5] *Parker v Clark* [1960] 1 W.L.R. 286, 292–294 (not a mere family arrangement).

[6] *MacPhail v Torrance* (1909) 25 T.L.R. 810 (to make ample provision: too vague).

[7] Law Reform (Miscellaneous Provisions) Act 1989 s.2(1).

[8] *Maddison v Alderson* (1883) 8 App.Cas. 467; *Re Gonin* [1979] Ch.16. But T's estate may be liable on a *quantum meruit* to P for services rendered to T, *Deglman v Guaranty Trust Co of Canada* [1954] 3 D.L.R. 785. For a recent case, where the contract was made in 1984 and the requirements of s.40 were satisfied, see *Irani v Irani* [2006] W.T.L.R. 1561.

[9] *Wakeham v MacKenzie* [1968] 1 W.L.R. 1175 (T promised to leave house and contents to

Similarly, a contract by which T promises P not to revoke or alter T's existing will, or a particular gift in it, is valid.[10] Such a contract is construed as prohibiting intentional revocation by T[11] but not automatic revocation of his will if T marries[12]: thus if T marries, thereby automatically revoking his will, T does not commit any breach of contract.[13] A contract not to revoke may be drafted in such wide terms as to purport to prohibit automatic revocation by marriage as well as intentional revocation. In so far as it operates in restraint of marriage, however, such a prohibition is void on grounds of public policy.[14]

2. Remedies for breach

6–02 If T commits a breach of his contract with P to leave specific property, a pecuniary legacy, or the whole or part of his residuary estate to P, after T's death P is entitled to recover damages from T's estate for loss of the promised benefit.[15] In appropriate circumstances in a claim for specific performance of the contract, the court may order T's personal representatives to transfer the property bound by the contract (e.g. T's house) to P.[16]

T commits a breach of his contract with P not to revoke T's existing will if T intentionally revokes it.[17] P cannot stop T from revoking his will by bringing a claim for specific performance or an injunction, but P is entitled to recover damages from T, or after his death from T's estate, for loss of the promised benefit under this will.[18]

3. Testator's duty during his lifetime

6–03 If T contracts with P to leave *specific* property to P, and later T during his lifetime disposes of the property to Q, T thereby repudiates the contract. P may at once sue T for damages which are assessed subject to a reduction for the acceleration of the benefit and also, if the benefit of the contract is personal to P, subject to a reduction for the contingency of his failing

P if P gave up her flat and moved in and looked after him for life; P did so: held part performance): see *Re Gonin* [1979] Ch.16, 30–31; Pettit (1968) 32 Conv. (N.S.) 384.

10 *Robinson v Ommanney* (1882) 21 Ch.D. 780; (1883) 23 Ch.D. 285.

11 Intentional revocation occurs where the revocation is effected by destruction, another will or codicil, or duly executed writing; see below, paras 7–15 et seq.

12 See below, para.7–03.

13 *Re Marsland* [1939] Ch.820.

14 *Robinson v Ommanney* (1882), above, where the contract not to revoke was held to be divisible, and valid in so far as it prohibited intentional revocation.

15 *Hammersley v De Biel* (1845) 12 Cl. & F. 45 (legacy); *Schaefer v Schuhmann* [1972] A.C. 572, 585 et seq.

16 *Re Edwards* [1958] Ch.168, 175–176 (contract to devise house to P): see *Coverdale v Eastwood* (1872) L.R. 15 Eq. 121 (contract to settle all T's property on P in strict settlement). The court may order any person holding the asset as T's successor in title to transfer it (*Synge v Synge* [1894] 1 Q.B. 466, 471) unless he is a purchaser without notice or protected by the registration provisions applicable to interests in land.

17 *Robinson v Ommanney* (1882) 21 Ch.D. 780; (1883) 23 Ch.D. 285.

18 *Robinson v Ommanney* (1882) 21 Ch.D. 780: probably in appropriate circumstances the court may order T's personal representatives to transfer the promised asset to P.

to survive T.[19] If P can intervene before a purchaser for value obtains an interest in the property, P can obtain a declaration of his right to have it left to him by will and an injunction to restrain T from disposing of it in breach of contract.[20]

On the other hand, a contract by T to leave by will *all* his assets (or a share of them) at his death to P does not impose on T a duty not to dispose of any of his assets during his lifetime, unless the contract contains a term to this effect. The contract does, however, impose on T a more limited duty not to make inter vivos dispositions which in substance have a testamentary effect, such as a voluntary settlement whereby T settles property on himself for life, remainder to Q.[21]

4. Effect of lapse

Normally a gift by T's will to P fails by lapse if P predeceases T.[22] It **6–04** is a question of construction of the contract between T and P whether (i) the benefit of the contract is personal to P, who takes the risk of lapse, so that T is discharged from liability if P predeceases T[23]; or whether (ii) the benefit of the contract is not personal to P but accrues for the benefit of P's estate, so that T ought to make provision in his will against lapse.[24]

5. Effect of insolvency

A contract to leave by will specific property or a pecuniary legacy to P **6–05** may merely impose an obligation on T to make a will containing such a gift; in that case P, like any other beneficiary under a will, takes the risk that T's estate may turn out to be insolvent, or insufficient to satisfy the gift; if it does, P takes nothing, or a reduced benefit.[25] Such a contract is, however, more likely to impose an obligation on T to make the gift effective; in that case, T commits a breach of contract if T's estate is insolvent, or insufficient to satisfy the gift, and P is entitled to be treated as a creditor for the value of the property[26] or the amount of the legacy,[27] and to rank for payment with T's other creditors of the same degree.[28] Thus the effect

[19] *Synge v Synge* [1894] 1 Q.B. 466; *Schaefer v Schuhmann* [1972] A.C. 572, 586: see *Parker v Clark* [1960] 1 W.L.R. 286.
[20] *Synge v Synge*, above, at p.471; *Schaefer v Schuhmann*, above.
[21] *Jones v Martin* (1798) 5 Ves.Jr. 266; *Fortescue v Hannah* (1812) 19 Ves.Jr. 67; *Logan v Wienholt* (1833) 1 Cl. & F. 611; *Re Bennett* [1934] W.N. 177 (Q the ostensible owner but T retained the income): cf. *Palmer v Bank of New South Wales* (1975) C.L.R. 150 (opening joint bank account with Q not testamentary).
[22] See below, paras 14–11 et seq.
[23] *Re Brookman's Trust* (1869) L.R. 5 Ch.App. 182; *Schaefer v Schuhmann* [1972] A.C.572, 586: see *Jones v How* (1848) 7 Hare 267; *Needham v Smith* (1828) 4 Russ. 318.
[24] See *Re Brookman's Trust*, above, at 191. See W. A. Lee (1971) 87 L.Q.R. 358, 361–362.
[25] See *Graham v Wickham* (1863) 1 D.J. & S. 474, 484–485; *Eyre v Monro* (1857) 3 K. & J. 305, 308.
[26] *Schaefer v Schuhmann* [1972] A.C. 572, 586.
[27] *Graham v Wickham* (1863) 1 D.J. & S. 474; *Eyre v Monroe* (1857) 3 K. & J. 305.
[28] For the order of priority of T's debts see below, paras 21–77 et seq.

of insolvency depends on the extent of the obligation imposed on T by the contract.

A contract by T to leave by will the whole or a specified share of his residuary estate to P is different because T's residuary estate available for distribution is only ascertained after T's debts and funeral and testamentary expenses have been paid. P takes the risk that T's estate may turn out to be insolvent; if it does, P takes nothing and has no claim as a creditor for breach of contract.[29]

6. Contracts (Rights of Third Parties) Act 1999[30]

6–06 Section 1 of the Act provides that a third party[31] may enforce a term of a contract if the contract expressly provides that he may, or if the term purports to confer a benefit on him, unless the contract itself makes it clear that the parties did not intend the term to be enforceable by the third party. Thus if T makes a contract with P to leave specific property to X and then breaks it, both P and X will have a claim in damages against T. Although s.1(5) provides that the third party has the benefit of any remedy which would have been available to him in an action for breach of contract, it is not clear whether a third party who has given no consideration can sue for specific performance. As a volunteer beneficiary who was a party to a deed was able to recover damages but not obtain specific performance,[32] it would seem strange if a third party were in a more favoured position.

B. PROPRIETARY ESTOPPEL[33]

1. Introduction[34]

6–07 As an alternative to making a claim in contract, someone who has relied upon an assurance given by the deceased to the effect that the deceased will dispose of some or all of his property in a particular way on his death may be able to bring a claim based on the equitable doctrine of proprietary estoppel.

[29] *Schaefer v Schuhmann* [1972] A.C. 572, 586; *Jervis v Wolferstan* (1874) L.R. 18 Eq. 18, 24.

[30] Section 10 provides that the Act does not apply to contracts entered into before the end of six months from 11 November 1999, i.e. 11 May 2000, unless the contract provides for the application of the Act.

[31] Although he need not be in existence when the contract is made, he must be expressly identified by name, as a member of a class, or as answering a particular description.

[32] See *Cannon v Hartley* [1949] Ch.213.

[33] See *Snell's Equity*, 3rd edn (London: Sweet & Maxwell, 2015), paras 12–032—12–053; Hanbury and Martin, *Modern Equity*, 20th edn (London: Sweet & Maxwell, 2015), paras 30–022—30–029; Megarry & Wade, *The Law of Real Property*, 8th edn (London: Sweet & Maxwell, 2012), Chap.16; Gardner (1999) 115 L.Q.R. 438 and (2006) 122 L.Q.R. 492; B. McFarlane, "Proprietary Estoppel: Undermining the Law of Succession?" Chap.4 in B. Häcker and C. Mitchell (eds), *Current Issues in Succession Law* (Oxford: Hart Publishing, 2016).

[34] For a comparative study of the position in England and New Zealand, and a discussion of the Law Reform (Testamentary Promises) Act 1949 (N. Z.), see Nield (2000) 20 L.S. 85.

The earlier cases where successful claims[35] were based on the doctrine of proprietary estoppel concerned assurances about existing rights, and they covered clearly identified property[36]; they did not cover promises to devise or bequeath all or part of someone's property on his future death. But in *Re Basham*[37] Edward Nugee QC[38] extended the doctrine of proprietary estoppel to cover promises which related to what would happen to the promisor's property when he died. He formulated the doctrine in the following way:

> "where one person, A, has acted to his detriment on the faith of a belief, which was known to and encouraged by another person, B, that he either has or is going to be given a right in or over B's property, B cannot insist on his strict legal rights if to do so would be inconsistent with A's belief."[39]

Since *Basham*, there have been eight Court of Appeal cases,[40] one House of Lords case[41] and one Privy Council case[42] in which the doctrine of proprietary estoppel has been held to cover promises to leave property on death.

2. Successful claims

In *Re Basham*[43] the claimant and her husband cared for her stepfather **6–08** after he made a series of promises to the effect that he would leave his property to the claimant when he died. In *Wayling v Jones*[44] the younger member of a homosexual partnership worked for the deceased for many years without being paid a proper wage. In *Gillett v Holt*[45] the claimant worked as a farm manager for modest reward following repeated statements and promises by the defendant that he would inherit the farm. In *Campbell v Griffin*[46] the claimant lived with an older couple, originally as their lodger, but the couple came to rely on the claimant to provide services such as cooking meals, shopping and so on. In *Jennings v Rice*[47] the

[35] Even before an attempt was made to extend the doctrine of proprietary estoppel to cover promises to leave property by will, different judges held differing views as to how far the doctrine could be taken. Contrast the restrictive approach of Fry J in *Willmott v Barber* (1880) 15 Ch.D. 96 with the more liberal approach of Oliver J in *Taylors Fashions Ltd v Liverpool Victoria Trustees Co Ltd* [1982] Q.B. 133.

[36] *Dillwyn v Llewelyn* (1862) 4 De G. F. & J. 517; *Inwards v Baker* [1965] 2 Q.B. 29.

[37] *Re Basham* [1986] 1 W.L.R. 1498.

[38] Sitting as a High Court judge.

[39] *Re Basham* [1986] 1 W.L.R. 1498, 1503 H.

[40] *Wayling v Jones* (1995) 69 P. & C.R. 170; *Gillett v Holt* [2001] Ch.210; *Campbell v Griffin* [2001] W.T.L.R. 981; *Jennings v Rice* [2003] 1 F.C.R. 501; *Grundy v Ottey* [2003] W.T.L.R. 1253; *Suggitt v Suggitt* [2012] W.T.L.R. 1607; *Bradbury v Taylor* [2013] W.T.L.R. 29 and *Southwell v Blackburn* [2015] W.T.L.R. 147.

[41] *Thorner v Major* [2009] 1 W.L.R. 776.

[42] *Henry v Henry* [2010] 1 All E.R. 988.

[43] *Re Basham* [1986] 1 W.L.R. 1498.

[44] *Wayling v Jones* (1993) 69 P. & C.R. 170.

[45] *Gillett v Holt* [2001] Ch.210.

[46] *Campbell v Griffin* [2001] W.T.L.R. 981.

[47] *Jenny v Rice* [2003] 1 F.C.R. 501.

claimant originally worked for the deceased as a part-time gardener, but he gradually took on more and more work for which he was not paid. He was told by the deceased that "this will all be yours one day". In *Grundy v Ottey*[48] the claimant and her lover lived together in a quasi-matrimonial relationship during the course of which she made extraordinary efforts to assist him overcome his addiction to alcohol and he promised her that, on his death, he would give her a life-interest in his houseboat and devise his flat in Jamaica to her. In *Thorner v Major*[49] the claimant spent most of his eighteen hour days, during a period of nearly 30 years, assisting his father's cousin on the cousin's farm, and for this he received no payment. The claimant understood, both from things said and done by the cousin, a childless widower, that the farm would be his on the cousin's death. In *Henry v Henry*,[50] the claimant was promised that he would inherit a plot of land if he cultivated it, and looked after its owner for the rest of her life. In *Suggitt v Suggitt*[51] a son gave his father assistance on the father's farm. In *Bradbury v Taylor*[52] the claimant gave up his home in Sheffield to move with his wife and two children to live in his uncle's large house in Cornwall to provide his uncle with company. In *Southwell v Blackburn*,[53] the claimant, on the basis of a representation that she would be provided with housing for the rest of her life, gave up her housing association tenancy to move in, with her children, to live with her lover in his house.

3. Formulating the rule

6–09 Lord Walker began his speech in *Thorner v Major*[54] by quoting an academic authority, Simon Gardner, "There is no definition of proprietary estoppel which is both comprehensive and uncontroversial (and many attempts at one have been neither)"[55] and he then went on to say that the doctrine is based on three main elements:

(i) a representation or assurance made to the claimant;
(ii) reliance on it by the claimant; and
(iii) detriment to the claimant in consequence of his (reasonable) reliance.

In *Gillett v Holt*[56] Robert Walker LJ, as he then was, had explained that the doctrine of proprietary estoppel should not be treated as subdivided into three or four water-tight compartments, so that it is necessary for the claimant to go through a list, ticking off the various elements. The

[48] *Grundy v Ottey* [2003] W.T.L.R. 1253.
[49] *Thorner v Major* [2009] 1 W.L.R. 776. For casenote, see [2009] All E.R. Annual Rev. para.29.29.
[50] *Henry v Henry* [2010] 1 All E.R. 988. For casenote, see [2010] All E.R. Annual Rev. para.26.54.
[51] *Suggitt v Suggitt* [2012] W.T.L.R. 1607. For casenote, see [2012] All E.R. Annual Rev. para.24.40.
[52] *Bradbury v Taylor* [2013] W.T.L.R. 29.
[53] *Southwell v Blackburn* [2015] W.T.L.R. 147.
[54] *Thorner v Major* [2009] 1W.L.R. 776.
[55] *An Introduction to Land Law*, 1st edn (Oxford: Hart Publishing, 2007), p.101.
[56] *Gillett v Holt* [2001] Ch.210.

quality of representations or assurances can influence the issue of reliance, which may then be intertwined with detriment. Detriment itself is not a narrow or technical concept and it need not consist of the expenditure of money or other quantifiable financial detriment: what must be proved is that the detriment was something substantial. The Court of Appeal in that case emphasised that all elements of the doctrine of proprietary estoppel are permeated by the fundamental principle that equity is concerned to prevent unconscionable conduct; so the court has to look at the matter in the round.[57]

4. Extending proprietary estoppel into the law of succession

6–10 Not everyone has been enthusiastic about the extension of the doctrine of proprietary estoppel into the law of succession.[58] A claimant does not need to make a claim based on proprietary estoppel if he can succeed in contract.[59] There is a danger that vague statements made by the deceased—to the effect that he intends to leave property to a particular person if that person behaves in a particular way—will become the basis for a claim. A will is ambulatory and if there is no contract, why should the testator be obliged to leave his property in a particular way?[60] On the other hand, if the deceased has made promises to leave property by will, on which reliance has been placed, the fact that a will is revocable is irrelevant to the detriment which has been suffered.

5. Special factors

6–11 It could also be suggested that in *Re Basham, Wayling v Jones, Grundy v Ottey* and *Thorner v Major*, there were particular factors which engendered sympathy for the claimants, but which were not directly relevant to the doctrine of proprietary estoppel. In *Basham* the claimant had not only cared for her stepfather, but the property he left on his death was inherited, in large part, from his wife, the claimant's mother. The claimant's moral claim to take all or part of the estate, even had she not cared for her stepfather, would have been strong.[61] In *Wayling v*

[57] The "in the round" approach does not always assist the claimant, see *Uglow v Uglow* [2004] W.T.L.R. 1183.

[58] *Re Basham* [1986] 1 W.L.R. 1498 was criticised by D. J. Hayton in [1987] C.L.J. 215 and by C. Sherrin in [1987] All E.R. Annual Rev. 263. The case was distinguished in *Taylor v Dickens* [1998] 1 F.L.R. 806; but the restrictive approach in *Taylor v Dickens* was criticised by the Court of Appeal in *Gillett v Holt* [2001] Ch.210.

[59] Claims under this heading are particularly likely to be formulated where claims in contract would fail because s.2(1) of the Law of Property (Miscellaneous Provisions) Act 1989 provides that "A contract for the sale or other disposition of an interest in land can only be made in writing and only by incorporating all the terms which the parties have expressly agreed in one document or, where contracts are exchanged, in each."

[60] Hayton said of *Basham*: "the decision seems to open the floodgates to all sorts of competing claims of disappointed relatives or friends of the deceased, and to make the lot of the personal representatives more onerous and that of the lawyers more remunerative" ([1987] C.L.J. 215, 216).

[61] Compare the not dissimilar case of *Re Callaghan* [1985] Fam. 1, where an adult stepchild succeeded under the Family Provision legislation, rather than by proprietary estoppel.

Jones the deceased *had* made a will devising his hotel to the claimant, but had subsequently sold it, so that the gift had been adeemed.[62] The application of the doctrine of proprietary estoppel undid the effect of the doctrine of ademption and almost certainly gave a result of which the testator would have approved. In *Ottey*, a family provision claim by the claimant failed on the ground that the parties were not living together immediately before the lover's death, but the termination of the relationship had not been the claimant's fault. Again, in *Thorner v Major*, the deceased cousin had originally made a will under which the claimant would have inherited his farm, but had destroyed it after falling out with one of the pecuniary legatees and had, for no apparent reason, failed to follow his solicitor's advice to make another. In each of *Basham*, *Griffin*, *Jennings* and *Thorner* the deceased died intestate, having failed to make the wills which they intended to make. *Gillett* is different because the defendant—who had quarrelled with the claimant—was still alive when proceedings were brought.

6. Proving reliance—demonstrating effect of assurances on claimant's conduct

6–12 In proprietary estoppel cases, the parties are nearly always closely linked: if they are not members of the same family, they are usually united by ties of affection. In *Wayling v Jones*[63] the judge at first instance dismissed the claim because the claimant's evidence was to the effect that he would have acted as he did whether or not the deceased had made representations to him. The Court of Appeal allowed the claimant's appeal on the ground that, once it had been established that promises had been made by the deceased to the claimant and that the claimant had acted to his detriment, the burden shifted to those opposing the claim to prove that the claimant did not rely on the representations.[64] The trial judge[65] followed this approach in *Ottey* and was endorsed by the Court of Appeal.

This problem is in some respects similar to the difficulty which arises in family provision cases where there are claims by dependants.[66] It may seem harsh to penalise a claimant whose generosity of spirit would cause him to act to his own detriment even if no promise were made to him. On the other hand, what about the friend or family member who acts to his detriment having received no promise at all? Morally, he is deserving too. The distinction is that proprietary estoppel is designed to prevent the deceased from reneging on a promise which he has made.

Callaghan is discussed below at para.8–67. Quaere what the result would have been had *Basham* been fought as a family provision case.

[62] For ademption, see below, paras 14–35 et seq.

[63] *Wayling v Jones* (1993) 69 P. & C.R. 170.

[64] *Campbell v Griffin* is similar: the claim was dismissed by the judge at first instance on the same basis and, again, the claimant's appeal was allowed by the Court of Appeal.

[65] HH Judge Langan QC, sitting as a Deputy Judge of the High Court.

[66] See below, para.8–76.

7. Satisfying the equity

Suppose that X promises Y that, if Y looks after him, he will leave Y his property on death. If Y does look after X, is he then entitled to the whole of X's estate? The governing principle has been expressed in different words by different judges; but in essence equity intervenes to prevent an injustice being perpetrated. The remedy afforded is "the minimum equity to do justice".[67] In *Basham* the claimant's stepfather had promised her that he would leave her all his property when he died and, when the claimant succeeded in her claim, she was awarded the entire estate. *Wayling v Jones* was also relatively straightforward in terms of the equity. The deceased had promised his homosexual partner that he would leave him a hotel in his will. The gift was adeemed when the hotel was sold, but the court ordered that the proceeds of sale of the hotel were to be paid to the claimant. **6–13**

The later cases cause more of a problem in relation to the satisfaction of the equity. In *Taylor v Dickens*[68] a widow promised her handyman that she would leave him her bungalow if he worked for her without being paid a wage. She then made a will in his favour, but changed her mind and made a fresh will leaving her property elsewhere. The handyman's proprietary estoppel claim was dismissed. This decision is out of line with the later authorities[69]; but the court may have been influenced by the size of the claim in comparison with the detriment suffered by the claimant. It was subsequently established that, in cases where the claimant is successful, he will not necessarily be awarded the entire estate. Sometimes this is because it is not clear exactly what property was covered by the deceased's representations[70]; but, quite apart from this, there is a need for proportionality—it is not simply a question of awarding the expectation. In *Gillett v Holt*,[71] after the parties had quarrelled, and while the promisor was still alive, the promisee was awarded a farm and £100,000 as compensation for his exclusion from the rest of the farming business. In *Campbell v Griffin*,[72] where there were also claims against the estate by the County Council,[73] the claimant was awarded £35,000. In *Jennings v Rice*[74] where the deceased was a 93 year old childless widow, with an estate whose net value exceeded £1 million (including a house worth £435,000) the claimant was awarded £200,000 on the basis that, even though the claimant argued that his expectation was that he would receive the entire estate, he had had no idea what the deceased owned apart from the house and there had to be proportionality between the expectation **6–14**

67 Scarman LJ in *Crabb v Arun District Council* [1976] Ch.179, 198.

68 *Taylor v Dickens* [1998] 1 F.L.R. 806.

69 It seems clear that claimants in proprietary estoppel cases have generally fared better in the Court of Appeal than before first instance judges. The Court of Appeal allowed appeals by claimants in *Wayling v Jones; Gillett v Holt* and *Campbell v Griffin. Taylor v Dickens* was criticised by M. P. Thompson in [1998] Conv. 210, by W. J. Swadling in [1998] R.L.R. 220 and by the Court of Appeal in *Gillett v Holt.*

70 See *Jennings v Rice* and *Campbell v Griffin.*

71 *Gillett v Holt* [2001] Ch.210.

72 *Campbell v Griffin* [2001] W.T.L.R. 981.

73 The claims by the County Council related to the cost of looking after the couple while they were in residential accommodation toward the end of their lives.

74 *Jennings v Rice* [2003] 1 F.C.R. 501.

and the detriment. In *Grundy v Ottey*[75] the claimant's expectation was worth about £250,000 but this was out of proportion to the detriment she had suffered and the award made to her, upheld by the Court of Appeal, had a value of approximately £100,000.[76] Having said this, there are two more recent cases where the property awarded appears to be disproportionate to any detriment suffered by the claimant. In *Suggitt*[77] the trial judge awarded the claimant son his father's farm, valued at more than £3 million, on the basis of unpaid work done by the son for the father. In fact, the son, insofar as he had undertaken work, had done so only part time, and this had been at a time when the father was providing free board and lodging for him, for his partner and for their children. The Court of Appeal considered that the award was not perverse and upheld it, but it is not easy to see the detriment and harder still to discern proportionality.[78] *Bradbury v Taylor* is a less extreme example of disproportion, in that the trial judge awarded the claimant a house worth about £1 million; but, as the detriment consisted of moving from Sheffield to live rent free in Cornwall, it is not easy to understand why the Court of Appeal upheld the award. If it becomes difficult to predict what the courts are likely to do in this kind of case, it will be hard for the parties to settle and there is a danger that proprietary estoppel claims will be added in to bolster other potentially weak claims, so leading to unnecessary litigation.[79]

II. SECRET TRUSTS

6–15 A secret trust arises when X dies leaving property to Y, but Y has undertaken that he will hold the property on trust for Z. There are two kinds of secret trusts: fully secret and half-secret.[80] A fully secret trust may arise under a will or on an intestacy, but where it arises under a will there is no reference to it in the will, which simply leaves the property "to Y". A half-secret trust can arise only under a will which refers to the trust's existence, but does not indicate its terms or the beneficiary's identity. The will states that the property is left "to Y on the trusts which he knows about" or uses some equivalent phraseology.

1. The decision to enforce secret trusts

6–16 When the first cases of fully secret trusts came before the courts, the judges had three choices. On the basis that it was established that X had devised

[75] *Grundy v Ottey* [2003] W.T.L.R. 1253.
[76] See also *Thorner v Curtis* [2008] W.T.L.R. 155.
[77] See above, fn.51.
[78] See Mee fn.79, below.
[79] Profs Hayton and Sherrin expressed unhappiness about the doctrine of proprietary estoppel from the outset, see fns 58 and 60. In [2013] 77 Conv. 280, Prof Mee found it hard to discern any significant detriment in *Suggitt* or *Bradbury*, decisions he described as "indulgent and confused".
[80] Half-secret trusts are sometimes called semi-secret trusts.

or bequeathed property to Y and that Y had undertaken to hold it on trust for Z, but that there was no reference to this in any testamentary document,[81] the courts could have held:

(i) that Y took the property absolutely—that there was no trust; or
(ii) that Y held the property on trust for Z, the person whom the testator wanted to benefit; or
(iii) that Y held the property on a resulting trust for X or for his estate.

The courts opted for (ii), and decided that Y, the person who benefited under the will or on intestacy, held in trust for Z, the person whom the deceased had wanted to benefit but whom, for whatever reason, he had been unwilling openly to acknowledge.

The earliest cases upholding fully secret trusts date from the latter part of the seventeenth-century[82] and it was quite clear from the eighteenth-century onwards that fully secret trusts would be upheld and enforced. The courts were less enthusiastic about upholding half-secret trusts and it was not until 1929 that the House of Lords in *Blackwell v Blackwell*[83] finally and unequivocally confirmed their validity, rejecting the belief in some circles that to uphold half-secret trusts was to "give the go-by" to the Wills Act 1837.[84]

2. The justification for enforcing secret trusts

The enforcement of secret trusts appears, prima facie, to be in conflict both with the letter and with the spirit of s.9 of the Wills Act 1837, which requires a will, unless privileged,[85] to be in writing. All the policy reasons which require that wills should be in writing, and that they should be executed in a particular way,[86] speak against the enforceability of secret trusts.[87] Nevertheless three separate theories have been put forward as explaining, or justifying, their enforcement. None of them represents a sound logical basis. **6–17**

(a) *Secret trusts are enforced because they operate outside (or "dehors")*[88] *the will*

One way of justifying the enforceability of secret trusts is to say that they operate outside the will. X's will gives property to Y and the fact that Y is directed to hold it on trust for Z is not a matter of succession law, but part of the law of trusts.[89] There are several problems with **6–18**

[81] The evidence would be extrinsic—i.e. evidence from outside (or "*dehors*") the will.
[82] See, e.g. *Thynn v Thynn* (1684) 1 Vern 296.
[83] *Blackwell v Blackwell* [1929] A.C. 318.
[84] In fact, *both* fully *and* half-secret trusts "give the go-by" to the Wills Act; it is just more blatant in the case of half-secret trusts.
[85] For privileged wills see above, paras 4–29 et seq.
[86] See above, paras 4–01 et seq.
[87] See E. Challinor [2005] Conv. 388.
[88] The use of legal French here may indicate an awareness of weakness in the reasoning.
[89] In the days when all probate matters, including contentious probate, were dealt with by the Court of Probate, cases on secret trusts would have come before the Court of Chancery.

this, one of which is that, even if it could be said that a fully secret trust operates outside the will, a half-secret trust operates at least half inside. But there is a deeper problem: to attempt to justify the enforcement of secret trusts on the ground that they operate outside the will is to miss the point. Those who want to justify them need to explain not simply how they operate outside the will, but how they operate outside the Wills Act 1837.[90]

(b) *Secret trusts are upheld for the avoidance of fraud*

6–19 Another possible justification for upholding secret trusts is to say that, by enforcing them, the secret trustee will be prevented from committing fraud. But there is a problem with this too. When it is said that the secret trustee must be prevented from committing fraud, it is not made clear whom he is supposed to be prevented from defrauding. When X leaves property to Y, and Y promises X that he will hold the property on trust for Z, whom should Y be prevented from defrauding: X or Z? If the object is to prevent Y from defrauding X, it can—generally[91]—be achieved by obliging Y to hold the property on a resulting trust for X. By obliging him to hold it on trust for Z, the court is deciding that he has defrauded Z, but he can only be held to have defrauded Z if Z had some rights under the trust. Z can only have rights under the trust if the trust is enforceable, and at this point the argument in favour of enforcing it becomes circular.[92]

(c) *Half-secret trusts can be justified by analogy with the doctrine of incorporation by reference*

6–20 The least convincing attempt to provide a theoretical justification for enforcing half-secret trusts (and it applies only to half-secret trusts) is to suggest that they are enforced by some form of analogy with the doctrine of incorporation by reference.[93] The requirements of the doctrine of incorporation by reference were explained in chapter 4[94] but the doctrine has nothing to do with secrecy. A document which is incorporated into a will under the doctrine of incorporation by reference is admissible to probate as part of the will. It becomes, like the will, a public document. This is nothing like the doctrine of secret trusts where the whole object is secrecy.

[90] (1999) 115 L.Q.R. 631 at 641 (P. Critchley).

[91] "Generally", but not when Y is himself the residuary beneficiary under X's will or is the beneficiary on X's intestacy.

[92] As Oakley says: "such arguments are completely circular. To refer to the terms of the secret trust as the 'wishes of the testator' and to describe those entitled under the secret trust as 'beneficiaries' begs the question; only if evidence of the terms of the trust is admitted contrary to the provisions of the Wills Act is it appropriate to describe the terms of the secret trust as the wishes of the testator and to refer to those entitled thereunder as its beneficiaries. It is not possible to use as a justification for admitting evidence contrary to the provisions of the Wills Act facts which can only be proven if such evidence is admitted"; A. J. Oakley, *Constructive Trusts*, 3rd edn (London: Sweet & Maxwell, 1996), p.248.

[93] [1979] Conv. 360 (P. Matthews).

[94] See above paras 4–39 et seq.

To link half-secret trusts with the doctrine of incorporation by reference is both confused and confusing.[95]

3. Why were secret trusts not enforced as resulting trusts?

(a) *The advantage of treating secret trusts as resulting trusts*

A decision in favour of a resulting trust would avoid contravening the provisions of the Wills Act, would prevent fraud, and would appear to create only one difficulty. The difficulty occurs where Y (the secret trustee) is X's residuary beneficiary, and so would himself be the ultimate beneficiary under the resulting trust.[96] But there could always be a special, separate sub-rule to deal with this situation. It is submitted that the logical way in which to have dealt with secret trusts (apart from the rare cases where the trustee was the residuary beneficiary) would have been to instruct the secret trustee to hold the property on a resulting trust for the estate. The fact that this was not done when the earliest secret trust cases came before the courts may well be because they were decided before the doctrine of resulting trusts was fully developed.[97] **6–21**

(b) *Secret trusts in favour of charity*

There may have been another reason why the courts did not need to apply the doctrine of resulting trusts in one group of early secret trust cases. It is generally assumed nowadays that nearly all the early secret trust cases were concerned with testators who wanted to devise or bequeath property to persons whom they were too embarrassed openly to acknowledge as beneficiaries—their mistresses and their illegitimate offspring. In fact, this was by no means always the case. A significant group of secret trust cases during the latter part of the eighteenth century and the earlier part of the nineteenth century were concerned with attempts to avoid the consequences of the Mortmain Act 1736. This Act declared void any gift of land[98] to charity by will.[99] Someone who wished to bypass the Act might leave property to an individual, but the individual would promise to hold it on trust for an agreed charity.[100] The effect of upholding the secret trust in this sort of case was exactly the same as the effect of enforcing a **6–22**

[95] J. G. Fleming suggests that the decision in *Re Keen* (see para.6–24 below) represents an improper engrafting of the rules concerned with incorporation by reference onto the doctrine of secret trusts; see (1947) 12 Conv. (N.S.) 28, 39.

[96] See *Re Rees' W.T.* [1950] Ch.204; *Re Pugh's W.T.* [1967] 1 W.L.R. 1262.

[97] Secret trust cases came before the courts from the late seventeenth–century onwards, whereas the doctrine of resulting trusts, as we know it, was developed in the eighteenth– and nineteenth–centuries.

[98] Not only devises of realty.

[99] G. H. Jones, *History of the Law of Charity 1532–1827* (Cambridge: Cambridge University Press, 1961), pp.115 et seq.

[100] The person who made the promise was usually a clergyman, and the promise was to hold the property in trust for the church. The purpose of the Mortmain Act was to prevent testators from leaving any significant part of their property to the church.

resulting trust[101]: by upholding the secret trust the court would decree that the property was held in trust for charity. A gift in trust for charity would be void under the 1736 Act; and the property would then result back to the testator.

3. Possible distinctions between fully-secret and half-secret trusts

6–23 It has been suggested that there may be four distinctions between fully secret and half-secret trusts.

(a) *Half-secret trusts must be communicated before the will is made*

6–24 A fully secret trust must be communicated to the trustee before the testator's death, but it does not have to be communicated before he makes his will.[102] The doctrine may also apply where X has made a will leaving property to Y, then decides to alter his will and to leave the property to Z, but does not proceed with the alteration because Y promises to hold the property in trust for Z.

Although it is clear that a fully secret trust may be communicated at any time before death, it has been suggested that a half-secret trust must be communicated before or at the same time as the will is made. There is no clear authority for the suggestion. There are obiter dicta in *Blackwell v Blackwell*[103] but the case usually said to be authority for the rule is *Re Keen.*[104] In fact, the half-secret trust in *Re Keen* failed *not* because communication was after the will—it was not—but because of an inconsistency between the terms of the will and the half-secret trust.[105] The failure in *Keen* appears to have been a question of construction, not a question of secret trusts.[106] In *Re Bateman's Will Trusts*[107] it seems to have been assumed that *Re Keen* was authority for the proposition that communication in the case of a half-secret trust has to be before the will, and the point was not argued. The supposed rule that communication in the case of a half-secret trust must precede the will is not followed in Ireland, New South Wales or in most American jurisdictions.[108] It is also difficult to reconcile with *Gold v Hill*[109] which, although involving a trust of a life policy nomination, rather than a trust of a gift by will, appears to find no fault with communication after the nomination.[110]

[101] *Muckleston v Brown* (1801) 6 Ves.109; *Stickland v Aldridge* (1804) 9 Ves.516.

[102] A fully secret trust does not require that there is a will; it may apply where the deceased dies intestate and someone who benefits on his intestacy promises to hold what he receives in trust for someone else.

[103] *Blackwell v Blackwell* [1929] A.C. 318.

[104] *Re Keen* [1937] Ch.316.

[105] The will said that the communication would be after the will, whereas the communication was, in fact, prior to the will.

[106] As a question of construction, it *might* nowadays be decided differently—see Chap.10.

[107] *Re Bateman's Will Trusts* [1970] 1 W.L.R. 1463.

[108] See Hanbury and Martin, *Modern Equity*, 20th edn, (London: Sweet & Maxwell, 2015), para.6–032, fn.157–159.

[109] *Gold v Hill* [1999] 1 F.L.R. 54.

[110] To draw a line between a nomination and a gift by will would appear, in this context, odd.

The question whether, when there is a half-secret trust, communication needs to be before the making of the will was raised, but not answered, in the 2014 case of *Rawstron v Freud*.[111] Lucien Freud, a successful artist, left his residuary estate to two women, one of whom was his solicitor and who had prepared the will and the other of whom was one of his daughters. There was no mention of a trust in the clause containing the residuary gift, but the two women were nominated in an earlier clause as "executors and trustees of this Will." and the residue was left to them jointly. A *beneficial* joint tenancy in favour of a testator's solicitor and daughter would seem to make little sense. Another pointer to there being a trust was that a solicitor will be struck off if he takes, or attempts to take, a beneficial interest under a will which he has prepared.[112] The two executors[113] admitted that the gift to them of the residue was to be held in trust, but they claimed that the trust was fully secret, not half-secret. So, the case raised the question as to how a trust should be classified if the gift to the trustee is not specifically designated as being held "in trust" but where a trust is implied by wording elsewhere in the will and/or by other surrounding circumstances. Richard Spearman QC[114] held that the classification of the trust as fully or half-secret must depend on reading the will as a whole, but then went on, rather surprisingly, to decide that this trust was fully secret. He held that, in any case, communication had been before the making of the will,[115] so the challenger, one of the testator's illegitimate children, suffered a double defeat. **6–25**

If the will was read as a whole, and the judge did so read it, it would not have been difficult to hold that the trust was half-secret. At the very least, the case demonstrates that the line drawn between fully and half-secret trusts is not always as clear as might be supposed. And the question as to the timing of the communication may also raise difficulties. What if, for example, communication by the testator to the trustees was before the will but it was also agreed that the testator reserved the right (of which he did not avail himself) to alter his instructions after execution?

What *Freud* demonstrates, is that attempting to draw a distinction as to the validity of a secret trust on the basis of the time of communication combined with classification as to the degree of secrecy is illogical and can lead to all kinds of problems. By deciding the two issues of timing and classification in the way he did, the judge in *Freud* avoided having to deal with the unresolved problem as to whether, when a trust is half-secret, communication does have to be before the making of the will. Had he attempted to come to a decision on that it is probable that, whatever conclusion he reached, his decision would have been subject to appeal. The value of the residuary estate in this case, i.e. the amount at stake, was a sum in excess of £40 million.

[111] *Rawstron v Freud* [2014] W.T.L.R. 1453.

[112] See *Re a Solicitor* [1975] 1 Q.B. 475 discussed in para.5–37, above.

[113] The women were described in the will as "executors"—they should, in traditional terminology, have been described as "executrices".

[114] Sitting as a deputy High Court judge.

[115] There was no direct evidence that communication had been after the will—the challenger inferred it from the surrounding circumstances. But, if communication was before the will, would it not have been simpler to arrange for the trust to appear, openly, as half-secret, thus avoiding any problems created by the solicitor's appearing to take a beneficial interest?

(b) *Are secret trusts express or constructive?*

6–26 There is disagreement as to whether secret trusts are express or constructive. Some writers say that both fully and half-secret trusts are express, others that both are constructive, others that half-secret trusts are express, but that fully secret trusts are constructive. It is suggested that they are both express. In each case the trust is founded on the undertaking given to the deceased by the "trustee". The question whether a secret trust is express or constructive is only of significance where the property involved is land. *Re Baillie*[116] appears to assume that half-secret trusts are express; but the question whether a fully secret trust of land is express or constructive was not raised in *Ottaway v Norman*,[117] where a fully secret trust was upheld without written evidence. It is submitted that, if it were suggested that either a fully or a half-secret trust of land had not been evidenced by writing as required by s.53(1)(b) of the Law of Property Act 1925, the response should be that "equity will not allow a statute to be an instrument of fraud".[118] It is not necessary, for this purpose, to suggest that either a fully secret, or a half-secret, trust of land is constructive.

(c) *What happens if the trustee under a secret trust dies before the testator?*

6–27 A secret trust arises where X dies leaving property to Y, and Y has (secretly) undertaken that he will hold the property on trust for Z. But what happens if Y dies before X? If X leaves property *beneficially* to Y, and Y predeceases X, the gift lapses.[119] If X leaves property to Y on an *express* trust, set out in the will, then Y's death does *not* cause the gift to fail because of the principle that "Equity will not allow a trust to fail for want of a trustee". Another trustee will be appointed to take Y's place.[120] But what about the case of a fully or a half-secret trust? It was suggested, obiter, in *Re Maddock*[121] that, in the case of a fully secret trust, the gift would fail; but it is thought by some[122] that a half-secret trust would survive. There is no authority. The point cannot, of course, be tested unless someone—other than the trustee—knows the terms of the secret trust. But where this is the case, it is submitted that it should make no difference whether the trust is fully secret or half-secret. If secret trusts are to be upheld, the logic of upholding them is to treat all secret trusts, fully secret and half-secret, as trusts and, provided there is evidence of the terms of the trust, to apply the ordinary trusts rule whenever the trustee dies before the testator.[123]

116 *Re Baillie* [1886] 2 T.L.R. 660.

117 *Ottaway v Norman* [1972] Ch.698.

118 See *Rochefoucauld v Bousted* [1897] 1 Ch.196.

119 See below, Chap.14, paras 14–11 et seq.

120 *Re Smirthwaite's Trusts* (1871) L.R. 11 Eq. 251.

121 *Re Maddock* [1902] 2 Ch.220.

122 See, e.g. A. J. Oakley, *Constructive Trusts*, 3rd edn (London: Sweet & Maxwell, 1997), p.250—Oakley's view is based, at least in part, on the assumption that fully secret trusts operate "outside the will", a view which represents a strained attempt to justify secret trusts.

123 Cozens-Hardy LJ suggested, obiter, in *Re Maddock* [1902] 2 Ch.220 that a fully secret trust would fail if the secret trustee disclaimed his legacy. This does appear to follow logically

(d) *What happens if the secret trustee witnesses the will?*

Section 15 of the Wills Act 1837 states that any beneficial devise, legacy or gift by will to a witness or to the husband or wife of a witness shall be "utterly null and void".[124] A devise or legacy to someone to be held on the terms of a trust, the terms of which are set out in the will, is not void. Some writers[125] appear to think that, in the case of a fully secret trust, the gift would be void, but that in the case of a half-secret trust it would not. This reasoning is, again, based on the supposition that a fully secret trust operates "outside the will". It is submitted that this distinction is impossible to justify. If secret trusts are to be enforced, a devise or legacy to a secret trustee (whether fully secret or half-secret) is held in trust and should fall outside the mischief of s.15 of the Wills Act 1837—it is simply *not* "beneficial". **6–28**

Re Young[126] holds that where a beneficiary under a half-secret trust attests a will, he will not forfeit his beneficial interest, because his rights are derived not from the will but from the trust.

4. Secret trusts to evade tax

One of the problems which appears never to have been properly discussed in relation to secret trusts is what happens where a secret trust has been created with the object of evading tax. The question was raised in *Kasperbauer v Griffith*,[127] but it was held that there had been no secret trust,[128] so no decision was needed. **6–29**

5. Standard of proof

The final problem in relation to secret trusts concerns the standard of proof required. In *Re Snowden*[129] Megarry VC held that, in the absence of fraud or other special circumstances, the standard of proof required to establish a secret trust was the ordinary civil standard of proof to establish an **6–30**

if it is assumed that a secret trust operates "outside the will". The suggestion appears, on the face of it, to be wrong and this is another reason for not accepting that secret trusts do operate "outside the will". There are dicta of Lord Buckmaster in *Blackwell v Blackwell* [1929] A.C. 318 to the effect that a secret trustee *cannot* disclaim; Lord Buckmaster did not accept the "outside the will" approach, preferring the fraud approach. Jamie Glister in [2014] 78 Conv. 11 supports the view that a fully secret trustee cannot disclaim.

124 See Chap.14.

125 e.g. A. J. Oakley, *Constructive Trusts*, 3rd edn (London: Sweet & Maxwell, 1997), p.250.

126 *Re Young* [1951] Ch.344.

127 *Kasperbauer v Griffith* [2000] W.T.L.R. 333.

128 The testator's will left most of his estate to his widow. Property left to a spouse is exempt from inheritance tax (see Chap.16). His children claimed that the widow had promised the testator that she would make inter vivos gifts of the property to them after his death. Inter vivos gifts by her to them would also be free of inheritance tax, provided she lived for another seven years and provided that they were her gifts and were not dispositions effected under a trust. Had there been a secret trust in this case, and had the Revenue not detected it, it would have operated in such a way as to evade tax. But the trial judge held, as a fact, that there was no secret trust and he was upheld by the Court of Appeal.

129 *Re Snowden* [1979] Ch.528.

ordinary trust.[130] He appears—clearly—to have assumed that secret trusts are upheld on the basis that they operate outside the will—if they operate for the prevention of fraud, it is hard to see how he could have inserted the caveat "in the absence of fraud". In any case, he decided, that on the facts, there had been no secret trust.[131]

6. Should testators be discouraged from making secret trusts?

6–31 Although it would have been better if, when secret trusts first came before the courts, the decision had been taken not to uphold them, but to direct that the property supposedly held on secret trust should be held on a resulting trust for the testator's estate, this did not happen. Once the decision was taken to enforce secret trusts, it would have been better if the courts had been consistent and had enforced fully secret trusts and half-secret trusts in exactly the same way. There was, and is, no point in drawing fine lines between them, which are confusing and logically indefensible.

6–32 In some cases it will be easy to distinguish between a fully secret and a half-secret trust. Where X has left property in his will to Y outright, with no further wording, and Y has promised secretly to hold the property in trust for Z, this is clearly a fully secret trust. Similarly, where X has left property to Y "to hold on the trusts which I have communicated to him, but the details of which I am not setting out in my will", there is plainly a half-secret trust. But where, as in *Freud*,[132] X leaves property to Y and uses words in the will which hint at a trust, but do not make it entirely clear whether there is a trust, but also gives Y clear instructions—outside the will—which state that the property is to be held on trust, is this fully secret or half-secret? It should not matter, but if fine lines are drawn between fully secret and half-secret trusts, this sort of case will have to be classified one way or the other.[133]

It is too late now for the courts to decide that they will not uphold secret trusts; so, if they are going to uphold fully secret trusts, they should uphold half-secret trusts on exactly the same basis.[134] But the making of secret trusts should certainly not be encouraged. There are several good policy reasons for enacting that wills should be in writing[135] and there is much to be said for suggesting that the formalities rules should, in some respects, be tightened rather than relaxed. There appears to be no discussion in the cases of the potential fraud problem posed as a result of the enforcement of secret trusts.[136]

[130] A high standard of proof is required to prove fraud.

[131] Both *Kasperbauer v Griffith* and *Snowden* are cases where the trial judge held, on the facts, that no secret trust had been established. Each is a case where it would have been easy to have come to a different interpretation on the facts. This goes to show how dangerous secret trusts are, and that they should be avoided.

[132] See para.6–25, above.

[133] Three other cases which show that what looks, at first sight, to be a half-secret trust may actually be fully secret, or vice versa, are *Re Spencer* [1887] 3 T.L.R. 822; *Re Falkiner* [1924] 1 Ch.88; and *Re Gardner (No.1)* [1920] 2 Ch.523.

[134] Whatever that basis may be.

[135] See Chaps 4 and 5.

[136] There is an interesting point here in relation to the case of *Wintle v Nye*—see above,

The only advantage of a secret trust is that it suppresses unwelcome publicity; but the price paid, in terms of the risk of significant dispute, is high; and the testator who is squeamish about what is thought of him after he dies should cover his tracks while he is still alive. Lifetime gifts are not public—wills, for good policy reasons, are.[137]

III. MUTUAL WILLS[138]

The Court of Chancery created the doctrine of mutual wills in order to remedy the unconscionable revocation of a will in certain circumstances. There are three requirements which must be satisfied for the doctrine to apply: **6–33**

1. Mutual wills made pursuant to an agreement

The first requirement of the doctrine is that two or more persons make an agreement as to the disposal of some or all of their property on death and execute wills pursuant to the agreement.[139] The persons are often husband and wife but the principle is not restricted to husbands and wives.[140] The mutual wills may take the form of a joint will or separate wills.[141] Usually, each of the mutual wills makes provision for the other person in some way. A relatively straightforward agreement would be where each will gives the other person a life interest, with remainder to the same beneficiary.[142] Sometimes, each will gives the other person an absolute interest, with an alternative gift in case the other dies first.[143] But it is not essential that the **6–34**

para.5–34. Nye, the solicitor, appeared to suggest at one stage in the proceedings that the property given to him by Miss Wells's will was to be held on a secret trust. Had he persisted in this, he *might* well have won the case. Steve Evans in [2014] 78 Conv. 229 suggests that most secret trusts nowadays appear either to be designed to defraud the DWP or are linked with matrimonial breakdown. He goes on to suggest that *Larke v Nugus* statements will probably make the insertion of half-secret trusts in professionally drawn wills ineffective. For *Larke v Nugus* statements see fn.112 in para.19–39, below.

[137] Once a will has been granted probate, it becomes a public document and anyone can, for a fee, inspect it. There should, at least, be no secrets, even though there may be surprises.

[138] See generally J.D.B. Mitchell (1951) 14 M.L.R. 136; R. Burgess (1970) 34 Conv. (N.S.) 230; T.G. Youdan (1979) U. of Toronto L.J. 390; A. Braun in Chap.12 of *Exploring the Law of Succession*, Vol. 5 of Edinburgh Studies in Law, 2007; Y. K. Liew, "Explaining the Mutual Wills Doctrine", Chap.5 in B. Häcker and C. Mitchell (eds), *Current Issues in Succession Law* (Oxford: Hart Publishing, 2016).

[139] A definite agreement—as opposed to an understanding, arrangement or compact—is required: *Re Goodchild* [1996] 1 W.L.R. 1216, 1224.

[140] In *Charles v Fraser* [2010] W.T.L.R. 1489 two widowed sisters made mutual wills in favour of members of their family.

[141] *Re Hagger* [1930] 2 Ch.190 (joint will); *Re Green* [1951] Ch.148 (separate); *Re Cleaver* [1981] 1 W.L.R. 939 (separate). A joint will is a single instrument whereby two (or more) persons give effect to their testamentary dispositions.

[142] *Re Hagger* [1930] 2 Ch.190 (joint will).

[143] *Re Green* [1951] Ch.148; *Re Cleaver* [1981] 1 W.L.R. 939: cf. *Re Oldham* [1925] Ch.75, 84 and 87–88.

other person receives a benefit. In *Re Dale*[144] Morritt J held that if two testators, e.g. husband and wife, agreed that each should leave his or her property to particular beneficiaries, e.g. their children, the surviving testator's property would be subject to a trust[145] for the beneficiaries named in the wills.[146] There is also no reason why remainders to different, but agreed, beneficiaries in the two wills should not suffice if this is the arrangement.[147]

2. Agreement for survivor to be bound

6–35 The second requirement is that the parties agree that the survivor shall be bound by the arrangement. This requirement normally takes the form of an agreement by the parties not to revoke their mutual wills. For instance, in *Re Hagger*[148] a husband and wife made a joint mutual will which contained a declaration by them that it should not be altered or revoked save by their mutual agreement: it was implicit in this declaration that the parties agreed that the survivor should be bound by this agreement. This requirement can also be satisfied by an agreement to leave property by will. Thus in *Re Green*[149] a husband and wife made mutual wills which recited an agreement between them that, if the survivor had the use of the other's property for life without any liability to account, the survivor would provide by will for the carrying out of the wishes expressed in the other's will.

The agreement by the parties that the survivor shall be bound by the arrangement can be proved by declarations to this effect in the mutual wills, or by clear and satisfactory extrinsic evidence.[150] A "mere honourable engagement" between the parties does not suffice.[151] In order to bring the agreement to the knowledge of any interested beneficiary and to facilitate proof of it in the future, it is advisable for the mutual wills to contain declarations that they are mutual or for the parties to hand to any interested beneficiary a signed declaration of their agreement.

6–36 The fact that the parties agreed to make, and did make, wills at the same time and in substantially identical terms is not sufficient to establish that they agreed that the survivor should be bound. In *Re Oldham*[152] a husband and wife made their wills on the same day, each giving the other an

[144] *Re Dale* [1994] Ch.31. See A.H.R.Brierley (1995) 58 M.L.R. 95.

[145] Morritt J called it an "implied trust", but "constructive trust" seems more appropriate.

[146] This is phrased hypothetically, "if two testatorsetc" because the matter was raised as a preliminary issue. There was no decision as to whether there *was* an agreement which was intended to be binding and irrevocable.

[147] It may be that the significant element in the agreement is that X is *not* to benefit, rather than that Y *is* to benefit.

[148] *Re Hagger* [1930] 2 Ch.190.

[149] *Re Green* [1951] Ch.148.

[150] *In the Estate of Heys* [1914] P. 192; *Re Cleaver* [1981] 1 W.L.R. 939 (proof on balance of probabilities). An agreement made after 26 September 1989 will be void if it relates to land and is not in writing and signed by each of the parties: Law Reform (Miscellaneous Provisions) Act 1989 s.2(1).

[151] *Re Cleaver*, above, at 945, 947–948.

[152] *Re Oldham* [1925] Ch.75: see also *Gray v Perpetual Trustee Co Ltd* [1928] A.C. 391; *Re Cleaver* above.

absolute interest with the same alternative gift in case the other died first. The husband died first and the wife took her husband's property under his will. She later remarried and died, having made a new will which provided for her second husband and which departed entirely from the terms of her earlier will. Astbury J held that the doctrine of mutual wills was not applicable and upheld the wife's new will, saying that "the fact that the two wills were made in identical terms does not necessarily connote any agreement beyond that of so making them."[153] *Re Goodchild*[154] was a virtually identical case. A husband and wife executed simultaneous wills in identical form in favour of the survivor of them, and then in favour of their son. On the wife's death her estate passed to the husband. He remarried and then made a new will leaving everything to his new wife. The Court of Appeal held that there was no agreement not to revoke the wills and so the doctrine of mutual wills did not apply.[155]

3. Binding event occurs

There was, until recently, considerable controversy as to when the binding event occurred. It was suggested[156] that there were four possibilities: **6–37**

- (i) when the agreement was made;
- (ii) when the first party died leaving his mutual will unrevoked;
- (iii) when the survivor received a benefit under the first will; or
- (iv) when the survivor died.

Of these four possibilities, there were strong arguments against the first and the fourth but almost equal support, based on dicta,[157] for the second and the third. But the decision in *Re Dale*[158]—to the effect that the doctrine of mutual wills may apply even where the survivor receives no benefit under the will of the first party to die—implies that the binding event *must* be the death of the first party, i.e. the second possibility suggested above.

Clearly, this third requirement is not satisfied if the first testator dies having revoked his mutual will before his death.[159] Again, it is not satisfied if the first testator dies knowing that the agreement to be bound no longer stands because the other has already repudiated it. To quote Lord Camden in *Dufour v Pereira*,[160]

[153] *Re Oldham* [1925] Ch.75, 88–89. See also *Birch v Curtis* [2002] 2 F.L.R. 847.
[154] *Re Goodchild* [1997] 1 W.L.R. 1216.
[155] It was also held that the son was entitled to financial provision under the Inheritance (Provision for Family and Dependants) Act 1975—see below Chap.8, para.8–61.
[156] See J. D. B. Mitchell (1951) 14 M.L.R. 136 at 137.
[157] See Parry and Clark, *The Law of Succession*, 9th edn (London: Sweet & Maxwell, 1988), p.13, fn.94 for details.
[158] *Re Dale* [1994] Ch.31.
[159] *Stone v Hoskins* [1905] P. 194; *Re Hobley* [2006] W.T.L.R. 467, (husband did not revoke his will but executed codicil which made significant change to it—same effect). And see C. E. F. Rickett (1991) 54 M.L.R. 581.
[160] *Dufour v Pereira* (1769) 1 Dick. 419; the quotation is from 2 Hargr.Jurid.Arg. 304, 308.

"A mutual will is a revocable act. It may be revoked by joint consent clearly. By one only, if he gives notice, I can admit. But to affirm that the survivor (who has deluded his partner into this will upon the faith and persuasion that he would perform his part) may legally recall his contract, either secretly during the joint lives, or after at his pleasure, I cannot allow."

Each is under an obligation not to revoke his will without giving notice to the other during the other's lifetime.[161]

4. Remedy of constructive trust

6–38 If the three requirements are satisfied, equity enforces the agreement against the survivor by treating him as holding the property concerned on a constructive trust, to be applied in accordance with his mutual will.[162] To quote Lord Camden again[163]:

"He, that dies first, does by his death carry the agreement on his part into execution. If the other then refuses, he is guilty of a fraud, can never unbind himself, and becomes a trustee of course. For no man shall deceive another to his prejudice. By engaging to do something that is in his power, he is made a trustee for the performance, and transmits that trust to those that claim under him."

This constructive trust takes effect when the binding event occurs.[164] Hence a beneficiary under the mutual wills, who survives the first but predeceases the second testator, does not lose his benefit by lapse. In *Re Hagger*[165] a husband (H) and wife (W) made a joint mutual will by which they gave their properties (held by them jointly) to trustees upon trust for the survivor for life, and after the survivor's death to divide the proceeds of sale of the properties among certain named beneficiaries including P. The will included a declaration that it should not be altered or revoked save by their mutual agreement. The arrangement between them was incompatible with the right of survivorship applicable to their joint tenancy; accordingly the arrangement severed their joint tenancy and henceforth they held the properties as beneficial tenants in common.[166] W died in 1904 and H accepted his life interest under the will in her share of the properties. P died in 1923; and H died in 1928, having made a different will in 1921. Clauson J decided that from W's death H held his share of the properties "on trust to apply it so as to carry out the effect of the joint will"[167]; thus from W's death

[161] *Birmingham v Renfrew* (1937) 57 C.L.R. 666, 682.
[162] *Birmingham v Renfrew* (1937) 57 C.L.R. 666; *Re Cleaver* [1981] 1 W.L.R. 939.
[163] *Dufour v Pereira*, 2 Hargr.Jurid.Arg. 304, 310.
[164] i.e. when the first party dies; see above, para.6–37.
[165] *Re Hagger* [1930] 2 Ch.190.
[166] *Re Wilford's Estate* (1879) 11 Ch.D. 267; *In the Estate of Heys* [1914] P. 192; *Szabo v Boros* (1967) 64 D.L.R. (2d) 48; *Re Woolnough, Perkins v Borden* [2002] W.T.L.R. 595; *Carr v Isard* [2007] W.T.L.R. 409.
[167] *Re Hagger* [1930] 2 Ch.190, 195.

P was entitled to a vested interest in remainder in H's share (as well as W's share) of these properties and there was no lapse by reason of P's death in H's lifetime.

6–39 This constructive trust does not stop the survivor from revoking his mutual will which, like any other will, is by its very nature revocable until his death. If the mutual will of the survivor is revoked and he makes a new will, any appointment of executors in his new will is effective (even if the executors are not the executors named in his mutual will), and on his death the new will must be admitted to probate.[168] But the survivor's personal representatives take the property concerned subject to the constructive trust, and to that extent the new will is ineffective.[169] In short, equity does not prevent, but frustrates, the unconscionable revocation of a mutual will.

Where the equitable doctrine of mutual wills applies, it has the merit of making the arrangement enforceable by any beneficiary under the constructive trust: a contract not to revoke is enforceable by the contracting parties and may only be enforced by a beneficiary if he can bring himself within the provisions of the Contracts (Rights of Third Parties) Act 1999, which applies to contracts entered into on or after 11 May 2000.[170]

5. Property bound

6–40 The property which is bound by the constructive trust depends on the construction of the agreement embodied in the mutual wills. The agreement may apply only to certain identified property; or it may apply to a part,[171] or the whole,[172] of each person's residuary estate.[173]

If the constructive trust applies to a part, or the whole, of each person's residuary estate, the question then arises as to the extent to which the survivor is free to dispose, during his lifetime, of: (i) the other's property, and (ii) the survivor's own property (including his after-acquired property).[174] As regards the other's property, this question arises only if the survivor took an absolute interest, as opposed to a life interest, under the other's

[168] *In the Estate of Heys* above.

[169] *Re Cleaver* [1981] 1 W.L.R. 939.

[170] It applies to contracts entered into after a period of six months beginning on the day on which it was passed, and to contracts entered into within that six months if they specifically provide for the application of the Act. The Act was passed on 11 November 1999.

[171] *Re Green* [1951] Ch.148, 156. See also *Re Gillespie* (1968) 69 D.L.R. (2d) 368 (assets of H and W at death of first to die held bound).

[172] *Re Cleaver* [1981] 1 W.L.R. 939.

[173] In *Healey v Brown* [2002] W.T.L.R. it was held that the property bound was only the half-share in the matrimonial home of the first testator to die, because s.2 of the Law of Property (Miscellaneous Provisions) Act 1989 prevented the doctrine affecting the property of the survivor. Sed quaere, in the light of s.2(5) which provides that "nothing in this section affects the operation of resulting, implied or constructive trusts." The effect of s.2 was discussed in *Re Walters* [2008] W.T.L.R. 339, but Norris J concluded there that the section did not apply, because there was a direction to convert the estate into cash; he did not need to express a view as to what the position would otherwise have been.

[174] *Re Walters* [2009] Ch.212 was an unusual case, in that the survivor was still alive when it was heard. In most mutual wills cases, both parties are dead. The position while the survivor was still alive was not covered as clearly as might have been wished.

will. In the Australian case of *Birmingham v Renfrew*[175] Dixon J suggested that often the purpose of such an arrangement is to allow the survivor full enjoyment of both the capital and income of the property for his own benefit during his lifetime, subject to his not making inter vivos gifts calculated to defeat the intention of the arrangement. "I do not see any difficulty in modern equity in attaching to the assets a constructive trust which allowed the survivor to enjoy the property subject to a fiduciary duty which, so to speak, crystallized on his death and [during his lifetime] disabled him only from voluntary dispositions inter vivos"[176] which were calculated to defeat the intention of the agreement.[177] This floating constructive trust finally attaches to such property as the survivor leaves at his death.

6. Remarriage of surviving spouse

6–41 If the parties to mutual wills are a husband and wife,[178] what happens if, after the first has died and the mutual wills have become binding, the survivor remarries? The point did not arise in *Re Oldham*[179] or *Re Goodchild*[180] because, in each case, it was decided that the wills were not mutual; but in *Re Goodchild* Carnwarth J suggested that had the wills been mutual, the floating trust which would have been created would not have been "destroyed by remarriage of the second testator after the death of the first".[181]

7. Conclusion

6–42 It is rarely sensible for persons to make mutual wills.[182] If they insist on doing so, they ought to record that fact in the wills themselves and carefully consider what provision should be made in their agreement for possible future events, such as the remarriage of the survivor or the birth of children to the survivor. Again, mutual wills ought clearly to define the property of each person which is intended to be bound by the arrangement and the powers which are intended to be conferred on the survivor to dispose of such property during his lifetime.[183] A will draftsman who

[175] *Birmingham v Renfrew* (1937) 57 C.L.R. 666. See J. D. B. Mitchell (1951) 14 M.L.R. 136 and R. Burgess (1970) 34 Conv. (N.S.) 230 and 240 et seq.

[176] *Birmingham v Renfrew*, above, 666 at 689–690: approved in *Re Cleaver* [1981] 1 W.L.R. 939, 945–947.

[177] *Re Cleaver*, above, at 947. ("No objection could normally be taken to ordinary gifts of small value"); *Carvel Foundation v Carvel* [2007] 4 All E.R. 81.

[178] As in most cases they will be.

[179] *Re Oldham* [1925] Ch.75, see above, para.6–36.

[180] *Re Goodchild* [1997] 1 W.L.R. 1216 see above, para.6–36.

[181] *Re Goodchild* [1996] 1 All E.R. 670, 678. This is consistent with *Re Green* [1951] Ch.148; but see Law Reform Committee's 22nd Report, *The Making and Revocation of Wills*, Cmnd.7902 (1980), p.26. The suggestion seems reasonable, when dealing with older testators, but may seem less so when dealing with younger ones.

[182] See Law Reform Committee's 22nd Report, *The Making and Revocation of Wills*, Cmnd.7902 (1980), p.26; *Lewis v Cotton* [2001] W.T.L.R. 1117, C.A (N.Z.); M. Pawlowski and J. Brown [2012] Conv. 467.

[183] In *Carvel Foundation v Carvel* [2007] 4 All E.R. 81 the parties had specifically agreed that while they were both alive neither should make gratuitous transfers unless the other consented, and that once the first had died the survivor should make no gratuitous transfers.

fails to address all these issues will run the risk of exposing himself to an action in negligence.[184]

8. Reform

In July 2014, the Law Commission published their Twelfth Programme of Law Reform. One of their projects was to review the law of wills and it was announced that they would focus "on four key areas that have been identified as potentially needing reform". One of these four was mutual wills.[185] It had been planned that the project would be commenced early in 2015, but it has now been postponed and will not be begun until the Commission have published a scoping paper on marriage, when a revised timetable on the wills project will be outlined. The wills project, when it is begun, is expected to take "around three years". **6–43**

IV. DONATIONES MORTIS CAUSA[186]

A *donatio mortis causa*[187] *(d.m.c.)* is "a singular form of gift"[188] derived in part from civil law. It is neither a gift inter vivos nor a gift by will. It has its own distinct requirements which are: **6–44**

(1) it must be intended by the donor to be conditional on his own death;
(2) it must be made by the donor in contemplation of death;
(3) before his death the donor must part with "dominion" over the subject matter of the *donatio*[189]; and
(4) finally, the subject matter must be capable of passing by *donatio mortis causa*.

The burden of proof of these requirements lies on the donee. A *donatio mortis causa* may be established by the sole evidence of the donee if the court, after sifting it carefully, considers his evidence trustworthy.[190]

184 See below, Chap.15. In *Charles v Fraser* [2010] W.T.L.R. 1489 the trial judge criticized the draftsman of the wills for failing to make a clear note of the fact that they were mutual and for not including a recital of it in the wills. A very unusual recent case, where it was held that there were mutual wills, was *Fry v Densham-Smith* [2011] W.T.L.R. 387. In that case, the wills were prepared by separate firms of solicitors, and there was no direct proof that one of the parties made a will at all—the trial judge, correctly it is submitted, inferred that there had been such a will, or at least a promise to make one.

185 The other three are capacity, formalities and rectification.

186 See A. Borkowski, *Deathbed Gifts: The Law of Donatio Mortis Causa* (London: Blackstone, 1999).

187 The Latin expression *donatio mortis causa* (of which the plural is *donationes mortis causa*) translates literally as "gift on account of death"; though a rough translation might simply be "deathbed gift".

188 per Buckley J in *Re Beaumont* [1902] 1 Ch.889, 892. He continued, "It may be said to be of an amphibious nature, being a gift which is neither entirely inter vivos nor testamentary."

189 For explanation and further discussion, see below, paras 6–50 et seq.

190 *Re Dillon* (1890) 44 Ch.D. 76, 80; *Re Farman* (1887) 57 L.J. Ch. 637.

A. REQUIREMENTS OF A *DONATIO MORTIS CAUSA*

1. Intended to be conditional on death

6–45 The donor must intend the gift to become absolute only at his own death; meanwhile, the gift is revocable. There must be "a clear intention to give, but to give only if the donor dies, whereas if the donor does not die then the gift is not to take effect and the donor is to have back the subject-matter of the gift."[191]

(a) *Proof of intention*

6–46 The donor need not express his intention in words; it may be inferred from the circumstances in which the gift was made. In *Gardner v Parker*[192] X, who was seriously ill and confined to his bed, gave to Y a bond for £1,800, saying, "There, take that and keep it." X died two days later. Leach VC held that this was a valid *donatio mortis causa*, inferring from the circumstances that X intended the gift to be conditional on his own death. Even if the donor knows that he is certain to die within a short time, there seems no reason why he should not show the necessary intention that the gift should become absolute only at his own death.[193]

(b) *Other forms of intention*

6–47 There can be no *donatio mortis causa* if the donor intends to make an immediate gift inter vivos. In that case the gift stands or falls as an ordinary gift inter vivos[194]: if it is invalid as a gift inter vivos, it may become effective after the donor's death under the rule in *Strong v Bird*[195] which is considered later.[196]

Again, there can be no *donatio mortis causa* if the donor intends to make a gift by will, i.e. intends the wishes he expresses to take effect at his death but does not intend to part with dominion over the asset during his life.[197] In order to make a valid *donatio mortis causa*, the donor must part with dominion over the asset in his lifetime, which involves a mental intention on his part to do so.

2. Contemplation of death

6–48 Of course, the donor cannot form the necessary intention that the gift should become absolute only at his own death without contemplating

[191] *Re Craven's Estate (No.1)* [1937] Ch.423, 426, per Farwell J.
[192] *Gardner v Parker* (1818) 3 Madd. 184; see also *Re Lillingston* [1952] 2 All E.R. 184 and *Re Mustapha* (1891) 8 T.L.R. 160.
[193] See *Wilkes v Allington* [1931] 2 Ch.104, 111.
[194] *Edwards v Jones* (1836) 1 My. & Cr. 226; *Tate v Hilbert* (1793) 2 Ves.Jun. 111.
[195] *Strong v Bird* (1874) L.R. 18 Eq. 315.
[196] See below, paras 6–69 et seq.
[197] *Solicitor to the Treasury v Lewis* [1900] 2 Ch.812; cf. *Re Ward* [1946] 2 All E.R. 206.

death. But it is not sufficient for the donor to contemplate the possibility of death at some vague time in the future. This second requirement is only satisfied if he contemplates death "within the near future, what may be called death for some reason believed to be impending."[198] In *Wilkes v Allington*[199] this requirement was satisfied because, at the time of the *donatio*, the donor knew that he had cancer and believed himself to be a doomed man: he did not know precisely how long he had to live, but understood that he was likely to die soon. A month later he caught a chill on a bus journey on his way home from market and died from pneumonia. The court held that the *donatio mortis causa* was valid because it was not conditional on his death from the particular cause contemplated by him.

In the recent case of *King v Chiltern Dog Rescue*[200] the judge at first instance followed the slightly earlier decision in *Vallée v Birchwood*[201] and held that there could be a valid *donatio* where the donor had handed over the deeds to her house to her nephew some months before her death. The Court of Appeal in *Chiltern* reversed the trial judge and overruled *Vallée*. As Jackson LJ put it, the deceased in *Vallée* "like many elderly people, was approaching the end of his natural life span. But he did not have reason to anticipate death in the near future from a known cause."[202] *Vallée* was wrongly decided and should not have been followed. This is an important decision on *donationes mortis causa* and will be discussed further below.[203] **6–49**

3. Parting with dominion[204]

Before his death the donor must part with dominion over the subject matter of the *donatio*. Two elements are required—(a) the donor's intention to part with dominion; and (b) a sufficient delivery or transfer of the subject matter of the gift, or of something representing it, to the donee. **6–50**

(a) *The donor's intention*

The donor must intend to part with dominion over the asset to the donee.[205] **6–51**
In *Reddel v Dobree*[206] X, when in declining health, delivered a locked cash box to Y, telling her that the box contained money for her, that he wanted the box from her every three months whilst he lived, and that at his death Y was to go to his son for the key. The court held that there was no *donatio mortis causa*. X intended to retain dominion over the contents of the box during his lifetime: he had kept control of the key and had reserved to himself in advance the right to deal with the contents. Again, there is no

[198] *Re Craven's Estate (No.1)* [1937] Ch.423, 426, per Farwell J.
[199] *Wilkes v Allington* [1931] 2 Ch.104; see also *Re Richards* [1921] 1 Ch.513 (contemplation of death from critical operation but died without operation: *d.m.c.* held valid).
[200] *King v Chiltern Dog Rescue* [2015] W.T.L.R. 1225.
[201] *Vallée v Birchwood* [2014] Ch.271.
[202] *King v Chiltern Dog Rescue* [2015] W.T.L.R. 1225 at para.56.
[203] See paras 6–60 and 6–64.
[204] See W. H. D. Winder (1940) 4 Conv. (N.S.) 382.
[205] *Birch v Treasury Solicitor* [1951] Ch.298, esp. at pp.304–306; *Hawkins v Blewitt* (1798) 2 Esp. 662.
[206] *Reddel v Dobree* (1834) 10 Sim. 244.

donatio mortis causa if X merely intends Y to have custody of a locked box and its key in her capacity as X's housekeeper.[207]

The donor may, however, have the requisite intention to part with dominion even though he imposes on the donee a trust; for instance, a trust to make a certain payment to another person, or to pay the donor's funeral expenses.[208]

(b) *Delivery*

6–52 There must be a sufficient delivery in the donor's lifetime.[209] If the donor does not part with dominion in his lifetime, the *donatio mortis causa* fails. In *Bunn v Markham*[210] X, believing himself near death, directed that the words, "For Mrs. and Miss C" should be written on sealed parcels containing money and securities, and declared that the parcels were to be delivered to Mrs. and Miss C after his death. X then directed that the parcels should be put back in his iron chest of which he kept the keys. Following X's death the court held that there was no *donatio mortis causa* because there had been no act of delivery and the donor had not parted with dominion over the parcels in his lifetime.

Delivery in the donor's lifetime is essential but it does not matter whether the delivery is made before, or after, the donor expresses his intention to make the *donatio*. For instance, in *Cain v Moon*[211] a daughter delivered a deposit note to her mother for safe custody. Two years later when the daughter was seriously ill she told her mother, "the bank-note is for you if I die." The court held this to be a valid *donatio mortis causa*: the antecedent delivery sufficed, and it was not necessary for the mother to hand back the deposit note and for the daughter to re-deliver it when she expressed her intention to make the *donatio*.

6–53 **(i) Parties to the delivery.** The delivery may be made by the donor or by his duly authorised agent,[212] and it may be made to the donee or to an agent for the donee.[213] But delivery by the donor to his own agent does not

[207] *Trimmer v Danby* (1856) 25 L.J.Ch.424 (box contained X's securities, including bonds indorsed by X as belonging to Y: no *d.m.c.* as no delivery of bonds to Y); *Wildish v Fowler* (1892) 8 T.L.R. 457 ("Take care of this" by sick lodger to landlady: no *donatio mortis causa*).

[208] *Hills v Hills* (1841) 8 M. & W. 401; *Hudson v Spencer* [1910] 2 Ch.285; *Birch v Treasury Solicitor* [1951] Ch.298, 304.

[209] *Ward v Turner* (1752) 2 Ves.Sen. 431; *Cant v Gregory* (1894) 10 T.L.R. 584 (no delivery of mortgage deed as donee refused to accept it).

[210] *Bunn v Markham* (1816) 7 Taunt. 224: see also *Hardy v Baker* (1738) West t. Hard. 519 (donor told his servant to deliver property to donee after donor's death: no *d.m.c.*); *Bryson v Brownrigg* (1803) 9 Ves. 1 (donor told his wife to move securities intended for his daughter to another drawer in his bureau: no *d.m.c.*); *Miller v Miller* (1735) 3 P.Wms. 356 (oral gift of coach and horses to wife but no delivery: no *d.m.c.*); *Re Miller* (1961) 105 S.J. 207 (insurance policy sent by letter, letter postmarked after death: no *d.m.c.*).

[211] *Cain v Moon* [1896] 2 Q.B. 283: see also *Re Weston* [1902] 1 Ch.680.

[212] *Re Craven's Estate (No.1)* [1937] Ch.423.

[213] *Moore v Darton* (1851) 4 De G. & Sm. 517, 520 (sed quaere whether on the facts the donor's lady's maid was the donee's agent).

suffice.[214] If the donor intends to make a *donatio* to two donees, H and W, jointly, delivery may be made to W both for herself and as agent for H.[215]

(ii) Delivery of a chattel. There must either be actual delivery of a chattel (e.g. the donor hands his watch to the donee) or delivery of the means of obtaining the chattel (e.g. the donor hands to the donee the key of the box which contains the watch)[216]: the latter suffices because the donor thereby parts with dominion over the chattel. A merely symbolic delivery, such as the delivery of a watchstrap as a symbol for the watch, does not suffice.[217] Handing over the key to the box which contains the watch is sufficient even though the donor does not hand over the box itself.[218] On the other hand, it probably does not suffice if the donor delivers to the donee one of two keys to the box but keeps the other key,[219] or delivers the box but keeps the only key to it,[220] because such conduct generally indicates that the donor does not intend to part with dominion. In *Woodard v Woodard*[221] the Court of Appeal upheld a decision that there had been a valid *donatio* where one set of car keys had been handed over and the whereabouts of the duplicate set was unknown. The case appears to be close to the borderline.[222] 6–54

In *Re Lillingston*[223] L, in contemplation of death, handed to P a packet of jewellery and the keys to her trunk, telling her that the trunk contained the key to her Harrods safe deposit, which in turn contained the key to her city safe deposit. L said that she wished P to have all her jewellery and that after L's death P could go and get the jewellery in these safe deposits. L and P agreed that the packet of jewellery should be kept in the trunk, which was in L's room, and P placed the packet in the trunk. L then said, "Keep the key: it is now yours." The court held that there had been a valid *donatio mortis causa* of the packet of jewellery and of the jewellery in the two safe deposits. As Wynn-Parry J put it, it did not matter "in how many boxes the subject of a gift may be contained or that each—except the last—contains a key which opens the next, so long as the scope of the gift is made clear."[224] Again, it did not matter that, under the terms of the contract between L and Harrods, P also needed L's signed authority to withdraw the jewellery

[214] *Farquharson v Cave* (1846) 2 Coll.C.C. 356, 367; *Powell v Hellicar* (1858) 26 Beav. 261; *Re Kirkley* (1909) 25 T.L.R. 522.

[215] *Birch v Treasury Solicitor* [1951] Ch.298, esp. at pp.303–304.

[216] See generally A. C. H. Barlow (1956) 19 M.L.R. 394, where the *d.m.c.* cases are discussed.

[217] *Ward v Turner* (1752) 2 Ves.Sen. 431.

[218] *Re Craven's Estate (No. 1)* [1937] Ch.423, 428. The delivery of the means of obtaining the chattel suffices even though the chattel is not bulky and is capable of manual delivery, *Jones v Selby* (1710) Prec.Ch.300 (key delivered to trunk containing government tally); *Re Mustapha* (1891) 8 T.L.R. 160.

[219] *Re Craven's Estate (No.1)*, above at 428.

[220] *Re Johnson* (1905) 92 L.T. 357.

[221] *Woodard v Woodard* [1995] 3 All E.R. 980.

[222] The Court of Appeal appeared not to want to encourage any further litigation in a case where both parties were legally aided and the value of the chattel in dispute (the car) was not great.

[223] *Re Lillingston* [1952] 2 All E.R. 184.

[224] *Re Lillingston* [1952] 2 All E.R. 184, p.191: see also *Re Mustapha* (1891) 8 T.L.R. 160 (key delivered to wardrobe which contained key to safe which contained bonds).

from the Harrods safe deposit—L had transferred partial dominion to P and this sufficed.[225]

6–55 **(iii) Delivery or transfer of a chose in action.** Similar rules apply if the subject matter of a *donatio* is a chose in action which is transferable by delivery. Thus, in the case of bearer bonds, there must be either actual delivery of the bonds to the donee or delivery of the means of obtaining them, such as the key of the box which contains the bonds.[226]

If the chose in action is not transferable by delivery, there must be either a valid transfer[227] or the delivery of a document "amounting to"[228] a transfer. In *Birch v Treasury Solicitor*[229] B, in contemplation of death, handed to H and W her Post Office Savings Bank book, London Trustee Savings Bank book, Barclays Bank deposit pass book, and Westminster Bank deposit account book, intending that the money in these banks should belong to H and W in the event of her death. The Court of Appeal held that this was sufficient delivery to establish a *donatio mortis causa* of each of these bank accounts. The test to apply was to ask,

> "whether the instrument 'amounts to a transfer' as being the essential indicia or evidence of title, possession or production of which entitles the possessor to the money or property purported to be given".[230]

This test was satisfied because in the case of each bank the production of the bank book was necessary upon any withdrawal from the account. It was, however, held to be unnecessary for the document to express the terms of the contract out of which a chose in action arose, i.e. in this case the terms of the contract between B and each bank.

6–56 4. Property capable of passing by donatio mortis causa

In general, most—if not all—pure personalty is capable of being the subject matter of a *donatio*. Thus bonds,[231] an insurance policy,[232] a banker's

[225] See also *Re Wasserberg* [1915] 1 Ch.195.

[226] *Re Wasserberg*, above, (key to bank box containing bearer bonds); *Re Harrison* [1934] W.N. 25 (delivery of key but no intent to part with dominion).

[227] *Staniland v Willott* (1850) 3 Mac. & G. 664 (*d.m.c.* by valid legal transfer of shares in public company). For the requirements for a valid transfer inter vivos see *Re Rose* [1952] Ch.78; and see *Pennington v Waine* [2002] 1 W.L.R. 2075.

[228] The phrase used by Lord Hardwicke LC in the leading case of *Ward v Turner* (1752) 2 Ves. Sen. 431, 444.

[229] *Birch v Treasury Solicitor* [1951] Ch.298: see also *Re Dillon* (1890) 44 Ch.D. 76 (delivery of banker's deposit note) and *Moore v Darton* (1851) 4 De G. & Sm. 517.

[230] *Birch v Treasury Solicitor* [1951] Ch.298, 311: cf. *Delgoffe v Fader* [1939] Ch.922 (production of bank book unnecessary for withdrawal: no *d.m.c.* by delivery of book).

[231] *Snellgrove v Baily* (1744) 3 Atk. 214 (donor delivered bond to donee saying, "in case I die it is yours": held *d.m.c.*); *Gardner v Parker* (1818) 3 Madd. 184 (bond for £1,800); *Re Wasserberg* [1915] 1 Ch.195 (bearer bonds).

[232] *Witt v Amis* (1861) 1 Best & Sm. 109 (insurance policy on donor's life); *Amis v Witt* (1863) 33 Beav. 619.

deposit note,[233] and savings certificates[234] have all been held capable of passing by *donatio mortis causa*.

The following categories of property need separate consideration:

(a) *Cheques and Promissory Notes*

A cheque or promissory note drawn by a third party may pass by *donatio*: this is so even though it is not transferable at law by delivery, having been made payable to the donor and not having been indorsed by him.[235] But a cheque drawn by the donor upon his own bank cannot be the subject of a *donatio* because it does not constitute property, but is merely an order to his bank which is revoked by the donor's death.[236] Similarly, there cannot be a *donatio* of a promissory note drawn by the donor himself because it does not constitute property but is merely a promise to pay money.[237] There may, however, be a valid *donatio* if the donee receives payment on the cheque from the bank in the donor's lifetime[238] (or even afterwards before the bank is apprised of the donor's death),[239] or if the donee negotiates the cheque for value in the donor's lifetime.[240] **6–57**

(b) *Company Shares*

In *Ward v Turner*[241] Lord Hardwicke held that the delivery of receipts for the purchase price of South Sea annuities was not a sufficient delivery of the annuities to the donee by way of *donatio*. He said that a *donatio mortis causa* of company stock could not be made, "without a transfer, or something amounting to that," and the receipts were "nothing but waste paper."[242] He certainly never suggested, however, that company stock was incapable of passing by *donatio*. In *Staniland v Willott*[243] the donor, in contemplation of death, made a valid legal transfer of company shares to the **6–58**

233 *Re Dillon* (1890) 44 Ch.D. 76: cf. *Re Mead* (1880) 15 Ch.D. 651.

234 *Darlow v Sparks* [1938] 2 All E.R. 235 (war and national savings certificates); *Beatrice Finch* (1958) in Charles Lawton, *Guide to the Law of Trustee Savings Banks*, 3rd edn (London: Savings Banks Institute, 1969), p.1026 (*d.m.c.* of premium savings bond). See also *Re Lee* [1918] 2 Ch.320 (registered Exchequer bond: *d.m.c.* by delivery of Exchequer bond deposit book) and *Re Richards* [1921] 1 Ch.513 (*d.m.c.* of registered Victory Bonds), and distinguish *Re Andrews* [1902] 2 Ch.394.

235 *Veal v Veal* (1867) 27 Beav. 303 (*d.m.c.* of unindorsed promissory notes payable to donor or order); *Re Mead* (1880) 15 Ch.D. 651 (*d.m.c.* of unindorsed bills of exchange payable to donor or order); *Clement v Cheesman* (1884) 27 Ch.D. 631 (*d.m.c.* of unindorsed cheques payable to donor or order). The Cheques Act 1992 does not appear to make any difference here.

236 *Re Beaumont* [1902] 1 Ch.889: see also *Re Swinburne* [1926] Ch.38, 47.

237 *Re Leaper* [1916] 1 Ch.579.

238 *Bouts v Ellis* (1853) 17 Beav. 121, affirmed 4 De G.M. & G. 249; it suffices if the bank accepts the cheque during the donor's lifetime. *Re While* [1928] W.N. 182; *Re Beaumont* [1902] 1 Ch.889, 895 (may be sufficient if bank gives undertaking to donee to hold amount of cheque for donee).

239 *Tate v Hilbert* (1793) 2 Ves.Jun. 111, 118.

240 *Rolls v Peare* (1877) 5 Ch.D. 730.

241 *Ward v Turner* (1752) 2 Ves.Sen. 431.

242 *Ward v Turner* (1752) 2 Ves.Sen. 431 at 443–444.

243 *Staniland v Willott* (1850) 3 Mac. & G. 664: see also *Re Craven's Estate* (No.1) [1937] Ch.423 (*d.m.c.* of shares transferred to donee).

donee and the Lord Chancellor held that this constituted a *donatio mortis causa*, which had been revoked by the donor's recovery from his illness.

Unfortunately, in *Moore v Moore*[244] the court misunderstood the effect of *Ward v Turner* and held that railway stock could never be the subject of a *donatio*. This decision was followed in *Re Weston*[245] where the court held that building society investment shares could not be the subject of a *donatio*. The decision in *Staniland v Willott* was not cited in either *Moore v Moore* or *Re Weston*, and both these first instance decisions must be regarded as of doubtful authority. Almost certainly, company and building society investment shares are capable of passing by *donatio mortis causa* if the donor makes a valid transfer of them to the donee or, perhaps, delivers a document which amounts to a transfer.

(c) *Land*

6–59 In *Duffield v Elwes*[246] Lord Eldon LC held that a mortgage can be the subject of a *donatio* by delivery of the mortgage deed: the mortgage debt passes under the *donatio* and it carries the mortgage security with it.[247] Nevertheless, he seemed to take the view, obiter, that land itself could not be the subject of a *donatio*[248]; and for more than a century and a half this view was generally assumed to be correct.[249] But in *Sen v Headley*[250] the Court of Appeal decided that land can be the subject matter of a valid *donatio*. In this case the claimant had visited the deceased in hospital and the deceased told her that his house and its contents were hers. The deceased went on to say that the deeds to the house were in a steel box to which the claimant had the keys. She later found that the deceased had slipped the keys to the box into her handbag. The Court of Appeal held that land could be the subject matter of a *donatio* and upheld her claim, by way of a constructive trust. The Appeal Committee of the House of Lords gave leave to appeal, but the parties came to terms; so the appeal was not heard.

6–60 Since *Sen v Headley* there have been two further cases concerning *donationes mortis causa* of land, *Vallée v Birchwood*[251] and *King v Chiltern Dog Rescue*.[252] In each of these cases judges at first instance followed *Sen* and upheld the claims, but the Court of Appeal allowed an appeal in *Chiltern* on the ground that the deceased did not anticipate death in the near future from a known cause and it went on to overrule *Vallée* on the same

[244] *Moore v Moore* (1874) L.R. 18 Eq. 474.

[245] *Re Weston* [1902] 1 Ch.680: contrast *Griffiths v The Abbey National B.S.* (1947) [1938–1949] Reg. Rep. 14 (delivery of building society shares pass book; held *d.m.c.* by Registrar of Friendly Societies).

[246] *Duffield v Elwes* (1827) 1 Bli., N.S. 497, 542–543.

[247] *Duffield v Elwes* (1827) 1 Bli., N.S. 497, 541, quoting Lord Mansfield in *Martin v Mowlin* (1760) 2 Burr. 969, 979.

[248] *Duffield v Elwes* (1827) Bli., N.S. 497 at 530 and 539.

[249] See C.E.F. Rickett in (1989) 53 Conv. 184 where he discusses the position in the Commonwealth.

[250] *Sen v Headley* [1991] Ch 425; see case note by P.V.B. in (1993) 109 L.Q.R. 19.

[251] *Vallée v Birchwood* [2014] Ch 271.

[252] *King v Chiltern Dog Rescue* [2015] W.T.L.R. 1225.

ground.[253] It was not suggested in the Court of Appeal in *Chiltern* that there was cause to question the decision in *Sen* itself, though the court did express misgivings about attempts to extend the doctrine of *donatio*.[254] These misgivings are discussed below.[255]

B. EFFECT OF A *DONATIO MORTIS CAUSA*

1. Revocable until death

A *donatio mortis causa* is revocable until the death of the donor. Revocation is automatic if the donor recovers from the illness from which he contemplated death.[256] Alternatively, the donor may expressly revoke the *donatio* by resuming dominion over the property[257] or, perhaps, by merely informing the donee of the revocation.[258] There is, however, no revocation if the donor resumes possession of the property in order to hold it in safe custody for the donee but does not resume dominion over it.[259] The donor cannot revoke a *donatio* by his will.[260] **6–61**

If the *donatio* transferred the donor's title to the property to the donee, then, on revocation, the donee holds the property on trust for the donor and must re–transfer it to the donor.[261]

2. Death of the donor

Assuming there has been no revocation, on the death of the donor the *donatio* becomes absolute. **6–62**

Often a *donatio* vests the donor's title to the property in the donee. This occurs where the donor makes a "complete" delivery or transfer, such as would suffice in the case of a gift inter vivos. In this case the donee's title becomes unconditional at the donor's death and no action on the part of the donor's personal representatives is needed to perfect the donee's title. But there may be a valid *donatio* even though the delivery or transfer does not vest the donor's title in the donee. In the case of a chattel or a chose in action transferable by delivery, the donor may make a delivery which suffices for a *donatio mortis causa* but would not suffice to support an inter vivos gift.[262] Again, a *donatio* of a chose in action not transferable

[253] See para.6–49, above.

[254] It was probably unfortunate that the doctrine of *donatio mortis causa* was extended to land in *Sen*. The facts in that case, like those in *Vallée*, though unlike those in *Chiltern*, were such as to engender sympathy for the claimant. Hard cases make bad law.

[255] See para.6–66, below.

[256] *Staniland v Willott* (1850) 3 Mac. & G. 664.

[257] *Bunn v Markham* (1816) 7 Taunt. 224: see also *In the Estate of Mulroy* [1924] 1 I.R. 98.

[258] *Jones v Selby* (1710) Prec. Ch.300, 303.

[259] *Re Hawkins* [1924] 2 Ch.47 (*d.m.c.* by delivery of envelope containing money to donee; envelope then placed in donor's deed box for safe custody).

[260] *Jones v Selby*, above.

[261] *Staniland v Willott* (1852) 3 Mac. & G. 664.

[262] *Re Wasserberg* [1915] 1 Ch.195.

by delivery may be made by the delivery of a document which amounts to a transfer, even though it does not effectively transfer the donor's title to the donee. For instance, a valid *donatio* may be made by the delivery to the donee of a mortgage deed, even though the legal title to the mortgage debt and the mortgage security remains vested in the donor.[263] The same principle will apply to a *donatio* of land. Where the donor makes a *donatio* by an "incomplete" delivery or transfer, the donor's personal representatives hold the legal title on a trust imposed by law for the donee. If need be, the donee is entitled to require the personal representatives to lend their names to any necessary claim, on receiving an appropriate indemnity from the donee.[264] In short, if the requisites for a valid *donatio* are satisfied, equity perfects an incomplete delivery or transfer to the donee after the donor's death. "The [equitable] principle of not assisting a volunteer to perfect an incomplete gift does not apply to a *donatio mortis causa*."[265]

3. Comparison with a legacy

6–63 The basic differences between a *donatio mortis causa* and a legacy given by will are that a *donatio* must be made by the donor in contemplation of death, whereas a will can be made at any time; and that a *donatio* requires the donor to part with dominion over its subject matter before his death which is not the case with a will. There are also some subsidiary differences: for instance, the methods of revocation are different; and if the *donatio* vested the donor's title to the property in the donee, no action on the part of the donor's personal representatives is needed to perfect the donee's title.[266] In some respects, however, *a donatio mortis causa* resembles a legacy:

(i) A *donatio* fails if the donee predeceases the donor[267]: similarly a legacy normally fails by lapse if the legatee predeceases the testator.[268]
(ii) Property given by *donatio* is liable for the debts of the donor, but only on a deficiency of the assets of his estate.[269]
(iii) The subject of the *donatio* forms part of the estate for the purposes of family provision.[270]
(iv) In general, a *donatio mortis causa* is subject to the rules of satisfaction.

[263] *Duffield v Elwes* (1827) 1 Bli., N.S. 497.
[264] *Duffield v Elwes*, above; *Re Wasserberg*, above; *Re Lillingston* [1952] 2 All E.R. 184.
[265] per Lindley LJ in *Re Dillon* (1890) 44 Ch.D. 76, 83.
[266] As to the rules of private international law governing the validity of a *d.m.c.* see *Re Korvine's Trust* [1921] 1 Ch.343 (cf. *Re Craven's Estate (No. 1)* [1937] Ch.423) and Dicey, Morris & Collins, *The Conflict of Laws*, 15th edn (London: Sweet & Maxwell, 2015), para.24–014.
[267] *Tate v Hilbert* (1793) 2 Ves.Jun. 111, 120; *Walter v Hodge* (1818) 2 Swans. 92, 99.
[268] See below, paras 14–11 et seq.
[269] *Smith v Casen* (1718) 1 P.Wms. 406; *Ward v Turner* (1752) 2 Ves.Sen. 431, 434; *Tate v Leithead* (1854) Kay 658, 659; *Re Korvine's Trust* [1921] 1 Ch.343, 348; cf. Warnock-Smith [1978] Conv. 130: see below, para.21–08. As to the liability for debts of general and specific legacies see below, paras 21–31 et seq.
[270] Inheritance (Provision for Family and Dependants) Act 1975 s.8(2). See below, para.8–89.

A *donatio* may therefore be satisfied by a legacy given to the donee by the donor's later will if the donor intended the legacy to be in satisfaction of the *donatio*.[271]

It has been held that the mere fact that the legacy is of an amount equal to the *donatio* does not raise a presumption that the donor intended it to be in satisfaction of the *donatio*.[272]

C. AN ANOMALOUS DOCTRINE

In the recent case of *King v Chiltern Dog Rescue*[273] the Court of Appeal reversed the trial judge and held that there could be no valid *donatio* where the deceased did not anticipate death in the near future from a known cause; and the court then went on to overrule the slightly earlier case of *Vallée v Birchwood*[274] on the same ground. In *Vallée* the deceased, who had been born in the Ukraine, died intestate in England in 2003, leaving an only child, a daughter, who lived in France. The daughter had been adopted by third parties when she was a teenager, so, under the English intestacy rules, the deceased's estate passed not to her, but to the deceased's brothers who still lived in the Ukraine and with whom he seems to have had no contact for many years. The daughter appears not originally to have realized that the effect of her adoption was to disinherit her, but, when she discovered that it was, she claimed that, when she had visited her father a few months before his death, he had handed her the deeds to his house and had indicated that he was making her a *donatio mortis causa* of the property. **6–64**

In *King v Chiltern Dog Rescue*[275] a single woman[276] died in 2011 leaving a will made thirteen years earlier in favour of various members of her family and of animal charities. One of her nephews was living with her at the time of her death and he claimed that she had given him the deeds to her house and had expressed the wish to make a *donatio* of it to him. His claim was upheld at first instance. **6–65**

It is easy to understand the sympathy felt by the court for the claimant in in *Vallée*, less so in *King*, where he had previous convictions for fraud. But, what was needed in these cases, was proper consideration of the dangers of permitting wholesale evasion of the basic rules applicable to testate succession without any discussion as to why those rules were introduced in the first place. A will needs to be witnessed by two supposedly independent witnesses.[277] *Donationes mortis causa* may be authenticated by **6–66**

[271] *Jones v Selby* (1710) Prec. Ch.300; *Hudson v Spencer* [1910] 2 Ch.285: for satisfaction see below, Chap.13.

[272] *Hudson v Spencer*, above (delivery of £2,000 deposit notes to housekeeper; two days later donor made will giving £2,000 legacy to her: held she took both *d.m.c.* and legacy).

[273] *King v Chiltern Dog Rescue* [2015] W.T.L.R. 1225.

[274] *Vallée v Birchwood* [2014] Ch 271.

[275] *King v Chiltern Dog Rescue* [2015] W.T.L.R. 1225.

[276] She was divorced and had no children.

[277] It was suggested in Chap.5 paras 5–32 et seq. that the protection afforded to testators is sometimes inadequate. But the position here is worse.

the donee without any other proof. What if, in *Vallée*, the facts had been very slightly different. Suppose that the deceased's daughter had *not* been adopted, but that she did live in France and did (like many adult children) visit her father infrequently. Suppose that, on his death intestate, it was not she who claimed that there had been a *donatio mortis causa*, but it was the old man's carer, or his cleaner, or next door neighbour? And why, in both *Vallée* and *Chiltern*, did the deceased not make wills? It does not require a high degree of cynicism to give rise to misgivings over upholding *donatines* in cases of this sort. Having said this, the Court of Appeal in *Chiltern* did allow the appeal against the first instance judge's decision in favour of the *donatio* and it overruled *Vallée v Birchwood*. The *ratio* of the decision of the Court of Appeal in *Chiltern* was that the deceased "did not have reason to anticipate death in the near future from a known cause"[278] but there are obiter dicta in the case which indicate concerns as to whether the doctrine of *donatio* can itself be justified. Note the following passages from Jackson LJ's judgment:

> "51. As many judges have observed, the doctrine of DMC in the context of English law is an anomaly. It enables D to transfer property upon his death without complying with any of the formalities of section 9 of the Wills Act or section 52 of the Law of Property Act. Thus the doctrine paves the way for all of the abuses which those statutes are intended to prevent.
>
> 52. The Lord Chancellor in *Jones v Selby*[279] and Lord Chelmsford in *Cosnahan*[280] drew attention to this risk. They stressed the need for the strictest scrutiny of the factual evidence. The Court of Appeal rightly stressed in *Birch* that the courts must not allow DMCs to be used as a device in order to validate ineffective wills.
>
> 53. I see much force in all of these observations. Indeed I must confess to some mystification as to why the common law has adopted the doctrine of DMC at all. . .it serves little useful purpose today, save possibly as a means of validating death bed gifts. Even then considerable caution is required. What D says to those who are ministering to him in the last hours of his/her life may be a less reliable expression of his/her wishes than a carefully drawn will.
>
> 54. In my view therefore it is important to keep DMC within its proper bounds. The court should resist the temptation to extend the doctrine to an ever wider range of situations."

6–67 The approach taken to *donationes* by the Court of Appeal in *King v Chiltern Dog Rescue* is welcome. The upholding of the *donatio* by the trial judge, when the only evidence to support it came from the beneficiary, a convicted fraudster, was startling even by the standards of the law of succession, where there has long been an odd reluctance to subject to proper scrutiny evidence produced by beneficiaries in their own favour. It is to be hoped (though not

278 *King v Chiltern Dog Rescue* [2015] W.T.L.R. 1225 at para.56.
279 *Jones v Selby* (1710) Prec. Ch.300.
280 *Cosnahan* (1862) 15 Moo P.C. 215.

necessarily expected) that not only will the law of *donationes mortis causa* be kept within its proper (narrow) bounds, but that the approach taken by the Court of Appeal in *Chiltern*, and, in particular the emphasis on "the need for strictest scrutiny of the factual evidence" may spread to other related areas—including beneficiary-made "suspicious" wills.

Having said this, the problem of *donationes mortis causa* of land may diminish in the future in that the three cases just discussed were all ones where the delivery consisted (according to the claimants) of the handing over of the title deeds to unregistered property. It is not clear if it would be possible to effect a transfer by handing over a land certificate in the case of registered property, and, in any case, where a title has been acquired since 2002 there will be no land certificate. The Land Registatation Act 2002 has introduced electronic transfers of land. There will, when transfers have been effected since 2002, be no paper Land Certificates and so, it would appear, no document, or equivalent, to be handed over. This may make future *donationes mortis causa* of land impossible, and some will hope that it will. **6–68**

V. THE RULE IN STRONG V BIRD[281]

A. THE ORIGIN OF THE RULE

1. Forgiveness of a debt

Strong v Bird[282] was decided in 1874 and concerned the forgiveness of a debt. B borrowed £1,100 from his stepmother, who was living in his house and paying him £212 10s. each quarter for her board. They agreed that B should repay the loan by a deduction of £100 from the stepmother's next 11 quarterly payments. The stepmother deducted £100 from her next two quarterly payments but then refused to make any further deductions and expressly forgave B the debt. She continued to make quarterly payments of £212 10s. to B until her death. By her will she appointed B her sole executor and B proved her will. When she forgave B the debt there was no release of the debt at law because her forgiveness of the debt was not made by deed or supported by valuable consideration.[283] But B—as executor—could not sue himself for the debt and therefore, as from his stepmother's death, B was no longer liable for the debt at common law.[284] Normally equity compels a debtor executor to account for the amount of his debt at the instance of the deceased's creditors or the beneficiaries **6–69**

[281] See *Jaconelli* [2006] Conv. 432.

[282] *Strong v Bird* (1874) L.R. 18 Eq.315.

[283] *Pinnel's Case* (1602) 5 Co.Rep. 117a; *Foakes v Beer* (1884) 9 App.Cas 605: in some circumstances the debtor may have a defence under the doctrine of promissory estoppel, see Cheshire, Fifoot and Furmston, *Law of Contract*, 16th edn (Oxford: Oxford University Press, 2012), pp.129 et seq.

[284] *Jenkins v Jenkins* [1928] 2 K.B. 501.

under the deceased's will or intestacy.[285] Jessel MR held, however, that B was not liable to account because his stepmother had a continuing intention to forgive him the balance of the loan. The debt was released at law and there was "no equity against him" to make him pay the debt. So, the stepmother's continuing intention to forgive the debt rebutted the equity of the deceased's creditors or beneficiaries to make him pay the debt.[286]

2. Imperfect gift of property

6–70 The rule in *Strong v Bird* has been extended from the forgiveness of a debt to an imperfect gift of property made by the deceased during his lifetime. In *Re Stewart*[287] a few days before his death, the deceased bought and paid for three bearer bonds through his brokers. He then handed his wife an envelope which contained the brokers' letter announcing the purchase and the bought note, and said to her, "I have bought these bonds for you." The bonds were not, however, delivered to the wife and immediately before his death she had no legal or equitable interest in the bonds. The wife was one of his executors and she and the other executors proved his will. Neville J held that the wife was beneficially entitled to the bonds under the principle of *Strong v Bird*, which he stated in this way[288]:

> "Where a testator has expressed the intention of making a gift of personal estate belonging to him to one who upon his death becomes his executor, the intention continuing unchanged, the executor is entitled to hold the property for his own benefit. The reasoning by which the conclusion is reached is of a double character—first, that the vesting of the property in the executor at the testator's death completes the imperfect gift made in the lifetime, and, secondly, that the intention of the testator to give the beneficial interest to the executor is sufficient to countervail the equity of beneficiaries under the will, the testator having vested the legal estate in the executor."

This reasoning is unconvincing. The legal title to the bonds vested in the wife in her *fiduciary* capacity as one of the executors appointed by the deceased, and not as intended donee. Why should this complete the imperfect gift made in the deceased's lifetime? *Re Stewart*—although extending *Strong v Bird*—has, however, been followed at first instance,[289] has been considered by the Court of Appeal[290] and has never been judicially doubted. In the present state of the case law authorities

[285] *Berry v Usher* (1805) 11 Ves. 87.

[286] *Re Applebee* [1891] 3 Ch.422, 429–430; *Re Pink* [1912] 2 Ch.529: see also *Re Gonin* [1979] Ch.16, 34.

[287] *Re Stewart* [1908] 2 Ch.251: see also *Re Griffin* [1899] 1 Ch.408, 412.

[288] *Re Stewart* [1908] 2 Ch.251, 254.

[289] *Re James* [1935] Ch.449 (imperfect gift of a house); *Re Comberbach* (1929) 73 S.J. 403; *Re Nelson* (1947) 91 S.J. 533. See also *Carter v Hungerford* [1917] 1 Ch.260: *Re Ralli's W.T.* [1964] Ch.288; *Re Gonin* [1979] Ch.16, 35 ("a simple rule of equity").

[290] *Re Freeland* [1952] Ch.110: see also *Cope v Keene* (1968) 42 A.L.J.R. 169 (High Court of Australia).

the rule in *Strong v Bird* is applicable to an imperfect immediate gift of any property, whether real or personal, made by the deceased during his lifetime.[291]

B. REQUIREMENTS OF THE RULE

1. Deceased's intention

For the rule in *Strong v Bird* to apply, the deceased must show during his lifetime a present intention of forgiving a debt or of making a gift of particular property (as the case may be), and this intention must continue unchanged until his death. It is not enough if the deceased merely intends, or promises, to make a gift on a future occasion.[292] **6–71**

(a) *Not a testamentary intention*

If the deceased's intention is to forgive the debt, or to make the gift, at his death or by his will, the rule in *Strong v Bird* does not apply. Such an intention is testamentary and has no effect unless the deceased shows such an intention in his duly executed will. In *Re Hyslop*[293] the deceased by his will appointed X, who owed him £100, to be one of his executors. After his death a letter written by the deceased to X was found; the letter showed that the deceased intended to cancel the debt due from X. The will—but not the letter—was admitted to probate. The court held that X was liable in equity to pay the debt to the deceased's estate. The rule in *Strong v Bird* did not apply because the deceased's intention to cancel the debt was testamentary. The letter was not duly executed as a will and was, therefore, not admissible in evidence and had to be disregarded. **6–72**

(b) *No change of intention*

The deceased's intention of forgiving the debt, or of making the gift, must continue unchanged until his death. This requirement is not satisfied if the deceased later takes security from X for the debt which she has previously **6–73**

[291] In *Blackett v Darcy* [2006] W.T.L.R. 581 the Supreme Court of N.S.W. applied the rule where a cheque made payable to a donee had not been cleared before the donor's death and the donee was the donor's executor.

[292] *Re Innes* [1910] 1 Ch.188; *Re Freeland*, above, (promise to give car when put in running order: rule not applicable); *Cope v Keene*, above, (High Court of Australia); *Simpson v Simpson* [1992] 1 F.L.R. 601 at 623 (promise to give proceeds of sale of cottage when sold, rule not applicable). *Re Goff* (1914) 111 L.T. 34 is out of line: the donor intended to forgive the debt only if the donor predeceased the donee.

[293] *Re Hyslop* [1894] 3 Ch.522: see also *Re Pink* [1912] 2 Ch.529, 536 and 538–539; *Re Greene* [1949] Ch.333 and *Brown v Selwin* (1735) Cas.t.Talb. 240 (also reported in 3 Bro.P.C. 607 sub nom. *Selwin v Brown*).

forgiven,[294] or later lends to Y the car which she previously intended to give to X.[295]

2. Property vests in done

6–74 The other requirement of the rule in *Strong v Bird* is that the debt, or the subject matter of the gift, must become vested in the intended donee. It suffices if it becomes vested in him as sole executor (as in *Strong v Bird* itself): and in *Re Stewart*[296] it was held that the rule applied to one of several proving executors.[297]

Does it suffice if it becomes vested in him as administrator? In *Re James*[298] it was held to be sufficient that it had vested in the intended donee as one of two administratrices appointed by the court. In that case S became entitled to his father's house on the latter's death intestate. S "gave" the house to his father's housekeeper, handing her the title deeds, but he did not convey the house to her. She occupied the house as donee and S had a continuing intention to give the house to her until his own death intestate nine years later. The housekeeper was appointed to be one of two administratrices of S's estate. The legal estate in the house therefore vested in the housekeeper jointly with the other administratrix. Farwell J held that under the rule in *Strong v Bird* this perfected the imperfect gift of the house made by S in his lifetime. But in *Re Gonin*[299] Walton J doubted whether the rule ought to apply to an administrator who (unlike an executor) is appointed by the court and not by the deceased: it would seem "an astonishing doctrine of equity" that the gift is perfected if the intended donee manages to obtain a grant of letters of administration, but is not perfected if another person equally entitled to a grant does so.[300]

Several other problems still need to be resolved.[301] For instance, does the rule apply to an executor by representation?[302] And is the rule binding

294 *Re Eiser's W.T.* [1937] 1 All E.R. 244.

295 *Re Freeland*, above, at 121; *Re Wale* [1956] 1 W.L.R. 1346. See Kodilinye [1982] Conv. 14, 26–28.

296 *Re Stewart* [1908] 2 Ch.251.

297 In *Re Stewart* the other executors took probate and the wife later took a grant of double probate (below, para.18–32). In *Simpson v Simpson* [1992] 1 F.L.R. 601, 623 it was suggested that an intended donee who was not the sole executor could, at least since 1925, not claim the benefit of the rule in *Strong v Bird*. The point was reserved and did not have to argued because it was held that there was no intention to make a present gift. In any case quaere whether the rule applies if the executor does not prove, see Kodilinye [1982] Conv. 14, 18–19.

298 *Re James* [1935] Ch.449: see also *Re Ralli's W.T.* [1964] Ch.288 (H made imperfect gift of her interest under T's will to her marriage settlement trustees of whom X was one; later X was appointed trustee of T's will; H died; X held H's interest on the trusts of the marriage settlement).

299 *Re Gonin* [1979] Ch.16, 34–35.

300 *Re Gonin* [1979] Ch.16, 34–35 at 35; but see (1977) 93 L.Q.R. 486; Kodilinye [1982] Conv. 14, 16–17. As to persons entitled in the same degree to a grant, see below, para.17–38.

301 For the effect of the Inheritance (Provision for Family and Dependants) Act 1975, see below, para.8–89, fn.320.

302 See below, para.17–11.

on the deceased's creditors, as well as on the beneficiaries entitled under his will or intestacy? The answer to each of these questions is probably no; because, at common law, the extinguishment of a debt by the debtor's appointment as executor did not avail against creditors.

C. AN IMPERFECT RULE

There may be something to be said for not perfecting any imperfect gift made by the deceased in his lifetime, so that at his death all his assets pass under his will or intestacy. There may perhaps be more to be said for perfecting all the imperfect gifts made by the deceased in his lifetime, provided his intention to give continues unchanged until his death; this gives effect to the deceased's intention when he is no longer able to perfect the gifts himself. But what is there to be said for the rule in *Strong v Bird* under which an imperfect gift (or the forgiveness of a debt) is perfected only if the property (or debt) vests in the donee in a *different capacity*, and in a *fiduciary capacity* at that?[303] **6–75**

[303] In *Day v Royal College of Music* [2014] Ch.211 there were a number of disputes between Sir Malcolm Arnold's children and his carer relating to property in Sir Malcom's estate. One of these disputes was settled in the carer's favour by deciding that some of the deceased's manuscripts passed to the carer (who was one of the executors) under the rule in *Strong v Bird*. This appears to have been a simple, but illogical, way of disposing of one element in a much larger quarrel, which, like many such feuds, had generated considerable bad feeling.

CHAPTER 7

REVOCATION, ALTERATION, REVIVAL AND CONFIRMATION OF WILLS

I. REVOCATION

A will is, by its very nature, revocable by the testator until his death.[1] There are four methods of revocation: marriage (or formation of a civil partnership), destruction, another will or codicil, or duly executed writing declaring an intention to revoke. The *legal* burden of proof of revocation lies on the party alleging it.[2] 7–01

The effect of divorce or annulment of marriage (or dissolution or annulment of a civil partnership) on a will is considered later.[3]

A. MARRIAGE

1. Civil partners

The Civil Partnership Act 2004—which came into force on 5 December 2005—puts same-sex couples who register their partnerships in the position of married couples in relation to matters of succession.[4] 7–02

2. The general rule

As a general rule, marriage automatically revokes any will made by either party before the marriage. It is immaterial whether the party intends the will to be revoked by the marriage. This rule is enacted both by the original s.18 of the Wills Act 1837 (which, together with s.177 of the Law of 7–03

[1] See above, Chap.3, para.3–06.

[2] *Harris v Berrall* (1858) 1 Sw. & Tr. 153; *Sprigge v Sprigge* (1868) L.R. 1 P. & D. 608; *Benson v Benson* (1870) L.R. 2 P. & D. 172. For rebuttable presumptions see below, paras 7–23 et seq.

[3] See below, Chap.14, paras 14–28 et seq.

[4] To avoid the need for repetition, all references in this chapter to husbands, to wives, or to spouses, include civil partners; all references to marriages include civil partnerships; references to void and voidable marriages include void and voidable civil partnerships; and references to wills made in contemplation of marriage include wills made in contemplation of the formation of a civil partnership.

Property Act 1925, is applicable if the will was made before 1 January 1983) and by the new s.18 as substituted by the Administration of Justice Act 1982 (which is applicable if the will was made after 31 December 1982).[5]

3. Void and voidable marriages

7–04 A *void* marriage is treated as never having taken place and so it does not revoke any will already made by either party.[6] But a *voidable* marriage does revoke any will already made by either party and this is so whether the voidable marriage is subsequently annulled or not.[7] The position where a marriage is voidable on the ground of absence of consent is now unsatisfactory. Before 1971, lack of consent made a marriage void.[8] But the Nullity of Marriage Act 1971[9] enacted that the effect of absence of consent was, from 1 August 1971, to make a marriage voidable not void.[10] This means that it is possible for someone who lacks testamentary capacity[11] to contract a voidable marriage which will revoke a will he made when he had capacity.[12] A graphic illustration of this is *Re Davey*,[13] the case of the 92 year old woman who married the nurse from the nursing home where she lived.[14] The problem was solved, just in time, by the execution of a statutory will[15]; but the woman died within a week of the execution of that will and few cases will be dealt with in this way. A standard illustration of the application of the post-1971 rule is *Morley-Clarke v Brooks*[16] where a stroke victim, who was suffering both from dementia and cancer, married his Russian "carer", who then left for Russia and did not return. The man's sons applied to have the marriage annulled, but were too late. He died before they were able to obtain an annulment and so his death put an end to any possibility of challenging the validity of the marriage.[17] The Law Reform Committee in their

[5] Administration of Justice Act 1982 ss.18(1), 73(7), 75(1), 76(11) and Sch.9, Pt I. Section 18 covers marriage, s.18B, added by the Civil Partnership Act 2004 s.71 and Sch.4(1) para.2, covers civil partnerships.

[6] *Mette v Mette* (1859) 1 Sw. & Tr. 416: see also *Warter v Warter* (1890) 15 P.D. 152.

[7] This is the position since 1 August 1971. Before the enactment of the Nullity of Marriage Act 1971, the effect of a decree of annulment on a voidable marriage was to deem it never to have existed. The 1971 Act did *two* things. It reclassified marriages where there was absence of consent as voidable rather than void *and* it enacted that a voidable marriage which was annulled should henceforth be treated as having existed during the period between the ceremony and the decree absolute of nullity.

[8] *In the Estate of Park dec'd* [1954] P.112.

[9] Subsequently re-enacted in the Matrimonial Causes Act 1973.

[10] Section 50 of the Civil Partnership Act 2004 states the grounds on which a civil partnership is voidable; these include lack of valid consent and mental disorder.

[11] See above, paras 5–04 et seq.

[12] *Re Roberts* [1978] 1 W.L.R. 653.

[13] *Re Davey* [1981] 1 W.L.R 164.

[14] For a more detailed account see above, Chap.5, para.5–13.

[15] See above, paras 5–10 et seq.

[16] *Morley-Clarke v Brooks* [2011] W.T.L.R. 297.

[17] For another recent case, illustrating the opportunities open to "carers", see *ABC v XY* [2013] W.T.L.R. 187 where a rich elderly widower, who was suffering from dementia, and who lacked the capacity to manage his affairs, was held to have sufficient capacity to marry his carer, whom he had known for three months.

twenty-second Report[18] considered various suggestions and concluded that the preferred solution would be that, where a deceased person had entered into a marriage while incapable through mental disorder of managing and administering his property and affairs, the court should have a discretion under the Family Provision legislation to make provision for persons who would have benefited under any will which was revoked by the marriage. This proposal has not been implemented.[19]

4. Exceptions to the general rule

There are two exceptions to the rule that marriage revokes any will 7–05
already made by either party: the first relates to wills made in contemplation of marriage, and the second to certain appointments made by will. The scope of each of the two exceptions depends on whether the will was made before 1983 or after 1982.

(a–1) *First exception to the general rule—will made before 1983—will expressed to be made in contemplation of a marriage*

Where a will is made after 1925 and before 1983, the relevant section is s. 7–06
of the Law of Property Act 1925 which provides that "a will expressed to be made in contemplation of a marriage shall not be revoked by the solemnisation of the marriage contemplated." Whether this exception applies depends on the true construction of the will.[20]

(i) Contemplation of the particular marriage. The will must be expressed 7–07
to be made in contemplation of the particular marriage which is later celebrated. If the testator makes a will giving his entire estate to a named beneficiary referred to in the will as "my fiancée" X, or X "my future wife", this suffices and the will is not revoked by his subsequent marriage to her,[21] although it would be revoked by his subsequent marriage to anyone else. If, on the other hand, the testator merely declares in his will "that this will is made in contemplation of marriage", this does not suffice to save the will from revocation by his subsequent marriage because it refers to marriage generally and not to a particular marriage.[22]

In *Pilot v Gainfort*[23] a testator made a will by which he gave "to Diana Featherstone Pilot my wife all my worldly goods." At that time he was

[18] *The Making and Revocation of Wills*—Cmnd.7902 (1980), pp.16–18; (1981) 125 S.J. 317.

[19] And was not discussed, as it should have been, in either of the Law Commission Reports, Law Coms No.s 187 and 331, on the reform of Intestacy. See Chap.2.

[20] *Re Coleman* [1976] Ch. 1, 11: for the admission of extrinsic evidence see below, Chap.10, paras 10–43 et seq.

[21] *In the Estate of Langston* [1953] P. 100 ("I give unto my fiancée Maida Edith Beck"); *Re Knight*, unreported but mentioned in *In the Estate of Langston*, P. 103 ("to E.L.B. my future wife"); *Re Coleman* [1976] Chs 1, 6–8 and 10–11. Cf. *Burton v McGregor* [1953] N.Z.L.R. 487 ("my fiancée" a mere word of description, and no intent that will should operate after marriage): followed in *Public Trustee v Crawley* [1973] 1 N.Z.L.R. 695 and *Re Whale* [1977] 2 N.Z.L.R. 1.

[22] *Sallis v Jones* [1936] P. 43.

[23] *Pilot v Gainfort* [1931] P. 103: not followed in *Re Taylor* [1949] V.L.R. 201. See also *In the Estate of Gray* (1963) 107 S.J. 156 and *Re Coleman*, above, at pp.5–6.

living with her and later he married her. Lord Merrivale P. decided that the will was not revoked by this marriage because the will "practically" expressed contemplation of his marriage to her. The decision has been questioned on the ground that the will did not express that the marriage was in contemplation but implied that it had already taken place.[24]

7–08 *(ii) Will expressed to be made.* A clause in a will stating "This will is made in contemplation of my marriage to X" satisfies s.177.[25] But need the whole will be expressed to be made in contemplation of the particular marriage? In *Re Coleman*[26] the testator made a will giving his personal chattels, his stamp collection, £5,000 and his dwelling-house to "my fiancée" X, and his residuary estate to Y and Z equally. Two months later the testator married X and a year later he died. Megarry J held that the will had been revoked by the testator's subsequent marriage. Although he said that it would suffice if each beneficial disposition made by the will was expressed to be made in contemplation of the testator's marriage to X, he decided that s.177 did not apply where only some parts of the will were expressed to be made in contemplation of the particular marriage, even if those parts were substantial, unless they amounted to substantially the whole of the beneficial dispositions made by the will.

It seems unlikely that the decision in *Re Coleman* will be followed. This construction of s.177 by Megarry J was criticised as "unduly narrow" by the Law Reform Committee,[27] which suggested: (i) that the courts in practice usually treat the words "in contemplation of a marriage" as equivalent to "with the intention that the will should survive the impending marriage"[28]; (ii) that if a gift in a will is made in contemplation of a marriage (in the sense of intending that it should survive the marriage), it seems illogical to suppose that the testator did not intend the will to survive the marriage, for the gift cannot survive unless the will survives; and (iii) that the use of the word "fiancée" ought not to be conclusive. Thus, a will ought not to be construed as expressed to be made in contemplation of a marriage if it contains only one trivial gift to "my fiancée" X.[29]

(a–2) *First exception to the general rule—will made after 1982—will (or disposition) not intended to be revoked by particular marriage.*

7–09 Where a will is made after 1982, the relevant provisions are contained in ss.18(3) and (4) of the Wills Act 1837 as substituted by s.18 of the Administration of Justice Act 1982.[30] These provisions give effect to

[24] *Theobald on Wills*, 17th edn (London: Sweet & Maxwell, 2010), para.8–004.

[25] *Re Coleman* [1976] Chs 1, 8.

[26] *Re Coleman* [1976] Ch. 1.

[27] Law Reform Committee's 22nd Report, pp.14–16. See also R. J. Edwards and B. F. J. Langstaff (1975) 39 Conv. (N.S.) 121.

[28] See *Burton v McGregor* [1953] N.Z.L.R. 487; *Public Trustee v Crawley* [1973] 1 N.Z.L.R. 695; *Re Whale* [1977] 2 N.Z.L.R. 1: cf. *Re Coleman*, above, at p.10.

[29] See *Public Trustee v Crawley*, above, at p.700.

[30] The corresponding provisions in the case of the formation of a civil partnership are ss.18B (3)–(6).

the recommendations of the Law Reform Committee[31] and are a great improvement on s.177 of the Law of Property Act. The substituted subsections apply if it appears from a will: (i) that at the time it was made the testator was expecting to be married to a particular person,[32] and (ii) that he intended that the will,[33] or a disposition in the will,[34] should not be revoked by the marriage. If these two requirements are satisfied, the will is not revoked by his marriage to that person, and the disposition takes effect notwithstanding the marriage; so does any other disposition in the will, unless it appears from the will that the testator intended the disposition to be revoked by the marriage. Whether these two requirements are satisfied depends on the true construction of the will.

(b–1) *Second exception to the general rule—will made before 1983—certain appointments by will.*

Under the original s.18 of the Wills Act 1837, an appointment[35] made by will is not revoked by the subsequent marriage of the testator if: **7–10**

> "the real or personal estate thereby appointed would not in default of such appointment pass to his or her heir, customary heir, executor, or administrator, or the person entitled as his or her next of kin under the Statute of Distributions."

The underlying purpose of s.18 was to allow the appointment by will to be revoked by the testator's subsequent marriage only in circumstances where the testator's new family might benefit under the gift in default of appointment.[36] In order to determine whether this exception applies it is necessary to ascertain who would take in default of the appointment made by the will. The appointment is not revoked by the subsequent marriage if persons taking in the specified capacities would not in any event be entitled in default of the appointment.[37]

(i) Taking in the specified capacities. Apart from the testator's executor or administrator, the other specified capacities all refer to succession on a death intestate before 1926 when realty passed to the heir, copyhold land **7–11**

[31] Law Reform Committee's 22nd Report, pp.16 and 27: see also G. M. Bates (1979) 129 New.L.J.547.

[32] As under the original section, it must appear from the will that the testator was expecting to the married to (or was expecting to form a civil partnership with) a particular person. A general reference to the possibility that the testator might be about to marry, or to form a civil partnership, does not suffice, *Court v Despallieres* [2010] W.T.L.R. 437.

[33] Subs.18(3).

[34] Subs.18(4).

[35] For powers of appointment, see Hanbury and Martin, *Modern Equity*, 20th edn (London: Sweet & Maxwell, 2015), Chap.7.

[36] See *In the Goods of Fitzroy* (1858) 1 Sw. & Tr. 133: *In the Goods of McVicar* (1869) 1 P. & D. 671; *In the Goods of Russell* (1890) 15 P.D. 111; *Re Paul* [1921] 2 Ch. 1.

[37] *In the Goods of Fenwick* (1867) L.R. 1 P. & D. 319; *In the Goods of Worthington* (1872) 20 W.L.R. 260.

to the customary heir, and personalty to the next of kin under the Statutes of Distribution 1670 and 1685.[38]

Ought the phrase "next of kin under the Statute of Distributions" in s.18 to be construed since 1925 as referring to the persons entitled on intestacy under the Administration of Estates Act 1925? It seems that the Interpretation Act may have updated s.18 in this way, see M. J. Russell (1952) 68 L.Q.R. 455 but the position remains uncertain.

7–12 *(ii) Remainder of will revoked.* Where this exception applies it saves the appointment, but not the remainder of the will, from revocation by the testator's subsequent marriage.[39]

(b–2) *Second exception to the general rule—will made after 1982—certain appointments by will.*

7–13 The substituted s.18(2) updates this exception, so that it no longer refers to the pre-1926 intestacy rules, and saves an appointment by will from revocation by subsequent marriage unless the property appointed would in default of appointment pass to the testator's estate.[40]

5. Pension scheme nominations

7–14 A nomination in respect of a lump sum benefit under a pension scheme may, in the light of the rules applicable to the scheme in question, not be a testamentary disposition.[41] Marriage will not revoke such a nomination.

B. DESTRUCTION

7–15 Under s.20 of the Wills Act 1837 the whole or any part of a will or codicil is revoked:

> "by the burning, tearing, or otherwise destroying the same by the testator, or by some person in his presence and by his direction, with the intention of revoking the same."

Two distinct elements are required: an act of destruction, and an intention to revoke. "All the destroying in the world without intention will not revoke a will, nor all the intention in the world without destroying: there must be the two."[42] Moreover, both elements are required for the

[38] Ought the phrase "next of kin under the Statute of Distributions" in s.18 to be construed since 1925 as referring to the persons entitled on intestacy under the Administration of Estates Act 1925? It seems that the Interpretation Act may have updated s.18 in this way, see M. J. Russell (1952) 68 L.Q.R. 455, but the position remains uncertain.

[39] *In the Goods of Russell* (1890) 15 P.D. 111.

[40] See Law Reform Committee's 22nd Report, pp.13–14.

[41] See above, para.1–05 and *Baird v Baird* [1990] 2 A.C 548.

[42] per James LJ in *Cheese v Lovejoy* (1877) 2 P.D. 251, 253, quoting Dr. Deane in the court below.

revocation of each will or codicil. The revocation of a will by destruction does not revoke a codicil to that will.[43]

1. An actual act of destruction

There must be an actual, and not merely a symbolic, "burning, tearing, or otherwise destroying." Cancelling a will by striking the body of it through with a pen and crossing out the name of the testator is not an act of destruction.[44] In *Cheese v Lovejoy*[45] a testator drew his pen through some lines of his will, wrote on the back of it, "All these are revoked," and threw it among a heap of waste paper in the corner of his sitting room. His housemaid retrieved it and kept it in the kitchen until the testator's death seven years later. The Court of Appeal held that the will was not revoked as there was no act of destruction. **7–16**

(a) *Extent of destruction*

In order to revoke it entirely, the whole will need not be destroyed, but there must be a destruction of so much of it as to impair the entirety of the will.[46] Accordingly it suffices if the signature of the testator is cut out,[47] or the signatures of the testatrix and attesting witnesses scratched away with a penknife[48] or scored out with a ball-point pen[49] so that it is impossible to see that they are signatures. It appears to suffice if the signatures of the attesting witnesses are destroyed by any of these methods.[50] There will, however, be no revocation where, for example, the signature has been scratched but remains legible.[51] It was suggested obiter in *Hobbs v Knight*[52] that it would suffice if the testator's signature were burnt or torn off and this is almost certainly correct. **7–17**

The testator must complete all he intends to do by way of destruction. In *Doe d. Perkes v Perkes*[53] the testator, being angry with a devisee named in his will, began to tear it up with the intention of revoking it, and tore it into four pieces before he was stopped, partly by a bystander who seized his arms and partly by the apologies of the devisee. The testator then became calm and fitted the pieces together saying, "It is a good job it is

[43] *In the Goods of Savage* (1870) L.R. 2 P. & D. 78; *In the Goods of Turner* (1872) L.R. 2 P. & D. 403 (codicil not revoked by destruction of will, although codicil gave legacy to be held under conditions stated in will). cf. *In the Goods of Bleckley* (1883) 8 P.D. 169 (both on same piece of paper).

[44] *Stephens v Taprell* (1840) 2 Curt. 459: see also *In the Goods of Brewster* (1859) L.J.P. 69 ("cancelled" written across signature: no revocation).

[45] *Cheese v Lovejoy* (1877) 2 P.D. 251. See Law Reform Committee's 22nd Report, pp.22–23.

[46] *Hobbs v Knight* (1838) 1 Curt. 768, 778.

[47] *Knight*, (1838) 1 Curt. 768, 778. *In the Goods of Gullan* (1858) 1 Sw. & Tr. 23.

[48] *In the Goods of Morton* (1887) 12 P.D. 141.

[49] *Re Adams* [1990] 1 Ch. 601.

[50] *Hobbs v Knight*, (1838) 1 Curt., p.781 (obiter as to erasure); *In the Goods of Dallow* (1862) 31 L.J.P.M. & A. 128 (torn off).

[51] *In the Goods of Godfrey* (1893) 69 L.T. 22.

[52] *Hobbs v Knight* (1838) 1 Curt. 781.

[53] *Doe d. Perkes v Perkes* (1820) 3 B. & Ald. 489: see also *Elms v Elms* (1858) 1 Sw. & Tr. 155.

no worse." The court held that the will had not been revoked because the testator had not completed all that he originally intended to do by way of destruction. On the other hand, if the testator's original intention had been to tear the will into four pieces, it would have been revoked.

(b) *Destruction by another person*

7–18 The act of destruction must be carried out by the testator himself or by another person in his presence[54] and by his direction.[55] If a testator instructs a third party by telephone to destroy his will as he wishes to make a new one, and the third party does so in the testator's absence, the will is not revoked.[56] A will destroyed by another person in the testator's presence but without the testator's direction to do so is not revoked even if the testator subsequently ratifies the destruction.[57]

2. Intention to revoke[58]

7–19 The testator must have the intention of revoking the whole, or part, of the will whilst the act of destruction is carried out.

(a) *Mental capacity to revoke*

7–20 Destruction whilst the testator is of unsound mind does not revoke a will.[59] The same standard of mental capacity is required for revocation by destruction as for the making of a will.[60]

(b) *Accident or mistake*

7–21 A will destroyed by accident is not revoked.[61] Again, there is no revocation if the act of destruction is done with the intention of destroying but not of revoking the will. Thus a will was not revoked where it was destroyed under the mistaken belief that it was invalid,[62] or that it was useless,[63] or that it had already been revoked.[64] The testator

[54] *In the Goods of Dadds* (1857) Dea. & Sw. 290.
[55] *Gill v Gill* [1909] P. 157 (will torn up in testator's presence by his wife in a fit of temper: no revocation as not done by his direction).
[56] *In the Estate of de Kremer* (1965) 110 S.J. 18 ("considerable professional error" of solicitor who destroyed will). The solicitor in *Re Adams* [1990] 1 Ch. 601 acted correctly in *not* complying with his client's telephoned instructions to destroy her will.
[57] *Mills v Millward* (1890) 15 P.D. 20, 21; *Gill v Gill*, above; *Re Booth* [1926] P. 118, 132 and 133.
[58] For conditional revocation see below, paras 7–39 et seq.
[59] *Brunt v Brunt* (1873) 3 P. & D. 37 (delirium tremens); *In the Goods of Hine* [1893] P. 282 (softening of the brain); *In the Goods of Brassington* [1902] P. 1 (drunk).
[60] *Re Sabatini* (1969) 114 S.J. 35; see above, paras 5–04 et seq.
[61] *Burtenshaw v Gilbert* (1774) 1 Cowp. 49, 52; *In the Goods of Taylor* (1890) 63 L.T. 230.
[62] *Giles v Warren* (1872) 2 P. & D. 401; *In the Goods of Thornton* (1889) 14 P.D. 82.
[63] *Beardsley v Lacey* (1897) 78 L.T. 25; *Stamford v White* [1901] P. 46.
[64] *Scott v Scott* (1859) 1 Sw. & Tr. 258; *Clarkson v Clarkson* (1862) 2 Sw. & Tr. 497 (in both cases mistaken belief that later will had already revoked it).

"may have merely torn it up, thinking that it was no longer worth the paper it was written upon. For myself, in those circumstances, I should have thought the right inference to draw was that he did not intend to revoke it at all; he was merely disposing of what he thought was rubbish."[65]

(c) *Whether intention to revoke whole or part*

It is necessary to decide whether the testator intended to revoke the whole or, alternatively, only a particular part of a will. There may be evidence of his expressed intention. If need be, the court infers the testator's intention from the state of the will after the act of destruction. If, for instance, the testator's signature is destroyed, this raises an inference that the testator intended to revoke the whole will.[66] If a portion of the will not necessary to its validity as a testamentary instrument is destroyed, the question arises whether the portion destroyed is so important as to raise the inference that the rest cannot have been intended to stand without it.[67] Thus, destruction of a clause at the commencement of a will, or cutting out various legacies, or a clause appointing executors, does not revoke the rest of the will.[68] Again, the cutting away of half a page, which contained details of the residuary trust, only revoked that part of the will, because sufficient remained to lead to the inference that the testator intended that what remained should be effective.[69] On the other hand, where the first two sheets of a will made on five sheets of paper had been destroyed, it was inferred that the testator intended to revoke the whole will, because the last three sheets were practically unintelligible in the absence of the first two sheets.[70] **7–22**

3. Presumptions

Two rebuttable presumptions may apply: **7–23**

(a) *Will missing at death*

A will last known to be in the testator's possession but which cannot be found at his death is presumed to have been destroyed by the testator **7–24**

[65] per Buckley LJ in *Re Jones* [1976] Ch. 200, 205.

[66] *Hobbs v Knight* (1838) 1 Curt. 768 (T's signature cut out: whole will revoked); *In the Goods of Gullan* (1858) 1 Sw. & Tr. 23; *Bell v Fothergill* (1870) 2 P. & D 148; in *Re Adams* [1990] 1 Ch. 601: cf. *Christmas v Whinyates* (1863) 3 Sw. & Tr. 81 (only part revoked, though signature cut off, due to manner in which cut).

[67] *Clarke v Scripps* (1852) 2 Rob. 563 (part only); *Re White* (1879) 3 L.R.Ir. 413 (whole); *Leonard v Leonard* [1902] P. 243 (whole).

[68] *In the Goods of Woodward* (1871) 2 P. & D. 206; *In the Goods of Nelson* (1872) 6 I.R. Eq. 569; *In the Goods of Maley* (1887) 12 P.D. 134; *In the Goods of Leach* (1890) 63 L.T. 111; *In the Estate of Nunn* (1936) 154 L.T. 498 (strip in middle of will cut out and remainder stitched together: only strip revoked).

[69] *Re Everest* [1975] Fam. 44.

[70] *Leonard v Leonard* [1902] P. 243: see also *Treloar v Lean* (1889) 14 P.D. 49; *In the Estate of Green* (1962) 106 S.J. 1034; *Re White* (1879) 3 L.R.Ir. 413.

with the intention of revoking it.[71] But the strength of the presumption varies according to the security of the testator's custody of the will: the safer the security, the stronger the presumption. The presumption may be rebutted by evidence of non-revocation, such as evidence that the will was destroyed by enemy action or accident, or by evidence showing the testator's intention to adhere to the will. The contents of the missing will may be proved by means of a draft or copy or by oral evidence.[72]

The leading case is *Sugden v Lord St Leonards*.[73] Lord St. Leonards, the former Lord Chancellor, died in 1875 aged 93. He had made a holograph will in 1870 and had then made eight codicils to it between 1870 and 1873. The will and codicils were kept in a deed box in Lord St. Leonards' sitting room; the box was locked but there was a spare key to it and the spare key was not kept securely; almost anyone in the house could have obtained access to the deed box. During Lord St. Leonards' final illness, his daughter, who lived with him, removed the deed box to her room, for safekeeping. After his death the box was opened: the codicils were in the box but the will was missing. There was no copy of the will, but the daughter had read it over to her father on a number of occasions and was able to give a reasonably full account of its contents. The case raised two questions: first, whether there was a presumption on these facts that Lord St. Leonards had destroyed his own will, with the intention of revoking it; and secondly, if there were no such presumption, whether the court could accept evidence from the daughter who was herself a beneficiary under the will. Sir James Hannen P. had no hesitation in finding that there was no presumption, on these facts, that Lord St. Leonards had destroyed his own will. No careful Chancery lawyer would be likely to destroy his will without destroying the codicils to it and without making another will. As to the daughter's evidence, it was entirely consistent with the codicils and was accepted. Sir James Hannen's judgment was upheld by a unanimous Court of Appeal.[74] Neither Sir James Hannen nor the members of the Court of Appeal chose to speculate on what had happened to the will, which remains a mystery.[75]

7–25 Given the ease with which wills may be photocopied nowadays, proving the contents of a missing will is generally not the problem it was in the nineteenth-century. In *Dickson v Dickson*[76] the deceased was a meticulous man who kept neat files and was not the sort of person who would have been expected to mislay his will, but he had made statements shortly

[71] *Eckersley v Platt* (1886) L.R. 1 P. & D. 281; *Allan v Morrison* [1900] A.C. 604.

[72] *Re Webb* [1964] 1 W.L.R. 509; *In the Estate of Yule* (1965) 109 S.J. 317: see below, paras 19–21 et seq.

[73] *Sugden v Lord St Leonards* (1876) 1 P.D.154.

[74] Some great lawyers thought, at the time, that the court would not grant probate to a will thus proved; i.e. proved on the basis of secondary evidence of contents given by an interested witness. Sir William Holdsworth, *A History of English Law* (London: Sweet & Maxwell), Vol.16, p.46.

[75] They did not speculate, but the judgments hint at what they thought. The will was probably removed from the deed box, while the box was in Lord St. Leonards' sitting room, by a servant who wanted to know what provision it made for him. When Lord St. Leonards' daughter took the box to her room, the servant could not replace the will, and so destroyed it. But this is only speculation.

[76] *Dickson v Dickson* [2002] W.T.L.R. 1395.

before his death which were inconsistent with his having destroyed it. The trial judge refused probate, but he was reversed by the Court of Appeal.[77] In *Rowe v Clarke*,[78] another case where probate of a missing will was granted,[79] the trial judge did not accept a suggestion that the will had been deliberately destroyed by a third party. Judges in succession cases tend not to be enthusiastic about accepting allegations of misbehaviour[80]: holding that a will has been mislaid by the testator is a way of avoiding unpleasantness.[81] But the judge in *Re Zielinski, Korab-Karpinski v Lucas-Gardiner* held that a member of the testatrix's family had "destroyed or suppressed [her last] will or procured its destruction or suppression".[82]

(b) *Will found mutilated at death*

A will, which has been in the testator's possession but which is found to be torn or mutilated at his death, is presumed to have been torn or mutilated by the testator with the intention of revoking it in whole or in part.[83] Again, the presumption may be rebutted by evidence to the contrary.[84] **7–26**

If the testator executed the will whilst of sound mind but was insane during any part of the period when the will was in his possession, there is no presumption that the destruction, or the tearing or mutilation, was carried out by the testator at a time when he was of sound mind. Unless the party alleging revocation proves that the testator was of sound mind (and thus capable of revoking the will) at the time of destruction, the will is admissible to probate.[85]

C. WILL OR CODICIL

Under s.20 of the Wills Act 1837, the whole or any part of a will may be revoked by another duly executed will or codicil.[86] **7–27**

[77] This is a 1984 case, reported late.
[78] *Rowe v Clarke* [2006] W.T.L.R. 347.
[79] Probate of missing wills was also granted in *Wren v Wren* [2006] 3 F.C.R. 18, and *Nicholls v Hudson* [2007] W.T.L.R. 341.
[80] In *Ferneley v Napier* [2011] W.T.L.R. 1303 it was held that the burden of proof, in a case where it is alleged that a will has been suppressed, is not the criminal burden (beyond all reasonable doubt) but the civil burden (the balance of probabilities). Nevertheless, "serious allegations" such as conspiracy to suppress a will "must be fully and properly proved". The effect is to impose a relatively heavy burden on the challenger and, in this case, the challenge failed.
[81] Such a finding may, however, have an effect on costs and so may be not only of moral, but also of practical significance; see *Rowe v Clarke (costs)* [2007] W.T.L.R. 373. In *Re Ciebrant, Van Kwawagen v* RNLI [2009] W.T.L.R. 69, a missing will was granted probate under the rule in *Sugden v Lord St Leonards* without its being clear what the judge thought had happened to it. It had, almost certainly, been deliberately suppressed.
[82] *Re Zielinski, Korab-Karpinski v Lucas-Gardiner* [2007] W.T.L.R. 1655 at 1671.
[83] *Lambell v Lambell* (1831) 3 Hag.Ecc. 568; *Bell v Fothergill* (1870) L.R. 2 P. & D. 148.
[84] *In the Estate of MacKenzie* [1909] P. 305; *Re Cowling* [1924] P. 113.
[85] *Harris v Berrall* (1858) 1 Sw. & Tr. 153 (tearing); *Sprigge v Sprigge* (1868) L.R. 1 P. & D. 608 (destruction).
[86] For conditional revocation see below, paras 7–39 et seq. For the rules of private international

1. Express revocation by will or codicil

7–28 Most wills contain a revocation clause in general terms by which the testator expressly revokes "all wills codicils and other testamentary dispositions heretofore made by me." Such a revocation clause normally operates to revoke all previous testamentary instruments[87] just as if they had never existed, and it will therefore revoke an appointment made by the testator in a previous will or codicil.[88] The advantage of inserting such a revocation clause is that it makes it unnecessary to consider whether, or to what extent, an earlier will or codicil is revoked by implication. A revocation clause may be much narrower in its ambit. Thus, in a codicil, a revocation clause may revoke a single clause, or even a single word, in a previous will or codicil. No particular form of words is required for express revocation. However, the usual form of commencement of a will—"This is the last will and testament of me"—is not construed as an express revocation of previous wills.[89]

On its proper construction a revocation clause in general terms may not revoke all previous testamentary instruments. In *Re Wayland*[90] a testator made a will in accordance with the law of Belgium dealing only with his Belgian property. Later he made a will in England which contained a revocation clause but which declared that "this will is intended to deal only with my estate in England." The court construed the revocation clause to mean that the testator revoked all former wills dealing with English property and admitted both the Belgian and the English wills to probate.[91]

A revocation clause does not operate at all if:

(i) the clause is contained in a conditional will which is inoperative owing to the specified condition not being satisfied[92];
(ii) the clause is rejected for want of knowledge and approval by the testator.[93] The clause is not admitted to probate if the testator did not know and approve of it,[94] but the clause must be admit-

law governing revocation by will or codicil see Dicey, Morris & Collins, *The Conflict of Laws*, 15th edn (London: Sweet & Maxwell, 2006), paras 27–128 et seq.; *Theobald on Wills*, 16th edn (London: Sweet & Maxwell, 2010), Chap.2).

87 But not statutory nominations, see above, para.1–08.

88 *Sotheran v Dening* (1881) 20 Ch.D. 99 (general power); *Re Kingdon* (1886) 32 Ch.D. 604 (special power); *Cadell v Wilcocks* [1898] P. 21, 26.

89 *Cutto v Gilbert* (1854) 9 Moo.P.C. 131; *Lemage v Goodban* (1865) L.R. 1 P. & D. 57; *Simpson v Foxon* [1907] P. 54 ("This is the last and only will and testament of me" not an express revocation); *Kitcat v King* [1930] P. 266.

90 *Re Wayland* [1951] 2 All E.R. 1041.

91 A similar result was reached in the Jersey case of *In the Estate of Vickers* (2001–02) 4 I.T.E.L.R 584, but in *Lamothe v Lamothe* [2006] W.T.L.R 1431 a revocation clause in a Dominican will was held to have revoked an earlier English will. The question is one of construction.

92 *In the Goods of Hugo* (1877) 2 P.D. 73; *In the Estate of O'Connor* [1942] 1 All E.R. 546: see para.3–10.

93 See above, paras 5–23 et seq.; and C. H. Sherrin (1972) 122 New L.J. 6.

94 *Re Phelan* [1972] Fam. 33, see above, para.5–29; *In the Goods of Oswald* (1874) L.R. 3 P. & D. 162 (included *per incuriam* without instructions); *In the Goods of Moore* [1892] P. 378; *Smith v Thompson* (1931) 47 T.L.R. 603. But cf. *Lowthorpe-Lutwidge v Lowthorpe-Lutwidge* [1935] P. 151

ted even if it was included as a result of a mistake as to its legal effect[95];

(iii) the clause itself is subject to a condition which is not satisfied.[96]

2. Implied revocation by will or codicil

A prior will or codicil is impliedly revoked by a later will or codicil so far as the latter contains provisions inconsistent with or merely repeating the former. If the provisions of the later will or codicil are wholly inconsistent or repetitive, the prior will or codicil is completely revoked.[97] If they are only partially inconsistent or repetitive, those parts of the prior will or codicil not affected by the inconsistency or repetition remain unrevoked.[98] The question to ask is not which of his wills or codicils did the testator desire to be admitted to probate: the true question is which provisions did the testator intend to take effect at his death.[99] This is a question of construction.[100] **7–29**

3. Proof of revocation

(a) *By lost will or codicil*

Revocation of an earlier will or codicil by a later will or codicil takes effect when the latter is executed, and it is immaterial that the latter is not forthcoming at the testator's death.[101] But in order to establish revocation by a will or codicil which has been lost or destroyed, it is necessary to prove: (i) that the later will or codicil was duly executed, and (ii) that by its contents it did expressly or impliedly revoke the earlier will or codicil. The second requirement may be proved by production of a copy or written instructions, or by clear and satisfactory oral evidence.[102] **7–30**

(b) *By will or codicil inadmissible to probate*

In *Re Howard*[103] a testator first executed a will leaving his estate to his son and later executed two wills on the same day, one in favour of his wife **7–31**

(no evidence of want of knowledge and approval of revocation clause); *In the Goods of Swords* [1952] P. 368.

95 *Collins v Elstone* [1893] P. 1 (T knew that her will contained revocation clause, but had been wrongly advised that it would not revoke her previous will).

96 This is considered below, at para.7–44.

97 *In the Estate of Bryan* [1907] P. 125 (wholly inconsistent even though later will did not dispose of residue); *In the Goods of Howard* (1869) L.R. 1 P. & D. 636.

98 *Curati v Perdoni* [2013] W.T.L.R. 63.

99 *Lemage v Goodban* (1865) L.R. 1 P. & D. 57; *In the Goods of Petchell* (1874) L.R. 3 P. & D. 153.

100 See below, Chap.10.

101 *Brown v Brown* (1858) 8 E. & B. 876; *Wood v Wood* (1867) L.R. 1 P. & D. 309.

102 *Cutto v Gilbert* (1854) 9 Moo.P.C. 131 ("oral evidence ought to be stringent and conclusive"); the ordinary standard of proof applies, i.e. a reasonable balance of probabilities, *Re Wipperman* [1955] P. 59: evidence that it was solicitor's usual practice to insert a revocation clause is insufficient by itself; *Re Wyatt* [1952] 1 All E.R. 1030 (contents of later will unknown; it had been drawn by a solicitor whose usual practice was to insert revocation clause: earlier will held not revoked); *Re Rear* [1975] 2 N.Z.L.R. 254, 267; cf. *In the Estate of Hampshire* [1951] W.N. 174.

103 *Re Howard* [1944] P. 39.

and the other in favour of his son. Each of these two wills contained a revocation clause in general terms. The court held that these two wills were effective to revoke the earlier will. However, neither of them could be admitted to probate as they were inconsistent and there was nothing to indicate the order in which they were executed. The deceased therefore died intestate.

D. DULY EXECUTED WRITING DECLARING AN INTENTION TO REVOKE

7–32 Under s.20 of the Wills Act 1837 the whole or any part of a will may be revoked by "some writing declaring an intention to revoke the same" and duly executed in the same manner as a will.

A statement at the foot of an obliterated codicil, "We are witnesses to the erasure of the above," signed by the testator and attested by two witnesses, was held to be a "writing declaring an intention to revoke."[104] Again, in *Re Spracklan's Estate*[105] the Court of Appeal held this requirement to be satisfied by the words, "will you please destroy the will already made out," in a letter signed by the testatrix and duly attested, and addressed to the manager of a bank having custody of her will. The will was therefore revoked as soon as the letter was duly executed.

E. AN ALTERATION IN CIRCUMSTANCES DOES NOT REVOKE

7–33 The general rule that marriage revokes a will ensures that a testator starts married life with a clean slate.[106] Apart from marriage, no other alteration in circumstances, such as the birth of children, revokes a will.[107]

F. REVOCATION BY A PRIVILEGED TESTATOR

7–34 The four methods of revocation already considered apply to a privileged testator subject only to the differences arising from his ability to make an informal will.[108]

[104] *In the Goods of Gosling* (1886) 11 P.D. 79.

[105] *Re Spracklan's Estate* [1938] 2 All E.R. 345, following *In the Goods of Durance* (1872) L.R. 2 P. & D. 406, where Lord Penzance said at p.407, "If a man writes to another 'Go and get my will and burn it,' he shows a strong intention to revoke his will."

[106] See Law Reform Committee's 22nd Report, pp.11–18, recommending no change in the general rule.

[107] See Wills Act 1837 s.19. For the effect of divorce or annulment of marriage see below, paras 14–28 et seq.

[108] *In the Estate of Gossage* [1921] P. 194 (the misleading headnote states the *ratio* of Younger LJ, and not that of the majority of the Court of Appeal).

1. Marriage

In the Estate of Wardrop[109] Shearman J decided that the will of a privileged testator was revoked by his subsequent marriage. He said that s.18 (which provided that "every will made by a man or woman shall be revoked by his or her marriage") was "a very sweeping enactment and it must be held to apply to soldiers' and sailors' wills." The two exceptions to the rule that marriage revokes a will also apply in the case of a privileged testator. **7–35**

2. Destruction

This method is applicable to an informal will[110] unless it was made orally so that destruction is impossible. **7–36**

3. Will or codicil

A privileged testator may revoke any previous will (whether or not made when he was privileged) by an informal will or codicil.[111] **7–37**

4. Writing declaring an intention to revoke

A privileged testator may revoke any previous will by informal writing declaring an intention to revoke.[112] There is a dictum that such informal writing does not revoke a formal will made when not privileged,[113] but it ought to be irrelevant whether the previous will was made when privileged.[114] **7–38**

II. CONDITIONAL REVOCATION

Revocation of the whole or part of a will or codicil by destruction, or by another will or codicil or by duly executed writing, requires an intention to **7–39**

[109] *In the Estate of Wardrop* [1917] P. 54: this decision was doubted in earlier editions of Williams, Mortimer and Sunnucks on the ground that *In the Estate of Gossage*, above, by implication overrules it. But it is only the judgment of Younger LJ which may carry this implication and the latest, the 20th edition of Williams, Mortimer and Sunnucks, *Executors, Administrators and Probate* (London: Sweet & Maxwell, 2015), para.16–16, fn.80 now agrees that the view taken in earlier editions of the work does not represent the true position.

[110] *In the Estate of Gossage*, above, at 196 Bailhache J at first instance apparently decided that a privileged will had been revoked by its destruction by another person in the testator's absence: no member of the Court of Appeal relied on this ground and the majority treated s.20 as applicable.

[111] Wills Act 1837 ss.11 and 20: Wills (Soldiers and Sailors) Act 1918: see *In the Goods of Newland* [1952] P. 71.

[112] *In the Estate of Gossage* [1921] P. 194 (letter from privileged soldier in South Africa to sister in England asking her to burn will "for I have already cancelled it": held letter revoked his previous will).

[113] *In the Estate of Gossage*, above, at 201–202 (writing must be "executed in the manner required for the execution of the will which it is intended to revoke").

[114] Wills Act 1837 s.20 refers to the manner in which "a will," not "the will", is hereinbefore required to be executed.

revoke. The testator's intention to revoke may be absolute or conditional. If it is absolute, revocation takes place immediately. If it is conditional, revocation does not take effect unless the condition is fulfilled. Often the condition makes revocation dependent upon the validity of another will or codicil and this particular type of conditional revocation has in the past been referred to as the doctrine of dependent relative revocation. It seems preferable, however, to use the less cumbersome term *conditional revocation* in all cases.[115]

Whether the testator's intention to revoke is conditional is a question of fact where revocation is by destruction,[116] and evidence as to the testator's declarations of intention is therefore admissible.[117] On the other hand, it is a question of construction[118] where revocation is by another will or codicil[119] or by duly executed writing.

1. Conditional revocation by destruction

7–40 The testator's intention to revoke by destruction may have been absolute (in the sense that the testator intended the revocation to take effect at once) or conditional (in the sense that he intended the revocation to take effect only if some condition were fulfilled).

(a) *Conditional upon due execution of new will or codicil*

7–41 If T formed the intention of making a new will in favour of B, and T destroyed his old will in favour of A, T's intention to revoke his old will may have been absolute or conditional. This is a question of fact to be decided after T's death upon all the evidence before the court. Evidence that T had formed the intention of making a new will does not, of itself, necessarily lead to the conclusion that T's intention to revoke was conditional.[120] For instance, the court may infer that T said to himself, "I cannot get on with making a new will in favour of B until my solicitor returns next week, but at least I will here and now get rid of this one, so that A shall not benefit". If, as in this instance, T's intention to revoke was absolute, T's destruction of his old will would have revoked it immediately.[121] It is irrelevant that

[115] "The name of this doctrine seems to me to be somewhat overloaded with unnecessary polysyllables. The resounding adjectives add very little, it seems to me, to any clear idea of what is meant. The whole matter can be quite simply expressed by the word 'conditional'," per Langton J in *In the Goods of Hope Brown* [1942] P. 136, 138; *Re Jones* [1976] Ch. 200, 212; Law Reform Committee's 22nd Report, p.24. The expression "conditional revocation" is clearly neater than "dependent relative revocation" but it could be suggested that not all instances of so-called "conditional revocation" are, in fact, conditional. Some of them may be instances of revocation induced by *mistake*—see J. Warren 33 Harv. L.R. (1920) 337.

[116] *Dixon v Solicitor to the Treasury* [1905] P. 42; *Re Jones*, above, at pp.215 and 218.

[117] *Powell v Powell* (1866) L.R. 1 P. & D. 209.

[118] The construction of wills is discussed below, Chap.10. Where revocation is by another, later will, the condition is almost always that the dispositive provisions in this later will are effective. The person construing the later will reads into the revocation clause in it a condition that the revocation clause shall operate only *if* the dispositive provisions in the later will are effective. For an example of this, see *Re Finnemore* [1991] 1 W.L.R. 793, discussed below, para.7–44.

[119] *Att Gen v Lloyd* (1747) 1 Ves.Sen. 32, 34.

[120] *Re Jones* [1976] Ch. 200; and see F. H. Newark 71 L.Q.R. (1955) 374.

[121] *Re Jones* [1976] Ch. 200 at pp.219–220.

this results in an intestacy which it is difficult to believe T intended.[122] On the other hand, the court may infer that T said to himself, "I believe that it is necessary for me to revoke my old will before I can make a new will". If, as in this instance, T's intention to revoke was conditional on his duly executing his new will, T's destruction of his old will would not have revoked it unless the condition was fulfilled.[123]

Similarly, if T believed that he had already made a new will (but had not done so because the "new will" had not been properly executed) and he then destroyed his old will, T's intention to revoke his old will might have been absolute (in which case his old will would have been revoked immediately)[124] or conditional on his new will having been duly executed (in which case his old will would not have been revoked unless the condition was fulfilled).[125] Alternatively, T may have had no intention to revoke, because he mistakenly believed his old will was useless or had already been revoked; in these cases his old will would not be revoked.[126]

(b) *Conditional upon revival of former will*

A will which has been revoked by a later will cannot be revived by the subsequent revocation of that later will.[127] It follows that if the testator destroys the later will, intending to revoke it conditionally on the revival of the former will, the revocation of the later will is ineffective.[128] **7–42**

(c) *Conditional upon particular devolution on intestacy*

In *In the Estate of Southerden*[129] a testator made a will giving all his property to his wife. Later he burned it, intending to revoke it conditionally on his wife being entitled to all his property on his death intestate. This condition was not satisfied and the Court of Appeal held that the will had not been revoked and its contents were admissible to probate. **7–43**

The doctrine of conditional revocation is not confined to these instances. It is of general application and applies if the testator's intention to revoke

122 *Re Jones* [1976] Ch. 200 at pp.213–214 and 217–218. It will, in some cases, be hard to be sure what the testator intended. An example of a recent case where a testator destroyed his will, intending to make another, but then failed to make it, is *Thorner v Major* [2009] UKHL 18; [2009] 1 W.L.R. 776, see para.6–09, above. In *Thorner*, the principal beneficiary under the destroyed will made a successful claim for proprietary estoppel, but quaere, could he have argued, in the alternative, that the revocation of the will was conditional?

123 *Dixon v Solicitor to the Treasury* [1905] P. 42: see *In the Estate of Bromham* [1952] 1 All E.R. 110. For evidence of conditional revocation of a will missing at death see below, para.19–22.

124 See *In the Estate of Green* (1962) 106 S.J. 1034.

125 *Dancer v Crabb* (1873) L.R. 3 P. & D. 98; *In the Estate of Davies* [1951] 1 All E.R. 920; *Sterling v Bruce* [1973] N.I. 255. Though quaere whether some cases where the revocation was held to be conditional should not have been dealt with as cases of revocation by mistake—see above para.7–39, fn.115.

126 See above, paras 7–19 et seq.

127 See below, para.7–58.

128 *Powell v Powell* (1866) L.R. 1 P. & D. 209; *Cossey v Cossey* (1900) 82 L.T. 203; *In the Estate of Bridgewater* [1965] 1 W.L.R. 416.

129 *In the Estate of Southerden* [1925] P. 177.

is conditional on the existence, or future existence, of a particular fact: if this condition is not satisfied, the will is not revoked by destruction.[130]

2. Conditional express revocation by will or codicil

7–44 A revocation clause may be subject to an express condition. If, for example, a testator inserts in a codicil a revocation clause expressed to take effect conditionally on his wife's predeceasing him, the clause does not operate if she survives him.

Even in the absence of an express condition, a revocation clause may be construed as conditional. An early instance is the decision in *Campbell v French*[131] where the testator, by his will, gave legacies to his sister's grandchildren living in America and then, by a codicil, revoked the legacies "they being all dead." In fact, they were still alive. Lord Loughborough held that the revocation was ineffective as it was conditional on the legatees being dead. A more recent instance is *Re Finnemore*[132] where a testator made three wills in succession. In each of the three wills the testator gave his house, the contents of his house, and three-quarters of his residuary estate to C. The three wills differed as to the way in which they disposed of the other quarter of the residuary estate. The two later wills contained standard clauses revoking all previous wills. Unfortunately, the gifts to C in the second and third wills were void because C's husband was an attesting witness to both of these wills.[133] Judge Micklem[134] held that the revocation clauses in the two later wills were conditional on the gifts to C in those wills being valid. As the gifts were void, the revocation clauses would not take effect insofar as they purported to revoke dispositions contained in the first will which gave benefits similar to those contained in the later wills.[135] The revocation clause in the last will was construed[136] distributively, so that it was effective in revoking the parts of the earlier wills which dealt with the quarter of the residue which did not pass to C; that quarter of the residue passed under the provisions of the last will.

3. Conditional implied revocation by will or codicil

7–45 Where a testator by a will or codicil gives property to X, and by a later will or codicil gives the same property to Y, the gift to X is

[130] *In the Estate of Southerden* [1925] P. 177; *Re Jones* [1976] Ch. 200, 213 and 216: see *Re Carey* (1977) 121 S.J. 173 (conditional on fact he had nothing to leave by will).

[131] *Campbell v French* (1797) 3 Ves. 321: see also *Doe d. Evans v Evans* (1839) 10 Ad. & El. 228; *Re Plunkett* [1964] I.R. 259: contrast *Re Feis* [1964] Ch. 106.

[132] *Re Finnemore* [1991] 1 W.L.R. 793.

[133] See below, paras 14–03 et seq.

[134] Sitting as a Judge of the High Court.

[135] See also *In the Goods of Hope Brown* [1942] P.136: *In the Estate of Cocke* [1960] 1 W.L.R. 491; *In the Estate of Crannis* (1978) 122 S.J. 489; see R.G. Henderson (1969) 32 M.L.R. 447; cf. *Re Luck* [1977] W.A.R. 148.

[136] The judge gave *two* alternative grounds for his decision. On the one hand, he *construed* the revocation clause as conditional. Alternatively (at p.826), he thought that the court could treat this as a case of *mistake*. The latter ground may appear more straightforward, but it raises difficulties. See J. Warren 33 Harv. L.R. (1920) 337.

impliedly revoked. But does this occur if for some reason the gift to Y fails? In that event it is a question of construction whether the testator has shown an intention to revoke the gift to X in any event (in which case X does not take) or conditionally on the gift to Y taking effect (in which case X does take on the failure of the gift to Y).[137] The answer therefore depends on the proper construction of the later will or codicil.

The decision in *Re Robinson*[138] is a useful illustration. The testatrix by will gave her estate upon trust to pay an annuity to her son, H, and after his death to divide her estate equally between her grandchildren who attained 21 years of age. By a later will she gave her whole estate to H absolutely, but the disposition was void as H's wife was an attesting witness.[139] The court held that the testatrix had not shown an intention to revoke the earlier will in any event. The later will contained no revocation clause and the only indication in it of an intention to revoke was in the disposition which had failed; the earlier will had therefore not been revoked. The intention to revoke was conditional on the absolute gift to H taking effect and this condition was not satisfied.

III. ALTERATION

Section 21 of the Wills Act 1837 lays down the rule for any alteration in a will: **7–46**

> "No obliteration, interlineation, or other alteration made in any will after the execution thereof shall be valid or have any effect, except so far as the words or effect of the will before such alteration shall not be apparent, unless such alteration shall be executed in like manner as hereinbefore is required for the execution of the will. . ."

In considering the effect of s.21 three main questions may arise and they should be considered in turn:

A. Was the alteration made before the execution of the will? If so, the alteration is valid and s.21 does not apply.
B. Was the alteration duly executed? If so, it is valid.
C. Has the alteration made any part of the will not "apparent"? If it is not apparent and the testator intended to revoke it, that part is revoked.

[137] *Ward v Van der Loeff* [1924] A.C. 653 (gift in later codicil void for remoteness: gift in earlier will held not revoked).
[138] *Re Robinson* [1930] 2 Ch. 332: see also *Re Davies* [1928] Ch. 24.
[139] See *Re Finnemore*, above, and see also below, paras 14–03 et seq.

A. ALTERATION MADE BEFORE EXECUTION OF WILL

7–47 An alteration made in a will before the will is executed by the testator is valid if the testator intends the alteration to form part of the will when it is executed. Thus the alteration is not valid if it is merely deliberative and not final. A rebuttable presumption arises that an alteration in pencil is merely deliberative and that an alteration in ink is intended to be final.[140]

1. Presumption as to time of alteration

7–48 There is a rebuttable presumption that an unattested alteration was made after the execution of the will[141] or any subsequent codicil.[142] This presumption may be rebutted by evidence, which may be internal evidence from the will itself, or extrinsic evidence, or both. If the alterations are trifling and of little consequence, the presumption may be readily rebutted.[143]

The presumption has been rebutted by internal evidence within the will itself where the alterations were made to fill blanks left in the will by the draftsman,[144] and again where interlineations written with the same ink as the rest of the will completed the otherwise unintelligible sentences of the will.[145]

Extrinsic evidence rebutting the presumption may take different forms; for instance, evidence from the draftsman of the will[146] or an attesting witness, or declarations by the testator showing that he made the alterations before executing the will.[147] The court considers all the evidence, both internal and extrinsic, in deciding whether the presumption is rebutted.

A different presumption applies if the will was made by the testator whilst privileged. In that case a rebuttable presumption arises that the alteration was made whilst the testator was still privileged and therefore entitled to make informal alterations.[148]

140 *Hawkes v Hawkes* (1828) 1 Hagg.Ecc. 321 (each presumption is stronger if there are both ink and pencil alterations); *In the Goods of Adams* (1872) L.R. 2 P. & D. 367.

141 *Cooper v Bockett* (1846) 4 Moo.P.C. 419; *In the Goods of Adamson* (1875) L.R. 3 P. & D. 253; *Luty v Magill* (2005) 246 D.L.R. (4th) 762.

142 *In the Goods of Sykes* (1873) 3 P. & D. 26, 27–28; *Lushington v Onslow* (1848) 6 N. of C. 183.

143 *In the Goods of Hindmarsh* (1866) 1 P. & D. 307 (testator a lawyer, alterations trifling and apparently written with same pen and ink as rest of will, and not very strong evidence of writing expert: presumption rebutted).

144 *Birch v Birch* (1848) 1 Rob.Ecc. 675 (blanks left for amounts of legacies); *Greville v Tylee* (1851) 7 Moo.P.C. 320, 327.

145 *In the Goods of Cadge* (1868) 1 P. & D. 543.

146 *Keigwin v Keigwin* (1843) 3 Curt. 607.

147 The admissibility of such declarations is now governed by the Civil Evidence Act 1995. It was formerly governed by the Civil Evidence Act 1968. Before that Act came into force, such declarations were not admissible if made by the testator after the execution of the will.

148 *In the Goods of Tweedale* (1874) L.R. 3 P. & D. 204 (soldier's will); *In the Goods of Newland* [1952] P. 71 (seaman's will).

2. Effect of confirmation

The confirmation[149] of a will by its re-execution with the proper formalities validates an alteration made in the will after it was executed but before it was confirmed, if the testator intends the alteration to form part of the will when it is confirmed.[150] The same result follows if, after the alteration is made, the will is confirmed by a duly executed codicil containing some reference to the will.[151] But the alteration is not validated by confirmation of the will if the alteration was merely deliberative and not final,[152] or if the codicil shows that the testator was treating the will as unaltered.[153] 7–49

As already explained,[154] the presumption is that an unattested alteration to the will was made, not only after the execution of the will, but also after the execution of the codicil.[155] Accordingly, unless this presumption is rebutted by evidence showing that the unattested alteration was made before the execution of the codicil,[156] the alteration is not validated by the confirmation of the will by the codicil.

B. ALTERATION DULY EXECUTED

1. Formalities

If the alteration is duly executed with the formalities required for the execution of the will, the alteration is valid. In this connection s.21 of the Wills Act 1837 provides that the signatures of the testator and the witnesses may be made "in the margin or on some other part of the will opposite or near to such alteration, or at the foot or end of or opposite to a memorandum referring to such alteration, and written at the end or some other part of the will." Accordingly an alteration is valid if the testator signs by writing his initials in the margin against the alteration, and the testator either makes or acknowledges this signature in the simultaneous presence of two witnesses, who then both sign in the presence of the testator by writing their initials in the margin.[157] 7–50

[149] See below, paras 7–65 et seq.: revival has the same effect, see below, paras 7–56 et seq.

[150] *In the Goods of Shearn* (1880) 50 L.J.P. 15 (alteration after execution: alteration invalid as will not properly re-executed): cf. *In the Goods of Dewell* (1853) 1 Sp.Ecc. & Ad. 103, which was wrongly decided.

[151] *In the Goods of Sykes* (1873) L.R. 3 P. & D. 26.

[152] *In the Goods of Hall* (1871) L.R. 2 P. & D. 256 (pencil alterations).

[153] *Re Hay* [1904] 1 Ch.317 (three legacies in will struck out by unattested alteration, later codicil revoked only one of them: held the other two stood, as testatrix was confirming her will without the alterations).

[154] See above, para.7–48.

[155] *In the Goods of Sykes*, above, at pp.27–28; *Lushington v Onslow* (1848) 6 Notes of Cases 183.

[156] *In the Goods of Heath* [1892] P. 253 (wording of codicil showed interlineation in will had already been made).

[157] *In the Goods of Blewitt* (1880) 5 P.D. 116 (initials suffice).

In *Re White*[158] the testator made a valid will in 1981, but in 1984 he decided that he wanted to alter it. A friend made alterations to the original will, in the testator's presence and at his dictation. The alterations were initialled by two witnesses, but the testator, who had signed the will in 1981, did not sign or initial any of the alterations in 1984. The alterations could not be held valid by virtue of s.21 and the *original* will was admitted to probate.[159]

An alteration is valid if a duly executed memorandum refers to the alteration.[160]

Two precautions are advisable in practice in connection with alterations:

- (i) Unless the testator is *in extremis*, it is advisable to restrict alterations to the correction of small errors, such as the misspelling of a name, and to give effect to all other alterations by the execution of a new will or a codicil. This reduces the likelihood that there will be problems of construction.[161]
- (ii) All alterations, whenever made, should be duly executed. This is advisable even though the alteration is made before the execution of the will, because it makes it unnecessary to rebut the presumption that an unattested alteration was made after the execution of the will.

2. Privileged testator

7–51 A testator who has made a will whilst privileged may make alterations to it without any formalities whilst still privileged[162] because no formalities are required for due execution under s.11.

C. PART OF WILL NOT APPARENT

7–52 An alteration after execution which makes any part of the will not "apparent" revokes that part if the testator has an intention to revoke it. Probate of the will must be granted with a blank space for the part not apparent.

1. The test of being not apparent

7–53 "Apparent" in s.21 means optically apparent on the face of the will itself.[163] A word in a will is not apparent if it cannot be deciphered by any "natural" means, such as holding the paper up to the light with a frame

[158] *Re White* [1991] Ch 1.
[159] See above, para.4–09.
[160] *In the Goods of Treeby* (1875) 3 P. & D. 242.
[161] Alterations and codicils both have the potential disadvantage that someone who has lost a benefit, or who has a benefit reduced, will find out that this has happened.
[162] *In the Goods of Tweedale* (1874) L.R. 3 P. & D. 204.
[163] *Townley v Watson* (1844) 3 Curt. 761, 768; *In the Goods of Itter* [1950] P. 130, 132: see Law Reform Committee's 22nd Report, pp.23–24 (recommending no change).

of brown paper around the portion attempted to be read[164] or by using a magnifying glass.[165] In determining whether a word is apparent, it is not permissible to ascertain the word by the use of extrinsic evidence,[166] or by physically interfering with the will by using chemicals to remove ink-marks, or removing a slip of paper pasted over the word,[167] or by making another document, such as an infra-red photograph.[168] If the word can only be ascertained by these "forbidden" methods it is not apparent.

2. Intention to revoke

The testator must make the alteration which renders part of the will not apparent with an intention to revoke that part.[169] A testator who accidentally obliterates part of his will by, for example, spilling ink over it does not, therefore, revoke that part. **7–54**

3. Conditional obliteration[170]

If the testator's intention to revoke is conditional, revocation does not take place despite the obliteration unless the condition is fulfilled. If the condition is not fulfilled, the word obliterated must be ascertained so that it can be admitted to probate. For this purpose the court has recourse to any means of legal proof, including any of the above "forbidden" methods,[171] because the question to be answered is not whether the word is apparent but, rather, whether the obliterated word can be ascertained. **7–55**

Usually the condition relates to the validity of a legacy of a different amount which the testator attempts to substitute in place of the original amount which he obliterates. For instance, T by his will gives to X a legacy of "one thousand five hundred pounds": later T obliterates the words "one thousand five hundred" (making them not apparent) and writes the words "two thousand" in their place. If, at the time he carries out this obliteration, T intends to revoke the original amount only if the new amount is effectually substituted, T's intention to revoke is subject to a condition which is not fulfilled (unless the alteration is duly executed

[164] *Ffinch v Combe* [1894] P. 191 (slips of paper pasted over words in will after execution).
[165] *In the Goods of Brasier* [1899] P. 36.
[166] *Townley v Watson* (1844) 3 Curt. 761, 768 (evidence of draftsman not admissible to prove what the obliterated words were).
[167] *In the Goods of Horsford* (1874) L.R. 3 P. & D. 211 (the same will came before the court in *Ffinch v Combe*, above). But a slip of paper may be removed in order to ascertain whether it covers words of revocation which took effect before being covered: *In the Goods of Gilbert* [1893] P. 183.
[168] *In the Goods of Itter* [1950] P. 130.
[169] *Townley v Watson*, above, at p.769.
[170] For conditional revocation by destruction see above, paras 7–40 et seq.
[171] *In the Goods of Horsford*, above, (strips of paper pasted over amount of legacy in codicil ordered to be removed as condition of revocation not fulfilled); *In the Goods of Itter*, above, *Sturton v Whetlock* (1883) 52 L.J.P. 29 (evidence of draftsman as to original words).

or T later confirms his will): accordingly the original amount is admissible to probate.[172] But if T merely obliterates the words "five hundred", intending to revoke them but not to substitute any new words, his intention to revoke is absolute: probate must be granted with a blank space for the words "five hundred" if these words are not apparent.[173] The same result follows even though T later changes his mind and attempts to substitute new words. Thus if T first obliterates the words "five hundred", intending to revoke them but not to substitute any new words, and later changes his mind and writes the words "nine hundred" in their place, probate must be granted with a blank space for the words "five hundred".[174]

Whether the testator's intention to revoke is conditional is a question of fact: evidence as to the testator's declarations of intention is, therefore, admissible.[175] If the testator attempts to substitute a legacy of a different amount, but leaves the name of the legatee untouched, the court may infer from this that his intention to revoke was conditional on the validity of the substituted amount.[176]

IV. REVIVAL AND CONFIRMATION

A. REVIVAL

7–56 A testator may revive a will or codicil, or any part of it, which has been revoked. He cannot, however, revive a will or codicil which is no longer in existence: once it has been destroyed it cannot be revived[177] and the testator must execute a new will or codicil in order to give effect to its provisions.

1. Two methods of revival[178]

7–57 Section 22 of the Wills Act 1837 provides that a will or codicil which has been wholly or partly revoked may be revived only: (i) by its

[172] *In the Goods of Itter* [1950] P. 130; *In the Goods of Horsford*, above. As to other conditions see *In the Goods of McCabe* (1873) 3 P. & D. 94 (T gave her residuary personalty to niece X, believing X's mother Y was dying, and later substituted Y for X after Y's recovery: held conditional obliteration of X, and "X" admitted to probate); *Sturton v Whetlock*, above, (gifts to grandchildren at age of twenty-one years; "one" erased and "five" substituted: held conditional obliteration).

[173] *In the Goods of Nelson* (1872) 6 I.R. Eq. 569; *In the Goods of Hamer* (1944) 113 L.J.P. 31.

[174] *In the Goods of Itter*, above, at p.133.

[175] *In the Goods of McCabe*, above, at pp.96–97; *In the Estate of Zimmer* (1924) 40 T.L.R. 502: see conditional revocation by destruction, above, paras 7–40 et seq.

[176] *In the Goods of Itter* [1950] P. 133.

[177] *Rogers v Goodenough* (1862) 2 Sw. & Tr. 342; *In the Goods of Steele* (1868) L.R. 1 P. & D. 575, 576–577; *In the Goods of Reade* [1902] P. 75. Quaere whether a testator may revive a will which has been destroyed without his knowledge.

[178] See Law Reform Committee's 22nd Report, p.25 (recommending no change).

re-execution with the proper formalities, or (ii) by a duly executed codicil showing an intention to revive it. No other methods of revival are available.

(a) *Revocation of revoking will cannot revive*

A will which has been revoked by a later will cannot be revived by the subsequent revocation of that later will. In *In the Goods of Hodgkinson*[179] a testator first made a will giving all his property to X and later made a second will giving his realty to Y: the second will impliedly revoked the first will as regards the testator's realty. Subsequently the testator revoked the second will by destruction. The Court of Appeal held that as regards the testator's realty the first will was not revived by the revocation of the second will: the first will disposed of the testator's personalty, but his realty passed on intestacy.[180] **7–58**

(b) *Revival by codicil showing an intention to revive*

The second method of revival requires the testator to execute, with the proper formalities, a codicil showing an intention to revive the revoked will or codicil. Whether a codicil shows the necessary intention to revive is a question of construction. The intention must **7–59**

> "appear on the face of the codicil, either by express words referring to a will as revoked and importing an intention to revive the same, or by a disposition of the testator's property inconsistent with any other intention, or by some other expressions conveying to the mind of the Court, with reasonable certainty, the existence of the intention in question."[181]

In construing a codicil, the normal rules as to the admission of extrinsic evidence apply.[182]

In the Goods of Davis[183] is a useful illustration. The testator made a will giving all his estate to Ethel Phoebe Horsley. A year later he married her, thereby revoking the will. Subsequently he wrote on the envelope containing the will, "The herein named Ethel Phoebe Horsley is now my lawful wedded wife", and this writing was duly signed and attested. As evidence of the surrounding circumstances, an affidavit by Ethel's

[179] *In the Goods of Hodgkinson* [1893] P. 339: see also *Major v Williams* (1843) 3 Curt. 432; *In the Goods of Brown* (1858) 1 Sw. & Tr. 32.

[180] The result would have been different if the testator had destroyed his second will, intending to revoke it *conditionally* on the revival of his first will as regards his realty—the condition would not have been fulfilled and the revocation of his second will would not have been effective, see above, para.7–41.

[181] *In the Goods of Steele* (1868) L.R. 1 P. & D. 575, at p.578. A codicil does not show an intention to revive a revoked will if it is merely attached to it by a piece of tape: *Marsh v Marsh* (1860) 1 Sw. & Tr. 528.

[182] See below, paras 10–43 et seq.; *In the Goods of Steele*, above, at p.576; *In the Goods of Davis* [1952] P. 279.

[183] *In the Goods of Davis* [1952] P. 279: see also *In the Goods of Terrible* (1858) 1 Sw. & Tr. 140.

sister was admitted, proving that, shortly before the testator wrote on the envelope, the sister had pointed out to him that the will had been revoked by his marriage. The court held that the writing on the envelope was a codicil showing the testator's intention to revive the will because it conveyed to the mind of the court with reasonable certainty the existence of this intention; both the will and the envelope were accordingly admitted to probate.

2. When a codicil refers to a revoked will by its date

7–60 Imagine the following sequence of events:

(i) The first will is dated January 1, 2010.
(ii) The second will is dated June 30, 2014 and expressly revokes all former wills.
(iii) Codicil "to my will dated January 1, 2010".
(iv) Death of testator.

If the codicil merely describes itself as a codicil to the testator's last will, but gives the date of the first will, it does not revive the first will or revoke the second will: the reference in the codicil to the date of the first will does *not* show an intention to revive it.[184] The cases which decide this may be supported on the ground that the description of the will by the codicil is ambiguous; the first will is not the testator's last will, or his will at all, as it has been revoked.[185]

7–61 If, on the other hand, the codicil not only refers to the first will by date, but also refers to the provisions of the first will, the codicil shows an intention to revive it.[186] Probate is granted of the first will and the codicil, and also of the second will, unless the second will was revoked by the codicil or by the first will. In doubtful cases, the question of the extent to which the second will was revoked may be left to a court of construction. The second will may be revoked expressly by a revocation clause in the codicil, or in the first will (which operates as if executed at the time of revival)[187]; or impliedly by provisions in the codicil and the first will which are inconsistent with the provisions in the second will.[188] If the codicil shows an intention to revive part, but not the whole, of the first will, probate is granted of that part of the first will and the codicil, and also of the second will, unless the second will is revoked by the codicil or the revived part of the first will.[189]

184 *In the Goods of May* (1868) L.R. 1 P. & D. 575; *In the Goods of Gordon* [1892] P. 228; *Jane v Jane* (1917) 33 T.L.R. 389; *Goldie v Adam* [1938] P. 85.

185 *In the Goods of Whatman* (1864) 34 L.J.P.M. & A. 17.

186 *In the Goods of Stedham* (1881) 6 P.D. 205; *In the Goods of Dyke* (1881) 6 P.D. 207; *In the Goods of Chilcott* [1897] P. 223.

187 *Re Pearson* [1963] 1 W.L.R. 1358: but see *Re Rear* [1975] 2 N.Z.L.R. 254, 264 (quaere from what date revocation clause speaks): for the effect of confirmation of a will containing a revocation clause see below, para.7–69.

188 *Re Baker* [1929] 1 Ch. 668; *In the Goods of Reynolds* (1873) 3 P. & D. 35.

189 *In the Estate of Mardon* [1944] P. 109.

Usually, if a codicil refers to a revoked will by its date, it is as the result of a blunder.[190] This could have been avoided by proper precautions if:

(i) after the second (or later) will was executed, the first (or earlier) will had been clearly marked to show that it had been revoked by the later will; and
(ii) the draftsman of the codicil had insisted on having the testator's last will before him.

3. Effects of revival

Under s.34 of the Wills Act 1837 a revived will is deemed for the purposes of the Act to have been made at the time of its revival.[191] A revived will operates as if it had been executed at that time.[192] **7–62**

(a) *Will revoked in stages*

Section 22 provides that if a will or codicil is first partly revoked and later wholly revoked, but is subsequently revived, the revival does not extend to the part first revoked unless an intention to the contrary is shown. **7–63**

(b) *Alteration and incorporation*

Revival may validate an unattested alteration made to the will or codicil before its revival.[193] Similarly, revival of a will or codicil may incorporate a document which came into existence prior to its revival, but which was not in existence when the will or codicil was first executed.[194] **7–64**

B. CONFIRMATION (OR REPUBLICATION)

A testator may confirm a will or codicil.[195] The traditional term tor this is "republication" but it has been an anachronism since s.13 of the Wills Act 1837 made publication[196] of a will unnecessary. It would **7–65**

[190] "If experience had not shown the fact, it would be almost incredible that mistakes should occur so constantly as they do in so simple a matter as reciting the true date of a will," per Lord Penzance in *In the Goods of Steele*, above, at p.580. For other mistakes, many of them incredible, see Chap.15.

[191] Section 34 may on its proper construction merely refer to the commencement of the Act (*Re Elcom* [1894] 1 Ch. 303, 309) but in *Goonewardene v Goonewardene* [1931] A.C. 647 the Privy Council treated it obiter as having general application.

[192] Confirmation generally has the same effect, see below, para.7–67.

[193] *Neate v Pickard* (1843) 2 Notes of Cases 406. Revival, like confirmation, does not validate a merely deliberative alteration; again the reviving codicil may show the testator was treating the revived will or codicil as unaltered; see below, para.7–67.

[194] Confirmation has the same effect, see above, para.4–38.

[195] See generally, J. D. B. Mitchell (1954) 70 L.Q.R. 353.

[196] Publication was a declaration by the testator in the presence of witnesses that the instrument produced to them was his will.

be better if the term "confirmation" came into general use instead, because this is the sense in which "republication" has been used since 1837.[197]

The difference between revival and confirmation is that revival revives a revoked will or codicil, whereas confirmation confirms an unrevoked will or codicil.

1. Two methods of confirmation

7–66 A will or codicil may be confirmed only (i) by its re-execution with the proper formalities,[198] or (ii) by a duly executed codicil containing some reference to it.[199] The codicil need not show an intention to confirm the previous will or codicil in the sense in which a codicil is required by s.22 to show an intention to revive a revoked will or codicil. In order to confirm a will, a codicil need only contain some reference to the will. Thus a will is confirmed by a codicil which describes itself as a "codicil to my will".[200] From such a brief reference the inference is drawn that, when executing the codicil, the testator considered the will as his will and thereby confirmed it. This has been termed constructive confirmation. It has the same effect as if the testator expressly confirmed the will, e.g. by using the phrase—"In all other respects I confirm my will"—which is usually found at the end of a codicil.

2. Effects of confirmation

7–67 Section 34 of the Wills Act 1837 applies to confirmation as well as to revival.[201] In general, a confirmed will operates as if it had been executed at the time of its confirmation.[202]

(a) *Confirmation must not defeat intention*

7–68 The doctrine of confirmation is not applied so as to defeat the testator's intention by, for instance, invalidating a gift which was

[197] *Berkeley v Berkeley* [1946] A.C. 555, 575–576. What is confusing is that s.13 of the Wills Act 1837 makes "publication" of a will unnecessary, but s.34 of the Act refers to "republication"; it is because of this that the term "republication" has remained in use.

[198] *Dunn v Dunn* (1866) L.R. 1 P. & D. 277.

[199] *Re Smith* (1890) 45 Ch.D. 632 (duly executed paper made no reference to previous will: no confirmation).

[200] *Re Taylor* (1880) 57 L.J.Ch. 430, 434: see also *Skinner v Ogle* (1845) 1 Rob.Ecc. 363; *Serocold v Hemming* (1758) 2 Lee 490 (revival prior to Wills Act 1837, and cited in *Re Smith*, above); *Re Harvey* [1947] Ch. 285 (where Vaisey J said "a codicil described as a codicil to a particular will republishes that will").

[201] See above, para.7–62, fn.192.

[202] For the effect of confirmation of a will which contains an appointment under a special power, which becomes exercisable after the will but before confirmation, see *Re Blackburn* (1890) 43 Ch.D. 75. For the exception relating to an illegitimate child see below, para.11–05, and for the exception relating to the age of majority see below, para.11–10.

valid at the date of the will.[203] As Barton J put it in the Irish case of *Re Moore*,[204]

> "The authorities lead me to the conclusion that the courts have always treated the principle that republication makes the will speak as if it had been re-executed at the date of the codicil not as a rigid formula or technical rule, but as a useful and flexible instrument for effectuating a testator's intentions, by ascertaining them down to the latest date at which they have been expressed."

(b) *Confirmation of will containing revocation clause*

The sequence of events in *In the Goods of Rawlins*[205] was: **7–69**

(i) execution of a will which contained a revocation clause in general terms;
(ii) execution of a codicil to the will; and
(iii) the testator deleted one clause in the will and then re-executed it.

The court held that the codicil was not revoked by the confirmation of the will containing the revocation clause. The will was re-executed so as to give effect to the deletion and it was not the testator's intention to revoke the codicil—"prima facie the re-execution of the will is a confirmation and not a revocation of the codicil, which became part of the instrument."[206]

(c) *Alteration and incorporation*

The effect of confirmation on an unattested alteration already made **7–70** to the will or codicil,[207] and on the incorporation of a document which came into existence prior to confirmation,[208] has already been considered.

(d) *Invalid gift to witness or spouse of witness*

Section 15 of the Wills Act 1837 deprives an attesting witness and **7–71** his spouse of any benefit under a gift in the will. But if the will is confirmed by a codicil not attested by that witness, this validates the gift.[209]

203 *Re Moore* [1907] 1 I.R. 315; *Re Heath's W.T.* [1949] Ch. 170; *Re Park* [1910] 2 Ch. 322.
204 *Re Moore* [1907] 1 I.R. 315; see also *Re Hardyman* [1925] Ch. 287, 291.
205 *In the Goods of Rawlins* (1879) 48 L.J.P. 64: see also *Wade v Nazer* (1848) 1 Rob. 627. If a will is confirmed by codicil, any alteration already made to the will by an earlier codicil between the execution and confirmation of the will stands (*Crosbie v MacDoual* (1799) 4 Ves. 610; *Green v Tribe* (1878) 9 Ch.D. 231) unless the confirming codicil shows an intention to revive a revoked part of the will (*McLeod v McNab* [1891] A.C. 471).
206 *In the Goods of Rawlins* (1879) 48 L.J.P. 64, 65.
207 See above, para.7–49.
208 See above, para.4–42.
209 See below, para.14–09.

(e) *Lapse and ademption*

7–72 The effect of confirmation on a gift which has lapsed,[210] or been adeemed,[211] is considered later.

(f) *Date from which a will speaks*

7–73 The effect of confirmation on the date from which a will speaks is considered later.[212]

[210] See below, paras 14–11 et seq.
[211] See below, paras 14–35 et seq.
[212] See below, paras 12–17 and 12–18.

CHAPTER 8

PROVISION FOR THE DECEASED'S FAMILY AND DEPENDANTS[1]

I. INTRODUCTION

From the sixteenth-century onwards, there was near total testamentary freedom[2] in England and Wales and in 1891, with the enactment of the Mortmain and Charitable Uses Act, this freedom became total. This meant that a testator could do whatever he liked with his property[3] and a rich testator could, if he wanted, leave his family destitute.[4] These four hundred years of testamentary freedom came to an end with the enactment of the Inheritance (Family Provision) Act 1938. **8–01**

Testamentary freedom is a concept which seems natural to lawyers brought up in the Common Law, as opposed to the Civil Law, tradition. Those accustomed to systems based on Roman Law are more likely to assume that the deceased must pass at least part of his property on to his descendants or to other members of his family. Such property is called in French Law the *réserve légale*[5] and in Scottish Law *legal rights*.[6] Common lawyers refer to the Civil Law concept that members of the deceased's family are entitled to part of his estate as "forced heirship".

The Inheritance (Family Provision) Act 1938 enabled four classes of "dependants" of a deceased person to apply to the court for a discretionary order for maintenance out of his estate. The four classes were the

[1] There are a number of monographs on Family Provision. See, e.g. Sidney Ross, *Inheritance Act Claims: Law and Practice*, 3rd edn (London: Sweet & Maxwell, 2011). See also R. Probert, "Disquieting Thoughts: Who Will Benefit When We are Gone?" Chap.2 in B. Häcker and C. Mitchell (eds), *Current Issues in Succession Law* (Oxford: Hart Publishing, 2016).

[2] Freedom to dispose of personalty at death dated back to the mid-fifteenth century. Freedom to dispose of realty derived from the Statute of Wills 1540.

[3] This refers, of course, to *his* property and not to property held in trust.

[4] Though it should not be forgotten that the widespread use of strict settlements and entails operated in such a way as to ensure that property stayed in the family.

[5] *Code Civil*, arts 913 and 914.

[6] Legal rights in Scottish law consist of the *jus relicti* for widowers, the jus relictae for widows, and *legitim* for children; see Gloag and Henderson, *The Law of Scotland*, 13th edn (London: Sweet & Maxwell, 2012) paras 39–08 et seq. and 40–36 et seq.

deceased's (i) wife or husband, (ii) unmarried or incapacitated daughter, (iii) infant son, or (iv) adult but incapacitated son. The 1938 Act applied only where the deceased had left a *will* but it was extended by the Intestates' Estates Act 1952 to intestacies. The Matrimonial Causes (Property and Maintenance) Act 1958, gave *former spouses* rights equivalent to those enjoyed by the four original classes.[7]

8–02 In 1973 the Law Commission produced a report, *Family Law: First Report on Family Property. A New Approach,*[8] in which it considered the possibility of introducing a system under which a surviving spouse would have had a legal right to inherit part of the estate of a deceased spouse. The Law Commission concluded, however, that it was neither necessary nor desirable to introduce such a principle; but it decided that, in so far as it was practicable in the differing circumstances, the claim of a surviving spouse upon the family assets should be at least equal to that of a spouse on a divorce.[9] This led, the following year, to a further Law Commission report, *Family Law: Second Report on Family Property. Family Provision on Death,*[10] which resulted in the enactment of the Inheritance (Provision for Family and Dependants) Act 1975.[11]

The 1975 Act made a number of important changes to the 1938 legislation: it added to the classes of applicants; it increased and amended the standard of provision for spouses; it added to the orders the court could make; it added to the property out of which financial provision could be ordered; and it introduced anti-avoidance provisions. Although cases decided under the 1938 Act should not be ignored,[12] the earlier authorities should be approached with caution because of the substantial changes which have occurred in the legislation.[13]

8–03 The 1989 Law Commission report, *Distribution on Intestacy*[14] recommended that cohabitants should not be provided for under the intestacy rules but that they should, instead, be provided for under the family provision legislation. In accordance with this recommendation, s.2 of the Law Reform (Succession) Act 1995 amended the 1975 Act by adding cohabitants as a further class of applicants.

The Civil Partnership Act 2004, which came into force on 5 December 2005, put same-sex couples who register their partnerships in the position of spouses.

In 2011 the Law Commission report *Intestacy and Family Provision Claims on Death*[15] recommended a number of relatively minor changes to the 1975 Act and also recommended that cohabitants *should* be entitled to benefit

[7] s.3 of the 1958 Act, which became s.26 of the Matrimonial Causes Act 1965.

[8] *Family Law: First Report on Family Property. A New Approach*, Law Com. No.52: H.C. 274.

[9] Law Com. No.52: para 61.

[10] *Family Law: Second Report on Family Property. Family Provision on Death*, Law Com. No.61: H.C. 324.

[11] For a more detailed history see K. Green in (1988) 51 M.L.R. 187, 190–195.

[12] *Re Coventry* [1980] Ch. 461, 474 and 487.

[13] *Moody v Stevenson* [1992] Ch 486, 502.

[14] Law Com. No.187.

[15] Law Com. No.331.

under the intestacy rules. Most of the minor changes have now been enacted by the Inheritance and Trustees' Powers Act 2014[16] and are discussed later in this chapter. The recommendation that cohabitants should be entitled to inherit on intestacy has not been enacted and is discussed further towards the end of the chapter.[17]

The 1975 Act, as amended by the Law Reform (Succession) Act 1995, the Civil Partnership Act 2004 and the Inheritance and Trustees' Powers Act 2014, applies on the death of any person on or after 1 January 1996.[18] Any of the following persons may apply for provision: **8–04**

> "1. (1) (a) the spouse or civil partner of the deceased;
> (b) a former spouse or former civil partner of the deceased, but not one who has formed a subsequent marriage or civil partnership;
> (ba) any person (not being a person included in paragraph (a) or (b) above) to whom subsection (1A) or (1B) below applies[19];
> (c) a child of the deceased;
> (d) any person (not being a child of the deceased) who, in relation to any marriage or civil partnership to which the deceased was at any time a party, or otherwise in relation to any family in which the deceased at any time stood in the role of parent, was treated by the deceased as a child of the family;[20]
> (e) any person (not being a person included in the foregoing paragraphs of this subsection) who immediately before the death of the deceased was being maintained, either wholly or partly, by the deceased.
>
> (1A) This section applies to a person if the deceased died on or after 1st January 1996 and, during the whole of the period of two years ending immediately before the date when the deceased died, the person was living–
> (a) in the same household as the deceased, and
> (b) as the husband or wife of the deceased.
>
> (1B) This subsection applies to a person if for the whole of the period of two years ending immediately before the date when the deceased died, the person was living—
> (a) in the same household as the deceased, and
> (b) as the civil partner of the deceased."[21]

[16] The Inheritance and Trustees' Powers Act 2014 s.6 and Sch.2.

[17] See below paras 8–82 et seq.

[18] Cohabitants within subs.1(1A) may apply only if the deceased died on or after 1 January 1996; there is no date specified in subs.1(1B). See, below, para.8–49. Members of the other classes may apply provided the deceased died on or after 1 April 1976.

[19] Paragraph (ba) was inserted by the Law Reform Succession Act 1995 and amended by the Civil Partnership Act 2004.

[20] s.1.(1)(d) was slightly amended in 2014. See below para.8–64.

[21] Each category of applicant is considered more fully below, at paras 8–33 et seq.

II. DOMICILE, JURISDICTION, TIME LIMIT AND PROTECTION FOR PERSONAL REPRESENTATIVES

1. Domicile

8–05 The Law Reform (Succession) Act 1975 Act applies only if the deceased died domiciled in England and Wales.[22] The legal burden of proof that the deceased died so domiciled lies on the applicant.[23]

2. Jurisdiction

8–06 An application under the Act may be made either to the Chancery Division or to the Family Division of the High Court, which has unlimited jurisdiction; or to the county court which now also has unlimited jurisdiction as a result of the High Court and County Courts Jurisdiction Order 1991.[24] Chancery masters in the High Court and district judges in the county court commonly hear applications; so the distinction between trial in the High Court and in the county court is not as significant as it might otherwise be.[25] As to the choice between the Chancery Division and the Family Division, some applications fall more conveniently within one jurisdiction and some within the other. If, for example, an application under the 1975 Act arises in relation to an estate where there is also a dispute over the construction of the deceased's will, it is best that the application be dealt with immediately after the construction summons by the same judge in the Chancery Division.[26] If, on the other hand, the application relates to the estate of someone who was previously subject to an order under the Matrimonial Causes Act 1973, it may be convenient to deal with it in the Family Division.[27]

[22] Law Reform (Succession) Act 1975 Act ss.1(1) and 27(2): for domicile see Dicey, Morris & Collins, *The Conflict of Laws*, 15th edn (London: Sweet & Maxwell, 2012), paras 6–001 et seq. There has, for many years, been dissatisfaction with domicile as the sole precondition to an application under the 1975 Act. The Law Commission's 2011 report *Intestacy and Family Provision Claims on Death* (Law Com. No.331) recommended change, but its proposals met with opposition. Other suggestions have also been opposed. As Professor Elizabeth Cooke, the member of the Law Commission who was responsible for the report, put it, in evidence to a Parliamentary Committee "a lot of people agree that something should be done, but very few agree on what."

[23] *Holliday v Musa* [2010] W.T.L.R. 839; *Sylvester v Sylvester* [2014] W.T.L.R. 111. Under the Domicile and Matrimonial Proceedings Act 1973, a married woman can acquire a domicile independent of her husband.

[24] SI 1991/724.

[25] The guidelines for the allocation of proceedings are contained in para.9 of the High Court and County Courts Jurisdiction Order 1991. See Williams, Mortimer and Sunnucks, *Executors, Administrators and Probate*, 20th edn (London: Sweet & Maxwell, 2015), paras 61–01 et seq.

[26] Similarly, if there is a claim by the applicant that he has an interest under a constructive (or resulting) trust and is seeking an order under the Trusts of Land and Appointment of Trustees Act 1996 s.14 (replacing LPA 1925 s.30).

[27] See Williams, Mortimer and Sunnucks, *Executors, Administrators and Probate*, 20th edn (London: Sweet & Maxwell, 2015), para.61–02. For a discussion of the (allegedly) different approaches taken in the two divisions, see F. Cownie and A. Bradney (2003) 23 LS 566.

3. Time limit for application

An application under the Act must be made no later than six months from the date on which a valid grant of probate or letters of administration to the deceased's estate[28] is first taken out.[29] The court has, however, an unfettered discretion to extend this time limit. In *Re Salmon*[30] a widow's application for an extension was refused by Sir Robert Megarry VC where her claim was more than four and a half months out of time and the fault was wholly on the widow's side.[31] The Vice-Chancellor laid down the following "guidelines": **8–07**

(i) the discretion must be exercised judicially;
(ii) the onus lies on the applicant to make out a substantial case for its being just and proper for the court to exercise its discretion to extend the time. He thought that the court should consider;
(iii) how promptly, and in what circumstances, the applicant applied to the court for an extension (and how promptly the applicant warned the defendants of the proposed application);
(iv) whether negotiations commenced within the time limit (if so, and time ran out while they were proceeding, this is likely to encourage the court to extend the time);
(v) whether the estate had been distributed before a claim under the Act was made or notified; and
(vi) whether a refusal to extend the time would leave the applicant without redress against anybody or, alternatively, whether she might have a claim against her own solicitors for negligence.[32]

There have been several cases where applications for leave to proceed out of time have been successful.[33] In *Adams v Schofield*[34] the application was made nineteen days after the end of the limitation period and, although the applicant's solicitor had been negligent, the estate had not been distributed and the executors had known that a claim was pending. In *Stock v Brown*[35] an 85-year-old childless widow was left a life interest in her husband's estate and sought no legal advice until five years after his death when the dramatic fall in interest rates, combined with the increasing cost of her care, caused her to consult solicitors. In *Re C*[36] the applica- **8–08**

[28] See below, paras 18–01 et seq. A grant limited to settled land or trust property is disregarded, as is a grant limited to real or personal estate unless a grant limited to the remainder of the estate has previously been made or is made at the same time. Grants made outside the UK are left out of account unless resealed under the Colonial Probates Act 1892. See s.23 of the 1975 Act and s.7 of and Sch.3 to the Inheritance and Trustees' Powers Act 2014.
[29] s.4. An application is made when the Pt 8 claim form is issued, and not when it is served: *Re Chittenden* [1970] 1 W.L.R. 1618.
[30] *Re Salmon* [1981] Ch.167, cf. *Stock v Brown* [1994] 1 F.L.R. 840.
[31] The fault lay either with the widow herself or with her solicitors
[32] An applicant must also show he has an arguable case, *Re Dennis* [1981] 2 All E.R. 140.
[33] cf. *Berger v Berger* [2014] W.T.L.R. 35, where the application failed.
[34] *Adams v Schofield* [2004] W.T.L.R. 1049.
[35] *Stock v Brown* [1994] 1 F.L.R. 840.
[36] *Re C* [1995] 2 F.L.R. 24. The case is reported as *Re W* [1995] 2 F.C.R. 689.

tion was made by an illegitimate child against the estate of her father who had been killed in a car accident when she was aged four. The father had a substantial estate, partly free and partly settled, but the child's mother took no steps to consult solicitors on her behalf until almost three years after the father's death. This was not the child's fault and there was, of course, no question of the child's being able to sue the mother who, in any event, had no means. In *McNulty v McNulty*[37] the application was made more than three years late by a widow who had been granted an annuity by the will but had no idea of the true value of land devised to others; this land had had a low value attributed to it for probate purposes, but had subsequently been sold for a vastly increased sum.

8–09 An application may be made under that Act *before* a grant of representation has been taken out. This is made clear by para.6 of Sch.2 to the Inheritance and Trustees' Powers Act 2014.[38] Before this amendment was made, it seemed that it might not have been possible to make such an application,[39] and this could have created difficulties where the deceased was a joint tenant of property which passed by survivorship[40] and nobody had applied for a grant of probate or letters of administration.

4. Protection for personal representatives

8–10 The personal representatives may safely pay the deceased's funeral, testamentary and administration expenses, debts and liabilities before the six months' time limit has expired, irrespective of whether any application under the Act has been made.[41]

After this time limit has expired, if no application under the Act has been made, the personal representatives may safely distribute the estate to the beneficiaries under the deceased's will or on his intestacy. The time limit is short so as not unduly to impede distribution by the personal representatives. The Act provides that after this time limit has expired the personal representatives can distribute without taking into account the possibility that the court might (i) extend the time limit, or (ii) vary its original order for the making of periodical payments to an applicant[42]; but this protection for the personal representatives does not prejudice any power to recover, by reason of the making of an order under the Act, any part of the estate so distributed.[43]

8–11 If an applicant does apply to the court, there is no rigid rule that the personal representatives must preserve the entire net estate intact until the

[37] *McNulty v McNulty* [2002] W.T.L.R. 737.
[38] Which inserts words at the end of s.4 of the 1975 Act.
[39] *Re McBroom* [1992] 2 F.L.R. 49, but cf. *Re Searle* [1949] Ch.73.
[40] The deceased's net estate, may, if the court so orders, include his severable share of any property of which he was a beneficial joint tenant immediately before his death, see below, para.8–90.
[41] See definition of the deceased's net estate, below, paras 8–88 et seq. As to the power of a personal representative to postpone performance of a contract which the personal representative has reason to believe the deceased entered into with the intention of defeating an application for financial provision under the Act, see below, para.8–128.
[42] See below, paras 8–109 et seq.
[43] s.20(1).

pending application has been heard by the court. Whether it is safe for the personal representatives to make any distribution depends on the circumstances. It may be safe, for instance, for them to pay a legacy to the applicant who is seeking more provision under the Act, or to some other legatee if there is no risk of the court's directing that any part of any provision ordered for the applicant should fall on the legacy because, for example, the legacy is trifling in comparison with the size of the estate, or because the legatee has a high moral claim on the testator's bounty and is in need of the money. If in doubt, personal representatives can seek the consent of the interested parties to such a payment being made and—if consent is not forthcoming—apply to the court for leave to make the payment.[44]

III. THE TEST OF REASONABLE FINANCIAL PROVISION

The court may order provision to be made under the Act for an applicant only if it "is satisfied that the disposition of the deceased's estate effected by his will or the law relating to intestacy, or the combination of his will and that law, is not such as to make reasonable financial provision for the applicant."[45] Exactly the same test applies whether the deceased died testate or wholly or partly intestate.[46] **8–12**

1. Two standards of reasonable financial provision

Section 1(2) of the 1975 Act sets two different standards of reasonable financial provision, which may be called "the surviving spouse standard" and "the maintenance standard". **8–13**

(a) *The surviving spouse standard*

Reasonable financial provision at the surviving spouse standard means "such financial provision as it would be reasonable in all the circumstances of the case for a husband or wife [or] civil partner to receive, whether or not that provision is required for his or her maintenance".[47] The standard is reasonable provision *in all the circumstances,* and not (as it was under the 1938 Act) reasonable provision for the *maintenance* of the husband or wife.[48] In setting this surviving spouse standard "the legislature had in mind a very much wider approach" than under the 1938 Act.[49] The Law Commission justified the introduction of this new standard on the ground that the claim of a surviving spouse upon the family assets should be at least equal to that of a divorced spouse, and the court's powers to order **8–14**

[44] *Re Ralphs* [1968] 1 W.L.R. 1522, 1525 where Cross J gave helpful guidance.
[45] s.2(1): see *Rajabally v Rajabally* [1987] 2 F.L.R. 390 (widow's application not defeated by unenforceable assurances by beneficiaries not to insist on their rights under will).
[46] *Re Coventry* [1980] Ch.461, 488–489: see also s.24.
[47] s.1(2)(a) and 1(2)(aa).
[48] *Re Besterman* [1984] Ch.458, 465–466, 470: see below, para.8–39.
[49] *Re Coventry* [1980] Ch.461, 468, 484–485.

provision for a surviving spouse should be as wide as its powers to order financial provision on a divorce.[50]

This surviving spouse standard is applicable on any application by the deceased's wife, husband or civil partner,[51] including a person who in good faith entered into a void marriage with the deceased,[52] but excluding a spouse who was judicially separated from the deceased at the latter's death and where the separation was continuing.[53]

(b) *Discretion to apply surviving spouse standard*

8–15 The court may in its discretion apply the surviving spouse standard on an application by a judicially separated spouse[54] or a former spouse who has not remarried[55] if (i) the deceased died within 12 months of the decree of judicial separation, or of the decree absolute of divorce or nullity of marriage (as the case may be), and (ii) at the deceased's death no order making (or refusing) provision for such spouse had been made in the matrimonial proceedings.[56] In this exceptional situation the court has discretion to apply the surviving spouse standard.[57] The Law Commission recommended this, in order to cope with cases where the death of the deceased has caused the judicially separated or former spouse to miss the opportunity to obtain a fair share of the family assets in the matrimonial proceedings.[58] This is the only situation in which the court has any discretion as to which standard of reasonable financial provision to apply.

(c) *The maintenance standard*

8–16 Reasonable financial provision at the maintenance standard means "such financial provision as it would be reasonable in all the circumstances of the case for the applicant to receive for his maintenance."[59] The same standard was applicable to all applications under the 1938 Act.

Reasonable provision for maintenance does not mean, on the one hand, merely the provision of the bare necessities of life, so as to keep an applicant at subsistence level[60]; on the other hand, it does not mean "anything which may be regarded as reasonably desirable for his general benefit or

[50] Law Com. No.61, paras 12–18 and 26–30.

[51] s.1(2)(a): see below, para.8–34.

[52] s.25(4): see below, para.8–34.

[53] The position is the same for civil partners where a separation order is in force.

[54] i.e. a spouse whose marriage with the deceased was the subject of a decree of judicial separation and at the date of death of the deceased the decree was in force and the separation was continuing, s.1(2)(a).

[55] s.1(1)(b): see below, para.8–43.

[56] s.14: no financial provision order or property adjustment order under ss.23 and 24 of the Matrimonial Causes Act 1973 must have been made or refused; it is immaterial that maintenance pending suit under s.22 has been ordered or refused.

[57] s.14(A) contains corresponding provisions for civil partners.

[58] Law Com. No.61, paras 59–63.

[59] s.1(2)(b).

[60] *Re Coventry* [1980] Ch.461, 485 and 494; *Re E.* [1966] 1 W.L.R. 709, 715; *Ilott v Mitson* [2015] W.T.L.R. 1399.

welfare."[61] In *Re Coventry*[62] Buckley LJ suggested it means "such financial provision as would be reasonable in all the circumstances of the case to enable the applicant to maintain himself in a manner suitable to those circumstances." In *Re Dennis*[63] Browne-Wilkinson J said that "'maintenance' connotes only payments which, directly or indirectly, enable the applicant in the future to discharge the cost of his daily living at whatever standard of living is appropriate to him."[64] The case concerned an application by an able-bodied adult son for £50,000 from the estate of his rich father, so that the applicant son could pay capital transfer tax on a lifetime gift[65] of £90,000 which his father had made to him and which the son had dissipated in spendthrift living. The son claimed that he could not otherwise pay the £50,000 tax and, if he did not pay it, he would be made bankrupt by the Inland Revenue. Browne-Wilkinson J held that payment of the capital transfer tax would not, directly or indirectly, contribute to the son's living expenses; so an application for payment of the tax was not an application for maintenance.[66]

The maintenance standard is applicable on an application by a judicially separated spouse or a former spouse or civil partner who has not remarried or formed a subsequent civil partnership, unless the court has,[67] and exercises, the discretion to apply the surviving spouse standard. The maintenance standard is always applicable on an application by a child of the deceased,[68] by a person treated by the deceased as a child of the family,[69] by a dependant of the deceased,[70] or by a cohabitant.[71]

2. No provision ordered unless test satisfied

The court cannot order provision to be made under the Act for an applicant unless it is satisfied that the disposition of the deceased's estate is not such as to make reasonable financial provision for the applicant, measured by the surviving spouse or maintenance standard as appropriate[72]: **8–17**

> "It clearly cannot be enough to say that the circumstances are such that if the deceased had made a particular provision for the applicant, that

[61] per Goff LJ in *Re Coventry* [1980] Ch.461, 485.

[62] *Re Coventry* [1980] Ch.461, 485 and 494 at 494: see also *Re Borthwick* [1949] Ch.395, 401 (a widow's application to which the surviving spouse standard would now be applicable); *Millward v Shenton* [1972] 1 W.L.R. 711 and 715 (married son suffering from a progressive illness: a lump sum to enable him to have a television set, or a car, or even a better house); *Malone v Harrison* [1979] 1 W.L.R. 1353, 1361.

[63] *Re Dennis* [1981] 2 All E.R. 140.

[64] *Re Dennis* [1981] 2 All E.R. 140, 145.

[65] For a brief explanation of capital transfer tax, see Chap.16.

[66] cf. *Re Abram* [1996] 2 F.L.R. 379 where provision was made for adult son, who had entered into an individual voluntary arrangement with his creditors, by settling 50% of his mother's estate on him on protective trusts.

[67] See above, para.8–15.

[68] s.1(1)(c).

[69] s.1(1)(d): see below, paras 8–64 et seq.

[70] s.1(1)(e): see below, paras 8–69 et seq.

[71] s.1(1)(ba), inserted by ss.2(2) and 2(3) of the Law Reform (Succession) Act 1995.

[72] s.2(1); *Re Coventry* [1980] Ch.461, 474–475, 494–495; *Re Fullard* [1982] Fam. 42, 46, 50 ("condition precedent").

would not have been an unreasonable thing for him to do and therefore it now ought to be done. The court has no carte blanche to reform the deceased's dispositions or those which statute makes of his estate [on his intestacy] to accord with what the court itself might have thought would be sensible if it had been in the deceased's position."[73]

Again, it is not the proper test to ask "how the available assets should be fairly divided?"[74]

3. The test is objective

8–18 The vital question whether the disposition of the deceased's estate is not such as to make reasonable financial provision for the applicant (measured by whichever standard is appropriate) is to be answered objectively from the point of view of the court and not subjectively from the point of view of the deceased.[75] As Megarry J put it in *Re Goodwin*,[76] "The statutory language is wholly impersonal." Accordingly it is irrelevant to consider whether the deceased acted unreasonably in making no provision, or no larger provision, for the applicant.[77] The question whether the deceased stands convicted of unreasonableness does not arise.[78]

This objective approach makes it irrelevant to consider whether the deceased knew of all the material facts. On an application by a former wife, for instance, there may well be some material fact which is proved in evidence but which was not known to the deceased. For example, though the deceased did not know it, his former wife may have fallen on ill-health or other ill-fortune and be no longer capable of self-support.[79] The court has regard to all the material facts irrespective of whether they were known to the deceased. Indeed, the court even takes into account material facts which occurred after the death of the deceased before the court hears the application.[80]

4. Two stages of an application

8–19 The court considers an application under the Act in two stages, because the court has to decide two key questions in turn.[81]

[73] *Re Coventry*, above at 475.
[74] *Re Coventry*, above at 486 and 493.
[75] ss.1(1) and 2(1); *Re Coventry*, above at 474–475 and 488–489 ("any view expressed by a deceased person that he wishes a particular person to benefit will generally be of little significance, because the question is not subjective but objective"): cf. *Re Christie* [1979] Ch.168, 174.
[76] *Re Goodwin* [1969] 1 Ch.283, 287 (on the similar language of the 1938 Act): see also *Re Shanahan* [1973] Fam. 1, 8.
[77] *Re Coventry* [1980] Ch.461, 474.
[78] *Re Goodwin* [1969] 1 Ch.283, 288; *Moody v Stevenson* [1992] Ch.486.
[79] *Re Shanahan*, above at p.4. See also *Re Franks* [1948] Ch.62 (son born two days before death of mother who had no opportunity to change her will and provide for him: held provision should be made for son).
[80] s.3(5).
[81] ss.2(1) and 3(1): *Re Coventry* at 469 and 486–487 above; *Re Sivyer* [1967] 1 W.L.R. 1482, 1486–1487.

(a) *First stage—the threshold question*

8–20 The court first decides whether it is satisfied that the disposition of the deceased's estate—effected by his will or the law relating to intestacy, or the combination of his will and that law—is not such as to make reasonable financial provision for the applicant, measured by the surviving spouse or the maintenance standard as appropriate. If the court decides that the disposition does make reasonable financial provision, the application fails at the first hurdle.[82] Thus if the will,[83] or the law relating to intestacy,[84] makes no provision at all for the applicant, and the court decides that reasonable financial provision is nil, the application fails. On the other hand, if the court is satisfied that the disposition is not such as to make reasonable financial provision for the applicant, the court proceeds to the second stage. This first stage involves a "value judgment, or a qualitative decision" by the trial judge.[85]

(b) *Second stage—quantum*

8–21 If the application passes the first hurdle, the court next decides whether, and in what manner, it shall order provision to be made for the applicant.[86] This is a question of discretion.[87] At this second stage the court quantifies the provision to be ordered for the applicant by reference to the test of reasonable financial provision, measured by the surviving spouse or the maintenance standard as appropriate.[88]

5. Facts as known to the court at the date of hearing

8–22 Section 3(5) of the Act directs the court "in considering the matters to which [it] is to have regard under [section 3] to take into account the facts as known to [it] at the date of the hearing." Thus the court must take into account events which occurred after the death of the deceased before the hearing of the application. For instance, the value of the deceased's net estate may have risen or fallen since his death and the court should consider its value at the date of the hearing. Similarly, the applicant may find himself in greater, or lesser, need at the time of the hearing than he was at the time of the deceased's death. Having said this, the way that s.3(5) fits into the overall scheme is potentially confusing and a contrast can be drawn between two different sorts of case.

[82] *Re Coventry*, above; *Re Fullard* [1982] Fam. 42.

[83] *Re Fullard* [1982] Fam. 42 (former wife): see below, para.8–46.

[84] *Re Coventry*, above, (adult child): see below, para.8–58.

[85] *Re Coventry*, above at 487 and 495.

[86] ss.2(1) and 3(1); *Re Coventry* at 469, 486 above; *Re Rowlands* (1984) 5 F.L.R. 813 (whether and in what manner poses two questions): for the orders which the court may make, see below, paras 8–83 et seq.

[87] *Re Coventry*, above at 487. Note that in *Ilott v Mitson* [2015] W.T.L.R. 1399 Arden LJ (at para.52) referred back to what Sir Nicholas Wall P had said at an earlier stage in the proceedings "there is plainly an overlap between the value judgment that the provision is unreasonable and the exercise of discretion in making an order."

[88] *Re Besterman* [1984] Ch.458: see para.8–39, below.

8–23 Suppose, on the one hand, that the deceased's adult daughter is a student at the time of the deceased's death and requires financial support for about a year to complete her studies. She is entitled, so it seems, at the time of the death, to make a modest claim against the estate. But, a month after the death, she is involved in an accident and is disabled. Under s.3(5), the award made to her will take her disability into account and the award made to her will be much greater than it would have been had she not been involved in the accident. This imaginary case should be contrasted with the case of a daughter who is a successful film star with a much larger income than the deceased himself, who would have had no grounds whatsoever for making a claim. But suppose one month after the death that the film star daughter is involved in an accident and is disabled so that she cannot work again. Can she make a claim?[89] And, if she can, how close in time does the change of circumstances have to be to the death? There is a distinction between the two cases: in the first, the claim exists at death and is increased or decreased by an event which occurs after the death but before the hearing; in the second the claim comes into existence only after the death. Cases of the second type will not arise very often, but one appeared to surface in *Re Hancock.*[90] The value of the deceased's estate increased dramatically after his death because land owned by the deceased turned out to have development value. The judge at first instance—who was upheld by the Court of Appeal— appeared to decide that, although it was not unreasonable for the deceased to have made no provision for the applicant daughter, on the facts as they were at the date of his death, she had a valid claim on the basis of assessing the relevant matters at the date of hearing. But if it was not unreasonable for the deceased to have made no provision for the applicant on the facts as they were at the date of his death, there appears to have been no foundation for her claim in the first place, because she should have failed at the first hurdle. In many cases, the court could avoid the problem by deciding that the failure of the deceased to make any provision at all was unreasonable, if only slightly; having decided that, there would be no difficulty in moving to the second stage. But this appears not to have been the way in which *Re Hancock* was approached and that is what creates the problem.

6. The general guidelines[91]

8–24 At both stages of an application, s.3 of the Act requires the court to have regard to (i) general guidelines, which are applicable on any application, and (ii) particular guidelines, which are specified for each different category of applicant. The particular guidelines are considered later.[92]

[89] This problem appears to have been noted first by Professor A. R. Mellows. See now *Mellows: The Law of Succession*, 5th edn (London: Lexis Law Publishing, 1993), p.217. Section 3(5) instructs the court to "take into account" facts known to it at the date of the hearing. It does not say that facts which occurred after the death are deemed to have occurred before the death.

[90] *Tibbs v Dick* [1998] 2 F.L.R. 346.

[91] The term "guidelines" was used in Law Com. No.61: the 1975 Act does not use this term, but refers to them as "matters."

[92] See below, paras 8–33 et seq.

(a) *Financial resources and needs*

The first three general guidelines are the financial resources and financial needs[93] which (i) the applicant, (ii) any other applicant for any order under the Act, and (iii) any beneficiary[94] has or is likely to have in the foreseeable future. **8–25**

In considering any person's financial resources, the court must take into account his earning capacity,[95] and not just his (perhaps low) current earnings.[96] Again, the court takes into account a person's pension, whether from the state or from former employment.[97] Other forms of state aid may also be relevant,[98] although the fact of state aid does not preclude consideration of whether reasonable financial provision has been made.[99]

A person's financial resources include his capital assets, such as his house or flat, company shares and money in the bank, and also (if applicable) the damages he has received for personal injuries.[100] It would, however, generally not be right to treat the value of a person's home as expendable capital which he should spend in maintaining himself.[101] The reference in the guideline to the financial resources which a person is likely to have in the foreseeable future covers, for instance, assets which he is likely to inherit under the will of an elderly relative.[102]

In considering any person's financial needs the court must take into account his financial obligations and responsibilities.[103] Again the guideline refers both to present financial needs and to needs which a person is likely to have in the foreseeable future.[104]

(b) *Obligations and responsibilities of the deceased*

The fourth general guideline is "any obligations and responsibilities which the deceased had towards any applicant or towards any beneficiary".[105] **8–26**

[93] For an example of a case where the claim failed because no satisfactory evidence was produced as to financial resources and financial needs, see *Patel v Vigh* [2013] EWHC 3403 (Ch).

[94] i.e. a person beneficially interested under the deceased's will or on intestacy, or a person who takes under a statutory nomination or a *donatio mortis causa* made by the deceased, s.25(1).

[95] s.3(6).

[96] *Re Ducksbury* [1966] 1 W.L.R. 1226, 1233: see also *Malone v Harrison* [1979] 1 W.L.R. 1353, 1359 and 1364–1365 (woman's earning capacity until age of 60).

[97] *Re Catmull* [1943] Ch.262 (widow's pension); *Re Charman* [1951] 2 T.L.R. 1095 (bank's voluntary pension unlikely to be withdrawn); *Re Clayton* [1966] 1 W.L.R. 969 (prospect of future pension from employer); *Re Crawford* (1983) 4 F.L.R. 273 (widow's pension).

[98] *Re E.* [1966] 1 W.L.R. 709; *Re Clayton* [1966] 1 W.L.R. 969; see below, para.8–29.

[99] *Re Collins* [1990] Fam. 56 and 61.

[100] *Daubney v Daubney* [1976] Fam. 267.

[101] *Malone v Harrison* [1979] 1 W.L.R. 1353, 1365. A house may yield income from lodgers, *Re E.*, above.

[102] See *Morgan v Morgan* [1977] Fam. 122.

[103] s.3(6).

[104] *Re Clayton*, above, (provision for crippled widower as employment might end); *Re Ducksbury* [1966] 1 W.L.R. 1226, 1233 (future needs when no longer able to earn her living).

[105] See above, fn.94.

Whether the deceased had any obligations and responsibilities towards an applicant or a beneficiary depends on all the circumstances.[106] Before the 1975 Act, these obligations and responsibilities were sometimes referred to as a moral claim on the deceased's bounty.

In *Re Jennings*[107] the Court of Appeal held that it was not possible to construe general guideline (iv) in such a way as to include legal obligations and responsibilities which the deceased had owed to his son during the son's minority, many years earlier, but which the deceased had failed to discharge. In this case, the applicant son had had no contact at all with the deceased from the time when the applicant was two years old and his parents were divorced. He was 45 years old when his father died. It was argued, on his behalf, that his father's failure to discharge legal obligations owed to the applicant during the applicant's minority formed the basis for a claim on the estate. The Court of Appeal[108] held that, as a general rule, guideline (iv) refers only to obligations and responsibilities which the deceased had immediately before his death: it neither revives defunct obligations and responsibilities as a basis for a claim for financial provision; nor does it turn the blood relationship between father and son into a continuing moral obligation which then forms the basis for an order under the 1975 Act.

8–27 The deceased's estate may be large enough to satisfy all his obligations and responsibilities[109]; but if it is not, the court may have to weigh in the balance the respective obligations which the deceased had towards each applicant and beneficiary in order to adjudicate on the conflicting claims of, for instance, a widow and a woman with whom the deceased was living at the time of his death,[110] or a widow and a former wife,[111] or a wife and the children of another marriage.[112] In doing so, the court considers all

[106] See cases cited below, fnn.110–111; *Re Simson* [1950] Ch.38, 40 (housekeeper, as beneficiary); *Re Andrews* [1955] 1 W.L.R. 1105 (father owed no moral obligation to daughter incapable of maintaining herself, who left home 42 years before to live with a married man): cf. *Millward v Shenton* [1972] 1 W.L.R. 711 (son aged 52 incapacitated from earning by progressive illness): *Re Clarke* [1968] 1 W.L.R. 415 (moral claims of applicant wife, and deceased's elderly mother as beneficiary, on his bounty: distant relatives no such claims); *Re Coventry* [1980] Ch.461, 475–477, 487–490 and 494–495 (father owed no moral obligations to adult son); *Re Fullard* [1982] Fam. 42 (no obligations to former wife); *Re Besterman* [1984] Ch.458 (duty to wife but not to main beneficiary Oxford University); *Re Rowlands* (1984) 5 F.L.R. 813 (some small moral obligation owed to wife despite 43 years' separation); *Re Debenham* (1986) 7 F.L.R. 404 (mother's moral obligation to unwanted daughter, aged 58 and epileptic). In *Re Harker-Thomas* [1969] P. 28, 31 Latey J said "the ties of blood and, indeed, the rights and benefits which the law itself provides on intestacy amount to a claim": sed quaere in what sense. See also *Re Pearce* [1998] 2 F.L.R. 705; *Re Goodchild* [1997] 1 W.L.R 1216; *Espinosa v Bourke* [1999] 1 F.L.R. 747; *Ilott v Mitson* [2015] W.T.L.R. 1399 (these cases are discussed further below, see paras 8–60 et seq.

[107] See *Jennings* [1994] Ch.286.

[108] Reversing the judge at first instance.

[109] *Malone v Harrison* [1979] 1 W.L.R. 1353, 1364.

[110] *Re Joslin* [1941] Ch.201 (T's moral obligation to woman with whom he was living at the time of his death and infant children by her); *Re E.* [1966] 1 W.L.R. 709; *Re Thornley* [1969] 1 W.L.R. 1037; *Jessop v Jessop* [1992] 1 F.L.R. 591.

[111] *Re Talbot* [1962] 1 W.L.R. 1113; *Roberts v Roberts* [1965] 1 W.L.R. 560 (moral claims of applicant first wife, and widow as beneficiary, on T's bounty).

[112] *Re Sivyer* [1967] 1 W.L.R. 1482 (applicant child, and third wife entitled on intestacy, had

the circumstances, including such factors as each person's resources and needs,[113] and the source of the deceased's assets. It may be material that one of the claimants had helped the deceased build up his business,[114] or that some or most of the deceased's assets had been inherited by him from the mother of one of the claimants.[115]

Two of the particular guidelines—which apply where an application is made by a person treated by the deceased as a child of the family, or by a dependant of the deceased—refer specifically to the assumption by the deceased of responsibility for the applicant's maintenance. These particular guidelines are considered later.[116]

(c) *Size and nature of the estate*

The fifth general guideline is "the size and nature of the net estate[117] of the deceased." If the deceased left a large net estate, reasonable financial provision for an applicant may well be considerably more than would be appropriate, or indeed possible, from a smaller net estate.[118] **8–28**

The 1975 Act does not impose any minimum limit on the value of the net estate in respect of which an application may be made. "The smallness of the estate neither excludes jurisdiction nor full consideration."[119] Nevertheless, the smallness of the estate may be significant in three different ways:

(i) It may be reasonable to make no provision for a needy applicant out of a small estate if the only effect of making provision would be to relieve the state from having to pay means-tested benefits.[120]

(ii) It may be reasonable to make no provision if the maintenance standard is applicable and the estate is too small to make an effective contribution to the applicant's maintenance, having regard to his means and standard of living. Where the maintenance standard is applicable, the purpose of the 1975 Act is to provide maintenance and not just a small windfall legacy for an applicant.[121] It

calls upon deceased's bounty); *Re Bellman* [1963] P. 239 (claims of applicant former wife, and sons as beneficiaries, on T's bounty); *Re Ducksbury* [1966] 1 W.L.R. 1226 (applicant daughter aged 29, and second wife as beneficiary).

[113] *Re Joslin*, above (applicant widow of small means; common law wife and children by her penniless); *Re Sivyer*, above; *Re E.*, above.

[114] *Re Thornley*, [1969] 1 W.L.R. 1037; see also *Re E.*, [1966] 1 W.L.R. 714 at p.714.

[115] *Re Sivyer*, above at 1488–1489; *Re Styler* [1942] Ch.387, 390: see *Re Canderton* (1970) 114 S.J. 208; *Jelley v Iliffe* [1981] Fam. 128: see below, para.8–30; *Espinosa v Bourke* [1999] 1 F.L.R. 747.

[116] See below, paras 8–66 and 8–71.

[117] For the meaning of net estate see below, paras 8–88 et seq.

[118] *Re Inns* [1947] Ch.576, 581; *Re Borthwick* [1949] Ch.395; *Malone v Harrison* [1979] 1 W.L.R. 1353, 1364; *Re Besterman* [1984] Ch 458 (£378,000 provision ordered for widow of millionaire).

[119] per Ungoed-Thomas J in *Re Clayton* [1966] 1 W.L.R. 969, 971.

[120] *Re E.* [1966] 1 W.L.R. 709, 715; *Re Clayton*, above at 971 and 974.

[121] *Re Clayton*, above at 971–972; *Re Vrint* [1940] Ch.920, 925–926; *Re Pearce* [1998] 2 F.L.R. 705.

may, however, be appropriate for maintenance to be ordered by way of a small lump sum payment to an applicant.[122]

(iii) "Claims in cases where the costs of establishing claims leave virtually nothing significant for the claimant deprive the claim of substance, and are to be discouraged."[123] One form of discouragement is for the court to make an order for costs against the claimant.[124]

(d) *Disability of any applicant or beneficiary*

8–29 The sixth general guideline is "any physical or mental disability" of any applicant or any beneficiary.[125] Such a disability may reduce the earning capacity and increase the financial needs of an applicant[126] or beneficiary (which is relevant under general guidelines (i), (ii) and (iii)). Again such a disability may give rise to—or strengthen—the obligations and responsibilities which the deceased had towards an applicant[127] or beneficiary (which is relevant under general guideline (iv)). Thus in *Millward Shenton*[128] the Court of Appeal held that a mother's will giving her whole estate to cancer research did not make reasonable provision for the maintenance of her married son, who was aged 52 and incapacitated from earning by a progressive illness.

The availability of state aid is a factor to be taken into account. It has been held reasonable to make only limited provision for a daughter incapable of maintaining herself by reason of mental disability, because the daughter could be maintained free of charge in a state mental hospital.[129] However, in such a case it may be unreasonable to make no provision for pocket money, so as to enable the applicant to buy extra comforts not provided by the state.[130]

(e) *Conduct and any other matter*

8–30 The seventh general guideline is "any other matter, including the conduct of the applicant or any other person, which in the circumstances of the case the court may consider relevant."

[122] *Re Clayton*, above (£400 lump sum from £1,271 estate).

[123] per Ungoed-Thomas J in *Re Clayton*, above, at 972; see *Re Coventry* [1980] Ch.461, 486.

[124] *Re Vrint*, above, (net estate £138: widow's application dismissed with costs): see *Re Fullard* (1982) Fam. 42, 46.

[125] i.e. a person beneficially interested under the deceased's will or on intestacy, or a person who takes under a statutory nomination or a *donatio mortis causa* made by the deceased, s.25(1).

[126] *Re Clayton* [1966] 1 W.L.R. 969 (widower crippled in both legs); *Millward v Shenton* [1972] 1 W.L.R. 711; *Hanbury v Hanbury* [1999] 2 F.L.R. 255.

[127] *Re Clayton*, above, *Millward v Shenton*, above: cf. *Re Andrews* [1955] 1 W.L.R. 1105.

[128] *Millward v Shenton* [1972] 1 W.L.R. 71 (estate £3,144: lump sum of eleven-twelfths of estate awarded to son): see also *Re Pointer* [1941] Ch.60.

[129] *Re Watkins* [1949] 1 All E.R. 695; *Re E.* [1966] 1 W.L.R. 709, 714–715 ("something might have been provided for comforts").

[130] *Re Pringle* [1956] C.L.Y. 9248 (£2,291 net estate: 10s. per week ordered for handicapped son resident in state mental hospital).

This reference to conduct is in wide terms.[131] It covers the conduct of the deceased[132] as well as that of an applicant or beneficiary. The court has considered, for instance, whether an applicant was a good and loving wife,[133] a deeply affectionate mistress,[134] or a dutiful child.[135] Again the court has considered to what extent an applicant widow and a mistress (who was a beneficiary under the will) each helped the deceased in his business.[136]

Another matter which the court may consider relevant is the source of the deceased's assets. Thus it was material that the deceased earned a death grant (the main asset in his estate) whilst living with his common law wife, to whom he gave the whole of his estate by his will.[137]

(f) *The deceased's reasons*

The 1938 Act required the court to have regard to the deceased's reasons for not making any provision for the applicant. The 1975 Act makes no such requirement, because it is based on the principle that what matters is not whether the deceased acted reasonably, or whether he believed himself to have acted reasonably: what has to be judged is not the deceased himself, but the disposition of his estate.[138] In *Williams v Johns*[139] the deceased left a statement with her will explaining why she had made no provision for the applicant, her adopted adult daughter, who had been independent of her for some years and was now impecunious. Judge Micklem[140] attached little significance to the deceased's recorded reasons, but as the applicant had failed to establish some sort of obligation to be maintained by the deceased, or at the expense of her estate, beyond the mere fact of an adoptive relationship, there was no foundation for her claim. The disposition of the deceased's estate was objectively reasonable. **8–31**

Although the Act does not *require* the court to have regard to the deceased's stated reasons, it may well be prudent to record them. In *Williams v Johns*[141] the applicant had, by her behaviour, caused the deceased distress. If the deceased's reasons for failing to make provision

131 per Hollings J in *Malone v Harrison* [1979] 1 W.L.R. 1353 and 1364.
132 *Re Thornley* [1969] 1 W.L.R. 1037 and 1042 (deceased manic-depressive and violent in drink: "human behaviour (and particularly the domestic variety) is contrapuntal. It is impossible to form a fair or intelligent view of the conduct of either party in a domestic or social relationship without also considering how the other behaved").
133 *Re Morris* [1967] C.L.Y. 4114 (applicant did not intend to carry out her responsibilities as a wife when she married and never did so); *Re Borthwick* [1949] Ch.395 (wife not at fault); *Re Blanch* [1967] 1 W.L.R. 987; *Re Thornley* [1969] 1 W.L.R. 1037 and 1042 (gravely wronged wife); *Re Snoek* (1983) 13 Fam. Law 18 (wife's atrocious and vicious behaviour): see below, para.8–42.
134 *Malone v Harrison* [1979] 1 W.L.R. 1353.
135 *Re Ducksbury* [1966] 1 W.L.R. 1226 and 1233; *Wright v Waters* [2015] W.T.L.R. 353. See also *Re B* [2000] Ch.662 (devoted mother).
136 *Re Thornley* [1969] 1 W.L.R. 1037.
137 *Re E.* [1966] 1 W.L.R. 709 (widow's application dismissed): for other instances see above, para.8–27; *Re Goodchild* [1997] 1 W.L.R. 1216; *Espinosa v Bourke* [1999] 1 F.L.R. 747.
138 See Law Com. No.61, para.105 and para.8–18, above.
139 *Williams v Johns* [1988] 2 F.L.R. 475.
140 Sitting as an additional judge of the High Court.
141 *Williams v Johns* [1988] 2 F.L.R. 475.

for the applicant are good reasons, based on truth, the court has regard to them under guideline (vii) or possibly one of the other guidelines. If they are bad or false reasons, the court disregards them.[142]

(g) *The deceased's state of mind*

8–32 The deceased's testamentary capacity is determined in probate proceedings and cannot be put in issue in an application under the 1975 Act.[143] The deceased's state of mind may, however, be a relevant matter to be considered. It may, for example, be relevant to the deceased's obligations that an applicant, or beneficiary, cared for the deceased during a long period of mental illness.[144]

IV. PERSONS WHO MAY APPLY AND THE PARTICULAR GUIDELINES

8–33 Each of the following persons who survived the deceased[145] may apply to the court for an order under the 1975 Act.[146]

1. The deceased's spouse or civil partner[147]

8–34 The burden of proof lies upon an applicant under this head to prove that at the deceased's death the applicant was the deceased's spouse or civil partner by a subsisting marriage or civil partnership.[148]

A judicially separated spouse falls within this category,[149] and so does a party to a voidable marriage which has not been annulled prior to the deceased's death. A party to a polygamous marriage falls within this category.[150]

A person who in good faith entered into a void marriage[151] with the deceased falls within this category unless during the deceased's lifetime

[142] *Re Borthwick* [1949] Ch.395; *Re Clarke* [1968] 1 W.L.R. 415; *Re Coventry* [1980] Ch.461, 488–489. The general rules of evidence—including those in the Civil Evidence Act 1995 making hearsay admissible—apply.

[143] *Re Blanch* [1967] 1 W.L.R. 987.

[144] *Re Blanch* [1967] 1 W.L.R. 987 at pp.991–992.

[145] If the applicant dies before an order is made, the application cannot proceed, *Whytte (or Whyte) v Ticehurst* [1986] Fam. 64 (widow); *Re R* (1986) 16 Fam. Law 58 (former wife).

[146] s.1(1).

[147] See *Miller* (1986) 102 L.Q.R. 445 and [1997] Conv. 442.

[148] *Re Peete* [1952] 2 All E.R. 599; *Re Watkins* [1953] 1 W.L.R. 1323.

[149] But a judicially separated spouse may be barred from applying for provision by an order of the court made on the application of the other spouse on or after the decree of judicial separation, ss.15(1) and (4), as amended by Matrimonial and Family Proceedings Act 1984 s.8: for similar order following overseas legal separation see s.15A as amended by 1984 Act s.25(3).

[150] *Re Sehota* [1987] 1 W.L.R. 1506.

[151] In *Gandhi v Patel* [2002] 1 F.L.R. 603 it was held that a ceremony at an Indian restaurant, presided over by a Brahmin priest, had not resulted in a "void marriage" but, for the purposes of English law, "no marriage at all". Moreover, the claimant had known that the

(i) the marriage was dissolved or annulled, or (ii) the person entered into a later marriage. Such a person cannot recover damages for breach of promise of marriage against the deceased's estate[152]; but, instead, is treated as the deceased's wife or husband for the purpose of an application under the 1975 Act.

(a) *The surviving spouse standard*

The surviving spouse standard is applicable on any application by the deceased's spouse or civil partner, including a person who in good faith entered into a void marriage or civil partnership with the deceased, but excluding a spouse who is judicially separated from the deceased at the latter's death, to whom the maintenance standard is applicable.[153] **8–35**

The same standard of provision and the same guidelines apply whether the applicant is a man or a woman.[154]

(b) *The particular guidelines*

The particular guidelines to which the court must have regard on an application by the deceased's spouse or civil partner are[155]: **8–36**

(i) the age of the applicant and the duration of the marriage or civil partnership[156];
(ii) the contribution made by the applicant to the welfare of the deceased's family, including any contribution made by looking after the home or caring for the family[157]; and
(iii) the provision which the applicant might reasonably have expected to receive if, on the day on which the deceased died, the marriage or civil partnership, instead of being terminated by death, had been terminated by a decree of divorce; but nothing requires the court to treat such provision as setting

deceased was married to someone else and, even had there been a void marriage, she had not entered into it in good faith. See Miller 2004 N.L.J. 252.

152 Law Reform (Miscellaneous Provisions) Act 1970 s.1 (agreement to marry not enforceable). Before 1971, the remedy *was* damages for breach of promise—see *Shaw v Shaw* [1954] 2 Q.B. 429.

153 Unless the court has, and exercises, the discretion to apply the surviving spouse standard, see above, para.8–15.

154 *Re Clayton* [1966] 1 W.L.R. 969 (widower crippled): provision for a widower was also ordered in *Re Lawes* (1946) 62 T.L.R. 231, *Re Bonham* (1962) 112 L.J. 634, *Moody v Stevenson* [1992] Ch. 486 and *Re Waite* [2009] 1 F.L.R. 747.

155 s.3(2).

156 See *Re Pugh* [1943] Ch.387 (two-and-a-half years' marriage); *Re Clarke* [1968] 1 W.L.R. 415, 425 (seven months together): a period of pre-marital cohabitation does not lengthen the duration of a marriage, *Campbell v Campbell* [1976] Fam. 347, 352, but see *Kokosinski v Kokosinski* [1980] Fam. 72, 83–88; *Foley v Foley* [1981] Fam. 160; *Re Krubert* [1997] Ch.97; *Adams v Lewis* [2001] W.T.L.R. 493.

157 See *H. v H.* [1975] Fam. 9, 16 (contribution made but job unfinished); *Re Rowlands* (1984) 5 F.L.R. 813.

an upper or lower limit.[158] This is the "imaginary divorce" guideline.[159]

(c) *The imaginary divorce guideline*

8–37 Guidelines (i) and (ii) set out factors to which the court must also have regard in applications under the Matrimonial Causes Act 1973.[160] The introduction of the imaginary divorce guideline (iii) was recommended by the Law Commission so as to enable the court "to adopt an approach similar to that adopted in divorce proceedings."[161] Unfortunately, the guideline does not set out all the hypothetical circumstances of the imaginary divorce and it is open to the criticism that it ignores an essential distinction between divorce proceedings and family provision proceedings: in the latter the deceased is dead and so has no future needs or future earnings. In *Re Bunning*[162] Vinelott J calculated that the maximum provision which the widow would have received in matrimonial proceedings would have been £36,000; yet on an application under the 1975 Act he awarded her £60,000. An award made on divorce would have had regard to the husband's likely future needs and would not have left him with insufficient funds to continue living in the former matrimonial home. Again, in *P v G*[163] Black J noted the difference between a divorce, where two spouses have to be provided for, and death where there is only one. She also pointed out that the tax position may not be the same on divorce as on death.[164]

8–38 Another distinction between divorce and death is that on divorce the courts often prefer the finality of a "clean break".[165] There is, however, not the same need for a clean break on death; so an application by a widow who has been granted, by the deceased's will, a life interest in the residue of his estate, may be dismissed on the basis that the life interest *was* reasonable provision.[166]

The 1975 Act does not require the court to treat the imaginary divorce guideline as decisive, or as laying down a minimum, or maximum[167] provision for the applicant. It is one guideline out of a number of general and particular guidelines, to all of which the court must have regard[168] and

[158] The reference to the upper or lower limit was added in 2014.

[159] Guideline (iii) does not apply on an application by a spouse who is judicially separated from the deceased at the latter's death unless the court has, and exercises, the discretion to apply the surviving spouse standard, s.14: see above, para.8–15.

[160] Matrimonial Causes Act 1973, s.25(2)(d) and (f) as amended by 1984 Act: for the case law on these guidelines under the Matrimonial Causes Act 1973 see Cretney, *Principles of Family Law*, 8th edn (London: Sweet & Maxwell, 2008), paras 13–040 et seq.

[161] Law Com. No.61, paras 33–34: see also paras 16–18.

[162] *Re Bunning* [1984] Ch.480.

[163] *P v G*. (Also known as *P v E*.) [2006] 1 F.L.R. 431.

[164] The principal distinction relates to capital gains tax: death gives a capital gains tax uplift: see below, para.16–37.

[165] *Minton v Minton* [1979] A.C. 593.

[166] *Davis v Davis* [1993] 1 F.L.R. 54, see comment by S.M. Cretney in [1993] Fam. Law 59. See also *Re Krubert* [1997] Ch.97; *Grattan v McNaughton* [2001] W.T.L.R. 1305; *Moore v Holdsworth* [2010] W.T.L.R. 1213.

[167] *Re Bunning* [1984] Ch.480.

[168] per Oliver LJ in *Re Besterman* [1984] Ch.458, 469.

which are not ranked in any order of priority. The key questions must be decided by applying the test of reasonable financial provision, measured by the surviving spouse standard. Thus "the overriding consideration is what is 'reasonable' in all the circumstances."[169]

(d) *Provision measured by the surviving spouse standard*

In *Re Besterman*[170] a wife, W, applied for provision to be made for her out of the estate of her deceased husband, H. They had been married for 18 years and W had been a faithful and dutiful wife. W was 66 years of age and she had only a widow's pension of £400 per annum. By his will H gave W his personal chattels and a yearly income of £3,500 for life. H left a net estate of over £1.4 million. Oxford University, the major beneficiary under his will, acknowledged that H's provision for W was not reasonable provision for a millionaire's widow accustomed to a high standard of living. The key question for the court was the amount of the provision to be ordered for W. The trial judge treated the maintenance of W as the paramount factor in fixing this amount, referring to the cost of purchasing an annuity sufficient to maintain W's standard of living, and awarded W a lump sum of £238,000 from H's estate. The Court of Appeal increased the lump sum to £378,000 because reasonable financial provision for W had to be measured by the surviving spouse standard and not by the maintenance standard. Moreover the sum awarded by the trial judge bore little relation to the sum which W might reasonably have expected to receive on divorce[171]; and took no real account of the need to cushion W against possible future contingencies, such as ill-health. **8–39**

In the case of an estate of more modest size, there are inevitably fewer assets available from which the court is able to make provision over and above what is required for the maintenance of the applicant spouse.[172] **8–40**

The House of Lords in *White v White*[173] rejected an approach based upon the "reasonable requirements" of the applicant in matrimonial proceedings, and suggested that a judge should check his tentative views when assessing a lump sum payment to a spouse against the yardstick of equality of division in cases where each party had contributed (in their respective ways) equally to the family.[174] This lead was followed in *Adams v Lewis*[175] where a widow, who had spent her married life of 54 years looking after the couple's eleven children, was awarded approximately half her

[169] per Oliver LJ in *Re Besterman* [1984] Ch.458, 469 And see *Singer v Isaac* [2001] W.T.L.R. 1045.

[170] *Re Besterman* [1984] Ch.458; see also *Re Bunning*, above, *Stead v Stead* [1985] 6 F.L.R. 16.

[171] The amount was a "matter of speculation" but counsel suggested £350,000 and Oliver LJ thought that this was "not excessive" [1984] Ch.458 and 478.

[172] *Stead v Stead* [1985] 6 F.L.R. 16.

[173] *White v White* [2001] 1 A.C. 596.

[174] The House of Lords stressed that there was no presumption of equal division, or a principle that in every case equality would be the starting point in relation to the division of assets. See also the later "big money" House of Lords divorce cases of *Miller v Miller* and *McFarlane v McFarlane* [2006] 2 A.C. 618. See also *Charman v Charman* [2007] 1 F.L.R. 1246.

[175] *Adams v Lewis* [2001] W.T.L.R. 493.

husband's estate.[176] By contrast, in *Cunliffe v Fielden*[177] the Court of Appeal reduced from £800,000 to £600,000 the provision for a widow from a net estate of £1.4 million. The marriage had lasted only a year and the claimant had made little or no contribution to the family wealth.[178]

(e) *Relevance of conduct*

8–41 Under the 1938 Act the court was required to have regard to the conduct of the applicant in every case.[179] Under general guideline (vii) of the 1975 Act, the court is to have regard to "any other matter, including the conduct of the applicant or any other person which in the circumstances of the case the court may consider relevant." The court may also need to consider conduct under other guidelines. The conduct of an applicant or beneficiary may be relevant to the deceased's obligations and responsibilities under general guideline (iv). Again some aspects of an applicant's conduct may be relevant in considering the applicant's contribution to the welfare of the deceased's family under particular guideline (ii).[180]

8–42 If, at the deceased's death, the marriage with the applicant had broken down, the court usually considers that the conduct of the parties which led to the breakdown is irrelevant.[181] This is the view adopted by the court in applications for financial provision in divorce proceedings[182] and a lengthy post-mortem to ascertain who was responsible for the breakdown of the marriage seems even less appropriate in family provision proceedings.[183] It is open to the court to take the same view in family provision proceedings because general guideline (vii) (unlike the other guidelines) requires the court to have regard to conduct only if it considers it a relevant matter in the circumstances of the case. But, as in divorce proceedings,[184] there will still be a minority of cases where the applicant's conduct is relevant because it would be inequitable to disregard it, so that reasonable financial provision for the applicant is either nothing at all or a reduced amount. Thus in

[176] There are some cases where "the yardstick of equality" means that a surviving spouse has no claim, see e.g. *Aston v Aston* [2007] W.T.L.R. 1349.

[177] *Cunliffe v Fielden* [2006] Ch. 261.

[178] For recent high value cases at first instance, see *Lilleyman v Lilleyman* [2012] W.T.L.R. 1007 and *F v F* [2012] W.T.L.R. 1079.

[179] Inheritance (Family Provision) Act 1938 s.1(6).

[180] See *H. v H.* [1975] Fam. 9 and 16.

[181] The Law Commission hoped the court would take this view, see Law Com. No.61, paras 35–36. For applications under the 1938 Act, see *Re Borthwick* [1949] Ch.395 (husband deserted wife); *Re Thornley* [1969] 1 W.L.R. 1037 (husband's cruelty); *Re Clarke* [1968] 1 W.L.R. 415 (husband's desertion); *Re Gregory* [1970] 1 W.L.R. 1455 (husband's desertion; 42 years' separation and virtually no payment of maintenance: wife's application failed).

[182] *Wachtel v Wachtel* [1973] Fam. 72: see generally Cretney, *Principles of Family Law*, 8th edn (London: Sweet & Maxwell, 2008), paras 13–082 et seq.

[183] *Re Bunning* [1984] Ch.480 and 489.

[184] Matrimonial Causes Act 1973 s.25(2)(g), as amended by 1984 Act; *Wachtel v Wachtel*, above, at p.90: per Cairns LJ in *Harnett v Harnett* [1974] 1 W.L.R. 219 and 224, "Where there is something in the conduct of one party which would make it quite inequitable to leave that out of account having regard to the conduct of the other party as well in the course of the marriage"; *Bateman v Bateman* [1979] Fam. 25; *Robinson v Robinson* [1983] Fam. 42.

Re Snoek[185]—where the wife's atrocious and vicious conduct towards her husband during the latter part of the marriage did not quite cancel out her contribution to the welfare of the family in the early part, when she managed the home and brought up their children—the court awarded her only a "modest" lump sum of £5,000 out of her husband's £40,000 estate.

It is possible that the deceased's conduct may be relevant. For instance, the deceased may have attacked and injured the applicant, disabling the applicant from working again, and this may justify an increased amount of financial provision.[186]

2. The deceased's former spouse or civil partner who has not remarried or formed a subsequent civil partnership[187]

A former spouse or civil partner means a person whose marriage or civil partnership with the deceased was dissolved or annulled during the deceased's lifetime *either* (i) by a decree of divorce or nullity granted under the law of any part of the British Islands, *or* (ii) by a divorce or annulment overseas which is recognised as valid by English law.[188] The deceased must, however, have died domiciled in England and Wales.[189] **8–43**

A former spouse or civil partner may be barred from applying under the 1975 Act by an order of the court made on the application of the other spouse or civil partner on or after the decree of dissolution or nullity.[190]

(a) *The maintenance standard*

The maintenance standard is applicable on an application by the deceased's former spouse or civil partner unless the court has, and exercises, the discretion to apply the surviving spouse standard.[191] **8–44**

(b) *The particular guidelines*

The particular guidelines to which the court must have regard are those applicable on an application by the deceased's spouse or civil partner, **8–45**

185 *Re Snoek* (1983) 13 Fam. Law 18. See also *Grattan v McNaughton* [2001] W.T.L.R. 1305 (persistence of widow in litigation reduced her award); *Parish v Sharman* [2001] W.T.L.R. 593.

186 See *Jones (M. A.) v Jones (W.)* [1976] Fam. 8 (divorce: "conduct of such a gross kind that it would be offensive to a sense of justice that it should not be taken into account").

187 Remarriage includes a marriage which is by law void or voidable and it is immaterial that the previous marriage was void or voidable, s.25(5).

188 s.25(1) as amended: British Islands means the UK, Channel Islands and Isle of Man, Interpretation Act 1978 s.5 and Sch.1.

189 See above, para.8–05.

190 s.15 and s.15ZA as amended by Matrimonial and Family Proceedings Act 1984 and Civil Partnership Act 2004: for similar order following overseas divorce or annulment see ss.15A and 15B. For an instance see *Kokosinski v Kokosinski* [1980] Fam. 72 and 88: see also *Re Fullard* [1982] Fam. 42 and 49–50; *Whiting v Whiting* [1988] 1 W.L.R. 565 and 577–578; *Cameron v Treasury Solicitor* [1996] 2 F.L.R. 717. Apart from s.15, it seems that the court's jurisdiction under the 1975 Act cannot be ousted by agreement with the deceased during his lifetime, see *Re M.* [1968] P. 174.

191 See above, para.8–15.

except that the imaginary divorce guideline does not apply unless the court has, and exercises, the discretion to apply the surviving spouse standard.[192]

(c) *Relevance of financial provision in matrimonial proceedings*

8–46 Any financial provision made in the matrimonial proceedings, whether by order of the court or by agreement between the parties, is a matter to which the court must have regard under the general guideline (vii). In view of the court's powers to make appropriate capital adjustments between spouses in matrimonial proceedings, there will be comparatively few cases where a former spouse or civil partner will succeed in an application under the 1975 Act. *Re Fullard*,[193] the applicant obtained a divorce from her husband and the parties settled their financial arrangements on the basis that the applicant paid £4,500 to her husband for the transfer to her of his share in the former matrimonial home. The husband moved out of the home and, about six months later, he died, leaving his entire estate (which consisted, for the greater part, of the £4,500 which the applicant had paid to him) to a friend. The applicant's appeal against a refusal to award her financial provision from her husband's estate was dismissed by the Court of Appeal. Had the applicant succeeded in her claim, she would, in effect, have been getting back the money she had paid to buy her husband's share in the former matrimonial home. In *Re O'Rourke*[194] the Court of Appeal held that the fact that there were no beneficiaries of the former husband's estate (so that it passed to the Crown as bona vacantia) was not a circumstance which could enhance or validate his former wife's claim.[195]

8–47 This is not to say that no application by a former spouse or civil partner will ever succeed. Such an application may succeed, for instance, where the deceased made periodical payments to the former spouse for a long time and leaves a reasonable amount of capital,[196] or where a substantial capital sum, such as the payment of an insurance policy, is unlocked by the death of the deceased.[197] It has been doubted whether the mere accretion of wealth by the deceased after the dissolution of the marriage would of itself justify such an application.[198] Again an application succeeded where the deceased died intestate less than a year after an order in divorce proceedings to make periodical payments to his former spouse.[199]

[192] ss.3(2) and 14: see above, para.8–15.

[193] *Re Fullard* [1982] Fam. 42: see also *Brill v Proud* [1984] Fam. Law 19.

[194] *Re O'Rourke* [1997] 1 F.C.R. 188.

[195] See also *Barrass v Harding* [2001] 1 F.L.R. 138; *Cameron v Treasury Solicitor* [1996] 2 F.L.R. 716.

[196] *Re Crawford* (1983) 4 F.L.R. 273. For the relevance of a secured periodical payments order see *Re Eyre* [1968] 1 W.L.R. 530: for the court's powers to vary or discharge such an order see below, paras 8–109 et seq.

[197] *Re Fullard*, above, at pp.49, 52.

[198] *Re Fullard*, above, at p.52: but see *Re Eyre*, above at 543.

[199] *Re Farrow* [1987] 1 F.L.R. 205.

(d) *Relevance of conduct*

Probably the court will consider the conduct of the parties which led to the breakdown of the marriage to be irrelevant except in a minority of cases where it would have been relevant in an application for financial provision in divorce proceedings.[200] **8–48**

3. A cohabitant[201]

An application may be made by any person (not being the deceased's spouse or civil partner, or former spouse or civil partner who has not remarried, i.e. a person within categories 1 and 2 above) who, during the whole period of two years ending immediately before the date when the deceased dies, was living in the same household as the deceased and as the deceased's husband or wife, or civil partner. If the applicant claims to have been living as the deceased's husband or wife, the deceased must have died on or after 1 January 1996.[202] If it is made by someone who was living as the deceased's civil partner, the amended section does not specify a date of death.[203] **8–49**

(a) *The maintenance standard*

The maintenance standard applies on an application by a cohabitant. **8–50**

(b) *The particular guidelines*

The particular guidelines to which the court must have regard are[204]: **8–51**

(i) the age of the applicant and the length of the period during which the applicant lived as the deceased's husband or wife or civil partner and in the same household as the deceased; and
(ii) the contribution made by the applicant to the welfare of the deceased's family, including any contribution made by looking after the home or caring for the family.

Guideline (i) is a slightly amended version of guideline (i) for spouses and former spouses; guideline (ii) is identical with guideline (ii) for spouses and former spouses; guideline (iii) is, of course, inapplicable to cohabitants.

[200] See above, paras 8–41 and 8–42.
[201] This description is a convenient shorthand, but the statutory definition in s.1(1A) has to be satisfied.
[202] s.1(1A).
[203] s.1(1B). This appears to be on the basis that a claim by someone who had been living "as [a] civil partner" could not have been made until the section was amended (on 5 December 2005, when the Civil Partnership Act 2004 came into force). Given that an application must be made within six months of a grant, it is improbable in the extreme that a situation could arise where the deceased in such a case could have died before 1996.
[204] s.3(2A), inserted by the Law Reform (Succession) Act 1995 s.2(4).

(c) *Living as the husband or wife or civil partner of the deceased*

8–52 The expression "living. . .as the husband or wife, [or civil partner] of the deceased" is, following the Law Commission's recommendation,[205] similar to the definition of cohabitant used in s.1(3)(b) of the Fatal Accidents Act 1976, but it is not entirely clear what it is supposed to mean.[206] In *Baynes v Hedger*[207] Lewison J held that it was not possible to establish that two persons had lived together as civil partners unless their relationship as a couple was an acknowledged one, "openly and unequivocally displayed to the outside world".[208] In *Re Watson (dec'd)*[209] Neuberger J dealt with a case where a middle-aged couple lived together and shared expenses but did not share a bedroom or enjoy sexual relations. He held that, given the multifarious nature of marital relations, the correct approach was to ask whether a reasonable person, with normal perceptions, would think that the couple were living together as husband and wife; he thought that they were. It is easy to understand the court's sympathy for the applicant in the *Watson* case, especially as there was no other claimant to the deceased's estate, except for the Crown claiming bona vacantia. If the applicant had been dependent on the deceased, the applicant would have fallen within the sixth category;[210] so applications by persons in the "living. . .as. . .husband or wife. . .or civil partner" category cover those who were not dependants.[211] The problem is that situations are likely to arise where the fact that the applicant is a brother or sister of the deceased, rather than a close friend, may be prejudicial to a claim; that seems to be illogical.[212] The problem is discussed further below, when considering reform of the family provision régime.[213]

(d) *Immediately before the date when the deceased died*

8–53 The applicant must show that he was living in the deceased's household, and as the deceased's husband or wife, during the whole of the period of two years ending immediately before the date when the deceased died. This is, in effect, similar to the condition which applies to dependants

205 Law Com. No.187, pp.15 and 16.

206 The underlying problem, or so it seems to the editor, is that, particularly in this age of growing economic equality between the sexes, there seems to be no obvious logical link between cohabitation (as such) and entitlement to economic support.

207 *Baynes v Hedger* [2008] W.T.L.R. 1719.

208 *Baynes v Hedger* [2008] W.T.L.R. 1719 at paras 124 and 150.

209 *Re Watson (dec'd)* [1999] 1 F.L.R. 878. See also *Swetenham v Walkley* [2014] W.T.L.R. 845.

210 See below, para.8–69.

211 An applicant may, of course, fall into both categories. Technically, someone who is both a cohabitant and a dependant, qualifies as a dependant; see the wording of s.1(1)(e) and see *Re Baker* [2008] W.T.L.R. 565. But, if he is a dependant, it will not generally matter whether or not he is a cohabitant; so the real importance of proving cohabitation will be in cases where there is no dependency.

212 Having said which, had the applicant in the *Watson* case been the deceased's sister, she would have inherited the whole estate on intestacy—but the sister's problem arises where the deceased has left a will giving all his property to (say) charity.

213 See below, paras 8–82 et seq.

and the interpretation of the phrase "immediately before the death of the deceased", as applied to them, is discussed further below.[214] In *Re Watson*[215] Neuberger J held that the two-year period of living together was not defeated by a short period of hospitalisation of the deceased shortly before his death.[216]

4. A child of the deceased[217]

This category includes a child of the deceased *en ventre sa mére* at the deceased's death,[218] an illegitimate child,[219] and a child adopted by the deceased[220]; but it does not include a child who was born to the deceased but has been adopted by someone else.[221] **8–54**

(a) *The maintenance standard*

The maintenance standard is applicable on an application by a child of the deceased.[222] **8–55**

(b) *The particular guideline*

The particular guideline to which the court must have regard is "the manner in which the applicant was being or in which he might expect to be educated or trained."[223] **8–56**

(c) *Application by adult son or daughter*[224]

Under the 1938 Act, a son who had attained the age of 21 years and a daughter who had been married were not eligible to apply for provision to be made for their maintenance out of the deceased's estate unless, by reason of some mental or physical disability, they were incapable of maintaining themselves.[225] Under the 1975 Act, there is no age limit or requirement that an applicant must not have been married.[226] **8–57**

The particular guideline points to one situation where it is appropriate for an adult child to bring a claim—the deceased dies whilst supporting his adult son or daughter in the process of acquiring some educational or

214 para.8–75.
215 *Re Watson* [1999] 1 F.L.R. 878.
216 cf. *Grundy v Ottey* [2003] W.T.L.R. 1253.
217 See *Miller* [1995] Conv. 22.
218 s.25(1).
219 s.25(1)
220 Adoption and Children Act 2002 s.67.
221 *Re Collins* [1990] Fam. 56, where the adoption took place after the deceased had died, but before the application.
222 See above, para.8–16. For an instance see *Re Chatterton*, unreported but referred to in [1980] Conv. 150 (daughter aged five, whom deceased had never seen).
223 s.3(3).
224 See G. Miller [1995] Conv. 22.
225 1938 Act s.1(1).
226 See Law Com. No.61, paras 71–79.

occupational qualification.[227] General guideline (vi)[228] points to another: by reason of physical or mental disability the applicant cannot maintain himself or herself,[229] or, perhaps, is seriously handicapped in earning capacity. Again, the deceased may have obligations and responsibilities under general guideline (iv) towards an applicant who gives up work in order to care for the deceased during illness or old age,[230] or to a daughter who is a widow with young children and who had not been provided for by her deceased husband.[231]

8–58 In *Re Coventry*[232] Oliver J commented that applications for maintenance under the 1975 Act "by able-bodied and comparatively young men in employment and able to maintain themselves must be relatively rare and need to be approached with a degree of circumspection."[233] In that case a son who was 46 years old, in good health and working as a chauffeur, applied for provision to be made for him out of his father's £7,000 net estate. His financial resources left him little or no margin for expenditure on anything other than the necessities of life. The father had died intestate, leaving his widow, who was 74 years old, solely entitled under the intestacy rules. She had lived apart from the deceased without any maintenance from him for 19 years. During that time, the son had lived rent-free with his father but had provided his father's food and contributed to the household outgoings. The Court of Appeal, affirming the decision of Oliver J, held that it was reasonable that the disposition of the deceased's estate effected by the intestacy rules made no provision for the son's maintenance and the son's application therefore failed at the first hurdle.[234] There was no "special circumstance" (such as a moral obligation upon the deceased to make provision for the son) which made this unreasonable.[235]

An application by an adult daughter, who has no disability and is able to maintain herself, will similarly fail at the first hurdle.[236] The same is

[227] *Re Coventry* [1980] Ch. 461, 469–470, 476.

[228] See above, para.8–29.

[229] *Re Wood* (1982) 79 L.S.Gaz. 774 (daughter mentally disabled, residing in hospital: £15,000 ordered for extra comforts such as electric wheelchair, outings and holidays); *Re Debenham* (1986) 7 F.L.R. 404 (married daughter, 58, with epilepsy); *Millward v Shenton* [1972] 1 W.L.R. 711 (see above, para.8–29); *Hanbury v Hanbury* [1999] 2 F.L.R. 255; *Gold v Curtis* [2005] W.T.L.R. 673: *Robinson v Bird* [2003] W.T.L.R. 529; *Challinor v Challinor* [2009] W.T.L.R. 931 (daughter suffering from Down's syndrome awarded approximately one third of £300,000 estate. This case is referred to in Chap.15, see below, para.15–31).

[230] *Re Coventry* [1980] Ch.461, 476–477; *Re B* [2000] Ch.662 (claim by mother against minor daughter's estate).

[231] Law Com. No.61, para.78.

[232] *Re Coventry* [1980] Ch.461.

[233] *Re Coventry* [1980] Ch.461 at 465. But there is no "especially heavy burden on a male applicant of full age beyond that which must, as a practical matter, necessarily exist when a person who applies to be maintained by somebody else is already capable of adequately maintaining himself," *ibid.*, Ch.461 at 474: see also *Re Dennis* [1981] 2 All E.R. 140, 145.

[234] See above, para.8–20.

[235] *Re Coventry* [1980] Ch.461, 187–489, 494–495. See also *Christofides v Seddon* [2014] W.T.L.R. 215.

[236] *Williams v Johns* [1988] 2 F.L.R. 475. See also *Re Garland* [2007] 2 F.L.R. 528, *Hope v Knight* [2011] W.T.L.R. 593 and *Wright v Waters* [2015] W.T.L.R. 353.

true of an application by a married daughter whose husband is supporting her.[237]

It appeared clear, after *Re Coventry*[238] and *Re Jennings*,[239] that claims by adult children who had earning capacity would fail except in special circumstances. There have been some recent cases, however, where claims have succeeded and the attitude of the courts appears to have become less strict than it once seemed. Having said this, it is not always easy to see what circumstances, or combination of circumstances, will encourage the courts to decide in favour of an adult child. *Re Jennings*[240] is a case where the judge at first instance found in favour of the applicant and where the estate, if it did not pass to the adult child, would go to charity; yet the Court of Appeal discharged the trial judge's order for payment of a lump sum. On the other side of the line, there appear to be three groups of cases where adult children are now succeeding. 8–59

(i) Cases where a child has worked for parent on an understanding. In *Re Abram*[241] a son worked for seventeen years at a low wage in the family business and his mother disinherited him when he left to get married. It was held that this was a case where there were special circumstances and a moral obligation, which meant that the son had an overwhelming case for provision. In *Re Pearce*[242] the son worked for very low wages on his father's sheep farm and the Court of Appeal held that there was a clear moral obligation on the part of the deceased in relation to the farm. 8–60

(ii) Source of estate. In *Re Goodchild*[243] the Court of Appeal[244] held that an understanding between the parents of an adult child, which was insufficient to found a claim for a constructive trust based on mutual wills,[245] was nevertheless sufficient to found a moral obligation entitling the child to make a claim under the 1975 Act. The child's mother had left her estate to the father on the understanding that he would give effect to what she believed to be their mutual intentions. The fact that the mother had left property to the father, expecting it then to pass on to the child, was also one of the reasons for the decision in *Espinosa v Bourke*.[246] 8–61

(iii) "Lame duck" cases. An adult child with earning capacity will almost always fail in a claim under the 1975 Act, but children who lack that capacity may succeed on the basis of their "financial needs and 8–62

[237] *Re Rowlands* (1984) 5 F.L.R. 813: see Law Com. No.61, paras 74 and 78.
[238] See above, para.8–58.
[239] *Re Jennings* [1994] Ch.286, see above, para.8–26.
[240] *Re Jennings* [1994] Ch.286, see above, para.8–26.
[241] *Re Abram* [1996] 2 F.L.R. 379. The beneficiaries under the will were charities.
[242] *Re Pearce* [1998] 2 F.L.R. 705. The son did not enjoy a good standard of living; and the beneficiary under the will was a woman with whom the deceased was not living at his death and who was not in need.
[243] *Re Goodchild* [1997] 1 W.L.R. 1216, see above, para.6–36.
[244] Upholding Carnwath J.
[245] See above, paras 6–33 et seq.
[246] *Espinosa v Bourke* [1980] Ch.461, see below.

resources". In *Re Hancock*[247] and *Espinosa v Bourke*[248] the Court of Appeal stated that there was no need for a moral obligation or other special circumstance in a claim by an adult child: and although a claim by a child who was capable of earning his own living would be unlikely to succeed, claims by less fortunate adults might do so. It is not entirely clear what this is going to mean in practice, or if the courts are really adopting a radically new approach. The decision in *Espinosa v Bourke*[249] appears to be based in part on the fact that the adult child's mother had expected her daughter to inherit money bequeathed by the mother to the father.[250] In this sense *Espinosa* is like *Goodchild*[251] and could be classified as a "source of the estate" type case.[252] Nevertheless, it seems that some members of the Court of Appeal have recently felt more sympathy for "lame duck" applicants than their predecessors did. The problem is that the cases involve so many variables, the child may have more than one ground on which to found a claim, and the question of who will benefit if the child does not succeed must play a part. This latter point is illustrated by *Ilott v Mitson*.[253] Here, the claimant daughter was the deceased mother's only child and was born just after her father had been killed in an accident at work. The father's employer had then made a substantial payment to the mother which the mother had used to pay off the mortgage on her home. The mother brought up the daughter, but there was friction between them and, aged 17, the daughter left home without her mother's knowledge or consent to live with her boyfriend whom she later married and by whom she had five children. Neither the daughter nor her husband had full time employment, they lived in property rented from a housing association, and in obviously straightened and needy financial circumstances. In spite of a number of attempts at reconciliation, the mother and daughter remained estranged until the mother's death, more than twenty five years after the daughter had left home. The mother's will left her entire £486,000 estate to charities with whom she had no close links, and she left a note explaining why she had done this. The application first came before a district judge who held that the dispositions made by the mother's will did not make reasonable financial provision for the daughter, i.e. the daughter succeeded at the first stagethe threshold stage.[254] He then went on to make an award of £50,000, but any benefit to the daughter from this award was effectively nullified by the loss of state benefits. The daughter appealed to the High Court, her appeal was on quantum. At that stage, the charities

[247] *Re Hancock* [1998] 2 F.L.R. 346 (upholding the decision of His Honour Judge Behrens but on different grounds.)

[248] *Espinosa v Bourke* [1999] 1 F.L.R. 747 (reversing the decision of Johnson J).

[249] *Espinosa v Bourke* [1999] 1 F.L.R. 747.

[250] There are also cases where an investigation into what happened to the other parent's estate operates in such a way as to explain or justify the deceased's decision *not* to make provision for the claimant. See, e.g. *Re Garland* [2007] 2 F.L.R. 528.

[251] *Goodchild* [1997] 1 W.L.R. 1216.

[252] There is another problem with the decision in *Re Hancock* which was discussed earlier in this chapter, see above, para.8–23.

[253] *Ilott v Mitson* [2015] 2 F.C.R. 547.

[254] See above, para.8–20.

cross appealed. King J held in favour of the charities, the mother's decision to leave nothing to the daughter had not been unreasonable. The daughter appealed to the Court of Appeal which held that King J had been wrong to allow an appeal against the district judge's decision on the threshold question, he had had grounds for reaching his conclusion and an appeal court should not have interfered with it. That still left the matter of quantum to be decided. The Court of Appeal expressed the hope that there would be no need for a further hearing. This was optimistic, there were, in fact, two further hearings. Parker J restored the award of the district judge, the daughter was again awarded £50,000. The daughter appealed again to the Court of Appeal who now awarded her approximately £184,000—being sufficient to buy her housing association home at a discount and to leave her with some spare cash. The award was drafted in such a way as to permit the daughter to retain her state benefits.[255] The case is a good example of one where the daughter was competing with charities who themselves had no particular call on the testatrix's bounty. But what is not clear, for those obliged to give advice in future in family provision cases, is what was really the basis on which this daughter succeeded, above and beyond the fact that she was a daughter, and was in need. The Court of Appeal (on the first occasion that the matter came before it) seemed to say that the district judge was engaged in making a value judgment and that, though he might have decided the matter differently, his decision was not open to appeal. The two High Court judges seem to have taken a clearly different approach—neither seems to have felt sympathy for this applicant. But, if this is a correct analysis of the position, it leads to a situation where cases like this may come to resemble a lottery.

And another the problem with the "lame duck" cases is the potential unfairness towards children, such as the son in *Re Jennings*,[256] who, having led virtuous lives, are then treated less generously than their prodigal brothers and sisters.[257]

(d) *Application by an infant child*

An infant child does not have to show special circumstances in order to make a claim because he has a moral and financial claim on his parents. In *Re Robinson*[258] the deceased had been married twice and had two children by his first wife as well as a child and a stepchild by his second wife. He was killed in a car crash and died intestate; his second wife took almost his entire estate. His children by his first marriage, who had been living with him and his second wife, then returned to live with their mother whose financial position was not as strong as that of their stepmother. It was held **8–63**

[255] *Wright v Waters* [2015] W.T.L.R. 1399. This is the reference for the last of the five hearings.
[256] *Re Jennings* [1994] Ch.286, see above, paras 8–26 and 8–59.
[257] There is a parallel here with the problem which used to exist in relation to dependants, where it became apparent that the more an applicant had done for the deceased, the harder it might be to make a claim. See below, paras 8–76 and 8–81.
[258] *Re Robinson* [2001] W.T.L.R. 267.

that provision for infant children depends simply on what is required for their maintenance.

5. A person treated by the deceased as a child of the family

8–64 Any person (not being a child of the deceased) who, in relation to any marriage or civil partnership to which the deceased was at any time a party, or otherwise in relation to any family in which the deceased at any time stood in the role of parent, was treated by the deceased as a child of the family.

This definition was slightly amended by the Inheritance and Trustees' Powers Act 2014. Before the amendment, a child qualified only if there had been a marriage or civil partnership, so a child of the deceased's cohabitant did not qualify.[259] The 2014 Act has also inserted an additional subs. (2A) which says:

> "The reference in subsection (1)(d) above to a family in which the deceased stood in the role of a parent includes a family of which the deceased was the only member (apart from the applicant)."

(a) *The maintenance standard*

8–65 The maintenance standard is applicable on an application by such a person.[260]

(b) *The particular guidelines*

8–66 The particular guidelines to which the court must have regard are "the manner in which the applicant was being or in which he might expect to be educated or trained"[261] and *also* the following four guidelines[262]:

- (i) whether the deceased maintained the applicant and, if so, the length of time for which and basis on which the deceased did so, and the extent of the contribution made;
- (ii) whether and, if so, to what extent the deceased assumed responsibility for the maintenance;
- (iii) whether in maintaining, or assuming responsibility for maintenance, the deceased did so knowing that the applicant was not his own child;
- (iv) the liability[263] of any other person to maintain the applicant.

[259] Though he might have qualified as a dependant.

[260] See above, para.8–16.

[261] This is the particular guideline which operates where there is an application by a child of the deceased. See above, para.8–56. *Re Andrews* [1955] 1 W.L.R. 1105.

[262] s.3(3): these four guidelines were very slightly amended by the Inheritance and Trustees' Powers Act 2014.

[263] This means any liability enforceable at law, whether or not an order has been made, *Roberts v Roberts* [1962] P. 212.

(c) *Application by an adult stepchild*

Obviously this category covers a young stepchild[264] whose mother or father married the deceased and who was brought up by the deceased as a child of the family after the marriage. This category is not, however, restricted to minor or dependent children. In *Re Callaghan*[265] the successful applicant was 35 years of age and living with his wife in their own home when his mother married the deceased. The deceased treated the applicant as a child (albeit an adult child) of the family in relation to this marriage by acknowledging his own role of grandfather to the applicant's children, placing confidences as to his property and financial affairs in the applicant, and depending upon the applicant to care for him in his last illness.[266] The deceased died intestate and the court held that the absence of provision for the applicant, under the intestacy rules, did not make reasonable financial provision for his maintenance; especially as the deceased's assets were derived from the applicant's mother (who had predeceased the deceased) who had herself derived them by way of gift from the applicant's paternal grandfather after the applicant's father had been killed on active service.[267] **8–67**

Treatment of a person as a child of the family refers to the behaviour of the deceased towards that person. The mere display of affection, kindness, or hospitality by a stepparent towards a stepchild does not by itself constitute such treatment.[268] The deceased must, expressly or impliedly, assume the position of a parent towards the applicant, with the attendant responsibilities and privileges of that relationship.[269] Normally the privileges of the quasi-parent tend to increase, and the responsibilities to diminish, as the years go by. In *Re Callaghan* the privileges of the elderly quasi-parent were more important than the responsibilities.[270] **8–68**

6. A dependant of the deceased

This category covers "any person (not included in the forgoing paragraphs of [the] subsection)[271] who immediately before the death of the deceased was being maintained, either wholly or partly, by the deceased." **8–69**

[264] Or, since 2014, the young child of a cohabitant.

[265] *Re Callaghan* [1985] Fam. 1: see *Re Leach* [1986] Ch.226 (step-daughter was 32 when her father married the deceased).

[266] per Booth J in *Re Callaghan* [1985] Fam. 1 at 6. Quaere whether treatment of the applicant as a child of the family before the marriage suffices, *ibid*.

[267] *ibid* at 7 (lump sum payment of £5,000 ordered from £31,000 estate to enable applicant to buy his council house). One of the things this case demonstrates is that the intestacy rules do not work well where there is a second marriage without issue, but surviving issue from a first marriage. See R. Kerridge [1990] 54 Conv. 358.

[268] *Re Leach* [1986] Ch. 226, 235.

[269] Treatment of the applicant as a child of the family *after* a marriage has ended by the death of the other spouse is a relevant factor if the treatment stems from the marriage, *Re Leach* [1986] Ch. 226 at 233–235.

[270] *Re Callaghan* [1985] Fam. 1 at 6.

[271] Someone who is both a cohabitant *and* a dependant succeeds only as a cohabitant: *Re Baker* [2008] W.T.L.R. 565.

Section 1(3) provides that a person is to be treated as being maintained by the deceased (either wholly or partly, as the case may be) only "if the deceased was making a substantial contribution in money or money's worth towards the reasonable needs of that person, other than a contribution made for full valuable consideration pursuant to an arrangement of a commercial nature."[272] The Law Commission, in 1974, recommended the introduction of this category of applicant,[273] whom it is convenient to call a dependant of the deceased.[274] Obviously this category is not confined to relatives of the deceased or to members of the deceased's household, and it covers persons who had no right to maintenance enforceable against the deceased during his lifetime.[275]

(a) *The maintenance standard*

8–70 The maintenance standard is applicable on an application by a dependant.[276]

(b) *The particular guideline*

8–71 The particular guideline to which the court must have regard is "(a) to the length of time for which and basis on which the deceased maintained the applicant, and to the extent of the contribution made by way of maintenance; (b) to whether and, if so, to what extent the deceased assumed responsibility for the maintenance of the applicant."[277] No minimum period of dependence on the deceased is prescribed.[278]

(c) *Burden of proof*

8–72 The burden of proof lies upon an applicant[279] to prove that immediately before the death of the deceased:

(i) the deceased was making a substantial contribution in money or money's worth towards the reasonable needs of the applicant,[280] and

[272] The wording of s.1(3) was slightly amended by the Inheritance and Trustees' Powers Act 2014, see below para.8–73.
[273] Law Com. No.61, paras 85–98.
[274] Because of the introduction of this category, a popular newspaper described the 1975 Act as a "mistress's charter"; see Green (1988) 51 M.L.R. 187, 195.
[275] See *Re Wilkinson* [1978] Fam. 22 (sister acting as companion); *Re Viner* [1978] C.L.Y 3091 (poor widowed sister); *Malone v Harrison* [1979] 1 W.L.R. 1353 (mistress); *Re C* (1979) 123 S.J. 35 (common law wife); *Jelley v Iliffe*, above, (common law husband); *Harrington v Gill* (1983) 4 F.L.R. 265 (common law wife); *Williams v Roberts* [1984] Fam. Law 210; *Bishop v Plumley* [1991] 1 W.L.R. 582 (common law wife); *Graham v Murphy* [1997] 1 F.L.R. 860 (common law husband); *Rees v Newbery* [1998] 1 F.L.R. 1041 (friend).
[276] See above, para.8–16.
[277] s.3(4), as slightly amended by the Inheritance and Trustees' Powers Act 2014.
[278] In *Witkowska v Kaminski* [2006] W.T.L.R. 1293 it did not matter that the dependant was an illegal over-stayer.
[279] *Re Wilkinson* [1978] Fam. 23 at 23.
[280] *Re Wilkinson*, [1978] Fam. 23 (board and lodging); *Re Viner* [1978] C.L.Y. 3091, (£5 per week);

(ii) the deceased was doing so otherwise than for full valuable consideration pursuant to an arrangement of a commercial nature.

(d) *Deceased's assumption of responsibility*

In *Re Beaumont*[281] Megarry VC held that an applicant must prove that before the deceased's death he had assumed responsibility for the applicant's maintenance. He arrived at this conclusion because of the original wording of the particular guideline applicable to a dependant—"the extent to which and the basis upon which the deceased assumed responsibility for the maintenance of the applicant". Unlike the particular guideline applicable to a person treated by the deceased as a child of the family, this made an implicit assumption that the deceased had assumed responsibiliy.[282] In *Jelley v Iliffe* the Court of Appeal decided that, as a general rule, proof that the deceased was maintaining the applicant raises a presumption that the deceased had assumed responsibility for the applicant's maintenance. There need be no other overt act to demonstrate the assumption of responsibility. **8–73**

To clarify matters, the guideline was slightly amended by the Inheritance and Trustees' Powers Act 2014 and the revised wording makes it clear that assumption of responsibility is not a condition under this heading, though it is a matter to which the court must pay regard. At one extreme the deceased may have assumed this responsibility for the rest of the applicant's life,[283] and, at the other, the deceased may have disclaimed any further responsibility beyond the contribution he made.[284] Again the deceased may have assumed responsibility for the applicant's complete maintenance on a generous scale,[285] or (on the other hand) grudgingly assumed responsibility for the applicant's partial maintenance.[286] **8–74**

(e) *Immediately before the death of the deceased*

Requirements (i) and (ii) of the burden of proof must be satisfied "immediately before the death of the deceased."[287] What if the situation immediately **8–75**

Malone v Harrison [1979] 1 W.L.R. 1353, (all living expenses paid; also flats in England and Malta in joint names, a car, £15,000 shares, and £5,500 furs and jewellery); *Re C* 1979) 123 S.J. 35, above, (lived as his wife); *Jelley v Iliffe* [1981] Fam. 128 (rent-free accommodation); *Harrington v Gil* (1979) 123 S.J. 35, (lived as his wife); *Graham v Murphy* [1997] 1 F.L.R. 860, (free accommodation and additional benefits); *Rees v Newbery* [1998] 1 F.L.R. 1041 (accommodation at very low rent).

281 *Re Beaumont* [1980] Ch.444.

282 *Re Beaumont* [1980] at pp.454–456: see above, p.8–60.

283 *Malone v Harrison* [1979] 1 W.L.R. 1353, 1358, 1364–1365 (cable to mistress, "I say to you you will have happiness and contentment with security for ever").

284 See *Re Beaumont* [1980] Ch.444, 458 ("it may be that would-be benefactors who wish to protect their families ought to obtain from anyone to whose maintenance they propose to contribute an acknowledgment that they are undertaking no responsibility for his or her [future] maintenance"): Law Com. No.61, para.97. See also *Baynes v Hedger* [2009] W.T.L.R. 759.

285 *Malone v Harrison* [1979] 1 W.L.R. 1353, 1358, 1364–1365, (at least £4,000 per annum, plus furs and jewellery and two flats in joint names).

286 *Re Viner* [1978] C.L.Y. 3091 (£5 per week paid for six months before death: provision ordered restricted to that made by deceased).

287 s.1(1)(e): see *Layton v Martin* [1986] 2 F.L.R. 227 (mistress dismissed two years before death of deceased: not dependent at death).

before the death differs from normal? For instance, A, who normally lives with and is fully maintained by B, falls ill and enters hospital for investigation: B dies whilst A is still in hospital. If only the abnormal situation at the instant before B's death is to be considered, A is not a dependant of B.[288] In *Re Beaumont* Megarry VC held that the court should consider the settled basis or arrangement at B's death, under which A was fully maintained by B, rather than any temporary variation owing to A's being in hospital.[289] In *Jelley v Iliffe*[290] the Court of Appeal took the same view. In *Kourkey v Lusher*[291] the applicant had been the deceased's mistress on an intermittent basis for about 12 years. She was not living with the deceased at the time of his death, nor had she been living with him for a few weeks before his death. Her claim for provision failed, but not simply on the basis that she was not living with the deceased for a matter of weeks: it failed because there had never been any settled pattern of dependence and there had always been a reluctance by the deceased to commit himself financially to the applicant during their relationship. In this case, there was no settled basis or arrangement to support her claim.

(f) *Weighing the contribution of each to the other's needs*

8–76 Here, the Inheritance and Trustees' Powers Act 2014 has made a change. If A and B live together and each of them makes some contribution towards the other's reasonable needs, on B's death A can claim as a dependant if B's contribution was substantially greater than A's.[292] Such a case is straightforward. But if the contributions were broadly equal, or A's contribution was greater than B's, A appeared, before 2014, not to be able to make a claim (unless he could bring himself within the cohabitant category).[293]

Even before 2014, the court took a broad commonsense view of the issue whether A was a dependant of B: the right question to ask was whether A was dependent on B for maintenance during B's lifetime, or did A give as good as A got?[294] In striking a balance between their respective contributions:

> "the court must use common sense and remember that the object of Parliament in creating this extra class of persons who may claim benefit from an estate was to provide relief for persons of whom it could truly be said that they were wholly or partially dependent on the deceased. It cannot be an exact exercise of evaluating services in pounds and pence.

[288] For this and other examples see *Re Beaumont* [1980] Ch.444 and 451–453.

[289] *Re Beaumont* [1980] Ch.444, 452–453: similarly, services rendered temporarily by A to B, such as nursing B during B's last illness, do not debar A from being a dependant because the court considers the settled arrangement, *ibid.* See also *Bishop v Plumley* [1991] 1 W.L.R. 582.

[290] *Jelley v Iliffe* [1981] Fam. 128: see also *Re Dix* [2004] 1 W.L.R. 1399.

[291] *Kourkey v Lusher* (1982) 12 Fam. Law 86.

[292] *Kourkey v Lusher* (1982) 12 Fam. Law 86.

[293] per Stephenson LJ in *Jelley v Iliffe*, above, at pp.138–139: see *Re Kirby* (1981) 11 Fam. Law 210.

[294] per Stephenson LJ in *Jelley v Iliffe*, above, at p.139. See also *Jennings v Rice* [2001] W.T.L.R. 87, which is discussed in Chap.6, as it raises issues of dependency and of estoppel.

By way of example, if a man was living with a woman as his wife, providing the house and all the money for their living expenses, she would clearly be dependent upon him, and it would not be right to deprive her of her claim by arguing that she was in fact performing the services that a housekeeper would perform and it would cost more to employ a housekeeper than was spent on her and indeed perhaps more than the deceased had available to spend upon her."[295]

In *Bishop v Plumley*[296] the deceased and the applicant cohabited for about ten years. For most of this time they pooled their modest resources; neither was maintained by the other. The deceased then inherited a substantial legacy and he bought a house in which he and the applicant went to live. Shortly after they moved into the house, the deceased became ill and the applicant looked after him. He died less than a year later. It was held by the Court of Appeal that the provision of the house *was* a substantial contribution and it was not balanced or cancelled out by care and attention, even of an exceptional kind, shown to the deceased by the applicant during the deceased's final illness. The care and attention could not be assessed in isolation from the mutual love and support of a couple living together. **8–77**

In any case, the 2014 amendment to s.1(3) of the 1975 Act consists of adding the words "pursuant to an arrangement of a commercial nature" to the words "other than a contribution made for full valuable consideration". This means that someone who contributed more than he received, but not under a commercial arrangement, can now qualify as a dependant. Salaried housekeepers and those who run nursing homes will not be able to claim as dependants, but someone who has lived with the deceased (but who does not qualify as a cohabitant) may be able to claim without having to go through a detailed assessment of who contributed what to their arrangements. How the change will operate in practice remains to be seen. It will make it easier to deal with some borderline cases, though it may also create difficulties about where to draw any final line.

(g) *Can a carer be a dependant?*

Re B, Bouette v Rose[297] raises the question whether a carer can be a dependant of the person for whom he is caring. A severely disabled child, who had been awarded £250,000 damages for medical negligence, was cared for by her mother in a bungalow which had been paid for as to 75 per cent by the child and as to 25 per cent by the mother. The child died intestate and, by the intestacy rules, her estate passed half to her mother and half to her father who had deserted her and her mother shortly after her birth. The mother made a family provision claim against the child's estate. At first instance, it was held that the mother was not a dependant of her daughter and the mother's application for leave to appeal out of time was dismissed. The Court of Appeal reversed this decision and ordered that **8–78**

[295] per Griffiths LJ in *Jelley v Iliffe*, above, at p.141.
[296] *Bishop v Plumley* [1991] 1 W.L.R. 582.
[297] *Re B, Bouette v Rose* [2000] Ch.662.

the application be restored. This is a case where there must be considerable sympathy for the mother, particularly given the father's desertion of her and of the child. Although one could argue that it is not entirely easy to see how the carer mother could correctly be classified as her disabled daughter's dependant, she had given up work and had no other source of income—except for social security benefits—besides the interest from the money invested for the daughter.

V. REFORM OF THE LAW—AND ADDING TO THE CLASSES OF APPLICANTS

1. Problems with the development of the law relating to family provision

8–79 The last major reform of the family provision legislation was more than forty years ago, but, since then, there have been a number of piecemeal, though significant, changes. In recent years, the problem areas have been the treatment of adult children, of dependants and of cohabitants.

2. Adult children

8–80 In spite of what was said in the Court of Appeal in *Ilott v Mitson*[298] it is not easy, when faced with an application by an adult child, to reconcile the approach taken by that court in *Re Coventry*[299] with the approach taken by the same court in *Re Hancock*[300] and in *Espinosa v Bourke*.[301] Eleanor King J, in *Mitson*, took the *Coventry* line, the Court of Appeal took the other approach, but is hard to see how, on the facts of *Ilott v Mitson*, where the mother and daughter had been estranged for the whole of the daughter's adult life, and where the daughter was not incapacitated, that the mother could be said to have acted in a way which was objectively unreasonable *unless* all parents who die having spare capital are now under some kind of obligation to make provision for such of their adult children who choose to adopt lifestyles which make them dependent on the state. The daughter's successful claim in *Mitson* seems ultimately to be based on some form of *welfarist* view of the position of the family—and, more than that, to create a great deal of potential work for the legal profession.

It could be suggested that the true choice in a case of this sort should be between adopting some form of forced heirship, or letting daughters like this fend for themselves. Until about a hundred years ago, most significant holdings of property were held in trusts or settlements and so "the family" were seldom entirely disinherited, even when parents and children did not feel great affection for one another. Freedom of testation

[298] *Ilott v Mitson* [2015] W.T.L.R. 1399.
[299] *Re Coventry* [1980] Ch.461.
[300] *Re Hancock* [1998] 2 F.L.R. 346.
[301] *Espinosa v Bourke* [1980] Ch. 461.

has its drawbacks, but the *Ilott v Mitson* solution will not seem to everyone to be the ideal countermeasure.

3. Dependants

Dependants were added as a class of applicant under the family provision legislation in 1975 and it seems probable that, at that time, it was generally assumed, both by those who favoured the addition of the class and by those who did not, that the great majority of those who qualified would be "common law wives".[302] But "common law wives" were not the only ones able to bring themselves within the statutory definition and there was then the probem of measuring contributions, the problem discussed above in paras 8–76 and 8–77. This problem was solved, in part, by the way in which the courts took a broad commonsense view of the matter[303]; and the 2014 amendment appears to dispose of this problem. But disposing of it in this way may create another difficulty. If someone can be a dependant, even if he has clearly contributed more than he has received, "dependency" is not going to be easy to recognise. **8–81**

4. Cohabitants

Cohabitants were added as a class in 1996[304] following one of the recommendations in the Law Commission's 1989 report *Family Law: Distribution on Intestacy*.[305] That report had considered whether cohabitants should be included as beneficiaries within the intestacy rules. The Commission decided that they should not be *but* went on to recommend that they should be included in the family provision legislation. The inclusion of cohabitants as a class of applicants within the family provision structure has solved one problem (dependants who cohabit do not need to prove dependency), but, again, it has created another. A relative—say a sister—who lived with the deceased will find that she is being treated less generously than a cohabitant. A sister who cares for the deceased *may* be entitled on the deceased's intestacy, but her entitlement will depend on which other members of the family survive the deceased.[306] **8–82**

And, even if one puts to one side the problem of the sister who cannot claim as a cohabitant, there is the potentially bigger problem of who is a cohabitant. Some of the cases on this topic were discussed in para.8–52. When dealing with a borderline case, it will be relatively easy for a judge to decide that the applicant is a cohabitant if there is no one else who has a strong claim to the deceased's estate. *Re Watson (dec'd)*[307] is an example. There was no other claimant to the deceased's estate, except for the Crown claiming bona vacantia. Another not dissimilar case is **8–83**

[302] See fn.274.

[303] There are those who consider that the "broad commonsense view" was actually a fudge.

[304] See para.8–03.

[305] *Family Law: Distribution on Intestacy*, Law Com. No.187 (1989).

[306] The deceased may be survived by many other undeserving brothers and sisters.

[307] *Re Watson (dec'd)* [1999] 1 F.L.R. 878.

Swetenham v Walkley.[308] The deceased was a childless bachelor, aged over eighty, who died intestate. For some years, he had been friendly with W, a widow. They did not have sexual relations, and each had his/her own house. But he had a bedroom at her house, where he often slept. She cooked for him and did his washing and ironing, but he did not tell her when he retired from work, and did not consult her when buying a new house. This is a borderline case, but, as he had no brothers or sisters (his next of kin were cousins with whom he appears not to have been in close touch) it is not hard to see why a judge would say that W should succeed in her claim for family provision as a cohabitant. W was awarded about a third of the deceased's £600,000 estate. But consider what the position would have been if he had been a widower with children, or if W had died first and it had been *he* who had made a claim. Would a court then have decided that he and W were cohabitants and that the survivor had a good claim? There are two interlinked problems here. What is cohabitation in this context[309] and why should a cohabitant who is not a dependant be considered deserving of a part of the deceased's estate?

8–84 That brings us back to something mentioned at the end of Chapter 2.[310] The Law Commission's 2011 report recommended that qualifying cohabitants should be entitled to benefit from the estate of a deceased partner under the intestacy rules. This recommendation has not been enacted. There will be those who will oppose its enactment on policy grounds and those who favour it, because they favour different policies. Politicians of various hues will adopt varying approaches.

Such discussion as there has been on the topic seems largely to have ignored the position of the deceased's children and grandchildren. The editor, when looking at the reform of intestacy, has always been concerned that the deceased's descendants by an earlier union should not be trumped by a later spouse (i.e. that the children of a first marriage should not see all their father's property passing to his second wife and then to her children).[311] *If* cohabitants were to obtain rights equivalent to those of spouses on intestacy, this would make things worse, potentially much worse. And disputes over whether someone was, or was not, a cohabitant, could become both prolonged and very bitter. A dispute between children and a cohabitant in these circumstances would not resemble the cases reported so far where (when there has been a dispute as to whether someone was a cohabitant) children are almost never involved. At the end of the day, borderline examples of what constitutes cohabitation will cause problems; and giving cohabitants rights on intestacy would be a recipe for much more litigation—not something to be welcomed.

308 *Swetenham v Walkley* [2014] W.T.L.R. 845.
309 Another borderline case on cohabitation is *Gordon v Legister* [2014] W.T.L.R. 1675.
310 See para.2–80.
311 See paras 2–76 et seq.

5. Beneficiaries under the wills of testators who become incapable and who then marry

The Law Reform Committee in their 22nd Report, *The Making and Revocation of Wills*,[312] considered, inter alia, the problem of the testator who married while he was mentally disordered. They recommended that where a testator entered into a marriage while incapable through mental disorder of managing and administering his property and affairs, the court should have a discretion to make financial provision for anyone who could show that he would have been a beneficiary under a will which was revoked by the marriage *and* that he was someone for whom the deceased might have been expected to provide by will if the deceased had not been mentally disordered.[313] This is discussed in Chapters 2 and 7.[314] If no other steps are taken,[315] it is suggested that the best course would be to implement this recommendation. **8–85**

6. The cost of family provision disputes

Litigation in England is expensive, and that is a good reason for attempting to arrive at rules which are clear. This is not the place to rehearse a list of arguments as to who is to blame for the increase in probate and family provision disputes in recent years. But there do seem to have been a relatively large number of prolonged disputes over family provision where the sums at stake have been relatively insignificant as compared with the costs involved in fighting over them. Apart from *Ilott v Mitson*, a case which may have caused the reader to draw breath, there have been a number of other cases which might be noted in this context, and which have been fought since the last edition of this book appeared.[316] This is not a welcome development and any proposals for reform should bear in mind the need for a system which does not promote unnecessary uncertainty. **8–86**

VI. A POTENTIAL CLAIMANT'S "INTEREST" IN THE ESTATE

In *O'Brien v Seagrave*[317] it was held that a person with a potential claim for financial provision under the 1975 Act has an "interest in the estate"[318] **8–87**

[312] Law Reform Committee, 22nd Report, *The Making and Revocation of Wills*, Cmnd.7902 (1980).
[313] Law Reform Committee's 22nd Report, para.3:25; and see *Re Davey* [1981] 1 W.L.R. 164, referred to above in paras 5–13 and 7–04.
[314] See paras 2–78 and 7–04.
[315] Other steps might be preferable.
[316] See, e.g. *Cattle v Evans* [2011] W.T.L.R. 947; *Patel v Vigh* [2013] EWHC 3403 (Ch); *Christofides v Seddon* [2014] W.T.L.R. 215; *Wright v Waters* [2015] W.T.L.R. 353; *Wright-Gordon v Legister* [2014] W.T.L.R. 1675.
[317] *O'Brien v Seagrave* [2007] 1 W.L.R. 2002.
[318] As required by C.P.R. 57.7(1).

sufficient to bring a probate claim seeking revocation of a grant of probate of a will in common form.

VII. ORDERS WHICH THE COURT MAY MAKE

1. The deceased's net estate

8–88 The deceased's "net estate", from which the court may order provision to be made for an applicant, is widely defined in the 1975 Act.

(a) *Property always included in the net estate*

8–89 The deceased's net estate always includes the following property[319]:

(i) All property of which the deceased had power to dispose by his will[320] (except by virtue of a special power of appointment) less the amount of his funeral, testamentary and administration expenses, debts and liabilities, including any inheritance tax payable out of his estate on his death. This category does not include property nominated under a pension fund trust deed[321] or benefits arising under assurance policies on the life of the deceased if the benefits are payable direct to a beneficiary and not to the deceased's estate.[322]

(ii) Any property in respect of which the deceased held a general power of appointment (not exercisable by will) which has not been exercised. This category does not apply if it has been exercised.[323] If the general power was exercisable by will, the property falls within category (i), whether or not the deceased exercised the power.

(iii) Any sum of money or other property nominated to any person by the deceased under a *statutory* nomination[324] or received by any person from the deceased as a *donatio mortis causa*,[325] less any inheritance tax payable in respect thereof and borne by the nominee or donee.[326] The legislation does not, however, permit

[319] s.25(1): "property" includes any chose in action, cf. the property which constitutes assets for the payment of the deceased's debts and liabilities, see below, Chap.21.

[320] Or would have had power to dispose by will if he had been of full age and capacity, s.25(2): it is immaterial that the estate passes as bona vacantia, s.24. Foreign property is included, provided the deceased died domiciled in England and Wales. Property, or a debt, subject to the Rule in *Strong v Bird* (see above, Chap.6) probably falls within category (i).

[321] *Jessop v Jessop* [1992] 1 F.L.R. 591.

[322] But category (v) may be applicable, see below, para.8–90. For occupational pension benefits see *Re Cairnes* (1983) 4 F.L.R. 225; Rosettenstein (1979) 123 S.J. 661.

[323] Again category (v) may be applicable.

[324] For statutory nominations see above, paras 1–06 et seq. In *Goenka v Goenka* [2014] EWHC 2966 (Ch) a nomination under the NHS pension scheme was treated as equivalent to a statutory nomination (as opposed to a pension fund nomination) and *was* included. The result may be technically correct, but seems odd.

[325] For *donationes mortis causa* see above, paras 6–44 et seq.

[326] ss.8 and 25(1): s.8 protects a person who pays money or transfers property in accordance with the nomination or *donatio mortis causa*. If any such inheritance tax is repaid

the court to order provision from property nominated under a pension fund trust deed.[327]

(b) *Property included if the court so orders*

The deceased's net estate also includes property in each of the following two categories if the court so orders: **8–90**

(iv) The deceased's severable share of any property of which he was a beneficial joint tenant immediately before his death.[328] If the deceased and X were beneficial joint tenants of (say) a house or a chose in action (such as a bank account) immediately before the deceased's death, X becomes absolutely entitled by operation of the right of survivorship at the deceased's death. But the court nevertheless has power to order that the deceased's severable share shall, to such extent as appears just in all the circumstances[329] and having regard to any inheritance tax payable in respect of that share, be treated as part of the deceased's net estate.[330]

An order under s.9 may be made only if an application is made to the court for an order under the 1975 Act within the six months' time limit[331]: if no application is made within this time limit, X cannot be deprived of the benefit of the right of survivorship because this category of property is not available on an application made out of time with the court's permission.

Of course, if the deceased and X were beneficial tenants in common, the deceased's undivided share falls within catagory (i).

(v) Any sum of money or other property which the court directs to be provided by any person under its powers to prevent evasion of the 1975 Act.[332] These powers are considered later.[333]

in consequence of an order making provision for an applicant, it forms part of the deceased's net estate, Inheritance Tax Act 1984 s.146(1), (4), (5) and (7): see below, para.8–98.

[327] *Jessop v Jessop* [1992] 1 F.L.R. 591—provision may not be ordered *from* such property, but the property may be relevant as a financial resource of a beneficiary of the deceased's estate (if provision is ordered from *other* property.)

[328] ss.9 and 25(1). For instances see *Re Crawford* (1983) 4 F.L.R. 273 (building society and bank accounts held jointly by deceased and second wife) and *Jessop v Jessop* [1992] 1 F.L.R. 591 (house in joint names of deceased and cohabitant, cohabitant ordered to pay £10,000 to widow.)

[329] For a case where it did not appear just, see *Murphy v Murphy* [2004] 1 F.C.R. 1 (insurance policy in names of deceased and former wife was intended to benefit survivor of them, no severance).

[330] Value is to be determined immediately before the death of the deceased, s.9(1); see *Dingmar v Dingmar* [2007] Ch.109; see also s.9(1A) (added in 2014) court may order that share is to be valued at different date.

[331] s.9(1): see above, para.8–07. Any person is protected for anything done by him before an order is made, s.9(3); e.g. the bank is protected if it pays the surviving joint tenant. If any inheritance tax borne by the surviving joint tenant is repaid in consequence of the order, it forms part of the deceased's net estate, Inheritance Tax Act 1984, ss.146(1), (4), (5) and (7): see below, para.8–104.

[332] ss.10, 11 and 25(1).

[333] See below, paras 8–115 et seq.

2. Forms of provision ordered for applicant

8–91 If the court is satisfied that the disposition of the deceased's estate is not such as to make reasonable financial provision for the applicant, measured by the surviving spouse or maintenance standard as is appropriate, the court may, in the exercise of its discretion, make any one or more of the following orders.[334]

(a) *Periodical payments*

8–92 Such an order may provide for periodical payments:

(i) of a specified amount[335] (e.g. £80 per week), or
(ii) equal to the whole, or a specified part, of the income of the net estate (e.g. one-half of the income of the net estate), or
(iii) equal to the whole of the income of such part of the net estate as the court directs to be set aside or appropriated.[336]

Alternatively, such an order may provide for the amount of the periodical payments to be determined in any other way the court thinks fit.[337]

8–93 Periodical payments are payable for the period specified by the court in the order.[338] Usually such payments are ordered to run from the death of the deceased (the court fixes the commencing date at its discretion)[339] and invariably the payments are ordered to terminate, at the latest, at the death of the applicant. An order for the making of periodical payments to a judicially separated spouse or former spouse of the deceased terminates automatically on the remarriage of that spouse.[340] The 1975 Act does not, however, specify any other event on which an order for periodical payments terminates.

(b) *Lump sum payment*

8–94 The amount of the lump sum is specified in the order and may extend to the entire net estate.[341] The lump sum may be made payable by instalments and the court may subsequently vary the number of instalments

[334] s.2(1).
[335] In that case the court may direct that a sufficient, but not excessive, part of the net estate be set aside or appropriated to meet the payments out of its income, s.2(3).
[336] s.2(2).
[337] See *Re Blanch* [1967] 1 W.L.R. 987, 992.
[338] s.2(1)(a): *Re Blanch*, above at 992–993.
[339] See *Askew v Askew* [1961] 1 W.L.R. 725 (former wife had received national assistance payments since death of former husband: order ran from death despite possible repayment); *Re Goodwin* [1969] 1 Ch.283, 292: cf. *Re Lecoche* (1967) 111 S.J. 136 (order from date of judgment to avoid sale of house); *Re Eyre* [1968] 1 W.L.R. 530, 544 (date of summons); *Lusternik v Lusternik* [1972] Fam. 125 (late application and proceedings over four years); *Re Debenham* (1986) 7 F.L.R. 404 (date of order, plus small lump sum to obviate need to backdate order as applicant had received social security).
[340] s.19(2); but any arrears are still payable, ibid. There are corresponding provisions for civil partners.
[341] s.25(3).

payable, and the amount of any instalment, but not the amount of the lump sum itself.[342] In the case of a small estate, a lump sum payment may well be the only practicable order.

(c) *Transfer of property*

The court may order the transfer to the applicant of specified property comprised in the deceased's net estate.[343] This may be preferable to an order for a lump sum payment if the latter would necessitate an improvident sale of assets. **8–95**

(d) *Settlement of property*

The court may order the settlement for the applicant's benefit of specified property comprised in the deceased's net estate.[344] **8–96**

(e) *Acquisition of property for transfer or settlement*

The court may also order the acquisition of specified property—for instance, a house—out of assets comprised in the deceased's net estate, and either the transfer of the acquired property to the applicant or the settlement of it for his benefit. **8–97**

(f) *and (g) Variation of marriage settlement or civil partnership settlement*

The court may order a variation of any ante-nuptial or post-nuptial settlement (including one made by will) made on the parties to a marriage to which the deceased was one of the parties. There is a corresponding provision for civil partners. **8–98**

(h) *Variation of the trusts on which the deceased's estate is held*

Finally, the court may order a variation of the trusts on which the deceased's estate is held. This heading was added in 2014. **8–99**

3. Quantum of provision ordered

If an application passes the first hurdle, the court determines whether it shall order provision to be made for an applicant and, if so, in what **8–100**

[342] s.7; *Re Besterman* [1984] Ch.458, 478 (if lump sum, court should take account of contingencies and inflation). Application for variation may be made by the person to whom the lump sum is payable, the personal representatives of the deceased, or the trustees of the property out of which the lump sum is payable, s.7(2).

[343] e.g. a house, *Re Christie* [1979] Ch.168. A weekly contractual tenancy is "property", *Hale v Hale* [1975] 1 W.L.R. 931 (private landlord); *Thompson v Thompson* [1976] Fam. 25 (local authority landlord).

[344] And confer on the trustees of the property such powers as appear to the court to be necessary or expedient, s.2(4)(c): see e.g. *Harrington v Gill* (1983) 4 F.L.R. 265 (house to be settled on applicant for life); *Hanbury v Hanbury* [1999] 2 F.L.R. 255 (discretionary trust).

manner. The only express requirement is that, in doing so, the court must have regard to the general and particular guidelines.[345] But it seems implicit that the court should use the surviving spouse, or maintenance, standard of reasonable financial provision (applicable at the first stage of the application) as a measure of the provision to be ordered for the applicant at the second stage.[346]

If the surviving spouse standard is applicable and the court orders a lump sum payment, in fixing the amount of that payment the court does not start with a bias against making a provision which may, ultimately, enable the applicant to make provision for somebody else who is not an applicant. That possibility is inherent in a lump sum order under the surviving spouse standard.[347] But the position is different if the maintenance standard is applicable because maintenance of the applicant is then a limiting factor.[348] In fixing the amount of a lump sum payment under the maintenance standard, the court assumes that the applicant will have to spend capital as well as income on maintenance during the period for which provision is being made.[349] Generally, however, it would not be right to treat the value of an applicant's home as expendable capital.[350] The possibility of marriage may also be a relevant factor in fixing this amount.[351]

4. Consequential and supplemental provisions

8–101 An order of the court may contain such consequential and supplemental provisions as the court thinks necessary or expedient for the purpose of (a) giving effect to the order, or (b) securing that it operates fairly as between the beneficiaries.[352]

(a) *Giving effect to the order*

8–102 In particular, the court has power to order any person who holds any property which forms part of the deceased's net estate to make such payment,

[345] s.3(1).

[346] See *Malone v Harrison* [1979] 1 W.L.R. 1353, 1365 (maintenance standard); *Re Besterman* [1984] Ch.458 (surviving spouse standard).

[347] *Re Besterman* [1984] Ch. 458 at pp.466, 470; *Adams v Lewis* [2001] W.T.L.R. 493.

[348] *Re Besterman*, see *Re Debenham* (1986) 7 F.L.R. 404 (periodical payments for applicant but not her husband).

[349] *Malone v Harrison*, above, (period of applicant's actuarial expectation of life, with possibility of marriage; "it is not my duty to provide for the beneficiaries under her will": estate large and multiplier calculation used to fix amount): for criticism of the multiplier calculation see Bryan (1980) 96 L.Q.R. 165 and cf. *Re Brown* (1955) 105 L.J. 169 ("a judge should not condescend to an analytical statement of how he has arrived at that figure"); *Re Pearce* [1998] 2 F.L.R. 705 (capitalisation of income).

[350] *Malone v Harrison* [1979] 1 W.L.R. 1353.

[351] *Malone v Harrison* [1979] 1 W.L.R. 1353. see also *Re Sivyer* [1967] 1 W.L.R. 1482, 1487–1488 (under 1938 Act).

[352] 1975 Act s.2(4). For the court's powers to vary or discharge a secured periodical payments order made under the Matrimonial Causes Act 1973, or the Civil Partnership Act 2004, and to vary or revoke a maintenance agreement, see 1975 Act ss.16 and 17: see also Matrimonial Causes Act 1973 ss.31 and 36, Pt II of Sch.5 to the Civil Partnership Act 2004, and the 1975 Act ss.18 and 18A. See generally Law Com. No.61, paras 263–276.

or to transfer such property, as is specified in the order.[353] This power is useful because the deceased's net estate may include property held by persons other than the deceased's personal representatives—for instance, property nominated by the deceased under a statutory nomination and (if the court so orders) the deceased's severable share of property of which he was a beneficial joint tenant.[354]

(b) *Incidence as between the beneficiaries*

The incidence of the provision ordered is of vital importance to the beneficiaries.[355] The court has power to vary the disposition of the deceased's estate effected by his will or the law relating to intestacy in such manner as the court thinks fair and reasonable, having regard to the provisions of the order and all the circumstances of the case.[356] Thus, if the court makes an order for the transfer to the applicant of property which was specifically given to a beneficiary by the will, the court may vary the disposition of the deceased's estate so as to make some other provision for that beneficiary. Again, if the court makes an order for periodical payments or a lump sum payment to an applicant, the court may direct from which part of the net estate this provision is to be made and which of the beneficiaries are to bear the burden of it.[357] The court has an unfettered discretion and is not bound by a direction in a will as to the incidence of any provision which may be ordered. **8–103**

5. Effect of an order

If the court makes an order making provision for an applicant, then for all purposes (including the inheritance tax legislation) the deceased's will or the law relating to intestacy (or both) shall be deemed to have had effect as from the deceased's death subject to the provisions of the order.[358] **8–104**

6. Interim order

The court has power to make an interim order in favour of an applicant. **8–105**

(a) *Two requirements*

It must appear to the court: **8–106**

[353] s.2(4)(a). But it appears that the court has no power to order a settlement of the applicant's own property, *Malone v Harrison* [1979] 1 W.L.R. 1353, 1366.
[354] See above, para.8–90.
[355] i.e. a person beneficially interested under the deceased's will or on intestacy, or a person who takes under a statutory nomination or a *donatio mortis causa* made by the deceased, s.25(1).
[356] s.2(4)(b): see also s.24.
[357] *Re Simson* [1950] Ch.38: *Re Jackson* [1952] 2 T.L.R. 90: *Re Preston* [1969] 1 W.L.R. 317.
[358] s.19(1): see also as to inheritance tax, Inheritance Tax Act 1984 s.146. See also *Tibbs v Dick* [1998] 2 F.L.R. 1118 (finality of the order): *Re Jennery* [1967] Ch.280.

(i) that the applicant is in immediate need of financial assistance, but it is not yet possible to determine what final order (if any) should be made; and
(ii) that property forming part of the deceased's net estate is or can be made available to meet the need of the applicant.[359]

In determining what interim order (if any) to make the court must have regard, so far as the urgency of the case admits, to the general and particular guidelines.[360]

(b) *Form of interim order*

8–107 By an interim order the court orders payment to the applicant out of the deceased's net estate of such sum or sums, and (if more than one) at such intervals, as the court thinks reasonable.[361] Such an order may impose conditions or restrictions[362] and may contain consequential and supplemental provisions.[363]

By its final order making provision for the applicant the court may direct to what extent any sum paid to the applicant under the interim order is to be treated as having been paid on account of any payment provided for by the final order.[364]

(c) *Protection of personal representative*

8–108 A personal representative who makes a payment under an interim order does not incur any liability by reason of the net estate not being sufficient to make that payment unless at the time of the payment he has reasonable cause to believe that the estate is not sufficient.[365]

VIII. VARIATION OR DISCHARGE OF A PERIODICAL PAYMENTS ORDER

8–109 Under s.6 of the 1975 Act the court has a wide power to vary or discharge any order already made for the making of periodical payments to an applicant.[366] The court exercises this power by making a new order, which it is convenient to call a variation order. On the other hand, apart from

[359] s.5(1).
[360] s.5(3).
[361] s.5(1). For instances see *Re Besterman* [1984] Ch.458 (£75,000 capital for widow to buy house and £11,500 income for her maintenance); *Stead v Stead* (1985) 6 F.L.R. 16.
[362] s.5(1) see *Re Ralphs* [1968] 1 W.L.R. 1522, 1524 (interim order directed payment of £10 per week to widow, to be brought into account against income to which entitled under will).
[363] s.5(2); see above, paras 8–101 et seq. The provisions as to periodical payments in ss.2(2) and (3) are also applicable.
[364] s.5(4).
[365] s.20(2).
[366] This power to vary applies to a periodical payments order made under the 1938 or 1965 Act, as well as one made under the 1975 Act s.26(4): see *Re Fricker* (1981) 11 Fam. Law 188.

its power to vary the instalments by which a lump sum has been made payable,[367] the court has no power to vary an order making any other form of provision for an applicant. This is in the interests of finality.

1. The relevant property

A variation order may affect only "relevant property."[368] There are two alternatives to consider: **8–110**

(i) The variation order is made *before* the periodical payments have ceased to be payable under the original order. In that case the relevant property means property the income of which is applicable wholly or in part for the making of the periodical payments at the date of the variation order.[369] The extent of this property depends on the terms of the original order. For instance, the original order may have directed part of the deceased's net estate to be set aside or appropriated and the periodical payments made out of its income: in that case the relevant property is that part of the deceased's net estate which has been set aside or appropriated.

(ii) The variation order is made *after* the periodical payments have ceased to be payable under the original order, i.e. after the occurrence of a terminating event specified in the original order[370] (e.g. the death of the applicant), or after the expiration of the period of payment so specified (e.g. the period during which the applicant was receiving full-time instruction at an educational establishment). In that case the relevant property means property the income of which was applicable wholly or in part for the making of periodical payments immediately before the occurrence of that event or the expiration of that period.[371] But this alternative applies only if application for a variation order is made within six months from the date of the occurrence of that event[372] or the expiration of that period.[373]

This rule—that a variation order may affect only relevant property—imposes a time limit beyond which a variation order either cannot be made (in alternative (i)), or cannot be applied for (in alternative (ii)).

2. Applicants for variation order

Any of the following persons may apply for a variation order: **8–111**

[367] See above, para.8–94.

[368] s.6(6).

[369] s.6(6)(a).

[370] Other than the formation of a subsequent marriage or civil partnership by a former spouse or former civil partner, s.6(3): for the meaning of former spouse and former civil partner see above, s.25(1) and para.8–43.

[371] s.6(6)(b).

[372] Other than the formation of a subsequent marriage or civil partnership by a former spouse or former civil partner, s.6(3): the remarriage of a judicially separated spouse is not referred to in s.6(3), though it is in s.19(2).

[373] s.6(3).

(a) a person who either did apply (whether successfully or not), or would but for the time limit have been entitled to apply, for an original order[374];
(b) the deceased's personal representatives;
(c) the trustees of any relevant property; and
(d) any beneficiary[375] of the deceased's estate.[376]

The applicant to whom the periodical payments are payable under the original order may apply for a variation order under category (a): such a person is referred to as "the original recipient".

3. Powers of the court

8–112 In exercising its powers the court must have regard to all the circumstances of the case, including any change affecting any of the general and particular guidelines which were applicable when the original order was made.[377]

By making a variation order the court may vary or discharge the original order, or suspend any provision of it temporarily, or revive the operation of any suspended provision.[378] The court may also provide for the making of periodical payments after the occurrence of a terminating event specified in the original order (other than the formation of a subsequent marriage or civil partnership by a former spouse or former civil partner) or after the expiration of a period so specified.[379]

8–113 Instead of (or in addition to) ordering periodical payments to be made, a variation order may direct the payment of a lump sum or the transfer of all or a specified part of the relevant property.[380] Moreover, a variation order is not restricted to making provision for the original recipient: it may provide for any person who either applied (whether successfully or not), or would but for the time limit have been entitled to apply, for an original order.[381] But, whatever new provision is ordered, a variation order may affect only the relevant property.[382]

Prior to the variation order the periodical payments may already have ceased to be payable to the original recipient: in that case any new provision made by the variation order cuts down the interest of the beneficiaries

[374] s.6(5)(a): see also s.26(4) for an order made under the 1938 or 1965 Act. If an application is made by one applicant and an order for periodical payments is made, a second applicant, who is out of time, can apply for its variation.
[375] i.e. a person beneficially interested under the deceased's will or on intestacy, or a person who takes under a statutory nomination or a *donatio mortis causa* made by the deceased, s.25(1).
[376] s.6(5).
[377] s.6(7): see also s.26(4) for an order made under the 1938 or 1965 Act.
[378] s.6(1): for the power to give consequential directions see s.6(8).
[379] s.6(10): for the meaning of former spouse and former civil partner see s.25(1) and para.8–43, above. The remarriage of a judicially separated spouse is not referred to in s.6(10), though it is in s.19(2).
[380] s.6(2): see also s.6(9).
[381] s.6(2).
[382] s.6(2) and (6).

in the relevant property. On the other hand, if the periodical payments had not ceased to be payable to the original recipient but the variation order makes new provision for another person, both the original recipient and the beneficiaries may be adversely affected.

4. Subsequent variation

The court has power subsequently to vary a variation order in so far as it provides for the making of periodical payments. **8–114**

IX. PREVENTION OF EVASION

1. Methods of evasion

Under the 1938 Act the court could order provision to be made for an applicant out of the deceased's net estate.[383] In order to avoid the Act, a person only needed to reduce the value of his net estate at his death—the smaller the value of his net estate, the less the provision which could be ordered by the court. There were essentially two methods of reducing the value of his net estate at his death: **8–115**

(a) *Reduction by the deceased of the property of which he had power to dispose by his will*

This could be done by means of dispositions made during his lifetime. **8–116**

(b) *Increase by the deceased of the debts and liabilities payable out of his estate on his death*

This could be done by means of contracts made during his lifetime. For instance, he might enter into a contract by deed with a "donee" to pay to the donee at his own death a sum of money large enough to exhaust his assets. Alternatively, he might enter into a contract with the "donee" to leave by his will a particular asset, or a pecuniary legacy, to the donee. **8–117**

2. Anti-evasion orders

The 1975 Act confers powers on the court in order to stop the evasion of just claims for provision by either of the methods outlined above. An applicant, who applies to the court for an order making provision for him, may also apply in the same proceedings for an anti-evasion order **8–118**

[383] Under the 1938 Act (and also the 1965 Act) the deceased's net estate meant all the property of which the deceased had power to dispose by his will (except by virtue of a special power of appointment) less the amount of his funeral, testamentary and administration expenses, debts and liabilities and estate duty (or capital transfer tax) payable out of his estate on his death, 1938 Act s.5(1) and 1965 Act s.26(6).

compelling the "donee" under such a disposition or contract to provide money or other property for the purpose of making financial provision for the applicant.[384] Such an anti-evasion order may also be made against the donee's personal representative or a trustee.

Before the court may make an anti-evasion order the court must be satisfied on four matters.[385]

3. Four requirements for the making of an anti-evasion order

(a) *Disposition or contract made by the deceased*

8–119 First, a disposition or contract must have been made by the deceased after the Act came into force: the Act does not apply to any disposition or contract made before 1 April 1976.[386]

8–120 **(i) Disposition.** A disposition means any inter vivos disposition of property made by the deceased, except an appointment made under aspecial power of appointment.[387] In Clifford v Tanner[388] the deceased owned a house in which he and his (second) wife lived. In 1977, the deceased transferred the title to the house to his daughter by his first marriage,[389] but subject to a covenant by the daughter to permit the deceased and his wife to continue living in the house for the rest of their lives. In June 1983, the deceased began divorce proceedings and in July he released his daughter from her covenant to permit his wife to live in the house. He died in September. The Court of Appeal held that the release, by the deceased, of his daughter from the covenant to permit her stepmother to live in the house (effectively, until the stepmother's death) was a disposition. The deceased was giving up a valuable right.

8–121 **(ii) Contract.** The Act applies to any contract by which the deceased agreed either to leave by his will a sum of money or other property to any person, or by which he agreed that a sum of money or other property would be paid or transferred to any person out of his estate.[390]

[384] ss.10–13: an application for such an order against a donee cannot be made in proceedings for variation of a periodical payments order. If an application for an anti-evasion order is made in relation to a disposition, the donee under that disposition (or his personal representative) or any applicant for provision may seek an anti-evasion order in relation to any other disposition made by the deceased, ss.10(5) and 12(4). See generally Sherrin [1978] Conv. 13. For an Australian case, see *Barns v Barns* [2005] W.T.L.R. 1093.

[385] ss.10(2) and 11(2).

[386] ss.10(8), 11(6) and 27(3).

[387] But neither a statutory nomination nor a *donatio mortis causa* constitutes a disposition, s.10(7).

[388] [1987] C.L.Y. 3881.

[389] This *may* (depending on the size of his estate) have been a tax-effective move, as it was effected during the capital transfer tax regime; see Chap.16.

[390] s.11(2)(a). See above paras 6–01 et seq.

A disposition must have been made less than six years before the deceased's death[391] but no such time limit is applicable to a contract. It follows that a disposition (but not a contract) made at least six years before death remains an effective means of avoiding the 1975 Act. For example, a settlement made at least six years before death effectively avoids the 1975 Act even though the settlor retains for himself both the income from the settled property until his death and a special power of appointment exercisable by deed or will over the settled property.[392]

(b) *Intention of defeating an application for provision*

Second, the deceased must have made the disposition or contract with the intention of defeating an application for financial provision under the Act.[393] This requirement is satisfied if the court is of the opinion that, on a balance of probabilities, the deceased's intention—though not necessarily his sole intention—was to prevent an order for financial provision being made or to reduce the amount of the provision which might otherwise be ordered.[394] **8–122**

A special rule applies to a contract made by the deceased for which no valuable consideration was provided by any person, e.g. a contract by deed or a contract where the only consideration provided was marriage or a promise of marriage, which is not valuable consideration for this purpose.[395] In that case a rebuttable presumption arises that the deceased made the contract with the required intention of defeating an application for financial provision under the Act.[396]

(c) *Full valuable consideration not given*

The third requirement is that full valuable consideration for the disposition or contract must not have been given by the "donee" or any other person.[397] "The donee" means the person to whom the disposition, or with whom the contract, was made or for whose benefit the disposition, or contract, was made.[398] Marriage or a promise of marriage is not regarded as valuable consideration for this purpose.[399] **8–123**

391 s.10(2)(a). See Law Com. No61, para.211 (which recommended this time limit so that the court would not need "to investigate a man's intentions at remote periods of time") and cf. para.237 (no time limit for contract).

392 Though such a settlement may not be very attractive from the tax viewpoint (looked at both in terms of income tax and inheritance tax), see Chap.16. For special powers see definition of net estate in s.25(1) and definition of disposition in s.10(7). But for the position at common law see *Cadogan v Cadogan* [1977] 1 W.L.R. 1041.

393 ss.10(2) and 11(2)(b).

394 s.12(1): and see *Hanbury v Hanbury* [1999] 2 F.L.R. 255.

395 s.25(1).

396 s.12(2).

397 ss.10(2)(b) and 11(2)(c): s.11(2)(c) provides that when the contract was made, full valuable consideration for that contract must not have been "given or promised" by the donee or any other person. See, e.g. *Re Dawkins* (1986) 7 F.L.R. 360, below, para.8–127.

398 s.10(2)(b).

399 s.25(1).

(d) *Facilitates financial provision for applicant*

8–124 The last requirement is that an anti-evasion order would facilitate the making of financial provision for the applicant.[400]

A disposition is widely defined in the first requirement but the second and third requirements are demanding and very much restrict the number of dispositions open to review after the deceased's death. The class of contracts is narrowly defined in the first requirement and is further restricted by the second and third requirements.

4. Anti-evasion order against the donee

8–125 If the court is satisfied as to these four requirements, the court in the exercise of its discretion may make an anti-evasion order against the donee. In deciding what order (if any) to make the court must have regard to the circumstances in which the disposition or contract was made, any valuable consideration which was given for the disposition, the relationship (if any) of the donee to the deceased, the conduct and financial resources of the donee and all the other circumstances of the case.[401]

(a) *Donee under a disposition*

8–126 The court may order the donee under a disposition to provide a specified sum of money or other property for the purpose of making financial provision for the applicant.[402] But the amount of the sum of money, or the value of the property, which the donee is ordered to provide must not exceed the statutory limit on the donee's liability. This statutory limit is:

(i) if the disposition consisted of the payment of money to or for the benefit of the donee, the amount of the payment made by the deceased *less* any inheritance tax borne by the donee in respect of the payment[403];

(ii) if the disposition consisted of the transfer of other property to or for the benefit of the donee, the value at the deceased's death of such property *less* any inheritance tax borne by the donee in respect of the transfer.[404]

8–127 *Re Dawkins*[405] is an example of a disposition by the transfer of property. The deceased died insolvent having sold his house worth £27,000 to the

400 ss.10(2)(c) and 11(2)(d).

401 ss.10(6) and 11(4): valuable consideration does not include marriage or a promise of marriage, s.25(1). For the effect of valuable consideration given for the contract see below, para.8–128.

402 s.10(2).

403 s.10(3). If any such inheritance tax is repaid in consequence of the order it forms part of the deceased's net estate, Inheritance Tax Act 1984, s.146(1)–(3), (5) and (7).

404 s.10(4); if such property has been disposed of, the value is taken at the date of disposal and not at the deceased's death, ibid. As to inheritance tax, see above, fn.403.

405 *Re Dawkins* (1986) 7 F.L.R. 360.

daughter of his previous marriage for £100. He did this 15 months before his death with the intention of defeating an application under the 1975 Act. His second wife applied under the 1975 Act and the court ordered the daughter to provide £10,000 for the purpose of providing a lump sum for the applicant.

The donee does not escape liability if, before the deceased's death, he spends all the money paid to him, or the proceeds of sale of other property transferred to him, by the deceased.[406] However, in deciding what order (if any) to make, the court has to consider the donee's financial resources and the court is unlikely to make any order against a donee who has meagre financial resources when the application is heard.

(b) *Donee under a contract*

By the time the application is heard the deceased's personal representatives may already have paid or transferred money or other property to or for the benefit of the donee in accordance with the contract. If so, the court may order the donee to provide a specified sum of money or other property for the purpose of making financial provision for the applicant.[407] The court may also order the personal representatives to make no, or no further, payment or transfer of property or only a reduced payment or transfer[408]: of course, such an order increases the value of the deceased's net estate from which provision may be directed for the applicant. **8–128**

Again there is a statutory limit. The court may exercise its powers only to the extent of the gift element in the contract, i.e. to the extent that the court considers that the amount of any money or the value of any property payable or transferable in accordance with the contract exceeds the value of any valuable consideration given or to be given for the contract.[409]

If the personal representatives have reason to believe that the deceased entered into such a contract with the intention of defeating an application for financial provision under the Act, the personal representatives have power to postpone the payment or transfer of money or property under the contract until the six months' time limit for the making of an application has expired or until any application made within that time limit has been determined.[410]

(c) *Consequential directions*

The court has a wide power to give consequential directions for the purpose of giving effect to its order or securing a fair adjustment of the rights of the persons affected by it.[411] **8–129**

406 s.10(2).
407 s.11(2).
408 s.11(2).
409 s.11(3): property must be valued as at the date of the hearing, ibid.
410 s.20(3).
411 ss.11(5) and 12(3).

5. Anti-evasion order against donee's personal representatives

8–130 If the donee has died, the court may make an order against the donee's personal representatives. The court must not, however, make an order in respect of any property forming part of the donee's estate which has been distributed by the personal representatives.[412]

6. Anti-evasion order against trustees

8–131 The deceased may have settled property less than six years before his death with the intention of defeating an application for financial provision under the Act: in that case an order may be made against the trustees for the time being of the settlement in respect of the disposition to the original trustees.[413] But any order against a trustee (whether or not he was an original trustee under the disposition) is subject to a special limit. A trustee is liable only to the extent of the value of the relevant assets in his hands at the date of the order, i.e. the assets which consist of, or represent or are derived from, the money or other property paid or transferred under the disposition.[414] Similar provisions apply in respect of any payment made or property transferred to trustees in accordance with a contract made by the deceased.[415]

[412] s.12(4): the donee's personal representative is not liable for having distributed before he has notice of the making of an application on the ground that he ought to have taken into account the possibility that such an application would be made.
[413] ss.13(1) and (3).
[414] s.13(1): a trustee is not liable for having distributed on the ground that he ought to have taken into account the possibility that such an application would be made, s.13(2).
[415] s.13.

CHAPTER 9

THE CONTENTS OF A WILL

I. A WILL PRECEDENT

The reader may find it helpful at this point to look at a specimen will.[1] **9–01**

THIS IS THE LAST WILL AND TESTAMENT of me EDWARD BURTENSHAW of 1 Sugden Street St. Leonards East Sussex journalist and author

1. I HEREBY REVOKE all former wills codicils and testamentary dispositions made by me

2. I DESIRE that my body may be buried

3. I APPOINT my wife Sophia Burtenshaw ("Sophia") to be the sole executrix and trustee of this my will but if she shall die in my lifetime or before proving this my will or shall renounce probate or for any reason be unable or unwilling to act then **I APPOINT** my brother Henry Richard Burtenshaw ("Henry") of 2 Copley Street Lyndhurst Hampshire and my son Frank Burtenshaw ("Frank") of 3 Smith Street Birkenhead Merseyside to be the executors and trustees of this my will in her place and they or my said wife or other the trustee or trustees for the time being of this my will are hereinafter referred to as "my Trustees"

4. IN the event of Sophia dying in my lifetime **I APPOINT** Henry to be the guardian of my minor children.

5. I GIVE (free of all duties and taxes) the following specific bequests absolutely:-

(a) To my godson Stephen Lushington of 4 Rolfe Avenue Cranworth Norfolk my collection of stamps together with all albums catalogues accessories loose stamp covers and other material relating to it

(b) To my goddaughter Caroline Wilde of 5 Thomas Street Truro

[1] All persons and places referred to in the will are, of course, fictitious.

Cornwall my late mother's diamond engagement ring and my mahogany framed Speed map of the County of Cornwall.

6. I GIVE (free of all duties and taxes) to Frank absolutely all my ordinary shares now standing in my name in Chancellors Limited and I declare that if at my death the said shares shall by virtue of any amalgamation reconstruction or reorganisation of the capital of the said company's business be represented by a different capital holding to which I am entitled or which I possess at my death then the said bequest shall take effect as if it had been a bequest of the capital holding or holdings which took the place of such shares.

7. I GIVE to my daughter Henrietta Brougham ("Henrietta") of Vaux Hall Bedfordshire the sum of Ten thousand pounds (£10,000) to be paid out of the money standing to my credit at the Caldecote Building Society at the date of my death and I declare that if this money shall be insufficient the balance of the said sum shall be paid out of my residue (as hereinafter defined).

8. I GIVE (free of all duties and taxes) the following pecuniary legacies absolutely:-

(a) To Henry the sum of Two thousand pounds (£2,000) if he acts as an executor and trustee hereof
(b) To Frank the sum of Four thousand pounds (£4,000) whether or not he acts as an executor and trustee hereof
(c) To the Retired Barbers' Benevolent Association of Sweeney Street Todley West Yorkshire the sum of Four thousand pounds (£4,000) (in memory of my late father) for its general charitable purposes and I declare that the receipt of the person who is or professes to be the treasurer or other proper officer for the time being thereof shall be a full and sufficient discharge to my Trustees

9. I GIVE (free of all duties and taxes) the freehold dwellinghouse and premises situate and known as The Thatched Cottage Wood Lane Hatherley Gloucestershire in which my sister Augusta Burtenshaw ("Augusta") is now living (or such other freehold or leasehold dwelling-house bungalow or flat owned by me in which Augusta is living at the date of my death) to Augusta absolutely provided that she shall still be living there at the date of my death

10. (a) **I GIVE** to my daughter Charlotte Burtenshaw ("Charlotte") of 1 Sugden Street St Leonards aforesaid for her life an annuity of Ten thousand pounds (£10,000) free of income tax at the basic rate payable by quarterly instalments from such date as my Trustees may decide but not later than six months from my death and then it shall accrue from day to day

(b) My Trustees may provide for this gift

(i) by appropriating a fund of such part of my residue (as hereinafter defined) as they consider appropriate to meet the cost; or
(ii) by buying an annuity of the equivalent amount from a reputable insurance company or public company; or
(iii) with the written consent of my daughter Charlotte by commuting it for a capital payment out of my residue.

(c) If my Trustees provide for this gift as mentioned in paragraph (i) of sub-clause (b) above then
(i) the powers of investment given to my Trustees by this will shall apply to the fund;
(ii) the rest of my estate shall be exonerated from the claims of Charlotte;
(iii) if the income of the fund is insufficient to meet the annuity my Trustees may resort to the capital thereof;
(iv) any excess income from the fund shall be applied as income of my residue; and
(v) after Charlotte's death the fund shall form part of my residue.

11. IN EXERCISE of the power of appointment conferred upon me by a Settlement made on the first day of July 1970 by my late grandfather Orlando Bridgeman ("the Bridgeman Settlement") **I HEREBY DIRECT** that the trustees of the Bridgeman Settlement shall stand possessed of the property subject at the date of my death to the trusts thereof upon trust for such of my children as shall be living at my death and if more than one in equal shares absolutely

12. SUBJECT as aforesaid **I GIVE** all my property whatsoever and wheresoever to Sophia absolutely if she shall be living on the twenty-eighth day after the date of my death

13. IF Sophia shall not be living on the said twenty-eighth day or if the gift to her in the preceding clause hereof shall lapse or for any reason fail to take effect then subject as aforesaid **I GIVE** all my property whatsoever and wheresoever to my Trustees **UPON TRUST** for sale (with full power to postpone) **AND I DIRECT** that my Trustees shall hold such property and the proceeds of sale thereof **UPON TRUST** to pay my debts and funeral and testamentary expenses and legacies and taxes payable in respect of my estate by reason of my death (including taxes on gifts made free of tax) and subject thereto to hold the same (hereinafter called "my residue") **IN TRUST** for such of them my children Frank Henrietta and Charlotte as shall survive me and attain the age of twenty-one years and if more than one in equal shares absolutely **PROVIDED ALWAYS** that if any of them Frank Henrietta and Charlotte shall die (whether or not in my own lifetime) before attaining a vested interest but leaving issue living at my death or born thereafter who attain the age of twenty-one years such issue shall take per stirpes and if more than one equally between them the share of my residue which Frank Henrietta or Charlotte would have taken had he or she survived me and attained a vested interest.

14. IF the trusts declared above shall fail or determine then subject to the trusts powers and provisions declared and contained in this will and to the powers by law vested in my Trustees and to every or any exercise of such powers my Trustees shall hold my residue **IN TRUST** for such of my nephews and nieces as shall be living at the date of such failure or determination and attain the age of twenty-one years and if more than one in equal shares absolutely

(N.B. At this point in a will, there would usually follow a clause containing a range of administrative provisions. Since the enactment of the Trustee Act 2000, many of the provisions which would previously have been inserted as a matter of routine will not be required, although in practice they may well still be included.)[2]

IN WITNESS whereof I have set my hand to this my will this

(day) of *(month)* Two thousand and eight

SIGNED by the said)
EDWARD BURTENSHAW SUGDEN)
as and for his last Will and)
Testament in the presence of)
us both present at the same) *(testator's signature)*
time who at his request)
in his presence and in)
the presence of each other)
have hereunto subscribed our)
names as witnesses:-)
(The two witnesses' signatures, addresses and occupations)

II. THE CONTENTS OF THE WILL

9–02 The will starts with a commencement which identifies the nature of the document.[3] This is not essential to its validity, but it obviously helps to make it clear that the testator knows, when he executes it, that this is his will.[4]

Clause 1 of the will is a revocation clause. It does not revoke a statutory nomination made by the testator.[5] If the testator has foreign property which is disposed of by a foreign will, this general revocation clause is not appropriate.[6]

[2] These provisions are outside the scope of this book. For trustee investments and powers of maintenance and advancement under ss.31 and 32 of the Trustee Act 1925, see Hanbury and Martin, *Modern Equity*, 20th edn (London: Sweet & Maxwell, 2015), Chaps 19 and 21.
[3] See above, paras 3–01 et seq.
[4] See above, paras 5–04 et seq.
[5] See above, paras 1–06 et seq.
[6] For further discussion of revocation, see Chap.7, paras 7–01 et seq.

This will is not made by someone contemplating marriage. If it were made in contemplation of marriage, and the testator wished to insert a declaration that it was not to be revoked by his marriage, such a declaration would be inserted at this point, after the revocation clause.[7]

Clause 2 is an expression of the testator's wishes as to the disposal of his body.[8] If a deceased has expressed wishes during his lifetime as to the disposal of his body, either in his will or otherwise, these wishes are generally not legally enforceable against his personal representatives, although they may well have effective moral force. For instance, wishes expressed in favour of, or against, cremation have moral, but not legal, force.[9] In any case, there is always the danger that the testator's will may not be read until after his funeral. A testator who has strong views as to the disposal of his body should, therefore, make these views widely known in his lifetime. **9–03**

The law recognises no property in the dead body of a human being.[10] It follows that a testator cannot by will dispose of his dead body[11]; and a direction in a will to the executors to deliver the testator's dead body to another person is void.[12] The executors are entitled to the custody and possession of the testator's dead body until it is buried,[13] and the duty of disposing of the body falls primarily on them,[14] at any rate if the testator leaves assets sufficient for this purpose.[15]

A testator needs to ensure that his wishes as to the disposal of his body are quickly brought to the notice of the person in possession of it after his death: indeed minutes count if his body is to be used for the purposes of a transplant. If he merely expresses his wishes in his will, there is a danger that no one will read it and learn of his wishes until after his funeral, particularly if the will is deposited for safe custody with a solicitor or bank. If the testator is unwilling to make his wishes known openly in his lifetime,

[7] For further discussion of revocation by marriage, see Chap.7, paras 7–03 et seq.

[8] See [2000] Conv. 517 (R. N. Nwabueze) for an article considering the nature of rights acquired by the purchaser of a grave space.

[9] Until 1965, reg.4 of the Cremation Regulations 1930 (S.R. & O. 1930 No.1016) made it unlawful to cremate the remains of any person who was known to have left a written direction to the contrary: this was revoked by the Cremation Regulations 1965 (SI 1965/1146), reg.7(a).

[10] *Buchanan v Milton* [1999] 2 F.L.R. 844. But see *R v Kelly* [1999] Q.B. 621 (the "no property rule" applies only to a corpse in its natural state, and not if it has acquired different attributes by virtue of preservation techniques).

[11] For a critical examination of the present position, and a suggestion that the law should be amended so that burial instructions given by the deceased should be legally binding, see H. Conway (2003) 23 L.S. 423.

[12] *Williams v Williams* (1882) 20 Ch.D. 659.

[13] *Dobson v North Tyneside Health Authority* [1997] 1W.L.R. 596. For a dispute as to the place of disposal of the ashes of a dead child, see *Fessi v Whitmore* [1999] 1 F.L.R. 767 (the issue was dealt with as if it were a dispute between two trustees, rather than the giving of directions as to the administration of an estate).

[14] But see *Lewisham Hospital NHS Trust v Hamuth* [2007] W.T.L.R. 309. (Dispute as to validity of will and, therefore, as to whether executor validly appointed. Impossible to resolve dispute within reasonable timescale, so hospital, as having lawful possession of body, given responsibility for deciding on its disposal.)

[15] *Rees v Hughes* [1946] K.B. 517, 524, 528. For the payment of funeral expenses see below, paras 21–09 et seq.

he needs to inform his executors and any persons who are likely to be with him at his death that his will contains these wishes. Alternatively he can express these wishes in a letter left with his executors and to be opened immediately after his death.[16] The Human Tissue Act 2004[17] provides that the use of a body, or the removed organs of a person, for transplantation is lawful if done with "appropriate consent"[18] and, in the case of an adult, this means his or her consent. Under s.4 of the Act a living adult may nominate a person or persons to give or refuse consent after his death, and where the deceased has not indicated his own wishes before his death, and has not nominated someone else to speak for him after death, the decision may then be taken by someone who stood in a "qualifying relationship" to him.

9–04 **Clause 3** is the appointment of executors and trustees. Executors are considered further in Chapter 17. The definition of "my Trustees" is inserted to ensure that any powers conferred by the will on "my Trustees" are not construed as personal to the original trustees. If the will contained only immediate absolute gifts, there would be no need to appoint trustees. If a bank is to be appointed, the bank will supply its current recommended form of appointment for use by the draftsman. If a bank, or a professional person, is to be appointed, it was, until the enactment of s.29 of the Trustee Act 2000, necessary to insert in the will provision for remuneration. This is no longer necessary,[19] but because of the limitations of s.29 most will draftsmen still include a charging clause.

If the testator's wife predeceases him, **Clause 4** appoints a testamentary guardian for the testator's minor children.[20] The law in relation to guardianship was modified and simplified by the Children Act 1989[21] A parent who has parental responsibility for his child may appoint another individual to be the child's guardian in the event of his death[22]; and a guardian may appoint someone else to take his place in the event of his own death[23]; *but* the guardian's appointment normally takes effect only when the child no longer has a parent who has parental responsibility for him.[24] In other words, the first parent to die may appoint a guardian, but the appoint-

[16] The NHS maintain an Organ Donor Register and would-be donors are urged to apply for registration.

[17] It has been suggested that the Human Tissue Act 2004 was "forced into service" as a result of unauthorised retention of tissues following post-mortem examination and that the rules covering transplantation are now less satisfactory than they might be. See Mason and McCall-Smith, *Law and Medical Ethics*, 8th edn (Oxford: Oxford University Press, 2010), pp.493–494.

[18] Human Tissue Act 2004 s.3.

[19] Trustee Act 2000 s.29 provides for the "reasonable remuneration" of trustees and personal representatives who are acting in a professional capacity.

[20] Including children born after the date of the will. For a general account of the appointment of testamentary guardians, see *Cretney's Principles of Family Law* edited by J. Masson et al, 8th edn (London: Sweet & Maxwell, 2008), paras 17–041 et seq.

[21] The Act followed the Law Commission's Report, Law Com. No.172 (1988); *Family Law, Review of Child Law, Guardianship and Custody*.

[22] Children Act 1989 s.5(3).

[23] Children Act 1989 s.5(4).

[24] Children Act 1989 s.5(8).

ment is effective only on the death of the second parent.[25] The appointment of a guardian may be made by will or in writing, signed and dated.[26] If an appointment is by will, it is revoked by revocation of the will[27] but an appointment by will is also revoked by a later written appointment.[28]

Clauses 5—14 contain the will's dispositive provisions, i.e. who is to inherit what property. **9–05**

Clause 5 contains a number of specific legacies or specific bequests; the terms "legacy" and "bequest" are interchangeable.

The classification of legacies as specific, general or demonstrative is discussed in Pt III B of this chapter. The different effects which follow from the classification are discussed in Pt III C.[29]

Clause 6 contains a specific legacy of shares. This specific legacy contains a provision designed to prevent ademption if, for instance, there is a reconstruction of the company's share capital or if the company is subject to a take-over before the testator's death. Ademption is discussed in Pt III C of this chapter and in Chapter 14. A direction designed to prevent ademption can give rise to difficulties in identifying which assets represent the original shares at the testator's death, but the omission of such a direction could amount to professional negligence on the part of a will draftsman.[30]

Clause 7 contains a demonstrative legacy. The advantages of demonstrative legacies to the legatees are explained in Pt III C of this chapter.[31] Demonstrative legacies are not often encountered in practice.

Clause 8 contains a series of general (pecuniary) legacies. The first is conditional and the third is to a charity.

Clause 9 contains a specific devise. The distinction between legacies and devises is explained in Pt III A of this chapter, and specific devises are explained in Pt III B.[32]

Clause 10 is a gift of an annuity. Annuities are nowadays uncommon. They are less popular than they once were because they lose their value with inflation; so an annuitant gradually finds that he has less and less real income as the years pass. Annuities are discussed in further detail in Pt IV of this chapter.[33]

Clause 11 executes a testamentary power of appointment given to the testator by a settlement created by the testator's grandfather many years earlier. Settlements containing powers of appointment exercisable by beneficiaries[34] were common during the nineteenth century but are rare nowadays. The settlement referred to in this will (the Bridgeman Settlement) would be a traditional settlement, giving the testator a life interest and

[25] Before the 1989 Act came into force, the guardian normally acted jointly with the surviving parent.
[26] Children Act 1989 s.5(5). Before 1989, the appointment had to be made by *deed* or will.
[27] Children Act 1989 s.6(4).
[28] Children Act 1989 s.6(1).
[29] See paras 9–11 et seq.
[30] See Chap.15.
[31] See paras 9–11 et seq.
[32] See paras 9–06 et seq.
[33] See paras 9–18 et seq.
[34] As opposed to those which can be exercised by trustees.

then giving him a power,[35] on his death, to appoint the capital by his will[36] among a defined class of beneficiaries. In this example, the donee's children constitute the defined class. The testator has the power to select which of his children will benefit on his death, but he cannot benefit other persons. In the specimen will, the testator (as donee of the power) has chosen to benefit all his children living at his death. The exercise of testamentary powers of appointment is discussed in Pt V of this chapter.[37] The construction of powers of appointment is discussed in Chapter 11.[38]

Clause 12 is a residuary gift to the testator's widow, provided that she survives him by twenty eight days. If she does not survive him for that period, the residue passes under **Clause 13** to the testator's issue, with stirpital substitution.[39] The stirpital substitution provided for in this will is slightly different from the provision made by s.33 of the Wills Act 1837, which is discussed in Chapter 14.[40] If the will made no express provision for substitution,[41] s.33 would apply.

The final dispositive provision in the will is **Clause 14**, which will apply only if the testator is survived neither by his widow nor by any issue who survive long enough to obtain vested interests. **Clause 14** is unlikely ever to come into operation, but is designed to avoid the possibility of the testator's dying wholly or partially intestate.

After the dispositive provisions, there would usually follow a clause containing a wide range of administrative provisions; but this clause has not been reproduced here as many of these provisions are outside the scope of this book.[42]

Finally come the testimonium and attestation clauses; the formal requirements for a valid will, including points relating to attestation, were discussed in Chapter 4.

III. LEGACIES AND DEVISES

A. INTRODUCTION

9–06 Legacies in wills may be classified as being either specific, general, or demonstrative.[43] Devises may be specific or general.

In the specimen will set out above, there were specific legacies in **Clauses 5** and **6**; a demonstrative legacy in **Clause 7**; general legacies in

[35] He would be the *donee* of a *special power of appointment*.
[36] The power might have been exercisable by deed or will.
[37] See para.9–26.
[38] See paras 11–33 et seq.
[39] i.e. if a child does not survive to take his share, his issue will take in his place, etc.
[40] See paras 14–22 et seq.
[41] Section 33 applies "unless a contrary intention appears by the will".
[42] These provisions have, in any case, become less necessary since the enactment of the Trustee Act 2000.
[43] See generally *Jarman on Wills*, 8th edn (London: Sweet & Maxwell, 1951), pp.1036 et seq.

Clause 8; a specific devise in **Clause 9**; and **Clauses 12—14** contained alternative gifts of residue.

Legacies (or bequests) are gifts of personal or moveable property. Devises are gifts of real property. Real property (or realty) is freehold land and certain rights in land. Leaseholds are personalty, but because of their kinship with realty they are sometimes known as "chattels real".[44] Sometimes the word "legacy" is used loosely to mean any gift by will, i.e. to include a devise; but this usage is not followed here. The term "gift" can cover both legacies and devises; and "I give" is quite legitimate shorthand for "I bequeath" or "I devise" or "I devise and bequeath". The expression "I give" is used in the specimen will.

B. CLASSIFICATION OF LEGACIES AND DEVISES

1. Specific legacies

A specific legacy is a gift by will of specified personal estate: e.g. "my collection of stamps" or "all my shares in Chancellors Ltd" or "my late mother's diamond engagement ring" or "my Speed map of the county of Cornwall". The item of property given: **9–07**

- (i) must itself be part of the testator's personal property, and
- (ii) must be a specified part, so that it is severed or distinguished by the testator from the general mass of his estate.[45]

If the testator uses the word "my" ("*my* shares in Chancellors Ltd"), or any other possessive word, this shows that the subject matter of the gift is itself part of the testator's property; so, too, does a reference to the acquisition by the testator of the subject of the gift, e.g. "I give to E the gold watch which my father gave me on my twenty-first birthday." The thing given may be specified in any way which distinguishes it from the remainder of his estate,[46] and it is immaterial whether the time for ascertaining it is the date of the will ("the cars which I own at the date of my will") or the date of death ("the cars which I own at the date of my death").[47]

[44] The distinction between real property and personal property is not of great significance since 1925 and the terminology is not always strictly adhered to: but leaseholds are personalty, while incorporeal hereditaments, such as easements, are realty: see Megarry & Wade, *The Law of Real Property*, 8th edn (London: Sweet & Maxwell, 2012), paras 1–011—1–013.

[45] *Bothamley v Sherson* (1875) LR 20 Eq. 304 (a gift of "all my shares or stock in the Midland Railway Company" held specific: a specific legacy must be "what has been sometimes called a severed or distinguished part" of the testator's personal estate); *Robertson v Broadbent* (1883) 8 App. Cas. 812, 815; *Re Rose* [1949] Ch.78 (reviewing some of the case law).

[46] Apart from other identical things, *Re Cheadle* [1900] 2 Ch.620 (gift of "my 140 shares" in C Co.; T had 40 fully paid and 240 partly paid shares: held legatee no right to select but entitled to 140 partly paid shares): see also *Re Tetsall* [1961] 1 W.L.R. 938, 943.

[47] *Bothamley v Sherson*, above, at 309–312. For the effect of Wills Act 1837 s.24 see below, paras 12–02 et seq.

Whether a legacy is specific, general, or demonstrative depends on the construction of the particular will.[48] However, in the absence of evidence to the contrary "the court leans against specific legacies, and is inclined, if it can, to construe a legacy as general rather than specific; so that if there is any doubt it should, on the whole, be resolved in favour of the view that the legacy is general."[49] The reason for this construction is to allow gifts to take effect, rather than to fail, wherever possible. A gift of "all my shares in Chancellors Ltd" or "my 5,000 shares in Chancellors Ltd" will be a specific legacy, but a gift of "5,000 shares in Chancellors Ltd" will be a general legacy.

2. General legacies

9–08 A general legacy, or general bequest, is a gift, not of any particular thing, but of something which is to be provided out of the testator's general estate. Its subject matter may or may not form part of the testator's property at his death.

> "A general bequest may or may not be a part of the testator's property. A man who gives £100 money or £100 stock may not have either the money or the stock, in which case the testator's executors must raise the money or buy the stock; or he may have money or stock sufficient to discharge the legacy, in which case the executors would probably discharge it out of the actual money or stock. But in the case of a general legacy, it has no reference to the actual state of the testator's property, it being only supposed that the testator has sufficient property which on being realised will procure for the legatee that which is given to him."[50]

The classic example of a general legacy is a gift of a sum of money, e.g. "I give £4,000 to my son F." Of course, a gift of a sum of money may be (but in practice seldom is) specific, e.g. "I give all the money in the safe in my study to G"[51] or "I give to H the money now owing to me from J."[52]

Sometimes the term "pecuniary legacy" is used as though it were synonymous with the term "general legacy." This can be confusing. If the term "pecuniary legacy" is used without stating whether the legacy is specific, general, or demonstrative, the sense in which the term is used should be ascertained from its context.[53] The term "pecuniary legacy" is

[48] For construction (the lawyers' word for interpretation) of wills, see Chap.10.

[49] *Re Rose* [1949] Ch.78 at 82. Quaere to what extent this rule of construction may have been modified by the enactment of s.21 of the Administration of Justice Act 1982, see below, Chap.10.

[50] per Jessel MR in *Bothamley v Sherson*, above, at 308.

[51] *Lawson v Stitch* (1738) 1 Atk. 507 (legacy of sum of money in a particular bag is specific).

[52] *Ashburner v Maguire* (1786) 2 Bro.C.C. 108; *Chaworth v Beech* (1799) 4 Ves. 555; *Nelson v Carter* (1832) 5 Sim. 530; *Davies v Morgan* (1839) 1 Beav. 405. See also *Re Wedmore* [1907] 2 Ch.277 ("I forgive my child all debts due from him to me on my death" held a specific legacy—"it really is a gift to the child of what he owes"); *Commissioner of Stamp Duties v Bone* [1977] A.C. 511, 519–520.

[53] See, e.g. *Re O'Connor's W.T.* [1948] Ch.628.

used in the Administration of Estates Act 1925,[54] which provides its own wide definition of the term when used in the Act.[55]

A gift of shares in a particular company is a general legacy unless there is something to show that the testator is referring to shares belonging to him.[56]

3. Demonstrative legacies

A demonstrative legacy is a hybrid, somewhere between a specific legacy and a general legacy. It is a gift which is in its nature a general legacy, but which is directed to be satisfied primarily out of a specified fund or specified part of the testator's property.[57] Examples include "I give £10,000 to H to be paid out of the money standing to my credit at the Caldecote Building Society" or "I give £1,000 to L out of my 2ø per cent. Consols."[58] But if the gift is directed to be satisfied *only* out of the specified fund or property, it cannot be demonstrative. An essential characteristic of a demonstrative legacy is that it should operate as a general legacy so far as it cannot be satisfied out of the specified fund or property[59]; so a legacy which can be satisfied only out of a particular fund is specific. **9–09**

4. Specific devises

A specific devise is a gift by will of specified real estate: e.g. "I give to my sister Augusta the freehold dwelling-house known as The Thatched Cottage Hatherley" or "I give to M in fee simple my farm Blackacre situated near High Top in the County of Durham," or "all my farms in the County of Durham," or "such of my houses at Sutton in the County of Norfolk as L shall select."[60] As in the case of a specific legacy, the property given: **9–10**

(i) must itself be a part of the testator's real property, and
(ii) must be a specified part, so that it is severed or distinguished by the testator from the general mass of his estate.

[54] Administration of Estates Act 1925 s.33(2) and Sch.1, Pt II: see below, paras 14–53 et seq. (abatement) and below, paras 21–87 et seq. (incidence of general legacies).

[55] Administration of Estates Act 1925 s.55(1)(ix), which is quoted below, para.21–39.

[56] It used to be said that there had to be something "on the face of the will" to show (where there was doubt) that the gift was not a general legacy. This was a traditional rule of construction (or interpretation). All traditional rules of construction (unless they depend on specific statutory provisions) now need to be applied with care. Section 21 of the Administration of Justice Act 1982 confirms that wills should be given an "intentional" (and not a literal) interpretation. See below, Chap.10. The rule that a legacy should be interpreted as a general legacy should no longer be applied mechanically.

[57] per Lord Thurlow L.C. in *Ashburner v Macguire* (1786) 2 Bro.C.C. 108, 109, "a demonstrative legacy, that is, a legacy in its nature a general legacy, but where a particular fund is pointed out to satisfy it."

[58] *Kirby v Potter* (1799) 4 Ves. 748; *Re Webster* [1937] 1 All E.R. 602 (I bequeath to K the sum of £3,000 to be paid to him out of my partnership share: held a demonstrative legacy).

[59] *Re O'Connor* [1970] N.I. 159; *Re Culbertson* (1967) 62 D.L.R. (2d) 134.

[60] *Springett v Jenings* (1871) L.R. 6 Ch.App. 333, 335–336 (gift of particular property in parish of Hawkhurst to X followed by gift of "the rest of my freehold hereditaments situate in the parish of Hawkhurst" to Y: both gifts were specific devises). For the effect of the Wills Act 1837 s.24 see below, paras 12–02 et seq.

It used to be said that all devises were by their nature specific: that was a loose and inaccurate way of stating that, before 1926, specific and residuary devises ranked *pari passu* for the purpose of the payment of the testator's debts.[61] Since 1925 a general or residuary devise no longer ranks *pari passu* with a specific devise.[62]

C. EFFECTS OF CLASSIFICATION

9–11 The classification of legacies as specific, general or demonstrative—and of devises as specific or general—is important because different rules apply in relation to:

(1) ademption;
(2) abatement;
(3) income and interest; and
(4) expenses.

1. Ademption of a specific legacy or of a specific devise

9–12 Ademption occurs when a specific legacy, or a specific devise, fails because its subject matter is no longer part of the testator's property at the time of his death.[63] For example, T may make a will leaving "the gold pocket watch my father gave me on my twenty-first birthday to A" This is a specific legacy. T has identified a particular pocket watch he owned when he made his will; if it has been sold, or given away, or stolen, before his death, the gift will be adeemed and A will not get a watch.

A specific legacy or specific devise fails by ademption if its subject matter is no longer part of the testator's property at the time of his death.[64] Take, by way of example, the specific legacy of "my 4,000 shares in Marks & Spencer plc to C"; if during his lifetime the testator sells, or otherwise disposes of, his 4,000 Marks & Spencer shares, the specific legacy fails by ademption. Furthermore, it is generally said[65] that C is not entitled to receive the proceeds of sale of these shares, even if the testator set the proceeds apart so that they can be traced at his death: the subject matter of the specific legacy was the testator's 4,000 Marks & Spencer shares, not their proceeds of sale.[66]

[61] *Hensman v Fryer* (1867) 3 Ch. App. 420; *Lancefield v Iggulden* (1874) 10 Ch.App. 136.
[62] A general or a residuary devise falls within para.2 and a specific devise falls within para.6 of the statutory order of application of assets. See below, para.21–31.
[63] *Ashburner v MacGuire* (1786) 2 Bro C.C. 108.
[64] *Ashburner v MacGuire* (1786) 2 Bro C.C. 108.
[65] By the writers of textbooks on Succession.
[66] *Harrison v Jackson* (1877) 7 Ch.D. 339. It is generally stated, but the assumption behind this may be open to question. The matter is discussed further in Chap.14, see paras 14–37 et seq. In any case, the testator may make provision against ademption by e.g. a take-over; see clause 6 of the specimen will. The safe course for a testator who wishes to avoid ademption in such circumstances is to insert such a clause.

Neither a general legacy nor a demonstrative legacy fails by ademption. If the testator gives general legacies of "£4,000 to F" and "4,000 shares in Marks & Spencer to G," it is immaterial whether the testator has, at his death, £4,000 in cash, or 4,000 shares in ICI. The subject matter of a general legacy must be provided by the personal representatives out of the testator's general estate.[67] So the personal representatives may need to realise assets in order to raise the £4,000, or the money needed to buy 4,000 shares in Marks & Spencer. In *Re O'Connor's Will Trusts*[68] T by his will bequeathed to his son 10,000 preference shares in a private company. When he died, T held only 9,000 of the shares. There was a dispute as to whether the legacy should be construed as general or specific. It was held that it was a general legacy. As it was a general legacy, T's son was entitled to have 1,000 shares (making up the 10,000) purchased for him by T's personal representative within 12 months from T's death: if it was not possible to purchase them in that time, the son was entitled to be paid a sum equal to the market value of 1,000 shares as at the end of 12 months from T's death.[69]

It was said above[70] that a gift of shares in a particular company is a general legacy unless there is something to show that the testator is referring to shares belonging to him.[71] So "I give 4,000 shares in Marks & Spencer to G" is a general legacy, unless there are sufficient indications[72] that the testator intended to refer to shares belonging to him.[73] The fact that the testator, at the date of his will, held exactly 4,000 shares in Marks & Spencer has been held, by itself, not to be a sufficient indication that he intended to give the particular shares which then belonged to him. In *Re Willcocks*[74] T by her will gave her father £948 3s. 11d. Queensland 3 1/2 per cent. Inscribed Stock. At the time she made her will, T held stock of this description to this exact value. Nevertheless, in the absence of anything to indicate that T intended to give a specific legacy, the court held that this was a general legacy. T's possession of stock to that exact value might have been her motive for fixing the size of the legacy, but T might still have intended to give it in the form of a general legacy.[75] T had sold her stock before she died; so if this had been a specific legacy, it would have been adeemed. As it was held to be a general legacy, it was not adeemed and T's executor was obliged to purchase stock to the value of £948 3s. 11d and to make it over to the legatee, T's father. **9–13**

[67] For the incidence of general legacies see Chap.22.
[68] *Re O'Connors' Will Trusts* [1948] Ch.628; see also *Robinson v Addison* (1840) 2 Beav. 515.
[69] T's son may also have been entitled to interest, see below, paras 22–08 et seq.
[70] See above, para.9–08.
[71] See above, para.9–08.
[72] The traditional rule (a rule of construction, or interpretation) was that the indications had to be found in the words of the will "construed as a whole in the light of relevant circumstances". This traditional rule has now been modified by s.21 of the Administration of Justice Act 1982, which allows in evidence of the testator's intention more freely. See below Chap.10. The case law now needs to be read in the light of s.21, and it should not be applied too rigidly or too mechanically.
[73] *Re Rose* [1949] Ch.78.
[74] *Re Willcocks* [1921] 2 Ch.327: see also *Re Gage* [1934] Ch.536; *Re O'Connor's W.T.* [1948] Ch.628; *Re Rose* [1949] Ch.78.
[75] *Re Willcocks*, above, at 329.

Another case which illustrates the court's reluctance to hold that a legacy is specific is *Re Gage*[76] where the will contained the following gifts:

> "I give and bequeath to my niece Eleanor R. the sum of £1,150 5% War Loan 1929/47 stock And to Marian G. the sum of £500 New South Wales 5% stock now standing in my name."

At the time when he made his will, the testator had exactly £1,150 five per cent War Loan 1929/47 stock and had exactly £500 New South Wales five per cent Stock. He sold the War Loan before he died and the question was whether the gift of the War Loan was adeemed. The fact that the gift was of an amount of stock which corresponded exactly with the amount he owned when he made his will was not taken to be an indication of a specific legacy, but there was still a problem with the words "now standing in my name". It was held, by Clauson J, that these words qualified only the gift of the £500 New South Wales stock and not the War Loan, so the gift of the War Loan was not adeemed. The result can be justified, technically, by pointing to the capital letter "A" at the start of the word "And", which emphasises the separateness of the two legacies.[77] Although this is a rather strained interpretation which seems to be carrying the presumption that a legacy is general to its furthest limits,[78] it can be justified on the basis that it is giving effect to what the testator probably intended.

9–14 Although a general legacy is never adeemed, it may fail. Thus, in the case of a general legacy of company shares, if the company is wound up so that it no longer exists at the testator's death, the gift fails because the personal representatives can neither purchase the shares nor ascertain their market value.[79]

A demonstrative legacy is treated as a general legacy so far as it cannot be satisfied out of the specified fund or the specified part of the testator's property primarily designated for its payment. Accordingly, in the case of a demonstrative legacy of "£10,000 to Henrietta to be paid from my account with the Caldecote Building Society", if T's account with the building society is closed at the date of his death, the demonstrative legacy to Henrietta does not fail by ademption, and Henrietta is entitled to have £10,000 provided for her by the personal representatives out of T's general estate.[80]

Ademption is dealt with further in Chapter 14.

[76] *Re Gage* [1934] Ch.536.

[77] Though there was no full stop before it.

[78] Given the new approach to the interpretation of wills (see below, Chap.10), it may well be that cases like this will not be followed in future.

[79] *Re Gray* (1887) 36 Ch.D. 205 (the general legacy "fails, not because of any ademption, but because it has become utterly impossible to determine what amount of money should be set apart" (for the legatee): cf. *Re Borne* [1944] Ch.190.

[80] *Mullins v Smith* (1860) 1 Dr. & Sm. 204, 210; *Fowler v Willoughby* (1825) 2 Sim. & Stu. 354; *Vickers v Pound* (1858) 6 H.L.C. 885; *Walford v Walford* [1912] A.C. 658, 662–663; *Re Webster* (1936) 156 L.T. 128.

2. Abatement

Abatement concerns the statutory order of the application of assets towards the payment of expenses, debts and liabilities. General legacies are used to pay expenses, debts and liabilites before resort is made to specific or demonstrative legacies. **9–15**

From the legatee's point of view, it is better if a legacy is classified as general, rather than specific, if there is any question of its being adeemed, but it will be better if it is classified as specific, rather than general, if the legacy may abate. Someone who is entitled to a demonstrative legacy gets the best of both worlds.[81]

Abatement is dealt with further in Chapter 14.

3. Income and interest

A specific legacy or devise generally carries with it all the income or profits accruing from its subject matter after the death of the testator. A general or demonstrative legacy carries interest (currently) at the rate of 4 per cent per annum from the time at which it is payable, i.e. usually from the end of one year (the executor's year) after the testator's death.[82] **9–16**

Income and interest are dealt with further in Chapter 23.

4. Expenses

Unless the testator directs otherwise by his will, any expenses incurred by the personal representatives in the upkeep and preservation of the subject matter of a specific legacy or specific devise during the period between the testator's death and the assent or transfer to the beneficiary must be paid by the beneficiary. In *Re Rooke*[83] T by her will made a specific gift of her freehold house and its contents to her friend M.H.G. and the executors incurred expenses in the upkeep and preservation of the house and contents. Maugham J held that these expenses were not payable out of T's estate as part of the administration expenses but had to be paid by M.H.G. A specific legatee or devisee is entitled to the income or profits accruing from his legacy or devise from the time of T's death,[84] and so it follows that he ought also to be made liable for the upkeep and preservation of the subject matter of the specific gift from the time of the death.[85] **9–17**

[81] See above, para.9–12, and below, paras 14–54 et seq.

[82] See below, paras 22–08 et seq. The rate of interest set by the court is now in para.15 of the Practice Direction to Pt 40 of the Civil Procedure Rules 1998, it is the basic rate payable on funds in court, unless the court directs otherwise.

[83] *Re Rooke* [1933] Ch.970: see also *Re Pearce* [1909] 1 Ch.819 (expenses of upkeep, care and preservation of furniture, horses and carriages, and yacht: held payable by specific legatee); *Re Wilson* [1967] Ch.53, 65. But if T by his will gives to B such articles of furniture and personal effects as B shall select, the expenses of preservation incurred prior to B's selection are not payable by B, *Re Collins' W.T.* [1971] 1 W.L.R. 37. If a contingent specific gift does not carry intermediate income, it does not bear these expenses prior to the occurrence of the contingency, *Re Eyre* [1917] 1 Ch.351, 356.

[84] See Chap.23.

[85] *Re Rooke* [1933] Ch.970, 974.

By contrast, any expenses incurred by the personal representatives in preserving other assets, i.e. those not specifically devised or bequeathed, are payable out of the testator's estate as part of the expenses of administration and are not payable by the general or demonstrative legatees.

IV. ANNUITIES

1. Classification of annuities

9–18 An annuity given by will is a legacy of money payable by instalments or, more accurately, viewing each instalment of the annuity as a separate legacy, "a series of legacies payable at intervals."[86]

Annuities given by will may be classified under the same three heads as other legacies:

(i) *A specific annuity*, i.e. a gift of an existing annuity belonging to the testator at his death[87] (e.g. "I give to A the perpetual annuity to which I am entitled under my father's will"), or a gift of an annuity or rent charge out of specified property belonging to the testator at his death[88] (e.g. "I give to B during her life an annuity of £6,000 to be charged upon and payable exclusively out of my farm Blackacre");

(ii) *A general annuity*, i.e. a gift of an annuity to be provided out of the testator's general estate (e.g. "I give to C during her life an annuity of £10,000 to begin from my death and to be payable by equal quarterly payments"); and

(iii) *A demonstrative annuity*, i.e. a gift of an annuity which is in its nature a general annuity, but which is directed to be satisfied primarily out of a specified fund or specified part of the testator's property.[89]

9–19 Under each of these three heads, whether an annuity is payable out of the corpus or only out of the income of the relevant property depends on the proper construction of the particular will.[90]

The duration of an annuity created by a will depends on the will's proper construction.[91] If, for instance, a testator gives A, an individual, an annuity, prima facie the annuity is only for A's life.[92] If, on the other hand,

[86] *Re Earl of Berkeley* [1968] Ch.154 and 165.

[87] *Smith v Pybus* (1804) 9 Ves. 566.

[88] *Creed v Creed* (1844) 11 Cl. & F. 491; *Long v Short* (1717) 1 P.Wms. 403; cf. *Re Trenchard* [1905] 1 Ch.82: see Rentcharges Act 1977 s.2(3).

[89] *Mann v Copland* (1817) 2 Madd. 223; *Livesay v Redfern* (1836) 2 Y. & C.Ex. 90; *Paget v Huish* (1863) 1 H. & M. 663, esp. at pp.667–671; *Re Briggs* (1881) 45 L.T. 249.

[90] See generally *Theobald on Wills*, 17th edn (London: Sweet & Maxwell, 2010), paras 20–16 et seq.

[91] See generally *Hawkins on the Construction of Wills* edited by R. Kerridge, 5th edn (London: Sweet & Maxwell, 2000) pp.253 et seq.

[92] *Blewitt v Roberts* (1841) Cr. & Ph. 274, 280: see also *Nichols v Hawkes* (1853) 10 Hare 342; *Blight v Hartnoll* (1881) 19 Ch.D. 294; cf. *Townsend v Ashcroft* [1917] 2 Ch.14.

a testator gives an annuity to a corporation or an unincorporated body capable of existing for an indefinite period of time, the annuity is prima facie perpetual.[93]

The differences in the effects of specific, general, and demonstrative annuities relate to ademption and abatement. In addition, it is necessary to consider what provision personal representatives should make for the payment of general annuities, from what date annuities are payable, and whether arrears of an annuity carry interest.

2. Ademption of a specific annuity

Like any other specific legacy, a specific annuity fails by ademption if its subject matter, or the specified property out of which it is payable, has ceased to exist as part of the testator's property at his death.[94] **9–20**

By contrast, neither a general annuity nor a demonstrative annuity fails by ademption. A demonstrative annuity is treated as a general annuity so far as it cannot be satisfied out of the specified fund or specified part of the testator's property primarily designated for its payment.[95]

3. Providing for payment of general annuities

(a) *Appropriation of assets*

In the ordinary case, where a general annuity is charged on the whole income, or the whole income and corpus, of the residuary estate, the annuitant is entitled to have sufficient assets appropriated to answer the annuity as will make it practically certain that the annuity will be fully paid: subject to this being done, the practice of the court is to direct that the remainder of the residuary estate shall be distributed to the residuary beneficiaries.[96] If the appropriated assets prove insufficient, the annuitant is nevertheless entitled to follow the assets so distributed into the hands of those entitled to them, because they are still subject to the annuity.[97] **9–21**

[93] *Re Jones* [1950] 2 All E.R. 239.

[94] *Cowper v Mantell* (No. 1) (1856) 22 Beav. 223 (T made will, giving a specific annuity to A out of T's leasehold property Blackacre; later T assigned Blackacre to trustees on certain trusts: held annuity was adeemed).

[95] *Mann v Copland* (1817) 2 Madd. 223 (the annuity "may stand, though the Fund out of which it is directed to be paid does not exist"); *Attwater v Attwater* (1853) 18 Beav. 330 (T gave X an annuity "from my funded property"; it was insufficient to pay it: held deficiency must be made good from his residuary estate).

[96] *Harbin v Masterman* [1896] 1 Ch.351 (annuity payable solely out of income: fund set aside to answer annuity by its income, and remainder of residuary estate ordered to be distributed to residuary beneficiaries); *Re Parry* (1889) 42 Ch.D. 570; *Re Coller's Deed Trusts* [1939] Ch.277, 284 ("in practice, and as a matter of administration, the distribution of the corpus or the income subjected to the annuity is not held up altogether in cases where the annuitant cannot be prejudiced by a partial distribution").

[97] *Re Evans and Bettell's Contract* [1910] 2 Ch.438. For the effect of an appropriation under Administration of Estates Act 1925 s.41, see below, para.23–25, fn.60.

(b) *Direction to purchase an annuity*

9–22 An annuitant for life is generally not entitled to require the capitalised value of his annuity to be paid to him.[98] The will gives him an annuity, not a legacy of a lump sum. But if by his will T directs that an annuity be purchased for A for life, A is entitled to take the purchase-money instead of the annuity.[99] A declaration by T in his will that A shall not be allowed to accept the value of the annuity,[100] or to alienate it,[101] is ineffective unless there is a valid gift over.[102]

If A survives T, but dies before T's personal representatives purchase an annuity for him, A's personal representatives are entitled to take the purchase-money because the right to take it vested in A at T's death.[103]

4. Date from which annuities are payable

9–23 An annuity given by will begins to run from the testator's death unless the testator shows a contrary intention in his will.[104] Thus the first payment is to be made (in arrear) at the end of one year from the death, unless the annuity is directed to be paid (say) monthly, in which case the first payment is to be made at the end of one month from the death.[105]

5. Interest on arrears of an annuity

9–24 The long-standing general rule is that no interest is payable on arrears of an annuity.[106] Interest is allowed by the court only in exceptional circumstances—for instance, "where the non-payment of the annuity has been the fault of the person out of whose income it would be payable."[107] This general rule is anomalous.[108] Without legislation[109] this rule can be

98 *Wright v Callender* (1852) 2 De G.M. & G. 652.

99 *Stokes v Cheek* (1860) 28 Beav. 620, 621; *Re Brown's Wills* (1859) 27 Beav. 324 (power for trustees to apply annuity for A's benefit if ill or incapacitated).

100 *Stokes v Cheek*, above.

101 *Woodmeston v Walker* (1831) 2 Russ. & M. 197.

102 See *Hunt-Foulston v Furber* (1876) 3 Ch.D. 285; *Re Mabbett* [1891] 1 Ch.707; *Hatton v May* (1876) 3 Ch.D. 148.

103 *Re Robbins* [1907] 2 Ch 8 (A died 16 days after T: held A's personal representatives entitled to purchase-money); *Re Brunning* [1909] 1 Ch.276 (T died on 21 September 1907; T's executors made quarterly payment of annuity to A up to 20 December 1907; A died before purchase of annuity: held A's executors entitled to purchase money required to purchase annuity on 20 December 1907, plus interest from that date).

104 *Gibson v Bott* (1802) 7 Ves. 89, 96; *Re Robbins* [1907] 2 Ch.8; *Pettinger v Ambler* (1866) 35 Beav. 321 (T by will gave annuity to A to be raised out of a reversionary interest of T: held annuity was payable from T's death).

105 *Houghton v Franklin* (1822) 1 Sim. & St. 390. But see below, para.23–02.

106 *Torre v Browne* (1855) 5 H.L.Cas. 555, esp. 577–580; *Re Berkeley* [1968] Ch.744, esp. at 760–762.

107 *Re Berkeley* [1968] Ch.154, 165. Another instance of exceptional circumstances is "where the annuitant has held some legal security which, but for the interference of the court, he might have made available for the obtaining of interest," *Torre v Browne* (1855) 5 H.L. Cas. 555, p.578.

108 *Re Berkeley* [1968] Ch.154: see also *Re Hiscoe* (1902) 71 L.J.Ch.347.

109 The Law Commission has advised that no action be taken on the proposal to abolish this

altered only by the House of Lords,[110] but a testator is, of course, free to override this anomalous rule by a direction in his will that interest is to be paid on arrears of an annuity.

6. Abatement of annuities

The abatement of annuities is discussed in Chapter 14.[111] **9–25**

V. EXERCISE OF TESTAMENTARY POWERS OF APPOINTMENT[112]

By his will the testator may exercise any power of appointment conferred on him and exercisable by will.[113] For instance, the testator may under a settlement have a life interest and a power to appoint the remainder interest in the settled property by will among his children or remoter issue. An example of the exercise of a testamentary power of appointment is **Clause 11** of the specimen will above. **9–26**

The testator may exercise a testamentary power of appointment either (i) by a will made in writing and duly executed in accordance with the formalities required by the Wills Act 1837[114] or (ii) by an informal will if the testator is privileged.[115] Occasionally, the instrument creating a power of appointment by will purports to require special formalities to be observed when the power is exercised, such as three witnesses to the will instead of the two required by the Wills Act 1837. To deal with this, s.10 of the Wills Act 1837 provides that, despite this special requirement, an appointment made by a will which is in writing and duly executed in accordance with the formalities required by the Act shall be valid "so far as respects the execution and attestation thereof". Section 10 thus makes it unnecessary to observe special formalities concerning execution and attestation; but any other requirements must be observed, otherwise an appointment is void.[116] Special formalities concerning execution and attestation must, however, be observed in an informal will, to which s.10 is not applicable.

rule; the Commission ascertained that there was a strong body of informed opinion in favour of retaining the rule because to abolish it would create "a disproportionate amount of work and expense": Law Commission, 5th Annual Report (1969–70) Law Com. No.36, para.63.

110 *Re Berkeley* [1968] Ch.744, 761.

111 See below, paras 14–58 and 14–59.

112 For powers of appointment, see Hanbury and Martin, *Modern Equity*, 20th edn (London: Sweet & Maxwell, 2015), Chap.7.

113 For the rules of construction governing the exercise of powers of appointment see below, paras 11–33 et seq.

114 Wills Act 1837 s.10: see also *Re Barnett* [1908] 1 Ch.402.

115 *Re Wernher* [1918] 2 Ch.82 (general power); *Re Earl of Chichester's W.T.* [1946] Ch.289 (special power over personalty: obiter as to special power over realty).

116 *Cooper v Martin* (1867) 3 Ch.App. 47 (requirement as to time of appointment). A requirement that the consent of a specified person be obtained to the appointment must, for instance, be observed.

Chapter 10

THE RECTIFICATION AND CONSTRUCTION OF WILLS

I. RECTIFICATION AND CONSTRUCTION

Construction is the process of interpretation, of ascertaining the meaning of the words in a document, in circumstances which have given rise to controversy.[1] **10–01**

Rectification consists of correcting, of altering, the words in a document. Although it has, traditionally, been possible to rectify most documents in order to cure errors in their production, it was (for reasons which are not now clear) not possible to rectify wills until 1983, when s.20 of the Administration of Justice Act 1982 came into force.

The two processes of construction and rectification are separate, but, if there is a doubt or dispute as to the meaning of the words in a will, either, or both, of them may assist in resolving it. In their Second Programme of Law Reform, in 1968, the Law Commission recommended that the rules governing the interpretation of wills should be examined by the Law Reform Committee and the Lord Chancellor accordingly requested the Committee to consider whether (a) it was desirable to amend the law relating to the admissibility of extrinsic evidence in relation to interpretation—the construction rules—and (b) whether (given that they had none at the time) the courts should be given powers to rectify wills. In 1973 the Committee produced their Nineteenth Report on *Interpretation of Wills*[2] and in due course ss.20 and 21 of the Administration of Justice Act 1982 were enacted to implement[3] their recommendations. These sections are discussed below, but, before looking at each of them in detail, it will be helpful to consider the order in which the two topics, construction and rectification, should be taken. The order in which the topics are dealt with may, in some instances, affect the outcome of cases.[4]

[1] This word "construction" is the noun derived from the verb "to construe", and it should not, of course, be confused with the noun "construction" derived from the verb "to construct".

[2] Cmnd.5301 (1973).

[3] Or, attempt to implement.

[4] See e.g. *Re Huntley; Brooke v Purton* [2014] W.T.L.R. 745, discussed below in para.10–13.

10–02 When the Law Reform Committee were given the task of reviewing the law relating to construction and rectification, the two topics were presented to the Committee in that order. In the final paragraphs of the Introduction to their Report[5] the Committee considered whether this was logical. They noted that two main views had emerged as to which ought to come first, but, notwithstanding the form of their terms of reference, they opted for the second—rectification should come before interpretation.

> "The court should first ascertain precisely what words the testator meant, or must be taken to have meant, his will to contain; if necessary it should rectify the words admitted to probate so as to make them conform with that intention. Then, and only then, should it proceed to the task of ascertaining what those words mean, in accordance with the rules of interpretation."[6]

In a number of recent cases,[7] the courts have not adopted this approach, but have chosen to discuss interpretation before rectification, though, usually without any explanation as to why they were doing this. In some cases, the court may have been influenced by the fact that an application for rectification has to be made within six months from the date when representation with respect to the estate was first taken out,[8] there is no equivalent problem if the question is one of interpretation. Nevertheless, the Law Reform Committee's approach is logical. If there is a doubt as to what are the words which a will should contain,[9] and if that doubt can be settled by rectification, the document should be rectified, so that it contains the appropriate wording, *before* any attempt is made to interpret the words.[10]

And so, in this chapter, rectification will be discussed before interpretation.

[5] Paras 15 and 16.

[6] Para.16.

[7] See *Parkinson v Fawdon* [2010] W.T.L.R. 79; *Rainbird v Smith* [2013] W.T.L.R. 1609; *Re Huntley: Brooke v Purton* [2014] W.T.L.R. 745; *Burnard v Burnard* [2014] EWHC 340 (Ch); *Reading v Reading* [2015] W.T.L.R. 1245.

[8] The court may grant an extension, but it may, in some cases, seem simpler to avoid dealing with arguments over this and to proceed to interpretation, and then to return to rectification afterwards, saying that it does not really matter. It may seem simpler, but it is not the correct way to proceed. An example of this approach is *Burnard v Burnard* [2014] EWHC 340 (Ch), a case of a straightforward clerical error.

[9] And, so much the more so, if it is clear that the will does not contain the correct wording.

[10] In *Marley v Rawlings* [2015] A.C. 129, Lord Neuberger appeared, at para.41, to avoid dealing with the question of the order. He discussed interpretation before rectification, but the discussion of interpretation appears to have been obiter and the decision is based on rectification. The case is discussed below, see para.10–66. In *Gledhill v Arnold* [2015] EWHC 2939 (Ch) there was an application to cure a solicitor's error by interpretation and, in the alternative, by rectification. Proudman J, correctly, held that the error should be cured by rectification. This was a straightforward clerical error and it is not clear why those who were attempting to put it right thought that interpretation should be looked at first. In *Reading v Reading* [2015] W.T.L.R. 1245 Asplin J took construction before rectification and may have come to the wrong conclusion on rectification, see below para.10–14.

II. POWER OF COURT TO ALTER WORDS IN A WILL

A. OMISSION OF WORDS FROM PROBATE

If a testator died before 1983, the court had no power, when admitting the will to probate, to *add* to it words intended by the testator.[11] In this respect the court was "enslaved" by the formalities required for a will by the Wills Act 1837. A probate court had power only to *omit* from the will words of which the testator did not know and approve, leaving a blank space in the probate copy. This power was discussed in Chapter 5.[12] **10–03**

B. RECTIFICATION

1. Section 20 of the Administration of Justice Act 1982

If a testator dies on or after 1 January 1983, and if a court is satisfied that his will is so expressed that it fails to carry out his intentions, s.20 of the Administration of Justice Act 1982 empowers it to order that the will shall be rectified, provided the court is satisfied, that the failure of expression is in consequence (i) of a clerical error or (ii) of a failure to understand his instructions.[13] If the court orders rectification under s.20, it may, of course, *add* to the will words intended by the testator. **10–04**

2. Clerical errors

A clerical error is an error of a clerical nature and not an error made only by a clerk; so a testator can make a clerical error in his home-made will.[14] **10–05**

The first reported case dealing directly with the application of s.20 appears to have been *Wordingham v Royal Exchange Trust Co Ltd*.[15] The testatrix's solicitor was instructed to draft a will which was to be based on an earlier will, but was to contain some alterations. He failed to include a clause which had been included in the earlier will and which he should have included. This *was* a clerical error. Had the testatrix died before 1983, her will could not have been rectified to include the clause, but under s.20, the clause could be inserted. And a recent, straightforward, example of a

[11] *Harter v Harter* (1873) 3 P. & D. 11, 19; *Morrell v Morrell* (1882) 7 P.D. 68; *In the Goods of Schott* (1901) P. 190 ("I can strike out words, but I cannot insert anything"); *Re Horrocks* [1939] P. 198, 216 (rule is "elementary"); *In the Goods of Swords* [1952] P. 368; *Re Morris* [1971] P. 62, 75; *Re Reynette-James* [1976] 1 W.L.R. 161, 166.

[12] See paras 5–20 et seq.

[13] In the High Court rectification is assigned to the Chancery Division, Senior Courts Act 1981 s.61(1) and Sch.I.

[14] *Re Williams* [1985] 1 W.L.R. 905, 912.

[15] *Wordingham v Royal Exchange Trust Co Ltd* [1992] Ch.412.

case involving a clerical error is *Joshi v Mahida*.[16] The solicitor preparing the will should have written "my one half share" of some buildings, but wrote instead "one half of my share". This was described by the trial judge as "an inadvertent slip".[17]

10–06 In *Joshi*, the trial judge referred back to *Re Segelman*[18] where Chadwick J suggested that s.20 requires the court to examine three questions. First, what did the testator intend? Secondly, was the will so expressed that it failed to carry out the testator's intentions? And, thirdly (if there was a failure to carry out his intentions) whether it was in consequence of (i) a clerical error, or (ii) a failure to understand his instructions, or (iii) had come about for some other reason. In order to answer the first question, the court could admit extrinsic evidence[19] of the testator's intentions and the second question then became one of interpreting the terms of the will.[20]

Segelman involved a testator who died, aged 92, leaving a will which he had executed two months before his death and which contained a clause including a proviso which had been drafted by the solicitor *before* he had been given the names of some of the beneficiaries. The clause did not carry out the testator's intentions, though it was not entirely clear whether this was the result of a clerical error or a failure to understand the testator's instructions. The error by the solicitor in this case might be described as somewhere between a clerical error and a failure to understand instructions; either way, the court had a power to rectify under s.20 and the will was rectified.

10–07 *Re Martin*[21] the testatrix's professionally drawn will provided that each of her godchildren should receive a one-twentieth share of her estate, but, as drawn, it did not dispose of all her property and there seemed to be something wrong somewhere. The trial judge held that, when giving instructions, it was probable that the testatrix had used the words "one twentieth", but had intended to say "20 per-cent". He allowed an application to rectify on the basis that this was a clerical error. It is submitted that it was not a clerical error, but it could, legitimately, be described as a failure to understand the testatrix's instructions.[22]

16 *Joshi v Mahida* [2013] W.T.L.R. 859.

17 Para.25 of the judgment—the testator was in hospital and the solicitor was probably in a hurry—in fact the testator survived for some years.

18 *Re Segelman* [1996] Ch.171.

19 Evidence from outside the will.

20 In this sense, a will needs to be interpreted before it can be rectified, but this is a preliminary interpretation and, if there has been a clerical error, that should be cured before the final interpretation. See above para.10–02.

21 *Re Martin* [2007] W.T.L.R. 329.

22 The solicitor who drafted the will admitted that he had been negligent and applied to rectify the will on the basis of a clerical error. See R. Kerridge and A.H.R. Brierley (2007) 71 Conv. 558. Calling this a failure to understand instructions is slightly generous to the testatrix, but the solicitor should have noticed that her apparent instructions, by creating an intestacy, seemed not to make sense. Another case where it is dubious whether the error was "clerical" is *Pengelly v Pengelly* [2007] W.T.L.R. 1619. A straightforward case of a failure to understand instructions is *Goodman v Goodman* [2006] W.T.L.R. 1807. Straightforward clerical error cases are *Wong v Wong* [2003] W.T.L.R. 1161; *Price v Craig* [2006] W.T.L.R.1873 and *Hobart v Hobart* [2007] W.T.L.R. 1213; in all these cases the draftsmen admitted fault. Whether

A case with which caused more of a problem was *Marley v Rawlings*.[23] 10–08
The facts were simple. Mr and Mrs Rawlings made mirror wills, but, at the time of execution the wills were switched and so each executed the will intended for the other. When Mrs Rawlings died, nobody noticed, but when Mr Rawlings died it was found that he had executed the document intended for his wife and the question was whether the error could be rectified. Was this a clerical error? Proudman J avoided answering the question. She held that the will which Mr Rawlings had executed was "not his will" and that there was, therefore, a failure of due execution under s.9 of the Wills Act. The Court of Appeal agreed. But the Supreme Court, unanimously, held that this was wrong. In effect, s.20 of the Administration of Justice Act, the rectification section, trumped s.9 of the Wills Act, the section concerned with due execution. This had to be right. If it were not, rectification would almost never be possible. The sole question in this case was whether the error (and there had clearly been one) was clerical, or some other kind of error. This *was* a clerical error.[24]

Lord Neuberger, with whom the other members of the Supreme Court agreed, put it this way:

"75 I accept that the expression "clerical error" can have a narrow meaning, which would be limited to mistakes involved in copying or writing out a document, and would not include a mistake of the type that occurred in this case. However. . . the expression also can carry a wider meaning, namely a mistake arising out of office work of a relatively routine nature, such as preparing, filing, sending, organising the execution of, a document (save, possibly, to the extent that the activity involves some special expertise).. and a mistake in connection with those activities, such as wrongly filing a document or putting the wrong document in an envelope, can properly be called "a clerical error".

76. . .it seems to me that the expression "clerical error" in section 20(1)(a) should be given a wide, rather than a narrow, meaning.

80 . . .If a solicitor is drafting two wills, and accidentally cuts and pastes the contents of B's draft will onto what he thinks is A's draft will, and hands it to A, who then executes it as his will, that will would be rectifiable under section 20(1)(a) . . ."

The result is to be welcomed. And will draftsmen (most of whom are worried about making mistakes) will have heaved a collective sigh of relief that the case ended as it did.[25]

the case is classified as one concerning a "clerical error" or as a failure to understand instructions" does not matter, provided it is certain that it is one or the other.

[23] *Marley v Rawlings* [2015] A.C. 129.

[24] After the Court of Appeal had heard the case, but before it reached the Supreme Court, the editor wrote a case note, suggesting that the Court of Appeal had reached the wrong conclusion. This case note *When a husband executes his wife's will* [2012] Conv. 505 was adopted and used in argument by the successful appellants in the case. See *Marley v Rawlings* [2015] A.C. 129 at 135, 136, 138. The case note contains a detailed exposition of what constititutes a "clerical error" in this context.

[25] The amount at stake in the case itself was relatively insignificant. But this was a test case and of great significance to the legal profession. The solicitor who had allowed this error to

3. Failure to understand the testator's instructions

10–09 The concept of what is a failure to understand the testator's instructions is less likely to cause a problem than the concept of a clerical error. There are some cases where there may be argument as to whether the error in question was a clerical error, or a failure to understand instructions, and an example of this is *Re Martin*[26] mentioned above in para.10–07. But, provided that it is certain that the error was either clerical, or a failure to understand instructions, it does not matter which of the two it was.[27]

What may be more of a problem in this regard is that, where there is an allegation of a failure to understand instructions, there is more likely to be a dispute as to the facts. In *Sprackling v Sprackling*[28] the solicitor who drafted the will insisted that she had not misunderstood her instructions, Norris J held that she had. *Martin v Triggs Turner Barton*[29] was similar in that the solicitor would not concede that he had been in error.

A case where there was no dispute on the facts, but where there might be genuine room for disagreement as to whether the mistake should be categorised as a failure to understand instructions is *Re Ryan, Gerling v Gerling*.[30] Here, the draftsman, a solicitor's clerk, drew up a will which resulted in a partial intestacy. This should not have been allowed to happen, but it may be that the testatrix had no intention in this regard, and that the draftsman's failure was not to fail to understand her, but to fail to warn her that she had not thought through what she really wanted. Having said this, the purpose of s.20 is to put right what has gone wrong and, in borderline cases such as this, it does no harm to classify as a failure to understand instructions something which a purist might not choose to classify in quite this way.[31]

10–10 The reference to the draftsman's carelessness in *Ryan* leads to an examination of the relationship between rectification and negligence. This will be discussed in Chapter 15, where it will be suggested[32] that all rectification cases involving professional will draftsmen are cases where the draftsmen have been negligent. Rectification can be obtained only if there has been *either* a clerical error *or* a failure to understand the testator's instructions. A clerical error—by a person paid to draft a will—must, by definition, constitute negligence. In the same way, it is suggested that a failure by a professional will draftsman to understand a testator's instructions will also constitute negligence. It is the duty of a professional will draftsman to understand the instructions he has been given and, if he is not certain

occur had (it was conceded) been negligent. Rectification (if it is allowed) is a damage limitation exercise by the negligent will-writer.

[26] *Re Martin* [2007] W.T.L.R. 329.

[27] For errors which are neither, see below, paras 10–11 et seq.

[28] *Sprackling v Sprackling* [2009] W.T.L.R. 897

[29] *Martin v Triggs Turner Barton* [2009] W.T.L.R. 1339.

[30] *Re Ryan, Gerling v Gerling* [2011] W.T.L.R. 1029.

[31] Compare this case with *Re Martin*, discussed above in para.10–07.

[32] See paras 15–18 et seq.

about his instructions, he should seek clarification or further instructions from the testator.[33]

If a solicitor, or other professional draftsman, admits that he has made a mistake and assists in the application for rectification, he is engaged in a form of damage-limitation exercise. He will usually have to pay all the costs incurred in relation to the rectification application, but these costs will generally be significantly less than the damages and costs which he or his insurers would have had to pay to disappointed beneficiaries if the will had not been rectified. Having said this, it may be simpler for a professional will draftsman to admit that he has made a clerical error than to agree that he had not understood the testator's instructions. *Sprackling v Sprackling*[34] and *Martin v Triggs Turner Barton*[35] are both examples of cases where solicitors insisted that they had correctly understood their instructions, but were held not to have done so. A problem, for the draftsman, in this kind of case is that, if there is a suggestion that he has not understood his instructions, it may be that the would-be beneficiaries who would have benefitted under the non-rectified provisions in the will, will seek to involve themselves in the dispute, in an attempt to prevent rectification.[36]

4. Errors which are neither clerical nor involve a failure to understand the testator's instructions

Section 20 of the Administration of Justice Act permits recfication where there has been either (i) a clerical error or (ii) a failure to understand the testator's instructions. So, what other kinds of error may occur in the production of a will, whereby the wording is somehow "wrong" but cannot be rectified? **10–11**

What cannot be rectified is a drafting error, that is to say an error whereby the draftsman (and the testator) know what words are in the will, but believe that they have an effect which they do not have; what the Law Reform Committee called a "failure to appreciate the effect of the words used".[37] This type of error may, possibly, be cured by construction, but it cannot be cured by rectification. Some lawyers appear to have had a difficulty identifying the type of error which occurred in *Marley v Rawlings*, but, in the context of rectification, there are, in reality, only three sorts of error, (i) a clerical error, (ii) a failure to understand instructions and (iii) a drafting error (i.e. a failure to appreciate the effect of the words used). On this basis, the error in *Marley* was clearly clerical.[38]

[33] See para.15–18 where the suggestion made in the Court of Appeal in *Walker v Medlicott* [1999] 1 W.L.R. 727 to the effect that there can be a non-negligent rectifiable error by a professional will draftsman is said to be wrong.

[34] *Sprackling v Sprackling* [2009] W.T.L.R. 897.

[35] *Martin v Triggs Turner Barton* [2009] W.T.L.R. 1339.

[36] *Sprackling v Sprackling* above is an example of a case where not all the potential beneficiaries were enthusiastic about the suggestion that the will should be rectified.

[37] Para.22 of the Law Reform Committee's Nineteenth Report on *Interpretation of Wills*.

[38] For a more detailed discussion of the distinction between clerical errors and drafting errors, see R. Kerridge [2012] Conv. 505.

10–12 The type of case in which a drafting error is most likely to occur nowadays is one involving a would-be tax-avoidance provision. If a draftsman has inserted a provision in a will, intending it to have a particular tax outcome, and he has made no error as to the words he has used, only as to their effect, it is not possible to correct this error by altering the words, by rectification.

Kell v Jones[39] is a straightforward example of a case, where an application for rectification was disallowed on the basis that the error was one of drafting. The solicitor's error was "not inadvertent" but in his "choice of words". He made no mistake as to the words he had used and ". . .he knew what he wanted to achieve and thought, wrongly, that he was doing so."[40]

10–13 And a case where discussing construction and rectification in the wrong order may have affected the outcome is *Re Huntley, Brooke v Purton*.[41] Here a solicitor copied a clause into a will without, it appears, fully understanding the tax implications. The trial judge dealt with construction first and held that, on the basis of a "liberal" approach he could interpret the will to have the desired effect. Then, as extra support for the conclusion he wanted to reach, he held that the will could be rectified, because there had been a clerical error. It is submitted that this was wrong. The error was not a clerical error, it was a drafting error. Rectification should have been taken before construction and the application to rectify should have been dismissed. As to construction, the editor is in favour of a liberal approach[42] but even ultra liberals may think that this case takes intentonalism too far.

Reading v Reading[43] is another case where rectification and construction were taken in the wrong order and the decision on rectification is again problematic.[44] Here, the solicitor who drafted the will used the word "issue" in one clause in it, when he knew that the testator intended that not only his descendants, but also his step children and step grandchildren should have been included. Asplin J dealt with construction first and held that the wording could be interpreted in such a way as to include the step children and grandchildren. This will be discussed further below.[45] But when she then proceeded to look at rectification, she decided that this was not a clerical error. Given her decision on construction, as far as the case itself was concerned, the point did not really matter. But was she right? This is a borderline instance. The solicitor admitted that he had made a mistake. But what kind of mistake was it? That was not entirely clear. Did he insert the word "issue" knowing that he had used the word, and believing that it included the step children and grandchildren? Or did he copy a passage from a precedent book

[39] *Kell v Jones* [2013] W.T.L.R. 507.

[40] *Kell v Jones* [2013] W.T.L.R. 507 at paras 30, 38, 39.

[41] *Re Huntley, Brooke v Purton* [2014] W.T.L.R. 745.

[42] See below, Pt II of this chapter–dealing with construction.

[43] *Reading v Reading* [2015] W.T.L.R. 1245.

[44] Though, this time, in the sense that the court held that the will could not be rectified, when it is arguable that it could have been.

[45] See below, para.10–70.

and, because he was not paying full attention, fail to note that the word was there in the precedent? The former would be a drafting error, the latter a clerical error. This may, after all, have been a clerical error. By taking construction before rectification, the wrong order, Asplin J drew attention away from the problem here. She should have conducted a full investigation as to how the error occurred. If, as is quite probable, it turned out to be clerical, she would have had no need to consider construction.

5. Time limit

An application for rectification must be made no later than six months from the date on which a grant of probate or letters of administration to the deceased's estate[46] is first taken out; the court has, however, an unfettered discretion to extend this time limit.[47] The purpose of this short time limit is to enable the personal representatives safely to distribute the estate to the beneficiaries entitled under the unrectified will as soon as six months have passed without any application having been made.[48] **10–14**

In *Chittock v Stevens*[49] the judge held that the guidelines set out by Megarry VC in *Re Salmon*[50]—relating to the decision whether the time limit for making an application under the Inheritance (Provision for Family and Dependants) Act 1975 should be extended—were capable of being transposed to applications under s.20 to seek rectification out of time. In applying the guidelines, the judge held that it was just and proper for the time limit to be extended in a case where a will had been negligently drafted by a solicitor, who had omitted a clause leaving the testator's estate to his wife. The wife had initially decided not to apply for rectification because she believed—mistakenly, as it turned out—that the matrimonial home was in the joint names of herself and her husband and passed to her by survivorship. The judge was particularly swayed by the fact that the assets had not been distributed on the faith of the will as unrectified. This outweighed the fact that, in all probability, the widow had a good claim in negligence against the solicitor who had drafted the will.[51]

46 See below, Chap.18.

47 Administration of Justice Act 1982 s.20(2). The following are disregarded: a grant limited to settled land or trust property; any other grant that does not permit any of the estate to be distributed; a grant limited to real or personal estate unless a grant limited to the remainder of the estate has previously been made or is made at the same time; and a grant made outside the United Kingdom (other than one sealed under s.2 of the Colonial Probates Act 1892). See ss.20(4) and 20(5) as amended in 2014.

48 For protection of the personal representatives in case the time limit is extended, see s.20(3).

49 *Chittock v Stevens* [2000] W.T.L.R. 643.

50 *Re Salmon* [1981] Ch.167.

51 In *Re Ryan, Gerling v Gerling* [2011] W.T.L.R. 1029 permission was given to make a claim outside the time-limit. Relevant considerations included the strength of the claim, the length of the delay, the reasons for the delay, the prejudice to which it might have given rise, the promptitude with which the claim was first notified, the existence of negotiations, and whether the estate had been distributed.

III. GENERAL PRINCIPLES OF CONSTRUCTION AND ADMISSIBILITY OF EVIDENCE[52]

A. THE LITERAL AND THE INTENTIONAL APPROACHES TO INTERPRETATION

10–15 A problem arises in relation to the construction, or interpretation,[53] of a will when the meaning of a word, or passage, in the will is not clear. Suppose that someone dies leaving a home-made[54] will giving "all my money to my nephews and nieces." There are at least two potential problems which may arise in relation to these words. "All my money" could be read restrictively to include only coins and bank notes ("money" in the narrowest sense) or to include also money deposited in a bank, or to include investments such as stocks and shares, or to include all personalty, or to include the whole of the testator's net wealth ("money" in the widest sense). "Nephews and nieces" could be read restrictively to cover only the children of the testator's brothers and sisters (nephews and nieces by a blood relationship) or the words could be read in a wider sense to include also the children of the testator's spouse's brothers and sisters (nephews and nieces by a marriage relationship).

1. The two approaches

10–16 When there is a doubt, or dispute, about the meaning of a word, or passage, in a will, there are two possible approaches. One is to look for the ordinary meaning of the word or passage; this is known as the *literal*, or *grammatical*, approach.[55] The other is to look for the meaning intended by the testator; this is known as the *intentional*, or *inferential*, or *purposive* approach.[56]

The difference between the two approaches is at the heart of almost all construction problems. It is when the ordinary meaning and the meaning intended by the testator differ that a problem of construction arises.[57]

[52] See, generally, *Hawkins on the Construction of Wills*, 5th edn (London: Sweet & Maxwell, 2000), Chap.2; *Theobald on Wills*, 17th edn (London: Sweet & Maxwell, 2010), Chap.15; Kerridge and Rivers (2000) 116 L.Q.R. 287; B. Häcker "What's in a Will?—Examining the Modern Approach Towards the Interpretation and Rectification of Testamentary Instruments", Chap.6 in B. Häcker and C. Mitchell (eds), *Current Issues in Succession Law* (Oxford: Hart Publishing, 2016).

[53] The words "construction" and "interpretation" are assumed here to be synonymous.

[54] It ought to be true (though the editor can point to no statistics) that the proportion of home-made wills which raises construction problems is higher than the proportion of professionally-drawn wills which raises them. Professional will draftsmen should be aware of the pitfalls and should avoid them. What is surprising is how often even they fail.

[55] It has also been called the *objective* approach: see T. G. Feeney, *The Canadian Law of Wills*, Vol.2, *Construction*, 3rd edn (Toronto: Butterworths, 1987).

[56] It has also been called the *liberal*, or *logical*, or *subjective* approach. This book uses the term *intentional*. It is of the essence of this approach that there is no "correct" word to convey meaning—what matters is that the reader understands a word in the way in which the writer uses it.

[57] "For what is it that gives rise to all questions of interpretation? Is it not that the meaning

By the beginning of the nineteenth-century, most English judges were demonstrating a general, though not entirely consistent, preference for the literal approach. The nineteenth-century lawyer who did most to champion the literal approach was Sir James Wigram who brought out the first edition of his book on the Construction of Wills in 1831.[58] The leading protagonist of the intentional approach was F. V. Hawkins, who also wrote a book about the Construction of Wills[59] but whose views on the general principles of construction were set out in a lecture which he gave to the Juridical Society in 1860.[60] **10–17**

2. The confusion between the two approaches

There have, over the years, been a number of examples of confusing the two approaches. A modern example can be found in the latest[61] edition of Halsbury's Laws of England: **10–18**

> Para.224. "The cardinal rule of English law as to the effect of a will is that the testator's intention. . .has effect given to it. . ."

> Para.225. "The first duty of a court of construction is to ascertain the language of the will. . .Where the will must be in writing, the only question is what is the meaning of the words used in that writing. The expressed intention is in all cases taken as the actual intention, whatever the testator in fact intended. . ."[62]

The first paragraph is intentional. The second paragraph is literal. The last sentence of the second paragraph says that the literal approach prevails. The end result is that the first paragraph is meaningless.

of the words fails to express the meaning of the writer?": Hawkins, Juridical Society's Papers 1858–1863, Vol.II, 298, 306.

[58] The full title was *An Examination of the Rules of Law Respecting the Admission of Extrinsic Evidence in Aid of the Interpretation of Wills*. The first edition appeared in 1831, the second in 1834, the third in 1840, the fourth in 1858 and the fifth in 1914.

[59] *Concise Treatise on the Construction of Wills* 1st edn 1863; 5th edition, as *Hawkins on the Construction of Wills* (London: Sweet & Maxwell, 2000).

[60] The lecture was published in Vol.II of the Papers of The Juridical Society at p.298. It was republished as Appendix C to Prof J. B. Thayer's *Preliminary Treatise on Evidence at the Common Law* (Boston: Little Brown, 1898). Thayer said that he knew "nothing on [the] subject so well worth reading."

[61] 2010 edition.

[62] These two paragraphs were paras 370 and 371 of Vol.50 of the 4th edition, which appeared in 1984. They became paras 423 and 424 of the 1998 reissue, then paras 513 and 514 of the 2005 reissue, and are now paras 224 and 225 of the 2010 reissue. The latest reissue does contain some extra wording (not included above) but that has no bearing on the fundamental self-contradiction between the two paragraphs; the effect of the extra wording is to give the two paragraphs a stronger bias towards the literal approach than they had previously. This is, of course, in conflict with the legislation and with the approach taken in recent cases. Approximately one hundred cases are cited in the footnotes to the two paragraphs, but only two are post-1983. For the significance of the year, in this context, see below paras 10–41 et seq.

3. The advantages of the literal approach

10–19 The literal approach seems at first sight to have three advantages over the intentional approach.

(a) *Guards against danger of speculation*

10–20 Those who favour the literal approach point out, first of all, that it guards against the danger of speculating on what the testator might have chosen to say in his will about something to which he had actually given no thought.[63]

(b) *Complies with the Wills Act*

10–21 The second point that literalists make in favour of their approach is that it complies with the Wills Act 1837. Section 9 of the Wills Act requires that a will must be in writing; so the interpreter must confine himself to what has been written.[64]

(c) *Words always have the same meaning*

10–22 A third advantage of the literal approach is said to be that, whenever a word appears in a will, it means the same thing. "Nephew" always means "nephew by blood", and so on. This has the virtue of certainty and clarity, and it is convenient for will draftsmen. That is why Chancery practitioners have tended to favour the literal approach.

4. These advantages can be countered

(a) *Guesswork and surmise*

10–23 But the three apparent advantages of the literal approach can all be countered. The difference between the literalist and the intentionalist is not that the intentionalist seeks the testator's unexpressed intention, but that he seeks the meaning given by the testator to the words he used, whereas the literalist seeks the meaning which would be given to those same words by somebody else, the fictitious ordinary man.

Both the literal approach and the intentional approach involve surmise in some circumstances. They both involve surmise in so far as they permit gap-filling rules of construction. The distinction between gap-filling rules of construction and sense-giving rules of construction is discussed further below.[65]

[63] See Lord Wensleydale (the leading literalist judge of the mid-nineteenth century) in *Abbott v Middleton* (1858) 7 HLC 68, 114: and see *Re Rowland* [1963] Chs 1, 11–12 and 17–18.

[64] See Lord Wensleydale in *Abbott v Middleton* (1858) 7 HLC 68 and in *Grey v Pearson* (1857) 6 HLC 106.

[65] See below, paras 10–48 et seq.

(b) *Compliance with the Wills Act*

The literalist's second point is also misconceived, because the Wills Act simply requires that a will be in writing, without indicating how the writing is to be interpreted. Some nineteenth-century judges go so far as to say that words have a "correct meaning".[66] But words gain their meaning from the way in which they are used. Different people in different groups, at different times and in different places, use words differently. Literalists do not usually refer to "correct" English, but they claim to interpret words in a will as though they had been written in "ordinary" or "normal" English. It is instructive to consider again the original hypothetical example suggested at the start of this chapter where someone makes a home-made will leaving property to "my nephews and nieces". The lawyers' interpretation of the phrase "nephews and nieces" will probably be blood nephews and nieces, but a looser popular meaning includes nephews and nieces by marriage. If it can be shown that, while the testator was alive, he habitually used the expression "my nephews and nieces" to include his nephews and nieces by marriage, by what logic is the phrase in his will to be restricted to the lawyers' meaning? **10–24**

(c) *Words always have the same meaning*

The third supposed advantage of the literal approach is purchased at a very high price: the meaning may not be the meaning intended by the testator. Given that virtually all construction problems arise because the literal meaning and the meaning the testator intended differ, it must follow that, in all these cases, the literal meaning is *not* what the testator intended. **10–25**

5. The advantages of the intentional approach

(a) *Simplicity*

The principal advantage of the intentional approach is that it is much simpler to operate. There is no need for technical rules concerning the non-admissibility of certain types of evidence; there is no need for detailed learning about the technical meaning of words. Of course, the reader of a will is entitled to assume that, when a testator uses words, he generally means by them what others would mean by them; he is also entitled to assume that the testator has used technical terms accurately. But all this is subject to evidence to the contrary. The question is, quite simply, what the testator meant by his words; it is not what someone else would have meant by his words. **10–26**

(b) *Gives effect to deceased's wishes*

Secondly, the intentional approach gives maximum effect to the expressed wishes of the deceased. In recent years, statutory interpretation has **10–27**

[66] In *Lowe v Thomas* (1854) 5 De G. M.& G. 315, Knight Bruce LJ spoke at p.317 of the "correct and proper" sense of a word and Turner LJ spoke at p.318 of the "proper and correct" sense.

become more purposive, and less literal, in an attempt to give effect to the presumed intentions of the legislator.[67] When interpreting statutes, there are reasons for adopting a literal approach which do not apply when interpreting wills. The literal interpretation of a statute protects the reliance of citizens upon it. There is no equivalent reliance by a beneficiary, or a would-be beneficiary, on the wording of a will. So the arguments for adopting an intentional approach to the interpretation of wills are even stronger than those for adopting a purposive approach to the interpretation of statutes.

B. ADMISSIBILITY OF EXTRINSIC EVIDENCE AND THE TWO APPROACHES

1. Three types of evidence

10–28 There are three types of extrinsic evidence[68] which could be admitted to assist in the interpretation of a will.

(a) *Linking words to subject-matter or to objects—evidence as to "reference"*[69]

10–29 First of all, there is evidence of circumstances surrounding the testator at the time he made his will, evidence which links him to particular things or particular people: evidence, for example, that he had one child, two step-children, no nephews by blood, two nephews by marriage etc. This sort of evidence links the words of the will to its subject-matter (the property devised and bequeathed) and to its objects (the persons who are to benefit). For example, the testator may refer in his will to "my wife Sophia Burtenshaw" or to "my late mother's diamond engagement ring" and this kind of evidence will prove that a particular woman is the person so described[70] and/or that a particular ring is the ring to which the testator referred.

(b) *The testator's use of language—evidence as to "sense"*[71]

10–30 Secondly, there is evidence as to the testator's use of language; for example, the fact that he habitually used the word "money" to cover investments,

[67] e.g. *Pepper v Hart* [1993] A.C. 593; See generally F. Bennion, *Statutory Interpretation*, 6th edn (London: Butterworths Law, 2013).
[68] Evidence from outside the will.
[69] The distinction between the first sort of evidence (evidence as to "reference") and the second sort of evidence (evidence as to "sense") was first drawn clearly by the German linguistic philosopher, Gottlob Frege. Having said this, Wigram, the leading English literalist (see above, para.10–17) anticipated Frege to a significant extent; it is essential for a literalist to be able to distinguish between reference and sense. It is to Wigram's credit that he understood this. This is explained in more detail in *Hawkins on the Construction of Wills*, 5th edn (London: Sweet & Maxwell, 2000), pp.31 et seq.
[70] i.e. "referred to".
[71] See fn.69.

or that he used the word "children" when speaking of step-children. This second sort of evidence is sometimes confused with the first; but it is, essentially, different. It is concerned with the testator's use of language, his dictionary, the sense in which he used words; and not, as such, with linking his words to particular persons or to particular things.[72]

(c) *Statements made by testator—evidence of dispositive intention*

Thirdly, there is evidence of the testator's dispositive intention, i.e. statements made by the testator as to the dispositions in his will. The testator may, for example, have told someone that in his will he had left his property to his nephews and nieces by marriage. **10–31**

2. Which types of evidence should be admissible?

Evidence as to reference, must be, and always has been, admissible— whether the approach has been literal or intentional. It is essential to admit evidence to identify a particular person as "my son" or "my son John" or to identify a particular ring as "my engagement ring". Intentionalists— but not literalists—have always been ready to admit evidence as to the sense of words. Literalists believe that they know the "ordinary meaning" of words—"nephew" means "blood nephew", "child" (in the nineteenth century) meant "legitimate child" etc., and so there is no need for them to enquire what a particular testator meant by such a word when he used it. Evidence of statements made by the testator was admissible before 1983 only when there was an *equivocation,* i.e. a form of ambiguity which occurred where someone or something was described in such a way as *correctly* to describe two or more objects, or two or more subjects. So a gift to "my grandson John" or a gift of "my grand piano" would create an equivocation if the testator had more than one grandson who was called John, or more than one grand piano. These cases were rare before 1983.[73] **10–32**

Having said that literalists believe that they know the "ordinary meaning" of words and that they have always opposed admitting evidence as to their sense, they were never entirely consistent. They were always willing to admit evidence *intrinsic* to a will[74] to show that a testator was using words in what they would otherwise consider an unusual sense. So, for example, although literalists would oppose admitting evidence from outside a will to show that a testator had used the word **10–33**

[72] There can, of course, be ambiguities and/or misunderstandings both of reference and of sense, and sometimes they overlap.

[73] There is a problem as to how this third sort of evidence should be described. Hawkins called it "direct evidence" of the testator's intention, but it is submitted that this is misleading. Matters are further confused if the first and second sorts of evidence are treated as though they are the same as one another and are then called "circumstantial". Some writers have traditionally so described them. The description is neat, but it is confusing. The first two sorts of evidence are different from one another and neither should be described as circumstantial. The third sort is not direct, and calling it "direct" makes it sound as though it is a persuasive form of evidence, which it has never been (though it is admissible in many more cases after 1982 than it was before 1983, see below, paras 10–41 et seq.

[74] Evidence from the will itself.

"nephew" in any other than its "ordinary" sense, they would be prepared to admit evidence that the testator had used the word in an unusual sense if that could be shown from the context of the will itself. If the will contained a "dictionary", *or* if the context in which the word was used in the will showed that it *had* to bear an unusual sense, then the literalists were prepared to accept this sense. The end result was that the literal rules, combined with the exceptions to them, ended up by being relatively complicated.[75] Whenever a literalist lawyer talked about the "context" of a will, that meant that he was going to give to a word a sense which he did not think was its ordinary sense—the "context" was an escape route for the literalist.

3. The approach taken by judges during the nineteenth-century

10–34 During the course of the nineteenth-century, most judges who had to deal with cases relating to the interpretation of wills, tended, most of the time, to adopt the literal approach. First instance judges who dealt with construction cases were Chancery lawyers; and Chancery lawyers were generally more likely than their Common Law counterparts to be literalists. But it followed from this that when cases reached the House of Lords—where there would be, relatively speaking, more Common lawyers—they were more likely to be decided according to the intentional approach.[76]

C. THE HOUSE OF LORDS ABANDONS LITERALISM

10–35 A particular problem with the literal approach was that lawyers who talked about giving words their "ordinary meaning" seemed sometimes not to realise that what they were really doing was to give them a "lawyers' meaning", i.e. the meaning the words would have had if they were being used by lawyers. But to give words in a home-made will the meaning they would have if they had been used by a lawyer, was not easy to justify. A direct challenge to the literal approach was bound to come; and it came in *Perrin v Morgan*.[77]

[75] Wigram compressed the literal rules into seven Propositions and his book was a discussion of these seven Propositions. They are set out in full in *Hawkins on the Construction of Wills*, 5th edn (London: Sweet & Maxwell, 2000), Chap.2.

[76] See, for example, *Gorringe v Mahlstedt* [1907] A.C. 225, where the Court of Appeal had adopted a literal approach, while the House of Lords found the sense of the words intended by the testator. The dividing line between the literalist Chancery lawyers and the intentionalist Common lawyers was certainly not rigid and there were a number of exceptions on both sides. The House of Lords judge who was the most enthusiastic supporter of the literal approach was Lord Wensleydale, a Common lawyer, who repeatedly insisted that the words in a will should be given their ordinary meaning. The judge who most enthusiastically championed the intentional approach was Lord St Leonards, a Chancery man. The contrast between the two approaches can be seen most clearly in the judgments of these two judges in the case of *Grey v Pearson* (1857) 6 HLC 106, 10 E.R. 1234, a two to one decision in favour of the literal approach.

[77] *Perrin v Morgan* [1943] A.C. 399.

1. *Perrin v Morgan*

A woman died leaving a home-made will in which she directed that "all moneys of which I die possessed shall be shared by my nephews and nieces now living."[78] Earlier case law[79] had established that the word "money" or "moneys" meant money held in cash, money in the bank, debts owed to the testator but *not* net residuary personalty. It was also quite clear that, in many of these cases, the literal approach had led to a result not intended by the testator. **10–36**

In *Perrin v Morgan* the testatrix's estate was worth more than £30,000 and consisted almost entirely of stocks and shares. She obviously intended the stocks and shares to pass under the word "moneys" because, if they did not, she would die almost wholly intestate. The House of Lords reversed the Court of Appeal[80]—which had (reluctantly) followed the earlier case law—and instead gave the word "moneys" a wide reading.

The decision was unanimous, but the result was reached by two different routes. No member of the House referred to any general theory. The focus was simply on reversing the earlier case law. But there was a straightforward split between the Chancery lawyers and the non-Chancery[81] lawyers. The former—Lords Russell of Killowen and Romer—gave a wide interpretation to the word "moneys" by finding it in the "context" of the will, i.e. by saying that the will had to be read as a whole and that the context showed that the word "money" in this particular will did not bear the meaning usually given to it. In other words, they were affirming that the word "money" had an "ordinary meaning" but that they were not going to adopt it in this particular case. This was the standard way of *appearing* to follow the literal approach, but escaping from it on the special facts of the case. The non-Chancery lawyers—Viscount Simon LC and Lords Atkin and Thankerton—simply decided that the word "moneys" had no strict and primary sense.[82] **10–37**

The decision in *Perrin v Morgan* could have, and should have, led to a completely different attitude towards the interpretation of home-made wills.[83] But the two Chancery lawyers had not agreed with the approach taken by the other three, and Chancery lawyers were reluctant converts to

[78] The problem over the meaning of "nephews and nieces" did not arise because the testatrix was unmarried.

[79] Starting with *Shelmer's case* (1725) Gilb Rep 200 and continuing through to *Jones v Collings* [1933] Ch.920 (Farwell J). One case stood against the line of the authorities: *Lynn v Kerridge* (1737) West temp Hard 172.

[80] Lord Greene MR, Luxmoore and Goddard LJJ. The Court of Appeal decision is reported at [1942] Ch.345.

[81] They were not all Common lawyers: Lord Thankerton was a Scot.

[82] Wigram used the phrase "strict and primary acceptation" to cover "ordinary meaning" or "correct meaning".

[83] The problem is usually with home-made wills. The literal approach generally works well enough for wills drafted by lawyers, provided they are competent lawyers, because lawyers use lawyers' language and the literal approach translates it as if it were lawyers' language. So, for wills drafted by lawyers, the literal and the intentional approaches should, generally, yield the same result.

the new approach. How reluctant was shown, twenty years after *Perrin v Morgan*, in *Re Rowland*.[84]

2. The reluctance of Chancery lawyers to abandon literalism—*Re Rowland*

10–38 Dr Trevor Rowland made a home-made will which contained a long-winded provision whereby he devised and bequeathed all his property to his wife: and then came the following words "in the event of the decease of the said Shirley Rowland preceding or coinciding with my own decease, I give and bequeath" and he then gave everything to his brother and to his infant nephew.

10–39 Dr Rowland and his wife both died in the same boating disaster. There was no indication that Mrs Rowland had died before her husband. The issue for determination was whether Mrs Rowland's death *coincided with* her husband's death. The judge at first instance[85] and two judges in the Court of Appeal,[86] decided that it had not. Their reasoning was that "coincided with" meant the same as "was simultaneous with"; as it was probable that Dr and Mrs Rowland had died seconds, or even minutes, apart, their deaths had not "coincided". Mrs Rowland was slightly younger than her husband; so she was presumed to have survived him[87] and she inherited his estate, which then passed under her will to her niece, not to Dr. Rowland's brother and nephew.

10–40 The dissenting judge in *Rowland* was Lord Denning MR, who adopted a purely intentional approach: Dr Rowland intended by his use of the words "coinciding with" to cover their dying together on the same occasion and by the same cause, not their dying at the very same moment.

D. THE ADMINISTRATION OF JUSTICE ACT 1982, SECTION 21

1. The Law Reform Committee's Nineteenth Report[88]

10–41 This Report is not an easy document to follow, but its main conclusion was clear: the literal approach (insofar as it had survived) should be abandoned and the intentional position should be adopted.[89] This was a re-affirmation of the position taken by the majority of the House of Lords in *Perrin v Morgan*. In effect, it meant that evidence as to the way in which

[84] *Re Rowland* [1963] Ch.1.

[85] Buckley J.

[86] Harman and Russell LJJ, both Chancery judges; Lord Denning MR dissented. Russell LJ, who later became a Lord of Appeal in Ordinary, was the son of Lord Russell of Killowen, who was one of the two members of the House of Lords in *Perrin v Morgan* who had not adopted an intentional approach.

[87] LPA s.184.

[88] Law Reform Committee's 19th Report, *Interpretation of Wills*, Cmnd.5301 (1973).

[89] Report, para.49.

the testator used language[90] should be admitted. There was, however, a further problem relating to the admissibility of evidence of the testator's dispositive intention[91] in relation to which the Committee were not agreed.

2. Section 21 of the Administration of Justice Act 1982[92]

The section needs to be set out in its entirety: 10–42

> **"Interpretation of wills—general rules as to evidence**
>
> **21.**—(1) This section applies to a will:
>
> (a) in so far as any part of it is meaningless[93];
> (b) in so far as the language used in any part of it is ambiguous on the face of it[94];
> (c) in so far as evidence, other than evidence of the testator's intention, shows that the language used in any part of it is ambiguous in the light of surrounding circumstances.[95]
>
> (2) In so far as this section applies to a will extrinsic evidence, including evidence of the testator's intention, may be admitted to assist in its interpretation."

The overall pattern of s.21 is that s.21(1)(a) covers cases where the testator has used a word or phrase which appears to have no meaning; s.21(1)(b) covers cases where he has used a word or phrase which appears to have several meanings; and s.21(1)(c) covers cases where he has used a word or a phrase which has an ordinary meaning in circumstances which indicate that he may have intended it to bear not its ordinary meaning, but some other idiosyncratic meaning. This is what the Law Reform Committee wanted to achieve.

3. What sort of evidence is, and what is not, admissible?

Evidence of the testator's use of language is always admissible. It is always 10–43
possible to show that the testator used the word "money", or the word "nephew", or the word "coincide", in a particular sense. Evidence of the testator's dispositive intention (evidence of what he said to someone about

[90] See above, para.10–30.
[91] See above, para.10–31.
[92] The section applies where the testator dies on or after 1 January 1983: Administration of Justice Act 1982 ss.73(6) and 76(11).
[93] "Is meaningless" must mean "appears to be meaningless" because if any part of a will "is meaningless" it cannot be interpreted. For an example, see *Kell v Charmer* (1856) 23 Beav. 195 (private marks used by a jeweller).
[94] This resembles the category of "patent ambiguity" in the existing law.
[95] This is an extension of the existing law relating to "latent ambiguities" or "equivocations". A classic example is *Re Jackson* [1933] Ch.237.

what he had put in his will) can be admitted if part of the will appears to have no meaning, or if it appears to have several meanings. Evidence of the testator's dispositive intention cannot be admitted where a word or phrase which has an ordinary meaning or meanings has been used and where there is no evidence (other than what the testator said about what he had put in his will) to indicate that he had used a word or phrase in an idiosyncratic sense.[96]

But what this should mean, in practice, is that, whenever a will is read and the reader can say (without needing to refer to what the testator said about what he had put in his will) that it contains a patent or a latent ambiguity, evidence of what the testator said was in his will, or should be in his will (including, especially, evidence of his instructions to a draftsman) *will* then be admissible. Put simply, if a professionally drawn will contains an ambiguity, the draftsman can, and should, give evidence of his instructions. It is not apparent that this has been properly understood, but the point becomes clearer when looking at the post-1983 case law.

4. The case law on section 21

10–44 The case law on s.21 will be discussed in Part III of this chapter—see below paragraphs 10–60—10–70.

IV. THE CONSTRUCTION OF THE WILLS OF TESTATORS WHO DIE ON OR AFTER 1 JANUARY 1983[97]

A. RULES OF CONSTRUCTION—RULES OF LAW—EQUITABLE PRESUMPTIONS

1. Rules of construction—rules of law

10–45 When attempting to understand the operation of rules of construction, it is important to distinguish between rules of construction and rules of law. According to Hawkins:

> "A rule of construction may always be reduced to the following form:—Certain words or expressions, which may mean either x or y, shall, prima facie, be taken to mean x. A rule of construction always contains

[96] Suppose that the testator bequeathed property in his will to "my niece" and that he had told someone that he intended to leave the property to the daughter of his friend. Suppose that he had *not* been in the habit of referring to this person as "my niece" and suppose also that he had a blood niece. Section 21 would not admit the evidence of his having said that he intended to benefit the daughter of his friend. But if he had no blood niece, or if he regularly called the daughter of his friend "my niece", the evidence could be admitted because there would be (a form of) ambiguity in the light of surrounding circumstances.

[97] See generally *Hawkins on the Construction of Wills*, 5th edn (London: Sweet & Maxwell, 2000), Chap.3.

the saving clause, 'unless a contrary intention appear ':. On the other hand a rule of law (as the rule in *Shelley's Case*, the rules as to perpetuity, mortmain, *etc.*) acts independently of intention, and applies to dispositions of property in whatever form of words expressed."[98]

One of the problems with the development of the rules of construction in the eighteenth-century and the early years of the nineteenth-century was that some lawyers, the arch—literalists, tended sometimes to confuse rules of law and rules of construction.[99] They created rules which they called rules of construction, but applied them in such a way that they were, effectively, not subject to the testator's intention. In so far as they did this, they were creating rules of law. When, for example, the judges decided that the perpetuity rules were going to apply irrespective of the testator's intention, they were creating rules of law. Conversely, when they decided that the class-closing rules[100] would be subject to the testator's intention, they were creating rules of construction. There was some confusion about this at some stages in the process, but it eventually became clear which rules were which.[101]

2. Equitable presumptions

Apart from rules of law and rules of construction, there are rules relating to equitable presumptions; and, in particular, to the equitable presumption of satisfaction.[102] The equitable presumption of satisfaction covers three sub-presumptions: (i) the presumption of satisfaction of a debt by a legacy; (ii) the presumption of satisfaction of a legacy by a legacy; and (iii) the presumption against double portions. The equitable presumption of satisfaction operates very much like a rule of construction; in fact, **10–46**

[98] This passage from *Hawkins* is quoted by Sir William Holdsworth in his *History of English Law* 4th edn (London: Methuen & Co Ltd, 1935) Vol.VII, p.395. In Vol.III, at pp.108–109, Holdsworth discusses the rule in *Shelley's Case* and notes that, although it had been recognised as a rule of law in the 17th century, there was a controversy during the 18th century as to whether it should be regarded as a rule of construction. Its status as a rule of law was finally confirmed by the decisions of the House of Lords in *Jesson v Wright* (1820) 2 Bligh. 1 and *Roddy v Fitzgerald* (1857–58) 6 H.L.C. 823.

[99] Holdsworth, *History of English Law*, 2nd edn (London: Methuen & Co Ltd), Vol.VII, p.174 and p.396.

[100] See below, Chap.11.

[101] There is one set of rules which *appear* to be rules of law but which should properly be regarded as rules of construction. These are the ademption rules. Most leading textbooks appear to assume that they are rules of law—see below, Chap.14 paras 14–37 et seq. and see *Ashburner v Macguire* (1786) 2 Bro.C.C. 108; *Stanley v Potter* (1789) 2 Cox. 180; and *Harrison v Jackson* (1877) 7 Ch.D. 339, 341. The rules relating to ademption appear to have become rules of law at a time when literalism was at its height and when some people were failing to distinguish properly between rules of construction and rules of law. Now that the distinction between rules of construction and rules of law is clear, it may be time to consider whether the rules relating to ademption should not be regarded as rules of construction.

[102] See Chap.13. It is clear that the presumption of satisfaction is an equitable presumption and not an ordinary rule of construction. But there is some doubt as to whether the rule that a legacy to an executor is conditional on his taking office is an equitable presumption or is an ordinary rule of construction. The distinction is of no significance if the testator dies on or after 1 January 1983.

it appears to be based on the presumed intention of the testator.[103] The distinction between what may be called ordinary rules of construction on the one hand, and the equitable presumption of satisfaction on the other, has been that *evidence of the testator's intention* has always been admissible to rebut,[104] or to support, the equitable presumption. So the equitable presumption of satisfaction has operated like a rule of construction, but subject to a more intentionalist régime than the ordinary rules of construction. Where a testator died before 1 January 1983, and where there was extrinsic evidence of his intention (i.e. of statements made by him) in relation to a provision in his will, such evidence could be admitted if it related to the equitable presumption of satisfaction (or to an equivocation)[105] but not if it related to some other kind of ambiguity. It can now be admitted in virtually all cases; so the person construing the will does not need to worry about drawing a line between the equitable presumption of satisfaction and other problems of construction.[106] This represents a simplification.[107]

B. WILLS DRAFTED PROFESSIONALLY AND HOME-MADE WILLS

1. Significance of the distinction

10–47 One effect of s.21 of the Administration of Justice Act 1982 is to emphasise the difference, for construction purposes, between wills drafted by lawyers[108] and home-made wills. It is surprising that in the pre-1983 cases very little is said about this distinction. Many judges interpreted home-made wills in exactly the same way that they interpreted wills which had been drafted professionally. The biggest problem with the rules of construction as they were applied by literalists before *Perrin v Morgan*[109] (and to some extent after *Perrin v Morgan* but before the enactment of s.21) was that literalists gave words in home-made wills the meaning, the sense, which those words would have had for lawyers. This is what happened in *Re Rowland*.[110] Section 21 of the Administration of Justice Act 1982 puts an end to this: and words in home-made wills should be given the sense (so far as one can establish it) which was intended by those who wrote them. On the other hand, wills drafted by lawyers will continue to be construed on that basis.

[103] *Re Cameron* [1999] Ch.386.
[104] *Re Tussaud's Estate* (1878) 9 Ch.D. 363.
[105] See above, para.10–32.
[106] There have not been many reported cases in recent years relating to the equitable presumption of satisfaction, but see *Re Cameron* [1999] Ch.386, discussed below in Chap.13.
[107] The equitable presumption of satisfaction is not a major problem, but getting rid of the distinction *is* a simplification. The equitable presumption of satisfaction is discussed further in Chap.13.
[108] The word "lawyers" in this context encompasses all those who provide a professional will-drafting service for clients.
[109] *Perrin v Morgan* [1943] A.C. 399 see above, paras 10–36 et seq.
[110] *Re Rowland* [1963] Ch.1 see above, paras 10–38 et seq.

2. Rules which state what sense words have—contrasted with gap-filling rules

There are two types of rules of construction which apply to wills. First, there are rules which specify, or attempt to specify, the sense which should be given to words in a will—for example, that "nephew" should be assumed to mean blood nephew.[111] Secondly, there are rules which attempt to fill gaps in the will: to provide what it is assumed that the testator intended when he has said nothing, or has appeared to say nothing, about a particular possibility; for example, the class-closing rules,[112] or the substitution rule whereby if a testator's child pre-deceases him, the child's issue take in his place.[113] The distinction between these two types of rules is not rigid; there is a shading between the extremes.[114] But it is significant in relation to the distinction between professionally-drawn wills and home-made wills.[115] Home-made wills will continue to be subject to the gap-filling rules. Home-made wills are, in fact, more likely to be subject to these rules than professionally-drawn wills, because home-made wills traditionally contain more gaps. **10–48**

Where a testator dies on or after 1 January 1983, and s.21 of the Administration of Justice Act 1982 applies, someone construing a will should first consider whether the will was drafted by a lawyer, or was home-made. If it was professionally drafted, the traditional rules applicable to discovering the sense of words will, by and large, apply. Lawyers use lawyers' language. Competent professional will draftsmen use language knowing that particular words or expressions have been held in the past to have particular meanings and intending them to have these meanings. They will avoid words or expressions which their training has taught them may lead to suggestions of ambiguity. They will also know about the gap-filling rules and will know how they will apply. **10–49**

If, on the other hand, a will is home-made, the gap-filling rules should apply[116] but the traditional rules which assist in deciding on the sense to be given to particular words or expressions should be applied, insofar as

[111] See *Hawkins on the Construction of Wills*, 5th edn (London: Sweet & Maxwell, 2000), Chap.12.

[112] See below, Chap.11, paras 11–11 et seq.

[113] See below Chap.14, paras 14–22 et seq.

[114] At one end of the spectrum, some rules lay down the sense in which particular words or expressions are to be understood. For example, s.26 of the Wills Act 1837 says that "land" includes leases. That is a straightforward rule of construction. At the other extreme, s.18A of the Wills Act says that a former spouse is deemed (for most purposes) to have died at the date when the marriage was dissolved. That is not truly a rule of construction. It is a rule imposed on the basis that it is assumed that that is what the testator would have put in his will, if he had been asked to think about something to which he had (at the time when he made his will), almost certainly, given no thought at all. It is suggested that s.24 of the Wills Act, which says that a will speaks from death, is essentially a construction section, but s.33, the substitution section, is more or less speculative. s.25, covering lapsed and void devises, falls somewhere in between.

[115] Where, again, the distinction may not be rigid, and there may be some shading.

[116] This is, of course, on the assumption that there is no indication of a contrary intention—but if there were such an indication, there would be no true gap.

they are applied at all, only with extreme caution.[117] This is because these rules tend to give a lawyers' sense, possibly an old-fashioned sense, to words and phrases; and what needs to be sought is not the lawyers' sense but the testator's sense.

3. The use of technical legal expressions by testators who draft their own wills

10–50 There is a line of pre-1983 cases which holds that where someone has, in his will, used a lawyer's term of art, he will be assumed to have used it as a lawyer would have used it. The cases do not, in general, appear to distinguish between wills drafted by lawyers and wills which are home-made; it is submitted that a clear line should, for this purpose, be drawn.

When a legal term of art appears in a will drafted by a lawyer, it should be assumed, as a question of construction, that he has used it as a lawyer would use it and has given it the lawyers' meaning.[118] But in relation to home-made wills, it is submitted that the approach should be to construe legal expressions to mean what the testator meant, not what a lawyer[119] would have meant. The fact that the expression is a technical legal expression is not something which a layman necessarily realises. The common-sense result was reached in some pre-1983 cases by relying on "context".[120] But there are other pre-1983 cases where judges took a resolutely literal line.[121] If there ever was a rule to the effect that when a layman has used a lawyer's term of art, he will be assumed to have used it as a lawyer would have used it, it has been abolished by s.21 of the Administration of Justice Act 1982.

4. Wills drafted by incompetent professional draftsmen

10–51 When a legal term of art appears in a will drafted by a lawyer, it should be assumed, as a question of construction, that he has used it as a lawyer would use it and has given it the lawyers' meaning. But if it can be shown that the professional draftsman was incompetent and used a word with a lawyers' meaning in a different sense, the word he has used should be given the meaning he intended it to have, not the ordinary lawyers' meaning. An example where this sort of problem can

[117] *Re Minchell's W.T.* [1964] 2 All E.R. 47 "one testator's nonsense is no guide to another testator's nonsense."

[118] It should be assumed, as a question of construction, but, even in this case, where the will has been drafted by a lawyer, it should be possible to demonstrate that the particular draftsman did *not* use the terms as a lawyer would ordinarily use them. This is discussed further below, see para.10–51.

[119] A competent lawyer—an incompetent lawyer might not have meant it anyway; see fn.117, above.

[120] See *Re Bailey* [1945] Ch.191 "residuary legatee" construed as "residuary beneficiary" so that "residuary legatee" took not only personalty but also realty (most of the residue was realty).

[121] See *Re Cook* [1948] Ch.212 "all my personal estate whatsoever" held *not* to include realty (most of the residue was realty).

occur is where an incompetent professional draftsman drafts a legacy which is intended to be a legacy to charity, but he uses wording which is technically inappropriate. If the testator and the draftsman intend the gift to be a gift to charity, it should be a valid gift to charity, even if the wording is technically inapt. This means, of course, that there is no absolute dividing line between professionally-drawn wills and home-made wills.[122]

5. Speculation

It was noted above that those who favour the literal approach claim that it guards against the danger of speculating about what the testator might have chosen to say in his will about something to which he had actually given no thought.[123] But the problem is then to distinguish between (i) the case where the testator has thought about something, and has intended to cover the situation in his will, but has given poor expression to his intentions; and (ii) the case where he has not thought about something at all, or has forgotten to cover the situation in his will. The dividing line between the two is not quite as rigid as it might at first appear. **10–52**

Even before the enactment of s.21 of the Administration of Justice Act 1982, it was possible to find different judges taking different attitudes to the problem of speculation. An example of a refusal to speculate is *Re James's Will Trusts*,[124] where the testator's children took life interests in his residuary estate, each child taking an equal share. As each child died, his share passed to his issue, but if a child died without issue his share passed to "my surviving children". The straightforward meaning of these words was that the share passed to the deceased child's surviving brothers and sisters but *not* to the issue of other brothers and sisters who had died before him. The result seems arbitrary and it is probable that the testator, who had begun by adopting a stirpital distribution, would not, had he thought about it, have intended it. Nevertheless, the ordinary meaning of the words was clear and that was the meaning Buckley J gave them.[125] But *Re James's Will Trusts* can be contrasted with *Re Whitrick*,[126] where T left her entire estate to her husband and provided that "in the event of my husband and myself both dying at the same time" it should be held upon trust for X, Y and Z equally. T's husband predeceased her and consequently, according to the literal meaning of the words used, the gift to X, Y and Z failed and T's entire estate passed as on her intestacy. The Court of Appeal[127] held that it was clear from the will as a whole that T intended, by means of the gift to X, Y and Z, to provide for the contingency of her husband's not surviving her.[128] The **10–53**

[122] See below, para.10–79.
[123] See above, para.10–20.
[124] *Re James's Will Trusts* [1962] Ch.226, 234.
[125] The will had been drafted by a solicitor.
[126] *Re Whitrick* [1957] 1 W.L.R. 884.
[127] Reversing Harman J.
[128] See also the very similar Canadian case of *Re Harmer* [1964] 42 D.L.R. (2d) 321 (Ontario CA) affd sub nom *Kilby v Myers* [1965] S.C.R. 24.

will was therefore read as if it had directed that X, Y and Z were to take if T's husband predeceased her, as well as if they both died at the same time.[129]

10–54 *James* and *Whitrick* are both pre-section 21 cases and it is worth comparing and contrasting them with two cases decided since 1983. In *Re Owen*[130] a home-made will contained a gift to the testator's wife and then a substitutionary gift in the case of her dying "together with me". Although the judge thought that the words were unambiguous, it is submitted that he was wrong and they should have been construed to include the wife's predecease. This was, after all, not a professionally-drawn will. A more difficult case is *Folds v Abrahart*[131] where another home-made will contained a provision as to what should happen if the testator and his wife should "die together". They did not "die together" but were divorced. The provision was held to be a condition, which, it is submitted, was correct; but it was then held that the condition had not been fulfilled. This result is questionable, because "die together" could, in a home-made will, be construed to cover pre-decease.[132]

10–55 There is a final point which needs to be noted in relation to speculation. Gap-filling construction rules are rules of speculation. The class-closing rules[133] say that, although the testator has expressed no intention in relation to the relevant matter, it will be assumed that he would have wanted to put a particular provision in his will. This *could* be justified on the basis that it is assumed that the testator had thought about the problem, but had not given clear expression to his thoughts; but it is highly probable that in most cases the testator has given the matter no thought at all. The truth is that these are situations which occur repeatedly: testators do not think about them, and rules have to be invented to deal with them.[134] A purist might object that they are, in fact, not true construction rules, but quasi construction rules: speculation rules which may be ousted by proof that the testator did not intend them to apply.[135]

[129] *Whitrick* like *Re James's W.T.*, is a case of a professionally-drawn will. In each of the two cases, something odd seems to have happened, though it is not entirely clear what. *Whitrick* seems to be a case where words had been omitted, probably by clerical error, and were facts like this to recur today it might well be a case for rectification. *James* is more likely to be a case where neither the testator nor his draftsman thought things through properly. *Whitrick* is a case where the problem was solved by a form of construction which amounted to rectification—see above, paras 10–04 et seq.

[130] *Re Owen* [2002] W.T.L.R. 619 (Stanley Burnton QC, sitting as a deputy High Court judge).

[131] *Folds v Abrahart* [2004] W.T.L.R. 327.

[132] This would then raise the question whether divorce is equivalent to pre-decease. For this, see s.18A of the Wills Act, which is discussed in Chap.14 at paras 14–32 et seq. This case is discussed again there.

[133] See below, paras 11–11 et seq.

[134] Section 18A of the Wills Act, referred to in the previous paragraph, is an example of a gap-filling rule.

[135] It is not particularly helpful to spend time discussing whether these are true construction rules or quasi-construction rules, but it is true that there is a significant element of speculation in them. Insofar as they are regarded as rules of construction, they appear to contradict the rule that an interpreter must never speculate. Both literalists and intentionalists permit speculation when they adopt gap-filling construction rules. An intentionalist must do so on the basis that he is adopting an objective-purposive (or "assumed intentional") approach to fill the gap. In fact, the more one attempts to classify detailed rules of construction, the

C. PRE SECTION 21 CASES WHICH WOULD HAVE BEEN DECIDED DIFFERENTLY HAD THE TESTATOR DIED AFTER 1982

1. *Re Sykes*[136] and *Re Lewis's Will Trusts*[137]

One significant advantage of the intentional approach to the interpretation of wills is that it is not necessary for the interpreter to distinguish between "reference" and "sense".[138] Where testators died before 1983, literalists needed to distinguish between the two sorts of evidence and, where there appeared to be a conflict between them, they would find themselves in difficulties. They usually decided that the "correct" sense of the testator's words would prevail over what they knew he was referring to, and so they ended up by making a nonsense of the will. Two good examples of this are *Re Sykes*[139] and *Re Lewis's Will Trusts*.[140] In *Sykes* the testator bequeathed "all my horses" to his wife. He had, at one time, owned some racehorses outright, but two years before he made his will he had registered his wife with the Jockey Club as a part-owner of the horses and, from then on, he and his wife were tenants in common. The question was whether the testator's interest as a tenant in common passed to his wife under the bequest of "all my horses". Bennett J held that it did not. He dealt with the case on the basis that the correct *sense* of the words "my horses" was "the horses which I own outright" and he then made this sense prevail over the reference which he must have known the testator intended—a reference to the interest which the testator had in the horses which he did not own outright. The result in *Sykes* is as incomprehensible to the non-lawyer as the result in *Rowland*.[141] **10–56**

In *Re Lewis's Will Trusts*[142] the testator left "my freehold farm" to his son. The farm was, in fact, owned by a company in which the testator held 75 per cent of the shares. His son held another 20 per cent and the son's wife the remaining 5 per cent. Scott J held that the testator's 75 per cent shareholding did not pass, despite the fact that there was no genuine dispute as to the meaning (i.e. the *sense*), of the word "farm". This was *not* a case where, for example, there was a problem as to whether the word "farm" included neighbouring woodland, which would have been a genuine dispute as to sense. This was a problem about what was meant by "my freehold farm" when the testator had no freehold farm, but held 75 per cent of the shares in a company which owned one. The case can **10–57**

more obvious it becomes that many of them are based, at least in part, on speculation. It was always an exaggeration for literalists to claim that they did not permit speculation. They were, in truth, selective about when they would permit it.

136 *Re Sykes* [1940] 4 All E.R. 10.

137 *Re Lewis's Will Trusts* [1985] 1 W.L.R. 102.

138 See above, paras 10–28 et seq.

139 *Re Sykes* [1940] 4 All E.R. 10. The will was professionally-drawn.

140 *Re Lewis's Will Trusts* [1985] 1 W.L.R. 102.

141 Had the husband not transferred an interest in the horses to his wife before he made his will, his will would have given her the horses; because he made her a co-owner while he was alive, she ended up with less than if he had done nothing.

142 *Re Lewis's Will Trusts* [1985] 1 W.L.R. 102. The will was professionally drawn.

only be justified by saying that the sense of the expression "my freehold farm" must prevail over what everyone knows was the reference intended by the testator—to whatever interest he had in the farm. This case is an example of an extreme literalist approach. It can well be argued that the case was incorrectly decided, even on the basis of the law as it stood before 1983; but it would not have been decided in the way it was if the testator had died after 1982,[143] when the words "my freehold farm" would be given the meaning which the testator intended them to have.

2. The *NSPCC* case

10–58 *NSPCC v Scottish NSPCC*[144] was almost certainly wrongly decided, even on the basis of the law as it stood before s.21 of the Administration of Justice Act 1982 was enacted. The result would certainly be different today.[145]

The testator was a Scotsman who had lived all his life in Scotland. He made a will, in Scottish form,[146] in which, inter alia, he bequeathed a number of legacies to Scottish charities. Among these legacies was a legacy to the National Society for the Prevention of Cruelty to Children. The question was whether the legacy belonged to an English charity called the National Society for the Prevention of Cruelty to Children, or to a Scottish charity called the Scottish National Society for the Prevention of Cruelty to Children. The House of Lords held, unanimously, in favour of the English charity.[147]

Before the enactment of s.21, the approach adopted by English law and Scottish law to the construction of wills was the same: the literal approach.[148] The decision was that, as the testator had correctly described the English charity, there was no ambiguity.

10–59 Those who argued in favour of the Scottish NSPCC appear to have accepted that where a person who is not a charity is "accurately described" that is normally the end of the matter. They claimed, however, that charities should be treated differently. It is submitted that the House was correct to reject this supposed distinction. Nevertheless, the House was wrong to adopt an uncritical application of the literal approach. The problem in the *NSPCC* case was *not* a problem of *sense*, but a problem of *reference*. Suppose that a testator leaves a number of bequests in his will to friends and former colleagues at work. Among these bequests is one to (say) Edwin Smith—with no further description or identification. Let it be supposed that the testator had a friend who was known as Edwin Smith but whose name on his birth certificate was Frederick Edwin Smith. Let it

[143] The testator died in 1978.

[144] *NSPCC v Scottish NSPCC* [1915] A.C. 207.

[145] At least, it would be different *if* it were an English case. It was a Scottish case and s.21 does not apply in Scotland. Nevertheless it is submitted that it should be decided differently even if s.21 were not to apply—see below, para.10–59 and fn.149.

[146] The report of the case does not specifically state whether the will was professionally drawn or home-made, but it was implicit in everything which was said about it that the will was professionally drawn.

[147] Reversing the Court of Session—[1913] S.C. 412.

[148] Scottish law still adopts this approach; see Gloag and Henderson, *The Law of Scotland*, 12th edn (Edinburgh: W. Green & Son, 2007), para.40–14.

also be supposed that someone else called Edwin Smith, and only Edwin Smith, could be found. Who would get the legacy? Of course Frederick Edwin Smith would get it. That *is* this case—a case of reference, which has nothing to do with s.21.[149]

D. CASES DECIDED SINCE SECTION 21 CAME INTO FORCE

1. Cases decided since section 21 came into force, but before *Marley v Rawlings*

The case law on s.21 has, so far, not been particularly helpful. It seems **10–60** that some lawyers have still not appreciated that the literal approach to the interpretation of wills has been abandoned. Just as two judges in the Court of Appeal in *Re Rowland*[150] paid no heed to the decision of the House of Lords in *Perrin v Morgan*, so some judges have ignored, or attempted to circumvent, s.21, in whole or in part. The section is not particularly well drafted, but its import is clear and its effect is radical.[151]

Sammut v Manzi[152] was an appeal from the Bahamas to the Privy Council. The case involved a will which, on a straightforward reading, had no clear meaning. Oddly, there was no enquiry or explanation as to who had drafted it, but the guess is that it was a lawyer. The case is of no assistance in the English context, because there was, in Bahamian law, no section equivalent to s.21. This is a case in a time warp. The Privy Council reached a conclusion different from that reached in the Bahamas, either at first instance, or on appeal. What the case does show is how useful it would have been to have been able to call s.21 in aid. *Sammut* has been cited, by counsel in argument, in at least one subsequent English case,[153] but it is of no assistance and should be ignored.

Beard v Shadler[154] concerned an English will which had been professionally drafted and where the meaning of certain clauses—principally relating to the disposition of intermediate income from residue—was unclear. There was no mention in the judgment of s.21, and the cases referred to were both pre-1983. This is another case in a time warp, but without any obvious excuse. What is clear here is that the will had been negligently prepared. No professionally drafted will should cause construction problems, it is the duty of a draftsman to understand the testator's instructions and to draft the will in such a way as to carry them out. In a case like

[149] Were this sort of case to arise in England today, it would be covered by s.21, but it has been suggested above that it should have been decided in favour of the charity intended by the testator, even before s.21 was enacted. The point would not be academic if the case were to arise (again) in Scotland, because Scotland has no legislation equivalent to s.21. For a recent English case see *Pinnel v Anison* [2006] W.T.L.R. (the testator's misdescribed sister took the gift intended for her).

[150] See above, para.10–38.

[151] See above, paras 10–42 et seq.

[152] *Sammut v Manzi* [2009] 1 W.L.R. 1834.

[153] *Reading v Reading* [2015] W.T.L.R. 1245.

[154] *Beard v Shadler* [2011] W.T.L.R. 1147.

this, the draftsman should have been called to give evidence—that is what s,21(2) provides for. He may not be enthusiastic about this, but it is he who has caused the problem.

10–61 *Curati v Perdoni*[155] was worse, s.21 was not ignored, it was mentioned, but misunderstood. The dispute here was as to whether a later will, written in Italian, revoked an earlier will, written in English. In paragraph 21 of his judgment, Sales J said:

> "...A will is a document which controls the disposition of property after someone dies. It is to be interpreted objectively, so everyone can know with confidence where they stand after the testator has gone. Evidence of the subjective understanding of the testator will not usually be relevant to that exercise. Since, judged on an objective basis, there is no ambiguity in the meaning of the 1980 will and the 1994 will (cf s 21 of the Administration of Justice Act 1982), the evidence of [an English solicitor who had advised the testator] cannot affect the proper interpretation of their meaning."

This passage is classically mistaken. To say that a will "is to be interpreted objectively" it to return four square to the literal approach. The reference in brackets to s.21 is, at first sight, not easy to understand, but it means that the judge thinks that certain words are "objectively unambiguous". This is wrong. Depending on context, any word can be ambiguous. Patent ambiguities are covered by s.21(1)(b) and latent ones by s.21(1)(c). The later will was clearly ambiguous. Had it not been ambiguous, there would have been no dispute, no case. The evidence of the solicitor would almost certainly have assisted in explaining the testator's meaning and it should have been heard.[156] This is exactly the sort of situation where s.21(2) would have assisted.[157]

10–62 In *Harris v Cooper*[158] the approach taken was over complicated and old fashioned. The problem here related to a home-made will which included the words "any money to be divided equally between my surviving relatives". There was no disagreement as to the meaning of the word "money", it was agreed that "money" in the context of this will included all the testarix's residuary estate. But who were her "relatives"? Here, Norris J looked at three pre-1983 cases and at an out of date (pre-1983) edition of *Hawkins and Ryder on the Construction of Wills*. After he had done this, he looked at s.21. His interpretation of the word "relatives" in the context of this will was almost certainly correct, but why did he need to look at pre-1983 cases and

155 *Curati v Perdoni* [2012] W.T.L.R. 505, Sales J (case then called *Perdoni v Curati*), CA ref [2013] W.T.L.R. 63. See note by editor in All E.R. Rev. 2012 at 446–448.

156 This is a case where the solicitor was *not* to blame for what had gone wrong. She had not drafted the document which was causing the problem. But she would have known about the testator's intentions.

157 The case involved other matters, including domicile and choice of law, the question of interpretation was not given much prominence in the Court of Appeal. The passage quoted from Sales J's judgment seems to have been based in part on a concession made by counsel: but it is still hard to understand how anyone can, today, speak of an objective lack of ambiguity.

158 *Harris v Cooper* [2010] EWHC 2620 (Ch). See note in All E.R. Rev. 2010 at 465–467.

an out of date edition of a book on Construction to reach his conclusion? The bigger question is why did a judge need to look at this will at all? Once it is accepted that what is being looked for is the testatrix's meaning, what she intended by the reference to her "relatives", it should have been possible to work this out without any need to involve the Chancery lawyers.

RSPCA v Sharp[159] is another case where there was no attempt to seek the **10–63** assistance of s.21 when construing a post-1983 will. Why not? Here, the dispute was as to whether the will had been intended to be especially tax-efficient, in which case it would have favoured a charity, or whether it had been meant to benefit the testator's brother, in which case it would have involved the payment of inheritance tax. Peter Smith J, at first instance, held in favour of the brother, but the Court of Appeal reversed him. What seems completely obvious in this case is that the will was badly drafted. Whatever was intended, it should have been clear. The draftsman should either have applied for rectification, or should have explained what the words he had used were intended to mean. So why did this not happen? The part-answer to this question is to be found in paragraph 16 of the judgment of the Court of Appeal:

> "16. . .it was common ground at the hearing that no extrinsic evidence should be admitted as an aid to the construction of the will. The judge did not therefore hear any evidence about the actual instructions given to the solicitors on behalf of the testator or what they intended by their drafting of the will. We therefore have to assume that the contents of the will properly construed represent what the testator intended to achieve."

The last sentence here contains a confusion. Why does the court "have to assume that the contents of the will properly construed represent what the testator intended to achieve"? What if the will could not be "properly construed"? What if it had been drafted in such a way that there was no "proper construction"? Everyone involved in the discussion of this will in this case assumed that the will had been intended to achieve *either* result X *or* result Y. But what if this was not so, and that it was actually intended to achieve *both* results at the same time. That would, in fact, have been impossible, but that does not mean that it was not intended, by the draftsman. Clearly, he made some kind of error. The question is, what error? Was X intended, or was Y intended, or were both intended? The way to find out was to call the draftsman to explain. The fact that he might have been embarrassed is not a reason for not calling him. As to the results reached at first instance and the Court of Appeal, Peter Smith J held for the brother, and the Court of Appeal for the charity. It may be that they were both wrong, but, if one had to choose between the two outcomes, Peter Smith J's construction seems, on the face of it, the more straightforward. What is clear here is that something was seriously wrong.

Where there is a professionally drafted will and there is a problem with

[159] *RSPCA v Sharp* [2011] 1 W.L.R. 980.

its interpretation, the standard approach should be to call the draftsman to explain. That follows straightforwardly from s.21(2).

10–64 Then there is yet another case which, at first glance seems similar—though this time the judge deserves to be congratulated. This was *Scarfe v Matthews*.[160] Bernard Matthews was the founder of a very successful turkey farming business and he left a substantial estate. He had property in England and in France and was survived by a wife from whom he was separated, by a cohabitant, by adopted children and by a natural son. Complications arose from the interrelationship of the French forced heirship provisions[161] with the need to provide for the payment of tax, and these complications led to a dispute among the beneficiaries. One possible suggested way of solving the dispute was by resorting to the doctrine of election,[162] and this was the route adopted by one of the parties. But it was Nicholas Strauss QC, sitting as a deputy judge of the High Court, who suggested, instead, opting for construction. What he said about construction was totally consistent with the intentional approach and he did mention s.21. All that was fine. But he might have gone further than he did, in that he could have suggested that s.21(2) should have been invoked, to introduce evidence of exactly what the testator said to those who drafted his will. This, again, is a case where s.21(2) would probably have been of real assistance.[163]

10–65 The major problem with the cases referred to above in paragraphs 10–61—10–64 is that they have either ignored s.21 altogether, or, if they have mentioned it, they have, for no clear reason, made no attempt to seek the assistance of s.21(2). But, once it becomes clear that there is a problem with the interpretation of a professionally drawn will, s.21(2) should be central to its resolution. Once it is apparent that the will contains either a patent or a latent ambiguity, s.21(2) allows the court to hear evidence of the testator's intention. And who should be able to give that evidence? The draftsman. He may have drafted the will incompetently, but he should surely know, from what the testator said to him, what the testator intended.[164] Section 21(2) allows him to give evidence of the testator's intention, ie to disclose his instructions to the court. It should be so straightforward.

And s.21(2) has not, in fact, been completely ignored. When *Frear v Frear*[165] reached the Court of Appeal in 2008, Wilson LJ, with whom the other members of the court agreed, included in his judgment[166] a reference to

[160] *Scarfe v Matthews* [2012] W.T.L.R. 1579. See note by editor in All E.R. Rev. 2012 at 451–454.

[161] For "forced heirship" see Chap.8, para.8–01.

[162] For the doctrine of election see Williams, Mortimer and Sunnucks, *Executors, Administrators and Probate*, 20th edn (London: Sweet & Maxwell, 2013), Chap.74. The doctrine is not covered in this book. It is old-fashioned and would, in earlier centuries, have been used from time to time to overcome problems caused by the literal approach to interpretation.

[163] Quaere, could there have been an application to rectify in this case. Probably not. The error by the person who prepared the will was probably a drafting error, rather than a clerical error, or a failure to understand instructions. See above, para.10–11.

[164] If he does not even know what the testator intended, his admission of such incompetence will at least have the advantage of telling everyone that the will cannot be interpreted and that there is no point in attempting the exercise.

[165] *Frear v Frear* [2009] 1 F.L.R. 391.

[166] At para.38. The point appears to have been raised by Wilson J himself, not by counsel.

latent ambiguity under s.21(1)(c), and then, in consequence, to s.21(2) and to evidence of statements by the testatrix which threw light upon her intention.

In *Esson v Esson*[167] Kevin Prosser QC[168] faced with a patent ambiguity under s.21(1) (b) admitted evidence of what the testatrix had said to her sister and to others.

2. *Marley v Rawlings*

The significance of *Marley v Rawlings*[169] in the present context, is that it was a case in the Supreme Court and it is probable that what was said in *Marley* will be quoted in later cases. *Marley* is, of course, the case of the switched wills, the case concerned with clerical errors and rectification. But, in *Marley*, Lord Neuberger, with whom the other members of the court agreed, set out his views on construction as well as on rectification. He began, in para.19 of his judgment by suggesting that wills should be interpreted in much the same way as contracts; the court should be concerned to seek the intention of the parties: "Whether the document in question is a commercial contract or a will, the aim is to identify the intention of the party or parties to the document by interpreting the words used in their documentary, factual and commercial context."[170] At the end of paragraph 19, he said that the court had to ignore "subjective evidence of any party's intentions", but he then qualified that in paragraph 24 by mentioning s.21 of the Administration of Justice Act, though rather as if it were an afterthought. **10–66**

He summed up in paragraphs 25 and 26:

> "25 In my view, section 21(1) confirms that a will should be interpreted in the same way as a contract, a notice or a patent. In particular, section 21(1)(c) shows that evidence is admissible when construing a will, and that that includes the surrounding circumstances. However, section 21(2) goes rather further. It indicates that, if one or more of the three requirements set out in section 21(1) is satisfied, then direct evidence of the testator's intention is admissible, in order to interpret the will in question.
>
> 26 Accordingly, as I see it, save where section 21(1) applies, a will is to be interpreted in the same way as any other document, but, in addition, in relation to a will, or a provision in a will, to which section 21(1) applies, it is possible to assist its interpretation by reference to evidence of the testator's actual intention (e g by reference to what he told the drafter of the will, or another person, or by what was in any notes he made or earlier drafts of the will which he may have approved or caused to be prepared)."

This passage is to be welcomed, and yet the welcome is slightly qualified. There was, in fact, no need at all for Lord Neuberger to say anything **10–67**

[167] *Esson v Esson* [2010] W.T.L.R. 187.
[168] Sitting as a deputy judge of the High Court.
[169] *Marley v Rawlings* [2015] A.C. 129.
[170] Para.20.

about construction in this case. It was concerned with rectification and was solved by rectification. Anything said about construction was, strictly, obiter. And, like so many other judges, he dealt with construction *before* looking at rectification. That was the wrong order.[171] Furthermore, wills are not like contracts, they are, in a very real sense, easier to construe, because one only needs to seek the intention of the testator, one is not looking for the intention of two or more parties. But the real problem with Lord Neuberger's approach is that he appears to see s.21 as somehow secondary. It is not, it is central. Of course, his approach is infinitely to be preferred to the literal approach, but there is, for those interpreting wills, no particular advantage in adopting rules which mirror those applicable to multi party documents. What is really needed in this context is guidance from the judges as to the introduction of evidence under s.21(2). This has no equivalent in contract.

It was suggested above[172] that, once it becomes clear that there is a problem with the interpretation of a professionally drawn will, s.21(2) should be central to its resolution and that the draftsman should give evidence of the testator's intention. It should be so straightforward. Incompetent draftsmen will not be enthusiastic about this, they will prefer to remain in the shadows. *RSPCA v Sharp*[173] seems to be the best example of this and it would be helpful if a senior judge could give an indication as to the obligation of a draftsman to put right what has gone wrong, whenever a will involves a construction problem.

10–68 In the days before 1983, lawyers who misdrafted wills somehow hid behind the literal approach. No one criticized the draftsman, in public at least. When a will has to be rectified, the draftsman has to admit that he has made a mistake. He should do the same when there is a problem with construction, but he should welcome the opportunity to put things right quite simply, by using s.21(2). The problem with Lord Neuberger's comments concerning construction, in *Marley*, is that, in an effort to standardize the law, they appear to leave the rules applicable to wills in a more complex state than they need to be—though certainly in a much better state than they were when literalism was truly dominant.

And, where wills are home-made (not that the editor wishes to encourage home-made wills) there should be less enthusiasm than there has been in the past for seeking the assistance of lawyers in interpreting them. If the words in a will are those of a layman, it may well be that other laymen, particularly among his friends and family, can work out what he meant quite as well as lawyers could.

3. Cases decided since *Marley v Rawlings*

10–69 There have been only two reported construction cases since *Marley*. The first of these is *Loring v Woodland Trust*[174] It is not typical, and not of great

[171] See above, para.10–02.
[172] See above, para.10–65.
[173] *RSPCA v Sharp* [2011] 1 W.L.R. 980.
[174] *Loring v Woodland Trust* [2015] 1 W.L.R. 3238.

assistance. Here, the will left to members of the testatrix's family "...such sum as is at the date of my death the amount of my unused nil-rate band for Inheritance Tax ..." The residue went to charity. After the making of the will, but before the testatrix's death, the inheritance tax rules were amended, to introduce the transferable nil-rate band.[175] In order to qualify for the transfer, the executors had, after the testatrix's death, to make a claim, which they did. The question of construction then became, was "such sum as is at the date of my death the amount of my unused nil rate band for Inheritance Tax" the single band, or the double band, including the transfer (£325,000 or £650,000)? The problem was that the will had to be construed to cover a situation which neither the testatrix not the draftsman could have contemplated, and it was necessary to choose one or other of two options.[176] Asplin J interpreted the will to mean that the larger sum and her construction was upheld by the Court of Appeal. Section 21 was, in effect, irrelevant to this situation. Asplin J adopted an essentially intentional approach, though she did refer, more than once to the testatrix's "expressed intention". The word "expressed", in this context, does sometimes have links with literalism. In the Court of Appeal, Lewison LJ spoke of "the purposes and values which are expressed or implicit in [the] wording". He took these words from an earlier judgment of Mance LJ in a case concerning a lease. His approach was clearly intentional and he won over the two other members of the court[177] who both indicated that they had originally been tempted to allow the appeal. The final result is clearly intentional (i.e. purposive), it certainly did not depend on a literal reading of the words in the will, but neither did it assist in demonstrating the use to which s.21 might be put.

The other construction case decided since *Marley v Rawlings* is *Reading v Reading*[178] and it has already been mentioned in the context of rectification.[179] Here, the solicitor who drafted the will used the word "issue" in one clause in it, when he knew that the testator intended that not only his descendants, but also his step children and step grandchildren should have been included. Asplin J looked at construction before rectification and it was suggested above that this was the wrong order.[180] Rectification should have been discussed first and, if this was a clerical error, which it may have been, rectification would have solved the problem.[181] This is the sort of case where the order of discussion matters, because it assists in interpreting words if it is known how they found their way into the will. Here, at least, and in contrast with some of the other cases discussed earlier, it was clear that the solicitor who drafted the will had made a mistake. The form of the mistake was not entirely clear, but it was clear that he had made one. **10–70**

175 For an explanation of the transferable nil-rate band, see below, para.16–19.

176 This is not a case where the testatrix has failed to contemplate a situation which was possible, but improbable, at the time the will was drafted. This situation could not have been envisaged, and the will had to be interpreted one way or the other.

177 Sir Colin Rimer and Christopher Clarke LJ.

178 *Reading v Reading* [2015] W.T.L.R. 1245.

179 See above, para.10–13.

180 See above, para.10–02.

181 See above, para.10–13.

Taking construction before rectification, Asplin quoted at length from Lord Neuberger's judgment in *Marley* and, following his approach, did correct the solicitor's error by construction. It was clear from reading the will as a whole that it included patent ambiguities and it was not hard to come to the conclusion that, in its overall context, the word "issue" could be read as including the step children and step grandchildren. The ultimate result was clearly correct. But the manner of getting there was slightly questionable. Apart from the question whether rectification or construction should have been considered first, and even if this had been a case of construction alone, there may have been too little emphasis on s.21. Following Lord Neuberger's approach, there was a tendency to insert s.21 into the discussion almost as an afterthought, and it was not clear how much part s.21(2) played in the final result. This made the relatively simple seem more complicated than it was.

4. A human rights case and construction

10–71 In *Re Erskine Trust, Gregg v Piggott*,[181A] the court, when construing a particular phrase in an inter vivos settlement, followed the decision of the European Court of Human Rights in *Pla and Puncernau v Andorr*[181B] and held that the phrase in question should not be construed as it would otherwise have been construed because that interpretation was "discriminatory".

The decision in *Pla and Puncernau* is wrong, and completely at odds with the intentional approach to the construction of wills. *Re Erskine* should not have followed it, and neither case should be followed when construing English wills. Freedom of testation necessarily involves freedom to discriminate.[182]

5. Errors of drafting in professionally drawn wills—questions of negligence

10–72 These are discussed further in Chapter 15.

V. CONSTRUCTION OF GIFTS TO CHARITY[183]

10–73 There remains one significant problem of interpretation, and it relates particularly to home-made wills.

[181A] [2013] Ch.135.
[181B] [2004] 2 F.C.R. 630.
[182] See note by the editor in All E.R. Rev. 2012 at 449. The *Pla and Puncernau* decision is illogical. The European Court of Human Rights appeared to see nothing wrong with the fact that the will in question treated males more favourably than females and treated legitimate descendants more favourably than illegitimate ones, but it took exception to the fact that the Andorran Court of Appeal had, in a judgment which was a model of the intentional approach to construction, held that a patent ambiguity in the will should be resolved in favour of the blood line, as opposed to an adopted descendant.
[183] See generally *Hawkins on the Construction of Wills*, 5th edn (London: Sweet & Maxwell, 2000), Chap.4.

1. Objects of charitable trust must be exclusively charitable

In English law, a gift in trust for charitable objects is good, but a gift to objects which are not exclusively charitable is void.[184] A charitable trust does not require certainty of objects provided all potential objects are exclusively charitable.[185] This requirement raises potential construction problems.[186] What words will suffice in a home-made will to demonstrate that the testator intended his gift to be exclusively charitable? 10–74

2. *Morice v Bishop of Durham*

In *Morice v Bishop of Durham*[187] the testatrix bequeathed her residuary personalty to the Bishop of Durham[188] upon trust to pay her debts and legacies and dispose of the ultimate residue "to such objects of benevolence and liberality as the Bishop in his own discretion shall most approve of." Sir William Grant MR held that the gift failed[189] because it was not exclusively charitable. The Bishop appealed to Lord Eldon, who upheld the Master of the Rolls.[190] 10–75

3. Gifts to ecclesiastical charities in the late eighteenth and early nineteenth centuries

During the latter part of the eighteenth-century and the earlier part of the nineteenth-century, judges who had to resolve disputes between charities (especially ecclesiastical charities) and testators' families usually found in favour of the families. The laity feared the wealth of the Church[191] and the judges reflected public feeling. The Mortmain Act, passed in 1736, had been designed to prevent testators from devising land to charity and it 10–76

[184] There are exceptional cases of non-charitable purpose trusts, but it seems that their scope will not be extended, *Re Astor's S.T.* [1952] Ch.534; in any case, they are not true trusts, but appear to operate as quasi powers.

[185] *Tudor on Charities*, edited by W. Henderson and J. Fowles, 10th edn (London: Sweet & Maxwell, 2015), para.3–013.

[186] The rule that a charitable trust does not require certainty of objects provided all potential objects are exclusively charitable is a rule of law, part of the law of charitable trusts: but when it is a question as to what words make a gift exclusively charitable, *that* is a question of construction.

[187] *Morice v Bishop of Durham* (1804) 9 Ves 399; (1805) 10 Ves 522.

[188] Whom she appointed as her sole executor.

[189] *Morice v Bishop of Durham* (1804) 9 Ves 399.

[190] *Morice v Bishop of Durham* (1805) 10 Ves 522. At first instance there were three issues: (i) was the gift for the personal benefit of the Bishop? (ii) was it a valid charitable trust? (iii) if it was not, was it a valid non-charitable purpose trust? It was clearly not a gift for the personal benefit of the Bishop, who disclaimed the application of any part of the property to his own use. And Sir William held that English law does not generally recognise non-charitable purpose trust s. It is in relation to this issue (the non-recognition of non-charitable purpose trusts) that the case is best remembered and usually cited. But the issue which is of concern in the present context is the charity issue—did the words which appeared in this will create a trust which was exclusively charitable?

[191] G. H. Jones, *History of the Law of Charity 1532–1827*, (London: Cambridge University Press, 1969), p.409.

remained in force until the end of the nineteenth-century.[192] *Morice* was not a case of a devise of land, but a gift of residuary personalty; so the bequest would have been valid *if* it was a valid bequest to charity. It was declared invalid on the basis that the gift was not exclusively charitable[193] and this result was reached by taking a very literal approach to the wording of the bequest in order to invalidate a bequest to which the judges were not sympathetic.

Even after the attitude of the courts towards charities in general seemed to soften, there appears to have been a residual anti-clericalism which manifested itself in some harsh decisions.[194] The cases are not easy to follow.[195]

4. Gifts for "benevolent", "philanthropic", or "public" purposes

10–77 The gift in *Morice* had been declared void on the basis that the words "benevolence" and "liberality" were wider than "charity". It was subsequently held that gifts for "benevolent",[196] or "philanthropic",[197] or "public" purposes[198] were also non-charitable. A line then began to be drawn between disjunctive and conjunctive constructions. Where there were objects which were "charitable *or* benevolent", such gifts would normally be void,[199] but gifts for purposes which were "charitable *and* benevolent" were normally valid.[200] What was clear was that the line between what was held to be charitable and what was held not to be charitable was a fine one; and some judges drew distinctions which most laymen, and many lawyers, found hard to understand.

5. *Chichester Diocesan Fund and Board of Finance v Simpson*[201]

10–78 In his professionally-drawn will, Caleb Diplock directed his executors to apply the residue of his estate "for such charitable institution or

[192] Until the enactment of the Mortmain and Charitable Uses Act 1891. Even under the 1891 Act, land devised to charity had normally to be sold within a year of the testator's death—though the charity could retain the proceeds of sale. The 1891 Act was repealed by the Charities Act 1960 and since 1960 charities have not been required to sell land which has been devised to them.

[193] During the latter part of the eighteenth-century and most of the nineteenth-century, a gift of land by will *to charity* would be void, and so those arguing in favour of the testator's family did not need to claim that such a gift was not exclusively charitable: they could argue that the gift *was* charitable and it would fail. This may explain why the judges were, on the whole, willing to find that gifts of land by will *were* gifts to charity (and, therefore, void) while gifts of pure personalty were not validly made *to charity*.

[194] See *Re Rumball* [1956] 1 Ch.105; *Re Garrard* [1907] 1 Ch.382; *Dunne v Byrne* [1912] A.C. 407; *Re Davies* (1932) 49 T.L.R. 5; *Re Stratton* [1931] 1 Ch.197; *Farley v Westminster Bank* [1939] A.C. 430.

[195] "in this notoriously difficult field some degree of fineness of distinction is, I think, inevitable"; Lord Evershed MR in *Re Rumball* [1956] 1 Ch.105 at 113.

[196] *James v Allen* (1817) 3 Mer. 17.

[197] *Re Macduff* [1896] 2 Ch.451.

[198] *Vezey v Jamson* (1822) 1 S. & S.69.

[199] *Re Jarman* (1878) 8 Ch.D 584.

[200] *Re Best* [1904] 2 Ch.354.

[201] *Chichester Diocesan Fund and Board of Finance v Simpson* [1944] A.C. 341.

institutions or other charitable or benevolent object or objects in England" as they should in their absolute discretion select. Farwell J held that this was a valid charitable bequest[202] by reading the will as a whole and by trying to see what the testator intended by the words "or benevolent" in the context of the will. But Farwell J was reversed by a unanimous Court of Appeal[203] and the Court of Appeal was upheld by a 4–1 majority in the House of Lords.[204]

At first sight, the decision of the House of Lords in *Simpson* was much like many other literal decisions. But *Simpson* was different: the challenge was launched by Caleb Diplock's cousins *after* almost all the money had been distributed to over 100 charities. The personal representatives were liable, and the recipients were also liable to the extent that the personal representatives were unable to pay.[205]

6. Where testator dies on or after 1 January 1983 leaving property to "benevolent" purposes

On the supposition that Caleb Diplock's intention was to leave the money to charity it is submitted that the words he used should be given the meaning *he* intended them to have. **10–79**

Caleb Diplock's will was professionally-drawn and the mistake should not have been made, because the draftsman should have used the formula "charitable and benevolent purposes" rather than "charitable or benevolent purposes" in order to achieve a valid charitable bequest. It is submitted, however, that even in the case of a professionally-drawn will, if it is clear that the testator intended his property to go to charity, such a gift should be interpreted to give it validity. The presumption that words used by lawyers should be interpreted to give them the lawyers' sense should not be carried so far as to mean that they should be given the lawyers' sense when the lawyers' sense is to invalidate the gift and it is known that neither the testator nor draftsman could have intended such an outcome.

A good example of the sort of problem which *could* arise is *Re Atkinson's Will Trusts*[206] where a solicitor drafted a will in which, inter alia, the testatrix bequeathed her residuary estate to be divided "between such worthy causes as have been communicated by me to my trustees in my lifetime". No causes were communicated and the question was whether the testatrix had shown general charitable intent. Had the word "charitable" been substituted for the word "worthy" there is no doubt that general charitable intent would have been found. The question was whether "worthy" **10–80**

[202] [1940] 1 Ch.988.
[203] The judgment of Goddard LJ is well worth reading for its expression of his distaste for the literal approach which he felt compelled by authority to adopt.
[204] As Professor Scott put it in (1945) 58 Harv. L.R. 548. "The Lord Chancellor, Viscount Simon, regretted the result but felt bound by prior decisions. Lord Macmillan and Lord Porter discussed the authorities and concurred, without expressing regret. Lord Simonds concurred and seemed to take an intellectual satisfaction in invalidating the bequest. Lord Wright dissented."
[205] See *Ministry of Health v Simpson* [1951] A.C. 251. This case is discussed below, in Chap.25.
[206] *Re Atkinson's Will Trusts* [1978] 1 W.L.R. 586.

could be read as meaning the same as "charitable". Megarry VC held that it could not. This is the traditional, pre-1983, approach. It is suggested that if a similar case were to arise where the testator dies on or after 1 January 1983, the court should, relying on s.21, hold that the clause was intended to cover objects which were exclusively charitable.[207]

VI. SPECIFIC RULES OF CONSTRUCTION

Interpretation sections in the Wills Act and in other legislation (other than section 21)

10–81 There are a number of sections, in the Wills Act 1837 and in other legislation, which lay down the sense which is prima facie to be given to words, or which fill gaps if the testator has failed to cover something in his will.

Sections 24–33 of the Wills Act 1837 are interpretation sections,[208] each of which contains the proviso "unless a contrary intention shall appear by the will".[209] Section 21 of the Administration of Justice 1982 allows the person interpreting the will to seek the testator's intention outside it, but these other sections lay down rules of interpretation which have to be followed unless a contrary intention shall appear *by the will*. What happens if one of these sections lays down a presumption as to what the testator intended and it can be shown by evidence extrinsic to the will that he did *not* intend this? In this sort of case—and it is not one which is likely to arise very often—the other sections should prevail, on the basis of the rule of statutory interpretation that a specific provision (in this case, the provision in the Wills Act) prevails over a general one, even if the general one is later.[210]

10–82 By contrast, sections in more recent legislation which are relevant to the interpretation of wills do *not* contain provisos such as "unless a contrary intention shall appear by the will"; instead, they use expressions such as "subject to any contrary intention".[211] These sections are not in conflict with s.21 and, when these sections apply, the interpreter may seek the tes-

[207] *A-G for the Cayman Islands v Wahr-Hansen* [2001] 1 A.C. 75 is not a case concerning the interpretation of a badly drafted will. It concerns a memorandum of agreement in which funds were settled (inter alia) on "organizations operating for the public good"—there was also mention of "worthy individuals". It was held that the beneficiaries were not exclusively charitable. The case is, it is submitted, correctly decided: but this is not an example of an incompetent draftsman who has intended to create a charitable trust and failed to use the "correct" wording; it is a case of an attempt to hide funds from the Norwegian banking and Revenue authorities.

[208] They are interpretation sections in the broad sense (some are gap-filling sections). S.32 has been repealed. See also LPA 1925 s.61 and AEA 1925 s.35.

[209] The proviso to s.33 is worded slightly differently—that is because the section has been substituted—but the substance is the same, see below Chap.14, paras 14–22 et seq.

[210] See F. R. Bennion, *Statutory Interpretation*, 5th edn (London: Butterworths, LexisNexis, 2008), s.88.

[211] See e.g. Legitimacy Act 1976 s.5(1).

tator's intention inside or outside the will. These sections merely give a prima facie indication of the meaning to be given to the words in the will.

The conflict between the sections in the Wills Act and s.21 is more apparent than real. The Wills Act sections were, in the main, inserted to give certain words and phrases meanings different from those which had been given to them prior to that Act's coming into force. It seems ironic, therefore, that these sections, originally designed to be liberal, now represent the last vestige of a semi-literal approach.

CHAPTER 11

THE CONSTRUCTION OF WILLS: SPECIFIC RULES OF CONSTRUCTION: THE CONSTRUCTION OF POWERS

I. GIFTS TO CHILDREN—THE AGE OF MAJORITY—ASCERTAINING CLASSES—ABSOLUTE/LIFE GIFTS

A. ADOPTED, LEGITIMATED AND ILLEGITIMATE CHILDREN[1]

The position of adopted, legitimated and illegitimate children for the purposes of intestacy was considered in Chapter 2.[2] Now it is necessary to turn to gifts by will. **11–01**

1. Adopted child

Under the Adoption and Children Act 2002 an adopted child is to be treated as if born the child of his adopters or adopter. If he is adopted by a couple he is treated as their legitimate child and otherwise he is treated as the legitimate child of his adopter,[3] not as the child of his natural parents.[4] This principle applies to the construction of the will of a testator who dies after 31 December 1975, subject to any contrary indication,[5] and it is immaterial whether the adoption order is made before or after the **11–02**

[1] See generally *Hawkins on the Construction of Wills*, 5th edn (London: Sweet & Maxwell, 2000), Chap.12.

[2] See above, paras 2–38 et seq.

[3] Adoption and Children Act 2002 s.67: ("couple" is defined in s.144(4)): this rule applies to an adoption order made by a court in any part of the UK, the Isle of Man or the Channel Islands, and to certain foreign adoptions, ibid s.66. For the protection of personal representatives see below, para.23–10.

[4] *Re Collins* [1990] Fam. 56; as to the effect of adoption by one of the child's natural parents, see Adoption and Children Act 2002 s.67(4) and Legitimacy Act 1976 s.4. The adopted child retains any interest vested in possession in him before the adoption, Adoption and Children Act 2002 s.69(4). Although a child who has been adopted by a third party or parties, is, prima facie, no longer within the description of "my child" in his natural father's will, in *Hardy v Hardy* [2013] EWHC 83 (Ch) the words "my children" in a natural father's will *were* construed to include such a son, because there was a contrary indication in the will.

[5] Adoption and Children Act 2002 s.69(1). In the case of a testator who died before 1 January 1976, the Adoption Act 1958 ss.16, 17 and provisions containing references to those sections

testator's death.[6] Thus, if T dies in 2015, having by his will given property upon trust for his son X for life and after X's death for X's children in equal shares absolutely, any child adopted by X (whether before or after T's death) will be entitled to take, unless there is a contrary indication. If X is T's daughter, the same result follows, subject to an exception which may be applicable in the case of a child adopted by a woman after she has attained 55 years of age.[7]

11–03 The Adoption and Children Act 2002 sets out two rules of construction (complete with statutory examples) which are applicable to the will of a testator who dies after 1975, subject to any contrary indication. The rules relate to a disposition[8] by will which depends on the date of birth of a child or children. The disposition is to be construed as if:

(i) the adopted person had been born on the date of adoption,[9] and
(ii) two or more people adopted on the same date had been born on that date in the order of their actual births,

but these rules do not affect any reference to the age of a child.[10] To take the statutory example of a gift by T's will to the children[11] of X "living at my death or born afterwards". T dies in 2008 and after T's death X adopts

continue to apply, Adoption and Children Act 2002 s.139 and Sch.4, para.17: *Re Upton* [2004] W.T.L.R. 1339 (will made in 1936).

6 ibid s.67(6). If the testator T died before 1 January 1976, the adoption order must have been made before T's death (Adoption Act 1958 ss.16(2) and 17(2)): but if T's will or codicil was executed before 1 April 1 1959, (i) the adoption order must have been made before its execution, unless it was confirmed by codicil executed after 31 March 1959 (Adoption Act 1958 Sch.5, para.4(3) and (4)), and (ii) the adopted child cannot take if T's will or codicil was executed before 1 January 1950 (ibid Sch.5, para.4(1) and (2)) unless, exceptionally, the child is entitled to take at common law, *Re Fletcher* [1949] Ch.473; *Re Gilpin* [1954] Ch.1; *Re Jebb* [1966] Ch.666, but see J. H. C. Morris (1966) 82 L.Q.R. 196. The position may now appear to be complicated by the first instance decision in *Re Erskine Trust, Gregg v Piggott* [2013] Ch.135, where the court, when construing the phrase "statutory next of kin" in an inter vivos settlement made in 1948, followed the decision of the European Court of Human Rights in *Pla and Puncernau v Andorra* [2004] 2 F.C.R. 630 and held that adopted children were within the phrase, because, to decide otherwise, would be "discriminatory". The decision in the *Pla and Puncernau* case is wrong, and completely at odds with the intentional approach to the construction of wills. *Re Erskine* should not have followed it, and neither case should be followed when construing English wills. Freedom of testation necessarily involves freedom to discriminate, see note by the editor in All E.R. Rev. 2012 at 449.

7 Adoption and Children Act 2002 s.69.(5) provides that "Where it is necessary to determine for the purposes of a disposition of property effected by an instrument, i.e. T's will, whether a woman can have a child—(a) it must be presumed that once a woman has attained the age of 55 years she will not adopt a person after execution of the instrument [this may mean after T's death, s.73(4)], and (b), if she does so, then that person is not to be treated as her child or (if she does so as one of a couple) as a child of the other one of the couple for the purposes of the instrument." If T's daughter X disclaims or releases her life interest, it may be necessary to determine whether X can have a child: quaere in what other circumstances it is "necessary".

8 ibid 2002 s.73.

9 As to the effect of adoption by one of the child's natural parents, see ibid s.70 (which sets out a statutory example).

10 ibid s.69(2).

11 *Or* grandchildren. Another statutory example is to X for life "until he has a child," and then to his child or children.

a child, who was born in 2006. This child is entitled to take under the gift as a child of X born (applying rule (i)) after T's death, though the child does not answer to the description of a child of X living at T's death. The second statutory example is another gift by T's will to the children[12] of X "living at my death or born afterwards before any one of such children for the time being in existence attains a vested interest and who attain the age of 21 years." X's adopted child is entitled to take under this gift if he is adopted before any other child attains a vested interest and if he attains the age of 21 years, which is measured from his true date of birth and not from the date of his adoption. Finally, consider a gift by T's will to the eldest son of X. At T's death in 2008 X has a natural son (born in 2006) and an adopted son (born in 2005 and adopted in 2007). If "eldest" is a reference to the age of a child, the adopted son takes; but probably it is not and, if so (applying rule (i)), the natural son takes.

By way of exception, an adoption does not affect the devolution of any property limited (expressly or not) to devolve along with any peerage or dignity or title of honour, unless a contrary intention is expressed in the will.[13]

2. Legitimated child[14]

Under the Legitimacy Act 1976 a legitimated person—and any other person—is entitled to take any interest under the will of a testator who dies after 31 December 1975 as if the legitimated person had been born legitimate, subject to any contrary indication.[15] As in the case of adoption, it is immaterial whether the legitimation occurs before or after the testator's death.[16] Again, in the case of legitimation, similar rules of construction are applicable to a disposition by will which depends on the date of birth of a child or children as apply (as explained above) in the case of adoption.[17] For instance, if T dies in 2008 having by his will—which was made before 1970—made a gift to the children of Z "living at my death or born afterwards," a child of Z who is legitimated after T's death by his parents' marriage is entitled to take under the gift as a legitimate child of Z born (under the rule of construction—on the date of his legitimation.[18] **11–04**

[12] *Or* grandchildren.

[13] ibid s.71; adoption does not affect the descent of any peerage or dignity or title of honour.

[14] A legitimated child is one who was illegitimate at the time of his birth, but who becomes legitimate by his parents' subsequent marriage. Legitimation was introduced into English law by the Legitimacy Act 1926.

[15] Legitimacy Act 1976 ss.5(1), (3) and (6) and s.10. In the case of a testator who died before 1 January 1976, the Legitimacy Act 1926 ss.3 and 5 continue to apply, Legitimacy Act 1976 Sch.1, para.2: *Re Upton* [2004] W.T.L.R. 1339.

[16] If the testator T died before 1 January 1976, the legitimation must have occurred before T's death, Legitimacy Act 1926 s.3(1).

[17] Legitimacy Act 1976 ss.5(4) and (5): as to the effect of posthumous legitimation see ibid s.5(6), and as to devolution of property limited to devolve along with any dignity or title of honour see ibid Sch.1, para.4.

[18] Legitimacy Act 1976 s.5(4). If T's will had been made after 1969, an illegitimate child of X would have been entitled to take: ibid s.5(5) gives statutory examples but in each example legitimation appears to have no practical effect if T's will was made after 1969, because

3. Illegitimate child

11–05 At common law a gift by will to children, or other relations, was prima facie construed as referring only to legitimate children, or persons tracing their relationship exclusively through legitimate links.[19] This rule of construction was reversed by s.15 of the Family Law Reform Act 1969, which applies to a disposition of property by a will or codicil made after 31 December 1969 and before 4 April 1988. If the will or codicil was executed before 1970, it is not, for this purpose, treated as made after 31 December 1969, even if it is confirmed by a codicil executed after that date.[20]

(a) *Rules of construction under the Family Law Reform Act 1969*

11–06 Section 15(1) of the Act lays down two rules of construction:

- (i) Any reference (express or implied) to the child or children of any person X is to be construed as, or as including, a reference to any illegitimate child of X. If T's will (made after 1969) gives property upon trust for X for life and after X's death for X's children in equal shares absolutely, any illegitimate child of X (whether born before or after T's death)[21] is entitled to take.
- (ii) Any reference—express or implied—to a person or persons related in some other manner to any person X is to be construed as, or as including, a reference to anyone who would be so related if he, or some other person through whom the relationship is deduced, had been born legitimate. A gift by T's will (made after 1969) to X's grandchildren therefore includes both the illegitimate child of a legitimate child of X and the legitimate child of an illegitimate child of X.[22]

(b) *Exceptions*

11–07 These rules of construction apply only to references to a child or other relation, where the reference is to a person who is to benefit, or who is capable of benefiting under the disposition; or where (when such person is being designated) someone else is referred to as being someone to or through

the illegitimate child, or a person related through him, would have been entitled to take anyway, unless a contrary intention appeared in the will, Family Law Reform Act 1969 s.15; Legitimacy Act 1976 ss.6(1) and (3).

[19] For this rule, and the exceptions to it, see generally *Hawkins on the Construction of Wills*, 5th edn (London: Sweet & Maxwell, 2000), Chap.12.

[20] Family Law Reform Act 1969 s.15(8): see also ibid s.1(7). For the general rule that a confirmed will or codicil operates as if it had been made at the time of its confirmation see above, para.7–67.

[21] ibid s.15(7) abolishes any rule of law that a gift to illegitimate children born after T's death is void as contrary to public policy.

[22] Quaere whether it also includes the illegitimate child of an illegitimate child, see E. C. Ryder (1971) 24 C.L.P., 163–164; Law Commission Report on Illegitimacy, Law Com. No.118, p.104. See also Prichard [1981] Conv. 343 ("as on intestacy" in will).

whom that person is related.[23] So these rules do not apply to a gift to X absolutely "if he dies without leaving children"; the word "children" in this case means legitimate children and, if X dies leaving one illegitimate child but no legitimate children, X takes absolutely.[24]

These rules of construction apply "unless the contrary intention appears". The contrary intention does not need to appear in the will itself.[25]

(c) *Rules of construction under the Family Law Reform Act 1987*

Section 19 of the Family Law Reform Act 1987 changes these rules of construction and abolishes most of these exceptions.[26] It applies to dispositions[27] by will or codicil made after 3 April 1988.[28] Under s.19 references (whether express or implied) to any relationship between two persons are to be construed without regard to whether the father and mother of either of them, or the father and mother of any person through whom the relationship is deduced, were married to each other at any time. This new rule of construction applies whether or not the reference is to a person who is to benefit or is capable of benefiting under the disposition.[29] **11–08**

The new rule of construction applies "unless the contrary intention appears". The contrary intention does not need to appear in the will.[30]

4. Change of gender

Section 9 of the Gender Recognition Act 2004 states that once a full gender recognition certificate is issued to a person, the person's gender becomes for all purposes the acquired gender; so if the acquired gender is male, the person's sex becomes that of a man and, if female, it becomes that of a woman. It follows that a gift in a will to an "eldest daughter" will benefit someone who was previously a son, but s.15 of the Act provides that the fact that a person's gender has become the acquired gender does not affect the devolution of property under a will made before 4 April 2005.[31] **11–09**

[23] Family Law Reform Act 1969 s.15(2).

[24] See E. C. Ryder, *loc. cit.* pp.164–166. And these rules of construction do not affect the construction of the word "heir" or "heirs" or of any expression which is used to create an entail, or the devolution of any property which would (apart from these rules) devolve along with a dignity or title of honour, Family Law Reform Act 1969 s.15(2) and s.15(6) No new entails may be created after 1996, Trusts of Land and Appointment of Trustees Act 1996 s.2.

[25] See above, Chap.10, paras 10–57 and 10–58.

[26] See Law Commission Second Report on Illegitimacy, Law Com. No.157.

[27] Including an oral disposition, Family Law Reform Act 1987 s.19(6), e.g. a privileged will made orally.

[28] Family Law Reform Act 1987 (Commencement No.1) Order 1988 (SI 1988/425). A will or codicil executed before, but confirmed by codicil executed on or after, 4 April 1988, is not treated as made on or after that date, Family Law Reform Act 1987 s.19(7).

[29] It also applies to the construction of the word "heir" or "heirs" and to any expression which is used to create an entailed interest (no new entails may be created after 1996, Trusts of Land and Appointment of Trustees Act 1996 s.2) but it does not apply to the devolution of any property which would otherwise devolve along with a dignity or title of honour, Family Law Reform Act 1987 s.19(2) and 19(4).

[30] See above, Chap.10, paras 10–81 and 10–82.

[31] The date when the Act came into force (SI 2005/54).

B. AGE OF MAJORITY

11–10 In a will the expressions "full age", "infant", "infancy", "minor", "minority" and similar expressions are to be construed by reference to the provision that a person attains full age on attaining the age of 18.[32] This construction applies, in the absence of a definition or of any indication of a contrary intention, if the will was made after 31 December 1969. A will or codicil executed before 1970 is not treated as made after 1969 even if it was confirmed by a codicil executed after 1969.[33]

The construction of any expression specifying a particular age (for example, "twenty-one") is not altered by the Family Law Reform Act 1969.[34]

C. RULES FOR ASCERTAINING CLASSES[35]

11–11 Wills often contain gifts to a class of beneficiaries. For example, T may give:

(i) £100 to each of the children of X (an individual gift to each member of a class, not a class gift in the strict sense);
(ii) £10,000 to the children of Y in equal shares absolutely (a class gift in the strict sense, because the size of a child's share depends on the number of children who fall within the class[36]); and
(iii) £10,000 to the children of Z who attain the age of 21 years in equal shares absolutely (again a class gift in the strict sense, but subject to a contingency).

In each of these examples the question may arise whether children who come into existence after T's death are eligible to take. Of course, T might have expressed his intention clearly in his will, e.g. by giving £100 to each of the children of X "who shall be living at my death." But if T has not done so, the question must be answered by applying certain rules of construction known as the class-closing rules.[37] Which rule is applicable depends upon whether the gift is:

(1) an individual gift to each member of a class (as in example (i) above); or
(2) a class gift where each member of the class takes a share at birth (as in example (ii) above); or

[32] Family Law Reform Act 1969 s.1.
[33] Family Law Reform Act 1969 s.1(7): for confirmation see above, paras 7–65 et seq.
[34] See E. C. Ryder (1971) 24 CLP pp.158–160; Cretney (1970) 120 N.L.J. 144, 145.
[35] See generally *Hawkins on the Construction of Wills*, 5th edn (London, Sweet & Maxwell, 2000), Chap.14.
[36] *Pearks v Moseley* (1880) 5 App.Cas. 714, 723. For the nature of a class gift see below, para.14–14.
[37] See J. H. C. Morris (1954) 70 L.Q.R. 61; S. J. Bailey [1958] C.L.J. 39.

(3) a class gift where a contingency is imposed on each member of the class (as in example (iii) above).

In the explanation which follows, reference will be made to persons who are "living" at a particular time or who "come into existence" before a particular time. In applying these rules it is necessary to remember that a child who is *en ventre sa mére* at that time (and who is subsequently born alive) is by a legal fiction treated as already "living", or as having already "come into existence", at that time if the child may thereby become entitled to benefit as a member of the class.[38]

1. Individual gift to each member of a class

In the case of an individual gift to each member of a class, the class closes at the testator's death. If T by his will gives a legacy of £100 to each of the children of X, only children of X living at T's death take under the gift[39]; if no child of X is living at T's death, the gift fails. Similarly, if T gives a legacy of £100 to each of the children of X who attain the age of 21 years or marry, only children of X living at T's death are eligible to take. It is immaterial whether each of them satisfies the contingency before or after T's death; if no child of X is living at T's death the gift fails.[40] **11–12**

The object of this drastic class-closing rule is to enable the personal representatives to distribute T's residuary estate. The rule is a rule of convenience which fixes the maximum number of members of the class at T's death, so that the personal representatives may know the total sum required to meet the legacies and may safely distribute the remainder of T's estate.[41] If the class did not close at T's death, the personal representatives could not safely distribute T's residuary estate until it had become impossible for further children of X to be born.

The rule is modified if the will postpones payment of the legacies and distribution of the residue until the death of a life tenant, e.g. if T gives his estate upon trust for X for life, and after X's death to pay £100 to each of the children of X and to hold the remainder on trust for Y absolutely. In that case the class remains open until the death of the life tenant, X, and therefore embraces children of X who are living at T's death or who come into existence before X's death.[42] **11–13**

The rule is altogether excluded—so that any children of X coming into existence after T's death may take—if the inconvenience prevented by the rule either does not exist or is expressly contemplated by the testator.[43]

[38] *Trower v Butts* (1823) 1 S. & S. 181 (such a child is "within the reason and motive of the gift"); *Storrs v Benbow* (1853) 3 De G.M. & G. 390; *Re Salaman* [1908] 1 Ch.4 (such a child is treated as born if he thereby takes a direct benefit); *Elliot v Joicey* [1935] A.C. 209: cf. *Re Corlass* (1875) 1 Ch.D. 460 (child *en ventre* illegitimate, though legitimated before birth). But see *Re Gardiner's Estate* (1875) 20 Eq. 647 (which appears to be wrongly decided).

[39] *Ringrose v Bramham* (1794) 2 Cox 384.

[40] *Rogers v Mutch* (1878) 10 Ch.D. 25.

[41] *Re Bellville* [1941] Ch.414.

[42] *Att.-Gen. v Crispin* (1784) 1 Bro.C.C. 396.

[43] *Re Bellville*, above, at pp.418–419.

An instance of the first exception is where the testator directs a fund of a specified amount to be set aside out of which alone the legacies are made payable.[44] The second exception was held to be applicable in a case where the testator showed a clear intention that the class should include any children coming into existence after his death and directed a sufficient fund to be set aside for this purpose.[45]

2. Class gift where each member takes a share at birth

11–14 Under a class gift in the strict sense, the members of the class share the same subject-matter of the gift, whether equally or in specified proportions. If the class has not yet closed, the personal representatives cannot safely distribute a share to a person who is already a member of the class, because the minimum size of that share is not yet fixed. However, the personal representatives can safely distribute the remainder of the testator's estate.

A class gift where each member takes a share at birth may be (1) immediate or (2) postponed.

(a) *Immediate gift*

11–15 In the case of an immediate gift where each member takes a share at birth, the class closes at the testator's death if any member of the class is then in existence[46]; if no member of the class is then in existence, no class-closing rule applies and the class remains open indefinitely.[47] If T's will gives £10,000 to the children of X in equal shares absolutely, and one or more children of X are living at T's death, then the class closes immediately and they alone take under the gift. On the other hand, if no child of X is living at T's death, then the class remains open indefinitely and all the children of X born thereafter take under the gift. This rule that the class closes at the testator's death if any member of the class is then in existence applies to an immediate class gift which is vested, even though payment is directed to be postponed until the youngest member of the class attains full age,[48] or even though a member's share is liable to be divested in a certain event (e.g. on his death under 21 years of age).[49]

[44] *Evans v Harris* (1842) 5 Beav. 45.

[45] *Defflis v Goldschmidt* (1816) Mer. 417 (court directed master to inquire what would be a sufficient sum to set aside to answer legacies of £2,000 payable to each child of A who might thereafter be born, having regard to A's age): cf. *Butler v Lowe* (1839) 10 Sim. 317.

[46] *Viner v Francis* (1789) 2 Cox 190; *Re Chartres* [1927] 1 Ch.466, 471; *Re Manners* [1955] 1 W.L.R. 1096.

[47] *Shepherd v Ingram* (1764) Amb. 448; *Weld v Bradbury* (1715) 2 Vern. 705; *Harris v Lloyd* (1823) 1 T. & R. 310; *Re Chartres*, above; *Re Bleckly* [1951] Ch.740, 749.

[48] *Re Manners*, above, (gift by T's will to my grandchildren (the children of my son X) "to be administered towards their maintenance and education until the youngest is 21 and then distributed equally among them": held grandchildren alive at T's death alone took): see also *Scott v Harwood* (1821) 5 Madd. 332.

[49] *Davidson v Dallas* (1808) 14 Ves. 576; *Scott v Harwood*, above.

(b) *Postponed gift*

A class gift may be postponed by a preceding life or other interest,[50] e.g. a gift by T's will of £10,000 upon trust for X for life and after X's death for the children of Y in equal shares absolutely. In this case the class closes at the time when the postponement ends,[51] but if at that time there is as yet no member of the class, no class–closing rule applies and the class remains open indefinitely.[52] If one or more children of Y are living at T's death or come into existence before X's death, the class closes at X's death and embraces only children of Y who are living at T's death or who come into existence before X's death. If any such child dies after T's death but before distribution of the £10,000, the child's share passes as an asset of his estate to his personal representatives.[53] On the other hand, if no child of Y is living at T's death or comes into existence before X's death, then the class remains open indefinitely and all the children of Y born thereafter take under the gift. This rule—that the class closes at the time when the postponement ends—applies to a class gift which is vested, even though payment is directed to be postponed until the youngest member of the class attains full age,[54] or even though a member's share is liable to be divested in a certain event. **11–16**

Thus the same class-closing rule applies to any class gift where each member takes a share at birth, whether the gift is immediate or postponed, except that the crucial "class-closing time" is the testator's death in the case of an immediate gift, and the end of the period of postponement in the case of a postponed gift. This rule differs in one vital respect from the more drastic rule applicable in the case of an individual gift to each member of a class[55]: under this rule, if at the class-closing time there is as yet no member of the class, the class remains open indefinitely. **11–17**

This class-closing rule, in common with the other rules, is sometimes called a rule of convenience (though it may appear inconvenient to Y's children who come into existence after the class has closed). In truth, it is a rule of construction and it is based upon the supposition that T would not wish Y's children who are in existence at T's death (or, in the case of a postponed gift, who come into existence before the time when the

[50] e.g. a life interest which is determinable or subject to a condition subsequent, *Re Aylwin's Trusts* (1873) L.R. 16 Eq. 585 (life interest determinable on bankruptcy or insolvency): or an absolute interest subject to a gift over, *Ellison v Airey* (1748) 1 Ves.Sen. 111 (to X absolutely, but if X dies under 21 unmarried, to the children of B). See also *Oppenheim v Henry* (1853) 10 Hare 441 (gift to all my grandchildren, to be divided among them at the end of 20 years after my death, income to be accumulated meanwhile: held class closed at end of 20 years).

[51] *Ellison v Airey*, above; *Devisme v Mello* (1782) 1 Bro.C.C. 537; *Ayton v Ayton* (1787) 1 Cox 327; *Middleton v Messenger* (1799) 5 Ves. 136; *Walker v Shore* (1808) 15 Ves. 122; *Holland v Wood* (1871) L.R. 11 Eq. 91.

[52] *Chapman v Blisset* (1735) Cas.t.Talb. 145; *Hutcheson v Jones* (1817) 2 Madd. 124; *Re Chartres* [1927] 1 Ch.466, 471–472; *Re Bleckly* [1951] Ch.740, 749 and 755.

[53] *Devisme v Mello*, above: but if the child held as a joint tenant (which is not the case in the example in the text) the right of survivorship operates.

[54] *Smith v Jackson* (1823) 1 L.J.(O.S.) Ch.231 (gift to children of T's granddaughters to be paid when youngest attained 21 years).

[55] Where the gift fails if there is no class member living at the testator's death.

postponement ends) to have to wait for distribution of the capital until it is no longer possible for further children of Y to be born.[56]

(c) *Acceleration of class gift by failure of preceding interest*

11–18 To return to the gift by T's will of £10,000 upon trust for X for life and after X's death for the children of Y in equal shares absolutely. If X's life interest fails because (for instance) he predeceases T, the class gift to the children of Y is accelerated and becomes an immediate—and not a postponed—gift, so that the crucial class-closing time is the testator's death.[57]

If X survives T, but X disclaims his life interest and thereby accelerates the class gift to the children of Y, does this have the same effect on class-closing as if X had predeceased T? Probably the answer is no—the crucial class-closing time is still X's death. In *Re Davies*[58] X—who had three children—disclaimed her life interest under T's will, and Vaisey J held that the vested class gift in remainder to the issue of X was accelerated, and that X's three children took to the exclusion of any other issue of X who might come into existence prior to X's death. But in *Re Harker's Will Trusts*[59] Goff J refused to follow *Re Davies*. He decided that, despite the acceleration of the class gift in remainder, the class of beneficiaries must remain open until X's death. It appears likely that the decision in *Re Harker's Will Trusts* will be followed.[60] X, by disclaiming his life interest *after* T's death, cannot change the composition of the class of beneficiaries entitled under the class gift in remainder. The class-closing rules are rules of construction and the proper construction of T's will cannot be altered after T's death by X's disclaimer.

3. Class gift where contingency is imposed on each member

11–19 Where a contingency is imposed on each member of the class, the relevant class-closing rule is known as the rule in *Andrews v Partington*.[61]

(a) *Immediate gift*

11–20 In the case of an immediate gift where a contingency is imposed on each member, the class closes at the testator's death if any member of the class

[56] *Re Ward* [1965] Ch.856, 865. See generally for the basis of the rules S. J. Bailey [1958] C.L.J. 39, 45–48.

[57] *Sprackling v Ranier* (1761) Dick. 344: as to T's revocation of X's life interest by a codicil see *Eavestaff v Austin* (1854) 19 Beav. 591; *Re Johnson* (1893) 68 L.T. 20. For acceleration see below, paras 14–77 et seq.

[58] *Re Davies* [1957] 1 W.L.R. 922: see also *Re Taylor* [1957] 1 W.L.R. 1043, 1047–1048 and *Re Chartres* [1927] 1 Ch.466.

[59] *Re Harker's Will Trusts* [1969] 1 W.L.R. 1124 (X for life, on his death to X's children equally on attaining 21; X surrendered his life interest; later one child of X attained 21: held the remainder was accelerated but the class remained open until X's death): see also *Re Kebty-Fletcher's W.T.* [1969] 1 Ch.339.

[60] It was not followed by the N.S.W. Sup Ct in *Bassett v Bassett* [2005] W.T.L.R., but the court made reference to an out-of-date edition of *Hawkins and Ryder*, which preceded *Harker* and *Kebty-Fletcher*.

[61] *Andrews v Partington* (1791) 3 Bro.C.C. 401.

who has satisfied the contingency is then in existence[62]; if not, the class closes as soon as one member satisfies the contingency.[63] Thus, if T's will gives £10,000 to the children of Z who attain the age of 21 years in equal shares absolutely, the class closes at T's death if any child of Z who has attained the age of 21 years is then in existence; if not, the class closes as soon as a child of Z attains the age of 21 years. Once the class closes, any child already in existence may take under the gift if the child subsequently satisfies the contingency, but any child not already in existence is excluded from taking.

(b) *Postponed gift*

A class gift may be postponed by a preceding life or other interest,[64] e.g. a gift by T's will of £10,000 upon trust for Y for life and after Y's death for the children of Z who attain the age of 21 years in equal shares absolutely. In this case the class closes at the time when the postponement ends if any member of the class who was in existence after T's death has satisfied the contingency[65]; if not, the class closes as soon as one member satisfies the contingency.[66] Applying this rule to this example, the class closes at Y's death if any child of Z, who was in existence after T's death, has attained the age of 21 years; if not, the class closes as soon as a child of Z attains the age of 21 years. **11–21**

In short, the same class-closing rule applies to any class gift where a contingency is imposed on each member, whether the gift is immediate or postponed, except that the crucial class-closing time is the testator's death in the case of an immediate gift, and the end of the period of postponement in the case of a postponed gift. The rule differs in one vital respect from both of the rules so far considered: under this rule, if at the class-closing time there is as yet no member who has satisfied the contingency, the class does remain open but only until one member satisfies the contingency.[67]

This rule, like the other rules, is a rule of construction[68] and is based upon the supposition that T would not wish a child of Z

[62] *Picken v Matthews* (1878) 10 Ch.D. 264; *Balm v Balm* (1830) 3 Sim. 492.

[63] *Andrews v Partington*, above; *Re Mervin* [1891] 3 Ch.197. It is immaterial that no member of the class is in existence at the testator's death, *Re Bleckly* [1951] Ch.740, 749–750.

[64] e.g. a life interest which is determinable or subject to a condition subsequent, *Re Smith* (1862) 2 J. & H. 594 (life interest determinable on bankruptcy or insolvency); *Re Bleckly* [1951] Ch.740 (whilst wife or widow of X); or an absolute interest subject to a gift over, *Gillman v Daunt* (1856) 3 K. & J. 48. As to postponement by a direction to accumulate see *Watson v Young* (1885) 28 Ch.D. 436; *Re Stephens* [1904] 1 Ch.322; *Re Watt's W.T.* [1936] 2 All E.R. 1555.

[65] *Re Smith*, above; *Re Canney's Trusts* (1910) 101 L.T. 905; *Gillman v Daunt*, above. See also *Re Faux* (1915) 113 L.T. 81 (one-half of income to A for life and other half to B for life: held postponement did not end at A's death, B still being alive); *Re Paul's S.T.* [1920] 1 Ch.99.

[66] *Clarke v Clarke* (1836) 8 Sim. 59; *Re Smith*, above; *Locke v Lamb* (1867) L.R. 4 Eq. 372; *Re Emmet's Estate* (1879) 13 Ch.D. 484. It is immaterial that no member of the class comes into existence until after the time when the postponement ends, *Re Bleckly*, above.

[67] i.e. not definitely.

[68] *Re Bleckly*, above at 747 and 750.

who has satisfied the contingency to have to wait for distribution of the capital until it is no longer possible for further children of Z to be born.[69]

4. Gift of income to a class

11–22 The rules so far considered do not apply to a gift of income to members of a class, e.g. a gift by T's will of property upon trust to pay the income thereof to the children of X in equal shares during some defined period. In this case the class does not close and each instalment of income is payable to the children of X for the time being living.[70] For example, if X has three children at T's death, the first instalment of income is payable in third shares to X's three children; if another child of X is then born, the next instalment is payable in quarter shares to X's four children. This rule—that the class does not close—applies whether the members of the class take a share of income at birth[71] (as in the last example), or on satisfying a contingency[72] (e.g. a gift of income to the children of X who attain the age of 21 years in equal shares).

The class-closing rules which apply to gifts of capital are based on suppositions which are not applicable to gifts of income.[73]

5. Class gifts to which class-closing rules apply

11–23 The class-closing rules do not, of course, apply to gifts to particular persons individually; for instance, a gift of property by T's will "to be divided equally between the children of X, namely B, C and D" is not a class gift.[74] Again, the class-closing rules do not apply in the case of a gift on trust for X for life and after X's death for X's children, because it is impossible for further children of X to come into existence after X's death: accordingly T cannot be taken to have intended a distribution before all X's children come into existence.[75]

The class-closing rules have been applied to a class gift made by T's will to a *limited* class of relatives, i.e. to a class which is not capable of infinite expansion, being limited to one or more particular generations. Instances include class gifts made by T's will to the children of X,[76] T's grandchildren,[77] T's brothers and sisters,[78] the nephews and nieces

[69] *Re Ward* [1965] Ch.856, 865.

[70] *Re Ward* [1965] Ch.856 (not following *Re Powell* [1898] 1 Ch.227).

[71] *Re Ward*, above.

[72] *Re Wenmoth's Estate* (1887) 37 Ch.D. 266.

[73] *Re Ward*, above, at 865.

[74] *Bain v Lescher* (1840) 11 Sim. 397 (B predeceased T and his share lapsed): see also *Havergal v Harrison* (1843) 7 Beav. 49 ("my brothers and sisters"): see below, para.14–14, below.

[75] *Re Harker's W.T.* [1969] 1 W.L.R. 1124, 1128; *Re Kebty-Fletcher's W.T.* [1969] 1 Ch.339. A child of X *en ventre sa mére* is treated as being in existence.

[76] *Viner v Francis* (1789) 2 Cox 190 (the children of my late sister X); *Re Bleckly* [1951] Ch.740 (children of my son X who attain 21).

[77] *Oppenheim v Henry* (1853) 10 Hare 441 (my grandchildren); *Gimblett v Purton* (1871) L.R. 12 Eq. 427 (such of my grandchildren as attain 21); *Re Manners* [1955] 1 W.L.R. 1096.

[78] *Re Gardiner's Estate* (1875) L.R. 20 Eq. 647.

of X,[79] T's great-nephews and great-nieces,[80] and T's cousins.[81] On the other hand, the class-closing rules have been held not to apply to a gift by T's will to an unlimited class of relatives, such as the issue—or the descendants—of X who attain the age of 21 years. T cannot have intended all X's issue, born in any generation at any time in the future, to take. Therefore, the question of construction inevitably arises—what class of issue did T intend should take? This question is to be answered without regard to the class-closing rules.[82] If the gift is to all of a limited class of relatives, it only raises the question as to when the class should be closed as a matter of convenience, and the class-closing rules provide the answer.

6. Rules excluded by contrary intention

The class-closing rules, being rules of construction, are not applicable if the testator has clearly shown a contrary intention. A gift by will to "all or any" the children of X who attain the age of 21 years is not sufficient by itself to indicate a contrary intention.[83] Again, a gift to all the children of X "whether now born or hereafter to be born" does not indicate a contrary intention because the words of futurity are capable of referring only to the period before the application of the relevant class-closing rule would close the class.[84] But the emphatic phrase children of X "whenever born" is a particular reference to the future expressly unlimited in time, and therefore excludes the application of the class-closing rules[85]: it is equivalent to the phrase "at whatever time they may be born", which has the same effect.[86] **11–24**

[79] *Dimond v Bostock* (1875) L.R. 10 Ch.App. 358 (nephews and nieces of my late husband X, who were living at his death, excepting P and Q).

[80] *Balm v Balm* (1830) 3 Sim. 492.

[81] *Baldwin v Rogers* (1853) 3 De G.M. & G. 649 (my first cousins by my mother's side).

[82] *Re Cockle's W.T.* [1967] Ch.690 (gift by T's will upon trust for X for life and after X's death for the issue of X who attain 21 years or being female marry in equal shares absolutely; X had no issue at T's death: held only issue in existence at X's death were intended to take); *Re Deeley's Settlement* [1974] Ch.454 (again a postponed gift); *Re Drummond* [1986] 1 W.L.R. 1096.

[83] *Re Bleckly* [1951] Ch.740, 751: see also *Prescott v Long* (1795) 2 Ves. 690 ("all and every the child and children of his son"); *Re Canney's Trusts* (1910) 101 L.T. 905; *Re Emmet's Estate* (1880) 13 Ch.D. 484 ("all and every the children" of X).

[84] i.e. in the case of an immediate gift, the period until T's death, *Sprackling v Ranier* (1761) 1 Dick. 344; *Dias v De Livera* (1879) 5 App.Cas. 123 (children which may hereafter be procreated): in the case of a postponed gift, the period until the end of the period of postponement, *Scott v Earl of Scarborough* (1838) 1 Beav. 154, 168: see also *Re Chapman's S.T.* [1977] 1 W.L.R. 1163.

[85] *Re Edmondson's W.T.* [1972] 1 W.L.R. 183 (an appointment by deed).

[86] *Re Edmondson's W.T.* above, at 188. See also *Scott v Earl of Scarborough*, above, (children of A, B and C "now born or who shall hereafter be born, during the lifetime of their respective parents": class-closing rule excluded); *Re Ransome* [1957] Ch.348 (such of the children of C as shall be living at time youngest child of C attains 21 years: class-closing rule excluded); *Re Tom's Settlement* [1987] 1 W.L.R. 1021 ("closing date" in deed); cf. *Re Clifford's S.T.* [1981] Ch.63 (compound class). As to the exclusion of the rules by a power of advancement applicable to vested presumptive shares, see *Re Henderson's Trusts* [1969] 1 W.L.R. 651.

D. WHETHER GIFT IS ABSOLUTE OR FOR LIFE

1. Presumption that devise passes fee simple

11–25 Section 28 of the Wills Act 1837 enacts that a devise of real estate to any person without any words of limitation shall be construed to pass the fee simple, or other the whole interest of which the testator has power to dispose, unless a contrary intention appears by his will.[87] The section applies to any will made or confirmed after 1837.[88] Thus, T's devise of Blackacre "to X" passes T's fee simple estate in Blackacre to X, unless a contrary intention is shown by T's will. The rule applies to a devise by T of any *existing* interest, e.g. a devise by T "to X" of a rentcharge (which is vested in T in fee simple at his death) passes the rentcharge to X in fee simple, unless a contrary intention is shown.[89] Since 1 January 1997, it has been impossible to create new entailed interests, although existing entails may continue to exist.[90] Any testator who wished to create an entail in any real or personal property by his will after 1925 and before 1997 had to employ the formal expressions which were effective to create an entail in a deed before 1926, i.e. the word "heirs" followed by words of procreation or the words "in tail".[91]

2. Presumption that bequest is absolute

11–26 A bequest by T of personal estate "to X" gives X an absolute interest, unless a contrary intention is shown by T's will. But if T's will also contains a direction that on X's death the same property is to go to Y, this shows T's intention to give X only a life interest.[92]

[87] *Gravenor v Watkins* (1871) L.R. 6 C.P. 500.
[88] Wills Act 1837 s.34.
[89] In general, no rentcharge may be created after 21 August 1977 and existing rentcharges will be extinguished at the end of 60 years from 22 July 1977 or 60 years from the date when they first became payable, whichever is the later: Rentcharges Act 1977. A devisee of a rentcharge which had been created by will (when that was possible) could take it only for life unless a contrary intention appeared: *Nichols v Hawkes* (1853) 10 Hare 342.
[90] Trusts of Land and Appointment of Trustees Act 1996 s.2.
[91] Law of Property Act 1925 s.130(1): see also s.130(3) and *Re Jones* [1934] Ch.315. For the effect since 1925 of informal expressions, which would have created an entail in a will before 1926 (e.g. "to X and his issue", "to X and his descendants", or "to X and his children"), see ibid s.130(2); *Hawkins on the Construction of Wills*, 5th edn (London: Sweet & Maxwell, 2000), pp.296 et seq. For the effect of a gift to X, but if he die without issue, to Y, see Wills Act 1837 s.29, and Law of Property Act 1925 s.134, as amended by Family Law Reform Act 1969 s.1(3) and Sch.1, Pt I; *Hawkins on the Construction of Wills*, 5th edn (London: Sweet & Maxwell, 2000), pp.362 et seq.
[92] *Re Russell* (1885) 52 L.T. 559; *Re Houghton* (1884) 53 L.J.Ch. 1018; *Sherratt v Bentley* (1833) 2 My. & K. 149.

3. Gift over of what remains[93]

Home-made wills sometimes contain a gift of property "to X," followed by a direction that on X's death *what remains* of the property (or words to that effect) is to go to Y. The decided cases indicate that at least three different constructions are possible: **11–27**

(i) One construction is that X takes absolutely, and the gift over to Y is void, either because it is repugnant to X's absolute interest[94] or because, construed as a trust, it fails for uncertainty of subject-matter.[95]
(ii) Another construction is that X takes a life interest, coupled with a power to dispose of capital (perhaps only inter vivos, or only by will), and subject thereto Y takes absolutely.[96]
(iii) A third construction is that X takes a life interest and subject thereto Y takes absolutely.[97] This construction treats the gift over to Y of *what remains* of the property as if it were a gift over to Y of *all* the property.

Obviously each of the decided cases turned on the particular wording in a particular will.[98] The same question arises in each case: what intention did the testator express in his will, read as a whole, with the aid of any admissible extrinsic evidence?

4. Presumption as to effect of gift to spouse

If a testator dies after 31 December 1982,[99] s.22 of the Administration of Justice Act 1982 provides that a gift by the testator's will to his spouse[100] shall be presumed to be absolute if two requirements are satisfied: **11–28**

[93] See generally *Hawkins on the Construction of Wills*, 5th edn (London: Sweet & Maxwell, 2000), pp.280 et seq.
[94] *Perry v Merritt* (1874) L.R. 18 Eq. 152 (gift of residuary personalty to X "for her own absolute use and benefit" with gift over to Y after X's death, held void for repugnancy); *Henderson v Cross* (1861) 29 Beav. 216 (gift to X to spend both principal and interest during his lifetime, gift over to Y should X not spend it, held void for repugnancy); *Re Jones* [1898] 1 Ch.438 (gift to X "for her absolute use and benefit so that during her lifetime for the purpose of her maintenance and support she shall have the fullest power to sell and dispose of my said estate absolutely").
[95] *Pushman v Filliter* (1795) 3 Ves. 7; *Bull v Kingston* (1816) 1 Mer. 314.
[96] *Re Stringer's Estate* (1877) 6 Ch.D. 1; *Re Pounder* (1886) 56 L.J.Ch.113 (X took for life with power to dispose of capital inter vivos but not by will); *Re Sanford* [1901] 1 Ch.939 (X took for life, with general power of appointment): cf. *Re Jones*, above.
[97] *Constable v Bull* (1849) 3 De G. & Sm. 411; *Bibbens v Potter* (1879) 10 Ch.D. 733 (gift over to Y was by codicil); *Re Sheldon and Kemble* (1885) 53 L.T. 527 (at the decease of X what might remain of my property to go to Y); *In the Estate of Last* [1958] P. 137 (at X's death "anything that is left" to go to Y).
[98] *Re Minchell's W.T.* [1964] 2 All E.R. 47, 49 (the will provided "an outstanding example of the toast of the Chancery Bar, 'Here's to the man who makes his own will.' He plainly did not brood on the rules of construction in his leisure time 'One testator's nonsense is no guide to another testator's nonsense'".
[99] Administration of Justice Act 1982 ss.73(6) and 76(11).
[100] Or civil partner; Civil Partnership Act 2004 Sch.4, para.5.

(i) The gift is made to the spouse "in terms which in themselves would give an absolute interest to the spouse,"—for instance, T gives "my house Blackacre to my wife Jane" *or* "all my property to my civil partner John." On the other hand, this requirement is not satisfied if T's gift is, for example, "to my wife Jane (*or* civil partner John) *for life*."[101]

(ii) The testator purports by the same instrument to give his issue an interest in the same property—for instance, "after her (*or* his) death I give Blackacre (*or* all my property *or* what remains of all my property) to my children equally." On the other hand this requirement is not satisfied if the gift over is, for example, to "my nephew George" *or* "the Oldcastle Dogs' Home."

If these two requirements are satisfied, under s.22 Jane takes Blackacre (*or* John takes all T's property) absolutely and T's children take nothing. However, s.22 is excluded where a contrary intention is shown—for instance, where T adds, "I direct that my wife Jane shall take only a life interest in Blackacre and after her death I give Blackacre to my children equally."

11–29 The purpose of s.22 is to prevent the creation of an "unintended" life interest for the spouse by a home-made will.[102] A testator who makes his own will often assumes—wrongly—that it is possible to give successive absolute interests in property, so that his spouse may first enjoy the full rights of an absolute owner and at her death these rights may pass to another person. Such a testator may well have no conception of the nature of a life interest, but he may nevertheless make his will in language which read as a whole—under the law applicable prior to 1983—expressed an intention to give a life interest, rather than an absolute interest, to his spouse. If the testator dies after 31 December 1982, s.22 applies but (rather oddly) only where the purported gift over is to the testator's issue.[103]

[101] In *Harrison v Gibson* [2006] 1W.L.R. 1212, Hart J read the words "in trust to my wife" in the context of the will as a whole and decided that the gift was not one which in terms gave her an absolute interest.

[102] See Law Reform Committee's, 19th Report, *Interpretation of Wills*, Cmnd.5301 (1973), paras 60–62 and 65.

[103] There is a slight element of self-contradiction in this part of the Law Reform Committee's 19th Report, because, once the Committee's principal recommendation as to the admissibility of extrinsic evidence had been accepted, it is possible to introduce extrinsic evidence, including all evidence of the testator's intention, to assist in the interpretation of any provision in the will. This is the only example in the 19th Report of an attempt to deal with a specific issue of construction. The Law Reform Committee appear to have wanted to insert a rule to cover the case where the testator has given the matter no thought. In that respect, they were proposing a rule to cover speculation about what the testator would have done if he had thought about something about which they considered he would not have thought. This element of self-contradiction contributed to the difficulties faced by Hart J in *Harrison v Gibson* [2006] 1 W.L.R. 1212.

5. The rule in *Lassence v Tierney*[104]

Under the rule in *Lassence v Tierney*[105] (more accurately called the rule in *Hancock v Watson*),[106] "it is settled law that if you find an absolute gift to a legatee in the first instance, and trusts are engrafted or imposed on that absolute interest which fail, either from lapse,[107] or invalidity, or any other reason, then the absolute gift takes effect so far as the trusts have failed, to the exclusion of the residuary legatee or next-of-kin as the case may be."[108] The rule applies to an absolute gift of realty as well as of personalty.[109] The rule reconciles two inconsistent provisions in T's will, e.g. **11–30**

(i) an initial gift of property to X absolutely, and
(ii) a subsequent provision that the property given to X shall be held upon trust for X for life and after his death for X's children absolutely as tenants in common in equal shares.

If X dies childless, so that the trust for X's children fails, under the rule the absolute gift to X takes effect; the property therefore passes under X's will or intestacy and does not pass under T's residuary gift or as on T's intestacy. The rule imputes to T an intention to modify the absolute gift to X only so far as is necessary to give effect to the trusts.[110]

(a) *Initial absolute gift*

The real difficulty usually lies in determining whether there is an initial absolute gift to X; this is a question of construction. If there is, the first requirement of the rule in *Lassence v Tierney* is satisfied. The rule applies whether the initial gift is made directly to X or to trustees on trust for X.[111] In *Hancock v Watson*[112] T gave his residuary personal estate to trustees upon trust for his wife for life and after her death to be divided into five portions, two of which he "gave" to X; his will continued: **11–31**

"But it is my will and mind that the two fifth portions allotted to [X] shall remain in trust, and that she be entitled to take only the interest of the shares so bequeathed to her during her natural life"

and after her death be held upon other trusts, which failed. The House of Lords held that there was an initial absolute gift of two fifth shares to X, because T used the words "I give" and referred to these shares as "allotted" to X. Accordingly, after X's death these two fifth shares formed part of X's estate.

[104] See generally *Hawkins on the Construction of Wills*, 5th edn (London: Sweet & Maxwell, 2000), pp.353 et seq.
[105] *Lassence v Tierney* (1849) 1 Mac. & G. 551.
[106] *Hancock v Watson* [1902] A.C. 14.
[107] See below, paras 14–11 et seq.
[108] per Lord Davey in *Hancock v Watson*, above, at p.22.
[109] *Moryoseph v Moryoseph* [1920] 2 Ch.33.
[110] *Fyffe v Irwin* [1939] 2 All E.R. 271, 282.
[111] *Re Harrison* [1918] 2 Ch.59 (rule applies to legacy bequeathed to trustees on trust for B).
[112] *Hancock v Watson* [1902] A.C. 14. For the extensive case law see *Theobald on Wills*, 17th edn (London: Sweet & Maxwell, 2010), paras 28–017 et seq.

On the other hand, this first requirement is not satisfied if the words of gift to X run straight on into a whole series of limitations, so as to form one system of trusts under which X takes only a limited interest.[113]

(b) *Engrafted trusts fail*

11–32 The other requirement of the rule in *Lassence v Tierney* is that the trusts engrafted on X's absolute interest in the property do not (in the events which happen) exhaust the whole beneficial interest in the property. These trusts may be declared later in T's will or in a codicil,[114] and the cause of their failure is immaterial.[115] Under the rule the absolute gift to X takes effect so far as the trusts do not exhaust the whole beneficial interest in the property.[116]

II. CONSTRUCTION OF POWERS[117]

1. General powers of appointment to which section 27 applies

11–33 Unless a contrary intention appears by T's will, s.27 of the Wills Act 1837 makes a general gift by his will of real or personal estate operate to exercise a power to appoint real or personal property, provided it is a power conferred on T to appoint such property "in any manner he may think proper". If s.27 is applicable, T need not expressly show an intention in his will to exercise the general power.

"It has been often said, and is now a platitude, that the object of the section was to abolish the distinction between property and a general power over property, because an ordinary man considers in the latter case that the property is his own."[118]

(a) *Powers within section 27*

11–34 Section 27 applies to any power of appointment[119] which satisfies the three following requirements:

[113] *Re Payne* [1927] 2 Ch.1; *Lassence v Tierney*, above: see also *Re Cohen's W.T.* [1936] 1 All E.R. 103 (estate to be equally distributed amongst T's seven named children "subject to the provisions and directions hereinafter contained": held no initial absolute gift to a child).
[114] *Norman v Kynaston* (1861) 3 De G.F. & J. 29.
[115] *Watkins v Weston* (1863) 3 De G.J. & S. 434 (B died childless); *Re Coleman* [1936] Ch.528 (trusts in part void for perpetuity).
[116] *Re Coleman*, above, (engrafted trusts after B's death were (i) discretionary trusts during life of B's widow and (ii) after her death trust for B's children: discretionary trust void for remoteness, and under rule income during widow's life formed part of B's estate).
[117] For an explanation of powers of appointment, see Hanbury and Martin, *Modern Equity*, 20th edn (London: Sweet & Maxwell, 2015), Chap.6: for the construction of powers, generally, see *Hawkins on the Construction of Wills*, 5th edn (London: Sweet & Maxwell, 2000), Chap.11. For a case involving alleged negligence in the preparation of a will exercising a power of appointment, see *Gibbons v Nelsons* [2000] W.T.L.R. 453 (discussed further in paras 15–36 and 15–37, below).
[118] *Re Jacob* [1907] 1 Ch.445, 449 per Parker J.
[119] But not to a power of revocation and new appointment, *Re Brace* [1891] 2 Ch.671: see also *Re Salvin* [1906] 2 Ch.459.

"(i) At T's death the power must be capable of being exercised by T by his will[120]; section 27 does not apply to a power exercisable by T by deed but not by will.[121] It does not matter whether the power had already been created at the date of the will, because under section 24 of the Wills Act[122] a will speaks from death as to property.[123]

(ii) The terms of the power must not impose any condition incompatible with the operation of section 27.[124]

(iii) T must be entitled to appoint "in any manner he may think proper," i.e. to any objects he may think proper. So section 27 does not apply to a special power of appointment among a limited class of objects, e.g. T's children[125]; and it does not apply to a "hybrid" power to appoint in favour of anyone except one or more excepted persons, *e.g.* except "her present husband, or any friend or relative of his."[126]

(b) *General gifts within section 27*

Section 27 applies to "a general devise of the real estate of the testator, or of the real estate of the testator in any place or in the occupation of any person mentioned in his will, or otherwise described in a general manner," and to "a bequest of the personal estate of the testator, or any bequest of personal property described in a general manner". The section applies both to residuary gifts of property[127] and to specific gifts of property described in a general manner.[128] **11–35**

Moreover, s.27 applies to a gift by T of general pecuniary legacies because this constitutes a "bequest of personal property described in a general manner". If and so far as T's own assets are insufficient for their payment,[129] the legacies are payable out of personal property over which T had a general power.[130]

[120] *Re Powell's Trusts* (1869) 39 L.J.Ch.188 (power to appoint to any persons by will only is within s.27); *Hawthorn v Shedden* (1856) 3 Sm. & G. 293.

[121] *Phillips v Cayley* (1890) 43 Ch.D. 222, 232 and 234.

[122] See Chap.12.

[123] *Boyes v Cook* (1880) 14 Ch.D. 53; *Airey v Bower* (1887) 12 App.Cas. 263. But s.27 does not apply to a power created after T's death, *Re Young* [1920] 2 Ch.427.

[124] *Phillips v Cayley*, above; *Re Tarrant's Trust* (1889) 58 L.J.Ch.780: see also *Re Davies* [1892] 3 Ch.63. But a condition imposing special formalities as to execution and attestation need not be observed in a formal will when a power is exercised, Wills Act 1837 s.10: see above, para.9–26.

[125] *Cloves v Awdry* (1850) 12 Beav. 604.

[126] *Re Byron's Settlement* [1891] 3 Ch.474; but see *Re Harvey* [1950] 1 All. E.R. 491. For an explanation of the difference between general, special and hybrid powers, see Hanbury and Martin, *Modern Equity*, 20th edn (London: Sweet & Maxwell, 2015), para.7–004.

[127] *Re Spooner's Trust* (1851) 2 Sim. (N.S.) 129 ("constituting my son my residuary legatee": held s.27 applied).

[128] *Re Jacob* [1907] 1 Ch.445; *Turner v Turner* (1852) 21 L.J.Ch.843: cf. *Re Brown's Trusts* (1855) 1 K. & J. 522. *Re Doherty-Waterhouse* [1918] 2 Ch.269 ("all my shares in the Halifax Corporation New Market consolidated stock": held s.27 applied.)

[129] For the rules governing the incidence of general legacies see below, Chap.22.

[130] *Hawthorn v Shedden* (1856) 3 Sm. & G. 293; *Re Wilkinson* (1869) L.R. 4 Ch.App. 587; *Re*

(c) *Contrary intention*

11–36 The operation of s.27 is excluded if "a contrary intention shall appear by the will", i.e. if it appears from the will that T, having the power in mind, did not intend to exercise it.[131] The onus of establishing such a contrary intention from the will lies on those who assert it.[132] In practice such a contrary intention very seldom appears from T's will.[133]

2. Powers of appointment to which section 27 does not apply

11–37 Section 27 does not apply to a special power, or to a hybrid power. In order to exercise such a power by will, there must be a sufficient indication in the will of an intention to exercise it.[134] In general, a reference either to the power or to the property subject to it constitutes a sufficient indication for this purpose.[135] The testator's intention is, of course, to be gathered from an examination of the whole of his will, with the aid of any admissible extrinsic evidence.[136]

3. Power to bar entail by will[137]

11–38 Under s.176 of the Law of Property Act 1925 a tenant in tail[138] has power to bar his entail in any real or personal property by will, and thus dispose of the fee simple in realty, or absolute interest in personalty, or any lesser interest[139] in such property. A testator may exercise this power to bar his entail if the following requirements are satisfied:

Seabrook [1911] 1 Ch.151. An express direction in T's will for the payment of his debts has the same effect, *Laing. Cowan* (1858) 24 Beav. 112; *Re Davies' Trusts* (1871) L.R. 13 Eq. 163, 166.

[131] *Scriven v Sandom* (1862) 2 J. & H. 743 (there must be something in T's will inconsistent with the view that the general gift was meant to exercise the power); *Re Thirlwell* [1958] Ch.146.

[132] *Re Jarrett* [1919] 1 Ch.366, 370; *Re Thirlwell*, above.

[133] *Re Jacob* [1907] 1 Ch.445 ("all stocks, shares and securities which I possess or to which I am entitled": held s.27 applied); *Re Doherty-Waterhouse* [1918] 2 Ch.269; *Re Spooner's Trust* (1851) 2 Sim.(N.S.) 129.

[134] *Re Ackerley* [1913] 1 Ch.510 (special power); *Re Upton* [2004] W.T.L.R. 1339 (special power); *Re Lawrence's W.T.* [1972] Ch.418, esp. pp.428–432 (hybrid power). If the instrument creating the power lays down any special requirement for its exercise, this must also be complied with, *Re Lawrence's* W.T., above, at 430. But a condition imposing special formalities as to execution and attestation need not be observed in a formal will when a power is exercised, Wills Act 1837 s.10, and see above, para.9–26.

[135] *Re Ackerley* above, at pp.514–515: see also *Re Holford's Settlement* [1945] Ch.21 (reviewing some of the case law: "the principle is clear. The difficulty lies in the application of it").

[136] *Re Knight* [1957] Ch.441.

[137] As a result of the Trusts of Land and Appointment of Trustees Act 1996, no new entails may be created after 1996, but existing entails may continue to exist. See Megarry & Wade, *The Law of Real Property*, 8th edn (London: Sweet & Maxwell, 2012), paras 3–031 and 3–070—3–083 for a discussion of the fee tail.

[138] Including an owner of a base fee in possession who has power to enlarge it into a fee simple without the consent of any other person, Law of Property Act 1925 s.176(3): but not a tenant in tail restrained by statute from barring his entail, or a tenant in tail after possibility of issue extinct, ibid s.176(2).

[139] If he merely disposes of a lesser interest such as a life interest, then, subject to the life interest, the entail devolves in the normal way, ibid ss.130(4) and 176(1).

(i) the testator is of full age and holds the entail in possession[140] (not in remainder) at his death;
(ii) his will is executed after 1925 (or confirmed by a codicil executed after 1925); and
(iii) his will refers specifically *either* to the property (e.g. "Blackacre"), or to the instrument under which it was acquired (e.g. "the property I acquired under my father's will"), *or* to entailed property generally (e.g. "all entailed property").[141]

[140] See the Law of Property Act 1925 s.205(1)(xix).

[141] *Acheson v Russell* [1951] Ch.67 ("the object of the section must surely be to avoid any risk of a disentail being effected by inadvertence or involuntarily").

CHAPTER 12

THE DATE FROM WHICH A WILL SPEAKS[1]

The question of the date from which a will speaks is a question of construction. It is dealt with here both because it is covered by a specific interpretation section in the Wills Act 1837[2] and because it is relevant to ademption and so, to some extent, depends on the classification of legacies and devises as specific or general.[3] **12–01**

A will is normally construed to speak from death when identifying, or describing, property; but from the date when it was made when identifying, or describing, the object of a gift, the legatee or devisee. So, if someone makes a will leaving "my I.C.I. shares to my butler" this will prima facie be construed as a gift of the I.C.I. shares owned by the testator at the time of his death to the person who was his butler at the time the will was made.

A. A WILL SPEAKS FROM DEATH AS TO PROPERTY

Before the Wills Act 1837, it was a rule of law that realty acquired after the date of the will could not be devised. So, until 1837, if an owner of freehold land who had a son and a daughter made a will devising his land to his daughter and then sold the land and bought some more land, the newly acquired land would not pass under his will but would go his heir, in this case his son. If the testator wanted his daughter to inherit the freehold land he had acquired after he made his will, he had, until 1837, to make another will. Section 3 of the Wills Act 1837 changed this rule and makes it lawful for a testator to devise his after-acquired realty. Section 24 of the Wills Act 1837 then goes on to provide that, **12–02**

> "Every will shall be construed, with reference to the real estate and personal estate comprised in it,[4] to speak and take effect as if it had been executed immediately before the death of the testator, unless a contrary intention shall appear by the will."

[1] See *Hawkins on the Construction of Wills*, 5th edn (London: Sweet & Maxwell, 2000), Chap.5.
[2] Wills Act 1837 s.24.
[3] For the classification of legacies as specific or general, see Chap.9, paras 9–06 et seq.
[4] *Langdale (Lady) v Briggs* (1856) L.J.Ch.27, 49 ("with reference to the real estate and personal estate comprised in it" means "so far as the will comprises dispositions of real and personal estate").

Thus, the description of the subject-matter of a gift is prima facie to be construed as comprising all the property which satisfies the terms of the description at the death of the testator, including property acquired by him after he made his will. For example, a devise by a testator of "all my freehold land" prima facie comprises all the freehold land to which the testator is entitled at his death, including any acquired by him between the date when he made his will and his death.[5]

1. General and residuary legacies

12–03 If someone leaves a general pecuniary legacy, there is no problem about construing it in terms of time. A legacy of "£10,000" is a legacy of money, which is the same in amount (if not in value) whether calculated at the time of the will or at the time of the death.[6] A gift of residue obviously means residue at the time of death and would have to be so construed even if s.24 had not been enacted. So, it seems at first as though s.24 has no application to general or residuary legacies, apart from stating the obvious. But s.24 does sometimes apply to general legacies. It applies when there is a legacy of, say, "10,000 shares in X.Y.Z. Ltd (a named company)" and the shares in X.Y.Z. Ltd have been reorganised or subdivided after the date of the will. It may be that any shareholder who had one old £1 share will, after a reorganisation or division, have 20 new 5p shares; so a shareholder who had 10,000 old shares will have 200,000 new ones. The effect of s.24 in this case, is, prima facie, to give the legatee 10,000 new shares, not 10,000 old shares.[7] The shares are described as at the date of death.

2. Specific legacies

12–04 Section 24 also applies to specific legacies.

Unless a contrary intention appears in his will, a specific legacy by T of "all my shares in Marks & Spencer plc" speaks from T's death and is construed as a gift of all the shares in Marks & Spencer to which T is entitled at his death.[8] Similarly, unless a contrary intention appears in the will, a specific devise by T of "all my lands in the county of Kent" is construed as a gift of all T's lands in the county of Kent at the date of his death.[9] These

[5] *Langdale (Lady) v Briggs* (1856) L.J.Ch.27, 49: and see *Re Kempthorne* [1930] 1 Ch.268.

[6] This would not be true if the currency were reorganised. If it were to happen, the legislation providing for the reorganisation of the currency would probably make specific provision for pecuniary legacies. If not, the same rule would apply as applies to shares (see para.12–10 below). If the pound is abolished and replaced by the euro, it is probable that the legislation which brings this about will provide for the translation of legacies expressed in sterling into specified euro equivalents.

[7] *Re Gillins* [1909] 1 Ch.345.

[8] *Goodlad v Burnett* (1855) 1 K. & J. 341 (gift of "my New Three-and-a-quarter per Cent. Annuities": held gift passed all Annuities of which T died possessed): see also *Trinder v Trinder* (1866) L.R. 1 Eq. 695; *Re Bancroft* [1928] Ch.577.

[9] *Re Evans* [1909] 1 Ch.784, 786; *Re Davies* [1925] Ch.642; *Castle v Fox* (1871) L.R. 11 Eq. 542, paras 12–12 and 12–13 below: cf. *Webb v Byng* (1855) 1 K. & J. 580. Where s.24 applies, a gift only passes after-acquired property which falls within the description of the subject-matter of the gift, *Re Portal and Lamb* (1885) 30 Ch.D. 50 (devise of "my cottage and all my land at S":

two examples are, respectively, of a specific generic legacy and a specific generic devise. In each case, the subject-matter is described in such a way as to be capable of increase or decrease between the date of the will and the date of T's death. There is no problem about the application of s.24 to specific generic legacies and devises.

3. Contrary intention

The problem cases in this area are concerned with specific legacies and devises which are not generic and the difficulty is to know when a contrary intention appears from the will. The cases are not easily reconciled. **12–05**

Some of the cases are concerned with whether or not a specific gift has been adeemed. The doctrine of ademption was explained, in outline, in Chapter 9 and will be discussed in further detail in Chapter 14. Ademption occurs when a specific legacy or devise fails because its subject-matter is no longer part of the testator's property at the time of his death. Section 24 is concerned with the time at which property is identified and so may be crucial in deciding whether a gift has or has not been adeemed.

Suppose that a testator makes a will leaving "my pocket watch to my nephew X". There can be no problem if the testator owned a pocket watch at the time when he made his will and owns the same pocket watch at the date of his death. The watch will pass. There can also be no problem if the testator owns no pocket watch at the time of his death, for in that case the legacy must be adeemed. But a problem arises if the testator owned a pocket watch at the time he made his will but owns a different pocket watch at the time of his death. Does a "contrary intention" appear by the will in this sort of case?

Section 24 lays down a rule which appears to be generally favourable to a specific legatee. By stating that the description of the subject-matter of a gift is to be construed as at the testator's death, it makes it less likely that a legacy will be adeemed. If the testator had two pocket watches—one when he made his will and a replacement one when he died—the straightforward application of s.24 will save the gift from ademption, while a finding that there is a contrary intention will cause the gift to be adeemed. It is, therefore, generally, in the legatee's interest to argue that the will shows no contrary intention. **12–06**

There are two elements in the description of property which appear to indicate a contrary intention under s.24. The first is a reference to the present time, i.e. the time when the will was made. The second is a detailed description, indicating a reference to a particular watch, or car, or whatever.

4. Reference in a will to the present time

A devise by a testator of "all my freehold land" prima facie comprises all the freehold land to which he is entitled at his death. But if T devises "all **12–07**

T later bought large house adjoining his small cottage: held s.24 applied but house did not satisfy description).

the freehold land of which I am possessed *at the date of this my will,"* s.24 is excluded and the devise does not pass any freehold land acquired by T after the date of his will. Some forms of wording are harder to construe. A reference in a will to property *"now"* or *"at present"* possessed by the testator may refer to the date of his will, or may refer to the date of his death. Such a reference to the present time makes it necessary to consider the language of T's will, in order to ascertain whether there is a contrary intention.[10] If a reference to the present time is an essential part of the description of the subject-matter of a specific gift, a contrary intention appears, s.24 is excluded and the reference is construed as referring to the date of T's will.[11] But if a reference to the present time is not an essential part of the description of the subject-matter of the gift—if it is merely intended as an additional form of identification—a contrary intention does not appear, s.24 applies and the reference is construed as referring to the date of death.

12–08 The latter construction was adopted in *Re Willis*.[12] T owned a house and garden and he devised to his wife "all that my freehold house and premises situated at Oakleigh Park, Whetstone and known as 'Ankerwyke,' and in which I now reside." After T had made his will, he bought two further plots of land next to the garden. He treated these two plots as an extension of the garden, so that while he was alive the house, the garden and the plots were all occupied as one unit. The question was whether the devise passed only the house and the original garden or whether it passed the plots as well. The problem lay with the words "and in which I now reside". If they were construed as an essential part of the description of the subject-matter of the devise, it would be restricted to the house and the part of the garden owned by the testator at the time he made his will. Eve J held that the phrase was not an essential part of the description of the subject-matter and so the devise passed the house and premises known as "Ankerwyke" at the date of T's death, including the two adjoining plots.

5. Detailed description of property devised or bequeathed

12–09 The subject-matter of a gift may be described with such particularity as to show that the testator intended to designate an object in existence at the date when he made his will. If this is so, a contrary intention appears in the will and s.24 does not apply. For example, the testator may bequeath "my gold watch, which I bought in Bond Street". If he were to lose that watch before his death and to buy another gold watch, but did not buy it in Bond Street, the replacement watch would not pass. This is clear because the replacement article does not satisfy the terms of the description of the original article: the more detailed the description, the more

[10] *Re Whitby* [1944] Ch.210; *Cole v Scott* (1849) 1 Mac. & G. 518; *Hutchinson v Barrow* (1861) 6 H. & N. 583.

[11] *Re Whitby*, above, (construction of exclusion clause).

[12] *Re Willis* [1911] 2 Ch.563: see also *Re Champion* [1893] 1 Ch.101 (where North J adopted the date of death construction and the C.A. relied on confirmation by codicil); *Re Horton* [1920] 2 Ch.1.

likely it is not to satisfy the description. But even if the replacement article does satisfy the terms of the description, the fact that the description is especially detailed may indicate a reference to a particular article and so indicate a contrary intention in the context of s.24. In the case of a bequest of "my gold watch, which I bought in Bond Street" if the testator were to lose his original gold watch and replace it with another gold watch bought in Bond Street (so satisfying the terms of the description of the original article), it could possibly be that a contrary intention would be found, on the basis that the description is of one particular gold watch. So what if the bequest were simply of "my gold watch"? Would there be a contrary intention in this case too? Or, to put the question another way, can s.24 ever save any specific gift from ademption other than a specific generic gift?

In *Re Gibson*[13] T bequeathed to his son Joseph "my one thousand North British Railway preference shares". He had, at the time he made his will, one thousand shares which fitted the description, but he sold these shares and later acquired some more shares, more than a thousand, which also fitted the description. Page Wood VC held that the gift had been adeemed. This was clearly a specific legacy and he held that the gift showed a contrary intention. He seemed to suggest, obiter, that s.24 would never apply to save from ademption any specific legacy other than a specific generic legacy.[14] He suggested a hypothetical example, **12–10**

> "Suppose a man to have, at the date of his will, a picture of the Holy Family by some inferior artist, and to give by his will 'my Holy Family.' He afterwards disposes of this picture, and subsequently acquires, by purchase or gift, a very much better one on the same subject, painted by an eminent artist. Would it not be a monstrous construction to hold that the picture in [his] possession at the time of his death would pass."

Page Wood VC's obiter view in *Re Gibson* is consistent with the decision of Clauson J in *Re Sikes*.[15] In this case, a testatrix bequeathed "my piano" to a friend. By the time of her death, the testatrix had sold her original piano and had acquired another piano. Clauson J, in a very brief judgment, held that the bequest did not cover the replacement piano because there was a contrary intention within the terms of s.24. Yet the only indication of a contrary intention appears to be the use of the word "my". So, *Re Gibson* and *Re Sikes* appear to say that no specific legacy, other than a specific generic legacy, will, by virtue of s.24, survive ademption. On their authority, a gift of "my watch" or "my car" will be adeemed whenever the testator has replaced his original watch or car.

Having said this, it is easy to understand why there would be reluctance to apply s.24 in a case where a specific article belonging to the testator had been replaced by another article of similar description but very different value; but it seems much less probable that there would be reluctance **12–11**

[13] *Re Gibson* (1866) L.R. 2 Eq 669.

[14] At p.672.

[15] *Re Sikes* [1927] 1 Ch.364.

to apply the section if the two articles were of approximately the same value. Page Wood VC's hypothetical example in *Re Gibson*[16] supposed a replacement picture worth much more than the one it replaced. The facts in *Re Sikes*[17] are also unusual. The testatrix sold her original piano for £5 to the husband of the friend to whom she had bequeathed it in her will. She then bought a replacement piano for £228. Either the original piano was worth much less than the new one, or the friend's husband had a bargain. Either way, it is not hard to see why Clauson J felt it inappropriate to apply s.24; had he applied it, the friend and her husband would have had two pianos. These cases do not really answer the question as to what would happen if there were a gift of "my watch" or "my car" and the watch or car were to be replaced with something of much the same type and value.

Section 24 says nothing about the value, but it is not unreasonable to suggest that the value will be thought significant, certainly in a case which would otherwise be regarded as borderline: and the more commonplace an article, and the more general the description of it, the more likely it is that s.24 will be held to apply. There seems to be no case which clearly establishes that a gift of "my watch" or "my car" or "my horse" can survive a change of watch or car or horse, under the terms of s.24; but there is no clear authority that it cannot, and a straightforward reading of s.24 would appear to favour the application of the section in this sort of case. The absence of cases on the point is probably due to a sensible avoidance, by testators and their will draftsmen, of specific legacies of this kind.

12–12 There are two further cases on s.24 which deserve noting. They are not cases on ademption but they both contain obiter dicta relating to ademption and they are not agreed as to what the correct rule should be. In *Castle v Fox*[18] the testator devised "my mansion and estate called Cleeve Court" and there was a dispute as to whether the devise covered land which was acquired, and added to the estate, after the will was made. A straighforward application of s.24 would say that it did, and Malins VC applied the section straighforwardly. He found no contrary intention. There seems little doubt that the decision is correct. But Malins VC went on to suggest, obiter, that a devise of "my house in Grosvenor Square" would not be adeemed if the testator disposed of his house in Grosvenor Square after he had made his will and then acquired another house in the same Square.[19] This is not so clear. *Castle v Fox* may be contrasted with *Re Evans*[20] in which T's will read as follows:

> "To my wife Agnes Evans I give and bequeath house and effects known as 'Cross Villa' situated at Templeton in the County of Pembroke."

At the time when the testator made his will, "Cross Villa" consisted of a house with a large garden. T later divided part of the garden from the

[16] *Re Gibson* (1866) L.R. 2 Eq 669.
[17] *Re Sikes* [1927] 1 Ch.364.
[18] *Castle v Fox* (1871) L.R. 11 Eq. 542.
[19] At p.551.
[20] *Re Evans* [1909] 1 Ch.784.

rest with a hedge and built two more houses in the part of the garden he had divided off. These newly built houses were known as "Ashgrove Villas". T continued to own all three houses. The question in the case was whether the devise passed only the one house known as "Cross Villa" at the time of the testator's death; or whether the devise passed all the land which would have been included within the description "Cross Villa" at the time the testator made his will. On the former construction, the widow would be entitled to one house, on the latter, she would be entitled to three houses. A straightforward reading of s.24 would construe the gift at the time of death and give her one house. Joyce J held that there was a contrary intention because the description was "so particular and precise." He suggested that the description was just the same as if the testator had used the expression "now known as 'Cross Villa'." This reasoning is not altogether easy to follow. The testator did not use the expression "now known as Cross Villa"; and even if it is correct that it would have made no difference if he had used it, that does not prove that the addition of the word "now" would show a contrary intention. In *Re Willis*[21] the expression "and in which I now reside" was *not* taken to indicate a contrary intention within the terms of s.24. In fact, *Re Evans* and *Re Willis* contrast oddly. In the former, the gift was construed as excluding s.24, in spite of the fact that there was no obvious reference to the date of the will; in the latter, s.24 was not excluded, even though there was a reference to the present time. The one thing the two cases have in common—and they share this with *Castle v Fox*—is that each of them adopts the construction most favourable to the specific devisee.

Castle v Fox, Re Evans and *Re Willis* are all cases where the issue was **12–13** not ademption, but the extent of the devise. But there are dicta in *Castle v Fox* and in *Re Evans* as to what would happen in cases of possible ademption. It has already been noted that in *Castle v Fox* Malins VC suggested that a gift of "my house in Grosvenor Square" would carry a house which fitted the description if the testator had sold one house in the Square and had bought another one. In *Re Evans* Joyce J suggested exactly the same example[22] but thought that the new house would not be covered by the gift. As in the case of a gift of "my gold watch", there appears to be no authoritative ruling.

6. Testator's later acquisition of a different interest

If T by his will makes a gift of "my leasehold house, 54 Narcissus Road," **12–14** of which T is the lessee at the date of his will, and T later acquires the freehold reversion, it was held in *Re Fleming's Will Trusts*[23] that the gift

[21] *Re Willis* [1911] 2 Ch.563, see above, para.12–08.

[22] *Re Evans* [1909] 1 Ch.784 at 786 (except that he changed "Grosvenor Square" to "Cavendish Square").

[23] *Re Fleming's Will Trusts* [1974] 1 W.L.R. 1552 (no merger occurred, but T's freehold estate and leasehold interest both passed under the gift): see also *Struthers v Struthers* (1857) 5 W.R. 809; *Miles v Miles* (1866) L.R. 1 Eq. 462; *Cox v Bennett* (1868) L.R. 6 Eq. 422; *Saxton v Saxton* (1879) 13 Ch.D. 359 (gift of "all my term and interest in the leasehold premises No.1, Berkeley

passes T's entire interest in the property at his death. To quote from Templeman J's judgment in this case,[24] "a gift of property discloses an intention to give the estate and interest of the testator in that property at his death; a mere reference in the will to the estate and interest held by the testator at the date of his will is not sufficient to disclose a contrary intention." On occasion the same result has been reached in reliance (at least in part) on s.24,[25] but the result is probably best explained as based on the testator's intention to pass whatever interest in the property he has at his death.

Similarly, if T by his will makes a gift of his share in a partnership business—in which he has a third share at the date of his will—and T later acquires his two partners' shares and carries on the business as sole owner until his death, the gift passes T's entire interest in the business at his death.[26]

If, however, T by his will shows an intention to give the leasehold interest in Blackacre which he holds at the date of his will, *and nothing else*, his intention must prevail. If at his death T no longer holds this leasehold interest, the gift fails by ademption; such a gift does not pass any other leasehold interest in Blackacre granted to T after the date of his will.[27]

B. A WILL SPEAKS FROM ITS DATE AS TO THE OBJECT OF A GIFT

12–15 Section 24 applies with regard to the subject-matter of a gift but it does not in any way affect the construction of a will with regard to the object of a gift.[28] In general, a will speaks from its date as to the object of a gift, unless a contrary intention appears in the will. Accordingly, words in a will indicating an existing person prima facie refer to a person in existence at the date of the will. Thus, where T by his will gave to "Lord Sherborne and his heirs my Oliver Cromwell cup for an heirloom," and the person who was Lord Sherborne at the date of the will died before T, the Court of Appeal held that the gift lapsed[29] and did not take effect in favour of the person who was Lord Sherborne at T's death.[30] Similarly, a gift by T to the "eldest son of my sister Frances" is a gift in favour of the person who answers the description at the date of the will, and the gift lapses if that person

Gardens subject to the payment of the ground rent and performance of the covenants affecting the same": held subsequently acquired freehold passed). As to renewal of a lease, see *Wedgwood v Denton* (1871) L.R. 12 Eq. 290.

[24] [1974] 1 W.L.R. 1552 at 1555.

[25] *Miles v Miles*, above; *Saxton v Saxton*, above: s.23 of the Wills Act 1837 was relied on (at least in part) in *Struthers v Struthers*, above; *Cox v Bennett*, above and *Saxton v Saxton*, above: sed quaere whether s.23 is relevant.

[26] *Re Russell* (1882) 19 Ch.D. 432 (s.23 relied on).

[27] *Cox v Bennett*, above, at 426; *Re Reeves* [1928] Ch.351.

[28] *Bullock v Bennett* (1855) 7 De G.M. & G. 283.

[29] For the doctrine of lapse, see Chap.14, paras 14–11 et seq.

[30] *Re Whorwood* (1887) 34 Ch.D. 446.

dies before T.[31] In *Peasley v Haileybury and I.S.C.*[32] the testatrix gave to her great-niece and "her husband"[33] the right to occupy a house. It was held that "her husband" meant the person who was the great-niece's husband at the time when the will was executed.[34]

The general rule that a will speaks from its date as to the object of a gift is, of course, excluded if a contrary intention appears in the will. For instance, a gift by T of a legacy to "the Lord Mayor of London for the time being" takes effect in favour of the person who holds this office at T's death.[35] Moreover, the general rule that a will speaks from its date as to the object of a gift does not apply to a class gift or to an individual gift to each member of a class.[36] **12–16**

C. EFFECT OF CONFIRMATION[37]

1. Subject of a gift

If a will speaks from its date as to the subject-matter of a gift (s.24 not being applicable because a contrary intention appears by the will), and later the will is confirmed by a codicil, the effect is to make the will speak *from the date of the codicil* as to the subject-matter of the gift, unless a contrary intention appears. In *Re Reeves*[38] a testator by his will made in 1921 gave to his daughter "all my interest in my present lease" of Blackacre. At the date of his will the testator held a lease granted in 1917 and due to expire in 1924. Later the testator took a new lease for a term of 12 years and by a codicil made in 1926 confirmed his will. The court held that the daughter was entitled to the new lease because the testator had confirmed his will. But confirmation does not make a gift pass property which does not answer the description in the will: if by his will the testator had given "my lease of Blackacre dated September 25, 1917," confirmation would not have made the will refer to the new lease.[39] Again, confirmation does not make the will speak from the date of the codicil if a contrary intention appears.[40] **12–17**

31 *Amyot v Dwarris* [1904] A.C. 268: see also *Foster v Cook* (1791) 3 Bro.C.C. 347 (gift by T's will to the child wherewith his wife was pregnant; this child was stillborn: held gift did not take effect in favour of another child with which wife was pregnant at T's death).
32 *Peasley v Haileybury and I.S.C.* [2001] W.T.L.R. 1365.
33 And the survivor of them.
34 *Re Coley* [1903] 2 Ch.102, is almost identical. The gift was to X for life and then to "his wife for her life"; held that "his wife" was the woman who was X's wife when the will was executed.
35 *Re Daniels* (1918) 118 L.T. 435: the general rule may not apply to a gift to the holder of an office, *In the Estate of Jones* (1927) 43 T.L.R. 324.
36 See above, paras 11–11 et seq.
37 For the requirements of confirmation (or "republication") see above, paras 7–65 et seq.
38 *Re Reeves* [1928] Ch.351: see also *Re Champion* [1893] 1 Ch.101 (land "now in my occupation" included land acquired by T between making and confirming his will); *Re Fraser* [1904] 1 Ch.726; *Grealey v Sampson* [1917] 1 Ir.R. 286; *Goonewardene v Goonewardene* [1931] A.C. 647.
39 *Re Reeves*, above at 357–358.
40 *Grealey v Sampson*, above, at 305.

2. Object of a gift

12–18 Similarly, if a will speaks from its date as to the object of a gift—and later the will is confirmed by a codicil—the effect is to make the will speak *from the date of the codicil* as to the object of the gift, unless a contrary intention appears. The decision in *Re Hardyman*[41] is an example of this. A gift was made by will to the wife of X. The testator confirmed the will by codicil after he knew that X's wife had died. It was held that a subsequent wife of X was entitled to take.

[41] *Re Hardyman* [1925] Ch.287.

CHAPTER 13

SATISFACTION[1]

A. EQUITABLE PRESUMPTIONS

13–01 It was said in Chapter 10[2] that, apart from rules of law and rules of construction, there are rules relating to equitable presumptions and, in particular, to the equitable presumption of satisfaction. The equitable presumption of satisfaction covers three sub-presumptions: (i) the presumption of satisfaction of a debt by a legacy; (ii) the presumption of satisfaction of a legacy by a legacy; and (iii) the presumption against double portions.[3] The equitable presumption of satisfaction operates very much like a rule of construction. In fact, it appears to be based on the presumed intention of the testator.[4] The distinction between what may be called ordinary rules of construction on the one hand, and the equitable presumption of satisfaction on the other, has been that *evidence of the testator's intention* has always been admissible to rebut,[5] or to support,[6] the equitable presumption. The equitable presumption of satisfaction has operated, therefore, like a rule of construction, but subject to a more intentionalist régime than the ordinary rules of construction. Where a testator died before 1 January 1983, and where there was extrinsic evidence of his intention in relation to a provision in his will, such evidence could be admitted if it related to an equitable presumption (or to an equivocation)[7] but not if it related to some other kind of ambiguity. It can now be admitted in virtually[8] all cases; so the person construing the will does not need to worry about drawing a line between the equitable

[1] See, generally, *Hawkins on the Construction of Wills*, 5th edn (London: Sweet & Maxwell, 2000), Chap.27.

[2] See above Chap.10 para.10–46.

[3] The presumption against double portions itself subdivides into three: see below, para.13–09.

[4] *Re Cameron* [1999] Ch.386.

[5] *Re Tussaud's Estate* (1878) 9 Ch.D. 363.

[6] If evidence is adduced to rebut the presumption of satisfaction, contrary evidence may be adduced to support it; *Re Tussaud's Estate* (1878) 9 Ch.D. 363; *Kirk v Eddows* (1844) 3 Hare 509, at 517, per Wigram VC (a case of satisfaction of a legacy by a portion, but the rule is stated in general terms).

[7] See above Chap.10 paras 10–32 and 10–33.

[8] See above Chap.10 paras 10–43 et seq.

presumption of satisfaction, or any other equitable presumption,[9] on the one hand, and other construction problems on the other. This represents a welcome simplification.

B. SATISFACTION OF A DEBT BY A LEGACY

1. The equitable presumption

13–02 If T owes C a debt, and T later makes a will or codicil giving C a pecuniary legacy of an amount equal to—or greater than—the debt, equity presumes that the legacy is intended to satisfy the debt. If at T's death C accepts the legacy, he cannot also claim payment of the debt[10]; and if—after T has made his will—he pays off the debt, the legacy is adeemed.[11]

Requirements

13–03 This equitable presumption arises[12] only if three requirements are fulfilled:

(i) T must already owe the debt to C before T makes the will or codicil giving C the pecuniary legacy. No presumption of satisfaction arises if T incurs the debt to C afterwards, because when he made the will or codicil T could not have intended the legacy to satisfy a non-existent debt.[13]

(ii) T must give C a *pecuniary legacy* of an amount equal to, or greater than, the debt.[14] No presumption of satisfaction pro tanto arises where the legacy is of a sum less than the amount of the debt.[15] A devise of land,[16] or a gift of residue or a share of residue,[17] raises no presumption of satisfaction.

(iii) The pecuniary legacy must be as beneficial to C as the debt. The presumption is not applicable if the debt is secured but the legacy is not,[18] or if the debt is immediately due at T's death but the

[9] There is some doubt as to whether the rule that a legacy to an executor is generally conditional on acceptance of office is an ordinary rule of construction, or an equitable presumption. There is no authority exactly in point, but if the testator dies on or after 1 January 1983, the distinction does not matter.

[10] *Talbot v Duke of Shrewsbury* (1722) Prec. Ch.394.

[11] *Re Fletcher* (1888) 38 Ch.D. 373 (legacy of same amount as debt).

[12] Subject to any contrary intention in the will, or extrinsic evidence to the contrary.

[13] *Cranmer's Case* (1702) 2 Salk. 508: see also *Horlock v Wiggins* (1889) 39 Ch.D. 142 (separation deed, containing covenant to pay £100, and will, giving £100 legacy, were contemporaneous: held no presumption of satisfaction).

[14] *Re Manners* [1949] Ch.613.

[15] *Eastwood v Vinke* (1731) 2 P. Wms. 613.

[16] *Richardson v Elphinstone* (1794) 2 Ves. 463.

[17] *Barret v Beckford* (1750) 1 Ves.Sen. 519; *Devese v Pontet* (1785) 1 Cox C.C. 188.

[18] *Re Stibbe* (1946) 175 L.T. 198: cf. *Re Haves* [1951] 2 All E.R. 928.

legacy is payable at a future time under an express term to this effect in the will.[19]

2. Rebutting the presumption

The presumption may be rebutted by extrinsic evidence that T did not intend the legacy to satisfy the debt, but intended to give the legacy regardless of his liability to pay the debt.[20] The presumption may also be excluded by T's expression of a contrary intention in a will or codicil made by T after he incurred the debt to C.[21] In *Chancey's Case*[22] it was held that a direction in T's will that his debts and legacies should be paid expressed a contrary intention and so C was entitled to the payment of both the debt and the legacy. It is now settled that a direction in T's will that his debts should be paid expresses a contrary intention.[23] As most wills contain such a direction, the presumption is usually excluded. **13–04**

C. SATISFACTION OF A LEGACY BY A LEGACY

1. Intention of the testator

If a testator gives two general legacies of the same amount to the same legatee, the question arises whether the legacies are cumulative (so that the legatee takes both of them) or substitutional (so that he takes only one of them). T may have expressed—when his will is read as a whole—his intention to make the legacies cumulative or (alternatively) substitutional. If not, the following rules apply: **13–05**

(a) *Legacies in the same instrument*

If by the same will (or the same codicil) T gives two general legacies of the same amount[24] to the legatee, an equitable presumption arises that the legacies are *substitutional* and that the legatee is intended to take only one of them.[25] Minor differences in the way in which the two legacies are given do not rebut this presumption.[26] **13–06**

[19] *Clark v Sewell* (1744) 3 Atk. 96 (legacy payable one month after T's death); *Adams v Lavender* (1824) M'Cle. & Yo. 41 (legacy payable within six months after T's death): see also *Re Van Den Bergh's W.T.* [1948] 1 All E.R. 935 (annuity given by will determinable on attempted alienation).

[20] *Wallace v Pomfret* (1805) 11 Ves. 542.

[21] *Gaynon v Wood* (1717) 1 P.Wms. 409n.

[22] *Chancey's Case* (1725) 1 P.Wms. 408.

[23] *Re Manners* [1949] Ch.613; *Re Huish* (1890) 43 Ch.D. 260: cf. *Re Hall* [1918] 1 Ch.562.

[24] If the two legacies are of different amounts, they are prima facie cumulative, *Curry v Pile* (1787) 2 Bro.C.C. 225.

[25] *Garth v Meyrick* (1779) 1 Bro.C.C. 30 (two legacies of £1,000 old South Sea annuities); *Holford v Wood* (1798) 4 Ves. 76 (two annuities of £30 for life); *Manning v Thesiger* (1835) 3 My. & K. 29.

[26] *Holford v Wood*, above, ("to B I give an annuity of £30 for his life payable quarterly. I give to B the butler £30 a year for his life": held B took only one annuity).

(b) *Legacies in different instruments*

13–07 If T gives two legacies of the same amount to B by different instruments (e.g. one legacy by a will and the other by a codicil), prima facie the legacies are *cumulative* and the legatee takes both of them.[27] This is a rule of construction and not an equitable presumption. It,

> "rests upon the perfectly sound basis, which is not to be weakened, that a testator intends each and every disposition which he makes to take effect where these are not mutually inconsistent."[28]

(c) *Legacies in different instruments given from the same motive*

13–08 If T gives two legacies of the same amount to one legatee but by different instruments, and T expresses the same motive in each instrument for giving each legacy, an equitable presumption arises that the legacies are *substitutional* and that the legatee is intended to take only one of them.[29] The court raises this presumption only where there is the double coincidence of the same amount and the same motive in each instrument, e.g. each instrument contains a legacy of £100 to the legatee "for his trouble as executor."[30]

The equitable presumptions in (a) and (c) above (that the legacies are substitutional) are not rules of construction and so it has always been possible to rebut them by extrinsic evidence that T intended the legacies to be cumulative; evidence of T's declarations of intention has always been admissible for this purpose.[31] But the rule in (b) above (that the legacies are cumulative) is a rule of construction and so evidence of T's declarations of intention was not admissible to rebut it if T died before 1983[32]: on T's death after 1982, s.21 of the Administration of Justice Act 1982 is applicable.[33]

D. THE PRESUMPTION AGAINST DOUBLE PORTIONS

13–09 The last of the three sub-presumptions (of the presumption of satisfaction) is the presumption against double portions and it itself

[27] *Hooley v Hatton* (1773) 1 Bro.C.C. 390; *Hurst v Beach* (1821) 5 Madd. 351, 358; *Roch v Callen* (1848) 6 Hare 531; *Re Davies* [1957] 1 W.L.R. 922.

[28] *Re Resch's W.T.* [1969] 1 A.C. 514, 548: see also *Wilson v O'Leary* (1872) L.R. 7 Ch.App.448, 454 (this rule "is not to be frittered away by a mere balance of probabilities"). For a summary of the case law as to what constitutes a clear indication of an intention to make the legacies substitutional see *Theobald on Wills*, 17th edn (London, Sweet & Maxwell, 2010), paras 17–020 et seq.

[29] *Benyon v Benyon* (1810) 17 Ves. 34 (£100 by will, and £100 by codicil, to B, in each case for his trouble as exector: held substitutional); *Hurst v Beach*, above, at 358–359; *Re Royce's W.T.* [1959] Ch.626. cf. *Wilson v O'Leary*, above, at 454–455.

[30] If the instruments merely describe him as "my servant," this is not construed as an expression of T's motive for giving each legacy and the legacies are prima facie cumulative, *Roch v Callen* (1848) 6 Hare 531.

[31] *Hurst v Beach*, at pp.360–361, above; *Hall v Hill* (1841) 1 Dr. & War. 94, 124–128:

[32] *Hurst v Beach*, above; *Hall v Hill*, above.

[33] See above, paras 10–42 et seq.

subdivides into three: (i) the presumption of satisfaction (or ademption)[34] of a legacy by a portion; (ii) the presumption of satisfaction of a portion debt by a legacy and (iii) the presumption of satisfaction of a portion debt by a portion. Only (i) and (ii) relate to wills and portion debts are rare nowadays,[35] so the relevant part of this presumption is (i).

1. The presumption of satisfaction (or ademption) of a legacy or devise by a portion

The presumption of satisfaction of a legacy or devise[36] by a portion is based on the assumption that a parent would wish to treat his children fairly and would not wish to make provision for one of his children twice over at the expense of his other children. A "portion is very broadly speaking, a gift intended to set up a child in life or to make substantial provision for him or her."[37] **13–10**

The presumption can apply only if the will containing the legacy to the child is made before the lifetime gift.

[34] Some judges (e.g. Lindsay J in *Re Cameron* [1999] Ch.386 at 409) prefer to use the term "ademption" where a legacy is satisfied (or adeemed) by a portion and the term "satisfaction" where a portion debt is satisfied by a legacy, or where a portion debt is satisfied by a portion. It may be helpful to distinguish between the last two cases (where the obligation being "satisfied" is a legal obligation) and the first case (where it is not); but the use of the term "ademption" rather than "satisfaction" in this context may lead to a different potential confusion, with the other form of ademption i.e. where property bequeathed by the testator has been disposed of before his death ("destruction ademption").

[35] Portion debts were usual in the days before the Married Women's Property Act 1882. At the time when his daughter was married, a woman's father might covenant to settle property upon her at some later date. The covenant constituted a portion debt and this portion debt might be satisfied by provision made under his will or by a portion paid during his lifetime.

[36] There had been doubt as to whether the rule against double portions applies to gifts of land. Where there is a specific devise of Blackacre in a will, followed by a lifetime gift of Blackacre to the would-be devisee, the question does not arise, there is nothing to pass under the will, see below, paras 14–35 et seq. But the question does arise if, for example, the testator makes a will in which he leaves his residuary estate, including Blackacre, to X and Y as tenants in common in equal shares, and afterwards conveys Blackacre to himself and X as tenants in common. This occurred in *Race v Race* [2002] W.T.L.R. 1193, where it was held that the rule does apply to land, not following *Davys v Boucher* (1839) 3 Y. & C. Ex. 397. The approach taken in *Race* appears to be correct as there is no logical reason why the rule against double portions should not apply to land.

[37] per Lindsay J in *Re Cameron* [1999] Ch.386 at p.407. See also Sir Wilfrid Greene MR in *Re Vaux* [1939] Ch.465 at 481–482 and the Earl of Selborne L.C. in *Re Pollock* (1885) 28 Ch.D. 552 at 555. It was held in *Taylor v Taylor* (1875) L.R. 20 Eq. 155 that paying for the son's entry into the Middle Temple, buying him a commission in the army (after he had given up the idea of a career in the law) and helping him to buy a mining business (after he had given up the idea of a career in the army) were all advancements (i.e. portions). Other lesser payments to assist the son, including helping him with his gambling debts, were not. Where an intestate dies on or after 1 January 1996, the rule as to advancements—the hotchpot rule—no longer applies—see above Chap.2 paras 2–59 et seq.

2. Testator must be parent or in loco parentis

13–11 It was held in *Re Cameron*[38] that for a gift to be a portion it sufficed that either the father or the mother[39] of the donee—or someone in loco parentis to the donee—made it to establish the child in life, or to make substantial provision for him; and that there was a rebuttable presumption that a donor would not intend to give two portions to the same donee.[40]

3. A stranger cannot benefit

13–12 Equity leans against double portions so as to achieve equality amongst children, not to benefit a stranger, i.e. a person who is neither a child of T nor a person to whom T stood in loco parentis. The presumptions of satisfaction and ademption which arise under this principle must not be applied to benefit a stranger; so where the residue is divisible between children and, say, a nephew or niece of the testator, the advances to be brought into account must be shared between the children alone.[41]

4. Rebutting the presumption

13–13 The equitable presumption may be rebutted:

(i) by intrinsic evidence from the different nature of the two provisions: or
(ii) by extrinsic evidence of T's actual intention.[42]

It is rebutted by intrinsic evidence if there are substantial differences between the limitations contained in the two provisions; this indicates T's intention to provide a double portion.[43] Moreover the presumption is rebutted if the provisions are not of the same type.[44] Thus, a legacy of a

[38] *Re Cameron* [1999] Ch.386.

[39] During the nineteenth-century, it seemed—though the position was not entirely clear—that only a gift by a father (or someone in loco parentis), and not a gift by a mother, could be a portion, see e.g. *Re Ashton* [1897] 2 Ch.574. Lindsay J took the view that, whatever the position might have been before the enactment of the Married Women's Property Act 1882, it suffices now for a gift to be capable of being a portion that it is made by *either* parent for the benefit of a child: [1999] Ch.386 at 405.

[40] There were particular problems in *Cameron* in that (i) the inter vivos gift was made by attorneys acting under an enduring power of attorney granted by the testatrix and (ii) the gift was not directly in favour of the testatrix's child, but of her grandchild (the child of the child to whom the bequest was made in her will).

[41] *Meinertzagen v Walters* (1872) L.R. 7 Ch.App.670; *Re Heather* [1906] 2 Ch.230; *Re Vaux* [1938] Ch.581 (not considered on appeal [1939] Ch.465). A grandchild is a stranger for this purpose: *Re Dawson* [1919] 1 Ch.102.

[42] *Weall v Rice* (1831) 2 Russ. & My. 251, 267–268.

[43] *Weall v Rice*, above, ("it is not possible to define what are to be considered as slight differences between two provisions"): cf. *Thynne v Earl of Glengall* (1848) 2 H.L.Cas. 131 (slight differences: presumption of satisfaction applied) and *Lord Chichester v Coventry* (1867) L.R.2 H.L. 71 (substantial differences: presumption of satisfaction rebutted).

[44] *Re Jacques* [1903] 1 Ch.267; *Casimir v Alexander* [2001] W.T.L.R. 939.

sum of money is not adeemed by a later gift inter vivos of stock-in-trade,[45] unless T puts a money value on the stock-in-trade at the time when he gives it so that it can be regarded as a gift of money.[46]

Evidence of T's declarations of intention has always been admissible as extrinsic evidence.[47] The testator's intention at the time he made his will is, generally, only indirectly relevant to the question of satisfaction in this sort of case. It is relevant that, at the time he made his will, he intended to treat his children equally, but the main problem is likely to relate to his intention at the time he made the (later) inter vivos gift.[48] Once one has double portions (which itself involves consideration of the donor's intentions) then, whether there is satisfaction, depends upon ascertaining the testator's intention at the time he makes the later inter vivos gift.[49]

5. The effect of the abolition of the hotchpot rule

There is one general issue in relation to the satisfaction—or ademption— **13–14**
of legacies by portions which has not yet been raised as an matter for discussion in the cases, but which could possibly be raised in the future. The doctrine—or presumption—of satisfaction of legacies by portions is based on the maxim that "Equity leans against double portions" and this maxim is linked with another, "Equality is Equity". These maxims were, of course, the foundation upon which the doctrine of hotchpot was based in relation to succession on intestacy.[50] Section 3 of the Statute of Distribution 1670[51] (the statute which dealt with intestate succession to personalty) provided that children should bring advancements by portion into account. The Statutes of Distribution were repealed in 1925, but s.47(1)(iii) of the Administration of Estates Act 1925 retained the requirement to bring advancements into account. The decision not to leave "the whole thing out" was criticised by Danckwerts J in *Re Morton*[52]; and the Law Commission in their 1989 Report, *Distribution on Intestacy*,[53] recommended that the hotchpot rules on intestacy and partial intestacy should be repealed. They were so repealed—for persons dying wholly or partially intestate on or after 1 January 1996—by s.1(2) of the Law Reform

[45] *Holmes v Holmes* (1783) 1 Bro.C.C. 555.

[46] *Re George's* W.T. [1949] Ch.154; *Bengough v Walker* (1808) 15 Ves. 507.

[47] *Re Tussaud's Estate* (1878) 9 Ch.D. 363 (satisfaction); *Kirk v Eddowes* (1844) 3 Hare 509 (ademption): see above, para.13–04. But failure by the testator to communicate to the donee his intention not to make double provision does not rebut the presumption, *Re Clapham, Barraclough v Mell* [2006] W.T.L.R. 203.

[48] In *Re Frost* [2013] EWHC 435 (Ch); [2013] W.T.L.R. 673, it was held that the alleged "gifts" to two of the testator's daughters were not portions but were partly repayments of money which they had spent in looking after him, and were otherwise made to cover anticipated future expenditure.

[49] *Re Vaux* [1939] Ch.465, 483. In *Casimir v Alexander* [2001] W.T.L.R. 939, it was held that the testator had not intended to treat all his children equally; he intended to show particular generosity to the daughter with whom he was living.

[50] See Sherrin and Bonehill, *The Law and Practice of Intestate Succession*, 3rd edn (London: Sweet & Maxwell, 2004) paras 13–016—13–039 and 15–012—15–029.

[51] Section 3 of the Statute of Distribution, 22 & 23 Car. 2, c.10.

[52] *Re Morton* [1956] 1 Ch.644 at 647. He described hotchpot as a "tiresome, irritating subject".

[53] *Distribution on Intestacy*, Law Com. No.187 (1989).

(Succession) Act 1995.[54] The question in relation to wills is whether the abolition of hotchpot on intestacy may lead to the suggestion that satisfaction—or ademption—of a legacy by a portion is somehow a dated concept, not in tune with the modern world. The point was not raised in *Re Cameron*[55] where the testatrix died in 1992 and the matter came before Lindsay J in 1999. It would, of course, be easier to make the suggestion in relation to a testator who dies on or after 1 January 1996,[56] but it was not made in *Race v Race*,[57] (where the testator died in 1999), or in *Re Clapham*,[58] (where he died in 2003).[59]

[54] See above, Chap.2, para.2–64.

[55] *Re Cameron* [1999] Ch.386.

[56] As to whether the abolition—as opposed to the reform—of the hotchpot rules (on total and partial intestacy) was a logical, or wise, step, see above, Chap.2 para.2–65.

[57] *Race v Race* [2002] W.T.L.R. 1193.

[58] *Re Clapham* [2006] W.T.L.R. 203.

[59] A form of quasi-hotchpot was introduced into the calculations in the proprietary estoppel case of *Evans v HSBC Trust Co* [2005] W.T.L.R. 1289; so there appears to be no sign that, other than in cases of intestacy, the satisfaction rule is losing ground.

Chapter 14

FAILURE OF GIFT BY WILL OR OF INTEREST ON INTESTACY

A gift by will may fail for any one or more of the following reasons, which are considered in turn in this chapter: **14–01**

I The beneficiary or his spouse is an attesting witness.
II The beneficiary predeceases the testator, causing the gift to lapse.
III The dissolution or annulment of the deceased's marriage to the beneficiary causes the gift to fail.
IV The gift fails by ademption.
V The gift abates.
VI The gift fails for uncertainty.
VII The beneficiary is guilty of the murder or manslaughter of the deceased.
VIII The beneficiary disclaims.

This list is not exhaustive. A gift by will may also fail because it infringes some rule of law, such as the rule against inalienability,[1] or is made for a purpose contrary to public policy.[2] A contingent gift by will may fail because the contingency is not satisfied.[3]

Heads VII and VIII are also applicable to a beneficiary on an intestacy. **14–02** Head II is not applicable on an intestacy but, of course, a person who predeceases an intestate cannot take on intestacy because the intestacy rules require the intestate's next-of-kin to survive the intestate in order to be eligible to take.[4] Similarly, head III is not applicable on an intestacy, but a former spouse, whose marriage to the intestate has been dissolved or annulled, cannot take on intestacy. Again, a contingent interest under the

[1] Sometimes called the rule against perpetual trusts: for this rule, see Megarry & Wade, *The Law of Real Property*, 8th edn (London: Sweet & Maxwell, 2012), paras 9–147—9–161.

[2] See, e.g. *Re Caborne* [1943] Ch.224 (provision void as tending to encourage break-up of existing marriage); *Re Johnson's* W.T. [1967] Ch.387.

[3] Sometimes this is referred to as failure by lapse; see e.g. *Re Parker* [1913] 1 Ch.162 and *Re Fox's Estate* [1937] 4 All E.R. 664.

[4] See Chap.2. The intestacy rules include, of course, the rules relating to the statutory trusts, so e.g. if a child of the intestate predeceases the intestate, the child's issue may take in his place: and a child *en ventre sa mére* at the intestate's death is treated as then living, see above, para.2–37, fn.54.

statutory trusts applicable on intestacy may fail because the contingency of attaining the age of 18 years or marrying is not satisfied.

The fact that a particular gift in a will fails, does not mean that the will as a whole is no longer valid. The failure of one gift—or of more than one gift—has no necessary effect on other dispositions contained in the will. The effect of the failure of a particular gift is considered at the end of this chapter; so, too, is the effect on an intestacy of failure under heads 7 and 8.

I. BENEFICIARY OR SPOUSE IS AN ATTESTING WITNESS

1. General rule

14–03 Section 15 of the Wills Act 1837 deprives an attesting witness[5] and his or her spouse[6] of any benefit under the will which the witness attests: the attestation is valid but any beneficial gift in the will to the witness or his or her spouse is "utterly null and void."[7] "[E]very time a beneficiary [or the spouse of a beneficiary] is an attesting witness, s.15 of the Wills Act 1837, deprives him of his benefit and defeats the testator's intention. This is considered necessary to ensure reliable, unbiased, witnesses of due execution."[8] Not surprisingly, critics have questioned whether this drastic rule is really justified.[9]

There are, however, several limits to the operation of the general rule.

2. Privileged will

14–04 The rule does not apply to a will intended to be an informal will and made by a privileged testator, because such a will does not require any attesting witnesses. Thus if a soldier—whilst in actual military service—makes a

[5] Presumably s.15 applies to a witness who acknowledges his signature under the amended s.9 of the Wills Act 1837, though such a witness is not required to attest: see above, paras 4–14 et seq.

[6] Para.3 of Sch.4 to the Civil Partnership Act 2004 equates civil partners to spouses for the purposes of s.15.

[7] The words of s.15. See *Ross v Caunters* [1980] Ch.297 (solicitor's negligence). As a result of the Trustee Act 2000 s.28(4) any payments to which a personal representative or trustee is entitled in respect of services are to be treated as remuneration for services and not as a gift for the purposes of Wills Act 1837 s.15.

[8] per Russell LJ in *In the Estate of Bravda* [1968] 1 W.L.R. 479, 492.

[9] See Law Reform Committee's 22nd Report, *The Making and Revocation of Wills*, Cmnd.7902 (1980), pp.6–7 (recommending no change); (1981) 125 S.J. 283; Davey [1980] Conv. 64, 75. For an account of the origins of the rule, a discussion of the policy behind it and of its present day utilily, see D.E.C.Yale (1984) 100 L.Q.R. 453. The Law Reform Advisory Committee for Northern Ireland discussed the witness beneficiary rule in their Report No.14, *Attestation of Wills*: this was their last report, before being disbanded and replaced, in April 2007, by the Northern Ireland Law Commission. They recommended following the approach taken in a number of other Commonwealth jurisdictions (they chose New South Wales as their model), and recommended that the court should be given a discretion not to apply the witness beneficiary rule where it was satisfied that the testator knew and approved of the gift and that it was made truly and voluntarily by the testator.

will intended by him to be an informal will, a gift in it to someone who happens to witness the will is valid.[10]

3. Superfluous attesting witness to a formal will

If the testator dies after 29 May 1968, the Wills Act 1968 provides that the attestation of his will by a beneficiary—or his spouse—is to be disregarded if without him the will is duly executed.[11] It follows that if a will is attested by three witnesses, only one of whom is a beneficiary—or the spouse of a beneficiary—the general rule is excluded and the beneficiary may take his benefit under the will. If, on the other hand, more than one of the three witnesses is a beneficiary (or the spouse of a beneficiary), the general rule is applicable and none of the witnesses (or their spouses) may take any benefit under the will. **14–05**

4. Beneficiary signed but not as a witness

The general rule does not apply if (which would be very unusual) the beneficiary (or his spouse) signed the will otherwise than as an attesting witness, for example, with the intention of recording his agreement with the gifts made by the testator in the will.[12] There is, however, a rebuttable presumption that any person (except the testator) whose signature appears at the end of a will signed as an attesting witness: so the general rule applies unless this presumption is rebutted.[13] **14–06**

5. Beneficiary not spouse of witness when will executed

A beneficiary who marries an attesting witness after the execution of the will may take a benefit under it: s.15 only disqualifies a beneficiary who is the spouse of an attesting witness when the will is executed.[14] **14–07**

6. Gifts on trust

The general rule only applies to beneficial gifts and not to gifts to an attesting witness (or his spouse) as trustee. If T by her will gives £200 to X and "£200 to Brompton Church, to be disposed of as X wishes," and X's wife is one of the two attesting witnesses, the first gift is void but the second gift is valid because X is a trustee for the purpose of directing the disposition of the legacy.[15] **14–08**

[10] *Re Limond* [1915] 2 Ch.240.

[11] Wills Act 1968 s.1. For the formalities required for due execution, see Chap.4. If the testator died before 30 May 1968, the general rule applies, even though there were two other attesting witnesses, *In the Estate of Bravda*, [1968] 1 W.L.R. 479.

[12] *In the Goods of Sharman* (1869) L.R. 1 P. & D. 661 (beneficiary's signature omitted from grant as she did not intend to attest testator's signature); *In the Goods of Smith* (1889) 15 P.D. 2 (wife, a beneficiary, signed will to verify its contents: her signature omitted from probate); *Kitcat v King* [1930] P. 266: but see *In the Estate of Bravda* [1968] 1 W.L.R. 479 at 488, 491 and 493.

[13] *In the Estate of Bravda* [1968] 1 W.L.R. 479.

[14] *Thorpe v Bestwick* (1881) 6 Q.B.D. 311: see *Re Royce's* W.T. [1959] Ch.626.

[15] *Cresswell v Cresswell* (1868) L.R. 6 Eq. 69: see also *Re Ray's* W.T. [1936] Ch.520 (gift by T's will

7. Gift made or confirmed[16] by another will or codicil

14–09 The general rule does not apply:

(i) if the gift to the beneficiary B is contained in a will or a codicil which was not attested by B or B's spouse, even though some other document was so attested[17]; *or*
(ii) if the gift to B is contained in a document which was attested by B or B's spouse, but this document was confirmed by a will or codicil not so attested.[18]

Consider situation (i). B is the residuary beneficiary under T's will, which was not attested by B or B's spouse. By a codicil, T revokes certain legacies given by his will, thereby swelling his residuary estate. It is immaterial that B or B's spouse attested this codicil—the general rule is not applicable because B takes the swollen residuary estate under T's will and not under the codicil.[19]

But the general rule is applicable if the will or codicil which contains the gift to B, and each document which confirmed this will or codicil, was attested by B or B's spouse. In this case B cannot take, because he cannot point to a document under which he claims which neither he nor his spouse attested.[20]

The application of the doctrine of conditional revocation in *Re Finnemore*,[21] to save a gift in an earlier will from revocation by a later will—which itself contained a gift which was void because the later will was witnessed by the beneficiary's husband—was discussed in Chapter 7.[22]

8. Witness or spouse takes under secret trust

14–10 If T by his will gives property to X, and X takes this property on a secret trust for Y, the general rule does not apply if Y or Y's spouse attested T's will.[23] This is said to be because Y does not take his beneficial interest

to the person who should be abbess at T's death; an attesting witness later became abbess: held gift was valid as she took in trust for the purposes of the convent—it was immaterial that she might, as a member of the convent, get some benefit in some shape or form out of the administration of the fund).

16 For confirmation (or republication), see above, paras 7–65 et seq.

17 *Re Marcus* (1887) 57 L.T. 399 (gifts to B and C by T's will; B attested codicils but not the will and C attested both the will and the codicils: held B could take but C could not); *Gurney v Gurney* (1855) 3 Drew. 208.

18 *Anderson v Anderson* (1872) L.R. 13 Eq. 381; *Re Trotter* [1899] 1 Ch.764 (B, a solicitor, attested will and second codicil: held B could take benefit of a charging clause in will under first codicil which confirmed will); see now Trustee Act 2000 s.28(4): cf. *Burton v Newbery* (1875) 1 Ch.D. 234 (confirmation of will by second codicil does not validate gift to attesting witness in first codicil not confirmed).

19 *Gurney v Gurney* (1855) 3 Drew. 208.

20 *Re Marcus*, (1887) 57 L.T. 399 at 400.

21 *Re Finnemore* [1991] 1 W.L.R. 793.

22 See above, para.7–44.

23 *Re Young* [1951] Ch.344; *O'Brien v Condon* [1905] 1 I.R. 51. For secret trusts, see above,

under T's will. He takes it by virtue of the secret trust imposed upon X who takes under the will.[24]

II. LAPSE

1. Doctrine of lapse[25]

Under this doctrine a gift by will lapses and fails if the beneficiary dies before the testator.[26] Similarly, a gift by will to a corporate body lapses if the corporate body is dissolved before the testator's death.[27] The doctrine of lapse is a consequence of the ambulatory character of a will, which has no effect until the testator's death and so confers no benefit on persons who die before him.[28] **14–11**

(a) *Declaration against lapse ineffective, but substitutional gift effective*

A testator cannot exclude the doctrine of lapse by declaring in his will that it is not to apply.[29] But he may provide that, if the original beneficiary predeceases him, the subject-matter of a gift shall be given to another beneficiary.[30] So, the testator may provide that if the original beneficiary predeceases him, the subject-matter of the gift shall be given to the original beneficiary's personal representatives, to be held as part of the original beneficiary's estate.[31] Or he may direct that if A dies in his lifetime, a gift to A shall operate as if A had survived him and had taken the gift but had died immediately afterwards (which achieves the same result).[32] Again—and this is much more common—the testator may make a gift to A, but if **14–12**

Chap.6, where it was suggested that there may be problems with the theories which are said to justify their enforcement.

24 *Re Young* [1951] Ch.344 at 350.

25 See generally Ford (1962) 78 L.Q.R. 88.

26 *Elliott v Davenport* (1705) 1 P.Wms. 83; *Maybank v Brooks* (1780) 1 Bro.C.C. 84 (legacy given to M, his executors, administrators, or assigns; M predeceased testator: held legacy lapsed).

27 *Re Servers of the Blind League* [1960] 1 W.L.R. 564; *Re Stemson's* W.T. [1970] Ch.16; *Re Finger's* W.T. [1972] 1 Ch.286. A gift by T's will to a corporation with charitable objects does not fail by lapse owing to its dissolution in T's lifetime if (i) it is really a gift for charitable purposes (unless the gift shows the corporation's continued existence is essential), or (ii) T shows a general charitable intention; see generally Hanbury and Martin, *Modern Equity*, 20th edn (London: Sweet & Maxwell, 2015), paras 15–067 et seq.

28 *Jarman on Wills*, 8th edn (London: Sweet & Maxwell, 1951), p.438.

29 *Re Ladd* [1932] 2 Ch.219 (T had a general testamentary power of appointment and by her will appointed to her husband "to the intent that this my will shall take effect whether I survive or predecease my husband"; the husband predeceased T: held the appointment to him failed by lapse and his executors did not take); *Browne v Hope* (1872) L.R. 14 Eq. 343 (declaration that gift to vest on execution of will does not prevent lapse).

30 *Sibley v Cook* (1747) 3 Atk. 572; *Re Greenwood* [1912] 1 Ch.393, 396.

31 For the consequences see *Re Cousen's* W.T. [1937] Ch.381: see also (1962) 78 L.Q.R. 88, 90 et seq.

32 *Re Greenwood*, above. The line between attempting to declare that the doctrine of lapse shall not apply, and providing that if the original beneficiary predeceases the subject-matter of the gift shall be given to his personal representatives, may not be easy to draw, see *Re Ladd*,

A shall die in his lifetime, he makes a substitutional gift to such of A's children living at his death who attain the age of, say, 21 years—or marry—in equal shares.[33]

(b) *Gift to joint tenants*

14–13 The nature of the gift made by the testator may exclude the doctrine of lapse. Thus if T by his will makes a gift to two or more persons as *joint tenants* (e.g. to A, B and C jointly), no lapse can occur unless all the beneficiaries die before the testator. If A and B both die before T, C takes the whole gift if he survives T[34]; but if C also dies before T, the gift lapses. The doctrine of lapse is, however, fully applicable if there are words of severance in T's will, so that the beneficiaries take as *tenants in common* (e.g. to X, Y and Z *equally*): in that case, if X dies before T, the gift of a third share to X lapses.[35]

(c) *Class gift*

14–14 The doctrine of lapse does not apply to a class gift made to persons who are to be ascertained at the testator's death.[36] It does not matter whether they take as joint tenants or as tenants in common. An instance is a gift by T's will "to all my children as tenants in common in equal shares." This is construed as a gift to all the persons coming within the description at the testator's death; they will take the subject-matter of the gift equally. If one of T's children predeceases him, there is no lapse because such child was never a member of the class.[37] A gift may be to a class, even though some individual members of the class are named: thus a gift "to my children including [or excluding] X" is a class gift.[38] But a gift "to Y and the children of Z" is prima facie not a class gift because Y falls outside the general description[39]: however, T's will may, on its proper construction, show that T intended this gift to take effect as a class gift, so that if Y predeceases T there is no lapse.[40]

On the other hand, if T by his will makes a gift "to my three brothers as tenants in common in equal shares," this is a gift to individuals and not a

above. The intentional approach to the construction of wills (see Chap.10, above) may save some gifts which might previously have failed.

33 Alternatively the substitutional gift may be in favour of A's children and remoter issue per stirpes in equal shares, so as to include descendants of a deceased child of A. See specimen will para.9–01.

34 *Morley v Bird* (1798) 3 Ves. 629.

35 *Page v Page* (1728) 2 P.Wms. 489; *Peat v Chapman* (1750) 1 Ves.Sen. 542; *Re Wood's Will* (1861) 29 Beav. 236. Of course, T may by his will provide that the gift is to such of X, Y and Z as shall survive him, and if more than one in equal shares. This prevents a lapse. See also Wills Act 1837 s.33 below, paras 14–22 et seq.

36 Or *after* the testator's death.

37 *Doe d. Stewart v Sheffield* (1811) 13 East. 526; *Shuttleworth v Greaves* (1838) 4 M. & Cr. 35. For the effect of the original, and the amended, s.33 of the Wills Act 1837 see below, paras 14–24 and 14–25.

38 *Shaw v M'Mahon* (1843) 4 D. & War. 431: see *Re Jackson* (1883) 25 Ch.D. 162. There may be a composite class gift—"to the children of A and the children of B."

39 *Re Chaplin's Trusts* (1863) 33 L.J. Ch.183; *Re Allen* (1881) 44 L.T. 240.

40 *Kingsbury v Walter* [1901] A.C. 187 (a "special" class gift).

class gift: each brother takes a distinct third share which is quantified from the beginning and which does not vary in size according to the number of the recipients. If one or more of the three brothers predeceases T, the gift to him of a third share lapses.[41] But if the gift is "to such of my three brothers as shall be living at my death as tenants in common in equal shares," there is no lapse if one of them predeceases T, because T has made provision for this event: the other two brothers living at T's death take the subject-matter of the gift equally.[42]

(d) *Effect of confirmation of will*

If T makes his will containing a gift to X, and after X's death T makes a codicil which confirms his will, this does not prevent the gift to X from lapsing or make it take effect as a gift to X's personal representatives.[43] The will is read as if it had been executed at the time of its confirmation[44] but this makes no difference: there is still a gift to X which fails by lapse. **14–15**

Occasionally, confirmation may alter the construction of a will as to the identity of the beneficiary and so save a gift which would otherwise have lapsed. In *Re Hardyman*[45] the testatrix by her will gave a legacy of £5,000 on trust for her cousin for life and then for "his wife" for life with remainders over. The will referred to the cousin's wife living at the date of the will. But this wife died and the testatrix—knowing of her death—made a codicil which confirmed her will. After the testatrix's death, the cousin married again. Romer J held that, as a result of its confirmation, the will referred to any woman whom the cousin might marry and not to the dead first wife. As a result of its confirmation, the will, said Romer J, "is a will which the testatrix tells me expressed her wishes as they were at the date of the codicil."[46] The cousin's second wife was therefore entitled to an interest in the legacy. If the will had not been confirmed, it would have been construed as referring to the first wife and any gift to her would have failed by lapse. Of course, if the will had referred to the first wife by name, any gift to her would have failed by lapse.

2. Presumption where there is uncertainty as to who survived whom

Owing to the doctrine of lapse, the order of deaths of T, a testator, and B, a beneficiary under T's will, is crucial. If B survived T for however short a time, B may take under T's will.[47] But if B predeceased T, the doctrine of lapse applies and B cannot take under T's will unless one of the exceptions **14–16**

41 *Re Smith's Trusts* (1878) 9 Ch.D. 117.

42 See *Re Woods* [1931] 2 Ch.138; *Re Peacock* [1957] Ch.310 (a gift to a group, having for purposes of lapse the characteristics of a class gift).

43 *Hutcheson v Hammond* (1790) 3 Bro.C.C. 127; *Re Wood's Will* (1861) 29 Beav. 236.

44 See above, paras 7–65 et seq.

45 *Re Hardyman* [1925] Ch.287.

46 *Re Hardyman* [1925] Ch.287 at 293.

47 Provided that the gift is absolute and not contingent. A gift may be made contingent on the beneficiary's surviving the testator by (say) 28 days.

to the doctrine of lapse[48] is applicable. The order of deaths may also be crucial (i) on an intestacy, (ii) on the death of joint tenants, in order to ascertain which of them benefits by the right of survivorship, and (iii) under the terms of a gift in a will—for instance, a gift by T "to X if my wife shall die in my lifetime," and T and his wife are both swept off a ship by the same wave and never seen again.[49]

Before 1926, if the evidence left the order in which people had died uncertain, there was no legal presumption that one person had survived another. If any person sought to establish a claim which depended upon B's having survived T, the onus of proof lay on the claimant to establish that fact by affirmative evidence: if he did not do so, his claim failed.[50] Thus if two people died in a shipwreck and the evidence left it uncertain which of them survived the other, a claim by the personal representatives of either of them to benefit under the other's will or intestacy necessarily failed.[51]

(a) *Death presumed in order of seniority*

14–17 Section 184 of the Law of Property Act 1925 now raises a presumption as to the order of deaths by providing as follows:

> "In all cases where, after the commencement of this Act, two or more persons have died in circumstances rendering it uncertain which of them survived the other or others, such deaths shall (subject to any order of the court), for all purposes affecting the title to property, be presumed to have occurred in order of seniority, and accordingly the younger shall be deemed to have survived the elder."

Accordingly, where s.184 applies, there is a statutory presumption that the deaths occurred in order of seniority, i.e. the eldest died first and the youngest died last. The words in brackets—"subject to any order of the court"—appear to be meaningless in this context.[52] They certainly give the court no discretion to disregard the statutory presumption on the ground that it would be unfair or unjust to act upon it.[53]

[48] See below paras 14–21 et seq.
[49] *Underwood v Wing* (1855) 4 De G.M. & G. 633; *Wing v Angrave* (1860) 8 H.L.C. 183: see also *Re Rowland* [1963] Ch.1.
[50] *Underwood v Wing* (1855) 4 De G.M&G 633; *Wing v Angrave*, (1860) 8 H.L.C. 183; *Re Phene's Trusts* (1870) 5 Ch. App.139 ("the true proposition is, that those who found a right upon a person having survived a particular period must establish that fact affirmatively by evidence").
[51] *Underwood v Wing*, (1855) 4 De G. M & G 633; *Wing v Angrave*, (1860) 8 H.L.C. 183.
[52] per Lord Simonds in *Hickman v Peacey* [1945] A.C. 304, 346–347, "I have tried in vain to give any reasonable meaning and effect" to the words. For other explanations see *Re Lindop* [1942] Ch.377, 382 (words make it clear presumption is rebuttable by evidence); *Re Grosvenor* [1944] Ch.138, 143 and see 148–149 (words may refer to subsequent orders of the court in the event of fresh evidence becoming available); *Hickman v Peacey*, above, at p.316 (words provide for case where insufficient evidence as to respective ages of deceased persons).
[53] *Re Lindop* [1942] Ch.377, 382.

(b) *Uncertainty as to who survived whom*

Section 184 applies where it is uncertain which of two or more persons survived the other. It applies when the deaths occurred in a common disaster[54] and it applies when the deaths occurred separately.[55] In *Hickman v Peacey*[56] five people were killed in the same house by a bomb dropped during a wartime air raid; two of them had made wills in favour of some of the others. The House of Lords held—by a majority—that s.184 was applicable in all cases where it could not be proved that one person had in fact survived the other, and it was immaterial whether the deaths appeared to be simultaneous or consecutive. As Lord Macmillan (speaking for the majority) put it:[57] **14–18**

> "Can you say for certain which of these two dead persons died first? If you cannot say for certain, then you must presume the older to have died first. It is immaterial that the reason for your inability to say for certain which died first is either because you think they both died simultaneously or because you think they died consecutively but you do not know in what sequence."

(c) *Exclusion of the statutory presumption*

(i) Intestate Spouses. By way of exception, the statutory presumption does not apply as between spouses if the older spouse dies *intestate*. Section 46(3) of the Administration of Estates Act 1925, as amended by s.1(4) of the Intestates' Estates Act 1952, states that if an intestate and his younger spouse die in circumstances rendering it uncertain which of them survived the other, the statutory presumption that the younger survived the older does not apply and the younger spouse is presumed not to have survived the older. Section 46(3) applies if the spouses die on or after 1 January 1952 and on or before 31 December 1995. If they die on or after 1 January 1996, a newly inserted s.46(2A) of the Administration of Estates Act 1925 provides that an intestate's spouse, in order to benefit on his intestacy, must survive him by 28 days.[58] **14–19**

(ii) Inheritance Tax. The statutory presumption is also not applicable for inheritance tax purposes; for inheritance tax, each of the deceased persons is assumed to have died at the same instant.[59] Take the case of T and his child B who are both killed in a road accident, in circumstances rendering it uncertain which of them survived the other: under the statutory presumption, B (the younger) is presumed to have survived T and may therefore take T's estate under T's will or on T's intestacy; but inheritance tax on T's estate is payable (if at all) only in respect of T's death and not, a

[54] *Re Bate* (1947) 116 L.J.R. 1409 (gas poisoning from gas oven in kitchen).
[55] e.g. the husband's ship may disappear at sea on an unknown date and the wife may die at home after the ship has sailed, *Hickman v Peacey* [1945] A.C. 304 at 314–315.
[56] *Hickman v Peacey* [1945] A.C. 304, 346–347.
[57] *Hickman v Peacey* [1945] A.C. 304, 346–347 at 323–324.
[58] Law Reform (Succession) Act 1995 s.1. See Chap. 2.
[59] Inheritance Tax Act 1984 s.4(2). For a further discussion of the tax position, see Chap.16.

second time, in respect of B's death.[60] On B's death, inheritance tax would be payable (if at all) in respect of B's property only, ignoring any property inherited from T.

(d) *Deficiencies of the presumption*

14–20 Where it is applicable, the statutory presumption has the merit of providing a definite (though arbitrary) solution, if the order of deaths is uncertain but there is sufficient evidence as to the respective ages of the deceased persons. This solution may, however, sometimes defeat the wishes which a testator would have expressed if he had thought about the problem. For instance, if T by his will gives his entire estate to his daughter D, and T and D die in circumstances rendering it uncertain which of them survived the other, under the statutory presumption D is presumed to have survived T and therefore takes T's estate, which then passes to the beneficiaries entitled under D's will[61] or to D's next-of-kin entitled on her intestacy (possibly her widower). It may well be a better solution for T to provide by his will that D shall take only if she survives T for (say) a period of one month: such a *commorientes* clause prevents D from taking under the statutory presumption and also guards against the possibility that D may only survive T for a very short time.

3. Exceptions to the doctrine of lapse

14–21 There are two exceptions to the doctrine of lapse: the first is a statutory exception under the Wills Act 1837, and the second is based on case law.

(a) *Gift to the testator's child or remoter descendant*

14–22 Section 33(1) of the Wills Act 1837 provides that:

> "where—
> (a) a will contains a devise or bequest to a child or remoter descendant of the testator; and
> (b) the intended beneficiary dies before the testator, leaving issue; and
> (c) issue of the intended beneficiary are living at the testator's death,
>
> then, unless a contrary intention appears by the will, the devise or bequest shall take effect as a devise or bequest to the issue living at the testator's death."

This section is quoted as substituted by s.19 of the Administration of Justice Act 1982, and it applies in its substituted form if the

[60] Under Inheritance Tax Act 1984 s.4(1) inheritance tax is charged in respect of B's death on the value of B's estate *immediately before B's death*: at that moment T would still be alive and B would not have inherited T's estate, s.4(2).
[61] See *Re Rowland* [1963] 1 Ch.1.

testator dies after 31 December 1982.[62] Section 33 in its original form applied if the testator died before 1 January 1983.[63] There are significant differences between the substituted section and the original section.

(i) The requirements of section 33(1). For the substituted s.33(1) to apply, T's will must contain a devise or bequest to B, who is T's child or remoter descendant. **14–23**

The original s.33 also required the devise or bequest to be for an interest not determinable at or before B's death, and therefore did not apply to a gift to B of a life interest, or an interest in joint tenancy,[64] or an interest contingent on B's attaining 25 years of age if B died under that age.[65] The substituted s.33(1) does not impose this additional requirement. Neither the substituted nor the original section applies to an appointment by will under a special power,[66] but each of them applies to an appointment by will under a general power.[67]

Both the substituted and the original section require issue of B to be "living" at T's death. For the purposes of the substituted section, any issue of B who is conceived before T's death and is born alive after T's death is treated as living at T's death.[68] This was probably not so under the original section.[69]

For the section to apply, B must leave issue living at B's own death and issue living at T's (later) death. But under neither the original section nor the substituted section do the issue need to be the same people. So, the section applies where T by her will gives all her property to her daughter B, who predeceases T leaving an only child C, who also predeceases T after bearing a child D who survives T.[70] Again, the section applies even though B is already dead at the date of T's will.[71]

The section applies unless a contrary intention appears by the will.[72]

[62] Administration of Justice Act 1982 ss.73(6) and 76(11).

[63] Administration of Justice Act 1982 s.33 in its original form read, "where any person being a child or other issue of the testator to whom any real or personal estate shall be devised or bequeathed for any estate or interest not determinable at or before the death of such person shall die in the lifetime of the testator leaving issue, and any such issue of such person shall be living at the time of the death of the testator, such devise or bequest shall not lapse, but shall take effect as if the death of such person had happened immediately after the death of the testator, unless a contrary intention shall appear by the will."

[64] *Re Butler* [1918] 1 I.R. 394.

[65] *Re Wolson* [1939] Ch.780: cf. *Re Wilson* (1920) 89 L.J. Ch.216.

[66] *Holyland v Lewin* (1883) 26 Ch.D. 266.

[67] *Eccles v Cheyne* (1856) 2 K. & J. 676: see Wills Act 1837 s.27 and above, paras 11–33 et seq. For an explanation of the difference between special powers and general powers, see Hanbury and Martin, *Modern Equity*, 20th edn (London: Sweet & Maxwell, 2015), para.7–004.

[68] Substituted s.33(4)(a).

[69] *Elliot v Joicey* [1935] A.C. 209, esp. at 229–233, disapproving *Re Griffith's Settlement* [1911] 1 Ch.246.

[70] *In the Goods of Parker* (1860) 1 Sw. & Tr. 523: see *Jarman on Wills*, 8th edn (London: Sweet & Maxwell, 1951), pp.463–464.

[71] *Mower v Orr* (1849) 7 Hare 473; *Wisden v Wisden* (1854) 2 Sm. & G. 396.

[72] *Ling v Ling* [2002] W.T.L.R. 553 (no contrary intention).

For the purposes of the substituted section, the illegitimacy of any person is to be disregarded.[73] This was so under the original section if T died after 1969, whenever he made his will.[74]

14–24 **(ii) The operation of section 33(1).** If the requirements of the original s.33 were satisfied, then, unless a contrary intention appeared by T's will,[75] T's gift to B did not lapse but took effect as if B had died immediately after T. The gift therefore fell into B's estate and had to be administered by B's personal representatives as an asset of B's estate. So, if B's estate was insolvent, the original s.33 increased B's assets and benefited his creditors.[76] If B's estate was solvent, the subject-matter of T's gift to him passed to the persons beneficially entitled under B's will[77] or on his intestacy[78] at the date when he actually died.[79] Thus, although B's issue living at T's death saved the gift to B from lapse, such issue only benefited if they were beneficially entitled under B's will or on his intestacy. Under the original s.33, B's issue living at T's death did not stand in B's shoes and take the gift in B's place—they merely enabled the gift to him to take effect.

14–25 The substituted s.33(1) operates differently. If the requirements of the substituted s.33(1) are satisfied, then, unless a contrary intention appears by T's will, the devise or bequest to B takes effect as a devise or bequest to B's issue living at T's death and B's issue take per stirpes, if more than one in equal shares.[80] If the class members have to satisfy a contingency—such as attaining a certain age—the issue included by s.33(2) must satisfy the contingency determining the date of distribution as much as any other member of the class.[81] In other words, under the substituted s.33(1), B's issue stand in his shoes and take the gift in his place. An example will illustrate the operation of the section. Suppose that T's will contains an absolute gift to his child B, who dies before T leaving issue, i.e. B's two children C and D. Then D has two children, E and F, and D dies. At T's death, B's issue C, E and F are living. Under s.33(1) the gift to B takes effect

73 Substituted s.33(4)(b).

74 Family Law Reform Act 1969 s.16(1). Before this Act s.33 applied if B was legitimated, *Re Brodie* [1967] Ch.818, and this is still so, Legitimacy Act 1976 ss.1–3 and 5(1) and (3), Sch.I, paras 1(1) and 2(1): for the status conferred by adoption, see Adoption and Children Act 2002 s.67, and above, paras 11–02 et seq.

75 *Re Meredith* [1924] 2 Ch.552.

76 *Re Pearson* [1920] 1 Ch.247 (T by his will made a gift to his son B, who predeceased T but left issue living at T's death; B died an undischarged bankrupt: held the gift passed to B's trustee in bankruptcy).

77 *Johnson v Johnson* (1843) 3 Hare 157; *Re Hayter* [1937] 2 All E.R. 110 (B by his will gave "everything I die possessed of" to X: held a general residuary gift which included property which passed to B under s.33 on the later death of T).

78 *Eager v Furnivall* (1881) 17 Ch.D. 115: see Ryder (1971) 24 C.L.P. 157, 174–177.

79 *Re Basioli* [1953] Ch.367 (reviewing the cases); *Re Hurd* [1941] Ch.196: see *Re Hone's Trusts* (1883) 22 Ch.D. 663. If T was the person beneficially entitled under B's will (or intestacy), this produced a "circle" which had to be broken at some point: see *Re Hensler* (1881) 19 Ch.D. 612.

80 Substituted s.33(3), which provides that B's issue shall take through all degrees according to their stock, in equal shares if more than one, any gift or share which their parent would have taken and so that no issue shall take whose parent is living at T's death and so capable of taking.

81 *Ling v Ling* [2002] W.T.L.R. 553, a badly drafted will. Etherton J held that s.33(2) applied.

as a gift to C (a one-half share), and E and F (a one-quarter share each). The substituted s.33(1) has the merit of operating in the same way as an express substitutional gift in a will commonly operates, i.e. benefiting B's issue and not his estate.[82]

(iii) Class gift to testator's children or remoter descendants. The original s.33 did not apply to a class gift because (as was explained earlier) the doctrine of lapse does not apply to a class gift to persons who are to be ascertained at T's death or subsequently.[83] Consider again the example of a class gift by T's will "to all my children as tenants in common in equal shares." If B, one of T's children, predeceased T but left issue living at T's death, the original s.33 did not apply and B's personal representatives did not take under the gift.[84] This was so even if B was T's only child.[85] **14–26**

If the testator dies after 31 December 1982, the substituted s.33(2) applies to a class gift to T's children or remoter descendants. The requirements are that:

- (i) T's will contains a devise or bequest to a class of persons consisting of T's children or remoter descendants;
- (ii) a presumptive member of the class[86] dies before T, leaving issue; and
- (iii) issue of that member are living at T's death.

If these requirements are satisfied, then, unless a contrary intention appears by T's will, the devise or bequest takes effect as if the class included the issue of its deceased member living at T's death, and the issue take the deceased member's share per stirpes, if more than one in equal shares.[87]

The substituted s.33(2) does not create an exception to the rule that the doctrine of lapse does not apply to a class gift. But where s.33(2) applies, it adds the issue of a deceased presumptive member to the class eligible to take, in order to give effect to the testator's likely intention, which he did not express in his will.

(b) *Gift to discharge a moral obligation*

If T by his will makes a gift to C in discharge of a moral obligation recognised by T in his will, and which still exists at T's death, the gift does not **14–27**

[82] See above, para.14–12. Given that the substituted s.33 operates in this way, the reader may wonder whether, since 1983, express provision in the will serves any purpose. The advantage of express provision is that it means that the testator's attention has been drawn to the point, and he may wish a provision to be inserted in his will, the effect of which is not in all respects identical with that of the substituted s.33.
[83] See above, para.14–14.
[84] *Olney v Bates* (1855) 3 Drew. 319; *Browne v Hammond* (1858) Johns. 210. The original s.33 of course applied to a gift to individuals, *Re Stansfield* (1880) 15 Ch.D. 84 (T's will gave "to my nine children as tenants in common in equal shares": held not a class gift and s.33 applied).
[85] *Re Harvey's Estate* [1893] 1 Ch.567.
[86] Substituted s.33(2)(b) refers to "a member of the class": in the context this means a *presumptive* member.
[87] Substituted s.33(3).

lapse, though C predeceases T, because the court infers that T intended the gift to pass to C's estate. As Farwell J put it in *Stevens v King*[88]:

> "I think that the cases have established the rule that, if the Court finds, upon the construction of the will, that the testator clearly intended not to give a mere bounty to the legatee, but to discharge what he regarded as a moral obligation, whether it were legally binding or not, and if that obligation still exists at the testator's death, there is no necessary failure of the testator's object merely because the legatee dies in his lifetime; and therefore death in such a case does not cause a lapse."

This exception to the doctrine of lapse is based on case law and its ambit is uncertain. The exception has been held applicable where T makes a gift in discharge of his own debt which is barred by limitation,[89] or by the law of bankruptcy,[90] or in discharge of his deceased son's debt.[91] It may be that the exception is confined to the express recognition by T in his will of a moral obligation to pay one or more debts, and that it does not extend to the recognition of any other form of moral obligation.

III. DISSOLUTION OF TESTATOR'S MARRIAGE TO BENEFICIARY

14–28 If a testator makes a will, is later divorced[92] and then dies without having remarried[93] and without having made a new will,[94] the rule governing the effect of the divorce on his will varies according to the date of his death. The original rule, which applied until 31 December1982, was that divorce had no effect on a will. The rule for testators dying between 1983 and 1995 was that a gift to the testator's former spouse would *lapse*. The rule for testators dying from 1 January 1996 onwards is that the former spouse will, for most purposes, be deemed to have pre-deceased the testator.

1. Testator dies on or before 31 December 1982

14–29 Before the enactment of the Matrimonial Causes Act 1857, divorce could be effected only by private Act of Parliament and there were on average

[88] *Stevens v King* [1904] 2 Ch.30, 33.

[89] *Williamson v Naylor* (1838) 3 Y. & C. 208.

[90] *Philips v Philips* (1844) 3 Hare 281; *Re Sowerby's Trust* (1856) 2 K. & J. 630; *Turner v Martin* (1857) De G.M. & G. 429.

[91] *Re Leach's* W.T. [1948] Ch.232.

[92] Section 18C of the Wills Act 1837, inserted by the Civil Partnership Act 2004, gives the same effect to the dissolution or annulment of a civil partnership as to the dissolution or annulment of a marriage. To avoid the need for repetition, the term "marriage", as used in this chapter, should be taken to include civil partnership; and the term "divorce" to include the dissolution of a civil partnership.

[93] (Re) marriage will revoke the will, see Chap.7.

[94] The new will will almost always contain a revocation clause.

about two divorces a year.[95] So, s.18 of the Wills Act 1837 provided that marriage would revoke a will,[96] but divorce had no effect. This remained the position until 1982 and covered all testators who died on or before 31 December 1982.

2. Testator dies on or after 1 January 1983 and before 1 January 1996

The Law Reform Committee's 22nd Report, *The Making and Revocation of Wills*[97] considered the position and a majority of the Committee's members recommended that the law should be changed so that a divorced spouse should be treated as having pre-deceased the testator. This led to the enactment of the Administration of Justice Act 1982 s.18(2) which inserted s.18A into the Wills Act. This section applies to testators who die on or after 1 January 1983 and before 1 January 1996, and reads as follows: **14–30**

> 18A.
> (1) Where, after a testator has made a will, a decree of a court of civil jurisdiction in England and Wales dissolves or annuls his marriage
>   (a) the will shall take effect as if any appointment of the former spouse as an executor were omitted; and
>   (b) any devise or bequest to the former spouse shall lapse,
>
>   except in so far as a contrary intention appears by the will.
> (3) Where
>   (a) by the terms of a will an interest in remainder is subject to a life interest; and
>   (b) the life interest lapses by virtue of subsection (1)(b) above, the interest in remainder shall be treated as if it had not been subject to the life interest"[98]

The problem with the original s.18A was that it did *not* enact the Law Reform Committee's recommendation, which was that the divorced spouse should be deemed to have pre-deceased the testator. The effect of s.18A(3) was that there was a deemed pre-decease where the divorced spouse was given a life interest; but in the more usual case, where the divorced spouse was given an absolute interest, s.18A(1)(b) enacted that a devise or bequest to the former spouse should *lapse*.

The difference between the Law Reform Committee's recommendation and the original s.18A became apparent in the case of *Re Sinclair*.[99] Mr Sinclair made a will in which he devised and bequeathed his whole estate to his wife. The will contained the following clause: **14–31**

[95] There were 184 Parliamentary divorces between 1715 and 1852—see Law Reform Committee's 22nd Report para.3.26, fn.11.
[96] See Chap.7.
[97] Law Reform Committee's 22nd Report, *The Making and Revocation of Wills*, Cmnd.7902 (1980).
[98] s.18A(2) makes it clear that the former spouse retains a right to make an application under the family provision legislation.
[99] *Re Sinclair* [1985] Ch.446.

> "If my said wife shall pre-decease me then I give the whole of my estate unto the Imperial Cancer Research Fund absolutely."

The Sinclairs were divorced but Mr Sinclair made no new will and did not remarry. He died in October 1983, survived by his former wife. Had Mr Sinclair remarried, his remarriage would have revoked his will. Had Mr Sinclair died before 1 January 1983, his former wife would have benefited under his will; but as s.18A had come into force, she did not benefit. The question arose as to who did benefit. It was suggested on behalf of the charity that "lapse" should be read to mean "fail with the same consequences as if the former spouse had died in the testator's lifetime"; but this was not accepted by the trial judge,[100] and his decision was upheld by a unanimous Court of Appeal. "Lapse" simply meant "fail". The gift to the former spouse failed, but there was nothing in the section to suggest that she was deemed to have pre-deceased the testator. The estate which she would have inherited accordingly passed not to the Imperial Cancer Research Fund but, on intestacy, to Mr Sinclair's brother.

3. Testator dies on or after 1 January 1996

14–32 It was generally agreed that *Re Sinclair* left the law in an unsatisfactory state and the Law Commission were asked to look at the problem. In September 1993 they presented a Report—*Family Law: The Effect of Divorce on Wills*[101] which recommended that the law should be amended so that, where there is a divorce or an annulment, the former spouse should—*for most purposes*—be deemed to have pre-deceased the testator: a *selective* deemed pre-decease rule.

The Law Commission's recommendations have been enacted as ss.3 and 4 of the Law Reform (Succession) Act 1995 which apply to persons dying on or after 1 January 1996 (regardless of the date of the will and of the date of the dissolution or annulment of the marriage).

Section 4 is straightforward. It causes the appointment of a former spouse as a testamentary guardian of the testator's infant children to be revoked. This will usually only apply where the former spouse is *not* the children's parent, but is a step-parent; if the former spouse is the children's parent he will (in most cases) have parental responsibility in any event.

14–33 Section 3 of the 1995 Act contains the significant change: the effect is to substitute new paras (a) and (b) for the original paras (a) and (b) in s.18A(1). Section 18A(1) as amended (and as applying to testators dying on or after 1 January 1996) now reads:

> "18A.
>
> (1) Where, after a testator has made a will, a decree of a court of civil jurisdiction in England and Wales dissolves or annuls his marriage
>
> (a) provisions of the will appointing executors or trustees or conferring a power of appointment, if they appoint or confer the

[100] Michael Wheeler QC, sitting as a deputy High Court judge.

[101] Law Com. No.217.

power on the former spouse, shall take effect as if the former spouse had died on the date on which the marriage is dissolved or annulled, and

(b) any property which, or an interest in which, is devised or bequeathed to the former spouse shall pass as if the former spouse had died on that date, except in so far as a contrary intention appears by the will."

The change effected by the substituted s.18A(1)(a) is to revoke the former spouse's appointment as the donee or appointor of a power of appointment, as well as revoking his appointment as executor or trustee. The substituted subsection also makes it clear that the former spouse is deemed to have pre-deceased the testator, so that any appointment of another person which is to take effect on the former spouse's death will be effective.

The substituted s.18A(1)(b) is the more important subsection, because it negatives the effect of *Re Sinclair*.[102]

Although the changes effected by the amendments to s.18A are clear **14–34** improvements, they seem to have been effected in a way that is more complicated than is necessary. Why did the Law Commission not suggest that the former spouse should be deemed to have pre-deceased the testator *for all purposes*, rather than for certain purposes? For at least two purposes he is treated as being still alive. First, the former spouse is treated as being still alive for the purpose of benefiting as an *appointee* under a *special* power of appointment.[103] Second, the former spouse will be treated as being still alive where a gift to a third party is somehow dependent on the former spouse's being alive, for example where a gift to a child is dependent on the child's living with the former spouse. Such gifts will be extremely rare and it would have been more straightforward if the amended s.18A had provided that the former spouse should be deemed to have predeceased for *all* purposes.[104]

A recent case which demonstrates this is *Folds v Abrahart*,[105] where the testator began his home-made will with the following words,

> "This is the last will and testament of me, G. R. M and my wife H. S. M. (if we should die together)."

There then followed a series of provisions for persons other than the testator's wife, who was not mentioned further in the will. The testator and his wife did not "die together" but were divorced. Patten J held that the words "if we should die together" were a condition. The testator had intended the will to take effect if he and his wife were to "die together", but if they did not "die together", he intended to die intestate. The judge

[102] The substituted s.18A(1)(b) is also wide enough to cover the ground formerly covered by s.18A(3), so s.18A(3) is repealed: Law Reform (Succession) Act 1995 s.5 and Schedule.

[103] General powers of appointment are covered by s.18A(1)(b) because "devised or bequeathed" has been held to include the exercise of a general power, but the words do not include the exercise of a special power; see Law Commission's Report para.2.11.

[104] See R. Kerridge [1995] Conv. 12.

[105] *Folds v Abrahart* [2004] W.T.L.R. 327, referred to in Chap.10, see para.10–54.

went on to hold that the condition had not been fulfilled; so the testator had died intestate. It would not be difficult for someone from the intentional school of interpretation[106] to suggest that the words "die together" could, in a home-made will, be thought ambiguous and could be construed to cover pre-decease. If the words were so construed, s.18A of the Wills Act would then come into play. Had s.18A been drafted in such a way as to provide that divorce was equivalent to a spouse's pre-decease for all purposes, the condition in *Folds v Abrahart* would then have been fulfilled; and it is virtually certain that the testator would have wanted it so. On the supposition, made (correctly) by the judge, that the will was intended to take effect if the testator and his wife died at the same time, it is logical to suppose that the testator would have wanted it to take effect if she died before him, or if they were divorced. The purpose of the condition was to provide for the wife; once the testator and his wife were divorced, it would lose that purpose and the judge's decision produced a result which the testator would not have intended.[107]

The best policy is, of course, for the divorced person to make a will, or a new will, following the dissolution of his marriage.

IV. ADEMPTION

1. Ademption of specific gifts

14–35 A specific legacy or specific devise fails by ademption if its subject-matter has ceased to exist as part of the testator's property at his death. As was explained in Chapter 9, neither a general legacy nor a demonstrative legacy fails by ademption in this way.

Consider some examples of ademption:

(i) A specific legacy by T of "my 200 shares in X.Y.Z. Ltd. to A"; if T sells or gives away his shares in X.Y.Z. Ltd. during his lifetime, the specific legacy fails by ademption.[108] If T sells his shares, A is not entitled to receive the proceeds of sale, because the subject-matter of the gift was the shares themselves and not their proceeds of sale.[109] If T sells or gives away some of his shares, the legacy fails to that extent.[110]

106 See Chap.10.

107 The conditional will benefitted one of the testator's daughters, his sister and his grandchildren. If he died intestate—having been divorced—the beneficiaries would be his two daughters. Upholding the will would benefit his sister at the expense of one of his daughters. If this is what he intended to happen if he and his wife died at the same time, there is no reason to suppose that he would have chosen to make any different provision if his wife had died before him, or if they were divorced. The judge made no reference to what the testator wanted to achieve.

108 *Ashburner v Macguire* (1786) 2 Bro.C.C. 108.

109 *Harrison v Jackson* (1877) 7 Ch.D. 339.

110 *Humphreys v Humphreys* (1789) 2 Cox. 184.

(ii) A specific legacy by T of a chattel, e.g. "the gold watch which my father gave me"; if T loses the watch,[111] or destroys it, or sells it, or gives it away, in each case the legacy fails by ademption.
(iii) A specific legacy by T of a debt, e.g. "I give to B the money now due to me from C"; if C pays the debt to T during his lifetime, whether voluntarily or under compulsion, again the legacy fails by ademption.[112] If C pays part of the debt to T, the legacy fails to that extent.[113]
(iv) A specific devise by T of "my farm Blackacre to D"; if T sells, or gives away, his farm Blackacre during his lifetime, the specific devise fails by ademption. Again, if T sells Blackacre, D is not entitled to receive the proceeds of sale.[114]

2. Failure of specific gifts speaking from death

A specific gift which speaks from the testator's death[115] is not subject to ademption in the strict sense of the doctrine. Examples include a specific gift of "the cars which I own at the date of my death", or "all shares in X.Y.Z. Ltd. of or to which I may be possessed or entitled at my death". Such a specific gift does, of course, fail if, at his death, the testator has no assets which answer the description in the will.[116] But such a specific gift does not fail under the doctrine of ademption in its strict sense, which applies only where the subject-matter of the gift is to be ascertained at some time prior to death (e.g. "the cars which I own at the date of my will" or "my 200 shares in X.Y.Z. Ltd."),[117] and has ceased to exist as part of the testator's property at his death. **14–36**

3. Is intention to adeem needed?

It is usually said that ademption occurs whether or not the testator intended it to occur.[118] It is certainly the case that the doctrine of ademption, as described in some of the cases, may defeat the intention which a testator would have expressed if he had appreciated how the doctrine operates.[119] Accordingly, commentators have inclined to the view that ademption is a rule of law, rather than a rule of construction.[120] On the **14–37**

111 *Durrant v Friend* (1852) 5 De G. & S. 343 (specific legacy of chattels; T and the chattels perished together at sea: held adeemed and insurance money for chattels fell into residue).
112 *Ashburner v Macguire*, above; *Re Bridle* (1879) 4 C.P.D. 336 (specific legacy of mortgage debt which was paid off in T's lifetime: held adeemed and immaterial T kept sum paid by mortgagor separate); *Gardner v Hatton* (1833) 6 Sim. 93: *Re Robe* (1889) 61 L.T. 497: *Sidney v Sidney* (1873) L.R. 17 Eq. 65 cf. *Re Heilbronner* [1953] 1 W.L.R. 1254.
113 *Aston v Wood* (1874) 43 L.J.Ch.715.
114 *Re Bagot's Settlement* (1862) 31 L.J.Ch.772, 774.
115 For specific gifts which speak from the death of the testator under the Wills Act 1837, s.24, see Chap.12, paras 12–04 et seq.
116 *Re Slater* [1907] 1 Ch.665.
117 *Re Gibson* (1866) L.R. 2 Eq. 669; some of the obiter dicta in *Re Gibson* may be open to question; see the discussion above, in paras 12–09 et seq.
118 *Ashburner v Macguire* (1786) 2 Bro.C.C. 108; *Stanley v Potter* (1789) 2 Cox 180.
119 *Harrison v Jackson* (1877) 7 Ch.D. 339, 341.
120 See *Jarman on Wills*, 8th edn (London: Sweet & Maxwell, 1951), p.1136 and Williams,

other hand, there is force in the argument that the ademption rule ought to be regarded as a rule of construction, but that because of the literal interpretation of wills formerly favoured by some judges, it has come to appear to be a rule of law. Nowadays, the construction of a will involves the court in seeking to discover the intention of the testator; and it may well be that the view that ademption is a rule of law—a view which causes complications, as can be seen from cases such as *Re Slater*[121] and *Banks v National Westminster Bank*[122]—will be successfully challenged.[123]

14–38 It is clear that, even if the ademption rule is a rule of law, a testator is entitled to insert a provision in his will which makes it clear that he wishes the beneficiary to inherit his shares in a particular company or the investments which represent those shares if they have been converted into other holdings.[124] If ademption is a rule of law, distinguishing between a gift which is subject to it, and one which is not subject to it, is likely to create difficulties and to lead to strained constructions in order to avoid hardship. If, on the other hand, it were to be regarded as a rule of construction, it would be easier to reach the just result in a more open and honest way.

4. A change in substance causes ademption, a change in name or form does not

14–39 In any case, quite apart from the fact that a testator may insert into his will a provision which has the effect of passing to the legatee the property into which the original gift has been converted,[125] it is also true that while a change in the substance of a specific gift causes ademption, a change which is only a change in name or form does not. This principle has been applied in cases where T gives a specific legacy of shares in a particular company and then, after T has made his will but before his death, the shares are altered in the course of an amalgamation or reconstruction.

In *Re Slater*[126] T's will contained a bequest to his wife during her life of "the interest arising from money invested in the Lambeth Waterworks Company". At the time when he made his will, T held a considerable amount of stock in the Lambeth Waterworks Company, but before he died the company was acquired by the Metropolitan Water Board (which also acquired other waterworks companies). Stock in the Metropolitan Water Board was issued to T before his death as compensation for the loss of his Lambeth Waterworks stock. T's widow claimed that this was a change only of form, that the Metropolitan Water Board stock was substantially the same investment as the Lambeth Waterworks stock, and that she was entitled to the Metropolitan Water Board stock. Her claim failed. It was

Mortimer and Sunnucks, *Executors, Administrators and Probate*, 20th edn (London: Sweet & Maxwell, 2013), paras 71–05 et seq.

[121] *Re Slater* [1907] 1 Ch.665, see below, para.14–39.

[122] *Banks v National Westminster Bank* [2006] W.T.L.R. 1693, see below, para.14–43.

[123] See also para.14–43 below, for discussion of *Re Viertel* [2003] W.T.L.R. 1075 and *Banks v National Westminster Bank* [2006] W.T.L.R. 1693.

[124] *Re Lewis's W.T.* [1937] Ch.118.

[125] See *Re Lewis's W.T.* [1937] Ch.118.

[126] *Re Slater* [1907] 1 Ch.665.

held that the Metropolitan Water Board stock differed in substance from the Lambeth Waterworks stock; it was different stock in a different concern operating over a much larger area.[127]

14–40 *Re Slater* may be contrasted with *Re Clifford*[128] in which T by his will gave "twenty-three of the shares belonging to me" in the L Co. Ltd. At the date of his will T held 104 £80 shares in the company and the gift was a specific legacy of 23 of these 104 £80 shares. Before T's death the company changed its name and sub-divided each £80 share into four new £20 shares so that at his death T held 416 new £20 shares in lieu of his 104 original £80 shares. Swinfen Eady J held that this change had not adeemed the specific legacy because the subject-matter remained the same in substance, though changed in name and form: the legatee therefore took 92 of the new £20 shares, which were "identical in all but name and form" with 23 original £80 shares. The same principle was applied in *Re Leeming*[129] where T gave a specific legacy of "my ten shares" in K Co. Ltd.: at the date of his will T held 10 £4 shares in this company. After the date of the will the company went into voluntary liquidation for the purpose of reconstruction as a new company with the same name, and at his death T held 20 £5 ordinary and 20 £5 preference shares in the new company in place of his 10 original £4 shares in the old company. The court held that the specific legacy had not been adeemed: the legatee took all T's shares in the new company because they were really in substance the same as the shares in the old company.

The line between a change of form and a change of substance has always been a fine—and artificial—one, and it is suggested that the legatee in *Re Slater* was particularly unlucky. It would have been perfectly possible for the court to have construed the words "the interest arising from money invested in the Lambeth Waterworks Company" as "the interest arising from money which is at the present moment invested in the Lambeth Waterworks Company" in order to give effect to what the testator probably intended.

5. Ademption by the exercise of an enduring, or lasting, power of attorney

14–41 Before the Enduring Powers of Attorney Act 1985 came into force,[130] a power of attorney was revoked by the subsequent mental incapacity of the donor. The 1985 Act created a régime whereby a donor might, while still capable of managing his affairs, select someone who could act on his behalf notwithstanding supervening incapacity. The 1985 Act has now been repealed and enduring powers of attorney have been replaced by

[127] *Re Slater* [1907] 1 Ch.665, 671–673 and 674–675; the Court of Appeal was affirming the decision of Joyce J. Statutes often provide that specific bequests of, e.g. government stock, shall not be adeemed by a conversion offer.

[128] *Re Clifford* [1912] 1 Ch.29: see also *Re O'Brien* (1946) 115 L.J.Ch.340.

[129] *Re Leeming* [1912] 1 Ch.828: cf. *Re Kuypers* [1925] Ch.244 (original shares given still existed though with rights curtailed: new shares issued in compensation for loss of rights did not pass).

[130] On 10 March 1986.

lasting powers of attorney.[131] Since 1 October 2007, no new enduring powers of attorney may be created, though existing enduring powers remain in force. Lasting powers of attorney may be personal welfare powers or property and affairs powers. Succession lawyers will be chiefly concerned with property and affairs powers and these are not markedly different from the enduring powers they replace.[132] But a problem arises where someone executes a will containing a specific legacy or devise, grants a lasting power of attorney, loses capacity, and the attorney, not knowing the contents of the will or of the existence of the specific gift, then sells the property which was the subject-matter of the gift. There is a statutory provision which deals with sales by deputies under the Mental Capacity Act 2005[133] and which should prevent ademption from occurring where a deputy disposes of property in this kind of situation, but there is no equivalent provision to cover a sale by an attorney. There is clearly a problem if ademption occurs as a result of the exercise of an enduring or a lasting power by a donor who knows nothing about its effect on a specific gift. Is there any way of avoiding the difficulty?

14–42 One possibility is to find that there has been no change of substance. This was how the legacy was saved in *Re Dorman*[134] where there was a specific legacy of "the balance of my Barclays higher deposit account No 10327719". After the testatrix had made her will, she gave X an enduring power and X, not knowing the terms of the will, closed the higher deposit account and opened another account, a capital advantage account, with a different number at the same branch of the same bank. X transferred into the new account all the money which had been in the old account. He opened the new account because a "capital advantage account" paid a higher rate of interest, though it was subject to special conditions as to notice of withdrawal of funds. On these "very unusual facts" and "after considerable hesitation" it was held[135] that the bequest was not adeemed.

14–43 But another—more radical—approach would be to suggest that a distinction should be drawn between (i) a case where a change is effected by the voluntary act of the testator and (ii) a case where a change is effected otherwise. Examples of the first category would be a disposal by the testator of an asset, or the exercise by him of an option to convert his shares into a different class of shares. In these circumstances it is not unreasonable to decide that the specific gifts must adeem because the testator himself has acted in such a way as to cause the original property no longer to exist. By contrast, where shares cease to exist as a result of a takeover of the company[136] it is arguable that there should be no

[131] Mental Capacity Act 2005 s.9.

[132] See *Cretney and Lush; Lasting and Enduring Powers of Attorney*, 6th edn (Bristol: Jordan Publishing Ltd, 2008) and T. M. Aldridge, *Powers of Attorney*, 10th edn (London: Sweet & Maxwell, 2007).

[133] Mental Capacity Act 2005 s.18, and Sch.2 para.8, replacing Mental Health Act 1983 s.101. A "deputy" under the 2005 Act would have been a "receiver" under the previous law.

[134] *Re Dorman* [1994] 1 W.L.R. 282.

[135] By David Neuberger QC sitting as a deputy High Court judge.

[136] In *Re Slater* the Lambeth Waterworks Company was acquired by the Metropolitan Water

ademption if the old shares can be traced into the new shares.[137] As *Re Slater* demonstrates, hardship can occur when a legatee loses property as a result of something over which the testator has either no, or very limited, control.[138] This approach would get to the same result as that reached in *Re Dorman*,[139] but would do so more straightforwardly. It was adopted by the Supreme Court of Queensland in *Re Viertel*,[140] a case involving an enduring power of attorney, and is entirely consistent with the English case of *Pennington v Waine (No.2)*,[141] referred to in para.14–47, below.[142] *Re Viertel* was not, however, followed in *Banks v National Westminster Bank*[143] where the sale of the testatrix's house by her daughter, under an enduring power of attorney, was held to adeem the devise of the house to the daughter. This decision raises a number of problems and may well be thought unfortunate.[144]

6. Ademption by contract (made after the will)

If T by his will makes a specific gift of his farm Blackacre to D, and T later enters into a binding contract to sell Blackacre to P, but T dies before completion, this adeems the specific gift to D and D is not entitled to the purchase price payable by P.[145] D is only entitled to enjoy Blackacre or its rents and profits from T's death until the time for completion of the sale to P.[146] This result follows from the equitable doctrine of conversion.[147] Under this doctrine T, by contracting to sell Blackacre, disposes of his beneficial interest in Blackacre except in so far as he remains entitled to enjoy it until the time for completion. **14–44**

Board under the provisions of the Metropolitan Water Act 1902. Nowadays the takeover is more likely to be as a result of the acquisition of shares on the market.

[137] Of course, a testator will receive a replacement share certificate in the event of a takeover and to that extent have knowledge of the need to revise his will; but there would seem to be a valid distinction between the passive reception of a new share certificate and the active step of disposing of his shares.

[138] Compare the approach adopted in *Re Fleming's W.T.* [1974] 1 W.L.R. 1152.

[139] If the testator could be shown to have had knowledge of, or instigated, the change, it is arguable that there would be an ademption. This would depend on the evidence.

[140] *Re Viertel* [2003] W.T.L.R. 1075.

[141] *Pennington v Waine (No.2)* [2003] W.T.L.R. 1011.

[142] See para.14–47, fn.153.

[143] *Banks v National Westminster Bank* [2006] W.T.L.R. 643.

[144] *Banks* involved a detailed examination of earlier authorities, but the result was not inevitable and *Pennington v Waine (No.2)* does not appear to have been cited. Judge Rich QC (sitting as a judge of the High Court) noted in *Banks* that the decision he reached could lead to all kinds of potential difficulties. What happens if the donee of a power suspects, or knows, that his exercise of the power may, or will, effect an ademption and that this may, or will, benefit X and so disbenefit Y? He may suspect, or know, that its exercise may or will, benefit, or disbenefit, himself.

[145] *Farrar v Earl of Winterton* (1842) 5 Beav. 1; *Watts v Watts* (1873) L.R. 17 Eq. 217; *Re Galway's* W.T. [1950] Ch.1; *Re Edwards* [1958] Ch.168; *Re Sweeting* [1988] 1 All E.R. 1016 (conditional contract): cf. *Re Thomas* (1886) 34 Ch.D.166 (contract not binding as T's title defective). See generally P. H. Pettit (1960) 24 Conv. (N.S.) 47.

[146] *Watts v Watts* (1873) L.R. 17 Eq. 217.

[147] See *Lysaght v Edwards* [1876] 2 Ch.D. 499 and Megarry & Wade, *The Law of Real Property*, 8th edn (London: Sweet & Maxwell, 2012), para.10–009.

7. Ademption by conditional contract (made after the will)

14–45 In *Re Sweeting*[148] it was held that a devise is adeemed by a conditional contract, in the same way that it is adeemed by an unconditional contract; provided, of course, that the condition is fulfilled and the contract is, in due course, completed.

8. Ademption by exercise of an option to purchase (granted after the will was made)

14–46 Under the anomalous, but well-settled, rule in *Lawes v Bennett*,[149] if T by his will makes a specific gift of Whiteacre to D, and then later grants to O an option to purchase Whiteacre, O's exercise of his option after T's death adeems the specific gift to D. D is not entitled to the purchase price payable by O[150]: he is only entitled to enjoy Whiteacre or its rents and profits from T's death until the option is exercised.[151] In other words, an option to purchase which is exercised after T's death adeems a specific gift in the same way as a binding contract for sale made by T before his death.

In the case of an option to purchase—unlike a binding contract for sale—T is, at his death, still entitled to his beneficial interest in Whiteacre, subject to O's interest which is contingent upon O's exercise of the option. After T's death, his beneficial interest passes to D under the specific gift, and O's subsequent exercise of the option should not—but does—adeem the specific gift retrospectively.

14–47 The decision in *Re Carrington*[152] is a classic instance of the application of this rule. T by his will made specific gifts of 420 shares held by him in C Ltd. Later T granted to O an option (exercisable within one month of T's death) to purchase all his shares in C Ltd. T died and O duly exercised the option. The Court of Appeal reluctantly held that the specific gifts of the 420 shares had been adeemed by O's exercise of his option after T's death and that the purchase price payable by O was not payable to the specific legatees but fell into T's residuary estate.

The rule in *Lawes v Bennett* is anomalous[153] and a potential cause of trouble both for testators and their advisers. It is almost certainly easier to overlook an option than it is to overlook a contract. Most contracts will be completed within a relatively short timescale, whereas it may be many years between the grant of an option and its exercise. In the case of an option, the devisee may well (either as a result of

[148] *Re Sweeting* [1988] 1 All E.R. 1016.
[149] *Lawes v Bennett* (1785) 1 Cox 167.
[150] *Weeding v Weeding* (1860) 1 J. & H. 424.
[151] *Townley v Bedwell* (1808) 14 Ves. 591.
[152] *Re Carrington* [1932] 1 Ch.1: see also *Re Rose* [1949] Ch.78.
[153] In *Pennington v Waine (No.2)* [2003] W.T.L.R. 1011 it was held that the rule in *Lawes v Bennett* would not be extended to cover the exercise of pre-emption rights over shares in a private company after the testatrix's death, as this was not equivalent to the exercise of a contractual option, and the testatrix herself had done nothing to trigger the exercise of the option while she was alive. See reference to this case in para.14–43, above.

ignorance or as a result of bad faith) fail to hand over the eventual proceeds of sale to the rightful beneficiaries after the option has been exercised.[154]

In *Clarke v Bruce Lance & Co*[155] a specific devisee attempted to sue a firm of solicitors because they had not warned their client, the testator, about the problems involved in granting to a third party a fixed price option to purchase land which he, the testator, had specifically devised. The devisee's claim was struck out as disclosing no reasonable cause of action. But the devisee appears to have attempted to base his claim on the fact that the solicitors did not warn the testator about the dangers of a *fixed price* option. But such a claim should have been instituted by the personal representatives, not by the devisee, who had no interest in the amount which would be paid under the option, because the money would not pass to him; that is the essence of the rule in *Lawes v Bennett*. But what if the devisee had attempted to sue the solicitors for failing to warn the testator about ademption? The court might well have been sympathetic to such a claim. The testator would have been very likely to have assumed that if he devised land to the devisee (who was his son) and later granted an option to a third party, then, if the third party exercised the option after his death, the purchase money would be paid to his son, the devisee. Given that this is not what happens because of the rule in *Lawes v Bennett*, testators should be made aware that the exercise of an option will effect an ademption and so deprive the specific devisee both of the property and of the proceeds of sale. **14–48**

9. Will made after contract, conditional contract or option

The rules set out above apply when T enters into the contract, the conditional contract, or the option after he has made his will. If, by contrast, T first enters into the contract, the conditional contract, or option and afterwards by his will makes a specific gift of the property, subject to the contract or option, to D, the gift is generally construed as passing to D all T's interest, whatever it may be, so that D is entitled to the purchase price payable by P.[156] The same result follows if the will is made before the **14–49**

[154] If an option relates to unregistered land, it is registrable by the option holder against the name of the grantor at the Central Land Charges Registry as an estate contract (a c (iv) land charge; Land Charges Act 1972 s.2(4)). An unprotected interest is void against a purchaser (s.4). If the title to the land is registered, the option is registrable by way of a notice/restriction against the land at the Land Registry (Land Registration Act 2002 ss.32–34) although if the holder of the option to purchase is in actual occupation (as he may well be, if the option is contained in a lease), he will have an overriding interest within the Land Registration Act 2002 Sch.3 para.2, *Webb v Pollmount Ltd* [1966] Ch.584. But quaere how many solicitors carry out a Central Land Charges Search against the deceased before they prepare an assent giving effect to a specific devise, to check whether a testator has granted an option over property which was specifically devised by a will made before the option was granted. The existence of the option should be apparent where the title to the land which is the subject of the specific devise is registered.

[155] *Clarke v Bruce Lance & Co* [1988] 1 W.L.R. 881. See R. Kerridge and A. H. R. Brierley [1999] Conv. 399 at 401–404.

[156] *Re Callow* [1928] Ch.710, esp at 714. *Drant v Vause* (1842) 1 Y. & C.C.C. 580: see generally *Hawkins on the Construction of Wills*, 5th edn (London: Sweet & Maxwell, 2000), pp.122 et seq.

contract or grant of the option, but is confirmed by a codicil which is made after it[157] or substantially contemporaneously with it.[158]

10. Effect of confirmation of will

14–50 If a specific gift in a will has been adeemed, and the testator later makes a codicil which confirms his will, in general this does not save the specific gift from ademption.[159] For instance, if T by his will makes a specific gift of Blackacre to D, and T sells Blackacre to P, and later T makes a codicil which confirms his will, this does not make the specific gift to D take effect as a gift of the proceeds of sale of Blackacre.

Nevertheless, confirmation may alter the construction of a will as to the subject of a specific gift, and thereby save a gift which would otherwise have failed by ademption. One instance has just been mentioned in relation to a contract of sale or an option to purchase.[160] Another instance is the decision in *Re Reeves*[161] which was discussed in Chapter 12.[162]

11. Simultaneous lapse and ademption

14–51 It may happen that a testator dies in a disaster which also destroys property which he has specifically bequeathed to X: and it may well not be clear which occurred first, the death or the destruction. If the death occurred or is deemed to have occurred first, the legatee will be entitled to the proceeds of any insurance claim, but, if the destruction occurred first, he will not. Where, as may well be the case, the order of events is uncertain, the destruction of the asset is taken to have occurred first.[163]

12. Ademption of legacies by portions

14–52 The ademption of legacies by portions under the principle that equity leans against double portions was considered in Chapter 13.

[157] *Emuss v Smith* (1848) 2 De G. & Sm. 722: for confirmation see Chap.7.

[158] *Re Pyle* [1895] 1 Ch.724 (T by will made specific devise of Whiteacre; T by codicil confirmed will and on same day granted lease to Q containing option to purchase Whiteacre; Q exercised option after T's death: held specific devisees took purchase price).

[159] *Drinkwater v Falconer* (1755) 2 Ves.Sen. 623, 626; *Powys v Mansfield* (1837) 3 My. & Cr. 359, 375–376; *Cowper v Mantell* (No.1) (1856) 22 Beav. 223; *Sidney v Sidney* (1873) L.R. 17 Eq. 65; *Macdonald v Irvine* (1878) 8 Ch.D.101, esp. at 108; *Re Galway's W.T.* [1950] Ch.1.

[160] See above, paras 14–44 et seq.

[161] *Re Reeves* [1928] Ch.351; see also *Re Champion* [1893] 1 Ch.101. For another instance see *Re Harvey* [1947] Ch.285, following *Re Warren* [1932] 1 Ch.42: cf. *Re Newman* [1930] 2 Ch.409 and *Re Galway's W.T.* above. And see J. D. B. Mitchell (1954) 70 L.Q.R. 353, 364 et seq.

[162] See above, para.12–17.

[163] *Durrant v Friend* (1852) 5 de G & Sm 343; *Re Mercer, Tanner v Bulmer* [1944] 1 All E.R. 759. The onus is on the specific legatee to show that the property bequeathed to him survived the testator, and he cannot do this. But, where someone is killed in a building which is destroyed at the same time, a devise of the building is probably not adeemed, because the devise is of the building and the land on which it stands, and so the destruction of the building does not constitute destruction of the asset, merely damage to it; *Re Clements* [2007] W.T.L.R. 1717.

V. ABATEMENT

1. Introduction

Abatement concerns the statutory order of application of assets to the payment of expenses, debts and liabilities. **14–53**

The distinction between specific, general and demonstrative legacies was explained in Chapter 9, where it was said that one of the reasons why it was necessary to distinguish between them was that general legacies are used to pay expenses, debts and liabilities before resort is had to specific or demonstrative legacies.

2. The order of abatement

Where the estate of a deceased person is solvent,[164] the burden of his expenses, debts and liabilities as between the beneficiaries is regulated by s.34(3) of the Administration of Estates Act 1925 which enacts that, unless the statutory order is varied by his will, his real and personal estate will be applicable towards the discharge of his funeral, testamentary and administration expenses, debts and liabilities in the order mentioned in Pt II of the First Schedule to the Act. This applies on the death of any person after 1925.[165] **14–54**

The statutory order consists of seven numbered paragraphs, starting with property undisposed of by will and ending with property appointed by will under a general power. The seven paragraphs are set out, and discussed, in detail, in Chapter 21.[166] The property described in each paragraph is to be applied towards the payment of expenses, debts and liabilities before the property described in the following paragraph.[167] The two paragraphs relevant to the present discussion are paras 5 and 6. Paragraph 5 covers "the fund, if any, retained to meet pecuniary legacies", but the expression "pecuniary legacy" is defined[168] to include a general legacy; so para.5 covers, in effect, the general legacy fund. Paragraph 6 covers "property specifically devised or bequeathed." This means that general legacies abate before specific legacies or devises.

A demonstrative legacy is treated as a specific legacy in so far as it can be discharged out of the designated property: to this extent it falls within para.6.[169] But in so far as it is not discharged out of the specified fund or specified part of the testator's estate primarily designated for its payment, **14–55**

[164] For insolvent estates, see below, paras 21–68 et seq.

[165] For the special rules applicable to debts charged on the deceased's property and to the incidence of inheritance tax see below, paras 21–44 et seq.

[166] See below, paras 21–31 et seq.

[167] See below, paras 21–32 et seq.

[168] By s.55(1)(ix) of the Act.

[169] See *Re Turner* [1908] 1 Ir. 274 (T's will gave specific legacies and devises, and demonstrative legacies payable out of specified railway stock held by T; T's other assets were insufficient to pay expenses and debts: held specific legacies and devises and demonstrative legacies so far as they could be satisfied from railway stock must all abate rateably).

it falls within para.5.[170] The justification for this distinction is that the testator is presumed to have intended the demonstrative legacy to be payable in priority to his general legacies so far as the demonstrative legacy can be satisfied out of the designated property.[171]

Summarising the liability to abatement under the statutory order, property falling within para.5 will be applied towards the payment of expenses, debts and liabilities before resort is made to property in para.6. A general legacy, and a demonstrative legacy so far as it is not discharged out of the designated property, both fall within para.5. On the other hand, a specific legacy, a specific devise, and a demonstrative legacy so far as it can be discharged out of the designated property, all fall within para.6. From the beneficiary's viewpoint, if there is any possibility of abatement, it is to his advantage to be entitled to property in paragraph 6 rather than in para.5.

In relation to ademption and abatement, a demonstrative legacy is said to have "the best of both worlds"[172] because it is immune from ademption (like a general legacy) and, so far as it can be discharged out of the designated property, is preferred (like a specific legacy) on abatement under the statutory order.

3. Gifts in the same class abate rateably

14–56 Paragraph 6 of the statutory order provides that property specifically devised or bequeathed is to bear the burden of expenses and debts falling on it "rateably according to value." It follows that any property specifically devised or bequeathed and any demonstrative legacy so far as it can be discharged out of the property primarily designated for its payment must abate rateably.[173] For the purpose of this rateable abatement under para.6, the property affected is valued as at the testator's death.[174]

Paragraph 5 of the statutory order does not refer to rateable abatement but there is a well-settled general rule that all general legacies abate rateably on the principle that "equality is equity."[175] Demonstrative legacies, so far as they cannot be discharged out of the designated property, are treated as, and therefore abate rateably with, general legacies. This general rule applies whenever the property from which general legacies are payable[176] is insufficient to satisfy them in full. For the purpose of this rateable abatement, a general legacy of something other than money (e.g. company shares) is valued 12 months after the testator's death.[177]

[170] Administration of Estates Act 1925 s.55(1)(ix) defines "pecuniary legacy" to include "a demonstrative legacy so far as it is not discharged out of designated property".
[171] *Acton v Acton* (1816) 1 Mer. 178; *Creed v Creed* (1844) 11 Cl. & F. 491, 509; *Livesay v Redfern* (1837) 2 Y. & C.Ex. 90; *Robinson v Geldard* (1851) 3 M. & G. 735, 745.
[172] *Snell's Equity*, 33rd edn (London: Sweet & Maxwell, 2015), para.35–008.
[173] *Re Turner*, above.
[174] *Re John* [1933] Ch.370; *Re Cohen* [1960] Ch.179: see below, para.21–40.
[175] *Miller v Huddlestone* (1851) 3 Mac. & G. 513, 523. Interest on a legacy is not an additional legacy for the purpose of abatement, *Re Wyles* [1938] Ch.313.
[176] For the incidence of general legacies see Chap.22.
[177] *Blackshaw v Rogers*, cited in *Simmons v Vallance* (1793) 4 Bro.C.C. 345; *Auther v Auther* (1843) 13 Sim. 422, 440: see also *Re Hollins* [1918] 1 Ch.503.

4. Testator's intention to give priority

The testator may—of course—by his will vary the statutory order or give priority to a particular legacy or devise. For instance, the testator may direct that a particular general legacy (e.g. to his wife) shall have priority over any other legacy or devise whatsoever contained in his will (i.e. taking priority over specific legacies and devises) *or* (alternatively) over any other general legacies given by his will.[178] **14–57**

In order to give priority to a particular legacy or devise the testator must show by his will a clear intention to do so.[179] Thus a direction by a testator that a legacy to his wife was to be paid to her immediately after his decease out of the first money to be received by his executors did not give her priority over the other general legacies, but merely specified the *time* for payment.[180] Again, a legacy given to an executor for his trouble did not take priority over other legacies.[181]

5. Abatement of annuities

(a) *Order of abatement under the statutory order*

Under the statutory order of application of assets, both a general annuity and a demonstrative annuity so far as it is not discharged out of the designated property fall within para.5, whereas both a specific annuity and a demonstrative annuity so far as it can be discharged out of the designated property fall within para.6. A demonstrative annuity is payable in priority to general legacies and annuities in so far as the demonstrative annuity can be satisfied out of the designated property.[182] **14–58**

(b) *Annuities in the same class abate rateably*

Property falling within para.6 of the statutory order abates "rateably according to value." This includes a specific annuity and a demonstrative annuity so far as it can be discharged out of the designated property. **14–59**

As to the abatement of general annuities[183] under para.5, if the property from which two general annuities (or a general legacy and a general annuity) are payable is insufficient to satisfy them in full, the general rule

[178] cf. *Marsh v Evans* (1720) 1 P.Wms. 668. See also *Re Compton* [1914] 2 Ch.119 (legacies by T of certain company stock "all now standing in my name as general and not as specific legacies": held T intended these specific legacies to be treated as general legacies and they must abate as such).

[179] *Miller v Huddlestone*, above. For the case law see Williams, Mortimer and Sunnucks, *Executors Administrators and Probate*, 20th edn (London: Sweet & Maxwell, 2013), para.76–12.

[180] *Blower v Morret* (1752) 2 Ves.Sen. 420; *Re Schweder's Estate* [1891] 3 Ch.44 (general legacy to be paid to wife within three months after death: no priority); *Cazenove v Cazenove* (1890) 61 L.T. 115.

[181] *Duncan v Watts* (1852) 16 Beav. 204.

[182] *Livesay v Redfern* (1836) 2 Y. & C.Ex. 90: see also *Creed v Creed* (1844) 11 Cl. & F. 491 (specific annuity payable in priority to general legacies charged in aid on same property).

[183] See generally *Theobald on Wills*, 17th edn (London: Sweet & Maxwell, 2010), paras 34–014 et seq.

applies to the effect that they must abate rateably unless the testator has shown by his will a clear intention to give priority to a particular legacy or annuity.[184] In order to achieve a rateable abatement, the rule of practice is to make an actuarial valuation of each annuity (so that the value can be treated as a legacy of a lump sum) and then abate this value (and also any general legacy) rateably, and pay this abated value to the annuitant.[185] Where this rule of practice applies, each annuitant is entitled to be paid a lump sum, by way of exception to the general rule against this.[186]

VI. UNCERTAINTY

14–60 A gift by will is void for uncertainty if, after applying any relevant rules of construction and considering any admissible evidence,[187] it is impossible to identify the subject-matter or the object of the gift.[188] Of course, the court tries to put a meaning on the words of a gift rather than "repose on the easy pillow of saying that the whole is void for uncertainty."[189]

1. Uncertainty of subject-matter

14–61 For instance, gifts by a testator's will of "some of my best linen"[190] and of "a handsome gratuity to be given to each of the executors"[191] have been held void for uncertainty as to their subject-matter. In *Asten v Asten*[192] T, who owned four houses in Sudeley Place, by his will made separate gifts to each of his four sons of "all that newly built house, being No.1, Sudeley Place" (using similar terms for each gift). The court held that the four gifts failed for uncertainty because the will showed that T intended to give a particular house to each of his sons (so the sons were not intended to select in turn), but the will did not indicate which house each was intended to take.[193]

By way of contrast, a direction by will to executors to let X enjoy a flat during her lifetime and "to receive a reasonable income from my other properties" was held valid on the ground that this required an objective

184 *Miller v Huddlestone* (1851) 3 Mac. & G. 513.

185 *Wright v Callendar* (1852) 2 De G.M. & G. 652; *Wroughton v Colquhoun* (1847) 1 De G. & Sm. 357; *Re Cox* [1938] Ch.556.

186 For the general rule and for exceptions to it, see above, para.9–22.

187 See above, Chap.10, paras 10–41 et seq.

188 *Anthony v Donges* [1998] 2 F.L.R. 775 ("such minimal part of my estate as she may be entitled to for maintenance purposes": void for uncertainty).

189 per Jessel MR in *Re Roberts* (1881) 19 Ch.D. 520, 529.

190 *Peck v Halsey* (1726) 2 P.Wms. 387 (if it were "so much of my bed linen, as they [the legatees] should chuse, or as my executors should chuse for them, this would be good, and by the choice of the legatees or executors is reducible to a certainty").

191 *Jubber v Jubber* (1839) 9 Sim. 503.

192 *Asten v Asten* [1894] 3 Ch.261.

193 cf. *Tapley v Eagleton* (1879) 12 Ch.D. 683 (T owned three houses in King Street; gift by T's will of "two houses in King Street" to X for life: held X was entitled to select); *Boyce v Boyce* (1849) 16 Sim. 476 (selector dead); *Re Knapton* [1941] Ch.428 (T by will gave "one house to each of my nephews and nieces:" held if they disagreed they must choose in turn, the order of the choice to be determined by lot).

assessment of reasonable income, which the court could undertake if need be.[194] In another case T's will read, "I give devise and bequeath unto my brother Mr. Harry Pateman [address] Also sister Mrs. Jane Slade [address] Also sister Mrs Ethel James [address]." The court inferred that the will was intended to deal with the whole of T's property and held that T's whole estate passed under this gift, even though T had omitted any mention of the subject-matter of the gift.[195]

2. Uncertainty of object

The decision in *Re Stephenson*[196] is an example of a gift failing for uncertainty of objects. T by his will gave his residuary estate "unto the children of the deceased son (named Bamber) of my father's sister share and share alike." This sister (as T was aware) had three deceased sons, each with the surname Bamber, and each had left children. The Court of Appeal held that the gift was void for uncertainty as it was impossible to ascertain which son's children were intended to take. **14–62**

By way of exception to the general rule about uncertainty of objects, "a charitable bequest never fails for uncertainty".[196A] This means that if the testator has shown a general charitable intention, a gift does not fail for uncertainty of objects merely because the testator has not indicated which particular charity he wishes to benefit. For instance a gift by will on trust for "the following charitable societies, *viz.* to be divided in equal shares among them" (the objects not being named) is valid and the court directs a scheme in order to give effect to the gift.[197]

This exception to the general rule is not, however, applicable if the gift is not exclusively charitable. The case of *Chichester Diocesan Fund and Board of Finance v Simpson*[197A] was discussed in Chapter 10[198] and it was suggested that were a will with wording similar to the wording in that case to be construed today, the gift should be construed as being exclusively charitable. There are, however, other cases where wording covers purposes which are not exclusively charitable and these cases would not be affected by the change in the construction rules.[199]

[194] *Re Golay* [1965] 1 W.L.R. 969: but see R. E. M. (1965) 81 L.Q.R. 481: see also *Talbot v Talbot* [1968] Ch.1 (option by will to purchase farm at "a reasonable valuation": option held valid).

[195] *Re Stevens* [1952] Ch.323.

[196] *Re White* [1893] 2 Ch.41, 53.

[196A] *Re Stephenson* [1897] 1 Ch.75.

[197] *Re White*, above, where the gift was "to the following religious societies"; this was treated as prima facie confined to charities. For application in accordance with the directions of the Crown under the Royal Prerogative where the gift is direct, and not by way of a trust, see *Re Bennett* [1960] Ch.18.

[197A] *Chichester Diocesan Fund and Board of Finance v Simpson* [1944] A.C. 341 "such charitable institutions or other charitable or benevolent objects as my executors may select."

[198] See above paras 10–78 et seq.

[199] See e.g. *A-G of the Cayman Islands v Wahr-Hansen* [2000] 3 W.L.R. 869. The rule that the objects must be exclusively charitable is a rule of the law of trusts and has always been good law. What has changed is the construction, or interpretation, of the words used by testators. Words which at one time would not have been construed as indicating an intention to settle property on trusts which are exclusively charitable would, it is suggested, now be so construed, see above, Chap.10, paras 10–79 and 10–80.

14–63 There is another point to note in relation to the *Chichester* case. In the judgments in the House of Lords there are dicta to the effect that a testator may not delegate his testamentary power. To quote, for example, from the judgment of Lord Simonds[200]:

> "It is a cardinal rule, common to English and Scots law, that a man may not delegate his testamentary power. To him the law gives the right to dispose of his estate in favour of ascertained or ascertainable persons. He does not exercise the right if in effect he empowers his executors to say what persons or objects are to be his beneficiaries. To this salutary rule there is a single exception. A testator may validly leave it to his executors to determine what charitable objects shall benefit, so long as charitable and no other objects may benefit."

Such dicta seem to go too far. A testator may by his will confer on another person,[201] or on the trustee of his will,[202] a power of appointment and thereby delegate his testamentary power.[203] In *Re Park*[204] T by his will gave his residuary estate to his trustee in trust to pay the income to such person (other than his sister Jane) or charitable institution as his sister Jane should from time to time during her lifetime direct in writing. Clauson J held that this "intermediate" power (i.e. intermediate between a general and a special power) was valid, and he referred in his judgment to "the well-settled principle" that a testator by his will may confer on any person a general or a special power.

Re Park was followed in *Re Beatty*[205] where the testatrix appointed executors and trustees, vested her personal chattels and cash to the value of £1,500,000 in them and then provided that they should distribute the chattels and cash "among such person or persons (whether individual or corporate) as they think fit," instructing them to observe any wishes as to distribution that she might express and providing that any chattels or cash not distributed within two years were to pass under the residuary gift in her will. Hoffmann J upheld these provisions and said that a

> "rule against testamentary delegation, in the sense of a restriction on the scope of testamentary powers, is a chimera, a shadow cast by the rule of certainty, having no independent existence."

He had no doubt as to the validity of testamentary powers whether special, general or intermediate.[206]

[200] *Chichester Diocesan Fund and Board of Finance v Simpson* [1944] A.C. 341 at p.371 (and see Viscount Simon L.C., at p.348, Lord Macmillan, at p.349, Lord Porter, at p.364): see also *Houston v Burns* [1918] A.C. 337, 342 and *Att.-Gen. v National Provincial and Union Bank of England* [1924] A.C. 262, 264 and 268.

[201] *Re Park* [1932] 1 Ch.580: see also *Re Hughes* [1921] 2 Ch.208, 212 and *Re Jones* [1945] Ch.105. cf. *Re Carville* [1937] 4 All E.R. 464 ("to each of my executors £100 The residue to be disposed of as the executors shall think fit": held by Clauson J residue went as on intestacy).

[202] *Re Abrahams'* W.T. [1969] 1 Ch.463, 474–476.

[203] See generally Gordon (1953) 69 L.Q.R. 334.

[204] *Re Park* [1932] 1 Ch.580.

[205] *Re Beatty* [1990] 1 W.L.R. 1503.

[206] See L. Smith, "What is Left of the Non-Delegation Principle?" Chap.9 in B. Häcker and

VII. MURDER OR MANSLAUGHTER OF THE TESTATOR OR INTESTATE[207]

1. Introduction

Before 1870, the property of a convicted felon was forfeited to the Crown.[208] **14–64** Murder and manslaughter were both felonies, so the property of anyone convicted of murder or manslaughter was forfeited. The Forfeiture Act 1870[209] abolished forfeiture to the Crown. A judge-made forfeiture rule,[210] a rule of public policy, then developed to the effect that someone who commits murder[211] or some forms of manslaughter[212] is debarred from taking any benefit under his victim's will or on his intestacy.[213] The rule does not apply if the killer is found not guilty by reason of insanity.[214] It has been applied where the killer has been convicted of manslaughter by reason of diminished responsibility,[215] but it may not apply to all cases of diminished responsibility.[216] In practice, the line between insanity and diminished responsibility has been rather a fine one and a reason for pleading insanity rather than diminished responsibility would, in some instances, have been to avoid forfeiture. It is not clear to which other manslaughter cases the forfeiture rule applies[217] and a complicating factor is that there may be different rules to cover (i) benefits derived under the deceased's will or on his intestacy; (ii) benefits derived under insurance policies and (iii) state benefits (such as the widow's pension).[218] It is probable—though not certain—that the forfeiture rule does not apply to other

C. Mitchell (eds), *Current Issues in Succession Law* (Oxford: Hart Publishing, 2016); but see also Davies in (1991) 107 L.Q.R. 211.

[207] See I. Williams, "How Does the Common Law Forfeiture Rule Work?" Chap.3 in B. Häcker and C. Mitchell (eds), *Current Issues in Succession Law* (Oxford: Hart Publishing, 2016).

[208] His realty would escheat to his feudal lord, but, by the nineteenth-century, this was equivalent to forfeiture.

[209] An Act to abolish Forfeitures for Treason and Felony: 33 & 34 Vict. c.23.

[210] It may be rather confusing to refer to the *pre*-1870 rule and to the *post*-1870 rule as both being "the forfeiture rule." But that is how they are referred to. The *pre*-1870 rule meant that the felon forfeited all his property to the Crown. The *post*-1870 rule, where it applies, is that the killer does not benefit from his victim's estate—he forfeits what he would have inherited and the property goes to someone else; see below paras 14–69 and 14–81 et seq.

[211] *In the Estate of Crippen* [1911] P. 108 (intestacy); *Re Sigsworth* [1935] Ch.89 (will or intestacy): as to burden of proof see *Re Dellow's* W.T. [1964] 1 W.L.R. 451.

[212] *In the Estate of Hall* [1914] P. 1.

[213] Or statutory nomination or *donatio mortis causa* of his victim. As to joint tenants see *Re K* [1985] Ch.85, 100 (forfeiture severs a beneficial joint tenancy); see also *Schobelt v Barber* (1966) 60 D.L.R. (2d) 519; *Re Pechar* [1969] N.Z.L.R. 574, 584–588.

[214] *Re Houghton* [1915] 2 Ch.173 (insane killer may take on his victim's intestacy); *Re Pitts* [1931] 1 Ch.546. There is a presumption of sanity, *Re Pollock* [1941] Ch.219.

[215] *Re Giles* [1972] Ch.544.

[216] See *Re H. (dec'd.)* [1990] 1 F.L.R. 441, discussed in para.14–66 below.

[217] Section 1 of the Forfeiture Act 1982 states that "the 'forfeiture rule' means the rule of public policy which *in certain circumstances* precludes a person who has unlawfully killed another from acquiring a benefit in consequence of the killing." The italicised words imply that the rule does not apply to all unlawful killings.

[218] *Gray v Barr* [1971] 2 Q.B. 554, 569 and 581 (manslaughter varies infinitely in its seriousness—but this is an insurance case); *R. v Chief National Insurance Commissioner, Ex. p.Connor*

cases of unlawful killing; for example, to cases where there is a conviction for causing death by dangerous driving.[219]

2. Forfeiture Act 1982

14–65 The Forfeiture Act 1982 gives the court the power to modify the effect of the forfeiture rule if the court is satisfied that the justice of the case so requires, having regard to the conduct of the offender and of the deceased and of any other material circumstances.[220] The power to modify the effect of the rule does not apply in the case of someone convicted of murder.[221] Under the power to modify, the court can grant complete or partial relief from the effect of the forfeiture rule.[222]

14–66 The 1982 Act is not well drafted. It is engrafted onto the earlier law and, as the earlier law is uncertain, the present position is uncertain too.[223] In *Re H*[224] a husband killed his wife while he was suffering from a form of mental disorder and was convicted of manslaughter by reason of diminished responsibility. Peter Gibson J held that the forfeiture rule did not apply in this case. He said that the proper test was whether the killer had been guilty of deliberate, intentional and unlawful violence or threats, and that it was for the court to determine, after careful scrutiny of the facts in each particular case, where the line should be drawn. He went on to hold that, if the forfeiture rule had applied, he would have granted relief from it under the 1982 Act. In *Dunbar v Plant*[224A] the judges in the Court of Appeal were unanimous in holding that the forfeiture rule applied to the survivor of a suicide pact,[225] but there was obiter disagreement as to whether the rule applied to all manslaughter cases. Mummery LJ thought

[1981] Q.B. 758, 765 (this is a state benefit case); *Re K* [1985] Ch.85, 95–98; *Re H.* [1990] above. See generally Youdan (1973) 89 L.Q.R. 235.

[219] See A. J. Oakley, *Constructive Trusts*, 3rd edn (London: Sweet & Maxwell, 1997), p.50. There appear to be no reported cases where it has been suggested that the rule applies to causing death by dangerous driving. Section 20 of the Road Safety Act 2006, which came into force in 2008, created an additional offence of "causing death by careless or inconsiderate driving". It is virtually certain that the forfeiture rule does not apply to someone convicted of this new offence.

[220] Forfeiture Act 1982 ss.1–2, 5 and 7. If the killer stands convicted, proceedings for modification cannot be brought more than three months after conviction, s.2(3); *Re Royse* [1985] Ch.22. Property acquired before 13 October 1982 by a person other than the killer in consequence of the forfeiture rule is protected, s.2(7); *Re K* [1985] Ch.85, 98–99, [1986] Ch.180 (only property actually transferred to other person, not property held by personal representative pending administration).

[221] Forfeiture Act 1982 s.5.

[222] Forfeiture Act 1982 s.2(1) and (5); see *Re K* [1985] Ch.85, [1986] Ch.180 (probation for H's manslaughter: W granted complete relief from forfeiture of her interests under H's will and in matrimonial home which H and W had held as beneficial joint tenants).

[223] See Cretney (1990) 10 O.J.L.S. 298; Matthews (1983) J.S.W.L. 141 "little short of a legislative disaster."

[224] *Re H* [1990] 1 F.L.R. 441.

[224A] *Dunbar v Plant* [1998] Ch.412.

[225] Who was guilty of aiding and abetting suicide contrary to the Suicide Act 1961 s.2(1). In the case of a joint tenancy the killing effects a severance and the killer holds the legal estate upon trust for himself and the deceased's estate in equal shares.

that it did not, and followed an approach close to that of Peter Gibson J in *Re H*, whereas Phillips LJ[226] appeared to think that the rule would now[227] apply to all manslaughter cases. In the event, full relief was given. Much the same result was reached by the same route in *Re K* [228] where Vinelott J held that the forfeiture rule did apply to a wife who had killed her husband with a single shot from a shotgun and who had been convicted of manslaughter[229]; she was granted relief under the Act and was permitted to inherit virtually the whole of her husband's substantial estate.

There have been several recent first instance decisions where it appears to have been held that the forfeiture rule applies to all those who are convicted of manslaughter. In *Jones v Roberts*[230] Judge Kolbert[231] held that a son who had killed his parents and who had been convicted of manslaughter by reason of diminished responsibility was subject to the forfeiture rule[232] and he cast doubt on the correctness of the decision in *Re H* on the ground that the earlier Court of Appeal decision in *Re Royse*[233] had not been cited to Peter Gibson J. In *Re Murphy, Dalton v Latham*,[234] Patten J, to whom *Re H* appears not to have been cited, also held that the forfeiture rule applied to someone convicted of manslaughter by reason of diminished responsibility and, in view of the manner in which the killer had taken advantage of his victim in the period before the killing took place,[235] he refused to grant any relief. In *Re Land*[235A] Judge Norris[236] referred briefly to *Re H* but he also seemed to think that the forfeiture rule applied to all cases of manslaughter.[237] In *Chadwick v Collinson*[238] Judge Pelling QC[239] held that the rule applied to all cases of manslaughter and refused to grant any relief to a man who had killed his lover and son while suffering from delusions.[240] **14–67**

[226] With whom Hirst LJ agreed.

[227] Though he also suggested that the rule would have been modified by the judges, had the 1982 Act not been passed.

[228] *Re K* [1985] Ch 85, Vinelott J; decision affirmed by C.A. [1986] Ch.180.

[229] It is not clear from the report of the case (dealing with the forfeiture) of which type of manslaughter the widow had been convicted; there was a dispute in the forfeiture proceedings as to whether remarks made by the trial judge in the criminal case implied that this was a case of reckless manslaughter, or whether it was a case of an intentional killing which was manslaughter because of provocation. In any event, the distinction, where there has been a shooting, is likely to be a very fine one.

[230] *Jones v Roberts* [1995] 2 F.L.R. 422.

[231] Sitting as a Deputy Judge of the High Court.

[232] He had not applied for relief from forfeiture under the 1982 Act—it is not clear why.

[233] *Re Royse* [1985] Ch.22.

[234] *Re Murphy, Dalton v Latham* [2003] W.T.L.R. 687.

[235] He had squandered much of his victim's money.

[235A] *Re Land* [2007] 1 All E.R. 324.

[236] Sitting as a judge of the High Court.

[237] It is not entirely clear, but *Land* appears to be a case of gross negligence manslaughter.

[238] *Chadwick v Collinson* [2014] EWHC 3055; [2015] W.T.L.R. 25, another case of diminished responsibility.

[239] Sitting as a judge of the High Court.

[240] The judge suggested that, in the light of the views of the majority in *Dunbar v Plant*, and of the decisions in *Dalton* and in *Land* it was now "entirely unarguable" that the forfeiture rule did not apply to all cases of manslaughter. This may be a slight overstatement. He had noted earlier in his judgment that "manslaughter is a crime that varies infinitely in its seriousness" and the case with which he was dealing was one where he thought that no relief at all should be granted.

Given that there appears to be some doubt as to when the forfeiture rule applies in manslaughter cases, it may seem that the safest course for the beneficiary/killer is to apply for relief under the Act. The problem is that this may involve unnecessary legal costs and, even if the applicant obtains relief under the Act, and so is able to inherit all or part of the estate of his victim, he may, by making an application under the Act, provoke potential problems in relation to insurance claims[241] and/or state benefits. The position is not satisfactory[242] and this branch of the law is in need of legislative clarification.

3. Application for provision for killer under the Inheritance (Provision for Family and Dependants) Act 1975

14–68 A particular problem arose in *Re Land* where a son who was convicted of his mother's manslaughter by gross negligence then applied for relief from forfeiture, but did so four days out of time. An application for relief under the 1982 Act must be made within three months of the killer's conviction; and the relevant section[243] gives the judge no discretion to extend this time limit.[244] However, the judge held that the son could make a valid claim under the Inheritance (Provision for Family and Dependants) Act 1975.[245] Emphasis was placed on s.3 of the 1982 Act, which states that the forfeiture rule shall not preclude anyone from making an application under the 1975 Act; but in this case the mother's will did make reasonable provision for her son. It was the forfeiture rule which deprived the son of that provision.

It is suggested that there were two ways in which the court in *Land* could, legitimately have overcome the problem of the late application: either it could have followed the lead taken by Peter Gibson J in *Re H*[246] and have held that the forfeiture rule does not apply to manslaughter by gross negligence; or, more simply, it could have held that the court has an inherent power to override the draconian effects of s.2(3) of the 1982 Act. Calling the 1975 Act into aid was unnecessary and wrong.[247]

[241] In *Re S* [1996] 1 F.L.R. 910 the court was asked to rule on what should happen to the proceeds of a joint-lives with-profits insurance policy, but the insurance company did not attempt to suggest that the policy moneys should not be paid out. It was held that the Act applied, and the forfeiture rule was modified so that the sum awarded was held in trust for the couple's minor child. Different issues would arise if the insurance company were to refuse to pay the proceeds to anyone.

[242] See N. Peart, *Reforming the Forfeiture Rule: Comparing New Zealand, England and Australia* [2002] Common Law World Review 1.

[243] Forfeiture Act 1982 s.2(3).

[244] Contrast Inheritance (Provision for Family and Dependants Act) 1975 s.4, which imposes a time limit of six months from the grant of representation "except with the permission of the court". See above, para.8–07.

[245] Contrast Inheritance (Provision for Family and Dependants Act) 1975 ss.3 and 5.

[246] See above, paras 14–66 et seq.

[247] S.1(1) of the 1975 Act is clear, and s.2(3) of the 1982 Act is not in conflict with it. S.2(3) covers the case where, for example, a cohabitant, for whom there is no provision in the deceased's will or on his intestacy, is convicted of his killing. And Judge Norris in *Re Land*, refused to follow dicta from the Court of Appeal in *Re Royce*, [1985] Ch.22: see above, para.14–68.

4. Consequences of Forfeiture

When a specific legacy or devise fails, it normally passes into residue or on intestacy, and a residuary gift which fails passes on intestacy.[248] It is submitted, however, that the rule is different in the case of failure under the forfeiture rule, where the beneficiary has been convicted of killing the person from whom he would have inherited. This is not a straightforward case of failure; it is a case of a constructive trust and is discussed further below.[249] **14–69**

VIII. DISCLAIMER[250]

1. Beneficiary is free to disclaim[251]

A beneficiary under a will may disclaim the gift to him. "The law certainly is not so absurd as to force a man to take an estate against his will."[252] Similarly a beneficiary entitled under the intestacy rules may disclaim his interest on intestacy.[253] The beneficiary may disclaim by a deed of disclaimer[254] or by conduct. **14–70**

If a beneficiary does disclaim a benefit under a will, he may subsequently retract his disclaimer provided that no one has altered his position in reliance upon it.[255] It is not possible for a beneficiary to disclaim a gift before the testator's (or intestate's) death.[256]

2. Limits on freedom to disclaim

There are, however, certain limits on a beneficiary's freedom to disclaim: **14–71**

(i) If the beneficiary has already unequivocally accepted the gift, he cannot disclaim it.[257]

(ii) In general the beneficiary is free to disclaim an onerous gift[258] in a will and accept another beneficial gift in the same will,[259] but

[248] See below, para.14–75.
[249] See below, paras 14–82 et seq.
[250] See, generally, J. Hill (2001) 117 L.Q.R. 127 esp. at pp.139 and 144.
[251] There may be tax advantages in a disclaimer, as there may be in a variation. See Chap.16, paras 16–45 et seq.
[252] per Abbot C.J. in *Townson v Tickell* (1819) 3 B. & Ald. 31.
[253] *Re Scott* [1975] 1 W.L.R. 1260; cf. Goodhart (1976) 40 Conv. (N.S.) 292; Oughton (1977) 41 Conv. (N.S.) 260.
[254] *Townson v Tickell*, above.
[255] *Re Cranstoun* [1949] Ch.523: see also *Re Paradise Motor Co* [1968] 1 W.L.R. 1125, 1143.
[256] *Re Smith* [2001] 3 All E.R. 552. If consideration is provided for the disclaimer of future property, it may be possible to treat the disclaimer as an agreement and enforce it accordingly.
[257] *Re Hodge* [1940] Ch.260; cf. *Re Wimperis* [1914] 1 Ch.502.
[258] e.g. a gift of a lease with an unduly heavy rent, or a gift subject to a condition imposing an onerous personal obligation, as in *Re Hodge*, above, (devise of Blackacre to H subject to personal obligation to pay £2 per week to S for life, and if H disposed of Blackacre to invest £2,000 on trust for S for life and after her death for S's children).
[259] *Warren v Rudall* (1861) 1 J. & H. 1.

occasionally the will requires him to take both or neither of the gifts.[260]

(iii) If a single gift includes two or more different assets, the beneficiary must take all the assets or none of them. For instance, a gift to B by T's will of his leasehold house Blackacre together with its contents constitutes a single gift, and not two separate gifts, and therefore B is not free to disclaim the gift of Blackacre and accept the gift of its contents.[261]

(iv) One of two or more joint beneficiaries cannot disclaim, though he can release his interest to the other joint tenants[262]—"the only disclaimer which can be made by joint tenants is a disclaimer which is made by them all."[263]

IX. EFFECT OF FAILURE

1. A legacy or specific devise which fails falls into residue or passes on intestacy

14–72 In general, the subject-matter of any legacy or specific devise which fails passes under the residuary gift (if any) contained in the testator's will or—if not effectively disposed of by the will—passes on intestacy.[264]

(a) *Residuary bequest*

14–73 Prima facie a residuary bequest includes the subject-matter of any legacy which fails for any reason.[265] As Grant MR put it in *Leake v Robinson*,[266]

> "I have always understood that, with regard to personal estate, everything which is ill given by the will does fall into the residue. It is immaterial how it happens that any part of the property is undisposed of ".

If T by his will gives "my 200 shares in X.Y.Z. Ltd." to A and "all the residue of my personal estate" to B, the word "residue" is *not* construed as referring to all T's personal estate except the 200 shares: instead, if the gift to A fails, the "residue" includes the 200 shares because the gift to B is a residuary bequest. The same result follows if T gives "all the rest of" or "all the remainder of" or "all other" his personal estate to B.[267] However, this

[260] *Talbot v Earl of Radnor* (1834) 3 M. & K. 252; *Fairclough v Johnstone* (1865) 16 Ir.Ch. 442.
[261] *Re Joel* [1943] Ch.311; *Guthrie v Walrond* (1882) 22 Ch.D. 573 ("all my estate and effects in the Island of Mauritius": held a single gift which could only be disclaimed as a whole).
[262] *Re Schär* [1951] Ch.280.
[263] *Re Schär* [1951] Ch.280 at 285.
[264] See generally *Hawkins on the Construction of Wills*, 5th edn (London: Sweet & Maxwell, 2000), Chap.9.
[265] *Cambridge v Rous* (1802) 8 Ves. 12 (lapsed legacies); *Blight v Hartnoll* (1883) 23 Ch.D. 218 (legacy void for remoteness); *Re Backhouse* [1931] W.N. 168 (disclaimed legacy).
[266] *Leake v Robinson* (1817) 2 Mer. 363, 393.
[267] *Re Mason* [1901] 1 Ch.619, 624–625; *Re Barnes'* W.T. [1972] 1 W.L.R. 587.

common law rule that a residuary bequest includes the subject-matter of any legacy which fails is not applicable if the will shows a contrary intention. Accordingly, the rule is not applicable if the testator shows an intention to exclude the subject-matter of a legacy from his residuary bequest in any event, irrespective of whether the legacy fails: in that event, if the legacy fails, the subject-matter passes on intestacy.[268]

(b) *Residuary devise*

Under s.25 of the Wills Act 1837, unless a will shows a contrary intention, a residuary devise[269] includes the subject-matter of any specific devise which fails for any reason. Thus, as a result of s.25, a residuary devise operates in the same way as a residuary bequest.[270] **14–74**

2. A residuary gift which fails passes on intestacy

If a residuary gift in a will fails completely, the residuary estate passes on intestacy. Again, if a gift of a share in the residuary estate fails, prima facie that share passes on intestacy. Accordingly, if T by his will gives his residuary real and personal estate to X and Y absolutely as tenants in common in equal shares, and the gift to X fails for any reason, prima facie X's share goes on T's intestacy and does not pass to Y. A residuary gift sweeps up property not effectively disposed of by any other form of gift, but it does not sweep up property not effectively disposed of by the residuary gift itself.[271] However, this rule is not applicable if the will shows a contrary intention. For instance, T may direct that if the disposition of a share of his residue fails, that share is to accrue to the other share, and under such a direction X's share does pass to Y.[272] **14–75**

3. Gifts which do not fail

The principles so far considered are not, of course, applicable if the gift—whether a legacy, specific devise or residuary gift—does not fail, even though one or more of the beneficiaries cannot take. This occurs: **14–76**

[268] *Re Fraser* [1904] 1 Ch.726; *Wainman v Field* (1854) Kay. 507, but see *Blight v Hartnoll*, above at 223. Also the subject-matter may, on the construction of the will, fall into a particular residue of that description of property, and not into general residue, *De Trafford v Tempest* (1856) 21 Beav. 564 and see *Hawkins on the Construction of Wills*, 5th edn (London: Sweet & Maxwell, 2000), pp.139–140.

[269] Wills Act 1837 s.25 only applies to general residuary devises, *Springett v Jenings* (1871) L.R. 6 Ch.App.333: cf. *Re Davies* [1928] Ch.24.

[270] *Re Mason* [1901] 1 Ch.619, C.A., [1903] A.C. 1, H.L. (specific devise to attesting witness fell into devise of "all other my freehold messuages and tenements at Wimbledon aforesaid and elsewhere," which was held to be residuary).

[271] *Skrymsher v Northcote* (1818) 1 Sw. 566, 570.

[272] For examples of contrary intention see *Evans v Field* (1839) 8 L.J.Ch. 264; *Re Palmer* [1893] 3 Ch.369 and *Re Allan* [1903] 1 Ch.276. For the effect of Wills Act 1837 s.15 see *Re Doland's W.T.* [1970] Ch.267 (trust of 2% share of residue for X, whose wife was an attesting witness; proviso that if "any of the trusts shall fail" gift to Y and Z equally: held under Wills Act 1837 s.15 the will must be treated as though it contained no trust in favour of X which could fail—X's share went on intestacy and not under proviso).

(i) in the case of a gift to X, Y and Z as joint tenants if X and Y both die before the testator, but Z survives him and takes the whole by survivorship[273]; and
(ii) in the case of a class gift to persons who are to be ascertained at the testator's death or subsequently.

If a presumptive member of a class dies in the testator's lifetime,[274] or is incapable of taking by reason of his being an attesting witness,[275] or forfeits because he is guilty of the testator's manslaughter,[276] this does not cause the gift to fail if at least one other member of the class takes. Again, if any property is given by will to X subject to a charge in favour of Y (e.g. charged with a legacy of £1,000 for Y), and the gift to Y fails, this causes the charge to fail and X takes the entire property free from the charge.[277] Finally, if any property is given by will to X absolutely, and trusts are engrafted on X's absolute interest which fail, under the rule in *Lassence v Tierney*[278] the absolute gift to X takes effect so far as the trusts have failed. This rule was considered in Chapter 11.[279]

4. Acceleration of subsequent interest

14–77 The doctrine of acceleration may be applicable if T by his will gives any real or personal property to X for life and this gift to X fails. It may fail because X or his spouse was an attesting witness, or X predeceased T, or T's marriage to X was dissolved or annulled, or X was guilty of T's murder or manslaughter, or X disclaimed the gift.

(a) *Gift in remainder vested*

14–78 If after X's life interest there is a vested gift in remainder (e.g. a gift in remainder to Y absolutely), the remainder is accelerated and takes effect in possession immediately.[280] "An interest is postponed that a prior interest may be enjoyed. If that prior interest is determined, whether by the death of a prior beneficiary or for any other cause, the reason for postponement disappears and there is no reason why there should not be acceleration."[281]

[273] *Morley v Bird* (1798) 3 Ves. 629.
[274] *Doe d. Stewart v Sheffield* (1811) 13 East. 526; *Shuttleworth v Greaves* (1838) 4 M. & Cr. 35: see also *Re Woods* [1931] 2 Ch.138 and cf. *Re Midgley* [1955] Ch.576.
[275] *Fell v Biddolph* (1875) L.R. 10 C.P. 701 (the headnote is wrong); *Re Coleman and Jarrom* (1876) 4 Ch.D. 165 ("the true rule is that those members of the class who are at the testator's death capable of taking take, and that those who become incapable of taking—whether by dying in the testator's lifetime, or by attesting the will, or by some other operation of law—do not take").
[276] *Re Peacock* [1957] Ch.310.
[277] *Tucker v Kayess* (1858) 4 K. & J. 339.
[278] *Lassence v Tierney* (1849) 1 Mac. & G. 551.
[279] See above, Chap.11 paras 11–30 et seq.
[280] *Lainson v Lainson* (1854) 5 De G.M. & G. 754 (X's life interest revoked by codicil: vested remainder accelerated); *Jull v Jacobs* (1876) 3 Ch.D. 703 (X an attesting witness: vested remainder accelerated); *Re Flower's Settlement Trusts* [1957] 1 W.L.R. 401, 405.
[281] *Re Hodge* [1943] Ch.300, 301–302 (X disclaimed: held annuities in remainder accelerated).

If the gift to Y is expressed to take effect "after the death" of X, this does not prevent acceleration: the gift to Y is construed as a gift taking effect on the death of X *or on any earlier failure or determination of X's interest*.[282] In short, the phrase "after X's death for Y absolutely" is construed in the same sense as the useful phrase "*subject as aforesaid* for Y absolutely." But T may by his will exclude the doctrine of acceleration by making it plain that the expression "after the death" of X refers to X's death in the literal sense and nothing else.

The doctrine of acceleration applies even though the vested gift in remainder is vested in Y subject to its being divested[283] (e.g. a gift in remainder to Y absolutely, but if Y dies before X and leaves issue, to Y's issue absolutely in equal shares per stirpes). In this case, under the doctrine of acceleration Y's interest takes effect in possession immediately, but Y's interest nevertheless remains liable to be divested in accordance with the terms of T's will.[284]

(b) *Gift in remainder contingent*

On the other hand, if after X's life interest there is only a contingent gift **14–79** in remainder (e.g. a gift in remainder to the first child of Y absolutely, and at T's death Y has no child), normally the remainder is not accelerated whilst the remainder remains contingent.[285] But if the gift in remainder subsequently becomes vested (i.e. in this example, if a child is born to Y), under the doctrine of acceleration the remainder is then accelerated and takes effect in possession.[286]

5. Failure of interest on intestacy by disclaimer

An interest on intestacy may fail because the beneficiary disclaims his **14–80** interest.[287] If the person who disclaims is a spouse, and if there are issue, the issue take the whole estate.[288] If the person who disclaims is a member of a class (such as issue) then the other members of the class take his share. So, if the testator were to die leaving four children and if one child were

[282] *Re Flower's Settlement Trusts* above.

[283] *Re Taylor* [1957] 1 W.L.R. 1043 (X disclaimed: held vested remainder accelerated but remained liable to be divested); *Re Conyngham* [1921] 1 Ch.491.

[284] *Re Taylor*, above; *Re Conyngham*, above.

[285] *Re Townsend's Estate* (1886) 34 Ch.D. 357 (X's wife an attesting witness; gift in remainder to X's child or children; X was childless: held no acceleration possible until X has a child—then "the interest of the children in remainder would be accelerated"); *Re Taylor*, above, at pp.1045 and 1049; *Re Scott* [1975] 1 W.L.R. 1260. But cf. *Re Dawson's Settlement* [1966] 1 W.L.R. 1456, esp. at pp.1465–1467 where Goff J held that a remainder which is contingent may be accelerated if the person contingently entitled is *in esse* and "the contingency is in no way related to the words of futurity or the determination of the prior interest," e.g. attaining 21 or marrying: see Prichard [1973] C.L.J. 246. If Y's interest in remainder was "contingent upon the termination of X's life interest," which lapsed by virtue of divorce or annulment, Y's interest is treated as if it had not been so contingent, Wills Act 1837 s.18A(3).

[286] *Re Townsend's Estate*, above; *Re Taylor*, above. For the effect of acceleration on class closing see above, para.11–18.

[287] See above, para.14–70.

[288] *Re Giles* [1972] Ch.544.

to disclaim, the other three would take his share.[289] If the child, in this example, were to want his share to go to someone other than his brothers and sisters, his correct course would be to effect a variation under s.142 of the Inheritance Tax Act 1984.[290] If all the members of the class of next-of-kin entitled under the intestacy rules disclaim, that class is disregarded and the next class of next-of-kin (of which there are members in existence capable of taking) is entitled.[291]

6. Consequence of failure under the forfeiture rule

14–81 In *Jones v Midland Bank*[292] a son killed his mother and was convicted of her manslaughter. She had left a will in which she had bequeathed her entire estate to him, but—if he predeceased her—to two nephews. Were she to have died intestate, her estate would not have passed to the nephews, but—supposing she had no son—it would have passed to her sister.[293] The son wanted to apply for relief from forfeiture but, in order for his application for relief to proceed, it was necessary to decide who (if he were not entitled) was entitled to his mother's estate. Both the first instance judge and the Court of Appeal treated this as a case of construction of the mother's will. The Court of Appeal ruled that the bequest to the nephews could not take effect because—given the way in which the will was drafted—the gift to them took effect only if the son predeceased his mother. She had not contemplated his killing her.

14–82 In *Re D.W.S* [294] a son murdered both his parents, who died intestate. The problem was as to whether the parents' property passed to the son' s son (the deceased parents' grandson), or to the parents' brothers and sisters, or to the Crown. Again, the Court of Appeal treated this case as a question of construing the intestacy legislation. The majority held that the property passed to the victims' brothers and sisters; Sedley LJ dissented and held that it passed as bona vacantia.

14–83 It is submitted that the Court of Appeal's approach of construing the words of the will—or the intestacy legislation—was, in each of these cases, misconceived. The Court of Appeal failed to appreciate that when the forfeiture rule operates, it operates by way of creating a *constructive trust*. This meant that the court was not bound to attempt to construe the will or the intestacy legislation in the ordinary way.[295] The court had a discretion as to the devolution of the property and should have attempted to guess[296] what the testator or the intestate would have

[289] But see also, the Estates of Deceased Persons (Forfeiture Rule and Law of Succession) Act 2011, discussed in para.14–83, below.

[290] See below Chap.16 paras 16–46 et seq.

[291] *Re Scott* [1975] 1 W.L.R. 1260 (brother and sister both disclaimed: next class of next-of-kin held entitled, not the Crown): see E. C. Ryder (1976) 40 Conv. (N.S.) 85.

[292] *Jones v Midland Bank* [1998] 1 F.L.R. 246.

[293] The deceased's sister was the mother of the two nephews; she had died after the deceased, leaving a will in which she had bequeathed her entire estate to her cohabitant.

[294] *Re D.W.S.* [2001] Ch.568.

[295] It cannot be construed in the ordinary way, because the case is, by definition, extraordinary—that is part of the problem. See R. Kerridge (2000) 117 L.Q.R. 371.

[296] This *is* a case of surmise, and should be recognised as such.

wanted had he been asked to contemplate this situation. In *Jones* it is reasonable to suppose that the testatrix would have wanted the nephews to take in preference to her sister and—*via* her—the sister's cohabitant; and in *Re D.W.S.* the victims would have wanted their estates to have passed to their grandchild (their son's son) rather than to their brothers and sisters.

In 2005, the Law Commission produced a Report, *The Forfeiture Rule and the Law of Succession*,[297] which recommended the introduction of a statutory deemed pre-decease rule to undo the effect of the decision in *Re DWS*.[298] In due course, the recommendation was enacted by the Estates of Deceased Persons (Forfeiture Rule and Law of Succession) Act 2011.[299] This Act covers both disclaimers[300] and forfeiture, and deems the person making the disclaimer, or forfeiting, as the case may be, to have died before the person or persons from whom he would have inherited. This puts right the problem created by the decisions in *Jones* and *DWS*, but it may be suggested that this new statutory rule creates too much of a straightjacket.[301]

The correct solution was to assert the existence (as it had previously **14–84** been asserted, in almost all the Trusts textbooks) of a constructive trust. The advantage of a constructive trust is that it gives the court a discretion, and a discretion is desirable in forfeiture cases. In *Jones*, and in *DWS*, a deemed pre-decease rule gives what is almost certainly the right result, but it will not always be so. Take the following hypothetical example. Suppose that X, a widower, has an adult only son, Y, who has an adult only son, Z. X discovers something about the conduct of Y and Z which causes him to decide that neither of them should inherit any part of his property. He instructs his solicitor to prepare a will for him, leaving his entire estate to charity. If this will is not executed, an earlier will will take effect, and that earlier will leaves his estate to Y (or, which is, in this context, the same thing, he will die intestate, and Y will take on his intestacy). X tells Y that he is about to execute a will disinheriting him, and Y murders X. Under the provisions of the 2011 Act, Z now inherits X's estate. But, if there were a constructive trust, the court would have a discretion which it would, almost certainly, exercise in favour of the charity already designated by X. So, the 2011 Act will generally operate fairly, but not always. In fact, there may be further complications. Grafting the 2011 rule onto the earlier law, when the earlier law had itself been misunderstood and misinterpreted, may well lead to other difficulties. What

[297] Law Com. No.295.

[298] It also, correctly, undoes the effect of *Jones v Midland Bank*, but this appears to have passed unnoticed.

[299] This Act, though it was modelled on the Law Commission's proposals, began life as a private member's bill.

[300] Although the Act covers disclaimers, it would appear to have relatively little significance in relation to them, because someone contemplating a disclaimer can always choose, instead, to effect a variation under s.184 of the Inheritance Tax Act 1984, and, in this case, he can choose who will take the property he would have inherited.

[301] There is another potential problem with the new statutory rule, in addition to that of the straightjacket. S.33A of the Wills Act 1837, newly inserted in 2011, applies "for the purposes of this Act" and the effect of these words is not entirely clear. See *Williams on Wills*, 10th edn (London: LexisNexis, 2014), para.9–17.

happens, for example, where the victim and murderer are beneficial joint tenants? The point does not appear to be covered by the 2011 Act, though it arose in a recent Irish case, *Cawley v Lillis*,[302] where it was held, consistently with the view expressed here, that this created a constructive trust.

302 *Cawley v Lillis* [2013] W.T.L.R. 559.

Chapter 15

DUTY OF CARE

I. SOLICITOR'S DUTY OF CARE IN PREPARATION OF A WILL[1]

1. Introduction

A solicitor or other professional will draftsman owes duties to his client, both in contract and in tort,[2] to carry out the task using reasonable skill and care. This duty survives the testator; so if the personal representatives, on behalf of the estate, can demonstrate that a breach of duty has occurred and that loss has been suffered as a result of that breach, they will be entitled to recover damages. The problem is, however, that the estate rarely suffers loss as a result of the draftsman's breach of duty; instead, the loss is suffered by the intended beneficiary, who either receives nothing or less than the testator had intended. In *Robertson v Fleming*[3] Lord Campbell LC opined that it was not the law of Scotland or of England or "of any country where jurisprudence has been cultivated as a science" to allow a disappointed beneficiary to sue the testator's solicitor. **15–01**

2. The duty

In *White v Jones*,[4] the House of Lords held, by a bare majority, that where a client had instructed a solicitor to prepare a will for execution, and where, as a result of the solicitor's negligence, an intended legatee was reasonably foreseeably deprived of a legacy, the solicitor was liable to the intended legatee for the loss of the legacy. The result was achieved by extending the assumption of responsibility principle, i.e. the assumption of responsibility by a solicitor towards his client in circumstances in **15–02**

[1] See generally, Frost, Reed and Baxter *Risk and Negligence in Wills, Estates and Trusts*, 2nd edn (London: Oxford University Press, 2014).

[2] The liability in the tort of negligence is under the principle in *Hedley Byrne & Co Ltd v Heller & Partners Ltd* [1964] A.C. 465; see *Midland Bank Trust Co Ltd v Hett, Stubbs and Kemp* [1979] Ch.384, approved in *Henderson v Merrett Syndicates Ltd* [1995] 2 A.C. 145.

[3] *Robertson v Fleming* (1861) 4 Macq. 147: the case was not a case on wills.

[4] *White v Jones* [1995] 2 A.C. 207. All members of the committee delivered speeches. Lords Keith of Kinkel and Mustill dissented; Lord Browne-Wilkinson and Lord Nolan expressed their agreement with the reasons given by Lord Goff, whose speech must, therefore, be regarded as containing the reasoning of the majority. See Chadwick LJ in *Carr-Glynn v Frearsons* [1999] Ch.326, 334 H–335 C.

which there was no confidential or fiduciary relationship; and neither the testator nor the estate had a remedy against the solicitor. In this way the common law was fashioning "a remedy to fill a lacuna in the law so as to prevent the injustice which would otherwise occur".[5]

In *Ross v Caunters*,[6] the testator's signature of his will had been attested by the spouse of one of the beneficiaries. The solicitors had sent the will to the testator for execution but had failed to warn him that, under s.15 of the Wills Act 1837,[7] attestation of the will by a beneficiary or a beneficiary's spouse would invalidate a gift to the beneficiary. The solicitors had also failed to notice that the testator's signature had been witnessed by a beneficiary's husband. Megarry VC held the solicitors liable to the disappointed beneficiary under the ordinary principles of the tort of negligence. The House of Lords in *White v Jones*, whilst approving the outcome in *Ross v Caunters*, rejected the reasoning, which posed a number of conceptual problems.[8]

15–03 The difficulty with this branch of the law is that "it lies at the interface of what has traditionally been regarded as the separate domains of contract and tort."[9] Lord Goff suggested in White v Jones that the imposition of liability was designed to do practical justice in a case where, in the absence of the remedy fashioned by the Court, neither the testator's estate nor the intended beneficiary would have a claim for the loss caused by the negligence. He thought that there had to be boundaries to the availability of a remedy in such cases, but that these boundaries would "have to be worked out in the future, as practical problems come before the courts".[10]

There are two important limitations on the liability of the solicitor to the disappointed beneficiary. The terms of the duty owed to the disappointed beneficiary depend upon the nature of the original instructions given by the testator. If, therefore, there is no breach of duty to the testator, the disappointed beneficiary—even if he suffers a loss—will have no claim. As Chadwick LJ pointed out in *Carr-Glynn v Frearsons*: "The duty owed by the solicitors to the specific legatee is not a duty to take care to ensure that the specific legatee receives his legacy. It is a duty to take care to ensure that effect is given to the testator's testamentary intentions."[11] The draftsman is, however, under a duty to make appropriate enquiries when taking instructions from the testator. Thus in *MacKenzie v MacKenzie*[12] the Novia Scotia Court of Appeal found the defendant solicitor liable for failing to ask about the extent of the testator's estate, his

[5] per Lord Goff at 268B.

[6] *Ross v Caunters* [1980] Ch.297. See also *Whittingham v Crease & Co* (1978) 88 D.L.R. (3d) 353; *Watts v Public Trustee for Western Australia* [1980] W.A.R. 97.

[7] See above, Chap.14, paras 14–03 et seq.

[8] See Lord Goff at *White v Jones* [1995] 2 A.C. 207, 261.

[9] per Steyn LJ in the Court of Appeal in *White v Jones* [1995] 2 A.C. 207, 235.

[10] *White v Jones* [1995] 2 A.C. 207, 269.

[11] *Carr-Glynn v Frearsons* [1999] Ch.326, 337 E. See also *Cancer Research Campaign v Ernest Brown & Co* [1998] P.N.L.R. 592; *Punford v Gilberts Accountants* [1998] P.N.L.R. 763, C.A.; *Sutherland v Public Trustee* [1980] 2 N.Z.L.R. 536. In *Gray v Buss Murton* [1999] P.N.L.R. 882, Rougier J held that where a client seeks advice in imprecise and non-legal terms, the solicitor is under a duty to clarify the extent and nature of the advice sought.

[12] *MacKenzie v MacKenzie* (1998) 162 D.L.R. (4th) 674.

earlier wills and why six of his children were excluded from benefit.[13] Secondly, the disappointed beneficiary will have no claim unless he can establish that it is the solicitor's negligence which has deprived him of the benefit. If the testator would not have followed the advice even if it had been given, or if the benefit which the testator intended would not have been received in any event, e.g. because the estate is insolvent[14] or the property is needed to pay debts and expenses,[15] the beneficiary will have no claim: not because there is no breach of duty, but because no loss has flowed from the breach.

3. Professional will draftsmen

The duty is owed not only by solicitors, but by all professional will drafts- **15–04**
men and by those who offer will-making services. In *Esterhuizen v Allied Dunbar*[16] a financial institution which offered a will-making service was held liable for the failure of its representative to ensure that a will was properly executed and attested.

4. Severing joint tenancies

The severance of a beneficial joint tenancy of a property is part of the law **15–05**
of succession, in the broad sense.[17] The failure of a solicitor to warn a client about the need to sever a joint tenancy and/or his failure to sever a joint tenancy when he has been instructed to do so, will make the solicitor liable to a beneficiary who does not then obtain a benefit[18] under the testator's will which the testator intended him to have.[19] The failure to sever a joint tenancy was also the essential element in the solicitor's negligence in *Carr-Glynn v Frearsons*.[20]

II. CASES WHERE TESTATOR FAILS TO EXECUTE A VALID WILL

Since *White v Jones*[21] there would appear to be no theoretical problem **15–06**
about cases where a would-be testator of full capacity is advised by a professional will draftsman and then fails to execute a valid will. Most of the cases are concerned with delay—or alleged delay—by the will draftsman: if the delay is unreasonable, and if the responsibility for the delay lies with

13 See also *Earl v Wilhelm* [2001] W.T.L.R. 1275, C.A. for Saskatchewan, (enquires should have been made of testator's accountant regarding precise ownership of land).

14 See Chap.21.

15 See Chap.21.

16 *Esterhuizen v Allied Dunbar* [1998] 2 F.L.R. 668.

17 See Chadwick LJ in *Carr-Glynn v Frearsons* [1999] Ch.326, 336A. "On a proper analysis, the service of a notice of severance was part of the will-making process."

18 He fails to obtain it because the property passes under a right of survivorship.

19 *Kecskemeti v Rubens Rabin & Co, The Times*, 31 December 1992.

20 *Carr-Glynn v Frearsons* [1999] Ch.326. It is suggested below (see paras 15–32 et seq.) that the decision of the Court of Appeal in this case may be open to question, but not on this point.

21 *White v Jones* [1995] 2 A.C. 207.

the draftsman, he will be liable to the beneficiary, or beneficiaries, for their loss. But there are other potential areas of difficulty.

1. Taking instructions

15–07 A draftsman who is asked to prepare a will for someone about whose capacity he has doubts, or in a case where he suspects that some kind of improper influence has been brought to bear upon the would-be testator, faces a dilemma. If he proceeds and prepares a will, and if the will is later set aside, an attempt may be made to claim from him the costs incurred in the challenge; if—on the other hand—he refuses to proceed, those who would have benefited under the will he has not made may allege that his conduct has caused them loss. The best course—when in doubt—is to seek the assistance of a doctor.

It was suggested in *Re Simpson*[22] that when making a will for an elderly and infirm testator, the draftsman should arrange for it to be witnessed and approved by a medical practitioner who satisfies himself as to the testator's capacity and makes a record of his examination and findings; and this "golden rule" was endorsed in *Re Morris, Special Trustees for Great Ormond Street Hospital v Rushin*.[23] If the draftsman follows this rule, it is hard to see how he can be criticised, provided that he tells the testator, or those around the testator, that he is doing this.[24] But there is a problem if the draftsman suggests a medical examination and the testator, and/or those close to the testator, oppose the suggestion. It may sometimes be hard to tell whether the testator is a completely free agent, and, in this kind of case it will be essential to keep a detailed written record, and advisable to write to the testator to record the advice which has been offered.

15–08 In the New Zealand cases of *Knox v Till*[25] and *Public Trustee v Till*,[26] it appears to be suggested that a draftsman who has been instructed to prepare a will should never refuse to do so, but this goes too far; it all depends on the circumstances. In the Canadian case of *Hall v Estate of Bruce Bennett*[27] an attorney refused to prepare a will for a dying testator from whom clear instructions could not be obtained: a claim against the attorney failed. In *Wood v Smith*,[28] a solicitor refused to proceed with the

[22] *Re Simpson* (1977) 121 S.J. 224. See also *Kenward v Adams*, *The Times*, 29 November 1975: both cases are decisions of Templeman J.

[23] *Re Morris, Special Trustees for Great Ormond Street Hospital v Rushin* [2001] W.T.L.R. 1137.

[24] In the New Zealand case of *Ryan v Public Trustee* [2000] 1 N.Z.L.R. 700, a non-legally qualified employee of the Public Trustee decided, without seeking a doctor's advice, not to proceed with the preparation of a will. He did not communicate his decision to the testatrix and he gave no advice about seeking a medical examination. The Public Trustee had to compensate those who would have benefitted under the will which had not been prepared.

[25] *Knox v Till* [2002] W.T.L.R. 1147 (will set aside for lack of capacity, costs of setting it aside were $430,000, costs claimed by beneficiaries from solicitors who prepared will, claim failed—see further reference to this case, and to *Public Trustee v Till*, in para.15–24 fn.106, below).

[26] *Public Trustee v Till* [2002] W.T.L.R. 1169 (same facts as *Knox v Till* above, but this claim, which also failed, was by personal representative, rather than beneficiaries).

[27] *Hall v Estate of Bruce Bennett* [2003] W.T.L.R. 827.

[28] *Wood v Smith* [1993] Ch.90. See also above at para.5–04.

preparation of a will, and no criticism was made of him. It is submitted that both these lawyers were right not to proceed. Furthermore, in *Sifri v Clough & Willis*,[29] a solicitor was held liable for part of the costs of a successful action to set aside a will on the ground that the testator had lacked knowledge and approval.[30]

Where testators are vulnerable, it is important that their wills are prepared by solicitors, or by properly qualified draftsmen. In *Fischer v Diffley*[31] a will was set aside for lack of capacity and for lack of knowledge and approval and one of the factors which told against it was that no solicitor had taken part in its preparation.[32] But, if wills are prepared by solicitors, or by other properly qualified draftsmen, they owe a duty to their clients to protect them. So, solicitors should be in a position to refuse to proceed, if they suspect that would-be testators either lack capacity or are being subjected to improper pressure.[33] A major source of difficulty in this area is that the Law Society has failed to lay down clear rules as to what is to happen if a solicitor suspects that a beneficiary is taking part in the will-making process and that the testator may not be a free agent. The hardest case to understand, in terms of the court's reaction to a solicitor's behaviour, in this regard, is *Burgess v Hawes*[34] where a will was refused probate for lack of capacity and lack of knowledge and approval, and the solicitor who prepared it received a mild rebuke from the judge at first instance. The solicitor deserved a rebuke, but not a mild one. The case then went to the Court of Appeal where there was an inexplicable hesitation about upholding the decision on the ground that the will had been prepared by someone described by that court as an "experienced and independent lawyer". Yet this solicitor had not only permitted the testatrix's daughter, who had been found by the trial judge to have been "the controlling force in the instructions given for the drafting of this will" to be present both when the instructions were given, and at the time of execution, but had kept no proper notes and had arranged for two of his partners to be executors. This was a will which disinherited the testatrix's son, and it was "suspicious" (i.e. it was a will in the preparation of which a beneficiary had been involved). Had the solicitor insisted on the beneficiary's absence while he was taking instructions, he would, almost certainly, have become aware of the testatrix's lack of capacity and the costs involved in setting this will aside would have been saved. This solicitor was fortunate to be treated as he was, but others would be unwise to follow his example. In any case, the approach taken in the Court of Appeal in *Burgess v Hawes*, to the effect that it will be assumed that a will prepared by a solicitor will have

[29] *Sifri v Clough & Willis* [2007] W.T.L.R. 1453.

[30] The claimants recovered only part of the costs because it was held that they had increased the costs of the action unnecessarily by challenging on grounds which had not been upheld.

[31] *Fischer v Diffley* [2014] W.T.L.R. 757.

[32] The will had been prepared by an accountant. Compare *Fischer* with *Re Devillebichot* [2013] W.T.L.R. 1701 where members of the testator's family arranged for the execution of his will as he lay dying and were criticised for not involving a solicitor in the process, but the will was upheld.

[33] Cases of undue influence are, of course, most likely to occur when the victims have limited capacity.

[34] *Burgess v Hawes* [2013] W.T.L.R. 453.

been properly prepared, even when there are clear indications that sensible precautions have not been taken, was not followed in *Re Ashkettle*[35] But *Ashkettle* then raises another issue, which is that some judges recognise that some solicitors tend to prepare wills in a hurry, and often for low fees, and this may also lead to their being treated with a degree of indulgence.[36] Proudman J remarked in *Re Boyes*[37] that not all solicitors are over-careful when they are concerned not to lose work. There is also a danger that if solicitor A, suspecting incapacity or improper pressure, quite reasonably refuses to go ahead with the preparation of will, then the would-be testator may be led away to another less scrupulous draftsman. There have been a number or examples of this, but a recent one is *Pearce v Beverley*.[38] The solicitor in this case acted correctly. He was not prepared to interview the testator while the would-be beneficiary was present, and then, following "the golden rule" he said that he was not willing to prepare a will until he had confirmation from a doctor as to the testator's mental capacity. The solicitor's services were then dispensed with and a will draftsman was instructed—he did go ahead, having allowed the beneficiary to remain in the room when instructions were being given. This will draftsman did not give evidence during the proceedings which led to the will which he had prepared being set aside on the grounds of lack of capacity and lack of knowledge and approval. There is no record as to whether any attempt was made to recover the costs of these proceedings from him, but he had certainly laid himself open to such a claim.

In *Couwenbergh v Valkova*,[39] in *Re Tociapski*[40] and in *Schomberg v Taylor*[41] wills prepared by solicitors were all set aside, but the solicitors escaped criticism. Another case where a solicitor seems to have been fortunate is *Re D*,[42] where a will which should never have been made was revoked by the making of a statutory will. Another borderline case, where the solicitors were not criticised, but could well have been, was *Vegetarian Society v Scott*.[43] The dispute here concerned the testator's capacity, but instructions for the will were taken by a bank employee and then forwarded to a firm

[35] *Re Ashkettle* [2013] W.T.L.R. 1331, where a judge at first instance, who would have been bound by a decision of the Court of Appeal, distinguished *Burgess* "on its facts". *Burgess* may also be contrasted with *Walters v Smee* [2009] W.T.L.R. 521, see para.15–09, below.

[36] *Scammell v Farmer* [2008] W.T.L.R. 1261 is an example of a solicitor who escaped criticism when he permitted a beneficiary to take part in the preparation of a will. He did not charge a high fee, and was treated leniently during the proceedings to set the will aside.

[37] *Re Boyes* [2013] EWHC 4027 (Ch).

[38] *Pearce v Beverley* [2014] W.T.L.R. 85.

[39] *Couwenbergh v Valkova* [2008] EWHC 2451. The will here was originally granted probate, and was set aside only after a series of cases; see discussion in Chap.5 at para.5–41. The solicitors who prepared the will did not see the testatrix, but took instructions from the beneficiary.

[40] *Re Tociapski* [2013] W.T.L.R. 1821.

[41] *Schomberg v Taylor* [2013] W.T.L.R. 1413. The solicitor permitted another retired solicitor to remain in the room while she took instructions from the testatrix. It was clear that the retired solicitor was linked to the beneficiary, and that there was no good reason for him to take any part in what was happening. The retired solicitor chose not to take part in the proceedings when the will was later set aside, so he did not have to explain himself.

[42] *Re D* [2012] Ch.57, this case was discussed in Chap.5 at para.5–14.

[43] *Vegetarian Society v Scott* [2014] W.T.L.R. 525.

of solicitors who, as far as can be ascertained, never themselves had any direct contact with the client. It is submitted that this is not a satisfactory way to proceed.

The cases just mentioned are ones where the solicitors were treated as though they were not to blame for the creation of wills which were later refused probate. But there have been cases where the judges have been less indulgent. In *Re Spalding*[44] solicitors who prepared three wills for a ninety-five year old woman, whom they had been warned might lack capacity, who took instructions which they were aware came from her window cleaner to benefit him, who did not properly investigate the terms of the woman's earlier wills, and who were executors under the wills they prepared, *were* criticised for their conduct when the wills were refused probate. In *Re Wilson, Turner v Phythian*[45] the trial judge directed thinly veiled criticism at a solicitor who was introduced to the testatrix by the beneficiary, and who permitted the beneficiary to be present when the will was being drafted.[46] **15–09**

Then there are two further cases where the draftsmen received clear rebukes. In *Re Key*,[47] a solicitor suggested to an eighty-nine year-old farmer whose wife had just died, that he should make a new will. The solicitor allowed the farmer's daughters to find out about the terms of his existing will (which favoured his sons) and took hurried instructions for the making of a new will, knowing that the daughters were playing a significant part in the process. He did not follow the "golden rule" of instructing a doctor and did not keep proper notes of what had happened. As Briggs J put it, when he refused probate of the new will on the grounds that the testator lacked capacity and that he did not know or approve of its contents:

> "I have tried, but without success, to understand how. . .[the solicitor] could have thought it to be sensible advice [that a new will should be prepared] to give at that time,. . .[the solicitor's actions transformed] the formerly close relationship between [the testator's] sons and daughters into one of mutual suspicion, recrimination and distrust. . .a significant element of responsibility for this tragic state of affairs lies with [the solicitor]."

In *Walters v Smee*[48] the judge, when pronouncing against a will made a month before the testatrix's death, on the ground that she lacked capacity, said this:

> "The will was duly prepared and executed. [The probate clerk who prepared it] said in her evidence that [the testatrix] was lucid, describing her as literally perfect. . .I did consider [the probate clerk's] evidence to be defensive though, and understandably so. . .I am surprised

[44] *Re Spalding* [2014] All E.R. (D) 73.
[45] *Re Wilson, Turner v Phythian* [2013] W.T.L.R. 899.
[46] Another case involving mild criticism is *Hubbard v Scott* [2012] W.T.L.R. 29 (Proudman J).
[47] *Re Key* [2010] 1 W.L.R. 2020.
[48] *Walters v Smee* [2009] W.T.L.R. 521 at paras 106 and 108.

that [she] did not enquire further as to why the previous will was being changed. . .In my judgment, [the testatrix] was ill-served on this occasion by [the probate clerk], who should have looked into the matter, as an experienced probate clerk, rather more cautiously in the light of the principles of law and practice with which she was well acquainted.

I am also surprised. . .that she did not enlist the services of a doctor to assess [the testatrix's] medical condition formally. Had she done so, who knows where we might be today?"

The last sentence carries the implication that, had the probate clerk done her job properly, the will which was now being successfully challenged might not have been made, and that, had it not been, the costs of having it set aside would have been saved.[49]

Given that a claim against a draftsman by those who incurred costs in setting aside a purported will, will be heard separately from the action to set the will aside,[50] such a claim may well not be reported, even if the challenge to the will itself is. Accordingly, it is hard to say how many cases there have been where those who have successfully challenged wills have attempted to recover their costs from the draftsmen.[51]

2. Cases of delay

15–10 There have been several cases since *White v Jones* which show that, once a solicitor has been instructed to draft a will, he should proceed

[49] There are significant parallels between the conduct of the solicitor in *Burgess v Hawes* (see para.15–08, above) and that of the probate clerk in *Walters v Smee*. Yet there was no criticism of the solicitor in *Burgess*, almost the contrary. The attitude of the court in *Burgess* is almost impossible to explain or to justify.

[50] Suppose that T dies leaving an earlier will and a later will. The later will is challenged and the challenge succeeds. The challengers may recover their costs from the propounders of the later will; but, if they do not, they may wish to issue proceedings against the draftsman of the later "will". He will usually not be a party to the first set of proceedings and the action against him can only begin once the challengers have succeeded in the validity proceedings. Whether a claim against the draftsman should be issued by the challengers themselves, who may be the beneficiaries under the earlier will, or by the personal representatives, is an issue which is discussed at para.15–24, below.

[51] Other cases where wills were successfully challenged and where those who challenged them might then have considered claiming costs from the draftsmen are *Buckenham v Dickinson* [2000] W.T.L.R. 1083 (client very deaf and almost blind, instructions fed to solicitor by wife); *d'Eye v Avery* [2001] W.T.L.R. 227 (will prepared by a bank for a man who had had a massive stroke and for whom a receiver had been appointed); *Richards v Allan* [2001] W.T.L.R. 1031 (solicitor had subconsciously viewed beneficiary, rather than testatrix, as his client); *Re Reynolds* [2005] All E.R. (D) 70 (draftsman took instructions from beneficiary); *Re Loxston* [2006] W.T.L.R. 1567 (draftsman prepared will for woman who was subject to a registered EPA and incapable of giving full instructions). In both *Re Key* and *Walters v Smee* the judges who set the wills aside came close to suggesting that those who had borne the costs of the contentious probate proceedings should attempt to recover them from the draftsmen. An earlier case concerning draftsmen who ought to have paid the costs of setting aside a will which should never have been prepared is *Re Stott* [1980] 1 W.L.R. 246, see Chap.5, para.5–37 fn.156 (solicitors had no direct contact with testatrix, but took instructions from a go-between, who happened to be the same person who appeared in the case of *Re Davey* [1981] 1W.L.R. 164).

with reasonable speed.[52] In *Bacon v Howard Kennedy*[53] solicitors were instructed to draft a will and failed to proceed. The would-be testator died eight years later. The person who would have benefited under the will sued the solicitors, who alleged both that there had been undue influence by the beneficiary and that the claim was statute-barred because the cause of action arose at the time when the will should have been drafted, and not at the date of death. Neither of these defences succeeded. It was not explained why the would-be testator took no action during the eight–year period. He could have instructed other solicitors, but did not. This shows how careful solicitors need to be: if they have not done what they have undertaken to do, they cannot then assume that their retainer has ceased simply because they do not hear from their client. A difficult case is *Feltham v Bouskell*[54] where a solicitor was instructed to prepare a will for a 90 year old childless widow, but did not proceed with its preparation. The problem here is that the instructions came from the beneficiary and the solicitor may have suspected that the testatrix lacked capacity and/or that there was the possibility of undue influence. He was held liable for the loss suffered by the beneficiary.[55]

Hooper v Fynmores[56] is more straightforward. The solicitor made **15–11** an appointment to see the testator in hospital for the execution of his will, which the solicitor failed to keep owing to his own ill-health. The deceased died without having executed the will and the solicitor was held liable in negligence to the disappointed beneficiary. The solicitor was not entitled to argue that his delay was reasonable—albeit caused by his own hospitalisation—when he could perfectly easily have arranged for the testator's signature to be attested by someone else.[57] *Fynmores* can be contrasted with *X v Woollcombe Yonge*[58] where the would-be testatrix died in hospital before her will was executed, but the delay was held not to be unreasonable. The solicitor had seen the testatrix in hospital, and had then prepared a will which would have been ready for execution eight days later. The solicitor had had no reason to believe that the testatrix was going to die within the week. In *Trusted v Clifford Chance*[59] the testator knew that the solicitor was going on sabbatical leave and specifi-

[52] What is reasonable will depend on the circumstances. In *White v Jones* [1995] 2 A.C. 207 the will instructions were received on 17 July, but an appointment to visit the testator on 17 September was too late: he died on 14 September.

[53] *Bacon v Howard Kennedy* [2000] W.T.L.R. 169.

[54] *Feltham v Bouskell* [2013] W.T.L.R. 1363.

[55] The solicitor in this case seems to have been in a dilemma. Had he simply refused to make the will, and had he said that he suspected lack of capacity, there was a good chance that the beneficiary would have found some other draftsman to prepare it. Shopping around by beneficiaries to find easy-going will draftsmen is a problem in this area, see para.15–08, above. Having said this, if the solicitor did suspect that the testatrix was not capable of making a will, he should have informed both the beneficiary and the testatrix, but should not have simply failed to proceed. The lack of protection afforded to vulnerable testators (see Chap.5) made this solicitor's position unenviable.

[56] *Hooper v Fynmores* [2001] W.T.L.R. 1019.

[57] See also *Smith v Claremont Haynes & Co*, *The Times*, 3 September 1991.

[58] *X v Woollcombe Yonge* [2000] W.T.L.R. 301.

[59] *Trusted v Clifford Chance* [2000] W.T.L.R. 1219.

cally told him that he was happy to wait until the solicitor returned to the office before his will was drafted. Although the testator died before this happened, the solicitor was held not to be negligent because he had warned his client about the delay and the client had himself chosen to proceed on this basis.[60]

3. Supervision of Execution

15–12 Not all clients will be able to attend the draftsman's office so that he may supervise the execution of the will he has prepared. In *Esterhuizen v Allied Dunbar*[61] Longmore J suggested that a draftsman should witness every will he has prepared, either in his office or at the testator's home. Although this may well be the counsel of perfection, it is not always practical.[62] Accordingly, the decision in *Gray v Richards Butler*[63]—which emphasises that the correct approach is to decide whether the client is capable of handling the execution himself—is to be preferred. Having said that, if the draftsman does send the will to the client for execution at home, it is incumbent upon him to provide the testator with clear instructions regarding execution; and maybe the draftsman should even require the testator to confirm—when returning the will—that the instructions have been followed.[64]

4. *Animus Testandi*

15–13 In *Corbett v Newey*[65] the Court of Appeal held that, where a testatrix executed a will subject to a condition which was not expressed on its face, the testatrix lacked *animus testandi* and so the will was invalid. This was another example of a solicitor's negligence. The testatrix had made it clear to her solicitor that she did not want her will to take effect until two inter vivos dispositions had been completed. She executed the will but did not date it, believing that it would not take effect until it was dated.[66] She made it clear to the solicitor what she had done, and he should have realised (but did not) that the dating of the will was irrelevant as to its taking effect. When the will was declared invalid—on the ground that the testatrix had lacked *animus testandi* at the time of its execution—those who would have benefited under it, and who did not benefit under an earlier will which now took effect, brought proceedings in negligence against the

[60] See *Smolinski v Mitchell* (1995) 10 B.C.L.R. (3d), Supreme Court of British Columbia—delay not the fault of solicitor.

[61] *Esterhuizen v Allied Dunbar* [1998] 2 F.L.R. 668.

[62] And, even when followed, things can, of course, still go wrong, see *Marley v Rawlings* [2015] A.C. 129.

[63] *Gray v Richards Butler* [2000] W.T.L.R. 143 (and [2001] W.T.L.R. 625). See also *Seale v Perry* [1982] V.R. 193 (Supreme Court of Victoria).

[64] See *Humblestone v Martin Tolhurst Partnership* [2004] P.N.L.R. 26 (will sent to client for execution and then returned to solicitors for safekeeping; solicitors negligent in failing to notice that, though will had been dated, and witnessed, it had not been signed by testator).

[65] *Corbett v Newey* [1998] Ch.57, see above, para.5–02.

[66] There is no statutory requirement that a will be dated. In practice, wills are dated so that it is clear on the face of them when they were executed and which is the testator's last will.

solicitor. These proceedings were settled on payment to the claimants of a sum representing what they would have obtained under this invalid will, together with interest.[67]

5. Marriage and divorce

In general, a will is revoked by the testator's marriage, unless it appears from the will that the testator did not intend the will, or a particular disposition within it, to be revoked by the marriage.[68] In *Hall v Meyrick*[69] it was alleged that a solicitor had been negligent because he did not draw to the attention of the deceased and the claimant—who wished to confer benefits upon one another—that, if they married, their marriage would revoke their wills. They did subsequently marry and the deceased died leaving considerable property and without having executed a new will. Although the action was dismissed for failure to plead the retainer properly, it has to be borne in mind that the case was decided before *White v Jones*. **15–14**

Solicitors who are instructed by a client who wants a divorce also need to advise that client to consider making a will—or a new will—and to sever any beneficial joint tenancies which may exist in the matrimonial home or other property. Section 18A (1) of the Wills Act 1837[70]—which provides that, on dissolution or annulment of a marriage, any property given to a former spouse shall pass as if the former spouse had died—applies only once the decree absolute has been obtained.

Draftsmen must also be careful when making wills for married or cohabiting couples with children from previous unions. In general, it would seem to be appropriate in such cases for properties to be held as beneficial tenants in common, so that provision can be made both for the survivor and for the children. In such cases, draftsmen may be liable in negligence if they do not give advice about the possibility of severing beneficial joint tenancies as part of the will-making process. **15–15**

Hines v Willans[71] illustrates problems a will draftsman may face if he makes a new will for one spouse, X, which alters the provision for the other spouse, Y, from that contained in previous wills made for each of them. Where there is a continuing professional relationship between the solicitor and Y—which will be a question of fact—it will be a breach of that relationship to prepare a new will for X which affects the entitlement of Y.[72]

[67] This claim in negligence is not reported—but the outcome is reported in *Corbett v Bond Pearce* [2001] 3 All E.R. 769, a case which represents a later stage in the saga. *Corbett v Bond Pearce* is discussed below, see para.15–25.
[68] Wills Act 1837 s.18 as substituted by Administration of Justice Act 1982 s.18(1). See above, Chap.7, paras 7–05 et seq.
[69] *Hall v Meyrick* [1957] 2 All E.R. 722, CA.
[70] See above paras 14–28 et seq.
[71] *Hines v Willans* [2000] W.T.L.R. 299, C.A.
[72] The solicitor was ordered to pay £115,000 plus interest and costs to Y, representing the sum of money which Y had to pay to X's children in return for being able to prove the earlier will. The Court of Appeal stressed that the facts of the case were quite exceptional.

III. RECTIFICATION AND CONSTRUCTION

15–16 The general principles which apply to the rectification and to the construction, or interpretation, of wills were considered in Chapter 10, and the changes effected by s.20 of the Administration of Justice Act 1982 (the rectification section) and s.21 (the interpretation section) were discussed there. Each of these sections has the effect of saving will draftsmen from potential negligence actions, because each can put right what has gone wrong.

A. RECTIFICATION

1. Where draftsman admits negligence

15–17 *Wordingham v Royal Exchange Trust Co Ltd*,[73] *Re Segelman*[74] and *Marley v Rawlings*[75] are all cases where solicitors made errors in drafting or preparing wills and then admitted that they had made mistakes; in each case it appears that the solicitors assisted in an application to the court for rectification.[76] If a solicitor admits that he has made a mistake and assists in the application for rectification, he is engaged in a form of damage-limitation exercise. He will usually have to pay all the costs incurred in relation to the rectification application, but these costs will be significantly less than the damages and costs which he or his insurers would have had to pay to disappointed beneficiaries if the will had not been rectified.[77]

2. Relationship between rectification and negligence

15–18 It seems that all rectification cases involving professional will draftsmen are cases where the draftsmen have been negligent. Rectification can be obtained only if there has been *either* a clerical error *or* a failure to understand the testator's instructions. A clerical error—by a person paid to draft a will—must, by definition, constitute negligence. In the same way, it is suggested that a failure by a professional will draftsman to understand a testator's instructions will also constitute negligence. It is the duty of

[73] *Wordingham v Royal Exchange Trust Co Ltd* [1992] Ch.412, see above, para.10–05.

[74] *Re Segelman* [1985] 1 W.L.R. 905, see above, para.10–06.

[75] *Marley v Rawlings* [2015] A.C. 129, see above, para.10–08.

[76] *Re Ryan* [2011] W.T.L.R. 1029 is another case where the solicitors, probably encouraged by their insurers, applied for rectification.

[77] In *Corbett v Bond Pearce* [2001] 3 All E.R. 769, it is reported that the defendant's insurers had to pay £275,000 to the disappointed beneficiaries i.e. the full amount of their claim plus interest. There would, in addition, have been the legal costs. *Marley v Rawlings* [2015] A.C. 129 is unusual in that the costs in the contested rectification proceedings would have been far greater than the amount at stake under the contested will. But the outcome was important, and the decision may well have a significant long term effect. It seems probable that those making the rectification application in *Marley* received encouragement from others who were concerned about the decision in the case.

a professional will draftsman to understand the instructions he has been given and, if he is not certain about his instructions, he should seek clarification or further instructions from the testator. In *Walker v Medlicott*[78] it appears to have been assumed by the Court of Appeal that it was possible to have a rectifiable but "non-negligent misunderstanding" between a testatrix and her solicitor. This led the court to hold that the defendant had not acted negligently, but that the claimant had a rectification claim which it was his duty to bring before embarking on negligence proceedings, because otherwise he would not be mitigating his loss.[79] It is respectfully suggested that this is incorrect. A misunderstanding can be rectified only if it amounts to a failure to understand instructions. A failure by a professional draftsman to understand instructions must constitute negligence. By contrast with *Walker v Medlicott*, the decision in *Horsfall v Haywards*[80] is consistent with the approach now being suggested, i.e. that it will be possible to rectify a professionally-drawn will only if the draftsman has been negligent.[81]

Where a professional will draftsman denies negligence, but a would-be beneficiary believes that he has been negligent and also believes that the error may be rectifiable, the appropriate course of action is for the would-be beneficiary simultaneously to bring a negligence action against the draftsman and to apply for rectification.[82] This approach was endorsed in *Grattan v McNaughton*[83] where the judge was scathing about the fact that rectification proceedings had been brought separately from negligence proceedings, on the same facts. In *Horsfall v Haywards*,[84] the defendant solicitors admitted, eventually, that they failed to draft the testator's will in accordance with his instructions. It was held that rectification proceedings did not have to be brought before negligence proceedings: partly because the rectification proceedings would, if successful, have required **15–19**

[78] *Walker v Medlicott* [1999] 1 W.L.R. 727. See Sir Christopher Slade at p.738.

[79] See below under double recovery, paras 15–22 et seq., and cf. *Pilkington v Wood* [1953] Ch.770.

[80] *Horsfall v Haywards* [1999] 1 F.L.R. 1182.

[81] See also *Grattan v McNaughton* [2001] W.T.L.R. 1305, where a widow brought separate negligence and rectification proceedings and failed in both; she succeeded in a claim for family provision.

[82] See further *Hawkins on the Construction of Wills*, 5th edn (London: Sweet & Maxwell, 2000), pp.8–14. If the draftsman admits that he has been negligent, and if his error can be rectified, it will be in his interest to apply for rectification, or, at least, to co-operate in a rectification application brought by someone else. In both *Sprackling v Sprackling* [2009] W.T.L.R. 897 and in *Martin v Triggs Turner Barton* [2009] W.T.L.R. 1339 it was alleged that solicitors had failed to understand their instructions, though in both cases they denied this. In each of the two cases it was held that they had failed to understand instructions, so, as it turned out, they would have saved themselves trouble by agreeing that they had been negligent and applying for rectification. The will in *Spracking* was rectified despite the solicitor's opposition. The solicitor in *Triggs Turner Barton* must be faulted for not keeping a proper attendance note. But these cases do illustrate a danger. A draftsman might possibly be tempted to agree to rectification in order to avoid a negligence claim, even though he does not believe it to be justified. This is all the more reason for instituting simultaneous negligence and rectification proceedings.

[83] *Grattan v McNaughton* [2001] W.T.L.R. 1305. Both the negligence proceedings and the rectification proceedings were dismissed. The will was fairly straightforward and all the evidence suggested that the testator was perfectly capable of understanding its terms and effect.

[84] *Horsfall v Haywards* [1999] 1 F.L.R. 1182.

the testator's widow—who had returned to her native Canada—to refund the net proceeds of sale of the testator's house, which she had made clear she would not be willing to do; and partly because the solicitors who had drafted the will and acted in the administration of the estate had neglected to advise the claimants of the possibility of bringing rectification proceedings before the expiration of the statutory time-limit[85] and before the net proceeds of sale had been remitted, wrongly, to the widow in Canada.[86]

B. CONSTRUCTION

15–20 The two possible approaches to the construction of wills—the literal approach and the intentional approach—were considered in Chapter 10. The literal approach consists in giving to the words in a will an "ordinary" or "correct" meaning; a meaning which the testator did not intend the words to bear.[87] *NSPCC v Scottish NSPCC*,[88] *Re Sykes*,[89] *Re Lewis's Will Trusts*[90] and *Chichester Diocesan Fund & Board of Finance v Simpson*[91] are all cases where some or all of the testator's property passed to persons whom he did not intend to benefit. All these cases were decided before *White v Jones*[92] and the beneficiary whom the testator intended to benefit appeared to have no cause of action; but, given that these are all cases where the wills were professionally drafted, he would now appear to have one.[93] If the facts of *Re Lewis* were to recur today, and if the court were to come to the same decision, i.e. that the son did not take anything under the gift of "my freehold farm", there is a high probability that the son would, under the principle in *White v Jones*, sue the solicitors who drafted the will. Happily for solicitors, the changes made to the interpretation rules by s.21 of the Administration of Justice Act 1982[94] mean that

[85] Six months from the date of the grant of representation, unless the court gives permission under Administration of Justice Act 1982 s.20(1)(b) to bring proceedings out of time.

[86] Quaere whether this would have been a rectification case anyway: it could be that it was a case of a failure to implement, as opposed to a failure to understand, the testator's instructions.

[87] In all cases where the literal meaning differs from the meaning intended by the testator—and this means in (virtually) all cases where there is a dispute as to the meaning of the words—the literal meaning must, by definition, be one which the testator did not intend the words to bear. See above, Chap.10.

[88] *NSPCC v Scottish NSPCC* [1915] A.C. 207, see above paras 10–58 and 10–59.

[89] *Re Sykes* [1940] 4 All E.R. 10 "all my horses", see above para.10–56.

[90] *Re Lewis's Will Trusts* [1985] 1 W.L.R. 102 "my freehold farm", see above para.10–57.

[91] *Chichester Diocesan Fund & Board of Finance v Simpson* [1944] A.C. 341 "charitable or benevolent objects", see above, para.10–78.

[92] *White v Jones* [1995] 2 A.C. 207.

[93] The only one of these cases in which an action was brought against the solicitors was the *Chichester* case. This was because the solicitors had distributed part of the estate to the beneficiaries whom the testator had intended to benefit—the charities—whereas it was held by the House of Lords that the gift to the charities was ineffective and so the estate passed to the next of kin, the Australian cousins. The charities were not able to bring successful actions against the solicitors claiming the loss which they had incurred as a result of the way in which the will had been drafted.

[94] See above, Chap.10.

the court should now interpret wills in such a way as to seek the testator's intention with the result that the son in *Re Lewis* would not now lose his intended benefit. In other words, the effect of s.21 will sometimes be to save draftsmen from negligence actions. The result is to be welcomed.[95] Given that it is suggested that cases such as *Chichester Diocesan Fund & Board of Finance v Simpson* would no longer be followed today,[96] it is not necessary to discuss whether an action would lie, on behalf of a charity, were the court to decide that a gift for "benevolent purposes" was not charitable.[97]

RSPCA v Sharp[98] is a recent case which appears, oddly, to have taken **15–21** no account of s.21 of the Administration of Justice Act. Here, there was a dispute as to whether the will was intended to be especially tax-efficient, in which case it would favour a charity, or whether it was meant to benefit the testator's brother, in which case it would involve the payment of inheritance tax. The judge at first instance held in favour of the brother, but the Court of Appeal reversed him. What seems obvious in this case is that the will was badly drafted. Whatever was intended, it should have been clear. The draftsman should either have applied for rectification, or should have explained what the words he had used were intended to mean. Either of these approaches would have saved trouble, and would have avoided a result whereby the interpretation of the will became a question of guesswork. It is not clear why, there having been no application for rectification, the draftsman was not called to explain the meaning of the words used.[99]

It was suggested in Chapter 10[100] that no professionally drafted will should cause construction problems; it is the duty of a draftsman to understand the testator's instructions and to draft the will in such a way as to carry them out. This means that if a construction problem reaches court, prima facie, the cost of the proceedings should be borne by the professional draftsman. Having said this, s.21(2) of the Administration of Justice

[95] The position in the nineteenth-century, when the literal approach to the interpretation of wills was at its zenith, was bizarre. One set of lawyers (solicitors) would draft wills for testators and then another set of lawyers (mainly barristers) would attempt to find fault with them and to invalidate dispositions made by them. In cases where dispositions in wills were declared invalid, the original draftsmen did not suffer. The only people who suffered were the intended beneficiaries. One lawyer would ask the testator to pay for the drafting of his will, and another lawyer would expect the estate to pay for upsetting it. An interesting example of a throwback case is *Sammut v Manzi* [2009] 1 W.L.R. 1834, an appeal to the Privy Council from the Bahamas. *Sammut* concerned a negligently drafted will, but the approach to construction was literal (s.21 of the AJA did not apply in the Bahamas) and nobody mentioned the fact that the draftsman must have been at fault.

[96] See above, para.10–79.

[97] The gift in *Chichester* was to "such charitable or benevolent objects as my executors may select". If such a gift were to fail after *White v Jones*, who could demonstrate loss? "Charity" would be the loser; it is submitted that the Attorney General could probably bring an action on behalf of "charity".

[98] *RSPCA v Sharp* [2011] 1 W.L.R. 980.

[99] It is possible that the draftsman had attempted to do what he could not do, and had tried both to benefit the brother *and* create an ultra tax-efficient will. But, if this was so, he should have been called on to explain. It would have assisted in the attempt at construction. See note in All E.R. Rev. 2011 at 431–433.

[100] See above, paras 10–60 et seq. Most of the cases referred to at this point in Chap.10 appear to have involved negligence by professional will draftsmen.

Act 1982 should make it possible to put things right much more speedily and much more simply than was the case in the past.

IV. DOUBLE RECOVERY

15–22 Cases like *White v Jones*—where the person who was supposed to draft a will has either failed to draft it, has not drafted it quickly enough, has failed to ensure that it was properly executed, or has failed to include within it effective dispositions reflecting the testator's intention—all involve double recovery. In *White v Jones* itself, the testator intended to make a will in favour of his daughters which was not executed in time; a previous will took effect in favour of other members of the testator's family. The daughters recovered damages from the solicitors; so the ultimate effect was that the daughters received from the solicitors (or their insurers) the entitlement they should have received from their father, whereas someone else in the family received from the estate benefits which the testator did not intend them to have.

1. Manufactured claims

15–23 There seems little doubt that some judges are concerned about double recovery and there may be a reluctance to apply *White v Jones* because its application may lead to situations where members of a family make false allegations of negligence by will draftsmen in order to obtain double recovery. There are references in *Walker v Medlicott*[101] to the "obvious possibility of abuse in this class of case".[102]

2. When estate itself suffers loss

15–24 The principle in *White v Jones* applies only to cases where the estate has suffered no loss and so cannot itself make a claim.[103] As Lord Goff put it in *White v Jones:*

> "In the forefront stands the extraordinary fact that, if such a duty is not recognised, the only persons who might have a valid claim (*i.e.* the testator and his estate) have suffered no loss, and the only person who has suffered a loss (*i.e.* the disappointed beneficiary) has no claim. . .it can therefore be said that, if the solicitor owes no duty to the intended beneficiaries, there is a lacuna in the law which needs to be filled."[104]

[101] See above, para.15–18.

[102] See *Walker v Medlicott* [1999] 1 W.L.R. 727 at 744 where Simon Brown LJ says that "there is always the risk of a family manufacturing a negligence claim in order to enhance the value of the estate I hasten to say that there has been no suggestion whatever in the present case of any such deceit".

[103] See A. Tettenborn [2005] Conv. 288 and *Daniels v Thompson* [2004] P.N.L.R. 638.

[104] *White v Jones* [1995] 2 A.C. 207 at 259–260.

An example of a case to which the principle in *White v Jones* is not, therefore, applicable is *Worby v Rosser*[105] in which proceedings were brought against a solicitor by three beneficiaries under a will which had been made in 1983. The solicitor had prepared a later will which, after contested proceedings, had been refused probate on the ground that the testator lacked capacity. The claimants sought to recover from the solicitor the substantial costs which had been incurred in successfully resisting probate of the later will. They alleged that the solicitor owed them a duty of care to ensure that the testator did not execute a will (the later will) at a time when he lacked testamentary capacity. The Court of Appeal rejected the claim on the ground that the estate had borne the costs and that if, owing to a breach of duty by the solicitor, the estate had suffered a loss, it was for the estate to sue the solicitor. There was no need for a *White v Jones* type action in this case.[106]

Corbett v Bond Pearce[107] is—in principle—a similar case. This is the third case in the *Corbett v Newey*[108] cycle. The first was *Corbett v Newey* itself, in which the will the testatrix had intended to make was set aside because of her lack of *animus testandi*.[109] She had not intended to execute that will until after she had made inter vivos dispositions of two farms which she owned. The second case was unreported, but involved a successful claim by the intended beneficiaries against the solicitors who had failed to ensure that the will was valid; they recovered the net value of the estate before the deduction of the costs of the probate action. The third case involved a claim by the administrator[110] of the testatrix's estate for those probate action costs.[111] Although this claim succeeded at first instance,[112] it failed in the Court of Appeal because the residue was going to pass to persons to whom the testatrix had not intended it to pass, for whom it was a windfall benefit. The duties owed by the solicitors to the testatrix in contract and to **15–25**

[105] *Worby v Rosser* [1999] Lloyd's Rep. P.N. 972. See also *Otter v Church Adams Tatham & Co* [1953] Ch.280; *McLellan v Fletcher* [1987] N.L.J. 593; *Lynne v Gordon Doctors and Walton* (1991) 135 S.J. 29.

[106] Having said this, it is not always self-evident whether the claim should be brought by the beneficiaries or by the estate. In *Sifri v Clough & Willis* [2007] W.T.L.R. 1453, it appears to have been one of the beneficiaries, and not the estate, who successfully claimed her costs from a solicitor who had prepared a will which had been refused probate. It appears that in *Sifri* letters of administration to the estate had not been obtained. The New Zealand case of *Knox v Till* [2002] W.T.L.R. 1147 seems to follow *Worby v Rosser* in suggesting that the estate should sue, but when (shortly afterwards), in *Public Trustee v Till* [2002] W.T.L.R. 1169, the estate did sue, it failed. It would be fair to say that there is some confusion in this area and that care should be taken. There may even be some cases where it might be best to join the estate and the beneficiaries as parties, to avoid the *Till* outcome(s). In *Chappell v Somers & Blake* [2004] Ch.19, Neuberger J held that an executrix had a right to claim damages from solicitors for prolonged delay in proving the estate; she would then account to the beneficiaries. The beneficiaries were willing to be joined as parties and he thought it would be best if they were so joined.

[107] *Corbett v Bond Pearce* [2001] 3 All E.R. 769.

[108] *Corbett v Newey* [1998] Ch.57, see above, paras 5–02 and 15–13.

[109] See above, para.5–02.

[110] He was an administrator with the will annexed. The surviving executors had renounced probate and he, the administrator, was entitled to half the residue.

[111] The costs amounted to some £150,000.

[112] *Corbett v Bond Pearce* [2000] Lloyd's Rep P.N. 805.

her intended beneficiaries in tort were not inconsistent, but complementary. Once the solicitors had compensated the intended beneficiaries, they could not be asked to compensate the estate, as representing the testatrix, for what was essentially the same loss.[113] Sir Christopher Slade said that he had "not found [this] an easy case"[114]; but it is hard to see how the court could have come to any other conclusion.[115]

3. Multiple claims

15–26 A trickier case is *Clarke v Bruce Lance*.[116] The testator—who owned a garage—instructed his solicitors to prepare a will under which, inter alia, he devised the garage to trustees to hold on trust for sale so that if his wife survived him the income should be paid to her for life and, on her death, the trustees were to hold the capital on trust for his son absolutely.[117] The testator's wife was the residuary beneficiary under his will. After the testator had executed his will, he leased the garage to a tenant and later still he granted to the tenant an option to purchase the garage for a fixed price—the option to be exercisable by notice within six months of the death of the survivor of the testator and his wife.[118] The testator died before his wife. While the testator's wife was still alive, his son sued the solicitors, alleging a breach of a duty of care both to his father and to him on the ground that they had failed to advise the testator that the grant of a *fixed price* option was an uncommercial and misconceived transaction. The solicitors applied to have the son's statement of claim struck out as disclosing no reasonable cause of action and they succeeded before the Court of Appeal. It was suggested in the Court of Appeal that, had the claimant son succeeded, the solicitors would have been at risk of having to pay damages twice over—double recovery.[119] *Bruce Lance* is confusing because, had the case been properly argued, it would have been seen that it involved not one, but two, potential claims. One of these claims belonged to the son, but he, mistakenly, attempted to bring the other. The problem was that those advising the son do not appear to have understood the rule in *Lawes v Bennett*[120]: that a gift in a will is adeemed by the exercise of an option granted subsequent to the execution of the will. This meant that, if the tenant exercised his option (and it is virtually certain

[113] Technically, the losses were not the same. The legal costs which the administrator was seeking to recover were an actual sum not available for distribution to the beneficiaries under the earlier will because of the solicitor's negligence. The disappointed beneficiaries recovered a notional sum which should have passed to them under the later will had it not been for the solicitors' negligence. In substance, however, the two sums represented the same monetary loss.

[114] *Corbett v Bond Pearce* [2001] 3 All E.R. 769, 782.

[115] The last, or last reported, case in the *Corbett v Newey* cycle appears to be *Corbett v Bond Pearce (damages)* [2006] W.T.L.R. 967; this deals with quantum, but also sets out the history of the various proceedings.

[116] *Clarke v Bruce Lance* [1988] 1 W.L.R. 881.

[117] This is a very slightly simplified version of the facts.

[118] i.e. it could be exercised only *after* the testator and his wife had both died.

[119] *Clarke v Bruce Lance* [1988] 1 W.L.R. 881 at 889E.

[120] *Lawes v Bennett* [1785] 1 Cox. 167—see above Chap.14, paras 14–46 et seq.

that he would exercise it when the testator's wife died), the proceeds of the exercise of the option would pass not to the devisee (the son) but to the residuary beneficiary's (the wife's) estate. The son's attempt to bring proceedings for negligence against the solicitors was misconceived because he, as the devisee of the garage,[121] was not in any way affected by the fact that his father had granted a *fixed price* option. Given the rule in *Lawes v Bennett*, the fact that the option was exercisable at a fixed price was, as far as he was concerned, irrelevant: as devisee, he would receive no part of the proceeds.

The correct course of action should have been (i) for the testator's estate (the residuary beneficiary of which was the widow) to have brought an action against the solicitors on the ground that they had been negligent in failing to warn the testator about the dangers of granting a fixed price option, while (ii) the son brought a separate action on the ground that the solicitors had failed to warn his father about the rule in *Lawes v Bennett*, i.e. they had failed to warn him that the exercise of the option would mean that the devise to the son would be adeemed and that the son would get nothing under it.[122] **15–27**

V. OTHER PROBLEM AREAS

There are several other potential problems in this field, but it seems that some judges are less enthusiastic than others about the approach in *White v Jones* and some may be more concerned than others about double recovery. Some areas of difficulty need to be examined. **15–28**

1. Suggesting to testators what provisions need to be included in their wills

Is it the duty of a professional will draftsman to suggest to a testator that he should include a particular provision in his will? Suppose that a testator informs the draftsman that he wants to leave his entire estate to his wife but fails to consider what would happen if (say) his wife predeceases him. It may be that the testator's wife is younger than he is and the testator simply does not consider the possibility that she might die before him. Is it then the draftsman's duty to point out the possibility and to suggest to the testator that he should insert in his will a provision to cover the possibility? **15–29**

This question arose in the New Zealand case of *Sutherland v Public Trustee*[123] where an 81 year old man, who was married to a 65 year old woman, made a will in his wife's favour. There was no provision in the will as to what should happen if his wife predeceased the testator. He had **15–30**

[121] He was, in effect, the devisee—the garage was left on trust for sale, but he was the ultimate beneficiary.
[122] See [1999] 63 Conv. 399 at 401–404.
[123] *Sutherland v Public Trustee* [1980] 2 N.Z.L.R. 536 (Supreme Court of New Zealand).

no children, but his wife had adult children by a previous marriage. In the event, the unexpected happened, and the testator's wife predeceased him. On the testator's death, the wife's children sued the will draftsman for failing to include in the will a provision that, if their mother predeceased their stepfather, they should become entitled to the property which their mother would have inherited. The stepchildren failed in their claim but only because the trial judge concluded, as a fact, that the will draftsman had drawn the testator's attention to the possibility that his wife might predecease him, and that the testator had consciously decided not to provide in his will for this eventuality. The careful will draftsman should now, therefore, draw a testator's attention to the possibility of deaths occurring in an improbable order and to the need to consider what further provision should be made where a gift to a residuary beneficiary lapses. He should record his advice in writing, preferably in the form of a letter to the testator. The problem for claimants in cases such as this is that not only do they have to establish that the will draftsman failed to give adequate advice, but also that, if the advice had been given, the testator would have made provision for them. It could well be, for example, that if the testator had been given proper advice, he would have preferred to allow the intestacy provisions to apply rather than to benefit the claimants.

15–31 When a will is being drafted, it is also good practice to point out to the testator the possibility that a particular person might, if not included as a beneficiary, have a claim against the estate under the family provision legislation.[124] If, for example, a testator were to instruct his solicitor to draft for him a will in which there was no provision for his widow, and if she were (as would then be probable) to make a successful claim for provision, the legal costs incurred as a result of such a claim would be likely to fall on the estate and, ultimately, on those whom the testator had wished to benefit. It is not far-fetched to suggest that whoever lost out as a result of the failure to anticipate the widow's claim (and so the failure to suggest to the testator that provision should be made for her in the will) should compensate those who had had to bear what should have been an unnecessary expense. There appears to be no English case law on this to date, but *Challinor v Challinor*[125] is an example of the sort of case where the point might have been raised—and where it may well be raised in the future. In *Challinor* the testator had been married twice. He had an adult disabled daughter by his first marriage, but made virtually no provision for her in his will, leaving almost everything to his second wife. The disabled daughter[126] made a claim against the estate and obtained an award equivalent to about one third of its total value. The costs position is not discussed in the case, but it is probable that the costs, as in many family provision cases, would have made a significant inroad into the estate.[127]

124 See Chap.8.
125 *Challinor v Challinor* [2009] W.T.L.R. 931.
126 Assisted by her sister.
127 The estate was worth about £300,000 and the daughter was awarded £100,000.

2. How far should clients be badgered about doing the right thing?

In *Carr-Glynn v Frearsons*[128] a solicitor who was advising a testatrix about her will was told by the testatrix that she owned a house jointly with her nephew. The testatrix wanted to leave her share of the house to her niece. The testatrix was not sure whether she and her nephew held the house as beneficial joint tenants or as beneficial tenants in common. The solicitor explained to the testatrix that if the tenancy were a beneficial joint tenancy, the testatrix's interest would pass automatically, by right of survivorship, to her nephew. The solicitor offered to investigate but the testatrix said that she would do so. The will was duly executed and the solicitor did not pursue the testatrix in relation to the beneficial ownership of the jointly owned property. When the testatrix died, it emerged that the house was held by the testatrix and her nephew as beneficial joint tenants, with the result that the niece took no share in it. The niece successfully sued the solicitor for negligence. **15–32**

Whilst it is reasonable that the duty of care owed by will draftsmen to disappointed beneficiaries should extend to acts and advice closely associated with the will-making process—such as the need to sever a beneficial joint tenancy so that a particular asset forms part of the testator's estate—the actual decision in *Carr-Glynn* seems to impose a very heavy burden on will draftsmen. The fact—emphasised by the Court of Appeal—that the service of a notice of severance is a very simple and straightforward exercise is, with respect, irrelevant. The effect of the decision is that the solicitor is now expected to do things for his client which the client has not asked him to do, and will be liable in negligence if he abides by the instructions which he has been given. Many clients will surely regard this as the unacceptable face of paternalism, particularly if they are expected to pay for work which has been done without their authority and contrary to their instructions.[129] By contrast, in *Atkins v Dunn & Baker*[130] the trial judge held that there was no duty owed by a will draftsman to a disappointed beneficiary who lost out because the testator had not executed a will which had been sent to him as a draft. The draftsman had not chased the client. The Court of Appeal made no reference to *Carr-Glyn* when dismissing the disappointed beneficiary's appeal. **15–33**

Carr-Glynn v Frearsons is a case in which the court's attitude towards the defendant solicitor seems harsh; by contrast, *Cancer Research Campaign v Ernest Brown*[131] is a case where the solicitors appear to have been lucky. **15–34**

[128] *Carr-Glynn v Frearsons* [1999] Ch.326.

[129] There may have been various reasons why the testatrix did not decide to proceed with the severance of the joint tenancy. Suppose that she had discovered that the house was held by her and her nephew as beneficial joint tenants; she would then have found that, in order to sever the tenancy, she would have to have served a notice upon him which would have alerted him to the fact that she intended that her half share would not pass to him when she died. She might have thought that this would generate unpleasantness within the family and she might have decided not to proceed with the severance. Why was the solicitor supposed to suggest to the testatrix that it was her duty to do the right thing and cause potential unpleasantness in this way? See [1999] 63 Conv. 399 at 404–411.

[130] *Atkins v Dunn & Baker* [2004] W.T.L.R. 477.

[131] *Cancer Research Campaign v Ernest Brown* [1997] S.T.C. 1425.

The testator died in December 1986, leaving a will in which he gave his residuary estate to his sister. She died in May 1988, leaving her residuary estate to seven charities. The defendant firm of solicitors had prepared the sister's will and an employee of the firm had acted as executor both of the brother's and of the sister's wills. Dispositions in a will may be varied after a testator's death[132] so that they are deemed to have been effected by the testator and become operative, for capital tax purposes, at the time of his death.[133] Gifts on death to charities are free of tax. Gifts to individuals are normally subject to inheritance tax.[134] The charities argued that the solicitors should have suggested to the sister that she should have varied her brother's will in such a way as to pass part of his estate direct to them.[135] In the alternative, they argued that the solicitors should have warned them, as soon as the sister died, that they were beneficiaries under her will, in order that they might apply to vary the brother's will. To be effective for inheritance tax purposes, post-death variations have to be made within two years of the death. The charities did not find out about the property passing to them under the sister's will until after it was too late to vary the brother's will. Harman J held that the solicitors owed no duty to the charities during the sister's lifetime; nor were they under any duty, when the sister died, to communicate with the charities and thereby enable them to arrange and execute a deed of variation themselves. He considered that the solicitors' retainer was limited to preparing the sister's will.

It is not difficult to understand why the solicitors were not under a duty to persuade the sister to make a variation during her own lifetime.[136] But the suggestion that the solicitors should have alerted the charities to the possibility of varying the brother's will *after* the sister's death seems better founded. Anyone who understands the tax system—and lawyers who are involved with wills and the administration of estates should understand the relevant parts of it—should realise that where there are two gifts in quick succession, so that property passes within a two year period from individual X to individual Y and then on to charity Z, it should be automatic to attempt to vary X's will,[137] so that the property bypasses individual Y and goes straight from individual X to charity Z. What appears to lie behind the decision in this case is an assumption that lawyers are not really expected to know anything about tax. This is an unhappy reflection on the legal profession, and is inconsistent with the decision in *Hurlingham Estates Ltd v Wilde*[138] where Lightman J considered that the relevant test

[132] Equivalent rules apply to an intestate.

[133] See below, Chap.16, paras 16–45 et seq.

[134] See below, Chap.16, paras 16–13 et seq.

[135] If it passed to her, it would suffer 40% inheritance tax; if it passed straight to the charities, no tax would be payable. Bypassing the sister would save the 40%.

[136] Though, if the approach taken by the Court of Appeal in *Carr-Glynn v Frearsons* (see above, para.15–32) is correct, they might be.

[137] The same reflex reaction should apply where X dies intestate leaving his estate to Y, who in turn dies intestate, leaving his estate to Z. A variation can ensure that the inheritance tax nil-rate band is used efficiently on both X's and Y's death.

[138] *Hurlingham Estates Ltd v Wilde* [1997] S.T.C. 627, a commercial case, rather than a wills case.

was whether the solicitor should reasonably have appreciated that his client needed his guidance in respect of the tax liabilities to which entry into the transaction would expose it.[139]

It is suggested that will draftsmen would be unwise to place too much reliance on the *Cancer Research* case and ought not to treat it as authority for the proposition either that they do not need to consider and advise upon mitigation of tax when acting in the administration of estates, or that they are under no duty to notify beneficiaries reasonably promptly[140] of the terms of the testator's will or the application of the intestacy provisions.[141] **15–35**

3. How much is a lawyer expected to anticipate things about which his client may not have thought?

Another curious case is *Gibbons v Nelsons*.[142] Two widowed sisters lived together in what had once been their parents' house. The house was the principal asset of a trust created on their father's death in 1945 and each sister had a life interest in a half share. Each sister's half share would pass, on her death, to her child or children but, if she had no child, she had a power of appointment, exercisable by deed or will, whereby she could appoint her half share to whomsoever she chose. The two sisters appear to have been close. The elder sister died childless leaving a will in which, inter alia, she left her residuary estate—including "any property over which I may have a general power of appointment"—to charity. The effect was to give her half of the house to charity, rather than to her sister (who was living in the house) or to her sister's son. The younger sister sued the solicitor alleging that the elder sister would not, had she realised what she was doing, have wanted to leave her half of the family house to charity.[143] **15–36**

[139] There is a problem with the *Cancer Research* case, which arises from the fact that the executor of the testatrix's will was also an employee of the solicitors who were dealing with the administration of her estate. By analogy with *Worby v Rosser* [1999] Lloyd's Rep. P. N. 972 (see above, para.15–24) it could be suggested that the sister's estate—rather than the beneficiaries—should have brought a claim against the solicitors in respect of the tax which was suffered because no variation of the brother's will was effected. But this would have meant that the executor would have had to sue his employers in respect of his own negligence!

[140] In *Cancer Research Campaign v Ernest Brown & Co* there were approximately six months within which the deed of variation could have been executed. Where the available time is limited, quaere whether this imposes a greater burden on the solicitors to notify the executor and the beneficiaries. See also *Chappell v Somers & Blake* [2004] Ch.19 (delay in administering an estate).

[141] cf. the majority decision of the High Court of Australia in *Hawkins v Clayton* [1988] 78 A.L.R. 69 where the solicitors were held liable to the estate for losses suffered as a result of estate property falling into disrepair and a fine being imposed for late payment of estate duty.

[142] *Gibbons v Nelsons* [2000] W.T.L.R. 453.

[143] There is no hint in this case of lack of capacity; the question is whether the testatrix understood the effect of the disposition. There is an interesting technical point. The 1994 will referred specifically to "a general power of appointment". There was no need for it to do this. The will would have executed the power of appointment even if it had not referred to it—this is the effect of s.27 of the Wills Act 1837. But the solicitor who inserted the provision had copied it from an earlier will which he had drafted in 1986, and he could not remember why he had inserted it in the earlier will. He had probably copied if from an even earlier will.

15–37 There were indications that the solicitor who drafted the elder sister's last will did not understand the effect of the combination of the trust (of which he was himself a trustee), of the power of appointment and of the will.[144] Blackburne J found in favour of the defendant solicitor, but his reasoning is not altogether convincing. He thought that it was the solicitor's duty to ascertain the testatrix's intention, but he also thought that there was no clear evidence as to what her intention had been. He considered that *White v Jones* was distinguishable because the solicitor in this case was unaware of the existence of any particular beneficiary. This seems odd, bearing in mind that the solicitor was clearly aware of the younger sister's existence and knew that she lived in the house. The defence in this case appears to rest, in part at least, on the solicitor's not having thought about what was going to happen when the testatrix died, and the decision is not easy to reconcile with *Sutherland*.[145]

4. Mutual wills

15–38 Mutual wills were discussed in Chapter 6 and it was suggested there that it is rarely sensible for people to make them.[146] But, if they do, they should record that fact in the wills themselves, and, to be on the safe side, it would be wise not only to record it when wills *are* mutual, but also, to avoid any subsequent dispute, to record (if it be the case) that wills are *not* mutual wherever it could be suspected that they might be. This is likely to assist in preventing later disputes, particularly where there are mirror wills. *Charles v Fraser*[147] is an unusual case in that it did not, like almost all mutual wills cases, involve a married couple, but two widowed sisters. They made mirror wills and it was held that they were mutual. The trial judge criticized the draftsman of the wills,[148] for failing to make a clear note of the fact that the wills were mutual and for not including a recital of it in the wills.[149] An even more unusual case was *Fry v Densham-Smith*[150] where the two wills were prepared by separate firms of solicitors, and there was no direct proof that one of the parties, the wife, had made a will at all. The trial judge, correctly it is submitted, inferred that there had been such a will, or at least a promise to make one. So, could the draftsman

The provision seems to imply that someone, at some stage, had noticed the relevance of the power of appointment. But there was no indication that the testatrix understood what was going to happen.

144 At *Gibbons v Nelsons* [2000] W.T.L.R. 453, 469 Blackburne J says: "I doubt whether even M [the solicitor] clearly understood what would happen to her [the elder sister's] half-share in the trust when [she] died." And in an internal office memorandum dated November 1989, M [the solicitor] referred (incorrectly) to the nephew as being "interested in the trust following the death of his mother *and* (the elder sister)."

145 It is suggested that *Sutherland* was correctly decided, *Carr-Glynn* seems harsh, and *Ernest Brown* and *Nelsons* were cases where the solicitors were lucky to succeed.

146 See para.6–42.

147 *Charles v Fraser* [2010] W.T.L.R. 1489.

148 A legal executive who had died before the case came to trial.

149 The effect of the decision in this case, that the wills *were* mutual, was to override a later will made by the surviving sister at a time when her capacity might have been in doubt.

150 *Fry v Densham-Smith* [2011] W.T.L.R. 387.

of the husband's will be blamed for failing to record that he was dealing with a mutual will, given that he had played no part in drafting the wife's will? It could be suggested that, once the husband had told the draftsman that the wife had made a will, and had stated or implied that the two wills were mutual, he should have noted this, either in the husband's will, or in some separate memorandum to be retained with the will. His failure to do this had the effect of prolonging the litigation which arose after the husband and the wife had both died.

Chapter 16

TAX

I. INTRODUCTION

This chapter is not intended to be a detailed account of the various taxes which are, or may be, relevant in relation to Succession. It is merely intended as an outline—an attempt to explain the overall position, to enable the reader to understand how the principal taxes operate in this field and how they interact with one another.[1] **16–01**

Tax avoidance and tax evasion

It may be best to begin by referring to a question of terminology. In everyday English, the words "avoidance" and "evasion" mean approximately the same thing. But in the world of tax they have taken on different meanings. "Tax evasion" is an expression used to refer to conduct which is unlawful. Essentially, it consists of misleading the Revenue[2] as to the facts, either by failing to disclose facts which should be disclosed or by making false disclosures: failing to declare income which should be declared is evasion of income tax; informing the Revenue that a deceased person's estate contains an asset which has a value less than its true value is evasion of inheritance tax.[3] Tax avoidance is different. It does not consist of misleading the Revenue, but of organising the taxpayer's affairs in such a way that, by taking advantage of the tax rules, the taxpayer pays less tax.[4] **16–02**

Tax avoidance schemes vary in their complexity and sophistication: some consist of taking advantage of rules which have clearly been inserted into the tax code to encourage taxpayers to act in particular ways; others consist of taking advantage of errors made by the Revenue or by the government when tax legislation has been enacted. Some judges,[5] and some

[1] See *Davies: Principles of Revenue Law*, 7th edn (London: Sweet & Maxwell, 2012).

[2] References to "the Revenue" are to Her Majesty's Revenue and Customs (H.M.R.C.).

[3] Evasion or attempted evasion, as it is possible that no income tax or inheritance tax would have been payable in any event.

[4] In the words of Lord President Clyde in *Ayshire Pullman Motor Services v I.R.C.* (1929) 14 T.C. 754, 763 "No man in this country is under the smallest obligation, moral or other, so to arrange his legal relations as to enable the Inland Revenue to put the largest possible shovel into his stores."

[5] In particular, Lord Templeman who, in the capital transfer tax avoidance case of

politicians, have attempted to draw distinctions between "tax avoidance", "tax planning" and "tax mitigation". In this chapter the expression "tax avoidance" will be used to describe the lawful avoidance of tax—no moral or political judgments are made or implied.[6]

II. INHERITANCE TAX

16–03 When someone dies, his property will pass, *via* his personal representatives, to someone else. It may pass under his will or by the rules of intestacy and it may pass to one other person or to several other persons. The disposition of the deceased's property effected by his will or by the rules of intestacy may be altered by the court under the family provision legislation[7] or by the beneficiaries themselves as a result of a deed of variation, or a disclaimer.[8]

A. TAXES PAYABLE ON DEATH

1. Taxes on death may be of a mutation character or of an acquisition character

16–04 If, on the death of a testator (or an intestate), his property passes to a number of beneficiaries, some of whom are members of his family and some of whom are not, such property could be charged to tax in one or other of two ways. It could be charged according to its total value, disregarding the way in which it is divided up between the beneficiaries; or it could be charged according to the value of the property acquired by each individual beneficiary. In the former case the tax may be said to be of a *mutation character* while in the latter it may be said to be of an *acquisition character*.[9] If the tax is a flat rate tax,[10] it will make no difference; but if it is a graduated tax, i.e. one where the percentage rate of tax rises as the sum involved gets bigger, it may be important. Suppose that a tax on death is graduated in such a way that the rate is 10 per cent on the first £10,000, 20 per cent on the next £10,000, 30 per cent on the next £10,000 and so on up to a maximum rate of 90 per cent. If the tax is calculated according to the total value of the

Fitzwilliam v I.R.C. [1993] 1 W.L.R. 1189 at 1126 described what the taxpayers had done as "no better than attempts to cheat the Revenue". But Lord Templeman was dissenting; see *Ingram v I.R.C.* [2000] A.C. 293 and *MacNiven v Westmoreland* (2001) 73 T.C. 293. The distinction between "tax avoidance" "tax mitigation" and "tax planning" is an extremely fine one. For a further discussion of "tax planning" see Pt VI of this chapter.

[6] For a brief account of the Disclosure of Tax Avoidance Schemes régime and the General Anti-Abuse Rule, see below para.16–62.

[7] See Chap.8.

[8] See I.H.T.A. 1984 s.142.

[9] *Beattie's Elements of Estate Duty*, 8th edn (London: Butterworths, 1974).

[10] A flat rate tax may also be described as a proportional tax—it is one where the amount paid is a fixed percentage which does *not* increase as the value of the property to be taxed increases.

property left by the deceased and he dies leaving an estate worth £100,000, it will make no difference whether he leaves all his property to one person, or whether he divides it between several members of his family. But if the tax is calculated according to the amount which passes to each beneficiary, it will effect a substantial reduction in tax if the estate is split.

This involves a question of social policy. Does a government want to encourage, or to discourage, or is it indifferent to, the splitting up of a deceased person's estate? There is a further, related, choice for those imposing the tax. If tax is to be charged on the beneficiary, rather than on the deceased, it could be imposed at different rates according to the relationship between the deceased and the beneficiary. In other words, there could be lower rates of tax for spouses or children than for beneficiaries who are either not members of, or are more remote members of, the deceased's family. It would be perfectly feasible to adopt a system whereby, for example, a beneficiary paid standard tax on the basis of a relatively steep graduation *but* the deceased's brother or sister might pay half the standard tax, a lineal descendant of the deceased might pay only a quarter of the standard tax and the deceased's spouse might pay a tenth of the standard tax or, possibly, no tax at all. **16–05**

There is then a further question. Should the tax be imposed only on property which passes on death or should it be imposed on lifetime gifts as well? It is generally easier for the Revenue to keep a record of property passing on death than it is for them to keep track of lifetime gifts; but if a tax is imposed only on property which passes on death, it will obviously be tempting to avoid the tax by making lifetime gifts.

2. Principal United Kingdom taxes on death have been of a mutation character

The principal United Kingdom taxes on property passing on death have all been, or have all essentially been, of a mutation and not of an acquisition character: they have been charged on the value of the total property passing from the deceased, disregarding how such property has been divided, or not divided, between the beneficiaries. This has certainly led to administrative simplicity. It is clearly easier for the Revenue to calculate and collect one sum of tax from the personal representatives than it is to calculate and collect a number of separate sums from a number of beneficiaries. **16–06**

The principal United Kingdom tax on succession is now inheritance tax. Inheritance tax is a hybrid, a mixture of two earlier taxes: estate duty and capital transfer tax.

(a) *Estate duty*

The main tax on death from 1894 until 1974/1975[11] was estate duty. It was introduced by the Finance Act 1894 and was payable, subject to certain exceptions and modifications, on all property passing on death. **16–07**

[11] The changeover from estate duty to capital transfer tax took place over a period between 1974 and 1975.

It was a graduated tax levied at increasing rates on successive slices of the deceased's estate. The top rate on the top slice during the final years of estate duty was 75 per cent.

(b) *Avoidance of estate duty*

16–08 There was one simple way of avoiding estate duty and that was for the owner of property to dispose of it during his lifetime. Accordingly, rules were enacted to the effect that property given away less than a certain time before death would be treated as though given on death and so would be subject to tax. The time limit for this was gradually extended to seven years.[12] Thus it was still possible to make an absolute gift of property, live for more than seven years and pay no tax at all, no matter how large the gift. But that led to further attempted avoidance and further anti-avoidance rules.

Suppose that someone aged 60 owned a house—the only substantial asset in his estate—and that he wanted to pass it on to his son when he died, but wanted to pay as little tax as possible. Suppose that he were to transfer the title to the house to his son while he was still alive but that he continued to live in the house. If he survived for more than seven years there would, if there were no further anti-avoidance rules, be no tax payable on the house on his death. Provided relations between father and son were good, this was an easy way of avoiding the tax. So, again, rules were enacted to levy estate duty on death on the value of property which had been given away during the deceased's lifetime where the deceased had reserved a benefit in property which he had given away.

16–09 Essentially, this is how estate duty operated. It taxed property which passed on death; property given away less than seven years before death; and property given away at any time if the donor had reserved a benefit in the property which he continued to enjoy until death. In that sense it was an easy tax to avoid; and avoidance was made easier by the use of discretionary trusts. Property could be transferred into a discretionary trust by someone who had a life expectancy of more than seven years and, provided the settlor had no interest in the settlement, i.e. provided he could not benefit from the property he had settled,[13] no estate duty would be payable.[14] It is not hard to see why some people thought that estate duty was a voluntary tax.

(c) *Capital transfer tax*

16–10 The Finance Act 1975[15] abolished estate duty and replaced it with capital transfer tax. It was a radical change. Like estate duty, capital transfer tax was a mutation tax *but* it was *not* a tax on property which passed on death.

[12] At a reduced rate, the longer the period of time between the gift and the death.

[13] In which case he would have fallen foul of the reservation of benefit rules.

[14] There were special anti-avoidance rules for discretionary trusts during the last years of estate duty, but the details are beyond the scope of this account.

[15] See below, fn.18.

It was, instead, a tax on *transfers of value* and these included lifetime gifts, death transfers and transfers into settlements. Capital transfer tax was not estate duty with some additional provision for taxing lifetime gifts, but a completely new tax.

As it was originally envisaged, capital transfer tax would have taxed life and death transfers at the same rate; but, by the time the tax was introduced, the original scheme had been modified and some lifetime transfers were taxed at a lower rate than death transfers. Nevertheless, capital transfer tax began life as a tax designed to tax both lifetime and death transfers and to ensure that there would be no substantial tax advantage in giving away property while the donor was alive. Under the estate duty régime, no tax was payable if someone made an absolute gift of property, with no reservation of benefit, and then survived seven years. Under the capital transfer tax régime, such a lifetime transfer was, in principle, subject to tax; whether tax would be payable would depend on the size of the transfer.

Although capital transfer tax was generally much harder to avoid than **16–11** estate duty, it was not harder to avoid in all circumstances. There were two ways in which capital transfer tax was an even more avoidable tax than estate duty had been. The first related to transfers between spouses. Under the capital transfer tax code, all transfers between spouses—whether lifetime transfers or transfers on death—were exempt from tax. The idea seems to have been that property should be subject to tax approximately once a generation, so it should be taxed as it passed from parents to children, but not as it passed between husbands and wives.

The other way in which capital transfer tax was easier to avoid than estate duty had been was in relation to reservation of benefit; there was no capital transfer tax rule forbidding reservation of benefit. Someone could, therefore, make an inter vivos gift of property in which he reserved a benefit, e.g. he could give his house to his son but could continue to live in it, and yet he would *not* be taxed on the gift when he died. The theory behind this approach was that it was not necessary to penalise reservations of benefit, because the donor who reserved a benefit in property he had given away would have paid tax on it at the time of the gift. The problem was that from the inception of capital transfer tax, some lifetime gifts had been subject to tax at different rates from property transferred on death and after 1979[16] the difference between the treatment of lifetime transfers and death transfers became more marked. Under the capital transfer tax régime which existed in the early 1980s, it was possible to make quite large lifetime transfers and to pay no tax. A transfer of the average family home presented no significant problem. So there was nothing to prevent a 60 year old parent from transferring his house to his child and continuing to live in it. That became, for a while, a reasonably easy way of avoiding tax on estates worth between £100,000 and £1,000,000.

Capital transfer tax had its own—rather complicated—régime for the **16–12** taxation of discretionary trusts. Discretionary trusts had been used so effectively for avoiding estate duty that those who devised capital transfer

[16] There was a change of government in 1979.

tax were determined to put in place a régime which would ensure that the use of discretionary trusts for the avoidance of this tax would not be possible. The general idea was to tax discretionary trusts at 10 yearly intervals at a special rate of tax designed to compensate for the fact that property settled on discretionary trusts would not, once it was settled, become subject to capital transfer tax in the ordinary way. Property not settled on discretionary trusts would, in theory and in the ordinary course of events, become subject to tax approximately once a generation, once every 30 years or so. So property settled on discretionary trusts was subjected to tax at about 30 per cent of the rate which would otherwise have applied and was paid once every ten years. The system was simple in its outline but complicated in detail; the complications arose largely because capital transfer tax was originally a highly graduated tax and it was difficult to translate a system of graduation which applied to individual transferors to trusts and settlements which were treated as having some characteristics derived from their own settlors.

B. OUTLINE OF INHERITANCE TAX[17]

1. Inheritance tax

16–13 The change-over from estate duty to capital transfer tax had followed a change of government and was not a surprise.[18] But the changeover from capital transfer tax to inheritance tax followed neither a general election nor a change of government and *was* a surprise.[19] Capital transfer tax had been introduced by the Finance Act 1975 and had then been consolidated in the Capital Transfer Tax Act 1984. When inheritance tax was introduced in 1986 its introduction did not even merit a fresh consolidation. The Capital Transfer Tax Act 1984 was renamed the Inheritance Tax Act 1984[20] and the new tax was created largely by adding extra sections to the capital transfer tax consolidation to turn what had been capital transfer tax into something much more like estate duty. The result is that inheritance tax has the *form* of capital transfer tax but more the *substance* of estate duty.

[17] There have—from time to time—been suggestions that taxing death transfers is unworkable and/or illogical. For an article suggesting that inheritance tax should be abolished, see N. Lee (2007) L.S. 678.

[18] Most major tax changes follow elections—capital transfer tax was introduced in 1975, the year after a general election; capital gains tax (see below, paras 16–36 et seq) was introduced in 1965, the year after a general election. *Or* they occur because there is an identifiable need to raise extra finance. Estate duty was introduced to pay for extra spending on the navy. Gladstone finally resigned as Prime Minister in 1894 because he did not wish to be associated with the policy. He liked neither raising taxes nor military expenditure.

[19] Days before the budget speech in which the Chancellor of the Exchequer announced that he was abolishing capital transfer tax and replacing it with inheritance tax, there were newspaper advertisements placed by organisations selling life assurance policies to the effect that "CTT is here to stay".

[20] The consolidation act for inheritance tax is two years older than the tax itself.

2. Inheritance tax combines the form of capital transfer tax with the substance of estate duty

The principal difference between estate duty and capital transfer tax was that estate duty taxed any property passing on death, whereas capital transfer tax taxed transfers of value. Inheritance tax, the hybrid tax, continues to tax transfers of value—just as capital transfer tax did—*but* it then *exempts* most lifetime transfers. Even calling the tax "inheritance tax" is confusing. The term "inheritance tax" implies a tax of an *acquisition* character, but this tax is *not* of an acquisition character.[21] **16–14**

3. Transfers on death under inheritance tax

Inheritance tax taxes transfers of value[22] and the principal charging section for the tax is s.4 which covers transfers on death. It provides that: **16–15**

> "(1) On the death of any person tax shall be charged as if, immediately before his death, he had made a transfer of value and the value transferred by it had been equal to the value of his estate immediately before his death."

Section 4(2) makes it clear that no tax will be payable as between *commorientes*, who shall be assumed to have died at the same instant. Therefore, if a parent and child die together in circumstances where it cannot be known who survived whom, the child will be deemed to have survived the parent,[23] but no inheritance tax will be payable on the child's death on property which has passed from the parent to the child.

4. Lifetime gifts under inheritance tax; potentially exempt transfers

Section 3A[24] states that *potentially exempt transfers* shall not be taxable. A potentially exempt transfer is an inter vivos transfer, which would otherwise be chargeable,[25] made by an individual on or after 18 March 1986[26] to another individual or to a trust in favour of a disabled beneficiary.[27] If **16–16**

[21] When the United Kingdom joined what was then called the European Economic Community (now the European Union) consideration was given to abolishing estate duty and replacing it with an acquisition tax which would have been called "inheritance tax". See "Taxation of Capital on Death: a possible Inheritance Tax in place of Estate Duty" Cmnd.4934 1972.

[22] Inheritance Tax Act 1984 ss.1, 2 and 3. In this chapter, all references to I.H.T.A. are to the Inheritance Tax Act 1984.

[23] L.P.A. s.184, see Chap.14, para.14–17.

[24] Inserted into the 1984 Act in 1986.

[25] Certain transfers, e.g. transfers within the annual exemption of £3,000, are exempt.

[26] 18 March 1986 was Budget Day—the day on which the introduction of inheritance tax was announced.

[27] The rules governing the inheritance tax treatment of trusts were amended by FA 2006 s.156 and Sch.20, and the changes (described in a Budget Press Notice as "an alignment") involved, inter alia, significant alterations to the provisions covering lifetime transfers into trusts. Before 22 March 2006, inter vivos transfers to interest in possession trusts, to accumulation and maintenance trusts (as defined) and to trusts in favour of disabled beneficiaries

the donor dies within seven years of the gift, it becomes chargeable to tax, just as it would have done under the estate duty régime. The expression *potentially exempt transfer* is really a misnomer because it is a transfer which is treated as if it were exempt from the tax but which may become chargeable *if* the donor dies within the relevant timescale. It would be better described not as a *potentially exempt transfer* but as a *potentially chargeable transfer* which is what it really is.[28]

5. Other features of inheritance tax

16–17 Because inheritance tax reintroduced the principle that a lifetime gift would normally be tax-free, it had also to reintroduce the rule that a lifetime gift, subject to reservation of benefit, would be taxable on the donor's death. Such a rule follows on inevitably from the scheme of exempting lifetime gifts from inheritance tax.[29]

Inheritance tax has retained two substantive rules, or sets of rules, from capital transfer tax. One set of rules is concerned with the taxation of discretionary trusts; the other covers transfers between spouses. Under the estate duty régime, transfers between spouses were taxable, unless they were made more than seven years before the transferor's death. Under capital transfer tax, transfers between spouses, whether inter vivos or on death, were tax-exempt and they *remain* tax-exempt for inheritance tax.[30]

6. The rate of tax

16–18 No tax is payable on the first "slice" of the testator's or intestate's property, which is known as the nil-rate band. Before 1988 it was payable at different rates on different slices above that band; the larger the estate, the higher the rate. When estate duty was first introduced there were twelve rate bands; and by the mid 1930s there were thirty-three rate bands.[31] In recent years the number of rate bands has gradually decreased and since

were all potentially exempt. Since 22 March 2006, the only lifetime transfers into trust which remain potentially exempt are those in favour of disabled beneficiaries. This means that, since 2006, almost all potentially exempt transfers will be transfers to individuals, and not into trusts.

[28] This was Professor Tiley's suggestion. Another condition of being a potentially exempt transfer is that the transfer must not otherwise be exempt. A gift which would be exempt anyway—for example, a gift to a spouse or to a charity (see below, para.16–21)—cannot be classified as potentially exempt. But the legislation would have been easier to follow if potentially exempt transfers had been called potentially chargeable transfers—then a simple rule could have been enacted that no exempt transfer could become chargeable. The way in which the rules are set out makes the scheme of the tax *seem* much more complicated than it really is.

[29] Gifts subject to reservation of benefit are dealt with in Finance Act 1986 s.102 and Sch.20.

[30] s.18. The s.18 exemption now includes civil partners and the term "spouse" in this chapter should be read as including a civil partner. In *Burden v UK* (2008) E.H.R.R. 38 the European Court of Human Rights held that there was no violation of the European Convention on Human Rights in denying to cohabiting sisters the tax privilege accorded to same sex cohabitants who had entered into a civil partnership.

[31] See *Oxford History of England, Vol.XIV* (Oxford: Oxford at the Clarendon Press, 1937), p.218, fn.1.

1988 there has been only one rate—40 per cent.[32] So there is now a nil-rate band[33] followed by one rate of tax.[34]

7. Inter-spouse transfers under inheritance tax

Looked at from the viewpoint of the potential taxpayer, inheritance tax combines the estate duty advantage of not taxing lifetime gifts, other than gifts into most forms of trusts, with the capital transfer tax advantage of not taxing inter-spouse transfers. Until October 2007, it was important for a husband and wife who between them owned property which exceeded the nil-rate band to try to ensure that each one used his or her nil-rate band. If, for example the nil-rate band was £300,000[35] and a married couple between them owned property with a total value of £600,000 it would have been good tax planning for the first to die to leave property to the value of the nil-rate band to their children[36] and the balance to the surviving spouse. This would have effected no saving on the first death—as there would have been no tax on that death if all the deceased's property passed to the other spouse—but it would have saved £120,000 tax on the second death.[37] **16–19**

The rules were changed by s.10 of, and Sch.4 to, the Finance Act 2008, which provide that such part of a deceased person's nil-rate band as has been unused on his death may be transferred to his spouse or civil partner. These changes take effect where the survivor's death occurs on or after 9 October 2007.[38] The changes make it much easier for a married couple to avoid paying inheritance tax without having to take artificial steps in order to reduce the tax burden.

8. The additional residence nil-rate band

Section 9 of the Finance (No.2) Act 2015 introduces an additional residence nil-rate band for inheritance tax where someone dies on or after 6 April 2017and his/her home is passed on to direct descendants. The maximum amount of the nil-rate band will increase in stages up to 2020–21 when it will be (£325,000 + £175,000 =) £500,000 for an individual, and so £1,000,000 **16–20**

[32] I.H.T.A. s.8(4) indexes the width of the nil-rate band, but this section may be overridden by a Finance Act, and has been so overridden since 2010.

[33] The nil-rate band has been fixed at £325,000 since 2009–10 and Finance (No 2) Act 2015 s.10 now freezes it at this figure until the end of the tax year 2020–21. This does not bind any future government.

[34] The 40% rate is for the charge on a death. When lifetime transfers are taxed the rate is 20%. These lifetime taxable transfers will be transfers into trusts and settlements.

[35] Which it was in the tax year 2007–08.

[36] Nil-rate band discretionary trusts were extremely popular, as the class of discretionary beneficiaries could include the spouse as well as the children and grandchildren. These wills may need to be reviewed in the light of the introduction of the transferable nil-rate band.

[37] It would, subject to inflation etc., reduce the surviving spouse's estate by £300,000, and tax on £300,000 at 40% = £120,000.

[38] The date, during the Party Conference season, when the proposed change was first announced.

for a married couple.[39] The benefit will be withdrawn[40] where the estates are valued at more than £2,000,000. Legislation has been promised for inclusion in the Finance Bill 2016 to extend the benefit of the new relief to the case where the deceased has downsized. Administering a relief of this nature could prove complicated, and its effect on the housing market remains to be seen.

9. Other inheritance tax exemptions

16–21 As well as the spouse exemption, there are several other exemptions which operate both for inter vivos and death transfers, including transfers to charities,[41] to political parties,[42] for national purposes,[43] and for public benefit.[44]

There are also several exemptions which operate only for lifetime transfers, including the annual exemption,[45] the small gifts exemption,[46] the normal expenditure out of income exemption[47] and the exemption for gifts in consideration of marriage.[48] The exemptions for inter vivos transfers are less important under inheritance tax than they were under capital transfer tax because most inter vivos gifts above the nil-rate band will be potentially exempt transfers. *But* if an inter vivos transfer is covered by an exemption, the gift will not become taxable even if the transferor dies within seven years.

10. Inheritance tax reliefs

16–22 In addition to the *exemptions*, there are *reliefs* from inheritance tax. The technical distinction between exemptions and reliefs is that *exemptions* depend upon the identity of the transferor or the transferee—for example, the inter-spouse exemption—whereas *reliefs* depend upon the nature of the property being transferred. Where exemptions apply, no tax is payable. Where a relief applies, it may be that tax remains payable, but that the amount payable is reduced by a percentage; as some reliefs operate at 100 per cent, they are effectively exemptions.

[39] When they take advantage of transferability.

[40] By means of a taper.

[41] I.H.T.A. s.23. Quite apart from the s.23 exemption, the F.A. 2012 further encouraged charitable giving: it enacted that where more than 10% of an estate is donated to charity, the remainder will be taxed at 36%, rather than 40%: see now I.H.T.A. Sch.1A.

[42] I.H.T.A. s.24.

[43] I.H.T.A. s.25.

[44] I.H.T.A. s.26.

[45] I.H.T.A. s.19. Currently £3,000.

[46] I.H.T.A. s.20. Currently £250 to any number of donees. It is not possible to combine the annual exemption with the small gifts exemption.

[47] I.H.T.A. s.21.

[48] I.H.T.A. s.22. The exemption for gifts made in consideration of marriage covers, for example, a gift of up to £5,000 made by a parent of a party to the marriage; if there are four living parents they can, between them, make exempt transfers to the couple totalling £20,000. Smaller exemptions apply in the case of donors who are not parents.

(a) *Agricultural relief and business relief*

The two most important reliefs are the relief for agricultural property[49] and the relief for business property.[50] A working farmer, a person who has vacant possession of agricultural land or the right to obtain it within 12 months, or an agricultural landlord who let the property on a lease which began on or after 1 September 1995, will be entitled to 100 per cent relief on the *agricultural value* of his farm. Thus the relief will not apply to any enhanced value attributable to development potential. In other cases the level of relief is 50 per cent.[51] Owners of relevant business property, where the business is a qualifying business, are also entitled to a 100 per cent relief. The 100 per cent relief applies to sole traders, partners and holders of unquoted shares; those with controlling holdings of quoted shares are entitled to a 50 per cent relief.[52] **16–23**

(b) *Woodlands and works of art*

There is also a woodlands relief[53] and a works of art and historic buildings relief.[54] **16–24**

(c) *Use of the reliefs*

It is, of course, important for someone drafting a will to try to take advantage of these reliefs. It is not generally good tax planning to give a farm to the testator's widow while at the same time giving property which would not be eligible for any relief to his children. Given that any transfer to the widow will be exempt anyway, it is, in tax planning terms, wasteful to give her something also covered by a 100 per cent relief. Imagine the case of a farmer entitled to 100 per cent relief who is also a partner in a qualifying business,[55] and who also has a flat in London and some cash in the bank. It will save tax if the farm and the interest in the business are left to the children while the flat and the cash go to the widow. On the supposition that he has made no potentially exempt transfers within the seven years before he dies, it would be possible to pass property to the value **16–25**

49 I.H.T.A. ss.115–124.

50 I.H.T.A. ss.103–114. See E Chamberlain, "Estate Planning for Businesses", Chap.11 in B. Häcker and C. Mitchell (eds), *Current Issues in Succession Law* (Oxford: Hart Publishing, 2016).

51 This is a simplified account—but it is the essential position.

52 The 50% relief will also apply to land, buildings, machinery or plant used for the purposes of a business carried on by a company controlled by the transferor or by a partnership of which he was a partner.

53 ss.125–130. This relief applies only on death. Commercial woodlands will often qualify for business property relief.

54 The works of art and historical buildings relief—which applies both to death and to lifetime transfers—is described as a "conditional exemption", ss.30–35, because it depends upon an application being made to postpone the payment of inheritance tax. Tax can be postponed indefinitely.

55 For example, a business breeding racehorses. The sort of "business" which will not qualify will be one whose purpose is basically investment.

of the nil-rate band, plus any property covered by a 100 per cent relief, to persons other than his widow and still pay no tax at all.

There may be all sorts of non-fiscal reasons for not drafting a will in the most tax-effective way. But it would be foolish (and possibly negligent for a professional adviser) not to consider the tax implications of the deceased's dispositions.[56]

C. PAYMENT OF INHERITANCE TAX: ACCOUNTABILITY AND INCIDENCE

16–26 Two questions arise in relation to the payment of inheritance tax. First of all, who is responsible for accounting to the Revenue—i.e. making payment—for the tax which is due? Second, on whom will the ultimate burden of the tax fall?

If someone dies domiciled in the United Kingdom, inheritance tax is chargeable on all the property comprised in his estate—it does not matter where such property is situated. If he was not domiciled in the United Kingdom, inheritance tax will be chargeable only on property which is situated in the United Kingdom.[57]

1. Accountability—who pays the Revenue?

16–27 Suppose that someone dies domiciled in the United Kingdom, having made no potentially exempt transfers within the seven years before his death and leaving an estate which exceeds the nil-rate band. Property subject to a 100 per cent relief drops out of account and property subject to a 50 per cent relief is reduced in value before calculating the tax.[58] If, *after* taking account of exemptions and reliefs, the testator has left an estate worth £575,000, tax will then be payable at 40 per cent on the amount by which it exceeds the nil-rate-band i.e. 40 per cent of (£575,000–£325,000 =) £250,000, which is £100,000. The responsibility for accounting to the Revenue for this tax on the deceased's estate in the United Kingdom lies on the personal representatives.[59] Tax has to be paid by the end of the sixth month after the end of the month in which the deceased died. In practice, the personal representatives will need to pay quickly because they must deliver an account and pay the tax *before* they can obtain probate or letters of administration. This means that they must raise the money to pay the tax *before* they can sell any of the deceased's property.[60] In practice, they will *either* (i) arrange with one or other of the banks or building societies at

[56] For a case where a will was drafted in such a way that there was confusion as to the interrelationship between the IHT nil-rate band and the charity exemption see *RSPCA v Sharp* [2011] 1W.L.R. 980, discussed above in Chap.15 at para.15–21.

[57] Property situated outside the UK is "excluded property" if the person beneficially entitled to it is an individual domiciled outside the UK, I.H.T.A. s.6.

[58] Because the 50% relief reduces the value of the transfer.

[59] s.200.

[60] They will need to obtain probate or letters of administration in order to sell.

which the deceased maintained an account for funds to be made available to pay the tax *or* (ii) borrow the money from a bank or other institution (in which case the interest payable on the borrowing is deductible for income tax purposes).[61]

2. Incidence—on whom does the burden ultimately fall?

When the tax has been paid by the personal representatives, the question then arises as to the person upon whom the burden ultimately falls. This should be provided for in the will. If the will makes no provision, tax is treated as part of the general testamentary and administration expenses of the estate[62] and will be payable from residue.[63] A particular danger is that a gift of the residue of an estate to a widow (itself exempt from tax) may be reduced by the tax payable on a specific devise or bequest to someone else. For example, the testator might leave legacies worth more than the nil-rate band to his daughters and the residue of his estate to his widow. The tax payable on the legacies to the daughters would reduce the widow's residue. It is usually best to stipulate in a will that a specific devise or bequest bears its own tax. The size of the gift can be adjusted, at the time when the will is drafted, to take account of the tax which is likely to be paid.[64] **16–28**

3. Partly exempt residue—a construction problem

There is a particular problem in relation to the burden of inheritance tax on partly exempt residue. Transfers to some transferees are exempt from inheritance tax.[65] In particular, transfers to spouses and to charities are exempt.[66] A special problem arises where there is a gift of residue which is to be divided between an exempt beneficiary and a non-exempt beneficiary, e.g. a spouse, or charity, on the one hand, and a child, or friend, on the other. **16–29**

Section 41 of the Inheritance Tax Act 1984 reads as follows: **16–30**

> **"41 Burden of tax**
> Notwithstanding the terms of any disposition—
> (a) none of the tax on the value transferred shall fall on any specific gift if or to the extent that the transfer is exempt with respect to the gift, and
> (b) none of the tax attributable to the value of the property comprised in residue shall fall on any gift of a share of residue if or to the extent that the transfer is exempt with respect to the gift."

[61] See below, para.16–56.
[62] s.211.
[63] See Chap.21, paras 21–31 et seq. and 21–55 et seq.
[64] The calculation of the tax, made at the time when the will is drafted, may well prove to be out of line with the tax payable at the time of death—but stipulating that specific bequests bear their own tax obviates the risk that the residue is all swallowed up in tax.
[65] See above, paras 16–19 et seq.
[66] There is no difference in principle between these cases and other cases of exempt transfers, but these are the ones most likely to occur in relation to the problem now being considered.

This means that none of the tax attributable to the value of property passing to the child—or friend—shall fall on the share which is exempt.

If a testator gives his residuary estate in such a way that it is to be shared equally between an exempt beneficiary and a non-exempt beneficiary, he should make it clear whether he wants the shares to be equal gross shares or equal net shares. If the shares are equal gross shares (the gross division approach), the non-exempt beneficiary's share will bear tax and the net shares will be unequal. If the testator wants the net shares to be equal (the net division approach), he needs to provide that the non-exempt beneficiary's share is grossed up so that, after tax has been deducted from it, it will equal the exempt beneficiary's share. An example may make this clearer. Suppose that a widowed testator bequeaths his residuary estate, worth £2 million, in such a way that half is to go to charity and half to his child. Suppose also that the rate of tax is 40 per cent and that (apart from the exemption) the entire residue is taxable at this rate.[67] If the testator provides for equal gross shares, the charity and the child will each get £1 million gross. The charity's share will pay no tax, so the charity will receive £1 million net. The child's share will pay 40 per cent tax, i.e. £400,000, and the child will receive £600,000 net. If the testator wants to provide for equal net shares, he will have to provide for the non-exempt beneficiary's share to be grossed up to £1,250,000. When tax at 40 per cent has been deducted from this, the non-exempt beneficiary will be left with £750,000[68] and the charity will also receive £750,000 so they will have equal net shares.[69]

16–31 A problem of construction arises where the testator has not made it clear whether he wants to opt for the gross division approach or for the net division approach. If he opts for the net division approach, the non-exempt beneficiary gains at the expense of the exempt beneficiary, but the total tax bill will be higher.[70] The problem has arisen in two cases.

(a) Re Benham

16–32 In *Re Benham's Will Trusts*[71] Robert Gray QC (sitting as a deputy judge of the High Court) held that a bequest of "the residue of my estate upon trust to pay the same to [(listed) exempt and (listed) non-exempt beneficiaries]

[67] This is a simple example; in practice the calculations may be more complicated because of the nil-rate band and/or because tax on other legacies and devises may fall on residue. Having said this, these additional complications *may* to some extent cancel one another out.

[68] Tax on £1,250,000 at 40% is £500,000.

[69] The "simplest" way of calculating this is probably to start by calculating the tax at 20% of £2 million, i.e. £400,000 and then to gross it up by five-fourths. This is on the basis that the total sum in question is £2 million and the tax is going to be at 40% on half of it, i.e. 20%. The tax then has to be grossed up by five-fourths because where the rate of tax is 20%, five-fourths (5 to 4) is the ratio of gross (tax plus net) to net. Overall, £100,000 more tax is payable if the net division approach is adopted.

[70] The testator *cannot* opt to pay only £400,000 tax on £2 million gross and then divide the balance equally between the two beneficiaries, exempt and non-exempt. This is precisely what s.41 of the Inheritance Tax Act is designed to prevent.

[71] *Re Benham's Will Trusts* [1995] S.T.C. 210.

as will bring about the result that the beneficiaries shall receive as much as [one another][72] in each case for their own absolute beneficial use and disposal" led to the net division approach so that the non-exempt beneficiaries received larger gross sums than the exempt ones and identical net sums.

(b) *Re Ratcliffe*

By contrast, in *Re Ratcliffe*[73] Blackburne J held that where the testatrix bequeathed her residuary estate to trustees upon trust, **16–33**

> "as to one half part thereof for [non-exempt beneficiaries] in equal shares absolutely. . . and as to the remainder of my estate upon trust for the following Charities in equal shares. . ."

the gross division approach should be adopted. The wording of the will in *Ratcliffe* is slightly more straightforward than in *Benham*. In *Ratcliffe*, an attempt was made[74] to argue that the net division approach was appropriate because s.211 of the Inheritance Tax Act[75] makes inheritance tax a testamentary expense; so the combination of s.211 with s.41 means that the net division approach is the standard approach, unless the testator expressly provides otherwise. Blackburne J did not agree. He did not follow *Benham* and thought that, although the testatrix would have been free to adopt the net division approach if she had so wished, "much clearer wording would be needed than the common form of wording actually used".[76]

(c) *Seeking the testator's intention*

In *Ratcliffe* Blackburne J made it clear that he was seeking the testatrix's intention. The problem is that the testatrix may well not have given any thought to the tax problem, and this is a good example of the sort of construction case which involves some degree of speculation as to what a testatrix would have said had she thought about something to which she had, in fact, not directed her attention. It is submitted that the result in *Ratcliffe* is to be preferred to the result in *Benham*: quite apart from making the calculations easier, it is likely to be the approach preferred by most testators. The will draftsman should, however, explain the position to the testator and, having received his instructions, draft the will in such a way that it is clear whether the gross division approach or the net division approach is to be followed. **16–34**

[72] The proportions in the case *were not* equal, but that only served to complicate the calculations—it had nothing to do with the principle.
[73] *Re Ratcliffe* [1999] S.T.C. 262.
[74] By those representing the non-exempt beneficiaries.
[75] See above, para.16–28.
[76] *Re Ratcliffe* [1999] S.T.C. 262, 268. He noted that to hold otherwise would mean that the net division approach would apply to an intestacy as well as on the wording of the will in *Ratcliffe* itself.

4. Accountability and incidence in relation to potentially exempt transfers and gifts subject to reservation

16–35 The liability for tax on a potentially exempt transfer, which becomes chargeable because the testator dies within seven years, falls on the donee, both as a question of accountability[77] and of incidence, although the Revenue may be able to recover tax from the personal representatives if they cannot obtain it from the donee.[78] Donees are also liable for tax on gifts subject to reservation. Trustees are generally liable for tax on trusts.[79]

III. CAPITAL GAINS TAX

1. Outline of capital gains tax

16–36 Capital gains tax was introduced in 1965[80] and is designed to levy tax on profit-making transactions which are not covered by income tax. A trader, such as a shopkeeper, pays income tax on his trading profits; but before capital gains tax was enacted, someone who could not be designated as trading for income tax purposes, but who was engaged in profit-making transactions—for example, buying and selling assets, such as shares and bonds—used to escape tax altogether. Capital gains tax was designed to close the gap, but it does it by throwing its net wide: it covers "chargeable gains accruing to a person on the disposal of assets".[81] Nevertheless, there are several exemptions and reliefs from the tax, the effect of which is that most transactions subject to capital gains tax will probably relate to shares, investment property, businesses or farms. There are exemptions or reliefs which cover owner occupied housing,[82] chattels worth less than £6,000,[83] ordinary motor cars[84] and debts.[85] It has to be said that some of these exemptions and reliefs appear to have been included in the capital gains tax régime with the primary object of ensuring that transactions which are likely to be loss-making

[77] I.H.T.A. s.216.

[78] I.H.T.A. s.199.

[79] I.H.T.A. s.201. When, during the settlor's lifetime, a "relevant property" trust (i.e., since 2006, any trust other than one in favour of a disabled beneficiary) is *created*, the transfer is *not* potentially exempt, but is immediately chargeable; and the *settlor* is primarily liable for the tax. This is outside the scope of this work. No tax will be payable if the trust fund has a value within the nil-rate band.

[80] It *was*—like capital transfer tax—introduced in the year following a general election.

[81] Taxation of Chargeable Gains Act 1992 s.1. This is the latest capital gains tax consolidation and references in this chapter to T.C.G.A. are to this act. "Disposal" is not defined but it covers not only cases where ownership of the asset changes—whether as a result of sale, gift or exchange—but other cases which would not naturally come within the normal meaning of the word, e.g. in relation to settlements.

[82] T.C.G.A. ss.222–226.

[83] T.C.G.A. s.262.

[84] T.C.G.A. s.263.

[85] T.C.G.A. ss.251–255.

will not be subject to tax; i.e. to disallow potential losses[86] and so to benefit the Revenue.

2. Capital gains tax and death

When capital gains tax was first introduced, *disposals* consisted of sales, gifts and *death*. Capital gains tax was chargeable at a flat rate, 30 per cent, and there was no relief for inflation.[87] So if, for example, someone bought some shares for £20,000 and later sold them for £30,000, he would pay tax at 30 per cent on the paper gain—taking no account of inflation. He would be liable to pay tax of £3,000.[88] It would have been the same if he gave the shares away, or if he died. If capital gains tax were payable on someone's death, it would be paid before calculating the value of the estate for estate duty purposes (estate duty being the death duty then payable) and the amount of capital gains tax payable would be deducted from the estate in calculating its net worth for estate duty. The rules were changed in 1971[89] and, since 1971, death has no longer been a chargeable event for capital gains tax purposes. In fact, death gives a capital gains tax uplift.[90] All gains made by the deceased before he died are freed from tax and the deceased's assets are revalued at his death, so that any future gains are calculated only as from death. This is effected by enacting that the personal representatives shall be deemed to have acquired the deceased's assets on his death, for their then market value, *but* that the deceased shall *not* be deemed to have disposed of such assets. There is no disposal and so no liability to tax; but there is an acquisition and a new base price.[91] 16–37

The governing section is s.62 which covers property owned by the deceased and devised or bequeathed under his will[92]; property which passes on intestacy[93]; property passing by *donatio mortis causa*[94]; property passing by survivorship on the death of a joint tenant[95]; and property of which the deceased was able to dispose under a general testamentary power of appointment.[96] 16–38

Returning to the earlier example, if someone owns property which he bought for £20,000 and which he sells or gives away when it is worth £30,000, he will prima facie be liable to tax on a gain of £10,000. If, however, he dies owning the property, there will be no liability to capital gains tax, actual or potential. So, if the owner of the property wants to pass it to a

[86] Chattels worth less than £6,000, ordinary motor cars and debts are *all* likely to be loss-makers. Owner-occupied housing was probably exempted from the tax, with a view to ensuring that the tax was acceptable to the middle-class voter.
[87] There was a rule whereby small gains made in any one tax year might be wholly or partly relieved from tax.
[88] 30% of (£30,000–£20,000 =) £10,000 is £3,000.
[89] Which was, again, the year after a general election.
[90] T.C.G.A. s.62(1).
[91] The tax jargon for this is "washing".
[92] T.C.G.A. s.62(1).
[93] T.C.G.A. s.62(1).
[94] T.C.G.A. s.62(5). See above, Chap.6.
[95] T.C.G.A. s.62(10).
[96] Whether or not he *did* so dispose of it, s.62(10).

member of his family, he will save capital gains tax by passing it on his death rather than by making an inter vivos gift. For capital gains tax purposes, the passing of the property from the personal representatives to the beneficiary entitled under the will or on intestacy is ignored,[97] and the beneficiary is deemed to have acquired the property from the deceased at his death and at its then value.

3. Interrelationship between inheritance tax and capital gains tax on death

16–39 The negative aspect of escaping capital gains tax on death is that the owner of the property will potentially be liable to inheritance tax instead. If that is so, it will seem to be an unattractive exchange. If there is a choice between paying one or other of the two taxes, inheritance tax would seem to be the less attractive option because, disregarding any difference in tax rates, inheritance tax is effectively levied on the *total* value of the property transferred whereas capital gains tax is levied only on any increase in its value since the date of acquisition.

When estate duty was replaced by capital transfer tax, capital transfer tax contained an exemption for transfers to the transferor's spouse and this exemption applied both to inter vivos transfers and to transfers on death. It still applies[98] under the inheritance tax régime. The system appears to have lost all logic: it is possible to pay *one* tax, or the *other* tax, or *both* taxes or *neither* tax. If someone makes an inter vivos transfer more than seven years before he dies, with no reservation of benefit, there will be a potential capital gains tax liability at the time of the gift but no liability to inheritance tax, either at the time of the gift or at the time of death. If someone dies leaving property which passes to his children (under his will, or by way of *donatio mortis causa*, or under the intestacy rules) such property will be subject to inheritance tax but any capital gains on such property will be washed on the death. Both taxes can become payable if there is a lifetime gift, subject to capital gains tax, followed by the donor's death within seven years; or if there is a lifetime gift, subject to capital gains tax, and the donor reserves a benefit in the gift. If an asset is transferred to the owner's spouse on death, there will be a capital gains tax uplift combined with an inheritance tax exemption. Since 1992, there has been the same effect where property which is subject to the 100 per cent (inheritance tax) business or agricultural property relief is transferred on death.

4. Planning to avoid a double tax charge

16–40 There are two very simple tax-planning rules to be followed when considering the inter-relationship between capital gains tax and inheritance tax. First, reservation of benefit should be avoided because it leads to a double

[97] T.C.G.A. s.62(4).

[98] And it has, in effect, been *extended* by allowing the nil-rate band to be transferred between spouses, see para.16–19, above.

tax charge.[99] Secondly, assets which are likely to attract a liability to capital gains tax, i.e. those which have shown substantial increases in value since they were acquired, should be retained until the owner's death. They need not necessarily attract a liability to inheritance tax because they may be covered by the spouse exemption, business relief, agricultural relief or the nil-rate band. Assets given away during the donor's lifetime should *generally* be those which are not going to be subject to capital gains tax, either because they are covered by capital gains tax reliefs or exemptions (e.g. owner-occupied houses) or because they have not shown gains which will attract the tax.

5. Allowing for inflation and calculating the rate of tax

Capital gains tax was originally imposed as a flat rate tax at 30 per cent on paper gains, making no allowance for inflation. In 1982, a partial allowance was given for inflation. The rules relating to the effect of inflation on gains were remodelled in 1988, since when only gains made since 1982 have been liable to capital gains tax.[100] The relief for inflation from 1982 until 1998 was an indexation relief and this was given by indexing the acquisition cost (or 1982 value, in the case of an asset acquired before 1982).[101] Indexation for the whole period of sixteen years from 1982 to 1998 gave a figure of approximately 100 per cent.[102] This meant that if a block of shares had been acquired in 1982 for £20,000 and had been disposed of in 1998 for £50,000, the acquisition cost for capital gains tax purposes would have been £40,000[103]; and the chargeable gain would have been £10,000.[104] This chargeable gain was then taxed at the individual taxpayer's *marginal rate of income tax* i.e. effectively the top rate at which he paid income tax. For most capital gains tax payers this meant 40 per cent.[105] **16–41**

In 1998 this system was changed from an indexation relief into a taper relief. Instead of indexing the acquisition cost, the new system reduced the gain by a percentage according to the length of time the asset had been held.[106] This taper relief was described[107] as being "simpler and fairer" than the indexation relief it replaced. It might have been simpler if it had completely replaced the earlier system, but, given that they both ran in parallel,[108] it was not. Another complication was that the amount of the relief varied according to whether the asset was or was not a business **16–42**

[99] It is generally more difficult to plan that someone shall *not* die within seven years of a gift, though there may be some cases where the donor's death within a short time of a gift is so probable that the making of the gift is almost an invitation to a double tax charge.

[100] T.C.G.A. s.35.

[101] T.C.G.A. ss.53–57. From 1994 onwards, indexation relief could not turn a gain into a loss—F.A. 1994 s.93.

[102] There were, of course, detailed rules for calculating the indexation, which was by reference to the month of acquisition and the month of disposal.

[103] £20,000 multiplied by 200% (100% being the original price plus another 100% for inflation).

[104] £50,000–£40,000.

[105] For income tax rates—see below, para.16–52.

[106] T.C.G.A s.2A and Sch.A1.

[107] By those who introduced it.

[108] Indexation relief covered gains made up to 1998 and taper relief covered gains made from

asset. Business assets held for more than two years attracted a 75 per cent relief; non-business assets attracted a maximum relief of 40 per cent, but only when the asset had been held for ten years. Moreover, the taper relief was not "fairer" than the indexation relief it replaced; it was, essentially, arbitrary.

The Finance Act 2008 contained provisions which abolished both indexation relief and taper relief and substituted a flat rate of tax of 18 per cent.[109] In 2010 this was raised to 28 per cent.[110] A 28 per cent rate, with no relief for inflation, means that the position now (post-2010) is almost exactly the same as it was between 1965 and 1982, though there is, in addition to the 28 per cent rate, an "entrepreneurs' relief" whereby business assets are subject to a rate of 10 per cent.[111]

In addition, an *individual* taxpayer (i.e. one who is not a personal representative and not a trustee) is also entitled to an annual exempt amount on which he pays no tax.[112] This now[113] stands at £11,100[114]; so if his net gains are less than £11,100, he will pay no tax, and if they exceed £11,100 he pays tax only on the excess over £11,100.

6. Payment of capital gains tax by personal representatives

16–43 For personal representatives the rules are different. The assets they acquire from the deceased are washed at the deceased's death, so there is no capital gains tax liability to the point of death. If an asset is then handed over to a "legatee"—which, for capital gains tax purposes, means a beneficiary under the deceased's will or on his intestacy[115]—the legatee is deemed to have acquired the asset at death and no tax is payable at the time of the transfer from the personal representatives to the legatee. The legatee is deemed to have acquired the asset at the time of the death and at the value at death. But if the personal representatives sell assets in order to raise money to pay debts, or to pay pecuniary legacies, they will be liable to pay capital gains tax, *but* only on the basis of gains made since the death; *and* they, like individuals, are entitled to an annual exempt amount for the year of death and for the next two tax years.[116] Thereafter they have no exemption; so it may not be bad tax planning for the personal representatives to realise assets which have made gains since the deceased's death by selling them over a three year period, but not over a longer period.[117] If they make gains in excess of the annual exempt amount, they pay tax at 28 per cent.[118]

1998 to 2008; where an asset was acquired before 1998 and was disposed of after 1998, but before 6 April 2008, they both applied.

[109] F.A. 2008 s.8 and Sch.2.

[110] F.(No.2) A. 2010 s.2.

[111] F.(No.2) A. 2010 s.2; but an individual has a lifetime limit of £10,000,000.

[112] T.C.G.A. s.3.

[113] Tax year 2015–16.

[114] It is normally adjusted each year, in line with inflation.

[115] T.C.G.A. s.64(2).

[116] T.C.G.A. s.3(7).

[117] It may be advantageous for the personal representatives to vest the assets in the beneficiaries prior to a sale if the annual exemption is not available to them.

[118] T.C.G.A. s.4.

7. Personal representatives and bare trustees

In some cases, the capacity in which personal representatives dispose of assets may be unclear. Were they acting as personal representatives or as "bare trustees"?[119] The Scottish case of *Cochrane*[120] seems to suggest that, in case of doubt, they will be treated as disposing of assets as personal representatives. On the whole, the advantage lies with the personal representatives. Suppose that the deceased owned shares which have gained considerably in value since the death. Some of these shares could be sold to pay debts or pecuniary legacies, or they could be appropriated to legatees in satisfaction of their entitlement under the deceased's will or on intestacy. The personal representatives can calculate how many shares to sell to use up their annual exempt amount, or they can appropriate shares to beneficiaries who are unlikely to dispose of them until their own deaths or who will dispose of them intermittently, thereby utilising their annual exemptions. Flexibility is an advantage.[121] **16–44**

IV. POST-DEATH VARIATIONS

An important form of flexibility for the tax planner is to be able to vary dispositions after a death and to backdate the variations so that they are deemed to have been effected at the time of the death—by the deceased. Such variations *are* permitted both for inheritance tax and for capital gains tax, but not for income tax. **16–45**

A. INHERITANCE TAX

1. Variations and disclaimers

After someone has died, it may be that those who have inherited his property under his will, or on his intestacy, decide that they would like to rearrange the distribution of the estate and divide up the assets differently. For example, an aged parent may leave all his property to his middle-aged children, but they may decide that they would prefer it to pass directly to their own adult children, the deceased's grandchildren, with a view to saving tax on their deaths. Section 142 of the Inheritance Tax Act[122] allows **16–46**

[119] When a bare trustee disposes of assets, the disposal is treated as being made by the person on whose behalf the bare trustee is holding; s.60. So, if a personal representative were to be treated as a bare trustee, a disposal by him would count as a disposal by the beneficiary.
[120] *Cochrane v IRC* (1974) 49 T.C. 299.
[121] Beneficiaries who have spouses may request the personal representatives to vest some of the shares in their spouses in order to take advantage of a second annual exempt amount.
[122] Combined with s.17. The section covers variations (where the beneficiary chooses the

the beneficiaries to alter the deceased's dispositions after his death; and any variation is then treated, for inheritance tax purposes, as if it had been the deceased's original disposition, provided an election is effected by an instrument in writing within two years of the death. The variation cannot be for money or money's worth.

16–47 The original beneficiaries must *agree* to any change; so if someone is, as a result of a variation, to receive a smaller share of the deceased's estate, that person has to consent.[123] The personal representatives of deceased beneficiaries can enter into variations and disclaimers.[124]

2. Two year discretionary trusts

16–48 Section 144 of the Inheritance Tax Act provides that a distribution from a testamentary discretionary trust within two years of the testator's death will be treated as though it had been made under the testator's will. This means that the testator can leave his trustees to decide how best to dispose of his property, taking into account the competing claims of the widow and children and all other considerations, including fiscal ones. Although such an arrangement confers a great deal of flexibility, some trustees may think that it imposes too heavy a burden upon them and may be unwilling to act as the trustees of such a discretionary trust unless they have reasonably clear instructions from the testator as to how he would expect them to act in given circumstances.[125]

As an alternative to creating a true trust, a testator may create a "precatory" trust, i.e. express a wish that the beneficiary should transfer some or all of his benefit to a third party; if he does so within two years after the testator's death, the transfer by the beneficiary is treated as if made by the testator to the third party.[126]

3. Other post-death alterations

16–49 Section 146 of the Inheritance Tax Act deals with orders of the court made under the Inheritance (Provision for Family and Dependants) Act 1975[127]: they are also backdated to the death and any property which passes under such an order is treated, for inheritance tax purposes, as if it had devolved in that way on the death. For example, if someone dies and leaves his substantial estate entirely to his mistress, this will result in a liability to inheritance tax. If the court then orders that part of the estate should be transferred to the deceased's widow, such property will be deemed to

person to take in his place) and disclaimers (where the disclaimed property passes in accordance with fixed rules of law).

[123] This may be a reason for using a two-year trust instead; see below, para.16–48.

[124] And this may be especially useful in terms of tax planning.

[125] A testator should leave his trustees a "letter of wishes" which indicates how he would like them to exercise their powers and discretions. This letter will not be legally binding on them (if it were, the trust would not be discretionary) and will not be admitted to probate, but it will be morally binding.

[126] I.H.T.A. s.143.

[127] See Chap.8.

have been bequeathed to the widow by the deceased, thereby reducing the inheritance tax burden.

B. CAPITAL GAINS TAX

1. Variations

Just as variations are possible for inheritance tax, so they are possible for capital gains tax. Section 62(6)–(10) of the Taxation of Chargeable Gains Act 1992 is essentially equivalent to s.142 of the Inheritance Tax Act 1984. Dispositions under a will or on intestacy may be varied for inheritance tax purposes under the one section[128] and for capital gains tax purposes under the other.[129] Those who effect the variation may want it to take effect for both taxes or only for one. In the ordinary course of events, a variation will be effected for inheritance tax purposes and an equivalent variation will be effected, simultaneously, for capital gains tax purposes. But there may be no need to effect a capital gains tax variation and in some cases a capital gains tax variation may not be advantageous. Suppose that the variation is that a block of shares in a public company[130]—worth £100,000 at the date of death, and £110,000 at the date of the variation—will, for inheritance tax purposes, pass to Y and not to X. The variation will be effected for inheritance tax purposes and the shares will be treated as though the deceased had bequeathed the shares to Y in his will. If the variation is effected also for capital gains tax, Y will be deemed to have inherited the shares from the deceased at £100,000. If the variation is not effected for capital gains tax, X will be treated as having inherited the shares from the deceased at £100,000 and as then having disposed of them to Y at £110,000. The gain is within X's annual capital gains tax exemption; so no tax will be payable by X, and Y will acquire the shares at a base cost of £110,000 as opposed to £100,000.[131] If, however, the shares had increased in value to, say, £140,000, an election by X will be made because of the capital gains tax liability which X will incur if there is no election.[132] **16–50**

A warning needs to be issued at this point. It would be a mistake to think that, because wills can be varied after death, there is no need to undertake planning before death. First of all, variations can take effect only with the consent of the beneficiaries, and beneficiaries may well not consent to variations which do not benefit them personally, even if such variations result in tax savings for others. Secondly, there is no guarantee that variations will always be possible. Without advance warning, the 1989 Finance Bill proposed their abolition; the proposal was subject to much adverse comment[133] and was withdrawn. But it is always possible that similar proposals may be implemented in the future. **16–51**

[128] I.H.T.A. s.142.
[129] C.G.T.A. s.62(6).
[130] *Not* covered by inheritance tax business property relief.
[131] This assumes X has his annual exemption available.
[132] Because the gain exceeds the annual exemption.
[133] See [1989] B.T.R. 113 and 211 where the proposal was described as "a mean piece of tinkering".

V. INCOME TAX

16–52 In the context of the Law of Succession, income tax is less significant than inheritance tax or capital gains tax. It is a tax on income[134] which is levied both on savings income and on non-savings income. It is a graduated tax: the more income an individual taxpayer has, in a particular tax year,[135] the more income tax he pays as a percentage of his income. He pays no tax on the first "slice", because of a "personal allowance",[136] he pays tax at the basic rate of 20 per cent on the next band,[137] then at the 40 per higher rate, and finally at the 45 per cent additional rate.

1. Deduction of income tax at source

16–53 Much income tax is collected by deduction at source, i.e. at the time when the income is received by the taxpayer. This is the case, for example, with most savings income and with employees' earnings.

2. Income tax owed for the period before death

16–54 Any income tax outstanding on death is a debt of the estate.[138] It will be the duty of the personal representatives to submit accounts to the Revenue, so that the tax can be calculated and paid. From the personal representatives' point of view, the most difficult type of case is probably that of a self-employed sole trader or partner, because accounts have to be furnished so that the income tax—which is a debt of the estate deductible from the gross estate when calculating its net worth for inheritance tax purposes—can be calculated.[139]

3. Income of the estate

16–55 Once the income of the deceased has been calculated, and the tax on it paid, it is then necessary to calculate the income of the estate. This income is generally, though not invariably, savings income. Sometimes, there may be room for argument as to whether income belonged to the deceased or belongs to the estate: the general rule is that income received after

[134] See Lord Macnaghten in *London County Council v Attorney General* [1901] A.C. 26, 35 "Income tax, if I may be pardoned for saying so, is a tax on income".

[135] The income tax year runs from 6 April to 5 April.

[136] In 2016–17 the personal allowance is £11,000; F (No.2) A 2015.

[137] In 2016–17, the basic rate band is the next £32,000 and the higher rate band goes from £32,001 to £150,000; F (No.2) A 2015. There is also a 0% starting rate for savings income, but this applies only if the taxpayer's non-savings income does not exceed a £5,000 limit.

[138] Taxes Management Act 1970 s.74(1). There was a time when, if the deceased was insolvent, the Revenue were preferential creditors: this is no longer the case.

[139] There is no difference of *principle* between a sole trader and other taxpayers, but the self-employed generally present problems—and once a sole trader is dead it may be particularly difficult to calculate his pre-death profits.

the deceased's death is taxed as income of the estate, whether or not it is apportioned for succession purposes.

Income of the estate, i.e. income *due* after the death but before the completion of the administration of the estate[140] is taxable in the hands of the personal representatives at the basic rate of income tax.[141] If and when the personal representatives pay such income over to the beneficiaries, the tax liability is recalculated to take account of the fact that basic rate tax has already been paid. Individual beneficiaries may owe tax on the top slice of their income or be entitled to a repayment of tax.[142]

4. Interest on money borrowed to pay inheritance tax

The personal representatives will need to pay inheritance tax *before* obtaining probate or letters of administration.[143] If they have to borrow the money to pay the inheritance tax, interest on such borrowing *is* deductible, for income tax purposes, from the estate income, provided that the loan is on a loan account and not merely by way of an ovedraft.[144] **16–56**

VI. TAX PLANNING

Someone who is drafting a will should bear the tax position in mind—particularly the inheritance tax position. Having said this, it is obviously not appropriate that saving tax should take precedence over everything else: to leave a widow, for example, with too little capital because this will save tax is neither fair nor sensible. **16–57**

This is not the place to go into further detail as to how to avoid tax. The general rule, however, is that the safest forms of tax planning are usually those which are the most straightforward—those which are based on a simple application of the rules.

For example, before the inheritance nil-rate band became transferable,[145] it was a simple application of the rules for someone who had an estate worth more than the inheritance tax nil-rate band to bequeath property to the value of the nil-rate band to his children and grandchildren[146] and the residue of his estate to his wife. If she were then to leave all her property to the children on her death, it would have been difficult to allege any impropriety, whether or not her net estate exceeded the nil-rate band at that stage. But not all cases are as simple as this: and the Revenue may

140 Corporation Tax Act 2009 Pt 10, Chap.3.

141 20%. The personal representatives are entitled to deduct administration expenses properly chargeable against income.

142 This *is* a simplified account.

143 See above, para.16–27.

144 Income Tax Act 2007 s.403.

145 See above, para.16–19.

146 Or to the trustees of a discretionary trust, of which the children and grandchildren—and possibly the spouse as well—were the discretionary beneficiaries.

invoke anti-avoidance rules in cases where they think that taxpayers are taking too much advantage.

1. Associated operations

16–58 The principal statutory anti-avoidance rule for inheritance tax is concerned with "associated operations". Section 272[147] of the Inheritance Tax Act 1984 provides that "disposition" includes a disposition effected by "associated operations" and s.268(1) provides a definition of "associated operations":

> "any two or more operations of any kind, being—
>
> (a) operations which affect the same property, or one of which affects some property and the other or others of which affect property which represents, whether directly or indirectly, that property, or income arising from that property, or any property representing accumulations of any such income, or
> (b) any two operations of which one is effected with reference to the other, or with a view to enabling the other to be effected or facilitating its being effected, and any further operation having a like relation to any of those two, and so on,
>
> whether those operations are effected by the same person or different persons, and whether or not they are simultaneous; and "operation" includes an omission."

It is not entirely clear what this section means and, when it was first enacted in 1975,[148] there were apparently contradictory statements made by ministers in Parliament[149] as to its intended effect. It probably would apply, for example, where someone dies leaving property to his widow on the understanding that she will transfer this property to the children by way of an inter vivos gift. If she makes the transfer without any such prior understanding, that is probably *not* an associated operation, particularly if the transfer takes place some time after the testator's death.

16–59 Nevertheless, there is one example of something which the Revenue are understood to *claim* would be an associated operation; although the matter has not been litigated. It is where property is left by will to someone other than the testator's spouse—say his adult child—and the child then varies the will to pass the property to the spouse (the child's mother), who then makes an inter vivos gift of that same property to the child.[150] This is a scenario to be avoided, although it can be avoided only by pre-death planning.

147 The interpretation section.
148 It was part of the original capital transfer tax legislation.
149 See [1976] L. S. Gaz p.650.
150 Since the F.A. 2008 the nil-rate band is transferable between spouses, see above, para.16–19, but the amount involved could exceed twice the nil-rate band, in which case avoidance still requires a transfer more than seven years before the death of the transferor.

2. Composite transactions

The tax planner also needs to be aware of what at one stage was regarded as the "new approach" to tax planning involving composite transactions which was adopted by the House of Lords in their decision in *Ramsay v IRC*,[151] extended in *Furniss v Dawson*[152] and then restricted in *Craven v White*,[153] *Fitzwilliam v IRC*[154] and *MacNiven v Westmoreland*.[155] This approach began by deciding that taxpayers could not, in capital gains tax cases, claim artificial losses which had been created by a pre-ordained series of self-cancelling transactions. At one stage it seemed to have been carried much further than this. Now that it appears to have been limited, it is not clear how far it applies to inheritance tax[156]; and it is not entirely clear how the inheritance tax rule about "associated operations" fits in with it. **16–60**

3. Contrasting reservation of benefit and severance

A gift with a reservation of benefit is subject to inheritance tax on the donor's death even if he dies more than seven years after the gift was made.[157] It is, therefore, important to try to ensure that the gift is not subject to reservation of benefit. But there is rather a fine dividing line between, on the one hand, giving something away, yet reserving a benefit in it, and on the other hand, splitting something up and then giving away one part while retaining another. In the latter case there is no reservation of benefit, but a severance: **16–61**

> " . . . by retaining something which he has never given, a donor does not bring himself within the mischief [of the reservation of benefit rule]. In the simplest analysis, if A gives to B all his estates in Wiltshire except Blackacre, he does not except Blackacre out of what he has given; he just does not give Blackacre".[158]

If, for example, a farmer owns a farm, including a farmhouse, and he gives the farm, including the farmhouse, to his son, but goes on living in the farmhouse, this will constitute reservation of benefit. If, by contrast, he transfers the farm *excluding* the farmhouse to his son, i.e. makes a gift of the fields and farm buildings only, and not the house, it will not be reservation of benefit if he goes on living in the farmhouse, because he has not given the farmhouse away. This is a straightforward case; others may be closer to the line.[159] The best advice will generally be to keep away from

[151] *Ramsay v IRC* [1982] A.C. 300.
[152] *Furniss v Dawson* [1984] A.C. 474.
[153] *Craven v White* [1989] A.C. 398.
[154] *Fitzwilliam v IRC* [1993] 1 W.L.R. 1189.
[155] *MacNiven v Westmoreland* [2001] 73 T.C. 1.
[156] *Fitzwilliam* makes it hard to see how it can be applied to inheritance tax schemes—see R. Kerridge (1994) 110 L.Q.R. 217. See also *Ingram v IRC*, below, fn.160.
[157] Finance Act 1986 s.102 and Sch.20.
[158] *St Aubyn v AG* [1952] A.C. 15, 29, Lord Simonds.
[159] The reader may think that this is an odd example, given that there will be a 100%

the line because any dispute with the Revenue will occur after the donor's death when it will be too late to change things.[160]

4. The Disclosure of Tax Avoidance Schemes régime and the General Anti-Abuse Rule

16–62 In addition to the "new approach", those involved in tax planning need to be aware both of the D.O.T.A.S. régime and of the G.A.A.R. The Finance Act 2004 Pt 7, i.e. ss.306–319, contains the Disclosure of Tax Avoidance Schemes (D.O.T.A.S.) provisions whereby certain "arrangements" have to be notified to the Revenue. This régime does not define "tax avoidance" but regulations under Pt 7 are made by statutory instrument and these may prescribe "arrangements".[161] The Finance Act 2013 Pt V, i.e. ss.206–215 introduced a General Anti-Abuse Rule (G.A.A.R.) which purports to counteract tax advantages from "arrangements" which are "abusive". The Revenue are producing, "guidance" on what they consider to be abusive. How exactly the D.O.T.A.S. régime and the G.A.A.R.[162] will operate, and how they will fit in with one another, and with other rules, has yet to be seen.

5. The taxation of trusts and settlements

16–63 One final point needs to be made. Little has been said in this chapter about the taxation of trusts and settlements, a topic which clearly overlaps with the taxation of lifetime and death disposals; but to venture into that territory would be to stray too far from the law of Succession.

agricultural relief and so no inheritance tax anyway—but that is not necessarily correct. Agricultural relief will apply only to the agricultural value: some, or all, of the farm may have development potential to which the relief will not apply. This said, if the farmhouse is separated from the farm, the *farmhouse* will lose agricultural relief. The planner needs to take care.

[160] In *Ingram v IRC* [2000] A.C. 293, the House of Lords upheld a severance in time (otherwise called a "horizontal severance" or a "carve out"), rather than space. The taxpayer had sailed very close to the wind and the Revenue then retaliated by inserting ss.102A and 102B into FA 1986. The reversing legislation applied only to gifts of interests in land made after 8 March 8 1999, but the Revenue followed this up by introducing an income tax charge on donors who would otherwise have escaped—see FA 2004 s.84 and Sch.15 (the Pre-Owned Assets régime). These latter provisions are retroactive and seem to cover virtually all attempts at time severance not previously dealt with. Geographical division, "vertical severance" is still possible.

[161] The D.O.T.A.S. régime applies, inter alia, to income tax, capital gains tax and inheritance tax.

[162] The G.A.A.R. is an anti-*abuse* rule, not (as the Revenue might have preferred) an anti-*avoidance* rule. There are likely to be differences of opinion as to when avoidance becomes abusive.

CHAPTER 17

EXECUTORS AND ADMINISTRATORS

The personal representatives of a deceased person are either executors or administrators.[1] **17–01**

An executor *de son tort* is not a personal representative, but he is liable to creditors and beneficiaries of the deceased as if he were a lawful executor.[2]

I. EXECUTORS

A. APPOINTMENT OF EXECUTORS

Executors may be appointed: **17–02**

(1) By the testator in his will. This is by far the most common method of appointment;
(2) Under a power conferred by the testator in his will. This method is rarely used;
(3) By the court, which has statutory powers to appoint executors in certain circumstances.

1. By the testator in his will

The appointment of executors by the testator in his will may be express or implied.[3] **17–03**

[1] Or, if female, executrices or administratrices. See Administration of Estates Act 1925 s.55(1)(i), (ii) and (xi).

[2] Administration of Estates Act 1925 ss.28 and 55(1)(xi): see below, paras 24–48 et seq.

[3] Or, in the case of settled land, statutory. For an explanation as to what "settled land" *is*, see Megarry & Wade, *The Law of Real Property*, 8th edn (London: Sweet & Maxwell, 2012), Chap.10. Since the beginning of 1997, it has not been possible to create *new* Settled Land Act settlements, but this does not affect settlements already in existence; see Trusts of Land and Appointment of Trustees Act 1996 s.2. See also Administration of Estates Act 1925 s.22 regarding special executors in regard to settled land. The court has power to appoint a special or additional personal representative in respect of settled land on the application of the trustees of the settlement or any person beneficially interested thereunder; see Administration of Estates Act 1925 s.23(2)–(5).

(a) *Express appointment*

17–04 Most wills contain an express appointment of one or more named, or otherwise identified, persons as the "executors" of the will.[4]

The appointment of an executor may be absolute, or it may be qualified in one or more respects, for instance:

(i) By a condition precedent or subsequent, e.g. "I appoint my nephew AB and also my son CD *if he shall have attained the age of 25 years at the time of my death* to be the executors of this will."[5]
(ii) As to the subject matter of the office, e.g. "I appoint EF *(hereinafter called 'my literary executor') to be the executor of this will to administer only the part of the estate bequeathed to him.*"
(iii) As to the time when the person appointed shall begin, or shall cease, to be executor, e.g. "I appoint my sister GH to be the executrix of this will *during the minority of my son* IJ."

The testator may, and often will, appoint one or more substituted executors to take office on a specified event in place of the first named executors, e.g.:

> "I appoint my wife PQ to be the executrix of this will *but if she shall die in my lifetime or shall renounce probate or for any other reason be unwilling or unable to act as such executrix* then I appoint my son RQ to be the executor in her place."

The event on which the substitution is to take place should be clearly specified.[6]

(b) *Implied appointment*

17–05 A person impliedly appointed executor by the testator in his will is usually called "an executor according to the tenor" of the will. A person is an executor according to the tenor if the testator has shown an intention that this person should act as executor of the will, without expressly nominating him as "executor". Whether the testator has shown such an intention is a question of construction. The following are examples of the appointment of an executor according to the tenor[7]:

(i) "I appoint my sister AB my executrix, only requesting that my nephews, CD and EF, will kindly act for or with this dear sister."[8]

[4] It is usual to appoint the same persons "to be the executors *and trustees* of this Will."
[5] A condition precedent. As to a minor who is appointed executor see below, para.17–18.
[6] *In the Goods of Foster* (1871) L.R. 2 P. & D. 304; *In the Goods of Betts* (1861) 30 L.J.P.M. & A. 167; *In the Goods of Lane* (1864) 33 L.J.P.M. & A. 185.
[7] For a summary of the case law see Williams, Mortimer and Sunnucks, *Executors, Administrators and Probate*, 20th edn (London: Sweet & Maxwell, 2013), paras 8–13 et seq.
[8] *In the Goods of Brown* (1877) 2 P.D. 110 (a combination of express and implied appointments).

(ii) "I desire GH to pay all my just debts."[9]
(iii) "I nominate as trustees to carry out this will JK and LM."[10] On the other hand, "I wish PQ to act as trustee to this estate" was not enough to make him executor according to the tenor: the will did not require him to pay the debts and generally to administer the estate.[11]

A person who is the universal devisee and legatee under a will (i.e. the sole beneficiary of the entire estate) is not entitled to probate as an executor according to the tenor unless the will shows an intention that he should act as executor.[12]

2. Under a power conferred by the testator in his will

The testator may, by his will, authorise another person to appoint executors of the will after the testator's death. For instance, the testator may, by his will, authorise his legatees to appoint two executors,[13] or direct that, on the death of one of two executors expressly appointed in his will, the surviving executor may appoint another executor.[14] **17–06**

3. By the court

The court has power to appoint executors[15] in the following circumstances: **17–07**

(a) *Substituted personal representative*

The court has a wide power to appoint a substituted personal representative in place of all or any of the existing personal representatives of the deceased. The power is exercisable on an application made by a personal representative of the deceased or a beneficiary under the deceased's will or intestacy.[16] As from the date of appointment, the substituted personal representative becomes an executor if he is appointed to act with one or more existing executors; otherwise he becomes an administrator. **17–08**

[9] *In the Goods of Cook* [1902] P. 115: see also *In the Estate of Fawcett* [1941] P. 85; *In the Goods of Adamson* (1875) L.R. 3 P. & D. 253, 254.
[10] *In the Goods of Russell* [1892] P. 380: see also *In the Goods of Laird* [1892] P. 381; *In the Goods of Way* [1901] P. 345; *In the Goods of Baylis* (1865) L.R. 1 P. & D. 21.
[11] *In the Goods of Punchard* (1872) L.R. 2 P. & D. 369: see also *In the Estate of Mackenzie* [1909] P. 305; *In the Goods of Wilkinson* [1892] P. 227; *In the Goods of Jones* (1861) 2 Sw. & Tr. 155.
[12] *Re Pryse* [1904] P. 301; *In the Goods of Oliphant* (1860) 1 Sw. & Tr. 525.
[13] *In the Goods of Cringan* (1828) 1 Hagg.Ecc. 548.
[14] *In the Goods of Deichman* (1842) 3 Curt. 123: see also *In the Goods of Ryder* (1861) 2 Sw. & Tr. 127; *Jackson & Gill v Paulet* (1851) 2 Rob. 344.
[15] In both (b) and (c) below the relevant legislation uses the generic term "personal representative"; see Williams, Mortimer and Sunnucks, *Executors, Administrators and Probate*, 20th edn (London: Sweet & Maxwell, 2013), para.8–32, fn.125 (not strictly executors).
[16] Administration of Justice Act 1985 s.50. In *Goodman v Goodman* [2014] Ch.186, it was held that s.50 could apply where the named executor had not yet obtained probate. For remuneration of the substituted personal representative, see below, para.20–71, and for appointment instead of a judicial trustee see s.50(4) and below, para.24–26.

(b) *Minority or life interest*

17–09 If at any time during the minority of a beneficiary or the subsistence of a life interest under a will or intestacy there is only one personal representative (not being a trust corporation), the court has power to appoint one or more additional personal representatives to act while the minority or life interest subsists and until the estate is fully administered.[17] The power is exercisable on the application of any person interested, or the guardian or deputy of any such person.[18]

B. TRANSMISSION OF THE OFFICE

17–10 In general, an executor cannot assign his office because it is an office of personal trust.[19] Section 7 of the Administration of Estates Act 1925 provides, however, for the automatic transmission of the office on death through proving executors.[20]

1. Executor by representation

17–11 If X is T's sole, or last surviving, executor and X has obtained probate of T's will, then if X dies, having by his will appointed Y to be his executor, and Y obtains probate of X's will, Y will be X's executor and T's *executor by representation*.[21]

If Y is unwilling to act as T's executor by representation, he should renounce probate of X's will. He cannot accept office as X's executor and renounce office as T's executor by representation.[22]

2. The chain of representation

17–12 The last executor in an unbroken chain of representation is the executor of every preceding testator.[23] So, if Y obtains probate of X's will (X being

[17] Senior Courts Act 1981 s.114(4): for trust corporations see below, para.17–20, and for the rules governing the number of personal representatives see below, paras 17–15 and 17–45.

[18] Senior Courts Act 1981 s.114(4). See also N.C. Prob. Rules 1987 r.26.

[19] *In the Estate of Skinner* [1958] 1 W.L.R. 1043.

[20] For another statutory transmission see Public Trustee Act 1906 s.6(2), which permits transfer of the estate by an executor or administrator to the Public Trustee with the sanction of the court.

[21] It suffices that the original executor obtained probate limited to certain property, *In the Goods of Beer* (1851) 2 Rob. 349: for limited probate see below, para.18–35. There is no chain of representation through a grant of probate limited to settled land, *Registrar's Direction*, 21 July 1936; or through an additional personal representative appointed under Senior Courts Act 1981 s.114(4), ibid. s.114(5); or through a substituted personal representative appointed under Administration of Justice Act 1985 ss.50(1) and (2). For Scottish confirmations and Northern Irish grants see below, paras 18–08.

[22] *In the Goods of Perry* (1840) 2 Curt. 655; *Brooke v Haymes* (1868) L.R. 6 Eq. 25. For possible reform see Law Reform Committee's 23rd Report, *The Powers and Duties of Trustees*, Cmnd.8733 (1982), pp.53–54 and 67.

[23] Administration of Estates Act 1925 s.7(2).

the executor of T) and later dies, having by his will appointed Z to be his executor, and Z obtains probate of Y's will, Z is the executor of Y and *the executor by representation of both X and T*. But the chain of representation is broken by:

(a) an intestacy, i.e. if Y dies intestate in the above example; or
(b) the failure of a testator to appoint an executor, i.e. if Y does not appoint an executor; or
(c) the failure to obtain probate of a will, i.e. if Y appoints Z to be his executor but Z does not obtain probate of Y's will.[24]

The chain of representation is not, however, broken by a temporary grant of administration to Y's estate if Z subsequently obtains probate of Y's will.[25]

3. Effect of representation

Section 7(4) of the Administration of Estates Act 1925 provides that every executor in the chain of representation to a testator— **17–13**

(a) has the same rights in respect of the testator's estate as the original executor would have had if living; and
(b) is, to the extent to which the testator's estate has come to his hands, answerable as if he were an original executor.

4. Double probate

Finally, consider the position if T by his will appoints (say) two executors, P and Q, and P alone obtains probate of T's will, power to prove being reserved to Q. P dies, having by his will appointed R to be his executor, and R obtains probate of P's will. R is P's executor and T's executor by representation. But if Q later obtains probate of T's will (called double probate),[26] R will thereupon cease to be T's executor by representation.[27] **17–14**

C. NUMBER AND CAPACITY OF EXECUTORS

1. Number of executors

Although a testator may appoint as many executors as he pleases, s.114 (1) of the Senior Courts Act 1981 provides that probate or administration **17–15**

[24] Administration of Estates Act 1925 s.7(3). If the chain of representation is broken, and X's or T's estate has not been fully administered, a grant of letters of administration *de bonis non administratis* with the will annexed is needed to each estate, see below, paras 18–36.
[25] Administration of Estates Act 1925 s.7(3).
[26] See below, para.18–32.
[27] Administration of Estates Act 1925 s.7(1).

shall not be granted to more than four persons in respect of the same part of the deceased's estate. If a testator appoints six executors of the same property, probate can be granted to not more than four of them, though power will be reserved to the others (if they have not renounced) to apply on the occurrence of any vacancy. Section 114 (1) does not, however, prohibit probate being granted to four executors in respect of a particular part of the deceased's estate and to four different executors in respect of the remainder of the estate.

17–16 Probate may be granted to one executor, whether or not there is a minority or a life interest which arises under the deceased's will or partial intestacy.[28] The rule is different for grants of administration.[29]

2. Capacity of executors

17–17 A testator is free to appoint any persons[30] as his executors, irrespective of their infancy, mental or physical incapacity, insolvency, criminal record, foreign nationality,[31] marital status,[32] or anything else.

(a) *A minor*

17–18 A minor cannot obtain probate until he attains the age of 18 years.[33] The testator's estate does not vest in the minor and the minor cannot act as an executor for any purpose until he obtains probate.[34]

(b) *Mental or physical incapacity*

17–19 A person who is incapable of managing his affairs by reason of mental or physical incapacity cannot act as executor—or take probate—while his incapacity continues.[35]

(c) *A corporation*

17–20 Three types of corporation need to be considered:

[28] For the court's power to appoint additional personal representatives see above, paras 17–07 et seq.

[29] See below, para.17–46.

[30] Including a corporation and members of a particular firm, *Re Horgan* [1971] P. 50 (partners in firm of solicitors). For what happens when a firm merges with another firm and then forms itself into an LLP, see *Re Rogers* [2006] 1 W.L.R. 1577. On 6 October 2011, the Law Society brought out a Practice Note entitled "Appointment of a Professional Executor".

[31] Status of Aliens Act 1914 s.17, as amended by British Nationality Act 1948 s.34 and Sch.4, Pt II.

[32] For married women see Law Reform (Married Women and Tortfeasors) Act 1935 s.1.

[33] N.C. Prob. Rules 1987 rr.32 and 33. For grants of administration for the use and benefit of a minor see below, paras 18–39 et seq.

[34] Senior Courts Act 1981 s.118.

[35] *Evans v Tyler* (1849) 2 Rob. 128: see also *In the Goods of Galbraith* [1951] P. 422; *In the Estate of Shaw* [1905] P. 92; N.C. Prob. Rules 1987 r.35.

(i) A corporation sole, such as the incumbent of a parish, may act as executor and take probate in his own name.[36]

(ii) Under s.115(1) of the Senior Courts Act 1981 a trust corporation[37] may also act as executor and obtain probate in its own name, either alone or jointly with another person.

(iii) By contrast, a corporation aggregate, such as a company, which is not a trust corporation, cannot take probate in its own name.[38] Letters of administration (with the will annexed)[39] for the corporation's use and benefit may be granted to its nominee or attorney.[40]

D. PASSING OVER AN EXECUTOR

Factors such as the insolvency or the criminal record of an executor do not disqualify him from acting as executor and taking probate.[41] But under s.116 of the Senior Courts Act 1981 the court has power to pass over an executor and appoint as administrator such other person as it thinks expedient if "by reason of any special circumstances" this appears to be necessary or expedient.[42] The grant of administration may be limited in any way the court thinks fit. Probably the "special circumstances" need not relate to the estate itself, or to the administration of it, but may extend to any other circumstances which the court thinks relevant.[43] **17–21**

In *In the Estate of S.*[44] the court passed over an executrix who was serving

[36] *In the Goods of Haynes* (1842) 3 Curt. 75 (Archbishop of Tuam for the time being): as to the effect of a vacancy in the office see Law of Property Act 1925 s.180(3).

[37] For the definition of "trust corporation" see Senior Courts Act 1981 s.128; a trust corporation includes the Public Trustee but also includes companies formed to take on the business of acting as trustees or P.R.s. Most trust corporations are, in fact, created by, and are subsidiaries of, the clearing banks. A trust corporation can also act as administrator, Senior Courts Act 1981 s.115(1).

[38] *In the Estate of Rankine* [1918] P. 134, 139; *In the Goods of Darke* (1859) 1 Sw. & Tr. 516.

[39] See below, para.17–35.

[40] If the corporation is appointed executor jointly with an individual, the latter must be cleared off, see N.C. Prob. Rules 1987 r.36(4).

[41] *Smethurst v Tomlin & Bankes* (1861) 2 Sw. & tr. 143 (conviction for felony did not disqualify executor). The court has no power of selection among executors not appointed by the court, as it has among administrators entitled in the same degree, below, para.17–38. The court does, of course, refuse probate to any executor who lacks capacity. It is not clear whether the murder or manslaughter of the testator by a sane executor automatically disqualifies him; in practice the court may pass over such an executor, and the issue of automatic disqualification does not arise.

[42] See N.C. Prob. Rules 1987 r.52, under which applications for passing over may be made to a district judge or registrar.

[43] *Re Clore* [1982] Ch.456 (conduct of executors in administration, and both executors abroad: passed over): cf. *In the Goods of Edwards-Taylor* [1951] P. 24, 27: both cases were decided under the 1925 Act: *Re Mathew* [1984] 1 W.L.R. 1011.

[44] [1968] P. 302: see also the following cases decided under the Court of Probate Act 1857; *In the Estate of Crippen* [1911] P. 108; *In the Estate of Drawmer* (1913) 108 L.T. 732 (executor serving 12 months' prison sentence for conspiracy: passed over); *In the Goods of Wright* (1898) 79 L.T. 473 (executor disappeared and warrant for arrest issued on embezzlement charge: passed over) and *In the Goods of Clayton* (1886) 11 P.D. 76.

a sentence of life imprisonment for the manslaughter of the testator, her husband. In *In the Estate of Biggs*[45] the court passed over two executors, a husband and wife, both elderly and infirm, and both of whom had steadfastly refused to take out a grant of probate. The court appointed another person as administratrix of the estate, with the will annexed. In *Khan v Crossland*[46] the executor operated a will-drafting business and had drafted the will, which permitted him to charge for administration services; the beneficiaries had requested him to renounce his role and he had refused. The relationship between the beneficiaries and the executor had broken down. The beneficiaries were of full age and mental capacity and were in agreement as to their proposed disposal of the deceased's estate. It was held that these constituted special circumstances under section 116, the executor was removed and one of the beneficiaries was appointed administrator.[47]

E. ACCEPTANCE AND RENUNCIATION

1. Executor may accept or renounce

17–22 A person who has been appointed executor is free to accept or renounce the office as he pleases.[48]

2. Citation to accept or refuse probate

17–23 The court has power to summon any person named as executor in a will to prove, or renounce, probate of the will.[49] The court exercises this power by issuing a citation at the instance of any person who would himself be entitled to a grant of letters of administration if the executor renounced.[50] The citation calls on the executor to enter an appearance and accept or refuse probate of the will. If the executor does not appear to the citation or renounces probate, his rights as executor wholly cease.[51]

[45] [1966] P. 118: see also *In the Estate of Potticary* [1927] P. 202 (intermeddling and misfeasance: executors passed over under the Court of Probate Act 1857); *In the Goods of Ray* (1927) 96 L.J.P. 37; *In the Estate of Leguia* [1934] P. 80; (1936) 105 L.J.P. 72; *Re D. and B.* (1979) 10 Fam. Law 55.

[46] *Khan v Crossland* [2012] W.T.L.R. 841.

[47] Contrast *Khan* with *AB v Dobbs* [2010] W.T.L.R. where the court refused to pass over someone appointed executor by the will and indicated that it was only in the most extreme cases, where the proposed executor was either in prison, demented, bankrupt or refusing point blank to carry out his task that the testator's will would be ignored.

[48] *Doyle v Blake* (1804) 2 Sch. & Lef. 231, 239; *Hargreaves v Wood* (1862) 2 Sw. & Tr. 602. This does not apply to personal representatives after their appointment by the court, see above, paras 17–07 et seq. But see N.C. Prob. Rules 1987 r.26(1) for prior consent of the person proposed for appointment by the court under Senior Courts Act 1981 s.114(4); Administration of Estates Act 1925 s.23(3). The Public Trustee is free to accept or renounce, subject to restrictions imposed by the Public Trustee Act 1906 ss.2 and 5.

[49] Senior Courts Act 1981 s.112.

[50] N.C. Prob. Rules 1987 r.47; see below, para.17–51.

[51] Administration of Estates Act 1925 s.5. If the executor appears, but does not apply

In *Re Stevens*, Vaughan Williams LJ said that he thought "no action would lie for neglect to take out probate—no such action appears ever to have been brought; and I think that the plaintiff's only remedy is by citing the executor."[52]

3. Acceptance of office

(a) *By taking probate*

An executor accepts office by taking probate and cannot thereafter renounce.[53] But an executor who has sworn the executor's oath[54] may still renounce if probate has not yet been granted to him.[55] **17–24**

(b) *By acting as executor*

An executor also accepts office if he does any act or acts in relation to the testator's assets which indicate an intention to take upon himself the executorship. Examples of such acts of inter-meddling include taking possession of the testator's goods; receiving or releasing debts due to the testator[56]; writing to request payment of money due upon an insurance policy on the testator's life[57]; and inserting an advertisement calling upon all persons who had any claim on the testator's estate to send in their accounts and to pay all money due to the estate to "his executors in trust."[58] Whether the executor's acts indicate an intention to take upon himself the executorship depends, however, on all the circumstances. An executor does not accept office if he deals with the testator's assets solely as the agent of another executor to whom probate has been granted.[59] Again, the executor's acts—though technically acts of administration—may be too trivial to indicate an intention on his part to take upon himself the executorship.[60] Section 36(5) of the Trustee Act 1925 provides that a sole or last surviving executor intending to renounce, or all the executors where they all intend to renounce, may appoint new trustees before renouncing probate without thereby accepting the office of executor. **17–25**

for probate, the citor may apply for a grant of administration to himself, N.C. Prob. Rules 1987 r.47(7).

[52] *Re Stevens* [1898] 1 Ch.162, 177; Chitty LJ expressed the same view, at 174, but see *Chappell v Somers and Blake* [2004] Ch.19.

[53] *In the Goods of Veiga* (1862) 32 L.J.P.M. & A. 9 ("once an executor, always an executor").

[54] See below, para.19–12.

[55] *Jackson & Wallington v Whitehead* (1821) 3 Phill. 577; *M'Donnell v Prendergast* (1830) 3 Hagg.Ecc. 212.

[56] *Pytt v Fendall* (1754) 1 Lee 553 (executor had released debt due to the testator: held he had accepted office and could not renounce).

[57] *Re Stevens* [1897] 1 Ch.422.

[58] *Long & Feaver v Symes & Hannam* (1832) 3 Hagg.Ecc. 771.

[59] *Rayner v Green* (1839) 2 Curt. 248.

[60] *Holder v Holder* [1968] Ch.353, 392, 397 and 401.

4. Citation to take probate

17–26 Any person interested in the estate may cite an executor to take probate if he has accepted office by acting as executor. Such a citation may be issued at any time after the expiration of six months from the testator's death unless proceedings as to the validity of the will are pending.[61] After the executor has been cited, the citor may apply for an order requiring the executor to take probate within a specified time,[62] and if the executor fails to do so he becomes liable to a fine and committal to prison for contempt of court.[63] Alternatively, the citor may apply for a grant to himself or some other person, pursuant to the court's power under s.116 of the Senior Courts Act 1981 to pass over an executor where special circumstances exist.[64] By adopting this latter course, the citor may avoid the difficulty and expense which is likely to be incurred in compelling an unwilling executor to take probate.

5. Renunciation

17–27 An executor who has not accepted office is free to renounce probate. Once he has done so, he may retract his renunciation only with the leave of the court.

(a) *Form of renunciation*

17–28 An executor renounces probate in writing signed by him and filed in a probate registry. A renunciation becomes binding on being filed.[65]

(b) *An executor cannot renounce in part*

17–29 An executor cannot renounce part of his office and accept the other part.[66] For instance, after the death of X—who is the sole or last surviving executor of T—X's executor, Y, cannot both accept office as X's executor and renounce office as T's executor by representation.[67]

(c) *Effect of renunciation*

17–30 If an executor renounces probate, his rights in respect of the executorship wholly cease.[68] But any right which the executor may have to a grant of

[61] N.C. Prob. Rules 1987 r.47(3).
[62] N.C. Prob. Rules 1987 r.47(5)(c) and (7)(c).
[63] *Mordaunt v Clarke* (1868) L.R. 1 P. & D. 4592: see Contempt of Court Act 1981 s.14.
[64] N.C. Prob. Rules 1987, r.47(5)(c) and (7)(c); *In the Estate of Biggs* [1966] P. 118 and see above, para.17–21.
[65] *In the Goods of Morant* (1874) L.R. 3 P. & D. 151.
[66] *Brooke v Haymes* (1868) L.R. 6 Eq. 25. See, however, Administration of Estates Act 1925 s.23(1) (executor who is not trustee of settlement may renounce with regard to settled land without renouncing with regard to other property.)
[67] See above, paras 17–10 et seq. Similarly an executor cannot refuse a worthless leasehold interest of the deceased; see below, paras 20–46.
[68] Administration of Estates Act 1925 s.5. See *Crawford v Forshaw* [1891] 2 Ch.261

administration in some other capacity (whether as a beneficiary or as a creditor) does not cease unless he expressly renounces that right as well.[69]

6. Retracting a renunciation

An executor who has renounced probate may with the leave of the court retract his renunciation and take probate.[70] **17–31**

(a) *Grounds for obtaining leave*

The court grants leave to an executor to retract his renunciation only if this will be for the benefit of the estate, or for the benefit of those interested under the testator's will. In *In the Goods of Stiles*,[71] leave was granted to an executor to retract his renunciation and take probate because his co-executor had absconded after taking probate. **17–32**

(b) *Effect of retraction*

Section 6 of the Administration of Estates Act 1925 provides that if an executor is permitted to retract his renunciation and prove the will, the probate shall take effect without prejudice to the previous acts and dealings of—and notices to—any other personal representative who has previously proved the will or taken out letters of administration. **17–33**

II. ADMINISTRATORS

An administrator is a person to whom the court has granted letters of administration of a deceased's estate.[72] He can only be appointed to his office by the court.[73] There is no transmission of the office on the death of a sole, or last surviving, administrator[74]; if by then the original deceased's estate has not been fully administered, one or more new administrators **17–34**

(executor who renounces is not entitled to exercise powers conferred on executors as such and not as individuals).

69 N.C. Prob. Rules 1987 r. 37(1); cf. effect of renouncing administration, below, para.17–54.

70 *In the Goods of Stiles* [1898] P. 12 (on Court of Probate Act 1857 s.79, the predecessor of Administration of Estates Act 1925 s.5): Administration of Estates Act 1925 s.6, now assumes that an executor may retract. See also N.C. Prob. Rules 1987 r.37(3); a district judge or registrar may give leave, but only "in exceptional circumstances" may leave be given to an executor to retract after a grant has been made to some other person entitled in a lower degree.

71 *In the Goods of Stiles* [1898] P. 12.

72 See Administration of Estates Act 1925 s.55(1)(i) and (ii): for a substituted personal representative, see below, para.24–27.

73 For the powers of a would-be administrator, before he obtains a grant, see *Caudle v I D Law* [2008] 1W.L.R. 1540.

74 cf. the automatic transmission of office on death through proving executors, above, para.17–10; and see above, para.17–12, fn.20, for statutory transmission to the Public Trustee.

may be appointed by a grant of letters of administration *de bonis non administratis*.[75]

A. ORDER OF PRIORITY TO ADMINISTRATION

17–35 The Non-Contentious Probate Rules 1987 regulate the classes of persons entitled to a grant of letters of administration in particular circumstances and the order of priority between them.[76] Two main heads need to be considered:

(1) Where the deceased left a will. In this case, if no executor takes probate, the court makes a grant of letters of administration with the will annexed.[77]
(2) Where the deceased died wholly intestate. In this case, the court makes a grant of letters of administration (or "simple" administration).[78]

1. Where the deceased left a will

(a) *The order of priority*

17–36 Rule 20 of the Non-Contentious Probate Rules 1987 specifies the order of priority to a grant of probate or administration with the will annexed. The order is as follows:

(i) The executor. The executor is, of course, entitled to a grant of probate: a person who falls within any of the later classes is entitled to a grant of administration with the will annexed. The later classes become relevant if, for instance, no executor was appointed, or the executor appointed has died,[79] or has renounced probate, or has not appeared to a citation to accept or refuse probate.[80] If T appoints P and Q to be executors of his will and P alone applies for a grant of probate, with power to prove being reserved to Q (who has not renounced), P must give notice of his application to Q.[81]

[75] See below, para.18–36.
[76] See Senior Courts Act 1981 s.127. For the rebuttable presumption that the deceased left no surviving relatives who are illegitimate, or whose relationship is traced through illegitimacy, see Family Law Reform Act 1987 s.21 (not applicable on death before 4 April 1988). For the special rules applicable where the deceased died domiciled outside England and Wales see N.C. Prob. Rules 1987, rr.28(2) and 30.
[77] Senior Courts Act 1981 s.119.
[78] See below, para.17–39.
[79] Unless he took probate before his death and the chain of representation continues; see above, para.17–10.
[80] See above, para.17–23.
[81] N.C. Prob. Rules 1987 r.27(1); a district judge or registrar may dispense with the giving of notice if this is impracticable or would result in unreasonable delay or expense, r.27(3); see *Practice Direction (Probate: Executor, Notice to)* [1988] 1 W.L.R. 195.

(ii) Any residuary legatee or devisee holding in trust for any other person, i.e. any person to whom the residuary personal or real estate is given by the will upon trust.

(iii) Any other residuary legatee or devisee[82] (including one for life) or where the residue is not wholly disposed of by the will, any person entitled to share in the undisposed of residue under the intestacy rules.[83]

For example, if T by his will gave his residuary real and personal estate to X and Y upon trust for his widow W for life and after her death upon trust for his three nephews A, B and C absolutely in equal shares, then X and Y fall within class (ii) and W, A, B and C fall within class (iii). If A predeceased T, so that the gift to A lapsed and A's share passed on T's intestacy, the persons entitled to it under the intestacy rules fall within class (iii).

(iv) The personal representative of any residuary legatee or devisee (but not one for life, or one holding in trust for any other person), or of any person entitled to share in any residue not disposed of by the will. For example, if C (in the above example) died soon after T's death, C's personal representative falls within class (iv).

(v) Any other legatee or devisee—including one for life or one holding in trust for any other person—or any creditor of the deceased.[84]

Class (v) covers all beneficiaries under the will other than residuary beneficiaries who fall within the earlier classes.

A creditor is entitled to a grant notwithstanding that his debt is barred by limitation[85] or was assigned to him after the death of the debtor.[86]

Where a gift by will to a beneficiary is void by reason of his (or his spouse's) having attested the will, the beneficiary has no right to a grant of administration as a beneficiary named in the will, though this does not prejudice his right to a grant in any other capacity, such as a person taking on intestacy or as a creditor.[87]

(vi) The personal representative of any other legatee or devisee—but not one for life or one holding in trust for any other person—or of any creditor of the deceased.

[82] Unless a district judge or registrar otherwise directs, a residuary legatee or devisee whose legacy or devise is vested in interest is preferred to one entitled on the happening of a contingency, r.20(c), proviso (i).

[83] Including the Treasury Solicitor (or Solicitor for the affairs of the Duchy of Lancaster and the Solicitor of the Duchy of Cornwall) when claiming bona vacantia on behalf of the Crown (or Duchy of Lancaster or Duke of Cornwall). For the power of the district judge or registrar to disregard the persons entitled as on intestacy where the testator has disposed of the whole or substantially the whole of the known estate see r.20(c), proviso (ii).

[84] Unless a district judge or registrar otherwise directs, a legatee or devisee whose legacy or devise is vested in interest is preferred to one entitled on the happening of a contingency, r.20(e), proviso.

[85] *Coombs v Coombs* (1866) L.R. 1 P. & D. 193 and 288.

[86] *In the Goods of Cosh* (1909) 25 T.L.R. 785 (statutory assignment), but see *Macnin v Coles* (1863) 33 L.J.P.M. & A. 175.

[87] N.C. Prob Rules 1987 r.21.

(b) *Clearing off*

17–37 Any applicant for a grant of administration with the will annexed must "clear off" all persons who have a prior right to a grant.[88] If in the previous example A and B, who fall within class (iii), survive T and wish to apply for a grant of administration with the will annexed, they must first clear off all persons who fall within classes (i) and (ii). If no executor was appointed by or under T's will, no one falls within class (i). If X predeceased T, this clears him off. A and B must also clear off Y, who falls within class (ii). Y must either renounce his right to administration[89] (if Y is willing to do so) or A and B must cite Y to accept or refuse a grant of administration. If Y does not appear to the citation, or appears but does not apply for a grant to himself, A and B may themselves apply for a grant of administration with the will annexed.[90]

(c) *Persons entitled in the same degree*

17–38 W, A, B and C all fall within class (iii) and are therefore entitled to a grant in the same degree. A grant of administration may be made to any person entitled without any notice being given to other persons entitled in the same degree.[91] Thus A and B do not need to give any notice to C or W. It is, however, open to C or W to enter a caveat, which ensures that no grant is sealed without notice to the person entering the caveat.[92]

Unless a district judge or registrar otherwise directs, administration must be granted:

(i) to a living person in preference to the personal representative of a deceased person, and
(ii) to a person of full age in preference to the guardian of a minor.[93]

If a dispute arises among persons entitled in the same degree as to which of them shall take a grant of letters of administration, the court[94] in its discretion selects the person or persons who are most likely to administer the estate to the best advantage in the interests of the creditors and beneficiaries.[95] Grounds of objection to an applicant include his bad character, bankruptcy or insolvency,[96] or ineptitude for business. An applicant who has an interest which conflicts with the proper administration of the

[88] N.C. Prob. Rules 1987 r.8(4). Alternatively persons having a prior right may be passed over by the court, see below, paras 17–49 et seq.
[89] See below, para.17–53.
[90] N.C. Prob. Rules 1987 r.47: see below para.17–51.
[91] N.C. Prob. Rules 1987 r.27(4): cf. the requirement of notice to another executor, see above, para.17–36.
[92] See below, paras 19–01 et seq.
[93] N.C. Prob. Rules 1987 r.27(5). For grants on behalf of minors see below, paras 17–48 and 18–38.
[94] On a summons before a district judge or registrar, N.C. Prob. Rules 1987 rr.27(6)–(8).
[95] *Warwick v Greville* (1809) 1 Phill. 123, 125.
[96] *Bell v Timiswood* (1812) 2 Phill. 22.

estate will not be selected.[97] If there is no ground of objection to any applicant, the court's usual practice is to select the applicant with the largest interest.[98] This practice is, however, not binding on the court.[99]

2. Where the deceased died wholly intestate

(a) *Order of priority*

Rule 22 (1) of the Non-Contentious Probate Rules 1987 specifies the order of priority[100] to a grant of administration where the deceased died wholly intestate after 1925: **17–39**

(1) The person or persons having a beneficial interest in the estate, in the following order:

- (a) the surviving spouse or civil partner;
- (b) the children of the deceased and the issue of any deceased child who died before the deceased;
- (c) the father and mother of the deceased;
- (d) brothers and sisters of the whole blood and the issue of any deceased brother or sister of the whole blood who died before the deceased;
- (e) brothers and sisters of the half blood and the issue of any deceased brother or sister of the half blood who died before the deceased;
- (f) grandparents;
- (g) uncles and aunts of the whole blood and the issue of any deceased uncle or aunt of the whole blood who died before the deceased.
- (h) Uncles and aunts of the half blood and the issue of any deceased uncle or aunt of the half blood who died before the deceased.[101]

The personal representative of any person has the same right to a grant as the person whom he represents.[102]

A person must have a beneficial interest in the estate in order to be entitled to a grant under para.(1) of this order of priority. For instance, **17–40**

[97] *Budd v Silver* (1813) 2 Phill. 115; *In the Goods of Carr* (1867) 1 P. & D. 291.

[98] *Dampier v Colson* (1812) 2 Phill. 54 (applicant beneficiary); *In the Goods of Smith* (1892) 678 L.T. 503 (applicant creditor).

[99] *Cardale v Harvey* (1752) 1 Lee 177, 179 and 180; *In the Goods of Stainton* (1871) L.R. 2 P. & D. 212.

[100] But subject to the court's power to pass over the person entitled under this order of priority, see below, para.17–49.

[101] This order corresponds with the order of entitlement on intestacy; see above, Chap.2.

[102] Subject to (i) the preference of a living person over the personal representative of a deceased person (above, para.17–38), and (ii) the preference of the persons mentioned in classes (b) to (h) over the personal representative of a spouse who has died without taking a beneficial interest in the deceased's whole estate as ascertained at the time of the application for the grant, see r.22(4).

if under the intestacy rules the surviving spouse is beneficially entitled to the whole estate, then the surviving spouse (or his or her personal representative) is the only person entitled to a grant under these paragraphs because no other person has a beneficial interest in the estate. In order to ascertain the person or persons who are entitled to a grant of administration, it is therefore necessary to apply the intestacy rules.[103]

(2) In default of any person having a beneficial interest in the estate, the Treasury Solicitor[104] if he claims bona vacantia on behalf of the Crown.
(3) If all prior persons entitled to a grant have been cleared off, a creditor of the deceased, or the personal representative of such a creditor,[105] or any person who may have a beneficial interest in the event of an accretion to the estate.

(b) *Clearing off*

17–41 Any applicant for a grant of "simple" administration to the estate of a deceased who died wholly intestate must clear off all persons who have a prior right to a grant.[106]

(c) *Persons entitled in the same degree*

17–42 The rules and practice already considered in connection with grants of administration with the will annexed also apply where two or more persons are entitled in the same degree to a grant of simple administration.[107]

3. Grants to assignees

17–43 If all the persons entitled to the deceased's estate under his will or intestacy have assigned their whole interest in the estate, the assignee replaces the assignor—or, if more than one, the assignor with the highest priority—in the relevant order of priority for a grant of administration.[108] If there are two or more assignees, administration may be granted with the consent of the others to any one or more—not exceeding four—of them.[109]

[103] See above, Chap.2.
[104] Including the Solicitor for the affairs of the Duchy of Lancaster and the Solicitor of the Duchy of Cornwall, N.C. Prob. Rules 1987 r.2(1).
[105] Subject to the preference of a living person over the personal representative of a deceased person, r.27(5).
[106] N.C. Prob. Rules 1987 r.8(4). Alternatively persons having a prior right may be passed over by the court, see below, para.17–49. If no persons are beneficially interested in the estate under the intestacy rules, the creditor must clear off the Treasury Solicitor who has a prior right to a grant.
[107] See above, para.17–38.
[108] N.C. Prob. Rules 1987 r.24.
[109] N.C. Prob. Rules 1987 r.24(2).

4. Foreign domicile

Rules 20 and 22 of the Non-Contentious Probate Rules 1987 do not normally apply if the deceased died domiciled outside England and Wales.[110] **17–44**

B. NUMBER AND CAPACITY OF ADMINISTRATORS

1. Number of administrators

Section 114(1) of the Senior Courts Act 1981 provides that probate or administration shall not be granted to more than four persons in respect of the same part of the deceased's estate.[111] **17–45**

Section 114(2) also lays down the important "minimum number" rule. If any beneficiary is a minor, or a life interest arises, administration must be granted *either* to a trust corporation (with or without an individual) *or* to no fewer than two individuals, *unless* it appears to the court to be expedient in all the circumstances to appoint an individual as sole administrator.[112] For instance, in order to comply with the rule on an intestacy under which a minority or a life interest arises, a grant of administration may be made to the deceased's spouse and a child of full age, or (if the deceased's spouse has been cleared off) to two of the deceased's children of full age.[113] The rule applies, of course, to a grant of administration with the will annexed as well as to a grant of simple administration.[114] On the other hand, the rule does not apply: **17–46**

(i) in the case of a grant to an administrator pending suit under s.117 of the Senior Courts Act 1981, which refers to "an administrator" in the singular[115]: and
(ii) in the case of a grant of administration (whether or not with the will annexed) limited to settled land.[116]

If, pursuant to the minimum number rule, administration is granted to two individuals and one of them subsequently dies, there is no requirement **17–47**

[110] N.C. Prob. Rules 1987 r.28(2): instead r. 30 regulates grants where the deceased died domiciled outside England and Wales.
[111] See above, para.17–15.
[112] On an application for administration the oath must state whether any minority or life interest arises under the will or intestacy, N.C. Prob. Rules 1987 r.8(4), and the court may act on the prescribed evidence, Senior Courts Act 1981 s.114(3).
[113] As to joinder of a second administrator with the person entitled to administration see N.C. Prob. Rules 1987 r.25.
[114] The rule applies to an insolvent estate, *Re White* [1928] P. 75; and where the court passes over the person otherwise entitled to a grant, *Re Hall* [1950] P. 156: but it may appear expedient to appoint a sole administrator in such circumstances under s.114(2).
[115] *In the Estate of Lindley* [1953] P. 203; *In the Estate of Haslip* [1958] 1 W.L.R. 583 (decided on similar wording in Judicature Act 1925 s.163): for administration pending suit see below, paras 18–48 et seq.
[116] See 12th edition, paras 18–45 et seq.

that a replacement must be appointed: the survivor can continue to act alone. But, if at any time during the minority of a beneficiary or the subsistence of a life interest there is only one administrator—not being a trust corporation—the court has the power to appoint one or more additional personal representatives to act while the minority or life interest subsists and until the estate is fully administered.[117] The power is exercisable on the application of any person interested, or the guardian or deputy of any such person.[118]

2. Capacity of administrators

17–48 A minor[119] or a person who is incapable of managing his affairs by reason of mental incapacity[120] cannot take a grant of administration. A trust corporation may take a grant of administration in its own name, either alone or jointly with another person.[121] Any other corporation aggregate cannot take a grant of administration: instead, letters of administration for its use and benefit may be granted to its nominee or attorney.[122] These rules are the same as those governing the capacity of executors.

C. PASSING OVER A PERSON ENTITLED TO ADMINISTRATION

17–49 The court has power under s.116 of the Senior Courts Act 1981 to pass over the person who would otherwise have been entitled to the grant of administration and to appoint another person if "by reason of any special circumstances" this appears to be necessary or expedient.[123] The grant of administration may be limited in any way the court thinks fit. Probably the "special circumstances" need not relate to the estate itself, or the administration of it, but may extend to any other circumstances which the court thinks relevant.[124]

The court has used its power to pass over a person entitled to administration in a wide variety of special circumstances[125] including bad character,[126]

[117] Senior Courts Act 1981 s.114(4), which also applies if there is only one executor, see above, para.17–09.

[118] Senior Courts Act 1981 s.114(4). See also N.C. Prob. Rules 1987 r.26.

[119] For grants of administration for the use and benefit of a minor see below, paras 18–39 et seq.

[120] N.C. Prob. Rules 1987 r.35 (mental incapacity).

[121] Senior Courts Act 1981 s.115(1): for trust corporation see above, para.17–20, fn.37.

[122] N.C. Prob. Rules 1987 r.36(4); see above, para.17–20.

[123] See N.C. Prob. Rules 1987 r.52, under which applications for passing over may be made to a district judge or registrar: see above, para.17–21, fn.42. For passing over executors, see above, para.17–21.

[124] *Re Clore* [1982] Ch.456: cf. *In the Goods of Edwards-Taylor* [1951] P. 24, 27; *Re Mathew* [1984] 1 W.L.R. 1011.

[125] For the extensive case law see Williams, Mortimer and Sunnucks, *Executors, Administrators and Probate*, 20th edn (London: Sweet & Maxwell, 2013), para.26–03.

[126] *In the Goods of Ardern* [1898] P. 147; *In the Estate of Paine* (1916) 115 L.T. 935 (widow who had propounded will found to be forged and had made claims against the estate passed over); *In the Estate of S.* [1968] P. 302. Contrast *In the Goods of Edwards-Taylor* [1951] P. 24.

absence abroad[127] and disappearance.[128] If a solicitor in practice on his own dies, the interests of his clients may be jeopardised if no grant of representation to his estate is obtained within a reasonable time after his death. In these circumstances the court may pass over the persons entitled and make a grant to a nominee of the Law Society.[129]

D. ACCEPTANCE AND RENUNCIATION

1. Person entitled to administration may accept or renounce

Like an executor, a person entitled to administration is free to accept or renounce office as he pleases. He cannot be compelled to take a grant of administration.[130] **17–50**

2. Citation to accept or refuse administration

Again, like an executor, a person entitled to administration may be cited by the court to accept or refuse a grant of administration: such a citation is issued at the instance of any person who would himself be entitled to a grant if the person cited renounced. If the person cited does not appear to the citation, or appears but does not apply for a grant, the citor may himself apply for a grant.[131] **17–51**

3. Acceptance of office

A person entitled to administration accepts office by taking a grant of letters of administration. But, unlike an executor, he does not accept office as administrator by doing acts in relation to the deceased's assets which indicate an intention to take upon himself the office.[132] The court has never issued citations to take administration.[133] **17–52**

4. Renunciation

(a) *Form of renunciation*

Like an executor renouncing probate, a person renounces his right to administration in writing signed by him and filed in a probate **17–53**

[127] *In the Goods of Cholwill* (1866) 1 P. & D. 192 (deceased a farmer: son in New Zealand passed over and administration granted to deceased's sister limited until son or his attorney obtained administration).

[128] *In the Goods of Callicott* [1899] P. 189; *In the Goods of Chapman* [1903] P. 192: see also *In the Goods of Peck* (1860) 2 Sw. & Tr. 506 (uncertain order of deaths); *In the Goods of Harling* [1900] P. 59.

[129] Practice Direction [1965] 1 W.L.R. 552.

[130] *In the Goods of Davis* (1860) 4 Sw. & Tr. 213.

[131] N.C.Prob Rules 1987 r.47.

[132] *In the Goods of Davis* (1860) 4 Sw. & Tr. 213; *In the Goods of Fell* (1861) 2 Sw. & Tr. 126: cf. para.17–25, above.

[133] *In the Goods of Davis* (1860) 4 Sw. & Tr. 213.

registry.[134] Unlike an executor, he need not declare that he has not intermeddled in the deceased's estate.[135]

(b) *Effect of renunciation.*

17–54 Renunciation of administration in one capacity (e.g. as a residuary legatee) precludes the person who has renounced from obtaining administration in some other capacity (e.g. as creditor) unless a district judge or registrar otherwise directs.[136] But renunciation of administration by a person does not bind that person's personal representatives; after his death they are free to take a grant of administration to the original deceased.

5. Retracting a renunciation

17–55 A renunciation of administration may be retracted with the leave of the court.[137] Retraction is permitted if necessary or expedient.[138]

[134] Above, para.17–28. Again, like an executor, he cannot renounce in part except under Administration of Estates Act 1925 s.23(1); see above, para.17–29.
[135] *In the Goods of Fell*, above.
[136] N.C. Prob. Rules 1987 r.37(2): cf. effect of renouncing probate, above, para.17–30.
[137] N.C. Prob. Rules 1987 r.37(3); a district judge or registrar may give leave.
[138] *In the Goods of Thacker* [1900] P.15 is an instance.

CHAPTER 18

GRANTS OF PROBATE AND LETTERS OF ADMINISTRATION

I. JURISDICTION OVER GRANTS

A. THE COURTS

Agrant of probate or letters of administration is an order under seal of the Family Division of the High Court of Justice, which has exclusive jurisdiction in England and Wales to issue a grant.[1] The High Court also has authority to determine all questions relating to the grant or revocation of probate or administration.[2] **18–01**

1. The High Court

Since 1971 the probate jurisdiction[3] of the High Court has been split between the Family Division and the Chancery Division: **18–02**

(1) non-contentious or common form probate business is assigned to the Family Division, and
(2) all other probate business—termed contentious or solemn form probate business—is assigned to the Chancery Division.[4]

(a) *Non-contentious or common form probate business*

This expression has a technical meaning[5] and means: **18–03**

[1] Senior Courts Act 1981 ss.25, 61(1) and 128, and Sch.1, para.3. For recognition of Scottish confirmations and Northern Irish grants of representation see below, paras 18–08 et seq.

[2] Senior Courts Act 1981 ss.19(2), 25 and 128; Judicature Act 1925 ss.20 and 175(1).

[3] "Probate jurisdiction" includes jurisdiction in relation to letters of administration as well as probates: Senior Courts Act 1981 s.25(1).

[4] Senior Courts Act 1981 ss.61(1) and 128, and Sch.1, paras 1 and 3. Probate had been dealt with by the Court of Probate from 1858 to 1875 and by the Probate, Divorce and Admiralty Division of the High Court from 1875 to 1971.

[5] Senior Courts Act 1981 s.128.

"the business of obtaining probate and administration where there is no contention as to the right thereto."

Most grants are issued "in common form" without any contention as to the applicants' right to the grant.[6] Moreover, even in contentious cases, once the contest as to (say) the validity of an alleged will has been terminated by an order of the Chancery Division (or the County Court) pronouncing for or against the validity of the will, any consequent grant is non-contentious business.

18–04 Non-contentious or common form probate business is regulated by the Non-Contentious Probate Rules 1987.[7] Most of this business is dealt with in the Principal Registry of the Family Division in London or in one of the district probate registries.[8] A small part of it may, however, come before a judge of the Family Division by summons[9]—for instance, an appeal from any decision or requirement of a district judge or registrar,[10] or a reference to a judge by a district judge or registrar who is doubtful whether a will was duly executed.[11]

(b) *Contentious or solemn form probate business*

18–05 Contentious or solemn form probate business is assigned to the Chancery Division and begins with the issue of a claim form.[12] Probate claims are usually classified into three categories:

(i) claims seeking a decree pronouncing for or against the validity of an alleged will; if the court pronounces for its validity, the will is said to be proved "in solemn form";
(ii) "interest claims" in which the interest alleged by a claimant to a grant of letters of administration is disputed (e.g. the dispute may be as to whether the claimant is the child of the intestate); and
(iii) claims for the revocation of a previous grant of probate or letters of administration.

These three categories are not mutually exclusive. A claimant may, as the son and only person entitled on intestacy to the deceased's estate, claim (i) to have the probate of an alleged will of the deceased granted in common form to the defendant as executor revoked; (ii) to have the alleged will

[6] A dispute between persons entitled to a grant in the same degree is determined by a district judge or registrar and is technically non-contentious, N.C. Prob. Rules 1987 r.27(6). So is a dispute as to passing over, *Re Clore* [1982] Fam. 113.
[7] See Senior Courts Act 1981 s.127. The 1987 Rules have been amended.
[8] Senior Courts Act 1981 ss.104–106; District Probate Registries Order 1982 (SI 1982/379). There are at present 11 district probate registries; all except one have one or more sub-registries attached.
[9] Unlike the former probate rules, the N.C. Prob Rules 1987 make no provision for motions; see Williams Mortimer and Sunnucks, *Executors, Administrators and Probate*, 20th edn (London: Sweet & Maxwell, 2013), para.32–07, fn.21.
[10] N.C. Prob. Rules 1987 r.65(1); *Re Clore*, above, is an instance.
[11] N.C. Prob. Rules 1987 r.61; *Re Bigger* [1977] Fam. 203 is an instance.
[12] CPR 57.3, 57 PD 2.

pronounced against (e.g. on the ground that the deceased lacked testamentary capacity); and (iii) to have a grant of letters of administration of the estate of the deceased. If the defendant denies that the claimant is the son of the deceased and seeks to uphold the validity of the will, the claim falls within all three categories.

2. The County Court

The County Court has jurisdiction over any contentious matter arising in connection with the grant or revocation of probate or administration.[13] Probate claims in the County Court are started by sending the claim to, or making the claim at (i) a County Court hearing centre where there is also a Chancery district registry; or (ii) the County Court at Central London.[14] All probate claims are allocated to the multi-track.[15] **18–06**

B. JURISDICTION TO MAKE A GRANT

Proof of a will

Assuming that there is property to be administered within England and Wales,[16] a will is admissible to proof: **18–07**

(i) if it appoints one or more executors, even though the appointed executor renounces probate[17]; or
(ii) if it contains a disposition of property within England and Wales.[18]

In *In the Goods of Coode*[19] the deceased left two wills, one of which disposed of his property in England and the other of his property in Chile. The court admitted the will of his English property to probate but refused probate of the other will because it did not dispose of any property within England and Wales. On the other hand, if in this case either will had incorporated the other will by confirming it, both would have been admitted to probate because together they would have constituted the deceased's will.[20] A later will which merely confirms an earlier will is admissible to probate.[21] A will or codicil, the whole of which is subject

[13] *In the Estate of Thomas* [1949] P. 336.
[14] CPR 57.2(3).
[15] CPR 57.2(4).
[16] The court may make a grant even if there is no property in England and Wales, if there is sufficient reason to do so: *Re Wayland* [1951] 2 All E.R. 1041; *Aldrich v Att.-Gen.* [1968] P. 281.
[17] *In the Goods of Jordan* (1868) L.R. 1 P. & D. 555; *In the Goods of Leese* (1862) 2 Sw. & Tr. 442.
[18] The will need not *effectively* dispose, *Re Cuffe* [1908] 2 Ch.500.
[19] *In the Goods of Coode* (1867) L.R. 1 P. & D. 449.
[20] *In the Goods of Howden* (1874) 43 L.J.P. & M. 26. If the foreign will is independent of the English will and is not admitted to probate, an attested copy of it is filed and its existence is noted on the probate, *In the Goods of Astor* (1876) 1 P.D. 150.
[21] *Weddall v Nixon* (1853) 17 Beav. 160.

to a condition which has not been satisfied, is not admissible to proof.[22] Again an instrument which does no more than completely revoke the previous will of the deceased is not admissible to proof[23]: of course, such a revoking instrument is effective for its purpose and is admissible in evidence in a probate claim in order to establish the revocation of the will. On the other hand, an instrument which effected only a partial revocation of the deceased's previous will is admissible to proof. A will which merely appoints a guardian of the testator's children is not admissible to proof under this head.[24]

C. RECOGNITION AND RESEALING OF GRANTS

1. Recognition of Scottish confirmations and Northern Irish grants

18–08 The Administration of Estates Act 1971 provides for the direct recognition in England and Wales of Scottish confirmations or Northern Irish grants of representation if the deceased died domiciled[25] in the country where the grant was issued.[26] Thus if the deceased died domiciled in Scotland or Northern Ireland leaving assets in England and Wales, the normal practice is for a grant of representation to be taken only in the country where he was domiciled.

2. Resealing of Commonwealth and Colonial grants

18–09 A grant of representation made in any country to which the Colonial Probates Act 1892 has been applied may be resealed with the seal of the Family Division of the High Court and thereafter has the same effect as an English grant.[27] The Act has been applied by Order in Council to the great majority of the countries within the Commonwealth.[28] It does not apply to the Republic of Ireland.

[22] *In the Estate of Thomas* [1939] 2 All E.R. 567; *In the Estate of O'Connor* [1942] 1 All E.R. 546: see above, paras 3–09 et seq.

[23] *In the Goods of Fraser* (1870) L.R. 2 P. & D. 40; *Toomer v Sobinska* [1907] P. 106: see also *Re Howard* [1944] P. 39. The revoking instrument must be filed in the registry and its existence is noted on the grant of letters of administration.

[24] *In the Goods of Morton* (1864) 3 Sw. & Tr. 422. For the appointment of guardians by will see above, para.9–04.

[25] For domicile see Dicey, Morris & Collins, *The Conflict of Laws*, 15th edn 2012, paras 6–001 et seq.; *Theobald on Wills*, 17th edn (London: Sweet & Maxwell, 2010), paras 20–004 et seq.

[26] Administration of Estates Act 1971 s.1. Under ss.2 and 3 English grants of representation are similarly recognised in Northern Ireland and Scotland if the deceased died domiciled in England.

[27] Colonial Probates Act 1892 ss.1 and 2. The deceased need not have been domiciled in the country where the grant was made. There is a chain of representation through a resealed probate.

[28] For a list of the countries covered, see Williams, Mortimer and Sunnucks, *Executors, Administrators and Probate*, 20th edn (London: Sweet & Maxwell, 2013), para.28–04, fn.28.

II. THE NATURE OF A GRANT

A. PROOF OF A WILL IN COMMON OR SOLEMN FORM

1. Proof in common form

If a will is proved in common form, a grant of probate or letters of administration with the will annexed is made in the absence of the interested parties. Indeed, if a will contains a proper attestation clause and does not on the face of it give rise to any doubt,[29] the executors need only support their application for probate by their own oath or affirmation[30] in order to obtain a grant of probate in common form. **18–10**

(a) *Revocation of a grant in common form*

Any grant made in common form may later be challenged in a claim for revocation of the grant brought by an interested party.[31] Thus one of the next of kin entitled under the intestacy rules may bring a claim for revocation of the probate of a will granted in common form to the executors, alleging that the will is invalid for some reason. If the court decides that the will is invalid, the probate is revoked. The next of kin cannot compel executors, who have obtained probate of a will in common form, to start a claim to establish the validity of the will in solemn form,[32] though the executors are at liberty to do so. **18–11**

If there is any doubt as to the validity of a will, or any possibility of its validity being challenged in the future, it is advisable for the executors—or the persons entitled to a grant of administration with the will annexed—to prove the will in solemn form, rather than take a grant in common form. Otherwise, there is a risk that the validity of the will may be challenged years later when material witnesses have died or cannot be traced.

(b) *Effect of delay or acquiescence*

An interested party is not barred from bringing a claim for revocation of a grant made in common form by lapse of time,[33] or his acquiescence in **18–12**

[29] See N.C. Prob. Rules 1987 rr.12 (doubt as to due execution), 13 (doubt as to testator's knowledge of contents of will at time of execution), 14 (terms, conditions and date of execution of will), and 15 (appearance of attempted revocation); see below, paras 19–23 et seq.
[30] See below, paras 19–12 et seq. A personal applicant must also produce a certificate of death, N.C. Prob. Rules r.5(5).
[31] Interested parties include any person entitled on an intestacy and an executor or beneficiary under any other will of the deceased. In *O'Brien v Seagrave* [2007] 1W.L.R. it was held that a person with a potential claim under the Inheritance (Provision for Family and Dependants) Act 1975 had a sufficient interest to permit her to proceed as a claimant. In *Randall v Randall* [2015] W.T.L.R. 99, the deceased's daughter's former husband, who wanted to allege forgery of her will, was held not to have an interest.
[32] *Re Jolley* [1964] P. 262.
[33] *Re Flynn* [1982] 1 W.L.R. 310 (obiter): a claim for revocation may be struck out by the court

the making of the grant,[34] or his acceptance of a legacy under the will he seeks to challenge.[35]

2. Proof in solemn form

(a) *Persons bound*

18–13 An order of the court pronouncing a will valid is, of course, binding on the parties to the claim.[36] The order is also binding on any person who, being sui juris, was aware (i) of the probate claim and (ii) of his own interest, which would have enabled him to apply to the court to be added as a defendant.[37]

On the other hand, a person who is aware of the probate claim but is not aware of his own interest in it is not bound by the order of the court.[38]

(b) *Grounds for setting aside*

18–14 Even a person bound by an order of the court in a probate claim may have the order set aside on one of the following grounds:

(i) that the order was obtained by fraud[39]—for instance, a "beneficiary" propounded a will which he had forged;
(ii) the discovery, after the order was made, of a will or of a later will than that previously pronounced for;
(iii) the discovery, after the order was made, that the will previously pronounced for had been revoked by the marriage or civil partnership of the testator.

A person not bound by an order of the court in a probate claim is not restricted to these narrow grounds and may re-open issues already

if the claim is frivolous or vexatious or otherwise an abuse of the process of the court, *ibid.* p.318.

34 *Bell v Armstrong* (1822) 1 Add. 365, 373; *Goddard v Smith* (1873) L.R. 3 P. & D. 7: see also *Williams v Evans* [1911] P. 175 (next of kin, who as executor of will had obtained probate in common form, may bring claim for revocation of probate). Acquiescence in a Chancery inquiry for next of kin has defeated an application for letters of administration made useless by the acquiescence, *Mohan v Broughton* [1899] P. 211, [1900] P. 56: cf. *Re Coghlan* [1948] 2 All E.R. 68.

35 *Bell v Armstrong*, above, at 374 (but the party challenging the will must bring the legacy into court); *Goddard v Norton* (1846) 5 N.C. 76 (legacy paid to infant).

36 Under CPR 39.3(3) the court has a discretion to set aside an order obtained where one party does not appear at the trial, see *Re Barraclough* [1967] P. 1, 11 (for instance, by unavoidable accident): as to compromise of a probate claim see Administration of Justice Act 1985 s.49; Sunnucks (1987) 137 N.L.J. 721.

37 This is the modern equivalent of the old right of intervention, under which such a person might apply to the court for leave to "intervene" in the claim. See *Newell v Weeks* (1814) 2 Phill. 224; *Ratcliffe v Barnes* (1862) 2 Sw. & Tr. 486; *In the Estate of Langston* [1964] P. 163. As to the effect of a compromise, see *Wytcherley v Andrews* (1871) 2 P. & D. 327; *Re West* [1948] W.N. 432.

38 *Young v Holloway* [1895] P. 87 (unaware of own interest under another will).

39 *Birch v Birch* [1902] P. 62, 130.

decided in that claim. If such an order of the court is subsequently set aside at the instance of a person not bound by it, this enures to the benefit of those persons bound by it who were adversely affected by it because "the will is either good or bad against all the world."[40]

B. DIFFERENT EFFECTS OF PROBATE AND LETTERS OF ADMINISTRATION

An executor derives his title from the testator's will, and not from a grant of probate.[41] By contrast, an administrator derives his title from the grant of letters of administration, whether with the deceased's will annexed or on intestacy. This distinction explains the differences which exist between the effects of probate and of letters of administration. **18–15**

In order to prove his title in any court, any personal representative must produce a grant of probate or letters of administration (as the case may be).[42] Even an executor is not permitted to prove his title in any other way.[43]

1. Time at which property vests

The deceased's real and personal property vests in an executor appointed by him in his will if the executor is of full age.[44] A subsequent grant of probate enables the executor to prove that this has occurred.[45] **18–16**

Section 9(1) of the Administration of Estates Act 1925,[46] provides that: **18–17**

> "Where a person dies intestate, his real and personal estate shall vest in the Public Trustee until the grant of administration."

The Public Trustee has no beneficial interest in, or duties to perform in respect of, property vested in him by s.9,[47] but a notice affecting land, which would have been served on the deceased but for his death, shall be sufficiently served, before a grant has been filed, if it is addressed to "The Personal Representatives of" (the named deceased) and left at, or posted to, his last known place of residence or business *and* a copy is then

[40] *Birch v Birch* [1902] P. 62. at p.138.

[41] *Chetty v Chetty* [1916] 1 A.C. 603 and 608; *Biles v Caesar* [1957] 1 W.L.R. 156, 159–160.

[42] For recognition of Scottish confirmations and Northern Irish grants of representation and resealing of Commonwealth and Colonial grants, see above, paras 18–08 et seq.

[43] *Chetty v Chetty* above, at 608–609. cf. *Re Crowhurst Park* [1974] 1 W.L.R. 583, 594 (unproved will of realty on death prior to Land Transfer Act 1897 admissible) and *Whitmore v Lambert* [1955] 1 W.L.R. 495 (unproved will admissible in Rent Act case).

[44] *Woolley v Clark* (1822) 5 B. & Ald. 744; *Chetty v Chetty*, above, (as to personalty); Administration of Estates Act 1925, ss.1(1) and 3 (as to realty). As to devolution of property on death see below, paras 20–02 et seq.

[45] *Whitehead v Taylor* (1839) 10 A. & E. 210, 212.

[46] As substituted by s.14 of the Law of Property (Miscellaneous Provisions) Act 1994. S.9(2) applies where there is a will, but no executor with power to obtain probate.

[47] S.9(3), as substituted.

served on the Public Trustee.[48] Service on the person(s) entitled under the intestacy rules is ineffective.[49]

The deceased's property vests in an administrator when letters of administration are granted to him in respect of that property.[50]

Relation back

18–18 A doctrine (or fiction) of relation back has been adopted by the courts for the limited purpose of protecting the deceased's estate from wrongful injury in the interval between his death and the grant of letters of administration to his estate. Under this doctrine, the grant relates back to the death of the deceased.[51]

The administrator may sue in respect of any wrongdoing to an asset of the deceased's estate during this interval between death and the grant of letters of administration—for instance, in respect of trespass to the deceased's land[52] or breaches of covenant by a lessee of the deceased's land.[53]

2. Litigation before grant

18–19 An executor may begin a claim in his representative character before obtaining probate and continue it until such time as he needs to prove his title, but at that stage he must produce a grant of probate.[54] It is immaterial that the defendant to the claim is willing to admit the claimant's title as executor. If the executor brings a claim against a defendant, who is willing to pay a debt due to the deceased as soon as the executor can prove his title to receive it, the court does not dismiss the claim but stays proceedings in the claim until the executor obtains probate.

18–20 An administrator, on the other hand, cannot begin any claim in his representative character before obtaining letters of administration.[55]

3. Acts of administration before grant

18–21 Before obtaining probate an executor[56] has power to do all the acts which are incidental to his office, except those acts for which he needs a grant of

[48] Law of Property (Misc Provs) Act 1994 s.18. Under s.17, a notice remains effective where the person serving it has no reason to believe that the deceased has died, and it would have been effective but for the death. *Earl of Harrowby v Snelson* [1951] 1 All E.R. 140 (notice to quit).

[49] *Edwards v Strong* [1994] E.G. 182 (C.S.), (option to purchase).

[50] *Woolley v Clark* (fn.44 above), as to personalty; Administration of Estates Act 1925 ss.1(1) and 3, (as to realty).

[51] *Foster v Bates* (1843) 12 M. & W. 226; *Thorpe v Stallwood* (1843) 5 M. & Gr. 760; *Re Pryse* [1904] P. 301, 305. The doctrine has no application to executors.

[52] *R. v Inhabitants of Horsley* (1807) 8 East 405, 410 (trespass to leaseholds); *Re Pryse*, above, (trespass to freehold land).

[53] *Fred Long & Son Ltd v Burgess* [1950] 1 K.B. 115, 121.

[54] *Easton v Carter* (1850) 5 Exch. 8, 14; *Chetty v Chetty* [1916] 1 A.C. 603, 608; *Re Crowhurst Park* [1974] 1 W.L.R. 583: see also *Biles v Caesar* [1957] 1 W.L.R. 156.

[55] *Ingall v Moran* [1944] K.B. 160; *Millburn Snell v Evans* [2012] 1 W.L.R. 41. An administrator with the will annexed, like an administrator on intestacy, cannot commence any claim in his representative character before obtaining letters of administration, *Phillips v Hartley* (1827) 3 Car. & P. 121.

[56] The executor must be of full age at the testator's death, above, para.17–18.

probate in order to prove his title.[57] For instance, before obtaining probate an executor may:

(i) take possession of any of the assets of the testator's estate and receive, or release, debts owing to the estate.[58] But if the holder of any asset refuses to hand it over, or any debtor refuses to pay, the executor cannot prove his title in a claim against him without producing a grant of probate.[59]

(ii) pay, or take releases of, debts owing from the estate;[60]

(iii) sell and transfer to a purchaser any of the assets of the testator's estate. A conveyance of the testator's land, the title to which is unregistered at HM Land Registry, by an executor vests the legal title to the land in the purchaser, but the purchaser can only establish the executor's authority to sell and convey by proving that the executor subsequently obtained probate.[61] A transfer of the testator's land, the title to which is registered at HM Land Registry, cannot be registered before probate is granted;[62]

(iv) pay legacies or transfer property given by the will to the person entitled.[63]

If an executor does any of these acts incidental to his office and dies without obtaining probate, such acts "stand firm and good."[64] The death of the executor without obtaining probate determines his executorship,[65] but does not invalidate acts done by him before his death whilst his authority as executor subsisted.[66]

A person entitled to administration has no power to do anything as administrator before letters of administration are granted to him.[67] **18–22**

In order to protect the assets of the estate before a grant of probate or letters of administration is made, the court may appoint a receiver pending **18–23**

[57] *Re Stevens* [1897] 1 Ch.422, 429–430, citing *Williams on Executors*, edited by F. Barlow et al, 9th edn (London: LexisNexis Butterworths, 2008, p.249; *Kelsey v Kelsey* (1922) 91 L.J.Ch.382, 384 (notice to be served on "personal representatives" validly served on executors before probate). For appointment of new trustees by an executor before probate see *Re Crowhurst Park* [1974] 1 W.L.R. 583, 593–594: see below, para.20–64, fn.192.

[58] *Re Stevens* [1897] 1 Ch.422, 429–430. He may also distrain for rent due to the testator, *Whitehead v Taylor* (1839) 10 A. & E. 210.

[59] Revenue Act 1884 s.11 as amended by Revenue Act 1889 s.19; Administration of Estates Act 1925 s.2(1).

[60] *Re Stevens* [1897] 1 Ch.422, 429–430.

[61] Or, if (say) the executor died without obtaining probate, by means of a grant to some other person of letters of administration with the will annexed, which establishes the appointment of the executor.

[62] Land Registration Rules 2003 r.163.

[63] *Re Stevens* [1897] 1 Ch.422, 429–430; *Re Crowhurst Park* [1974] 1 W.L.R. 583, 594, 95.

[64] *Re Stevens* [1897] 1 Ch.422, 429–430.

[65] Administration of Estates Act 1925 s.5.

[66] *Wankford v Wankford* (1704) 1 Salk. 299, 309.

[67] *Wankford v Wankford*, above, at 301; *Doe'd. Hornby v Glenn* (1834) 1 A. & E. 49; *Morgan v Thomas* (1853) 8 Exch. 302; *Holland v King* (1848) 6 C.B. 727 (notice to be served by administrator of deceased partner: intending administratrix cannot give notice before grant) and cf. *Kelsey v Kelsey*, above, fn.57; *Mills v Anderson* [1984] Q.B. 704 (settlement of claim on behalf of deceased's estate prior to letters of administration not binding).

the grant.[68] An application to the Chancery Division for the appointment of such a receiver may be made by any person interested, whether a creditor[69] or a beneficiary.[70] For example, the court appointed a receiver where an executor had carried on the deceased's solicitor's practice for three years without taking probate.[71]

4. Period after grant

18–24 The chain of representation through executors is continued by a grant of probate, but is not continued by a grant of letters of administration.[72] Apart from this single difference, s.21 of the Administration of Estates Act 1925 provides that every person to whom letters of administration are granted has[73] the same rights and liabilities, and is accountable in like manner, as if he were the executor of the deceased. Moreover, if letters of administration are granted in respect of a deceased's estate, s.15 provides that no person shall have power to bring any claim or otherwise act as executor of the deceased so long as the grant has not been recalled or revoked.

C. PAYMENTS FOR WHICH A GRANT MAY NOT BE NEEDED

18–25 The general rule is that a grant of probate or letters of administration must be produced in order to establish the right to recover or receive any part of the deceased's estate situated in the United Kingdom.[74] There are, however, a large number of provisions, made by statute or statutory instrument, under which payment of particular sums otherwise due to the deceased's estate may be made without the production of any grant of representation to the deceased's estate.[75] Obviously the scope and effect of each of these provisions depends on its own particular wording but some characteristics are common to most, if not all, of them.[76]

[68] For grants of administration *ad colligenda bona* and *pendente lite* see below, paras 18–47 et seq.
[69] *Re Sutcliffe* [1942] Ch.453.
[70] *Steer v Steer* (1864) 2 Dr. & Sm. 311 (receiver and manager of deceased's business appointed); *Re Oakes* [1917] 1 Ch.230; *Ingall v Moran* [1944] K.B. 160, 169, 171–172.
[71] *Re Sutcliffe*, above.
[72] See above, paras 17–10 et seq.
[73] But subject to any limitations contained in the grant: for limited grants see below, paras 18–34 et seq.
[74] Revenue Act 1884 s.11 (personalty) and extended to realty by Land Transfer Act 1897 s.2(2), now replaced by Administration of Estates Act 1925 s.2(1).
[75] Instances are: (a) Friendly Societies Act 1974 s.68: (b) Trade Union and Labour Relations (Consolidation) Act 1992 s.18; Trade Union (Nominations) Regulations 1977 (SI 1977/789), reg.6 (as amended by SI 1984/1290): (c) National Savings Bank Act 1971 s.9; National Savings Bank Regulations 1972 (SI 1972/764) reg.40 (as amended by SI 1984/602): (d) National Debt Act 1972 s.11; Savings Certificates Regulations 1991 (SI 1991/1031), reg.15: (e) Building Societies Act 1986 s.32 and Sch.7.
[76] The provision contained in the Revenue Act 1884 s.11 (as amended by Revenue Act

(i) Almost every such provision specifies that the sum payable must not exceed £5,000.[77] **18–26**

(ii) These provisions authorise, but do not compel, the payer to make the payment without the production of a grant of representation to the deceased's estate. **18–27**

These provisions may be contrasted with those applicable to statutory nominations[78]: on the death of a nominator, payment to his nominee is obligatory, subject only to satisfactory proof of the nominator's death.[79]

(iii) Many of these provisions expressly protect the payer against the risk of making a payment to a person who turns out not to be entitled.[80] **18–28**

(iv) The Law Commission's Report *Intestacy and Family Provision Claims on Death*[81] recommended that the Government should commission a review of the small payments regime.[82] This review should consider, inter alia, whether the £5,000 limit should be raised, the range of assets to which the rules should apply, formalities, and the protection afforded to asset holders. **18–29**

III. FORMS OF GRANTS

There are three types of grant of representation: **18–30**

(i) probate (which is granted when an executor proves a will);
(ii) administration with the will annexed (which is granted when a person other than an executor proves a will); and
(iii) administration or "simple" administration (which is granted when the deceased died wholly intestate).

1889 s.19) is exceptional: it provides that the production of a grant of representation from a UK court shall not be necessary to establish the right to receive money payable in respect of a life assurance policy effected with any insurance company by a person who dies domiciled outside the UK; there is no maximum limit on the money payable and payment is obligatory, see *Haas v Atlas Assurance Co* [1913] 2 K.B. 209 (foreign executor entitled to judgment for policy money less estate duty).

77 The Administration of Estates (Small Payments) Act 1965 made a £500 limit generally applicable by inserting this £500 limit in almost 50 such provisions listed in the First Schedule to the Act. The Treasury has power to fix a higher limit. In 1975 the Treasury fixed a £1,500 limit on the sum payable and in 1984 increased this to £5,000 (SI 1984/539). In practice, banks and building societies may pay out larger sums without sight of a grant, subject to appropriate indemnities being given.

78 For statutory nominations see above, paras 1–06 et seq.

79 e.g. Industrial and Provident Societies Act 1965 s.24.

80 e.g. Industrial and Provident Societies Act 1965 s.27.

81 Law Com. No.331 (2011).

82 Law Com. No.331 (2011) at para.5.43.

Each of these types of grant may be general or limited—for instance, limited as to the property[83] to which the grant extends, or as to the duration of the grant.[84]

A. GENERAL GRANTS

18–31 Most grants of probate or administration—whether or not with the will annexed—are general in the sense that the grant is not by its terms limited in any way. A grant may be general even though it was preceded by another grant in respect of the same estate.

1. Double probate

18–32 When probate of a will is granted to some but not all of the executors, it is the practice to reserve power to the other executors who have not renounced to apply later for probate. If such an executor later applies for probate, he receives a grant called double probate.[85] If he was a minor when the original grant was made, he must attain 18 years of age before he applies, and if the original grant was made to four executors (the maximum number permitted), he must wait for a vacancy to occur.

A grant of double probate is a general grant which runs concurrently with the original grant. Until the grant of double probate is made, the executors to whom probate was originally granted may exercise all the powers conferred by law on a personal representative.[86]

2. Cessate grant

18–33 Agrant of probate or administration which is limited as to its duration terminates at the end of its allotted span. For instance, where a minor is the sole executor of a will, administration with the will annexed may be granted to his guardian, limited until the minor attains the age of 18 years[87]: when he attains 18, the grant automatically terminates and a further grant called a cessate grant may be made. Similarly, where a grant has been obtained by an attorney, the donor may revoke the power and apply for a cessate grant, whereupon the original grant ceases to have effect.

[83] An example of a limited grant is a settled land grant. Such a grant is made to the deceased's special personal representatives. Settled land grants are now rare and are not discussed in detail in this edition of this book. For further information, see paras 18–45 et seq. of the 12th edition of this book.
[84] Senior Courts Act 1981 s.113.
[85] Such an executor may be cited to accept or refuse a grant at the instance of the executors who have proved, or the executors of the last survivor of them, N.C. Prob. Rules 1987 r.47(2).
[86] Administration of Estates Act 1925 s.8.
[87] See below, paras 18–39 et seq.

B. LIMITED GRANTS

1. Powers to make limited grants

Under s.113 of the Senior Courts Act 1981, the court has power to grant probate or administration in respect of any part of the deceased's estate, limited in any way the court thinks fit.[88] **18–34**

If the court exercises its powers under s.116 of the Act to pass over an executor, or to pass over a person who would otherwise have been entitled to the grant of administration, and it appoints some other person as administrator,[89] the court may limit its grant of administration in any way it thinks fit.[90] Thus, on passing over, the power to make a limited grant is not subject to any restriction.

If a grant is first made limited to particular property or a particular purpose, a grant may later be made *caeterorum*, i.e. of all the rest of the estate. If the grants are made in the reverse order, a grant is first made *save and except* the particular property or particular purpose, and a grant limited to that property or purpose may be made later.

2. Limited probate

The appointment by a testator of an executor may be qualified as to the subject matter of his office (e.g. limited to his copyrights and manuscripts), or as to time (e.g. during the minority of a particular person).[91] Such an executor may only take a grant of probate limited to the property, or the time, specified in the will.[92] **18–35**

3. Administration *de bonis non*

A grant of administration *de bonis non administratis*—usually known as a grant *de bonis non*—is made in respect of a deceased's unadministered estate and is designed to enable the administration of the estate to be completed. **18–36**

(a) *When made*

A grant *de bonis non* is made following the death of a sole, or last surviving, personal representative who died without having fully administered the deceased's estate. Two requirements apply: **18–37**

[88] See N.C. Prob. Rules 1987 r.51. This wide power to make limited grants is subject to only one restriction: where the deceased's estate is known to be insolvent. See below, paras 21–68 et seq. The section forbids severance of the grant of representation to it, except as regards a trust estate in which the deceased had no beneficial interest.

[89] See above, paras 17–21 and 17–49.

[90] For an instance see *In the Goods of Baldwin* [1903] P. 61 (will only made specific gift to X: next-of-kin passed over and letters of administration (with will annexed) granted to X limited to property specifically given to X by will).

[91] See above, para.17–04.

[92] *In the Estate of Falkner* (1915) 113 L.T. 927.

(i) there must have been a prior grant of probate or letters of administration in favour of the personal representative who has died,

(ii) any chain of representation[93] through proving executors must have been broken.[94]

A grant *de bonis non* is also made following the revocation by the court of a previous grant of probate or administration.[95]

(b) *To whom made*

18–38 The rules of priority which govern applications for original grants apply equally to applications for *de bonis non* grants. Thus r.20 of the Non-Contentious Probate Rules applies to an application for administration *de bonis non* with the will annexed, and r.22 to an application for simple administration *de bonis non*.[96] An applicant for a *de bonis non* grant must clear off all persons who have a prior right to a grant: alternatively, the court may pass them over pursuant to its power under s.116 of the Senior Courts Act 1981.

4. Administration for the use and benefit of a minor

18–39 A minor cannot take a grant of probate or letters of administration.[97] If the person to whom a grant of probate or administration would otherwise be made is a minor, administration is granted for the use and benefit of the minor until he attains the age of 18 years.[98] If a grant of probate or administration with the will annexed would otherwise be made, it is a grant of administration with the will annexed: if the deceased left no will, it is a grant of simple administration. This form of grant, formerly known as a grant *durante minore aetate*, is by its nature limited as to its duration and terminates automatically. When the minor attains the age of 18, probate or administration may be granted to him.

(a) *When made*

18–40 If the sole executor is a minor, a grant of administration for his use and benefit is made. But if there are two or more executors, of whom at least one is not under disability, probate may be granted to any executor not under disability, with power reserved to the executor who is a minor to

93 See above, para.17–12.

94 *In the Goods of Reid* [1896] P. 129 (chain not broken).

95 *In the Goods of Galbraith* [1951] P. 422 (executors becoming unfit, probate revoked); *In the Goods of Loveday* [1900] P. 154 (grant to administratrix who could not be traced, revoked); *In the Estate of French* [1910] P. 169.

96 See above, paras 17–35 and 17–39.

97 See above, paras 17–18 and 17–48. An infant is usually referred to as a minor in probate practice.

98 N.C. Prob. Rules 1987 r.32. As an alternative to a grant for the use and benefit of a minor, a trust corporation may sometimes take a limited grant until the minor applies for and obtains a grant, see r.36(3).

take probate on attaining full age[99]: in such a case a grant for the use and benefit of the minor cannot be made unless the executors not under disability either renounce or fail to take probate on being cited to accept or refuse a grant.[100]

In determining whether a minor is the person to whom a grant of administration would otherwise be made, r.27(5) of the Non-Contentious Probate Rules requires administration to be granted to a person of full age entitled thereto in preference to a guardian of a minor, unless a district judge or registrar otherwise directs.

(b) *To whom made*

Under r.32 a grant for the use and benefit of a minor is made to: **18–41**

(i) a parent of the minor who has, or is deemed to have, parental responsibility for him[101]; a person who has, or is deemed to have, parental responsibility for the minor by virtue of s.12(2) of the Children Act 1989; a step-parent who has parental responsibility in accordance with s.4A of the Children Act 1989; a guardian of the minor who is appointed, or is deemed to have been appointed, in accordance with s.5,[102] or a special guardian appointed in accordance with s.14A, of the 1989 Act; an adoption agency which has parental responsibility by virtue of s.25(2) of the Adoption and Children Act 2002; or a local authority which has, or is deemed to have, parental responsibility by virtue of section 33(3) of the 1989 Act.[103]
There is a single exception to this head (i). If a minor who is sole executor has no interest in the deceased's residuary estate, such a grant is made to the person entitled to the residuary estate, unless a district judge or registrar otherwise directs.[104]

(ii) any person appointed by a district judge or registrar to obtain administration for the use and benefit of the minor.[105]
The person so appointed may obtain administration for the use and benefit of the minor in default of, or jointly with, or even to the exclusion of, any person falling under head (i). Thus any person falling under head (i) may be passed over.

If any beneficiary is a minor, or a life interest arises under a will or on intestacy, administration must be granted either to a trust corporation—with or without an individual—or to no fewer than two individuals

[99] N.C. Prob. Rules 1987 r.33(1).
[100] N.C. Prob. Rules 1987 r.33(2).
[101] In accordance with (i) s.2(1), 2(2) or 4 of the Children Act 1989, (ii) para.4 or 6 of Sch.14 to that Act, or (iii) an adoption order within the meaning of s.46(1) of the Adoption and Children Act 2002.
[102] Or in accordance with paras 12, 13 or 14 of Sch.14.
[103] N.C. Prob Rules 1987 r.32(1) as amended.
[104] N.C. Prob Rules 1987 r.32(1) proviso.
[105] R32(2).

unless it appears to the court to be expedient to appoint an individual as sole administrator.[106] If there is only one person competent and willing to take a grant under heads (i) and (ii), that person may nominate a suitable person as co-administrator unless a district judge or a registrar otherwise directs.[107]

(c) *Renunciation*

18–42 A minor's right to administration may be renounced only by a person appointed administrator by a district judge or registrar and who is authorised to renounce by the district judge or registrar.[108] A minor's right to take probate as executor on attaining the age of 18 years may not be renounced by any person on his behalf.[109]

(d) *Accountability of administrator*

18–43 An administrator who takes a grant for the use and benefit of a minor has the same rights and liabilities as an ordinary administrator.[110] After his grant has terminated, he must account to the person who subsequently obtains a grant of representation to the deceased—often this person is the former minor.[111]

5. Administration in case of lack of mental capacity

18–44 A person who lacks capacity within the meaning of the Mental Capacity Act 2005 to manage his affairs cannot take a grant of probate or letters of administration. Instead, administration may be granted for his use and benefit, limited until further representation is granted or in such other way as the district judge or registrar may direct.[112] If the deceased left a will, it is a grant of administration with the will annexed, otherwise it is a grant of simple administration.

(a) *When made*

18–45 Unless a district judge or registrar otherwise directs, no such grant is made unless all the persons equally entitled in the same degree as the person who lacks capacity have been cleared off.[113] As in the case of a minor executor, probate may be granted to any other executor not under disability, with power reserved to the executor who lacks capacity to take

[106] Senior Courts Act 1981 s.114(2).
[107] N.C. Prob. Rules 1987 r.32(3).
[108] N.C. Prob. Rules 1987 r.34(2).
[109] N.C. Prob. Rules 1987 r.34(1).
[110] Administration of Estates Act 1925 s.21: see *Re Cope* (1880) 16 Ch.D. 49, 52; *Harvell v Foster* [1954] 2 Q.B. 367.
[111] *Fotherby v Pate* (1747) 3 Atk. 603; *Taylor v Newton* (1752) 1 Lee 15 (accounting to creditor administrator).
[112] N.C. Prob. Rules 1987 r.35(2). Such a grant is sometimes called a disability grant.
[113] N.C. Prob. Rules 1987 r.35(1).

probate if he regains capacity. Notice of an intended application for such a grant must be given to the Court of Protection, unless the applicant is the person authorised by the Court of Protection to apply for a grant.[114]

(b) *To whom made*

Under r.35 such a grant is made: **18–46**

(i) to any person authorised by the Court of Protection to apply for a grant,
(ii) where there is no person so authorised, to the lawful attorney of the person who lacks capacity acting under a registered enduring power of attorney or lasting power of attorney,
(iii) where there is no such attorney entitled to act, or if the attorney renounces administration, to the person entitled to the deceased's residuary estate.

If there is only one person competent and willing to take a grant under heads (i), (ii) and (iii), and a grant is required to be made to no fewer than two administrators, that person may nominate a co-administrator unless a district judge or registrar otherwise directs.[115]

A district judge or registrar may override this order of priority by ordering administration for the use and benefit of the incapable person to be granted to such other person as he may direct.[116]

6. Administration *ad colligenda bona*

A grant of administration *ad colligenda bona* is made to any suitable person **18–47**
for the purpose of preserving the assets of the estate until a general grant is made. Such a grant is useful, for instance, where urgent action is needed and the person entitled to a general grant cannot readily apply for it.[117] A grant *ad colligenda bona* is usually limited to the purpose of collecting, getting in and receiving the estate and doing acts necessary for its preservation, and is always limited until a further grant of representation is made. The grant is one of administration, and the will (if any) of the deceased is not annexed because no distribution to beneficiaries is authorised. A grant *ad colligenda bona* may specifically confer any wider power (such as a power to sell the deceased's farming stock) needed by the administrator. But if wider powers are needed, or it is not clear what action the administrator

114 N.C. Prob. Rules 1987 r.35(5). Persons acting under a registered power of attorney are not considered to be authorised by the Court of Protection. For proof of mental incapacity see *Practice Note* [1962] 2 All E.R. 613; *Practice Direction* [1969] 1 All E.R. 494.
115 N.C. Prob. Rules 1987 r.35(3).
116 N.C. Prob. Rules 1987 r.35(4).
117 *In the Goods of Bolton* [1899] P. 186 (next of kin in South America, goodwill of deceased's business as a newsagent needed to be sold before it became valueless; grant *ad colligenda* made to deceased's friend); see also *In the Goods of Stewart* (1869) L.R. 1 P. & D. 727; *In the Goods of Schwerdtfeger* (1876) 1 P.D. 424; *In the Goods of Ashley* (1890) 15 P.D. 120; *In the Goods of Roberts* [1898] P. 149; *Re Clore* [1982] Fam. 113, [1982] Ch.456 (capital transfer tax dispute: Official Solicitor, not executors, appointed): N.C. Prob. Rules 1987 r.52.

may have to take, it is preferable to apply for a grant to be made, limited as may be appropriate, under s.116 of the Senior Courts Act 1981.[118]

7. Administration pending determination of a probate claim (pending suit or *pendente lite*)

18–48 After a probate claim has begun[119] the court has power under s.117 of the Senior Courts Act 1981 to grant administration of the deceased's estate to an administrator. Such a grant of administration pending determination of a probate claim is limited to the duration of the claim and terminates at its conclusion.[120] The person entitled may then take a grant of probate or administration as appropriate.

(a) *When made*

18–49 Agrant of administration pending determination of a probate claim is made if this is proper in all the circumstances. In general, a grant is justified if there are assets of the estate to be collected and safeguarded.[121] An application for the appointment of an administrator pending determination of a probate claim may be made by any party to the probate claim or by any other interested person, such as a creditor.[122]

(b) *To whom made*

18–50 Usually such a grant is made to a person unconnected with the claim,[123] such as an accountant or a solicitor, and not to a party to the claim unless all parties consent.[124] A sole administrator pending determination of a probate claim may be appointed, even though there is the possibility of a minority or a life interest arising.

(c) *Function of administrator pending determination of a probate claim*

18–51 Section 117 provides that an administrator pending suit shall have all the rights, duties and powers of a general administrator,[125] subject to an

[118] See above, paras 17–21 and 17–49: *In the Goods of Wyckoff* (1862) 32 L.J.P.M. & A. 214; *In the Goods of Suarez* [1897] P. 82. For a discussion as to the need to give notice, the revocation of a grant *ad colligenda bona* obtained without notice, and the costs position in such circumstances, see *Ghafoor v Cliff* [2006] 1 W.L.R. 646.

[119] *Salter v Salter* [1896] P. 291 (caveator appearing to warning, but no claim form issued: no jurisdiction to grant administration pending determination of claim).

[120] *Weiland v Bird* [1894] P. 262 (probate claim terminates with decree); *Taylor v Taylor* (1881) 3 P.D. 29 (appeal extends probate claim).

[121] *Re Bevan* [1948] 1 All E.R. 271. In *Mortimer v Paull* (1870) L.R. 2 P.& D 85 the court refused to make such a grant where a probate claim had been begun to determine the validity of a codicil, but the appointment of executors by the deceased's will was not challenged.

[122] *In the Goods of Evans* (1890) 15 P.D. 215; *In the Estate of Cleaver* [1905] P. 319.

[123] *Stratton v Ford* (1755) 2 Lee 216; *Whittle v Keats* (1866) 35 L.J.P. & M. 54.

[124] *Re Griffin* [1925] P. 38 (claimant appointed without defendant's consent as appointment was clearly desirable).

[125] *Re Toleman* [1897] 1 Ch.866 (administrator *pendente lite* may be sued by a creditor of the deceased without any leave of the court).

important restriction—he must not make any distribution of the deceased's estate to any beneficiary without the leave of the court.[126] The administrator is subject to the immediate control of the court and acts under its direction[127]: he should, for instance, obtain the directions of the court as to any disputed debt.[128]

The administrator must submit such accounts to such parties as the court may direct[129] and he is entitled to such reasonable remuneration as the court thinks fit out of the deceased's estate.[130]

8. Representation in legal proceedings

If there is no personal representative of the deceased and it is necessary for **18–52** the estate to be represented in legal proceedings, a grant of administration limited to a claim (known as a grant *ad litem*) may be made under s.116 of the Senior Courts Act 1981.[131] Such a grant is limited to bringing, defending or being a party to particular legal proceedings. Thus an intending claimant, who wishes to bring a claim for damages against the deceased's estate in respect of the deceased's negligence in a motor accident, may apply for a grant to be made to the claimant's nominee, limited to defending the claim.[132]

Since 1971 there has been a simpler alternative procedure, which is applicable where any person against whom a claim would have lain has died but the cause of action survives.[133] If no grant of probate or administration has been made, the claimant may bring his claim against the "the estate of" the deceased, and then apply in the claim for an order appointing a person to represent the deceased's estate for the purpose of the proceedings.[134]

[126] *Or* in such circumstances as may be prescribed by rules of court, Senior Courts Act 1981 ss.117(2) and 151(1).
[127] Senior Courts Act s.117(2). *In the Estate of Lindley* [1953] P. 203; *In the Estate of Haslip* [1958] 1 W.L.R. 583.
[128] *Charlton v Hindmarsh* (1860) 1 Sw. & Tr. 519.
[129] CPR 69.4 (relating to receivers) applies (CPR 57 PD 8.2(1)).
[130] Senior Courts Act 1981 s.117(3): see also *Re Howlett* [1950] P. 177. See below, para.20–71.
[131] See above, paras 17–21 and 17–49.
[132] *In the Estate of Gunning* [1936] P. 40; *In the Goods of Knight* [1939] 3 All E.R. 928 (grant *ad litem* to Treasury Solicitor); *In the Estate of Newsham* [1967] P. 230.
[133] CPR 19.8.
[134] CPR 19.8(2): the deceased driver's insurers may be appointed in a running-down claim. As to the appointment of the Official Solicitor, see *Re Amirteymour* [1979] 1 W.L.R. 63.

Chapter 19

THE MAKING AND REVOCATION OF GRANTS

I. THE MAKING OF GRANTS

A. CAVEATS AND CITATIONS

1. Caveats

A caveat is a notice in writing to the Family Division of the High Court that no grant is to be sealed in the deceased's estate without notice to the caveator, the person who enters the caveat.[1] An index of caveats entered in any registry is kept and is searched on any application for a grant being made in any registry.[2] Thus the entry of a caveat stops the issue of any grant in the deceased's estate—except to the caveator himself[3]—until the caveat ceases to be effective. It gives the caveator time to take legal advice, or collect evidence, so that he may decide whether to oppose an application by another person for a grant. **19–01**

(a) *Warning of Caveat*

When an applicant for a grant finds that a caveat has been entered, he may issue a warning in the prescribed form to the caveator.[4] A warning states **19–02**

[1] Caveats are regulated by N.C. Prob. Rules 1987 r.44.

[2] Senior Courts Act 1981 s.108; N.C. Prob. Rules 1987 r.44(4) and r.44(1). The Non-Contentious Probate (Amendment) Rules 1998 introduced new rules and amendments as a result of computerisation of probate records. Rule 44(4) requires an index of caveats to be maintained, which is searched when an application for a grant is received by any probate registry or sub-registry. The senior district judge is required by r.57 to maintain an index of every pending application for a grant in any registry or sub-registry, which is updated when a caveat is entered. The caveat is instantly matched against pending applications.

[3] A caveat does not prevent the issue of a grant *ad colligenda bona*, or a grant pending suit: *Re Clore* [1982] Ch.456; nor does it prevent the sealing of a grant on the day on which it is entered: r.44(1).

[4] N.C. Prob. Rules 1987 r.44(5): any person interested may issue a warning. Caveats may be warned only at the "nominated registry" i.e. the registry nominated by the senior district judge and, in the absence of such nomination, the Leeds District Probate Registry (r.44(15)).

the interest of the applicant (e.g. that he is the executor of the will of the deceased, or interested on intestacy) and sets out two alternative courses of action open to the caveator:

(i) to enter an appearance to the warning, stating the caveator's contrary interest (e.g. that he is the executor of a different will of the deceased).[5] If the caveator enters an appearance, no grant can be issued without an order of the court.[6] Often the applicant or the caveator commences a probate action[7] at this point in order to obtain the decision of the court as to who is entitled to a grant,

(ii) to issue a summons for directions if the caveator has no contrary interest but wishes to show cause against the sealing of a grant to the applicant.[8] The caveator and the applicant may, for instance, be entitled to a grant in the same degree.

If the caveator does not follow either of these courses of action, the caveat ceases to be effective[9] and a grant of probate or administration may be issued to the applicant.

(b) *Duration of a caveat*

19–03 A caveat also ceases to be effective at the expiration of six months beginning with the date on which it was entered.[10] A caveator may lodge a written application for its extension during the last month of this six months' period: each time the caveator does this, the caveat remains in force for another six months.[11]

A caveat ceases to be effective if the caveator withdraws it before he enters an appearance to a warning.[12]

(c) *Standing search for a grant*

19–04 A person who wishes to commence family provision proceedings or to take action against an estate should not enter a caveat.[13] Instead, he should apply for a standing search to be made for any grant of representation to

[5] N.C. Prob. Rules 1987 r.44(10); appearance to a warning must be entered at the nominated registry.

[6] N.C. Prob. Rules 1987 rr.44(13) and 45(3): for the caveator's position in a consequent probate claim see *Rose v Epstein* [1974] 1 W.L.R. 1565: for caveats entered by a vexatious litigant see *Re Hancock* [1978] C.L.Y. 1443.

[7] N.C. Prob. Rules 1987 r.44(13).

[8] N.C. Prob. Rules 1987 r.44(6).

[9] N.C. Prob. Rules 1987 r.44(12); the caveator has at least eight days to do so, see rr.44(10) and (6).

[10] N.C. Prob. Rules 1987 r.44(3); but see rr.44(8) and (13).

[11] N.C. Prob. Rules 1987 r.44(3).

[12] N.C. Prob. Rules 1987 r.44(11).

[13] He will not be objecting to the validity of a will or to the issue of a grant: he will be claiming that the will does not make adequate financial provision for him, or that the estate is liable to him.

the deceased's estate issued within the previous 12 months or within the following six months.[14]

2. Citations

There are three types of citation.[15] Two have already been considered, namely a citation to accept or refuse a grant[16] and a citation to take probate.[17] The third type is a citation to propound a will. **19–05**

A person who is interested on intestacy—or under an earlier will of the deceased—may cite the executors and beneficiaries under an alleged will, or an alleged later will, to propound it. If they fail to enter an appearance and propound the alleged will, the citor may apply for an order for a grant in common form as if the alleged will were invalid.[18] A citation to propound a will is not, however, appropriate if the will in question has already been proved in common form. In this case, the person challenging the will may bring a probate claim for the revocation of the previous grant.[19]

This procedure by citation is useful where there is doubt as to the validity of a will.[20] The procedure cannot, however, be invoked by an executor of a will who doubts the validity of a later codicil. In this case the executor should apply for a grant of probate in solemn form and, if he has reason to believe that the codicil is invalid, should adduce evidence of its invalidity.[21]

B. TIME LIMIT FOR ISSUING A GRANT

1. Minimum time

Normally no grant of probate or letters of administration with the will annexed may be issued within seven days, and no grant of simple administration within 14 days, of the deceased's death. An earlier grant may be issued with the leave of a district judge or registrar.[22] **19–06**

[14] N.C. Prob. Rules 1987 r.43: for extension see r.43(3).
[15] For the issue of citations see N.C. Prob. Rules 1987 r.46.
[16] See above, para.17–23 (probate) and para.17–51 (administration).
[17] See above, para.17–26.
[18] N.C. Prob. Rules 1987 r.48: see also *In the Goods of Morton* (1863) 3 Sw. & Tr. 179; *In the Goods of Dennis* [1899] P. 191; *In the Goods of Bootle* (1901) 84 L.T. 570.
[19] *Re Jolley* [1964] P. 262.
[20] *In the Estate of Muirhead* [1971] P.263, following *In the Goods of Benbow* (1862) 2 Sw. & Tr. 488.
[21] *In the Estate of Muirhead* [1971] at 270. Cairns J also suggested obiter that his decision might apply in a case where there were two wills with the same executors, the later will if valid revoking the earlier.
[22] N.C. Prob. Rules 1987 r.6(2); "District judge" means a district judge of the Principal Registry; "registrar" means a district probate registrar; see also r.6(1) (inquiries to be answered before grant issued).

2. No maximum time

19–07 There is no maximum limit of the time within which a grant must be obtained. But penalties are laid down for administering an estate without obtaining a grant of representation.[23]

C. LIABILITY OF PERSONAL REPRESENTATIVES FOR INHERITANCE TAX

19–08 The overall tax position was discussed in Chapter 16. This part of this chapter is concerned only with the liability of the deceased's personal representatives for inheritance tax. The incidence of the tax on the beneficial interests under the deceased's will or intestacy is considered later.[24]

1. Liability of the personal representatives

19–09 Under s.200(1) of the Inheritance Tax Act 1984 the deceased's personal representatives are liable for the inheritance tax charged on his death on the value of:

(i) any property which was not immediately before his death comprised in a settlement; and
(ii) any land in the United Kingdom which immediately before his death was comprised in a settlement and which devolves upon or vests in the personal representatives.[25]

Head (ii) is relatively narrow whereas head (i) is very wide, including, not only the deceased's property which vests in his personal representatives, but also the deceased's severable notional share of property held jointly, and the deceased's foreign property which does not vest in them.

This liability of personal representatives for inheritance tax under s.200(1) is a personal liability—their own assets are liable to be taken in execution to satisfy the tax due to the Crown,[26] but only to the extent of assets which they received as personal representatives or might have received but for their neglect or default.[27]

[23] Stamp Act 1815 s.37 as amended by Finance Act 1975 ss.52(2), 59(5) and Sch.13 Pt I.
[24] See below, paras 21–55 et seq.
[25] For exceptions to the personal representatives' liability under s.200(1) see ss.30–35 (as amended), 125–130, and 207–208; the exceptions include heritage property and woodlands to which special accountability rules apply: for the definition of settlement see s.43. For the contingent secondary liability of personal representatives to tax in respect of lifetime transfers see s.199(2), as amended by Finance Act 1986 Sch.19, para.26.
[26] *I.R.C. v Stannard* [1984] 1 W.L.R. 1039 (order is in *de bonis propriis* form).
[27] Inheritance Act 1984 s.204, and see *Re Clore* [1982] Ch.456.

2. Delivery of Inland Revenue Account

The personal representatives[28] must deliver an account to the Commissioners for Her Majesty's Revenue and Customs (HMRC)[29] within 12 months from the end of the month in which the death occurs or (if this is later) within three months from the date on which they first acted.[30] Normally, no account needs to be delivered if the value of the deceased's estate does not exceed the inheritance tax nil-rate band.[31] The account specifies to the best of the personal representatives' knowledge and belief[32] the nature and value of all property which formed part of the deceased's estate immediately before his death.[33] They may submit a provisional estimate of value if they are unable to ascertain the exact value of any property and undertake to deliver a further account as soon as its value is ascertained. If the personal representatives discover that the account delivered by them is defective, they must deliver a corrective or supplementary account within six months of this discovery.[34] **19–10**

3. No grant before payment of tax

Personal representatives must pay all the tax for which they are liable on delivery of their account, unless they are entitled to, and do, elect to pay by instalments.[35] Although they have 12 months from the end of the month in which the death occurs to deliver their account, interest is charged on unpaid tax as soon as six months have passed from the end of the month in which the death occurs.[36] **19–11**

[28] This means executors, any person by whom or on whose behalf an application for a grant of administration or for the resealing of a grant made outside the UK is made, and an *executor de son tort*, see s.272: as to an *executor de son tort* see below, paras 24–48 et seq.

[29] HMRC, combining the Inland Revenue and Her Majesty's Customs and Excise, became a legal entity on 18 April 2005.

[30] ss.216(1) and (6) and 257. For delivery of the account to a probate registry instead see s.257(3).

[31] For the tax year 2015–16 the nil rate band is £325.000; see above, para.16–18. If the deceased dies on or after 6 April 2004 there is no obligation to file an HMRC Account if the estate is "excepted". The Inheritance Tax (Delivery of Accounts) (Excepted Estates) Regulations 2004, SI 2004/2543, as amended by SI 2006/2141, SI 2011/2226 and SI 2014/488 provide for three types of excepted estate. Whether or not an estate is "excepted" depends on a number of factors, including whether the estate includes settled property, whether it includes property situated outside the United Kingdom, whether the deceased made chargeable transfers within the seven years before his death and whether the deceased was domiciled in the United Kingdom. Where an estate qualifies as an "excepted estate" the relevant form is IHT 205. For further details, see the Regulations and see also Williams Mortimer and Sunnucks, *Executors, Administrators and Probate*, 20th edn (London: Sweet & Maxwell, 2013), para.21–53.

[32] *I.R.C. v Stype Trustees (Jersey) Ltd*. [1985] 1 W.L.R. 1290.

[33] s.216(3) (as amended); see also ss.5(1) and (2).

[34] s.217. For penalties in connection with accounts see ss.245–253 and *Robertson v IRC (No.1)* [2002] W.T.L.R. 885 and *Robertson v IRC (No.2)* [2002] W.T.L.R. 907.

[35] s.226(2). For their election to pay tax by 10 yearly instalments in the case of land, certain company shares or securities, a business or interest in a business, see ss.227–234.

[36] s.233; the rate of interest is calculated according to an algebraic formula, see Taxes (Interest Rate) Regulations 1989 SI 1989/1297, para.4(2). Interest payable is not deductible for income tax purposes, s.233(3).

The High Court cannot make any grant of probate or letters of administration, or reseal any grant made outside the United Kingdom, until the personal representatives have paid any inheritance tax payable on delivery of their account.[37]

Personal representatives find themselves in a practical difficulty over the payment of tax. The difficulty is circular. They cannot generally dispose of the deceased's assets without a grant and they cannot easily raise money without disposing of the deceased's assets. But they cannot obtain a grant without paying the tax and to pay the tax they need money. With effect from 3 March 2003, it has been possible to draw on funds owned by the deceased in a bank or building society, which are transferred directly to HMRC. If no or insufficient funds are available, the personal representatives may borrow money to pay the tax.[38]

D. OATH AND OTHER EVIDENCE

19–12 Every application for a grant must be supported by an oath sworn by the applicant and by such other papers as the registrar may require.[39]

1. The oath

19–13 The oath of the applicant is contained in an affidavit sworn by him. The form of oath varies according to the circumstances of the case.[40] An oath normally includes the following:

(a) *Death of the deceased*

19–14 The applicant swears to the name and dates of birth and death of the deceased.[41]

(b) *Domicile at death*

19–15 The oath states where the deceased died domiciled[42] and this is noted in the grant.

[37] Senior Courts Act 1981 s.109 as amended by Inheritance Tax Act 1984, Sch.8: this requirement may be dispensed with by arrangement between the President of the Family Division and the Revenue s.109(2) see *Re Clore* [1982] Fam. 113, 117.

[38] The interest is deductible for income tax purposes; see above, para.16–56.

[39] N.C. Prob. Rules 1987 r.8(1): the applicant may affirm instead of swearing the oath.

[40] See e.g. *Practice Direction* [1990] 2 All E.R. 576 where unnamed partners in firms of solicitors are appointed executors, and not all partners wish to apply for probate.

[41] N.C. Prob. Rules 1987 r.53 and Practice Direction (Fam Div: Probate Records: Deceased's Names) [1999] 1 W.L.R. 259.

[42] N.C. Prob. Rules 1987 r.8(2).

(c) *Will or intestacy*

The applicant swears that he believes "the paper writing now produced to and marked[43] by me to contain the true and original last will and testament" of the deceased (on an application for probate or administration with the will annexed), *or* that the deceased died intestate (on an application for simple administration). **19–16**

(d) *Title of applicant to grant*

The applicant shows his title to the grant for which he is applying— for instance, that he is the sole executor of the will (on an application for probate); the residuary legatee and devisee named in the will (on an application for administration with the will annexed); or the son and one of the persons entitled to share in the estate (on an application for simple administration). On any application for administration (whether or not with the will annexed), the oath must state in what manner all persons having a prior right to a grant have been cleared off, and whether any minority or life interest arises under the will or intestacy.[44] **19–17**

(e) *Settled land*

The oath must state whether, to the best of the applicant's knowledge, information and belief, there was land vested in the deceased which was settled previously to his death (and not by his will) and which remained settled land notwithstanding his death.[45] **19–18**

(f) *Duties of personal representative*

Section 25 of the Administration of Estates Act 1925[46] summarises the duties of a personal representative as being to: **19–19**

"(a) collect and get in the real and personal estate of the deceased and administer it according to law;
(b) when required to do so by the court, exhibit on oath in the court a full inventory of the estate and when so required render an account of the administration of the estate to the court;
(c) when required to do so by the High Court, deliver up the grant of probate or administration to that court."

[43] The will is "marked" by the signatures of the applicant and the person before whom the oath is sworn, N.C. Prob. Rules 1987 r.10.
[44] N.C. Prob. Rules 1987 r.8(4). For the minimum number of administrators see above, para.17–46.
[45] N.C. Prob. Rules 1987 r.8(3) (applicable if the deceased died after 1925); for grants to settled land see previous (i.e. 12th) edition of this book, paras 18–45 et seq. Since the Trusts of Land and Appointment of Trustees Act 1996 came into force on 1 January 1997, it is no longer possible to create a settlement for the purposes of the Settled Land Act 1925.
[46] As substituted by Administration of Estates Act 1971 s.9.

The applicant swears that he will carry out these duties which are set out in thc oath.

(g) *Value of the estate*

19–20 The applicant states (to the best of his knowledge, information and belief) the gross and net values of the estate passing under the grant, except where the estate is an excepted estate, in which case it is sufficient to specify the net value rounded to the next whole thousand.[47]

2. Will not available

19–21 Normally on an application for probate or administration with the will annexed, the applicant lodges the original will in the registry,[48] where a photostat copy is made and annexed to the grant.[49] Sometimes the original will is not available. It may be in the custody of a foreign court, in which case a duly authenticated copy of the will may be admitted to proof.[50] It may have been lost or destroyed, either during the testator's lifetime—without being revoked—or since his death. In that case, a district judge or registrar may make an order admitting to proof the will as contained in a copy or a reconstruction.[51] The district judge or registrar may require application to be made to a district judge or registrar or to a judge of the High Court,[52] who in turn may make such an order or, if there is opposition from persons entitled under an intestacy or an earlier will, require the will to be propounded in a probate claim. Usually the grant made is limited until the original will or a more authentic copy of it be proved.[53]

An applicant who seeks to prove a will which has been lost or destroyed needs to establish:

(i) that the will was duly executed. This may be proved, for instance, by the evidence of one or more of the attesting witnesses, or by proof that the will contained a proper attestation clause,[54]

[47] Practice Direction 27 October 2004. The fee payable for a grant of probate or administration is assessed on the net value N.C. Prob. Fees Order 2004 (SI 2004/3120) as amended by the N.C. Prob. Fees (Amendment) Order 2014 (SI 2014/876). A flat fee of £155 is payable where the value of the estate exceeds £5,000.

[48] The original will is then preserved in a place of deposit, Senior Courts Act 1981 s.124; *Re Greer* (1929) 45 T.L.R. 362 and cf. *In the Estate of White Todd* [1926] P. 173.

[49] For the lodging of an engrossment of the original will where a photographic copy would not be satisfactory, or where the will contains alterations not admissible to proof or has been ordered to be rectified, see N.C. Prob. Rules 1987 r.11.

[50] N.C. Prob. Rules 1987 r.54(2).

[51] N.C. Prob. Rules 1987. r.54(1): the rule also applies to a nuncupative will of a privileged testator.

[52] N.C. Prob. Rules 1987 r.61(1) and see *In the Estate of Nuttall* (Practice Note) [1955] 1 W.L.R. 847.

[53] *In the Goods of Lemme* [1892] P. 89 (French notary forbidden to part with original will); *In the Goods of Von Linden* [1896] P. 148.

[54] *In the Estate of Phibbs* [1917] P. 93 (proof that will contained a proper attestation clause sufficed though identity of attesting witnesses not known); *Re Webb* [1964] 1 W.L.R. 509

(ii) what the contents of the will were. There may, for instance, be a copy or draft of the will in existence, or the contents of the will may be proved by the evidence of a person who read the will before it was lost.[55]

In addition, if the will was last known to be in the testator's possession but could not be found at his death so that a presumption of revocation arises, the applicant needs to rebut this presumption by evidence of non-revocation,[56] or evidence showing the testator's intention to revoke subject to a condition which is not fulfilled,[57] or proving that the will was destroyed by enemy action or accident.[58] **19–22**

In *Re Webb*[59] the testatrix's sister found a completed draft of the testatrix's will in a tin trunk and the testatrix told her, "Don't throw that away; it's my will." After her death the original will could not be found and the sister (a beneficiary) propounded the draft in a probate claim. Faulks J held that the presumption of revocation was rebutted by what the testatrix said to her sister. He found that the original will had been destroyed by enemy action in 1940[60] and the completed draft was admissible as secondary evidence to prove its contents. But had the original will been duly executed? The completed draft contained an attestation clause. A witness (named as an attesting witness in the draft) testified that she did not remember signing the will but she did remember being called by the testatrix to her shop for some purpose and that "a little man in a homburg hat" was there. There was a solicitor who was named in the draft as the other attesting witness. Faulks J held, applying the maxim *omnia praesumuntur rite et sollemniter esse acta*, that this attestation clause—which spoke to the regularity of the execution of the will—was, in the absence of cogent negative evidence, sufficient evidence of due execution. He admitted the completed draft to probate.

3. Evidence of due execution

An attestation clause raises a presumption that the will was duly executed.[61] If a will contains no attestation clause or the clause is insufficient, or if it appears to the district judge or registrar that there is some **19–23**

(attestation clause in completed draft); *Harris v Knight* (1890) 15 P.D. 170 (no attestation clause, will signed by testator and two others, maxim *"omnia praesumuntur rite et sollemniter esse acta"* applied).

55 *Sugden v Lord St. Leonards* (1876) 1 P.D. 154; *In the Estate of Lintott* [1941] L.T.Jo. 115; *Re Webb* [1964]1 W.L.R. 50; *Re Dickson* [2002] W.T.L.R. 1395.

56 *Sugden v Lord St. Leonards*, above; *In the Estate of Wilson* (1961) 105 S.J. 531.

57 *In the Estate of Botting* [1951] 2 All E.R. 997 (conditional revocation, though no direct evidence of destruction of will), explaining *Homerton v Hewitt* (1872) 25 L.T. 854; *In the Estate of Bridgewater* [1965] 1 W.L.R. 416; *Sterling v Bruce* [1973] N.I. 255: for conditional destruction see above, paras 7–40 et seq.

58 *Rowe v Clarke* [2006] W.T.L.R. 347.

59 *Re Webb* [1964] 1 W.L.R. 509.

60 The court might have decided that the presumption was also rebutted by the will's destruction by enemy action.

61 See above, para.4–22.

doubt about the due execution of a will, he must require an affidavit as to its due execution before admitting the will to probate in common form.[62]

The affidavit of due execution is to be from one or more of the attesting witnesses[63] or, if no attesting witness is available, from any other person who was present when the will was executed.[64] If no such affidavit can be obtained, the registrar may accept evidence on affidavit from any person to show that the signature on the will is in the handwriting of the deceased, or of any other matter which may raise a presumption in favour of due execution and he may require notice of the application to be given to any person prejudiced by the will.[65] Normally evidence on affidavit as to the deceased's handwriting is accepted if accompanied by the consent of the persons prejudiced (if all are sui juris) or by evidence on affidavit as to the handwriting of the witnesses. If after considering the evidence the district judge or registrar is doubtful whether the will was duly executed, he may refer the matter to a High Court judge. If he is satisfied that the will was not duly executed he must refuse probate and mark the will "Probate Refused".[66]

19–24 The maxim *omnia praesumuntur rite et sollemniter esse acta* may apply if the observance of all the formalities required for due execution is not proved by the evidence of witnesses. To quote Lindley LJ in *Harris v Knight*,[67]

> "The maxim, *'omnia praesumuntur rite esse acta,'* is an expression, in a short form, of a reasonable probability, and of the propriety in point of law of acting on such probability. The maxim expresses an inference which may reasonably be drawn when an intention to do some formal act is established; when the evidence is consistent with that intention having been carried into effect in a proper way; but where the actual observance of all due formalities can only be inferred as a matter of probability."

The maxim applies with more or less force according to the circumstances of each case; for example, a formal attestation clause in a will which is regular in form raises a strong presumption,[68] but an informal clause,[69] or a formal clause in a will irregular in form,[70] raises a weaker presumption.[71]

The maxim may apply in the absence of any attestation clause. In *In the Estate of Denning*[72] the will consisted of a small sheet of writing paper.

[62] N.C. Prob. Rules 1987 r.12(1): see also r.16. For proof of a privileged will see rr.17 and 18.

[63] An attesting witness who refuses to make an affidavit may be required to attend for examination in open court, Senior Courts Act 1981 s.122; N.C. Prob. Rules 1987 r. 50(1): see *In the Goods of Sweet* [1891] P. 400.

[64] N.C. Prob. Rules 1987 r.12(1).

[65] N.C. Prob. Rules 1987. r.12(2).

[66] N.C. Prob. Rules 1987 r.12(1).

[67] *Harris v Knight* (1890) 15 P.D. 170, 179.

[68] *Sherrington v Sherrington* [2005] 3 F.C.R. 538; *Channon v Perkins* [2006] W.T.L.R. 269; *Re Walters* [2008] W.T.L.R. 339.

[69] *Vinnicombe v Butler* (1864) 3 Sw. & Tr. 580.

[70] *In the Estate of Bercovitz* [1961] 1 W.L.R. 892, 896.

[71] *Weatherhill v Pearce* [1995] 1 W.L.R. 592.

[72] *In the Estate of Denning* [1958] 1 W.L.R. 462: see also *In the Goods of Peverett* [1902] P. 205;

On one side (and occupying the whole of it) was written, "Sept. 3rd. Year of our Lord 1939. I give all I possess to my cousins Mary Jane and John Harnett in Parish of St. Feock, County of Cornwall" followed by the signature of the testatrix. On the other side—turning the paper upside down—two names were written in different hands, "Edith Freeman" and "Dorothy Edwards," one below the other. No person of either of these names could be traced. During her lifetime the testatrix had told John Harnett that she had made a will in favour of him and his sister: at her death no other will had been found. In a probate claim Sachs J held the maxim applicable and declared the will to be duly executed. He said that it seemed to him "that there is no other practical reason why these names should be on the back of the document unless it was for the purpose of attesting the will."

The maxim is not applicable if observance of the formalities is disproved by the evidence.[73]

4. Doubt as to knowledge and approval[74]

If a will appears to have been signed by a blind or illiterate testator, or by another person by the testator's direction, or for any other reason gives rise to doubt as to the testator's having had knowledge of its contents at the time of its execution, the district judge or registrar must, before admitting the will to proof, satisfy himself that the testator had such knowledge.[75] He may require affidavit evidence for this purpose. **19–25**

5. Alteration, incorporation and attempted revocation

(a) *Alteration*

The district judge or registrar must require evidence to show whether an unattested alteration was present in a will when it was executed.[76] There is a rebuttable presumption that an unattested alteration was made after the execution of the will.[77] The district judge or registrar also has a useful time-saving power to disregard any alteration which appears to him to be of no practical importance[78]—for instance, an alteration to a gift which has lapsed. **19–26**

Harris v Knight (1890) 15 P.D. 170; *Trott v Skidmore* (1860) 2 Sw. & Tr. 12: cf. *In the Estate of Early* [1980] I.R. 223.

[73] *In the Estate of Bercovitz* [1961] 1 W.L.R. 892, [1962] 1 W.L.R. 321.

[74] For a discussion of the way in which "suspicious" wills are attacked on the ground that the testator allegedly lacked knowledge and approval, and as to whether this is the correct form of attack, see above Chap.5, paras 5–32 et seq.

[75] N.C. Prob. Rules 1987 r.13; for the burden of proof of the testator's knowledge and approval see above, paras 5–37 et seq. In a professionally drawn will, the attestation clause should be amended to record the circumstances of the attestation.

[76] N.C. Prob. Rules 1987 r.14(1).

[77] See above, para.7–48.

[78] N.C. Prob. Rules 1987 r.14(2).

(b) *Incorporation of another document*

19–27 If a will contains any reference to another document in such terms as to suggest that it ought to be incorporated in the will, the district judge or registrar must require the document to be produced and accounted for by evidence.[79]

(c) *Attempted revocation*

19–28 Any appearance of attempted revocation of a will by burning, tearing or otherwise must be accounted for to the district judge's or registrar's satisfaction.[80] The person who found the will may swear an affidavit as to its plight and condition when found.

E. OMITTING WORDS FROM PROBATE

19–29 A particular passage or word in an otherwise valid will or codicil is omitted from probate if it was inserted:

(i) owing to an insane delusion on the testator's part[81];
(ii) without the testator's knowledge and approval[82];
(iii) as a result of undue influence or fraud[83]; or
(iv) as an alteration which was not duly executed by the testator.[84]

The court may also exclude from probate words which have no testamentary value[85] but which are offensive,[86] defamatory[87] or blasphemous. Such words are not expunged from the will itself but are omitted from the probate copy.[88]

[79] N.C. Prob. Rules 1987 r.14(3); see also r.14(4) if there is doubt as to the date on which the will was executed.
[80] N.C. Prob. Rules 1987 r.15.
[81] *In the Estate of Bohrmann* [1938] 1 All E.R. 271; see above, para.5–09.
[82] See above, paras 5–23 et seq: for rectification, see above, paras 10–04 et seq.
[83] See above, paras 5–15 et seq.
[84] See above, paras 7–46 et seq.
[85] *In the Estate of Rawlings* (1934) 78 S.J. 338 ("that rascal" her husband relevant to construction).
[86] *In the Goods of Bowker* [1932] P. 93 (offensive directions as to disposal of testator's remains and funeral excluded): cf. *In the Estate of Caie* (1927) 43 T.L.R. 697 (exhortation to become a Freemason not excluded). No application was made in *Fuller v Strum* [2002] 1 W.L.R. 1097 to exclude the offensive description of the residuary beneficiary.
[87] *In the Estate of White* [1914] P. 153; *In the Goods of Wortnaly* (1846) 1 Rob. 423; *Marsh v Marsh* (1860) 1 Sw. & Tr. 528; *In the Goods of Honywood* (1871) L.R. 2 P. & D. 251.
[88] *Re Maxwell* (1929) 45 T.L.R. 215: for the procedure see *Practice Direction* [1968] 1 W.L.R. 987.

F. PROBATE CLAIMS

In general, the same practice and rules of evidence are applicable in a probate claim as in other claims.[89] But a few significant differences may be mentioned. **19–30**

1. Administration pending suit

After a probate claim has begun, a grant of administration pending suit limited to the duration of the probate claim may be made. This type of grant has already been considered.[90] **19–31**

If the probate claim is for the revocation of a previous grant of probate or letters of administration, the previous grant must be lodged in court after the commencement of the claim.[91]

2. Lodging of testamentary documents and filing evidence about them

Any testamentary document of the deceased person in the possession of any party must be lodged with the court.[92] A testamentary document means a will, a draft of a will, written instructions for a will (e.g. a solicitor's attendance note recording the deceased's instructions), and any document purporting to be evidence of the contents, or to be a copy, of a will which is alleged to have been lost or destroyed. The claimant—and every defendant who acknowledges service—must in written evidence, describe any testamentary document of the deceased of which he has any knowledge.[93] **19–32**

This special procedure ensures that at an early stage in a probate claim any testamentary scripts in the possession of the parties are lodged in the safe custody of the court. The procedure is different from disclosure of documents, which takes place at a later stage.

3. Evidence of attesting witnesses

The party propounding a will in a probate claim must call one of the attesting witnesses to give evidence as to its due execution unless they are all unavailable,[94] e.g. dead. **19–33**

[89] The procedure is set out in Pt 57 of the Civil Procedure Rules 1998 (probate claims, rectification of wills, and substitution and removal of personal representatives), which has effect from 15 October 2001. C.P.R. Pt 57 is supplemented by a Practice Direction 57.

[90] See above, paras 18–48 et seq.

[91] C.P.R. 57.6.

[92] C.P.R. 57.5(1).

[93] C.P.R. 57.5(3).

[94] *Bowman v Hodgson* (1867) L.R. 1 P. & D. 362: see Evidence Act 1938 s.3. The rules in this section doubtless apply to a witness who acknowledges his signature under the amended s.9 of the Wills Act 1837, above, para.4–18.

(a) *Witness of the court*

19–34 An attesting witness is regarded as the witness of the court. Accordingly (and contrary to the general rule) he may be cross-examined by the party calling him on matters relating to the execution of the will,[95] and no claim of professional privilege may be made in respect of his previous statements to solicitors concerning execution.[96]

(b) *Not conclusive*

19–35 The evidence of the attesting witnesses is not conclusive for, or against, the due execution of the will. A formal attestation clause in a will raises a presumption of due execution[97] and the party propounding a will is free to call other evidence that it was duly executed.[98] The court decides whether the will was duly executed having regard to all the circumstances of the case.[99]

4. Costs[100]

19–36 Costs in a probate claim, as in other proceedings in the High Court and Civil Division of the Court of Appeal, are in the discretion of the court.[101] Generally costs follow the event,[102] i.e. the losing party is ordered to pay the costs of the successful party.[103]

(a) *Notice to cross-examine*

19–37 Rule 57.7(5) of the Civil Procedure Rules 1998 imposes a restriction on the court's discretion to order the payment of costs in a probate claim. A party who opposes a will in a probate claim may give notice in his defence that he does not raise any positive case, but insists on the will being proved in solemn form and, for that purpose, will cross-examine the witnesses who attested the will.[104] No order may then be made for him to pay the other side's costs unless the court considers that there was no reasonable ground for opposing the will.[105] This protection may generally be relied on

[95] *Oakes v Uzzell* [1932] P. 19; *Re Brock, Jones v Jones* [1908] 24 T.L.R. 839; *Re Webster* [1974] 1 W.L.R. 1641 (party calling attesting witness may cross-examine him on other issues, as well as due execution).

[96] *In the Estate of Fuld* [1965] P. 405.

[97] See above, para.19–23.

[98] *Re Vere-Wardale* [1949] P. 395.

[99] *Wright v Rogers* (1869) L.R. 1 P. & D. 678; *Weatherhill v Pearce* [1995] 1 W.L.R. 592.

[100] It was suggested in Chap.5 at paras 5–49 et seq. that the rules relating to burden of proof, and to costs, make it very difficult to challenge suspicious wills. It was suggested in para.5–58 that the rules should not be applied as they have been applied in the past. But whether there will be any change remains to be seen.

[101] Senior Courts Act 1981 s.51.

[102] C.P.R. 44; *Twist v Tye* [1902] P. 92.

[103] *Blackman v Man* [2008] W.T.L.R. 389.

[104] C.P.R. 57.7(5)(b).

[105] Rule 57.7(5) preserves the practice of the Prerogative Court (the Ecclesiastical Court which dealt with wills of personalty before the Court of Probate was established in 1857). When

if the party opposing the will pleads want of due execution, incapacity, or want of knowledge and approval,[106] but not if he pleads undue influence or fraud[107] or claims revocation of probate already granted in common form.[108]

(b) *Exceptions to the general rule*

Apart from this restriction, the court has an unfettered discretion as to costs. The general rule of practice is that costs follow the event, but in special circumstances a different order may be made. The special circumstances justifying a different order may be classified under three heads[109]: (i) fault of the testator or the residuary beneficiary, in which case costs come out of the estate; (ii) fault of the will draftsman, in which case, if he is a solicitor or other professional, he or his insurers may be ordered to pay the costs of either or both parties; and (iii) case for inquiry, in which case there is no order as to costs.[110] **19–38**

(i) Costs out of the estate. If the litigation has been caused by the conduct of the deceased, or of the residuary beneficiaries, the costs of both parties may be ordered to be paid out of the estate. Such an order was made where the litigation was caused by the confusion in which the deceased left his testamentary papers,[111] or by the deceased's habits and mode of life which gave grounds for questioning his testamentary capacity.[112] Again, such an order was made where the residuary beneficiaries were active in the preparation of a will in their own favour, thereby raising suspicions by their conduct,[113] and where the residuary beneficiary, despite inquiries, **19–39**

the Court of Probate was established, the pre-1857 practice became r.41 of the Contentious Probate Rules 1862, then it became R.S.C Ord 62 r.4(3) and it is now C.P.R 57.7(5). The wording of the Rule has changed slightly over the years. Examples of cases where the 1862 version of the Rule was in issue are *Davies v Jones* [1899] P. 161 (opposition to will failed, but reasonable ground for opposing, so no order as to costs) and *Spicer v Spicer* [1899] P. 38 (no reasonable ground for opposing, so costs followed event).

[106] *Cleare v Cleare* (1869) 1 P. & D. 655. But see *Sherrington v Sherrington (costs)* [2005] EWCA Civ 410; and see also Chap.5, esp para.5–03.

[107] *Ireland v Rendall* (1866) 1 P. & D. 194; *Harrington v Bowyer* (1871) 2 P. & D. 264.

[108] *Tomalin v Smart* [1904] P. 141.

[109] *Spiers v English* [1907] P. 122; *Mitchell v Gard* (1863) 3 Sw. & Tr. 275.

[110] *Re Cutcliffe's Estate* [1959] P. 6, 13; *Wylde v Culver* [2006] 1 W.L.R. 2674 (where this passage from 11th edn was quoted at p.2678); *Jarrom v Sellars* [2007] W.T.L.R. 1219.

[111] *Jenner v Ffinch* (1879) 5 P.D. 106 (doubt as to deceased's intention to revoke former will); *Lemage v Goodban* (1865) L.R. 1 P. & D. 57; *Orton v Smith* (1873) L.R. 3 P. & D. 23 (testator had patched up his signature); cf. *Re Wynn* [1983] 3 All E.R. 310, 315.

[112] *Davies v Gregory* (1873) 3 P. & D. 28 (deceased a recluse of strange habits); *Roe v Nix* [1893] P. 55 (testatrix of unsound mind); see also *Boughton v Knight* (1873) L.R. 3 P. & D. 64 (testator outwardly capable of managing his affairs); *Kostic v Chaplin (costs)* [2007] EWHC 2909 (Ch) (investigation of testamentary capacity justified); cf. *Blackman v Man* [2008] W.T.L.R. 389 (fact that will prepared by bank was *not* a ground for giving unsuccessful challengers their costs). Note also *Larke v Nugus* [2000] W.T.L.R. 1033 (solicitor draftsman ought to provide full information as to execution and surrounding circumstances).

[113] *Goodacre v Smith* (1867) L.R. 1 P. & D. 359; *Orton v Smith* (1873) L.R. 3 P. & D. 23; *In the Estate of Osment* [1914] P. 129 (conduct of legatees); *Re Good* [2002] W.T.L.R. 801 and 1305 (grounds for suspecting undue influence).

failed to produce the will after administration had been granted to the next of kin.[114]

19–40 **(ii) Costs payable by negligent will draftsman or by his insurers.** If the will was prepared by a solicitor, or other professional will draftsman, and an error on his part led to a reasonable challenge to the validity of the will, he, or his insurers may be ordered to pay the costs of the proceedings. In *Marley v Rawlings*[115] the solicitor who prepared their wills for a husband and wife allowed each to execute the will prepared for the other. When the husband died, an application was made to rectify the will he had executed on the basis that the error had been clerical. Rectification was refused at first instance and by the Court of Appeal, but the application succeeded in the Supreme Court. The case was discussed in Chapter 10.[116] When allocating costs, Lord Neuberger, with whom all other members of the court concurred, suggested that, had there been no question of negligence,[117] it would have been difficult to decide what order to make – whether to order that the loser should pay or that costs should come from the estate. Having thus hesitated, he opted for awarding costs from the estate. But, in the knowledge that the successful party (having thus been made to bear the loss) would then recover these costs from the solicitor, whose error had led to the problem in the first place, and that the solicitor would seek indemnity from his insurers, it was possible, pragmatically, to delete two steps from the process and so the order was that the solicitor's insurers should pay all the costs of both parties.[118]

Marley v Rawlings was a rectification case, but there is no reason to restrict the application of the costs rule in the case to rectification. It could, potentially, be applied to any case where a professional draftsman's error has been the cause of litigation. A draftsman's duty of care is, of course, discussed in Chapter 15. Having said this, there may have been two special interlinked factors in *Marley*. One was that the estate was relatively small, worth a mere £70,000 odd.[119] The other was that the Supreme Court had reversed a unanimous decision of the Court of Appeal upholding the judge at first instance. Ordering either of the parties to pay for litigation in a case of this nature might seem especially harsh, and shifting the burden to the insurers was a way out. Nevertheless, the principle in the case is likely to be adopted in the future, it follows on from *White v Jones*.[120]

19–41 **(iii) No order as to costs.** If the circumstances led reasonably to an inquiry into the issues raised, the losing party is left to pay his own costs

[114] *Smith v Smith* (1865) 4 Sw. & Tr. 3.
[115] *Marley v Rawlings* [2015] A.C. 129.
[116] See paras 10–08 et seq.
[117] Had there been no question of negligence, the situation would have been altogether different, so this reference seems slightly odd.
[118] *Marley v Rawlings* [2015] A.C. 157 at para.12. In fact, there was a further complication, in that the defendants had entered into a CFA to cover costs in the Supreme Court, but this is not directly relevant to Succession law and will not be considered here.
[119] The successful party and the deceased were beneficial joint tenants of the house in which the deceased lived.
[120] *White v Jones* [1995] 2 A.C. 207. See Chap.15, para.15–02.

but is not ordered to pay the costs of the successful party. It is therefore necessary to consider whether the losing party had reasonable grounds, looking to his knowledge and means of knowledge, for the issues he raised.[121]

No order for costs was made where the next of kin unsuccessfully opposed a will because the deceased's doctor, who was an attesting witness, stated that when the will was read over the testator approved it by gesture only and that he could not swear that the testator was in full possession of his mental faculties.[122]

(c) *Pleas of undue influence or fraud*

The generally accepted rule is that a party ought never to put forward a plea of undue influence or fraud unless he has reasonable grounds upon which to support it.[123] If he does plead undue influence or fraud—and loses the claim—he will normally be ordered to pay the costs of the successful party[124] unless special circumstances justify a different order.[125] There are a few reported cases where heads (i) or (iii) have been held applicable[126]; but a party who makes an unsuccessful plea of undue influence or fraud usually has to pay the costs of the successful party.[127] **19–42**

(d) *Executor's right to costs out of the estate*

An executor who proves a will in solemn form is entitled, unless the court orders otherwise, to take his costs of the probate claim out of the estate.[128] **19–43**

[121] *Mitchell v Gard* (1863) 3 Sw. & Tr. 257, 278.

[122] *Tippett v Tippett* (1865) 1 P. & D. 54: see also *Ferrey v King* (1861) 3 Sw. & Tr. 51 (conflicting evidence of attesting witnesses).

[123] *Spiers v English* [1907] P. 122, 124. The difficulty is as to what are reasonable grounds. Is it reasonable to suggest that the "suspicious circumstances rule" creates a presumption of fraud and/or undue influence? In *Wilson v Bassil* [1903] P. 239 Walton J thought that it did, so that someone who challenged a beneficiary-prepared will on the grounds of undue influence and fraud was entitled to his costs from the estate even though his challenge failed. But in *Spiers v English* Gorrel Barnes P. refused to follow him. The latter approach appears now to be the accepted one, but it is suggested that Walton J's manner of dealing with a "suspicious" will was both robust and logical. See also, above, Chap.5, para.5–58.

[124] *Spiers v English* ibid; *Re Cutcliffe's Estate* [1959] P. 6 (not special circumstances if T misled persons into false hopes of benefiting by his will). But see also *Wilson v Bassil* above, fn.123, and *Re Good* [2002] W.T.L.R. 801.

[125] See Chap.5, para.5–58, fn.254.

[126] e.g. costs out of the estate in *Mitchell v Gard* (1863) 3 Sw. & Tr. 75 and 275 (will prepared by solicitor in own favour, undue influence and three other pleas failed); in *Rowe v Clarke* [2007] W.T.L.R. 373 (will lost by testator); and in *Orton v Smith* (1873) L.R. 3 P. & D. 23 (undue influence, fraud, and other pleas failed): no order as to costs in *Smith v Smith* (1866) L.R. 1 P. & D. 239 (undue influence and two other pleas failed).

[127] In *Cummins v Murray* [1906] 2 I.R. 509 the judge had made an order allowing costs to a party who had unsuccessfully pleaded undue influence; on appeal, it was held that where there are any grounds on which a judge can base such a special order, there is no jurisdiction to interfere with it. The editor believes that the standard rule now operates in such a way as to make it very hard to challenge suspicious wills, see above Chap.5, paras 5–40 et seq.

[128] This was an equitable rule which was codified as R.S.C Ord. 62 r. 6(2). There is no corresponding provision in the C.P.R. but the omission cannot, it is thought, have altered the legal position; see Williams Mortimer and Sunnucks, *Executors, Administrators and Probate,*

He does not need an order of the court for this purpose.[129] The court may order otherwise if the executor has acted unreasonably—for instance, by carelessly losing the original will.[130] If the executor unsuccessfully propounds a will, the rules of practice already considered apply: costs follow the event[131] unless head (i) or (iii) applies.[132] To protect himself against the risk of being condemned in costs, a person appointed executor may find it advisable before he propounds the will to insist on an indemnity from the beneficiaries interested in upholding it.

II. THE REVOCATION OF GRANTS

A. GROUNDS FOR REVOCATION

19–44 A personal representative may be removed *either* by the revocation of his grant (which is considered in this section) *or* by the appointment of a substituted personal representative or by the termination of his appointment (which is considered later).[133]

The jurisdiction of the High Court to revoke a grant of probate or letters of administration is exercised by the Family Division as regards non-contentious or common form business, and by the Chancery Division as regards revocation claims.[134] The county court also has jurisdiction (limited in amount) over revocation claims.[135] In the Family Division a district judge or registrar may order a grant to be revoked or amended, but only on the application or with the consent of the person to whom the grant was made, unless there are exceptional circumstances.[136] The court has power to revoke a grant of its own volition where the grant ought not to have been made or contains an error.[137] But if the person to whom the grant was made opposes revocation, a revocation claim is normally necessary.

The main grounds for revocation of a grant may be classified into two categories.

20th edn (London: Sweet & Maxwell, 2013), para.66–02: see also *In the Estate of Plant* [1926] P. 139 (executors proved will but failed on codicil); *Re Barton* [1977] C.L.Y. 3182. C.P.R. 48.4 implies (at least) that the personal representative will be entitled to his costs out of the estate, and on an indemnity basis, except in rare cases. See also *D'Abo v Paget (No.2)* [2000] W.T.L.R. 863 (a trusts case).

[129] He is better off without an order, which necessitates assessment of his costs. *In the Estate of Cole* (1962) 106 S.J. 837.

[130] *Burls v Burls* (1868) 1 P. & D. 472.

[131] *Twist v Tye* [1902] P. 92.

[132] e.g. costs out of the estate in *Boughton v Knight* (1873) L.R. 3 P. & D. 64.

[133] See below, para.24–27.

[134] See above, para.18–02.

[135] See above, para.18–06.

[136] N.C. Prob. Rules 1987 r.41; see also r.26(2).

[137] Senior Courts Act 1981 s.121: the court may also cancel the resealing of a grant, s.121(3); for resealing, see above, paras 18–08 et seq.

1. Grant wrongly made

Usually a grant is wrongly made as a result of a false statement by the grantee, whether made fraudulently or in ignorance of the truth. For example, revocation is ordered where the "deceased" is found to be still alive[138]; where a will is discovered after a grant of simple administration has been made, or a later will is discovered after an earlier will has been proved; where an invalid, revoked or forged will has been proved[139]; where a grant has been made to a minor on the basis that he is of full age; where administration has been granted to a person who falsely claimed to be the deceased's surviving spouse,[140] or next of kin[141]; where it has been granted to someone who claimed that he was a chartered accountant and that he was a creditor of the estate but failed to disclose that he had been adjudicated bankrupt and struck off[142]; or where administration has been granted to the Treasury Solicitor and next of kin are discovered. Occasionally a grant is wrongly made as a result of an official error. For example, revocation is ordered where a grant has been made without special leave before the minimum time has elapsed from the deceased's death,[143] or where a grant has been made whilst a caveat was in force.[144] **19–45**

2. Subsequent events

A grant which was properly made may be revoked by reason of the occurrence of subsequent events. **19–46**

(a) *Grantee becomes incapable*

If there are at least two executors and one or more of them becomes incapable of managing his affairs by reason of mental or physical incapacity, the grant of probate is revoked. In *In the Goods of Galbraith*[145] a grant of probate made six years previously to two executors was revoked because both had become unfit to act in their old age, owing to their physical and mental infirmity. Instead the court made a grant of letters of administration *de bonis non* with the will annexed. If only one of the executors had become incapable, the court would have revoked the original grant and **19–47**

138 *In the Goods of Napier* (1809) 1 Phill. 83 (left for dead on the field of battle and appeared personally in court on revocation of probate).
139 *Vaccianna v Herod* [2006] W.T.L.R. 367.
140 *In the Goods of Moore* (1845) 3 Notes of Cases 601 ("widow" not married to deceased); *In the Estate of Evon* (1963) 107 S.J. 893.
141 *In the Goods of Bergman* (1842) 2 Notes of Cases 22: see also *In the Goods of Morris* (1862) 2 Sw. & Tr. 360 (grant to elected guardian of minors revoked as there was testamentary guardian).
142 *Shephard v Wheeler* [2000] W.T.L.R. 1175.
143 See above, para.19–06.
144 See *Re Davies* [1978] C.L.Y. 3095.
145 *In the Goods of Galbraith* [1951] P. 422.

made a fresh grant of probate to the other executor, with power for the incapable executor to take probate if he recovered.[146]

Similarly, if there are at least two administrators and one or more of them becomes incapable, the grant of administration is revoked and a new grant made.[147]

If, on the other hand, there is a sole, or sole surviving, executor or administrator and he becomes incapable, the grant to him is not revoked. Instead a grant of letters of administration *de bonis non* and for the use and benefit of the incapable grantee, limited during his incapacity, is made. The court no longer impounds the original grant in these circumstances.[148]

(b) *Grantee wishes to be relieved of duties*

19–48 A grant may be revoked if a grantee wishes to be relieved of his duties for some good reason, such as advanced age.[149]

(c) *Grantee disappears*

19–49 If a grantee disappears and the estate has not been fully administered, the grant is revoked and a new grant is made.[150]

(d) *Grantee commits breach of duty*

19–50 If the grantee commits a serious breach of his duties, probably his grant will be revoked and a new grant made where this is appropriate so as to secure the proper administration of the estate.

B. EFFECT OF REVOCATION

19–51 A grant of probate or letters of administration is in a sense a precarious title because the grant is liable to be revoked at some later date. The deceased may die apparently intestate so that a grant of simple administration is made, and years later a will appointing executors may be found; or the deceased may die leaving a "will" which is proved by the executors, but

146 *In the Estate of Shaw* [1905] P. 92.

147 *In the Goods of Newton* (1843) 3 Curt. 428.

148 Registrar's Direction (1985) 9 July.

149 *In the Goods of Thacker* [1900] P. 15 (grant to receiver in bankruptcy revoked after debts paid); *In the Goods of Hoare* (1833) 2 Sw. & Tr. 361 and cf. *In the Goods of Heslop* (1846) 1 Rob. Eccl. 457. A personal representative may not simply have a grant in his favour revoked because he has become bored with the administration. For reform to allow personal representatives to retire for good cause see Law Reform Committee's 23rd Report, *The Powers and Duties of Trustees*, Cmnd.8733 (1982), pp.53 and 67.

150 *In the Goods of Loveday* [1900] P. 154 (widow obtained administration and later disappeared); *In the Goods of Covell* (1890) 15 P.D. 8; *In the Goods of Bradshaw* (1888) 13 P.D. 18 (creditor administrator absconded): see also *In the Estate of Thomas* [1912] P. 177 (administrator emigrated to New Zealand but his address was ascertainable: grant revoked).

which years later is discovered to have been a forgery. In the meantime, before the revocation of the first grant, the personal representative may have administered the estate.

1. Purchaser from the former personal representative

A purchaser from a personal representative to whom a grant has been made is protected by two statutory provisions: **19–52**

(a) *Conveyance valid despite revocation of grant*

Section 37 of the Administration of Estates Act 1925 provides that a conveyance of any interest in real or personal estate made to a purchaser by a person to whom probate or letters of administration has been granted is valid, notwithstanding any subsequent revocation or variation of the grant.[151] The section has a wide application because "conveyance" is so widely defined by the Act—the expression includes "a mortgage, charge by way of legal mortgage, lease, assent, vesting declaration, vesting instrument, disclaimer, release and every other assurance of property or of an interest therein by any instrument, except a will."[152] But, to be protected under s.37, a purchaser must have acquired the interest in the property in good faith and for valuable consideration, which includes marriage but not a nominal consideration in money.[153] **19–53**

Section 37 does not apply to a disposition of property to a purchaser by a personal representative unless it was made by a "conveyance".[154] Most sales of goods by personal representatives will probably fall outside s.37 because the property in the goods is transferred without any written instrument. If this is so, the principle laid down in 1914 by the Court of Appeal in *Hewson v Shelley*[155] applies. The effect of applying *Hewson v Shelley* is much the same as s.37. In *Hewson v Shelley* a widow took a grant of simple administration to her husband's estate, believing that he had died intestate. The administratrix sold and conveyed the deceased's land to a purchaser. Eleven years later a will of the deceased was found in the back of a bureau, the letters of administration were revoked, and probate was granted to the claimants as executors. The claimants sued the purchaser for the return of the land, but the Court of Appeal held that the purchaser had a good title because he had bought the land in good faith. **19–54**

[151] Administration of Estates Act 1925 s.37 applies whenever the conveyance was made, or the grant was revoked or varied, or the testator or intestate died, but without prejudice to any order of the court made before 1926 ss.37(1) and (2). As to contracts made by a personal representative see Administration of Estates Act 1925 s.39(1) and the Law of Property (Misc Provs) Act 1994 s.16 below, para.20–56.
[152] s.55(1)(ii).
[153] s.55(1)(xviii).
[154] e.g. it does not apply to oral leases.
[155] *Hewson v Shelley* [1914] 2 Ch.13.

(b) *Grant conclusive as an order of the court*

19–55 A purchaser is also protected by s.204(1) of the Law of Property Act 1925 which reads:

> "An order of the court under any statutory or other jurisdiction shall not, as against a purchaser, be invalidated on the ground of want of jurisdiction, or of want of any concurrence, consent, notice, or service, whether the purchaser has notice of any such want or not."

A grant of probate[156] or letters of administration[157] is, of course, an order of the court and is, therefore, conclusive. Again, s.204(1) protects only a purchaser in good faith and for valuable consideration, which includes marriage but not a nominal consideration in money.[158]

2. Payments made to the former personal representative

19–56 Section 27(2) of the Administration of Estates Act 1925 provides that, where a grant of probate or letters of administration is revoked, all payments and dispositions made in good faith to a personal representative under the grant before its revocation are a valid discharge to the person making them. Thus, if the deceased's debtor pays his debt in good faith to the deceased's personal representative under a grant before it is revoked, the debtor is discharged.

3. Payments made by the former personal representative

19–57 Section 27(2) of the Act also enacts that a personal representative who acted under a grant before its revocation may retain and reimburse himself in respect of any payments or dispositions made by him, which the person to whom representation is afterwards granted might have properly made. The former personal representative should reimburse himself in this way before delivering the balance of the assets to the new personal representative.

4. Indemnity of former personal representative

19–58 Section 27(1) of the Administration of Estates Act 1925 provides that "Every person making or permitting to be made any payment or disposition in good faith under a representation shall be indemnified and protected in so doing, notwithstanding any defect or circumstance whatsoever affecting the validity of the representation." Presumably the section applies to

[156] *Re Bridgett & Hayes' Contract* [1928] Ch.163.
[157] *Hewson v Shelley* [1914] 2 Ch.13, 29–30 and 33.
[158] Law of Property Act 1925 s.205(1)(xxi), which also provides that "purchaser" includes a lessee, mortgagee, or other person who acquires an interest in property. S. 37 of the A.E.A. and s.204(1) of the L.P.A were both considered in *Re Bridgett & Hayes' Contract* [1928] Ch.163.

any payment or disposition made in good faith by the former personal representative before his grant was revoked, whether in discharging the deceased's funeral, testamentary and administration expenses, debts and liabilities, or in distributing the deceased's estate to the beneficiaries entitled under the former grant.[159]

Apart from any protection afforded by s.27(1), a personal representative who receives notice of a claim which casts doubt on the validity of the grant made to him, and subsequently makes payments in disregard of that claim, is liable to the deceased's estate if his grant is later revoked. Thus in a New Zealand case an executor, who obtained probate of a will and, knowing that next of kin were contemplating a claim for revocation on the ground that the testatrix lacked testamentary capacity, paid pecuniary legacies to beneficiaries under the will, was held liable by the Privy Council to the deceased's estate for the sums so paid, after probate had been revoked.[160] The same result would follow under English law unless an honest belief by the executor that the testatrix had testamentary capacity and that the claim for revocation would fail suffices for "good faith," so that the executor is protected by s.27(1).[161] **19–59**

5. Distribution to wrong beneficiary

If the former personal representative made a distribution to a beneficiary entitled under the former grant but not under the new grant, the beneficiary is not protected. The remedies available against him are considered later.[162] **19–60**

[159] See *In the Estate of Bloch, The Times*, 2 July 1959.

[160] *Guardian Trust & Executors Company of New Zealand Ltd v Public Trustee of New Zealand* [1942] A.C. 115; see p.123 where the Privy Council referred to "what befell another executor who paid the legacies given by a will that was afterwards declared to be invalid, and whose sad story was told by him to Sam Weller when they were fellow inmates of the Fleet prison," (*Pickwick Papers*, Chap.XLIV).

[161] But, in *Cobden-Ramsay v Sutton* [2009] W.T.L.R. 1303 the executor, who had obtained a grant of probate in common form, was entitled to distribute where there was an allegation that the testatrix lacked capacity, but the person making the allegation took no action to have the grant revoked.

[162] See below, paras 24–36 et seq.

CHAPTER 20

COLLECTION, REALISATION AND MANAGEMENT OF THE ESTATE

A personal representative has a statutory duty to "collect and get in the real and personal estate of the deceased and administer it according to law."[1] Normally the administration of the deceased's estate is carried out by the personal representatives out of court. If need be, the personal representatives may ask the court to decide any matters of difficulty which arise.[2] Very occasionally, the general administration of the estate is carried out under the direction of the court in an administration claim.[3] **20–01**

I. DEVOLUTION ON PERSONAL REPRESENTATIVES

1. Devolution of property on a death after 1925

The deceased's entire personal estate devolves on his personal representatives. As to the deceased's land, s.1(1) of the Administration of Estates Act 1925 provides that **20–02**

> "real estate to which a deceased person was entitled for an interest not ceasing on his death shall on his death devolve from time to time on the personal representative of the deceased"

in the same manner as chattels real (i.e. leaseholds) devolved before 1926. The personal representatives represent the deceased in regard to his real estate as well as in regard to his personal estate.[4] If there is any change in the personal representatives, the deceased's estate automatically devolves on the new personal representatives.[5]

[1] Administration of Estates Act 1925 s.25 as amended by Administration of Estates Act 1971 s.9.

[2] See below, para.24–28 and 24–29.

[3] See below, paras 24–22 et seq.

[4] Administration of Estates Act 1925 s.1(3).

[5] Administration of Estates Act 1925 s.55(1)(xi).

(a) *"Real estate" which devolves*

20–03 The "real estate" which devolves is defined to include chattels real (i.e. leaseholds), and land in possession, remainder, or reversion, and every interest in or over land to which the deceased was entitled at his death.[6] It includes:

(i) Land held on trust by the deceased, including settled land.[7] This head is only applicable where the deceased held the land at his death as the sole trustee, or as the sole tenant for life of settled land. It is not applicable where the deceased is survived by one or more co-trustees, or where the deceased held the land at his death in his capacity as a personal representative and not as a trustee.[8]

(ii) Land held by the deceased by way of mortgage or security.[9]

(iii) Land appointed by the deceased in his will under a general power of appointment.[10] By way of contrast, pure personalty appointed by the deceased in his will under a general power of appointment has never devolved on his personal representatives.[11]

(iv) Land in which the deceased held an entailed interest[12] which was barred by his will and which passes under a gift contained in the deceased's will: if not, the entailed interest does not devolve on the deceased's personal representatives.[13]

(b) *Interest ceasing on death*

20–04 An interest of the deceased which ceases on his death does not devolve on his personal representatives. Again, the interest of the deceased under a joint tenancy does not devolve where another joint tenant survives the deceased.[14] On the other hand, the interest of the deceased as an equitable tenant in common does devolve, unless it was a life interest. If the deceased was a legal joint tenant and an equitable tenant in common, his co-owner takes at law by operation of the right of survivorship but the deceased's equitable undivided share devolves on his personal representatives.

[6] Administration of Estates Act 1925 ss.3(1)(i) and 55(1)(xxiv).

[7] Administration of Estates Act 1925 s.3(1)(ii).

[8] See above, paras 18–36 et seq.

[9] Administration of Estates Act 1925 s.3(1)(ii).

[10] Administration of Estates Act 1925 s.3(2). For the exercise by will of a general power of appointment see above, paras 11–33 et seq.

[11] *O'Grady v Wilmot* [1916] 2 A.C. 231. But both real and personal estate appointed by the deceased in his will under a general power of appointment are assets for payment of his debts, see below, para.21–06.

[12] No new entailed interests may be created since the Trusts of Land and Appointment of Trustees Act 1996 came into force on 1 January 1997, but existing entails may continue to exist (as may existing Settled Land Act settlements).

[13] Administration of Estates Act 1925 ss.3(2) and (3); Law of Property Act 1925 s.176; see above, para.11–38.

[14] Administration of Estates Act 1925 s.3(4).

(c) *Assured tenancies*

In general, a tenancy of a dwelling-house let as a separate dwelling on or after 15 January 1989 is an assured tenancy under the Housing Act 1988 if and so long as the tenant is an individual and occupies the dwelling as his only or principal home.[15] **20–05**

When a fixed-term assured tenant dies, the tenancy will vest in his personal representatives and will devolve under his will or on his intestacy. When, however, a periodic assured tenant[16] dies, the tenancy will not devolve under his will or on his intestacy if the tenant is survived by his spouse or civil partner[17] who immediately before the tenant's death was occupying the dwelling-house as his or her only or principal home.[18] In such a case, provided that the tenant is not himself a successor,[19] the tenancy will vest in the spouse or civil partner. If the assured periodic tenancy does not vest in the spouse or civil partner, it will pass under the assured tenant's will or on his intestacy, but a mandatory ground of possession is available to the landlord.[20]

(d) *Corporation Sole*

On the death of a corporation sole (such as a bishop) his interest in the corporation's real and personal estate devolves on his successor and not on his personal representatives.[21] **20–06**

2. Causes of action

The general rule laid down by the Law Reform (Miscellaneous Provisions) Act 1934 is that any causes of action vested in the deceased at his death survive for the benefit of his estate. Similarly, any causes of action subsisting against him survive against his estate.[22] Where a cause of action **20–07**

[15] Housing Act 1988 s.1. The Act contains a number of exceptions and exclusions (s.1(1)(c)) and also provides for certain transitional cases (s.34). As a result of the Housing Act 1996, all assured tenancies created after 28 February 1997 are assured shorthold tenancies (save for important exceptions), s.19A. A tenancy entered into before 15 January 1989 is a protected tenancy for the purposes of the Rent Act 1977, if a dwelling-house is let as a separate dwelling. For the rules covering the succession to protected and statutory tenancies, the reader should consult the 11th edition of this book, or works on the law of landlord and tenant.

[16] Whether contractual, or statutory following the expiration of a fixed term tenancy: Housing Act 1988 s.5(2).

[17] This includes a person living with the tenant as his or her wife or husband, or civil partner: Housing Act 1988 s.17(4). See *Amicus Horizon Ltd v Mabbott's Estate* [2012] HLR 42.

[18] Housing Act 1988 s.17(1).

[19] As defined in Housing Act 1988 s.17(2). The definition is broad and includes not only a person in whom the tenancy vested by virtue of the statutory provisions or under a will or intestacy of a previous tenant, but also the survivor of joint tenants.

[20] Housing Act 1988 s.7(3) (as amended), Sch.2, Pt 1, Ground 7. Ground 7 is not available where the tenancy has vested in the spouse by virtue of s.17. For the succession provisions in relation to secure tenancies under the Housing Act 1985 ss.87–90. The rules are similar to those in the Housing Act 1988, save that there may be a succession in favour of another member of the tenant's family (as defined in s.113) where there is no spouse.

[21] Administration of Estates Act 1925 s.3(5).

[22] Law Reform (Miscellaneous Provisions) Act 1934 s.1(1): a cause of action is treated as

survives for the benefit of the deceased's estate two special rules as to damages apply:

(i) The damages recoverable never include any exemplary damages, or any damages for loss of income in respect of the "lost years" after death;[23] and

(ii) Where the deceased's death has been caused by the act or omission which gives rise to the cause of action, the damages recoverable must be calculated without reference to any loss or gain to his estate consequent on his death, except that a sum in respect of funeral expenses may be included.[24] Thus the damages recoverable must be calculated without reference to the *loss* arising in respect of the cost of administration of his estate, or the liability of his estate to inheritance tax; or the *gain* arising from the proceeds of an insurance policy on his life.[25]

(a) *Contract*[26]

20–08 The deceased's personal representatives may enforce a contract made by the deceased with X in his lifetime and obtain damages for X's breach[27] or, if appropriate, an injunction or specific performance.[28] The personal representatives may also carry out the performance of such a contract and then recover the contract price from X.[29] Conversely the personal representatives are liable to X (to the extent of the deceased's assets) for any breach of contract committed before or after the deceased's death.[30]

The Employment Rights Act 1996 provides that, where an employer or employee has died, any tribunal proceedings arising under any of the provisions of the Act may be defended, instituted or continued by a personal representative of a deceased employer or employee.[31] A claim for wrongful

subsisting against the deceased at his death though the damage necessary to complete the cause of action occurs at or after death, s.1(4): see *R. v Criminal Injuries Compensation Board, Ex p. Tong* [1976] 1 W.L.R. 1237; *Ronex Properties Ltd v John Laing Construction Ltd* [1983] Q.B. 398 (contribution); *Re Lane* [1986] 1 F.L.R. 283 (order on divorce). For claims under the Inheritance (Provision for Family and Dependants) Act 1975 see above, para.8–33, fn.145.

23 Law Reform (Miscellaneous Provisions) Act 1934 s.1(2)(*a*), as amended by Administration of Justice Act 1982 s.4(2) (in effect reversing *Gammell v Wilson* [1982] A.C. 27, H.L.).

24 Law Reform (Miscellaneous Provisions) Act 1934 s.1(2)(*c*); *Hart v Griffiths-Jones* [1948] 2 All E.R. 729 (funeral expenses include embalming of the body but not monument costing £225); *Stanton v Ewart F. Youldon Ltd.* [1960] 1 W.L.R. 543 (funeral expenses include simple gravestone but not marble memorial set up as a sign of love and affection).

25 *Gammell v Wilson* [1982] A.C. 27, 46–47, 69, 74, 77–78.

26 See P. M. North (1966) 116 N.L.J. 1364–1366.

27 *Otter v Church, Adams, Tatham & Co* [1953] Ch.280.

28 *Beswick v Beswick* [1968] A.C. 58.

29 *Marshall v Broadhurst* (1831) 1 Cr. & J. 403 (executors carried out contract for construction work).

30 *Wantworth v Cock* (1839) 10 Ad. & El. 42 ("like any ordinary case of goods ordered by a testator, which the executor must receive and pay for"); *Cooper v Jarman* (1866) L.R. 3 Eq. 98 (administrators liable on intestate's contract). For special defences of personal representatives see below, paras 24–31 et seq.

31 The Employment Rights Act 1996 s.206.

dismissal at common law also survives the death of the employer or the employee.

(b) *Tort*

20–09 The general rule that any causes of action vested in, or subsisting against, the deceased survive for the benefit of, or against, his estate is applicable to all torts with the exception of defamation.[32] The damages recovered by the personal representatives in respect of any cause of action vested in the deceased form part of his estate for all purposes.

(c) *Statutory Torts*[33]

20–10 Claims for compensation for discrimination contrary to the Race Relations Act 1976, the Sex Discrimination Act 1975 and the Disability Discrimination Act 1995 are causes of action within the Law Reform (Miscellaneous Provisions) Act 1934 and survive the death of the complainant; it is immaterial that these Acts do not expressly confer rights on a personal representative to pursue a deceased's claim for compensation.[34]

A cause of action which was vested in the deceased and which survives for the benefit of his estate must be distinguished from a cause of action for damages under the Fatal Accidents Act 1976.[35] Under this Act the personal representatives may recover damages on behalf of certain dependants of the deceased where the death was caused by a wrongful act in respect of which the deceased could have sued if he had not died.[36] The damages belong to the dependants for whose benefit they are awarded and are designed to compensate the dependants for the loss of their "breadwinner."[37] The personal representatives may also recover £10,000 damages for bereavement for the benefit of the deceased's wife or husband, or civil partner, or the deceased's parents if the deceased was an unmarried minor.[38] Damages recovered under the Fatal Accidents Act form no part of the deceased's estate.[39]

[32] Law Reform (Miscellaneous Provisions) Act 1934 s.1(1); Law Reform (Miscellaneous Provisions) Act 1970 ss.4–5: a claim for bereavement under Fatal Accidents Act 1976 s.1A does not survive for the benefit of a person's estate on his death, Law Reform (Miscellaneous Provisions) Act 1934 s.1(1A), as amended by Administration of Justice Act 1982 s.4(1).
[33] See *Sheriff v Klyne Tugs (Lowestoft) Ltd* [1999] I.R.L.R. 481.
[34] *Harris v Lewisham & Guy's Mental Health N.H.S. Trust* [2000] 3 All E.R. 769.
[35] Consolidating the Fatal Accidents Acts 1846–1959.
[36] Fatal Accidents Act 1976 ss.1 and 2–4, as amended by Administration of Justice Act 1982 s.3(1) and Civil Partnership Act 2004 s.83.
[37] Damages may also be awarded in respect of the deceased's funeral expenses if incurred by the dependants: Fatal Accidents Act 1976 s.3(5), as amended.
[38] Fatal Accidents Act 1976 s.1A: the specified sum of £12,980 damages may be varied by the Lord Chancellor by statutory instrument, s.1A(5); the sum was last varied in 2013 by SI 2013/510.
[39] In assessing damages under the Fatal Accidents Act 1976, benefits accruing to any person from the deceased's estate or otherwise as a result of his death are disregarded, Fatal Accidents Act 1976 s.4, as amended.

3. Tax

20–11 The personal representatives are liable for income tax and capital gains tax chargeable on the deceased.[40]

II. COLLECTION AND PRESERVATION OF THE ESTATE

1. Collection of the estate

20–12 The personal representatives must carry out their statutory duty to "collect and get in the real and personal estate of the deceased" with reasonable diligence.[41]

(a) *Unsecured debts*

20–13 Personal representatives should require payment of any unsecured debts due to the deceased and, if need be, bring legal proceedings in order to recover payment.[42] But a personal representative who has taken no steps to enforce a debt will not be liable if he can prove that there were reasonable grounds for believing that the debtor could not pay.[43]

(b) *Secured debts*

20–14 Personal representatives are not under any duty to call in and realise loans made by the deceased on mortgages of land which are authorised investments under the deceased's will,[44] unless the money is needed for the payment of funeral and testamentary expenses, debts and pecuniary legacies.[45]

(c) *Statutory powers*

20–15 Under s.15 of the Trustee Act 1925, a personal representative has power to allow time for the payment of any debt, to accept composition or any real

[40] Taxes Management Act 1970 ss.74(1) and 77(1).
[41] Administration of Estates Act 1925 s.25, as amended by Administration of Estates Act 1971 s.9; *Re Tankard* [1942] Ch.69 (personal representatives' duty to pay debts with "due diligence"): see below, paras 21–12 et seq. Note the statutory duty of care imposed on trustees and personal representatives by Trustee Act 2000 s.1.
[42] *Caney v Bond* (1843) 6 Beav. 486 (sum due on promissory note): see also *Lowson v Copeland* (1787) 2 Bro.C.C. 156 (sum due on bond); *Powell v Evans* (1801) 5 Ves. 839 (sums due on bond: "debts due upon personal security are what executors without great reason ought not to permit to remain longer than is absolutely necessary"); *Tebbs v Carpenter* (1816) 1 Madd. 290 (executor failed to collect rents); *Stiles v Guy* (1848) 16 Sim. 230, 1 M. & G. 422 (executors failed to compel their co-executor to account and pay the balance he owed).
[43] *Clack v Holland* (1854) 19 Beav. 262, 271–272; *Stiles v Guy*, above, (onus on executors to prove debtor could not pay); *Re Brogden* (1888) 38 Ch.D. 546.
[44] Trustee Act 2000 s.3 has now given trustees a wide general power of investment and s.35 states that it applies to personal representatives as it applies to trustees.
[45] *Re Chapman* [1896] 2 Ch.763, esp. at 773 and 778.

or personal security for any debt or property claimed, and to compromise, abandon or settle any debt or claim relating to the deceased's estate.[46] If the personal representative exercises this wide power,[47] provided he has discharged the duty of care set out in s.1(1) of the Trustee Act 2000,[48] he is not responsible for any consequential loss. But the personal representative is only protected by the section if he exercises an active discretion.[49]

2. The inventory and account

If required to do so by the court, the personal representative has a statutory duty to "exhibit on oath in the court a full inventory of the estate and when so required render an account of the administration of the estate to the court."[50] Any person interested[51] in the deceased's estate may apply to the court[52] for an order requiring such an inventory and account from the personal representative. An order may be made against a former administrator whose grant has been revoked by the court in a probate claim.[53] Lapse of time is not in itself a bar but the court has a discretion to refuse such an order.[54] **20–16**

Compared with an administration claim[55] an application for an inventory and account is a relatively inexpensive procedure but the scope of the remedy is limited. In essence, it enables the applicant to obtain information from the personal representative as to the property comprised in the estate and the manner in which the administration has been carried out.

3. Time for realisation of unauthorised investments[56]

Personal representatives have a duty to realise any investment, which it is not proper for them to retain, within a reasonable time, which prima **20–17**

[46] For the statutory powers in relation to reversionary interests, see Trustee Act 1925 ss.22 and 68(1)(17).
[47] See *Re Earl of Strafford* [1980] Ch.28.
[48] Prior to the amendment of the section by Trustee Act 2000, the test was one of good faith. See *Snell's Equity* by John McGhee (ed), 31st edn (London: Sweet & Maxwell, 2005), para.26–24.
[49] *Re Greenwood* (1911) 105 L.T. 509 (case decided under s.21 of the Trustee Act 1893, the predecessor of the Trustee Act 1925 s.15).
[50] Administration of Estates Act 1925 s.25, as amended by Administration of Estates Act 1971 s.9.
[51] *Myddleton v Rushout* (1797) 1 Phillim. 244 ("any kind of interest" suffices); *Hackman v Black* (1755) 2 Lee 251 (creditor); *Kenny v Jackson* (1827) 1 Hag.Ecc. 105 (residuary legatee).
[52] Application is made to a district judge or registrar, N.C. Prob. Rules 1987 r.61(2).
[53] *In the Estate of Thomas* [1956] 1 W.L.R. 1516; *Taylor v Newton* (1752) 1 Lee 15 (order made against former administrator whose grant had expired). Apparently an order may be made against the executors of a deceased administrator with the will annexed, *Ritchie v Rees* (1822) 1 Add. 144, 153, and against the executor of a deceased executor though the other original executor is still alive, *Gale v Luttrell* (1824) 2 Add. 234.
[54] *Burgess v Marriott* (1843) 3 Curt. 424, 426; *Ritchie v Rees*, above, (administration granted in 1777: application in 1822 for inventory and account refused as estate fully administered); *Scurrah v Scurrah* (1841) 2 Curt. 919; *Pitt v Woodham* (1828) 1 Hag.Ecc.247; *Bowles v Harvey* (1832) 4 Hag.Ecc.241.
[55] See below, paras 24–22 et seq.
[56] The Trustee Act 2000 significantly widens the investment powers of trustees and personal representatives.

facie means within the executor's year, i.e. within a year from the date of death.[57] But the executors will not be liable if, in the honest exercise of the reasonable discretion allowed them, they decide to postpone the sale beyond the end of the executor's year.[58]

4. Preservation of the estate

20–18 Personal representatives are under a duty to take reasonable care in preserving the deceased's estate.[59] If they take reasonable care, they are not liable for the loss of the testator's goods which are destroyed by an accidental fire,[60] or which are taken by a thief from the possession of the personal representatives or their agent, such as their solicitor or banker.[61] It was held in *Re Clough-Taylor*[62] that an executor was not obliged to engage in proceedings to recover an asset which had been removed from the testatrix's house after her death by someone who claimed that she had given it to him during her lifetime. The executor's duty was to assent to the specific legatee, and to assign to him the right to bring proceedings to recover the asset, so that the cost of such proceedings would fall on the specific legatee and not on the estate.

(a) *Power to insure*

20–19 A personal representative has power under s.19 of the Trustee Act 1925[63] to insure any property belonging to the estate against risks of loss or damage due to any event[64] and is not restricted as to the funds from which he may pay the premiums.[65] The original s.19 imposed no *duty* to insure, only a limited power. On the face of it, the substituted s.19 also imposes no duty; but the duty of care under s.1 of the Trustee Act 2000 may well have the effect of turning the s.19 power into a duty.[66]

[57] *Grayburn v Clarkson* (1868) 3 Ch.App. 605: see also *Hughes v Empson* (1856) 22 Beav. 181; *Sculthorpe v Tipper* (1871) L.R. 13 Eq. 232: cf. *Re Norrington* (1879) 13 Ch.D.654.

[58] *Buxton v Buxton* (1835) 1 My. & Cr. 80; *Marsden v Kent* (1877) 5 Ch.D. 598; *Re Chapman* [1896] 2 Ch.763.

[59] *Job v Job* (1877) 6 Ch.D. 562 (per Jessel MR, "an executor or administrator is in the position of a gratuitous bailee"); *Re Gunning* [1918] 1 Ir.R. 221.

[60] *Executors of the Lady Croft v Lyndsey* (1676) 2 Freem. Ch.1.

[61] *Jones v Lewis* (1751) 2 Ves.Sen. 240.

[62] *Re Clough-Taylor* [2003] W.T.L.R. 15.

[63] The Trustee Act 2000 s.34 substituted a new s.19, which applies to those who died before as well as after 1 February 2001, when the Trustee Act 2000 came into force.

[64] The original section restricted the property (to buildings or other insurable property), the risk (to loss or damage by fire), and the amount of cover (it could not exceed three-quarters of the value of the property).

[65] Under the original section, the premiums had, normally, to be paid out of income.

[66] The duty of care in Pt I of the Trustee Act 2000 applies to personal representatives, and will draftsmen need to consider whether the duty should be excluded or whether personal representatives should be protected by an exemption clause. Having initially recommended in a 2003 Consultation Paper (CP No.171) that professional trustees should not be permitted to exempt themselves for liability for negligence, the Law Commission then recommended in 2006 (Law Com. No.301) that they should – subject to non-statutory regulaton governing disclosure and the explanation of clauses. This latter recommendation was accepted by the Ministry of Justice in 2010. Rules of Practice are now being implemented by the bodies

(b) *Deposit of documents*

Section 18 of the Trustee Act 2000 [67] states that if a personal representative retains, or invests in, any securities payable to bearer,[68] he must appoint a person to act as a custodian of such securities. The appointment has to be evidenced in writing[69] and s.19 restricts the persons who may be appointed.[70] Apart from this duty to deposit securities payable to bearer, any assets of the estate *may* be deposited with a person appointed to act as a custodian.[71] **20–20**

III. REALISATION OF THE ESTATE

The original s.33(1) of the Administration of Estates Act 1925 imposed a trust for sale on each asset (other than money) as to which a person died intestate, although the personal representative had a power to postpone sale. Section 5(1)[72] of the Trusts of Land and Appointment of Trustees Act 1996 has substituted a new s.33(1) which replaces the trust for sale with a power of sale.[73] Nevertheless, it remains common for a testator by his will to direct his executors to hold his residuary estate upon trust for sale. **20–21**

1. Powers to sell

Powers of sale are conferred both (a) at common law and in equity, and (b) by statute. **20–22**

(a) *Common Law*

Both at common law and in equity a personal representative has power to sell the deceased's personal estate (including leaseholds) for the purpose of carrying out the administration of the deceased's estate. An unpaid creditor of the deceased,[74] or a beneficiary under his will or on intestacy,[75] **20–23**

which govern and influence the practice of trustees. STEP have produced a Practice Rule and Guidance Notes on it. The Law Society's Rules and Ethics Committee have also produced a Practice Rule.

67 Replacing s.7 of the Trustee Act 1925.

68 If a security is payable to bearer, the person in possession is entitled to demand payment.

69 Trustee Act 2000 s.18(3).

70 Persons who carry on business as nominees or custodians, or are bodies corporate controlled by the appointing trustees, or are solicitors' nominee companies recognized under s.9 of the Administration of Justice Act 1985.

71 Trustee Act 2000 s.17; a custodian is a person who undertakes the safe custody of the assets or of any documents or records concerning them.

72 Together with Sch.2.

73 See above, paras 2–03 (total intestacy) and 2–50 (partial intestacy). The 1996 Act came into force on 1 January 1997, by virtue of SI 1996/2974, but Sch.5(5) states that the substituted section applies whether the death occurs before or after the commencement of the Act.

74 *Nugent v Gifford* (1738) 1 Atk. 463; *Whale v Booth* (1784) 4 T.R. 625.

75 *Ewer v Corbet* (1723) 2 P.Wms. 148.

cannot reclaim the property sold from the purchaser; if this were not the rule, no one would ever buy from a personal representative.

Under s.2(1) of the Administration of Estates Act 1925 a personal representative has the same powers with respect to real estate[76] as were in force before 1926 with respect to leaseholds.[77]

(b) *Statute*

20–24 A personal representative also has a statutory power of sale under s.39(1) of the Administration of Estates Act 1925. This section, as amended by the Trusts of Land and Appointment of Trustees Act 1996,[78] provides that in dealing with the deceased's personal estate his personal representatives shall have all the powers and discretions that a personal representative had before 1926 with respect to personal estate, and as respects the real estate they shall have all the functions conferred on them by Pt I of the Trusts of Land and Appointment of Trustees Act 1996. The personal representatives have in relation to the land the subject of the trust "all the powers of an absolute owner",[79] including the power to sell or exchange land. Personal representatives have power to enter into a contract to make such a sale or exchange and any contract is binding on, and enforceable by, the personal representatives for the time being of the deceased.[80]

2. Powers to mortgage

(a) *Common Law*

20–25 At common law and in equity a personal representative has power to raise money required for purposes of administration by mortgaging[81] or pledging[82] (as may be appropriate) any of the deceased's personal estate.

(b) *Statute*

20–26 Under s.39(1) of the Administration of Estates Act 1925 this common law power "including power to raise money by mortgage or charge

[76] See Administration of Estates Act 1925 s.3, and above, para.20–03.
[77] The Land Transfer Act 1897 s.2(2) had the same effect on a death after 1897. See also *Re Chaplin & Staffordshire Potteries Waterworks Co Ltd's Contract* [1922] 2 Ch.824.
[78] Trusts of Land and Appointment of Trustees Act 1996 s.25.
[79] Trusts of Land and Appointment of Trustees Act 1996 ss.6 and 18.
[80] Administration of Estates Act 1925 s.39(1) (iii); for power to raise capital money see Trustee Act 1925 s.16. The powers conferred by s.39(1) are exercisable for purposes of administration and also "during a minority of any beneficiary or the subsistence of any life interest, or until the period of distribution arrives."
[81] *Mead v Orrery* (1745) 3 Atk. 235, 239–240; *Scott v Tyler* (1788) Dick. 712, 725; *M'Leod v Drummond* (1810) 17 Ves. 152, 154; *Earl Vane v Rigden* (1870) L.R. 5 Ch.663 ("it is a very common practice for an executor to obtain an advance from a banker for the immediate wants of the estate by depositing securities. It would be a strange thing if that could not be done").
[82] *Russell v Plaice* (1854) 18 Beav. 21, 28–29.

(whether or not by deposit of documents)" may be exercised by personal representatives over the personal estate of the deceased. Again, because under s.39(1), personal representatives have, as respects real estate, all the functions conferred on trustees by Pt I of the Trusts of Land and Appointment of Trustees Act 1996, they have all the powers of an absolute owner.[83]

Personal representatives also have power, for the purpose of paying inheritance tax for which they are liable on any property (or raising the amount of it when paid), to raise the amount of the tax by sale or mortgage of, or a terminable charge on, the property.[84]

3. Powers to lease

(a) *Common Law*

20–27 At common law and in equity a personal representative has power to grant a lease for purposes of administration.[85] For instance, if the deceased's estate includes a leasehold interest for which the personal representative cannot find a purchaser or negotiate a surrender to the landlord, he may grant an underlease. This common law power now applies to the deceased's real estate as well as to the deceased's leaseholds.[86]

(b) *Statute*

20–28 As already mentioned, under s.39(1) of the Administration of Estates Act 1925 personal representatives have, as respects real estate, all the powers of an absolute owner and these include powers to lease and to accept surrenders of leases.

4. Protection of purchaser

(a) *Propriety of the disposition*

20–29 Section 36(8) of the Administration of Estates Act 1925 provides protection for a purchaser of a legal estate in land as "a conveyance[87] of a legal estate by a personal representative to a purchaser shall not be invalidated by reason only that the purchaser may have notice that all the debts, liabilities, funeral and testamentary or administration expenses, duties, and legacies of the deceased have been discharged or provided for." For s.36(8) to apply, the purchaser (or mortgagee or lessee)[88] must have

[83] Trusts of Land and Appointment of Trustees Act 1996 s.6.

[84] Inheritance Tax Act 1984 ss.212(1) and (4) (tax includes interest and costs properly incurred in respect of tax).

[85] *Oceanic Steam Navigation Co v Sutherberry* (1880) 16 Ch.D. 236, 243.

[86] Administration of Estates Act 1925 s.2(1).

[87] "Conveyance" includes inter alia a mortgage, charge by way of legal mortgage, and a lease: see Administration of Estates Act 1925 s.55(1)(iii).

[88] Administration of Estates Act 1925 s.55(1)(xviii).

acquired a legal estate in land[89] in good faith[90] and for money or money's worth.[91]

(b) *Application of the purchase money*

20–30 Section 14 of the Trustee Act 1925 provides that the receipt in writing of a personal representative[92] for any money, securities or other personal property payable or transferable to him under any trust or power shall be a sufficient discharge to the person paying or transferring the same and "shall effectually exonerate him from seeing to the application or being answerable for any loss or misapplication thereof." The statutory protection of the purchaser cannot be excluded by a contrary direction in the deceased's will.[93]

(c) *Good faith essential*

20–31 Good faith on the part of the purchaser is always essential, whether the conveyance is of a legal estate in land (so that s.36(8) applies) or of an equitable interest in land or any interest in pure personalty (to which s.36(8) is not applicable). If the purchaser knows that the disposition to him is a breach of duty on the part of the personal representative, the purchaser's bad faith vitiates the disposition.[94] If the transaction is vitiated by bad faith on the part of the purchaser, a creditor or a beneficiary entitled under the deceased's will[95] or on his intestacy may have the transaction set aside unless the creditor or beneficiary is barred by laches.[96]

(d) *Previous assent*

20–32 A personal representative's powers are exercisable over the property for the time being vested in him in his capacity as personal representative. He cannot exercise his powers over property which he has already transferred to the trustees or the beneficiary entitled under the deceased's will or on his intestacy.[97]

Section 36(6) of the Administration of Estates Act 1925 provides some

[89] Administration of Estates Act 1925 s.55(1)(vii).
[90] Administration of Estates Act 1925 s.55(1)(xviii).
[91] Administration of Estates Act 1925 s.36(11): quaere whether a nominal consideration in money suffices, see s.55(1)(xviii); *Midland Bank Trust Co Ltd v Green* [1981] A.C. 513, 531–532.
[92] Trustee Act 1925 s.68(1)(17).
[93] Trustee Act 1925 s.14(3): see also ss.17 and 68(1) (7) and (17).
[94] *Doe d. Woodhead v Fallows* (1832) 2 Cr. & J. 481. In *Scott v Tyler* (1788) Dick 712, 715 Lord Thurlow gave some instances of bad faith on the part of the purchaser. He said that the transaction was vitiated if the purchaser "concerts with an executor by obtaining the testator's effects at a nominal price, or at a fraudulent undervalue, or by applying the real value to the purchase of other objects for his own behoof, or in extinguishing the private debt of the executor."
[95] *Hill v Simpson* (1802) 7 Ves. 152; *M'Leod v Drummond* (1810) 17 Ves. 152, 169–170; *Wilson v Moore* (1834) 1 M. & K. 337.
[96] *Elliot v Merriman* (1740) 2 Atk. 41; *Andrew v Wrigley* (1792) 4 Bro.C.C. 125.
[97] *Attenborough v Solomon* [1913] A.C. 76 (see below, para.20–58).

protection for a purchaser (or mortgagee or lessee)[98] of a legal estate in land[99] in good faith[100] and for money or money's worth.[101] A purchaser can rely on a statement in writing by a personal representative that he has not given or made an assent or conveyance in respect of a legal estate and a conveyance by a personal representative of a legal estate to a purchaser accepted on the faith of such a statement shall operate to transfer or create the legal estate expressed to be conveyed as if no previous assent or conveyance had been made. This protection is, however, "without prejudice to any previous disposition made in favour of another purchaser".

(e) *Revocation of grant*

The protection of a purchaser from a personal representative against any subsequent revocation of the latter's grant has already been considered.[102] **20–33**

IV. CARRYING ON THE DECEASED'S BUSINESS

On the death of the sole proprietor of a business, the assets of the business which were vested in the deceased devolve on his personal representatives. On the death of a partner, the assets of the partnership which were vested in the deceased (other than as a joint tenant)[103] devolve on his personal representatives: but such assets remain partnership assets and the surviving partner or partners may deal with them for the purposes of the partnership.[104] If the deceased was a shareholder in an incorporated company which owned the business, the deceased's shares, but not the assets of the business, devolve on his personal representatives. **20–34**

1. Authority to carry on business

The general rule is that personal representatives have no authority to carry on the deceased's business.[105] Similarly on the death of a partner, his personal representatives are generally under a duty to call in the deceased's share in the partnership business and they ought not to permit the deceased's share to be left outstanding in the business.[106] For instance, if under the partnership agreement (or under a contract made with the personal representatives after the deceased's death) the surviving partners **20–35**

98 Administration of Estates Act 1925 s.55(1)(xviii): s.36(6) applies to assents and conveyances made after 1925, whenever the deceased died, s.36(12).
99 Administration of Estates Act 1925 s.55(1)(vii).
100 Administration of Estates Act 1925 s.55(1)(xviii).
101 Administration of Estates Act 1925 s.36(11).
102 See above, paras 19–52 et seq.
103 Land vested in the partners has to be held by them as legal joint tenants, Law of Property Act 1925 s.34, but in equity the partners are presumed to be tenants in common, *Re Fuller's Contract* [1933] Ch.652.
104 *Re Bourne* [1906] 2 Ch.427.
105 *Barker v Parker* (1786) 1 T.R. 287, 295; *Kirkman v Booth* (1848) 11 Beav. 273.
106 *Kirkman v Booth*, above.

are bound to purchase the deceased's share, the personal representatives should require payment of the price due to the deceased's estate: if the surviving partners are not so bound, and if the surviving partners do not have an option to purchase the deceased's share,[107] the personal representatives should require the business of the partnership to be wound up.[108]

There are certain exceptions to the general rule that personal representatives have no authority to carry on the deceased's business.

(a) *Proper realisation*

20–36 Personal representatives have authority to carry on the deceased's business with a view to the proper realisation of his estate; for example, to carry out the deceased's obligations under a contract made by him,[109] or to enable the business to be sold as a going concern.[110] Thus, if selling the deceased's business as a going concern is a proper method of realisation, his personal representatives may carry on the business for such a reasonable period of time as is necessary to enable them to effect the sale. Normally this period is not much longer than the executor's year.[111]

(b) *Authority in the will*

20–37 The personal representatives have authority to carry on the deceased's business if they are directed, or empowered, to do so by the deceased in his will. If the personal representatives are empowered to postpone the sale of the deceased's business, they have by implication authority to carry on the business during the period of postponement.[112] It is desirable that a testator should specify in his will which assets of his estate may be employed by his personal representatives in carrying on his business.[113]

Personal representatives who carry on the deceased's business without authority are liable to make good any losses they incur. If personal representatives consider it expedient to carry on the deceased's business but lack the authority to do so, it may be advisable for them to apply to the court for an order authorising them to do so,[114] or to seek an indemnity from the beneficiaries (if they are ascertained and sui juris).

[107] It is not improbable that, under the terms of the partnership agreement, the surviving partners will either have a duty to purchase the deceased partner's share, or an option to purchase it. There may be tax implications in relation to business property relief, I.H.T.A. ss.103–114, see Chap.16, para.16–23.

[108] Partnership Act 1890 ss.33(1), 38–39 and 42: see *Barclays Bank Trust Co Ltd v Bluff* [1982] Ch.172.

[109] *Marshall v Broadhurst* (1831) 1 Cr. & J. 403 ("if a man makes half a wheelbarrow or a pair of shoes, and die, the executors may complete them"); *Edwards v Grace* (1836) 2 M. & W. 190.

[110] *Dowse v Gorton* [1891] A.C. 190, 199; *Garrett v Noble* (1834) 6 Sim. 504.

[111] *Re Crowther* [1895] 2 Ch.56, 60. Though what is reasonable must, to some extent, depend on general economic conditions and on the nature of the business.

[112] *Re Crowther* [1895] 2 Ch.56: cf. *Re Smith* [1896] 1 Ch.171; *Re Chancellor* (1884) 26 Ch.D. 42, 46.

[113] *Cutbush v Cutbush* (1839) 1 Beav. 184; *Re Slater* (1915) 113 L.T. 691; *M'Nellie v Acton* (1853) 4 De G.M. & G. 744.

[114] See Trustee Act 1925 s.57.

2. Liability of personal representative for debts incurred

A personal representative is personally liable on every contract which he makes in carrying on the deceased's business[115] even if he is expressed to make the contract as personal representative.[116] Thus, if the personal representative incurs a debt in carrying on the deceased's business, the creditor may sue the personal representative personally and enforce the judgment against the latter's assets. The creditor is not entitled at common law to payment out of the deceased's assets because the debt was not due from the deceased.[117] The creditor may, however, be entitled in equity to payment out of the deceased's assets by subrogation to the personal representative's own right of indemnity out of those assets. **20–38**

3. Indemnity of personal representative

The personal representative who incurs liabilities in carrying on the deceased's business may be entitled to an indemnity out of the assets of the deceased's estate if; **20–39**

(a) he had authority to carry on the business; or,
(b) one or more creditors of the deceased have assented to the carrying on of the business by the personal representative.

(a) *Effect of authority to carry on the business*

Under this head the extent of the personal representative's right of indemnity depends on the nature of the authority he exercised to carry on the business. **20–40**

(i) Proper realisation. If the personal representative carried on the business with a view to the proper realisation of the deceased's estate, his right of indemnity from the assets may be exercised against both the deceased's creditors and the beneficiaries.[118] In this case his right of indemnity takes priority over the claims of the deceased's creditors. **20–41**

(ii) Other authority. If, on the other hand, the personal representative carried on the business under an authority in the will but not with a view to proper realisation, his right of indemnity may be exercised against the beneficiaries but not against the deceased's creditors.[119] The reason for this distinction is that the beneficiaries are bound by the terms of the will but the creditors are not. Of course, under this right of indemnity the personal **20–42**

[115] *Owen v Delamere* (1872) L.R. 15 Eq. 134, 139.

[116] *Labouchere v Tupper* (1857) 11 Moo.P.C. 198; *Liverpool Borough Bank v Walker* (1859) 4 De G. & J. 24.

[117] *Re Morgan* (1881) 18 Ch.D. 93, 99: see also *Farhall v Farhall* (1871) 7 Ch. App. 123.

[118] *Dowse v Gorton* [1891] A.C. 190, 199.

[119] *Dowse v Gorton*, above; *Re Millard, Ex p. Yates* (1895) 72 L.T. 823; *Re East* (1914) 111 L.T. 101.

representative may only resort to assets which the will authorised him to employ in carrying on the business.[120]

(b) *Effect of assent by creditor*

20–43 If one of the deceased's creditors has assented to the carrying on of the business, the personal representative is entitled to be indemnified out of the deceased's assets in priority to that creditor.[121] This rule applies whether or not the personal representative had authority under the will to carry on the business.[122] If, on the other hand, a creditor of the deceased has not assented to the carrying on of the business, and the business has not been carried on with a view to proper realisation, that creditor may treat the continuance of the business as improper: if he does so, he is entitled to be paid out of the value of the assets which existed at the deceased's death and the personal representative has no right to be indemnified in priority to him.[123]

A creditor does not assent to the carrying on of the business if he merely knows of it and does nothing to stop it.[124]

4. Creditor's right of subrogation

20–44 If in carrying on the deceased's business the personal representative incurs a debt[125] in respect of which he is entitled to indemnity out of the assets, then, by subrogation to the personal representative, his creditor is entitled to claim the benefit of his right of indemnity. The creditor is therefore entitled in equity to stand in the personal representative's shoes and obtain payment out of the deceased's assets.[126]

The creditor may obtain payment out of the assets to exactly the same extent as the personal representative is entitled to be indemnified out of the assets.

This right of subrogation is most important to the creditor if the personal representative becomes insolvent.

5. Assets and profits of the business

20–45 Any assets acquired and any profits made by the personal representative in carrying on the deceased's business belong to the deceased's estate.[127] But a creditor of the deceased who is entitled to treat the continuance of the business as improper may not be entitled to invoke this principle. Such a creditor has a choice:

[120] *Ex p. Garland* (1804) 10 Ves. 110; *Cutbush v Cutbush* (1839) 1 Beav. 184.
[121] *Dowse v Gorton*, above.
[122] *Re Brooke* [1894] 2 Ch.600.
[123] *Re Oxley* [1914] 1 Ch.604; *Re East* (1914) 111 L.T. 101.
[124] *Re Oxley* [1914] 1 Ch.604.
[125] Or a liability for damages in tort, *Re Raybould* [1900] 1 Ch.199.
[126] *Ex p. Edmonds* (1862) 4 De G.F. & J. 488, 498; *Re Johnson* (1880) 15 Ch.D. 548; *Re Evans* (1887) 34 Ch.D. 597; *Re Owen* (1892) 66 L.T. 718; *Re Frith* [1902] 1 Ch.342.
[127] *Abbott v Parfitt* (1871) L.R. 6 Q.B. 346; *Moseley v Rendell* (1871) L.R. 6 Q.B. 338; *Gibblett v Read* (1744) 9 Mod. 459.

(i) If he treats the continuance of the business as improper, he may only make the personal representative accountable for the value of the assets which existed at the deceased's death: in that event the personal representative has no right to be indemnified in priority to him.[128]

(ii) If, on the other hand, he treats the business as properly continued, the personal representative is accountable to him for assets acquired and profits made in carrying on the business, but the personal representative is entitled to be indemnified in priority to him against liabilities incurred in carrying on the business.

V. THE DECEASED'S LEASEHOLDS

On the death of a tenant, his leasehold interest devolves on his personal representatives[129] without their having to enter the property.[130] The personal representatives cannot refuse the leasehold interest, because they cannot renounce part of their office.[131] This is so even if the tenant's interest is worthless because the rent exceeds the value of the land. If the lease contains a covenant prohibiting any assignment by the tenant without the landlord's consent, there is no breach of covenant when the leasehold interest devolves by operation of law on the tenant's personal representatives.[132] **20–46**

When considering the liability of a personal representative for rent or breach of the other covenants in a lease, it is vital to distinguish between two types of liability:

(1) Liability as personal representative (representative liability), which arises from his office; and

(2) Personal liability as assignee of the deceased's leasehold interest, which arises if the personal representative enters into possession of the demised premises.

1. Liability as personal representative

The personal representative is liable as such for rent due from the deceased at his death and for any subsisting breach of other covenants in the lease. **20–47**

[128] per Lord Macnaghten in *Dowse v Gorton* [1891] A.C. 190, 203–204 (such creditors may "make the executors accountable for the value of the assets used in carrying on the business, and they may also follow the assets and obtain a charge on the business in the hands of the executors for the value of the assets misapplied, with interest thereon; and they may enforce the charge, if necessary, by means of a receiver and a sale").

[129] See above, para.20–02.

[130] *Wollaston v Hakewill* (1841) M. & G. 297.

[131] *Billinghurst v Speerman* (1695) 1 Salk. 297; *Rubery v Stevens* (1832) 4 B. & Ad. 241, 244. For renunciation by a personal representative of his office in regard to settled land if he is not a trustee of the settlement, see Administration of Estates Act 1925 s.23(1).

[132] *Parry v Harbert* (1539) 1 Dyer 45b.

Similarly, the personal representative is liable as such for rent falling due and for any breach of covenant committed during the period for which he is liable after the deceased's death.[133] This "liability period" ends, of course, with the determination of the lease. If the lease was granted after 1995—or if the lease was granted before 1996 but the deceased was an assignee of the lease (and so liable under privity of estate, but not privity of contract)—this liability period usually ends with an assignment of the lease by the personal representative. The lease may, however, require the tenant to enter into an authorised guarantee agreement within section16 of the Landlord and Tenant (Covenants) Act 1995 as a condition of the landlord's giving consent to the assignment.[134] But if the lease was granted before 1996,[135] and if the deceased was the original tenant, his personal representative remains liable as such for rent and any breach of the other covenants during the entire unexpired term of the lease, despite any assignment of the lease by the tenant during his lifetime or by the personal representative.[136]

(a) *Extent of representative liability*

20–48 In his representative capacity the personal representative is liable only to the extent of the deceased's assets.[137] He does not incur any personal liability unless he enters into possession of the demised premises.[138] But a constructive entry into possession suffices: for example, a personal representative enters into possession if he accepts rent from a sub-tenant.[139]

(b) *Protection against representative liability*

20–49 If the lease was granted after 1995, or if the deceased was an assignee of the lease, the personal representative may end the liability period by assigning the lease.[140] If the lease is onerous (the rent exceeding the value of the land), the personal representative should try to end the liability period as soon as possible by negotiating a surrender

[133] *Youngmin v Heath* [1974] 1 W.L.R. 135.

[134] The guarantee must terminate on a subsequent assignment.

[135] The general rule is that tenants of leases granted on or after 1 January 1996 are released from covenants on assignment of those leases: Landlord and Tenant (Covenants) Act 1995 s.5. Section 11 provides for an exception if the assignment is in breach of covenant or by operation of law (e.g. on bankruptcy). Original tenants remain liable where leases were granted on or before 31 December 1995.

[136] *Coghill v Freelove* (1690) 3 Mod. 325; *Pitcher v Tovey* (1692) 4 Mod. 71, 76; *Brett v Cumberland* (1619) Cro.Jac. 521.

[137] *Wilson v Wigg* (1808) 10 East 315 (personal representative may plead *plene administravit*, whether breach of covenant was by the deceased or after his death); *Helier v Casebert* (1665) 1 Lev. 127; *Lydall v Dunlapp* (1743) 1 Wils. 4.

[138] *Rendall v Andreae* (1892) 61 L.J.Q.B. 630; *Wollaston v Hakewill* (1841) 3 M. & G. 297, 320–321.

[139] *Mayor, Aldermen and Burgesses of Stratford-upon-Avon v Parkes* [1914] 2 K.B. 562, 569.

[140] Subject to the landlord's requiring an authorised guarantee agreement as a condition of the assignment.

of the lease to the landlord, or an assignment of the lease to a third party.[141]

If the lease was granted before 1996, and if the deceased was the original tenant, an assignment by the personal representative does not end the liability period; but s.26 of the Trustee Act 1925 provides protection for the personal representative against any representative liability after he has assigned the lease to a purchaser or a beneficiary entitled to it.[142] Similar protection is afforded to a personal representative who has entered into, or may be required to enter into, an authorised guarantee agreement.[143]

2. Personal liability

20–50 If the personal representative[144] (as is usual) enters into possession of the demised premises, he becomes personally liable as an assignee of the deceased's leasehold interest.[145] A personal representative who enters is personally liable for rent falling due and any breach of the other covenants which touch and concern the land[146] and which are committed after his entry into possession and so long as the lease is vested in him.[147] He is not personally liable as assignee for breaches committed after he has assigned the lease.

(a) *Extent of personal liability*

20–51 There is an unusual upper limit on his personal liability for rent. The personal representative may, by proper pleading, limit his liability for rent to the letting value of the premises, i.e. the amount he received or might by the exercise of reasonable diligence have received from the premises during his period of liability as assignee.[148] It seems that this upper limit is meant to prevent hardship to the personal representative in a case where the rent reserved exceeds the actual value of the premises. But, illogically, this upper limit appears not to be appli-

[141] *Rowley v Adams* (1839) 4 My. & Cr. 534: cf. *Rendall v Andreae*, above, at 631. The landlord would probably require a premium to be paid on surrender.

[142] s.26 does not prejudice the right of the landlord to follow the deceased's assets into the hands of persons amongst whom they have been distributed, s.26(2): for this remedy see below, paras 24–36 et seq. The section also protects the personal representative against representative liability for a rentcharge or under an indemnity covenant, see ss.26(1) and (3).

[143] Trustee Act 1925 s.26(1A).

[144] The rule does not apply to an *executor de son tort* because the deceased's leasehold interest does not devolve on him. *Mayor, Aldermen & Burgesses of Stratford-upon-Avon v Parker* [1914] 2 K.B. 562; see below, para.24–51, fn.187.

[145] *Mayor, Aldermen & Burgesses of Stratford-upon-Avon v Parker*, above, at 567; *Tilney v Norris* (1700) 1 Ld.Raym. 553.

[146] If they touch and concern the land, they are binding on him as assignee under privity of estate. Examples of covenants which touch and concern the land are covenants to repair, to insure, and not to assign without the landlord's consent, see Megarry and Wade, *The Law of Real Property*, (8th edn (London: Sweet & Maxwell, 2012), paras 20–033 et seq.

[147] *Whitehead v Palmer* [1908] 1 K.B. 151.

[148] *Rendall v Andreae* (1892) 61 L.J.Q.B. 630, 633; *Re Bowes* (1887) 37 Ch.D. 128; *Hornidge v Wilson* (1841) 11 Ad. & E. 645 (executor liable for value he might have received if he had complied with covenant to repair); *Hopwood v Whaley* (1848) 6 C.B. 744. See also *Minford v Carse* [1912] 2 Ir.R. 245 (receiver in possession: executors not liable for rent).

cable to his personal liability for breach of other covenants, so that a personal representative who enters is apparently fully liable for breach of a repairing covenant in the lease, even though the lease is onerous.[149]

(b) *Protection against personal liability*

20–52 Section 26 of the Trustee Act 1925 provides protection for a personal representative against his representative liability but not against his personal liability.[150] A personal representative who incurs personal liability by entering into possession is entitled:

(i) to have a proper indemnity from the beneficiaries[151] (e.g. the beneficiaries may give security); or,
(ii) to set aside an indemnity fund out of the deceased's estate.[152]

The indemnity fund is for the protection of the personal representative and not of the lessor.[153] It is distributable to the beneficiaries when all possible claims against the personal representative have either been satisfied, or become statute-barred by lapse of time since the determination, or assignment by the personal representative, of the lease.[154] If the personal representative assigns the lease to the beneficiary entitled without taking a proper indemnity from him, the personal representative is not then entitled to set aside an indemnity fund out of the deceased's estate.[155]

VI. EXERCISE OF POWERS BY PERSONAL REPRESENTATIVES

1. Sole personal representative

20–53 A sole personal representative has the same powers as two or more personal representatives. This is so where a single personal representative was appointed initially or where only one of several personal representatives survives.[156] In particular, a sole personal representative, acting as such, may give a valid receipt for, or direct the application of, the

[149] *Rendall v Andreae*, above, at 633; *Tremeere v Morison* (1834) 1 Bing.N.C. 89; *Sleap v Newman* (1862) 12 C.B.(N.S.) 116: but see *Reid v Lord Tenterden* (1833) 4 Tyr. 111, 118, 120.
[150] *Re Owers* [1941] Ch.389.
[151] *Simmons v Bolland* (1817) 3 Mer. 547; *Dobson v Carpenter* (1850) 12 Beav. 370; *Hickling v Boyer* (1851) 3 Mac. & G. 635; *Dean v Allen* (1855) 20 Beav. 1.
[152] *Re Owers*, [1941] Ch.389.
[153] *King v Malcott* (1852) 9 Hare 692.
[154] *Re Lewis* [1939] Ch. 232.
[155] *Re Bennett* [1943] 1 All E.R. 467; *Shadbolt v Woodfall* (1845) 2 Coll. 30; *Smith v Smith* (1861) 1 Dr. & Sm. 384.
[156] Administration of Estates Act 1925 ss.2(1) and (2). For survivorship of powers see below, para.20–60.

proceeds of sale of land[157]: by way of contrast, a sole trustee may not do so unless the sole trustee is a trust corporation.[158]

A sole personal representative may contract in his representative capacity with himself as an individual[159]: normally a person cannot make a contract with himself.

2. Joint personal representatives

The general rule is that joint executors have joint *and several* authority: the act of one of them in exercise of their powers is therefore binding on the other executors and the deceased's estate.[160] This rule may also apply to joint administrators, though there is no decisive authority.[161] So: **20–54**

(i) A sale or other disposition of a chattel comprised in the deceased's estate by one of the executors is valid.[162]

(ii) One executor may pay a debt due from the deceased,[163] or accept payment of[164] or release[165] a debt due to the estate, or settle an account with a person liable to the estate.[166]

(a) *Statutory Exceptions*

This general rule is subject to significant statutory exceptions. **20–55**

(i) Interests in land. The rule does not apply to any "conveyance"[167] of freehold or leasehold land[168]: such a conveyance must not be made without the concurrence of all the personal representatives (still living) to **20–56**

[157] Law of Property Act 1925 s.27(2) as amended by Law of Property (Amendment) Act 1926 Sch.1.

[158] ibid; Settled Land Act 1925 s.18(1); Trustee Act 1925 s.14.

[159] *Rowley, Holmes & Co v Barber* [1977] 1 W.L.R. 371.

[160] *Jacomb v Harwood* (1751) 2 Ves.Sen. 265, 267; *Attenborough v Solomon* [1913] A.C. 76. The Law Reform Committee, in their 23rd Report, *The Powers and Duties of Trustees*, Cmnd.8733 (1982), suggested reform (see pp.55–56 and 68), but the recommendations of this Report were not enacted.

[161] *Fountain Forestry Ltd v Edwards* [1975] Ch.1, 10–14 (where Brightman J reviewed the case law).

[162] *Kelsack v Nicholson* (1596) Cro.Eliz. 478, 496; *Jacomb v Harwood*, above.

[163] *Jacomb v Harwood*, above, at pp.267–268.

[164] *Charlton v Earl of Durham* (1869) 4 Ch.App. 433.

[165] *Herbert v Pigott* (1834) 2 Cr. & M. 384.

[166] *Smith v Everett* (1859) 27 Beav. 446.

[167] "Conveyance" is defined to include "a mortgage, charge by way of legal mortgage, lease, assent, vesting instrument, disclaimer, release and every other assurance of property or of an interest therein by any instrument, except a will". Administration of Estates Act 1925 s.55(1)(iii). A denial of their landlord's title in a pleading on behalf of one of two executors is not a "conveyance" within this definition, *Warner v Sampson* [1958] 1 Q.B. 404 (reversed on other grounds [1959] 1 Q.B. 297).

[168] Administration of Estates Act 1925 s.3(1). If the deceased died before 1926 the general rule applies to his leasehold land, see Administration of Estates Act 1925 s.54; Land Transfer Act 1897 s.2(2) and *Anon.* (1536) 1 Dyer 23(b).

whom a grant has been made in respect of the land conveyed, or without an order of the court.[169]

A contract to sell land is not a "conveyance" and before the enactment of s.16 of the Law of Property (Miscellaneous Provisions) Act 1994[170] it seemed that one of two or more executors could enter into a contract to sell land to a purchaser and that this contract would be binding on the deceased's estate, even though he could not convey the land to the purchaser without the concurrence of his co-executors or an order of the court.[171] Section 16 now requires the concurrence of all personal representatives in any contract to convey real estate, as well as for the conveyance itself. The section applies to contracts made on or after 1 July 1995.[172]

20–57 **(ii) Shares and stock.** If a company is regulated by the Companies Acts, its articles usually require a transfer of its shares to be executed by all the personal representatives.[173] The Bank of England may decline to give effect to a transfer of government stock unless it is executed by all the personal representatives.[174]

(b) *Authority of trustees*

20–58 Trustees, as opposed to executors, must always act jointly.[175] This difference between the authority of executors and of trustees may make it essential to decide whether persons appointed to be executors and trustees held particular property as executors or as trustees at the time when one of them sold or otherwise disposed of it.[176]

3. Powers in the will annexed to an office

20–59 By his will a testator may confer powers on the persons who are appointed by him as his executors or his trustees. It is a question of construction whether such a power is intended to be (i) a bare power personal to those persons,[177] or (ii) a power annexed to their office, so

169 Administration of Estates Act 1925 ss.2(2) and 24.

170 This section amends s2(2) of the Administration of Estates Act 1925.

171 *Fountain Forestry Ltd v Edwards* [1975] Ch.1, 11–12.

172 Law of Property (Misc Provs) Act 1994 (Commencement No.2) Order 1995, SI 1995/1317.

173 Companies Act 1985 ss.8 and 182; Companies Act 2006, ss.544 and 773; Companies (Tables A to F) Regulations 1985 (SI 1985/805), Table A, arts. 29–31. If personal representatives are registered as the holders of shares or stock in a company incorporated under the Companies Clauses Acts, a transfer is invalid unless executed by all of them; *Barton v North Staffordshire Railway Co* (1888) 38 Ch.D. 458; *Barton v London and North Western Railway Co* (1889) 24 Q.B.D. 77.

174 Government Stock Regulations 1965 SI 1420, reg.6(2); Finance Act 1942 s.47(2) and Sch.11, Pt III.

175 *Luke v South Kensington Hotel Ltd* (1879) 11 Ch.D. 121, 125; see Hanbury and Martin *Modern Equity*, 20th edn (London: Sweet & Maxwell, 2015), para.18–007.

176 *Attenborough v Solomon* [1913] A.C. 76. See below, paras 23–47 et seq. for discussion as to whether persons, who are both personal representatives and trustees, are holding property in their capacity as personal representatives or in their capacity as trustees.

177 *Down v Worrall* (1833) 1 M. & K. 561; *Forbes v Forbes* (1854) 18 Beav. 552 (bequest of £2,000

as to be exercisable by the holders or holder of the office for the time being.[178]

4. Survivorship of powers

Under s.18(1) of the Trustee Act 1925,[179] where a trust or power is imposed on, or given to, personal representatives jointly, it may be performed, or exercised, by the survivors or survivor of them for the time being. In the absence of any contrary direction in the will,[180] this provision applies to all the statutory and common law powers of personal representatives and to all the powers conferred by will which are annexed to their office.[181] **20–60**

5. Effect of order for general administration

If in an administration claim the court makes an order for general administration (i.e. an order for the administration of the deceased's estate under the direction of the court),[182] the personal representatives must not exercise their powers without first obtaining the sanction of the court.[183] **20–61**

VII. DECEASED A SOLE TRUSTEE

1. Devolution of trust property

If, at his death, the deceased held property as a sole or last surviving trustee, the property devolves on his personal representatives.[184] To meet this situation s.18(2) of the Trustee Act 1925 provides that: **20–62**

> "Until the appointment of new trustees, the personal representatives or representative[185] for the time being of a sole trustee, or, where there were

to executors in trust to build a bridge over the river Don, the site "to be chosen by them": Romilly MR said power to choose site seemed to have been personal to original executors, who had died without choosing).

178 *Crawford v Forshaw* [1891] 2 Ch.261 (power for "my executors herein named" to select charities held annexed to office of executor: two executors who proved could, but renouncing executor could not, exercise power): see also *Lambert v Rendle* (1863) 3 New Rep. 247 (power for executor acting under his will to carry on testator's business; executor renounced: held power not exercisable by administratrix with will annexed). And see *Re Smith* [1904] 1 Ch.139, 144.

179 Applicable to personal representatives, Trustee Act 1925 ss.68(1)(17) and 69(1).

180 Trustee Act 1925 s.69(2).

181 But not to a bare power given to persons by name and not annexed to an office, *Re Harding* [1923] 1 Ch.182. See also Williams, Mortimer and Sunnucks, *Executors, Administrators and Probate*, 20th edn (London: Sweet & Maxwell, 2015), paras 55–80 et seq.

182 For administration proceedings see below, paras 24–22 et seq.

183 *Re Viscount Furness* [1943] Ch.415 (sanction is needed even if the accounts and inquiries ordered are not to be proceeded with except with the leave of the judge in person); *Minors v Battison* (1876) 1 App.Cas. 428. See generally A. J. Hawkins (1968) 84 L.Q.R. 64, 68–73.

184 See above, paras 20–02 et seq.

185 This does not include an executor who has renounced or has not proved, Trustee Act 1925 s.18(4).

two or more trustees, of the last surviving or continuing trustee, shall be capable of exercising or performing any power or trust which was given to, or capable of being exercised by, the sole or last surviving or continuing trustee, or other the trustees or trustee for the time being of the trust."

This provision applies to any trust unless a contrary intention is expressed in the trust instrument.[186]

2. Personal representative is not bound to act as trustee

20–63 The personal representative of such a deceased trustee is not bound to perform the trust.[187] He is only bound, in his capacity as personal representative, to collect and preserve the property of which the deceased was trustee[188]: he is not bound, for instance, to pay the income of that property to the beneficiary entitled to it under the trust. But under s.18(2), the personal representative may, if he chooses, perform the trust or exercise the power. There is only one restriction: a sole personal representative (who is not a trust corporation) cannot give a valid receipt for proceeds of sale or other capital money arising under a trust of land, or for capital money arising under the Settled Land Act 1925.[189]

3. Appointment of new trustees

20–64 The personal representative may only perform the trust or exercise the power under s.18(2) "until the appointment of new trustees." An appointment of new trustees may be made under s.36 of the Trustee Act 1925[190]:

(i) by the person or persons nominated for the purpose of appointing new trustees by the trust instrument.[191]
(ii) if there is no person nominated who is able and willing to act, by the personal representative.[192]

[186] Trustee Act 1925 s.69(1) and (2).
[187] He has "an absolute right to decline to accept the position and duties of trustee if he chooses so to do" *Re Benett* [1906] 1 Ch.216, 225.
[188] *Re Benett*, above, at 225, 227–228: see also Administration of Estates Act 1925 s.25 as amended by Administration of Estates Act 1971 s.9.
[189] Trustee Act 1925 ss.18(3) and 14(2) (as amended by Trusts of Land and Appointment of Trustees Act 1996 s.25(1), Sch.3, para.3(1), (3)).
[190] Subject to any contrary intention expressed in the trust instrument, Trustee Act 1925 ss.69(1) and (2).
[191] If the persons nominated make an appointment of new trustees but do not include the personal representative among the new trustees, this operates to displace the personal representative for all purposes from the trust, *Re Routledge's Trusts* [1909] 1 Ch.280.
[192] Trustee Act 1925 ss.36(1) and (4): for appointment by a renouncing executor see s.36(5). An executor who has not proved may appoint under s.36(1), but his title to appoint can only be proved by production of a grant of probate or letters of administration with the will annexed, *Re Crowhurst Park* [1974] 1 W.L.R. 583, 593–594. The personal representative may include himself among the new trustees he appoints; if he does not do so, his own appointment of new trustees displaces him for all purposes from the trust.

The personal representative cannot be compelled to exercise his power to appoint new trustees.[193] If need be, an appointment of new trustees may be made by the court.[194]

VIII. DELEGATION BY A PERSONAL REPRESENTATIVE

The rules applicable to delegation by personal representatives are virtually identical to the rules applicable to trustees.[195] There are two forms of delegation: collective delegation and individual delegation. Collective delegation occurs when the personal representatives of a deceased person, as a group, delegate some of their functions to an agent whom they ask to carry out some task on their behalf: a straightforward example would be where personal representatives request an auctioneer to sell some property which belongs to the estate. Individual delegation, by contrast, takes place when an individual personal representative delegates his powers and discretions to someone else because, for example, he is going abroad and is unable to act. There may be some occasions when the two forms of delegation appear to merge into one another—for example, where there is a sole personal representative—but the two forms are, essentially, and historically, distinct. **20–65**

The general principle is that a personal representative cannot delegate the tasks attached to his office, because his is a position of personal confidence. The underlying rule[196] is that a personal representative may not commit to another person the exercise of any task vested in him by virtue of his office, except as authorised by statute or by the will which appointed him.[197]

1. Collective delegation under the Trustee Act 2000[198]

Sections 11–15 of the Trustee Act 2000 give trustees and personal representatives, acting collectively, the power to appoint agents. Sections 16–20 are concerned with the appointment of nominees and custodians to hold property. Sections 21–23 deal with supervision and ss.24–27 contain supplementary provisions. This Part of the Trustee Act applies in relation to trusts (and wills) whether created before or after its commencement, and the powers conferred may be extended, restricted or excluded by the terms of the will.[199] **20–66**

[193] *Re Knight's Will* (1884) 26 Ch.D. 82.

[194] Trustee Act 1925 s.41(1) and Settled Land Act 1925 s.34.

[195] The statutory rules applicable to trustees (now to be found in the Trustee Act 2000—see below, paras 20–66 and 20–67) apply to personal representatives.

[196] See *Lewin on Trusts* edited by John Mowbray et al., 18th edn (London: Sweet & Maxwell, 2008), paras 36–09 et seq.

[197] The testator may, of course expressly give his executors powers to delegate.

[198] The Act came into force on 1 February 2001. See 12th edition of this book, para.20–67, for position prior to the 2000 Act.

[199] Trustee Act 2000 s.26.

The major change introduced by the Trustee Act 2000 is that it *is* now possible for trustees and personal representatives to delegate discretions—the discretions which matter are those relating to investments. Section 11 of the Act authorises trustees and personal representatives to delegate any or all of their "delegable functions" which are defined so as to include all functions other than functions relating to the distribution of assets; decisions as to whether fees should be paid out of income or out of capital; powers to appoint trustees or executors; and the powers of delegation themselves.

The statutory duty of care under the Trustee Act 2000 applies to personal representatives[200] and it applies not only to new trusts, but also to existing trusts.[201] The duty is laid down in s.1 of the 2000 Act and the scope of the duty depends on what is "reasonable in all the circumstances". A higher standard is expected of a professional executor than of someone who is not charging for his services.[202]

Section 22 of the Trustee Act 2000 instructs the trustees or personal representatives to keep under review the arrangements under which their agents are acting; but s.23 makes it clear that they will not be liable for any acts or defaults of their agents unless they failed to comply with the duty of care when appointing the agents and/or reviewing the arrangements.

2. Individual delegation

20–67 Section 25 of the Trustee Act 1925, as substituted by s.5 of the Trustee Delegation Act 1999, covers individual delegation of a trustee's, or personal representative's, functions by power of attorney.

This section enables a personal representative to delegate to any person by power of attorney for twelve months or any shorter specified period "all or any of the trusts, powers and discretions vested in him as trustee either alone or jointly with any other person or persons". Written notice must be given within seven days to each of the other personal representatives. The personal representative who delegates under s.25 remains liable for the acts and for the defaults of the person to whom he delegates.

If there are two personal representatives, delegation under this section may now be by one to the other.[203] The substituted s.25 takes effect as from 1 March 2000; prior to that date, it was not possible for one personal representative to delegate to his sole co-personal representative.

IX. REMUNERATION OF PERSONAL REPRESENTATIVES

20–68 It was a fundamental principle of equity that a personal representative, like a trustee, was not entitled to any remuneration for the work which

[200] Trustee Act 2000 s.13. The duty may be excluded or amended in the trust instrument: Sch.1, para.7.

[201] This means that it will apply to personal representatives whenever they took office.

[202] *Bartlett v Barclays Bank Trust Co Ltd (No.1)* [1980] Ch.515.

[203] s.25(3).

he did[204] unless there was some specific authorisation. If he accepted the office, then, in so far as he was not authorised to receive remuneration, he had to give his services gratuitously, although he was entitled to reimburse himself out of the deceased's estate for his out-of-pocket expenses.[205] There were, however, several different ways in which a personal representative might acquire authority to receive remuneration for his services.

The Trustee Act 2000 radically altered the position in relation to professionals who become personal representatives. But, before considering the 2000 Act, other ways in which personal representatives may be remunerated will be considered.

1. Legacy given to proving executors

The most obvious way of remunerating an executor is by the testator **20–69**
making a gift by will to each of his executors who proves his will or, alternatively (a wider form) who accepts office.[206] Such a gift encourages an executor to prove the will and not to renounce.

There is a presumption that any specific or general legacy given to a person appointed executor is meant to be conditional on his accepting office.[207] This presumption may, of course, be rebutted[208] and the presumption does not apply to a gift of residue.[209] For the avoidance of doubt, any gift made by will to a person appointed executor should be expressed either as conditional (e.g. "if he shall prove this will") or as unconditional (e.g. "whether or not he shall prove this will").

2. Charging clause in will

The testator may authorise his executors to charge and be paid remunera- **20–70**
tion for their services. Before the enactment of the Trustee Act 2000, such a "charging clause" had commonly to be inserted in a will, because otherwise a professional person, such as a solicitor or accountant, would have been unlikely to agree to act as an executor.

A charging clause was construed as a legacy to the executor, which meant that if the executor witnessed the will, the charging clause became void under s.15 of the Wills Act 1837 as a gift to an attesting witness.[210] It also meant that if the deceased's estate was insolvent, an executor was not

[204] *Robinson v Pett* (1734) 3 P.Wms. 249 ("It is an established rule, that a trustee, executor, or administrator, shall have no allowance for his care and trouble"); *Brocksopp v Barnes* (1820) 5 Madd. 90; *Re White* [1898] 2 Ch.217.

[205] See below, para.21–11.

[206] See above, paras 17–22 et seq.

[207] *Re Appleton* (1885) 29 Ch.D. 893; *Stackpoole v Howell* (1807) 13 Ves. 417. See generally *Hawkins on the Construction of Wills*, 5th edn (London: Sweet & Maxwell, 2000), pp.114–116.

[208] *Bubb v Yelverton* (1871) 13 Eq. 131 (gift of £1,000 to each executor "as a remembrance": held executor who did not act was entitled); *Cockerill v Barber* (1826) 2 Russ. 585.

[209] *Griffiths v Pruen* (1840) 11 Sim. 202; *Christian v Devereux* (1841) 12 Sim. 264; *Re Maxwell* [1906] 1 I.R. 386: but see *Barber v Barber* (1838) 3 My. & Cr. 688.

[210] *Re Pooley* (1888) 40 Ch.D. 1: cf. *Re Royce's W.T.* [1959] Ch.626 (solicitor appointed trustee of will after testator's death may rely on charging clause though an attesting witness).

entitled to any remuneration under the charging clause.[211] If the deceased's estate was solvent, but there were insufficient assets available to pay the pecuniary legacies in full, they abated rateably, and this included the payment to the executor. In *Gray v Richards Butler*[212] solicitors charged for work done on behalf of one of their partners who was an executor of a will which was subsequently declared invalid. Given that the charging clause was treated as a legacy, they were not entitled to payment, except in so far as the work they had done could properly have been undertaken in relation to an earlier valid will. The payment, like any legacy, depended on the validity of the will.

In the absence of a charging clause on which he could rely, or on any other authority to receive remuneration, a solicitor-executor, like any other executor, was, before the enactment of the Trustee Act 2000, entitled to no remuneration for his services, only to reimbursement for his out-of-pocket expenses.[213]

3. Order of the court

20–71 The court may, in the exercise of its inherent jurisdiction, authorise remuneration for a personal representative, in order to secure the competent administration of the estate.[214] Remuneration may be authorised for his past[215] and future[216] services, and the remuneration authorised by a charging clause in the will may be increased, whether or not he has already accepted office.[217] The court authorises remuneration only in a proper case,[218] where it is in the interests of the creditors[219] or the beneficiaries[220] to do so. Such cases will be rare.

Even before the enactment of the Trustee Act 2000, the court had a statutory jurisdiction to authorise remuneration for a corporation (other than the Public Trustee) where the court appoints the corporation to be a personal representative, either solely or jointly with another person.[221] Thus,

[211] *Re White* [1898] 1 Ch.297, [1898] 2 Ch 217; *Re Salmen* (1912) 107 L.T. 108.

[212] *Gray v Richards Butler* [2001] W.T.L.R. 625.

[213] *Moore v Frowd* (1837) 3 My. & Cr. 45; *Todd v Wilson* (1849) 9 Beav. 486.

[214] *Re Duke of Norfolk's S.T.* [1982] Ch.61 (reviewing the cases): see also *Forster v Ridley* (1864) 4 De G.J. & S. 452 (executors remunerated for managing deceased's leaseholds and carrying on business); *Re Freeman's* S.T. (1887) 37 Ch.D. 148 (remuneration for trustee). For possible reform see Law Reform Committee's 23rd Report, *The powers and duties of trustees*, Cmnd.8733 (1982), pp.29–30 and 64 (professional persons acting as administrators).

[215] *Re Macadam* [1946] Ch.73 (trustees holding company shares remunerated for exceptional work as directors); *Re Masters* [1953] 1 W.L.R. 81 (bank remunerated for acting as administrator and trustee); *Re Keeler's* S.T. [1981] Ch.157: see also *Boardman v Phipps* [1967] 2 A.C. 46, 104, 112.

[216] *Re Duke of Norfolk's S.T.*, above, (future services of trust corporation).

[217] ibid.

[218] *Re Worthington* [1954] 1 W.L.R. 526 (remuneration refused to solicitor-administrator in absence of exceptional circumstances); *Re Barbour's* S.T. [1974] 1 W.L.R. 1198, 1203.

[219] *Re Duke of Norfolk's S.T.*, above, at 77 (order of court authorising remuneration binds creditors of insolvent estate); *Re Worthington*, above.

[220] *Re Duke of Norfolk's S.T.*, above, at 79.

[221] Trustee Act 1925 ss.42, 68(1), (17) and 69(1).

on granting letters of administration to a bank, the court could authorise the bank to charge for its services.[222]

4. The Rule in *Cradock v Piper*

Under the Rule in *Cradock v Piper*[223] a solicitor who is a personal representative (or his firm) is entitled to profit costs for work done in connection with litigation on behalf of the personal representatives jointly, except so far as the costs have been increased by his being one of the parties. This Rule ceases to have any relevance in cases where the Trustee Act 2000 applies.[224] **20–72**

5. The Public Trustee

The Public Trustee has always been entitled to charge for its services.[225] **20–73**

6. The Trustee Act 2000

The Trustee Act 2000 radically alters the position in relation to the payment of personal representatives (and trustees) where the death occurs on or after 1 February 2001.[226] Under s.29, a personal representative who acts in a professional capacity is entitled to receive reasonable remuneration out of the estate for any services that he provides to or on behalf of the estate if each of the other personal representatives has agreed in writing that he may be remunerated for his services. **20–74**

Under s.28, except to the extent that the will makes inconsistent provision, the professional personal representative is to be treated as entitled under the will to receive payment in respect of services even if they are services which are capable of being provided by a lay personal representative. Furthermore, any payments to which the personal representative is entitled in respect of services are to be treated as *remuneration* for services (and not as a gift) for the purposes of s.15 of the Wills Act 1837[227] and s.34(3) of the Administration of Estates Act 1925 (the order in which the estate is to be distributed).

[222] *In the Estates of Young* [1934] W.N. 106; *Re Masters* [1953] 1 W.L.R. 81.
[223] *Cradock v Piper* (1850) 1 Mac. & G. 664.
[224] See below para.20–74.
[225] The Public Trustee has statutory authority to charge fees, Public Trustee Act 1906 s.9, as amended by Public Trustee (Fees) Act 1957 and fees orders made thereunder.
[226] The Trustee Act 2000 s.35(4).
[227] In other words, a charging clause will not be void if the would-be personal representative witnesses the will.

CHAPTER 21

PAYMENT OF EXPENSES AND DEBTS, AND INCIDENCE OF GENERAL LEGACIES

I. ASSETS, EXPENSES AND DEBTS

A. WHAT ARE ASSETS?

This chapter is concerned with the property which constitutes assets for the payment of the deceased's debts and liabilities.[1] Section 32(1) of the Administration of Estates Act 1925 defines two categories of property which constitute assets: the deceased's own property, and property over which he exercises a power of appointment by his will. **21–01**

1. Deceased's estate to the extent of his beneficial interest

The first category mentioned in s.32(1) is "the real[2] and personal estate, whether legal or equitable, of a deceased person, to the extent of his beneficial interest therein." If at his death the deceased held property as a sole or last surviving trustee so that the property devolves on his personal representatives, this trust property is not assets,[3] though any beneficial interest of the deceased therein (not ceasing on his death) constitutes assets. **21–02**

The following property constitutes assets in the hands of a personal representative, whether or not it falls within s.32(1).

(a) *Transactions defrauding creditors*

If the deceased entered into a transaction which is set aside after his death as defrauding his creditors,[4] any property recovered by his personal representatives constitutes assets in their hands. **21–03**

[1] See above, paras 20–02 et seq. for property which devolves on personal representatives.

[2] "Real estate" means real estate, including chattels real, which devolves on the personal representative: Administration of Estates Act 1925 s.55(1)(xix).

[3] *Re Webb* [1941] Ch.225; *Re Gordon* [1940] Ch.851; *Hassall v Smithers* (1806) 12 Ves. 119.

[4] Insolvency Act 1986 ss.423–425.

(b) *Income and assets arising after death*

21–04 Income arising after death from the deceased's beneficial interest in his real and personal estate is assets.[5]

(c) *Benefits for which personal representative is accountable*

21–05 A personal representative, like a trustee, is accountable for benefits received by him by virtue of his position as personal representative and such benefits constitute assets for the payment of the deceased's debts and liabilities.[6]

2. Property appointed by will under a general power

21–06 The second category of property mentioned in s.32(1) is realty and personalty of which the deceased "in pursuance of any general power[7] (including the statutory power to dispose of entailed interests) disposes by his will."

Section 32(1) applies only if the deceased by his will exercises a general power of appointment.[8] If he does not do so, the person who takes in default of appointment takes the settled property and it does not constitute assets for the payment of the deceased's debts and liabilities.[9]

3. Property appointed by deed under a general power[10]

21–07 Section 32(1) does not specifically mention property appointed by deed. There is nothing in the Administration of Estates Act 1925 to deprive a creditor of the equitable right he had before 1925 and so, on a death after 1925, a creditor is still entitled to resort, in the last instance, to property appointed by the deceased by deed under a general power provided (i) the appointment was made in favour of a volunteer and (ii) took effect only at the deceased's death.[11]

Property appointed by the deceased by will or deed under a special

[5] *Re Tong* [1931] 1 Ch.202 (C.A.).

[6] *Keech v Sandford* (1726) Sel.Cas. t. King 61. For a discussion of the rule in *Keech v Sandford*, see Hanbury and Martin, *Modern Equity*, 20th edn (London: Sweet & Maxwell, 2015), para.22–012. The rule applies to an executor *de son tort*, *Mulvany v Dillon* (1810) 1 Ball & B. 409. For another instance see *Re Edwards'* W.T. [1982] Ch.30.

[7] *Re Phillips* [1931] 1 Ch.347: see A. D. Hughes (1962) 26 Conv.(N.S.) 25, esp. at pp.32–34; Williams, Mortimer and Sunnucks, *Executors, Administrators and Probate*, 20th edn (London: Sweet & Maxwell, 2015), paras 49–23 et seq.

[8] As to the exercise by will of a general power of appointment see Wills Act 1837 s.27 above, para.11–33.

[9] *Holmes v Coghill* (1802) 7 Ves. 499, (1806) 12 Ves. 206. But it forms part of the deceased's net estate under the Inheritance (Provision for Family and Dependants) Act 1975 s.25(1): see above, para.8–89.

[10] For a discussion of the difference between general, special and intermediate powers, see Hanbury and Martin, *Modern Equity*, 20th edn (London: Sweet & Maxwell, 2015), para.7–004.

[11] *O'Grady v Wilmot* [1916] 2 A.C. 231; *Townshend v Windham* (1750) 2 Ves.Sen. 1; *George v Milbanke* (1803) 9 Ves. 190; *Pack v Bathurst* (1745) 3 Atk. 269; *Troughton v Troughton* (1747) 3 Atk. 656.

power is never assets[12] unless the deceased makes a valid appointment of it to himself.[13]

4. Donatio mortis causa

21–08 Property given by *donatio mortis causa* is liable for the debts of the donor, but only in the last resort on a deficiency of the assets of his estate.[14] If the donor makes the *donatio* by an "incomplete" delivery or transfer, the legal title to the property remains vested in the donor's personal representative. On the other hand, if the *donatio* vests the deceased donor's title in the donee, presumably a creditor may bring proceedings against the donee for payment of his debt out of the property.

It is probable that property to which the Rule in *Strong v Bird* applies is liable for the donor's debts.[15]

B. FUNERAL, TESTAMENTARY AND ADMINISTRATION EXPENSES

1. Funeral expenses

(a) *Personal liability of personal representative*

21–09 The personal liability of a personal representative for funeral expenses may arise under contract or quasi-contract:

(i) A personal representative who orders the funeral is personally liable in contract to the undertaker for the contract price or, if no price is fixed, on a *quantum meruit* for a reasonable price for the funeral which is ordered.[16] If another person orders the funeral and the undertaker gives credit to that person, the latter is liable in contract to the undertaker, but the personal representative is not.[17]

(ii) If no other person is liable in contract to the undertaker, a personal representative is personally liable in quasi-contract to the undertaker for reasonable funeral expenses. If another person ordered the funeral but without accepting liability for it, the law imposes an obligation on the personal representative to pay the

[12] *Townshend v Windham* (1750) 2 Ves.Sen. 1, 9–10.

[13] *Re Penrose* [1933] Ch.793. If the deceased may make a valid appointment to himself, the power may be classifiable as a general power.

[14] *Smith v Casen* (1718) 1 P.Wms. 406; *Ward v Turner* (1752) 2 Ves.Sen. 431, 434; *Tate v Leithead* (1854) Kay 658, 659; *Re Korvine's Trust* [1921] 1 Ch.343, 348: cf. Warnock-Smith [1978] Conv. 130. See above, para.6–63. Property given by *d.m.c.* is part of the deceased's "net estate" for the purposes of the Inheritance (Provision for Family and Dependants) Act 1975, see above, para.8–89.

[15] See above, para.6–74. As to property subject to a statutory nomination see *Bennett v Slater* [1899] 1 Q.B. 45, 52.

[16] *Corner v Shaw* (1838) 3 M. & W. 350, 356; *Brice v Wilson* (1834) 8 Ad. & E. 349 (executor ratified contract with undertaker).

[17] *Green v Salmon* (1838) 8 Ad. & E. 348, 350, explaining *Brice v Wilson*, above.

reasonable expenses of a funeral conducted in a manner suitable to the deceased's position and circumstances.[18] The personal representative is, however, liable only so far as he has available assets of the deceased to meet the expenses.[19]

(b) *Funeral expenses payable out of the deceased's estate*

21–10 Reasonable funeral expenses are payable out of the deceased's estate to the personal representative if he incurs liability to the undertaker in contract or quasi-contract. Similarly, another person who orders and pays for the funeral may recover reasonable funeral expenses from the personal representative out of the deceased's estate[20] unless that person paid for the funeral as an act of bounty.[21]

The reasonableness of the funeral expenses is a question of fact to be decided having regard to all the circumstances of the particular case.[22] The following factors may be material:

(i) the insolvency of the deceased's estate which makes a lower scale of expenses appropriate[23];
(ii) the deceased's position in life[24]; and
(iii) the deceased's religious beliefs[25] and any wishes expressed by him as to his funeral.

Social fund payments to meet funeral expenses are recoverable by the Department for Work and Pensions out of the deceased's estate, as if they were funeral expenses.[26]

2. Testamentary and administration expenses

21–11 Although the expression "testamentary and administration expenses" is not defined in connection with the administration of solvent[27] or insolvent[28] estates, it means, in general, expenses incident to the proper

[18] *Rogers v Price* (1829) 3 Y. & J. 28; *Tugwell v Heyman* (1812) 3 Campb. 298; *Corner v Shaw*, above, at 355–356; *Rees v Hughes* [1946] K.B. 517, 524–525 and 528.
[19] *Sharp v Lush* (1879) 10 Ch.D. 468, 472; *Re Walter* [1929] 1 Ch.647, 655.
[20] *Green v Salmon*, above.
[21] *Colely v Colely* (1866) 12 Jur.(N.S.) 496; cf. *Williams v Williams* (1882) 20 Ch.D. 659. See also *Shallcross v Wright* (1850) 12 Beav. 505.
[22] *Goldstein v Salvation Army Assurance Society* [1917] 2 K.B. 291. See also *Hart v Griffiths-Jones* [1948] 2 All E.R. 729; *Stanton v Ewart F. Youldon Ltd* [1960] 1 W.L.R. 543; *Gammell v Wilson* [1982] A.C. 27. Reasonable funeral expenses are deducted from the value of the estate for inheritance tax purposes; see Inheritance Tax Act 1984 s.172.
[23] At any rate if the personal representative knows of, or has any reason to anticipate, the insolvency: *Edwards v Edwards* (1834) 2 Cr. & M. 612; *Hancock v Podmore* (1830) 1 B. & Ad. 260; *Bissett v Antrobus* (1831) 4 Sim. 512; *Stag v Punter* (1744) 3 Atk. 119.
[24] *Stag v Punter*, above; *Re Walter* [1929] 1 Ch.647, 655.
[25] *Gammell v Wilson* [1982] A.C. 27, 43.
[26] Social Security Administration Act 1992 s.78: for these payments see Social Fund Maternity and Funeral (General) Regulations 2005 (SI 2005/3061), Pt III.
[27] Administration of Estates Act 1925 s.34(3): see below, para.21–29.
[28] Administration of Insolvent Estates of Deceased Persons Order 1986 (SI 1986/1999), paras 4(2) and 5(2): see below, paras 21–68 et seq.

performance of the duties of an executor or administrator.[29] By way of example the expression includes the following, if properly incurred:

(i) the expense of obtaining probate or letters of administration[30];
(ii) the cost of obtaining legal advice as to the administration of the estate[31];
(iii) the costs of an administration claim or other proceedings instituted for a proper purpose[32];
(iv) the expense incurred in collecting and preserving the assets of the deceased's estate[33]; and
(v) the expense incurred in ascertaining the deceased's debts and liabilities (including the cost of advertisements).

Testamentary and administration expenses also include any inheritance tax payable in respect of the deceased's death on his property situated in the United Kingdom which vests in his personal representatives.[34]

C. DEBTS AND LIABILITIES

1. Personal representatives' duty to pay debts

(a) *Nature of the duty*

To quote the classic statement of this duty by Uthwatt J in *Re Tankard*[35]: **21–12**

> "It is the duty of executors, as a matter of the due administration of the estate, to pay the debts of their testator with due diligence having regard to the assets in their hands which are properly applicable for that purpose, and in determining whether due diligence has been shown regard must be had to all the circumstances of the case. The duty is owed not only to creditors, but also to beneficiaries, for the ultimate object of the administration of an estate is to place the beneficiaries in possession of their interest and that object cannot be fully achieved unless all debts are satisfied."

Thus if personal representatives fail to pay a debt of the deceased with due diligence, despite having assets in hand properly applicable for that

[29] *Sharp v Lush* (1879) 10 Ch.D. 468.
[30] *Re Clemow* [1900] 2 Ch.182 and cf. *Re Prince* [1898] 2 Ch.225. For costs of a probate claim see above, paras 19–36 et seq.
[31] *Sharp v Lush*, above.
[32] *Sharp v Lush*, above; *Miles v Harrison* (1874) L.R. 9 Ch.App. 316; *Harloe v Harloe* (1875) L.R. 20 Eq. 471; *Re Hall-Dare* [1916] 1 Ch.272.
[33] *Peter v Stirling* (1878) 10 Ch.D. 279, 284; *Re Goetze* [1953] Ch.96, 111–113; *Re Sebba* [1959] Ch.166.
[34] See below, paras 21–55 et seq.
[35] *Re Tankard* [1942] Ch.69, 72.

purpose, they are liable not only to creditors but also to the beneficiaries for any consequent loss. A loss may result because the debt bears interest[36] or because the creditor brings proceedings to obtain payment.[37]

(b) *Time for payment*

21–13 To quote Uthwatt J again in *Re Tankard*[38]:

"There is, in my opinion, no rule of law that it is the duty of executors to pay debts within a year from the testator's death. The duty is to pay with due diligence. Due diligence may, indeed, require that payment should be made before the expiration of the year, but the circumstances affecting the estate and the assets comprised in it may justify non-payment within the year, but, if debts are not paid within the year, the onus is thrown on the executors to justify the delay."

The personal representatives may well be able to justify non-payment of a debt within the executor's year. For example, the personal representatives may never have had assets in their hands properly applicable for payment of the debt.[39] Again, if the deceased's estate is insolvent, or if it may turn out to be insolvent, the personal representatives may need more than one year in order to ascertain the assets and the extent of the debts, and to determine which debts are payable under the order of priority applicable to an insolvent estate.[40]

(c) *Modification of the duty by will*

21–14 Quoting again from Uthwatt J's judgment.[41]

"As against creditors, the provisions of the testator's will which relate to the realisation of his assets or otherwise bear on the payment of debts are irrelevant. As against beneficiaries, the position is different. Beneficiaries take their interest under the will only on the terms of the will. As respects them full effect has to be given to any provisions which, either in express terms or by implication, modify the executor's duty of paying debts with due diligence."

2. Debts unknown to personal representatives

21–15 Personal representatives who distribute assets to the beneficiaries remain liable for the unpaid debts and liabilities of the deceased to the extent of the assets which would have been properly applicable for their payment,

36 ibid at 72–73; *Hall v Hallett* (1784) 1 Cox. 134; *Re Stevens* [1898] 1 Ch.162, 168–169.
37 ibid.
38 *Re Tankard* [1942] Ch.69 at 72–73.
39 *Re Stevens*, above.
40 See below, paras 21–77 et seq.
41 *Re Tankard* [1942] Ch.69, 74.

even though the personal representatives had no notice of such debts and liabilities when they made the distribution to the beneficiaries.[42] But personal representatives may protect themselves against this liability (1) by advertising for claims in accordance with s.27 of the Trustee Act 1925, or (2) by obtaining the leave of the court to distribute on the footing that all the deceased's debts and liabilities have been ascertained.

(a) *Advertising for claims*

Under s.27 of the Trustee Act 1925[43] personal representatives may give notice of their intention to distribute, requiring any person interested to send in particulars of his claim[44] to the personal representatives within a stated time, not being less than two months. The notice is to be given: **21–16**

(i) by advertisement in the *London Gazette*[45]; *and*
(ii) by advertisement in a newspaper circulating in the district in which land to be distributed is situated; and
(iii) by "such other like notices, including notices elsewhere than in England and Wales,[46] as would, in any special case, have been directed by a court of competent jurisdiction in a claim for administration."[47]

Section 27(2) provides that nothing in the section **21–17**

> "frees the personal representatives from any obligation to make searches or obtain official certificates of search similar to those which an intending purchaser would be advised to make or obtain."

The meaning of this provision is not clear. In order to be certain of the protection of s.27, before distributing land personal representatives should probably carry out the same searches as an intending purchaser of land would be advised to make. In addition, before distributing any asset, personal representatives should search in bankruptcy against the deceased and against any beneficiary to whom the distribution is to be made.

After the expiration of the stated time for claims to be sent in, the personal representatives may distribute to the persons entitled, having

[42] *Knatchbull v Fearnhead* (1837) 3 My. & Cr. 122; *Norman v Baldry* (1834) 6 Sim. 621. For the defence of limitation see below, paras 24–13 et seq.
[43] As amended by Law of Property (Amendment) Act 1926 ss.7, 8(2) and Sch.1.
[44] This includes a claim to be a beneficiary under the deceased's will or intestacy as well as a claim to be a creditor, *Re Aldhous* [1955] 1 W.L.R. 459, see below, paras 23–05 et seq.: it is desirable for the notice to refer to both a creditor and a beneficiary (e.g. "any person having any claim against or any interest in" the deceased's estate), ibid at 462.
[45] Trustee Act 1925 s.68(4).
[46] *Re Holden* [1935] W.N. 52: cf. *Re Achillopoulos* [1928] Ch.433.
[47] Trustee Act 1925 s.27(1); *Re Bracken* (1889) 43 Ch.D. 1. For advertisement for beneficiaries under the deceased's will or intestacy see *Newton v Sherry* (1876) 1 C.P.D. 246, 256 (advertise in foreign country if claimant may be residing there). It is important for the personal representatives to satisfy this requirement because otherwise they lose the protection of s.27.

regard only to the claims (whether formal or not) of which the personal representatives then have notice.[48] It is advisable for personal representatives to advertise and make searches at an early stage in the administration of the deceased's estate, because s.27 does not protect them in respect of assets which they have already distributed before these requirements are satisfied.[49]

21–18 Section 27 does not protect personal representatives against any debt or liability of which they had notice at the time of distribution, even though the claimant did not respond to the advertisement.[50] Nor does s.27 protect personal representatives against a person who claims that they have "no right to administer the estate at all"[51]—for instance, against the next of kin entitled on intestacy, who claim that the grant of probate of the deceased's will to the executors should be revoked on the ground that the deceased lacked testamentary capacity.

A testator cannot by his will deprive his personal representatives of their protection under s.27.[52]

(b) *Leave of the court to distribute*

21–19 If the court gives personal representatives leave to distribute on the footing that all the deceased's debts and liabilities have been ascertained, this protects the personal representatives against any unknown debts and liabilities.[53]

Neither s.27 of the Trustee Act 1925, nor the leave of the court to distribute, prejudices the remedy of an unpaid creditor against a recipient of the deceased's assets.[54]

3. Future debts and liabilities

21–20 A debt or liability of the deceased may not fall due for payment until long after the deceased's death. For example, the deceased may have been the original tenant of a lease granted before 1996 which he assigned to a third party long before his death: his personal representatives will remain liable as such for rent and for any breach of covenant during the entire unexpired term of the lease.[55] There is no problem as long as the assignee and

[48] Trustee Act 1925 s.27(2); *Clegg v Rowland* (1866) L.R. 3 Eq. 368; *Re Frewen* (1889) 60 L.T. 953. For notice where a personal representative is acting for the purpose of more than one estate see Trustee Act 1925 s.28.

[49] *Re Kay* [1897] 2 Ch.518 (some assets distributed, before advertisement, to widow in need: personal representatives not protected, but relief against liability granted under Judicial Trustees Act 1896 s.3—now Trustee Act 1925 s.61): see below, para.24–21.

[50] *Re Land Credit Company of Ireland* (1872) 21 W.R. 1351.

[51] *Guardian Trust & Executors Company of New Zealand Ltd v Public Trustee of New Zealand* [1942] A.C. 115, 125 (a Privy Council decision on the New Zealand equivalent of s.27): see above, para.19–59.

[52] s.27(3).

[53] *Re Gess* [1942] Ch.37; *Re Benjamin* [1902] 1 Ch.723.

[54] Trustee Act 1925 s.27(2); *Re Gess*, [1942] Ch.37 at 39: and see below, paras 24–36 et seq.

[55] Before 1996, the original tenant remained liable to the landlord throughout the term by virtue of privity of contract. Subject to exceptions where there is an assignment by operation

his assigns continue to pay the rent and perform the covenants in order to avoid forfeiture of the lease. But if the assignee becomes insolvent, the liability of the original tenant for the rent and for other breaches of covenant can be onerous.

(a) *Order of the court*

If there is any possible future debt or liability of which the personal representatives have notice, the safest course is for them to apply to the court for directions. If the personal representatives make full disclosure of all the information they have, and act in accordance with the order of the court, they are fully protected.[56] The court generally authorises the estate to be distributed without making any provision for future contingent liabilities.[57] This protects the personal representatives and leaves the unpaid creditor (if the contingent liability arises) to pursue his remedy against a recipient of the deceased's assets.[58] This practice is not, however, appropriate if there is a reasonable probability that a liability will arise.[59] **21–21**

(b) *Distribution without an order of the court*

If the personal representatives distribute the assets of the estate without first applying to the court and acting in accordance with its order, and later the contingent liability arises, the personal representatives are liable to the unpaid creditor to the extent of the assets they distributed.[60] If this happens, the personal representatives may claim repayment from a beneficiary of the capital value of the assets which they distributed to him, unless at the time of distribution they knew that the claim had already fallen due for payment.[61] This right to claim repayment permits the personal representatives to distribute the assets of the estate provided the contingent liability is remote.[62] **21–22**

of law or in breach of covenant, the Landlord and Tenant (Covenants) Act 1995 s.5 releases the tenant from covenants on assignment of a tenancy if lease is granted on or after 1 January 1996; see Megarry & Wade, *The Law of Real Property*, 8th edn (London: Sweet & Maxell, 2012), paras 20–085 et seq.

[56] *Re King* [1907] 1 Ch.72 where Neville J reviewed the case law (possible future liability on deceased's company shares not fully paid up: order of the court directing distribution to residuary beneficiaries exonerates personal representatives from liability to company); *Re Nixon* [1904] 1 Ch.638 (leases formerly held by deceased: distribution directed and personal representatives not liable on leases thereafter).

[57] *Re King*, above; *Re Johnson* [1940] W.N. 195; *Re Sales* [1920] W.N. 54; *Re Yorke* [1997] 4 All E.R. 907; *Re K* [2007] W.T.L.R. 1007.

[58] See below, paras 24–36 et seq.

[59] *Re Arnold* [1942] Ch.272: cf. *Re Johnson*, above.

[60] *Taylor v Taylor* (1870) L.R. 10 Eq. 477 (executors liable for unexpected calls on company shares made after death); *Knatchbull v Fearnhead* (1837) 3 M. & C. 122; *Re Bewley's Estate* (1871) 24 L.T. 177. For the defence of limitation see below, paras 24–13 et seq.

[61] *Jervis v Wolferstan* (1874) L.R. 18 Eq. 18 (repayment of capital, but not of intermediate income, received by beneficiary); *Whittaker v Kershaw* (1890) 45 Ch.D. 320.

[62] *Jervis v Wolferstan*, above, at 25–26; *Whittaker v Kershaw*, above, at 326, 329.

21–23 In order to secure more protection without incurring the expense of an application to the court, personal representatives:

(i) may obtain a proper indemnity from the beneficiaries before distributing the assets (e.g. a beneficiary may give security[63] to repay his share of the assets if the contingent liability arises); or
(ii) may set aside an indemnity fund out of the deceased's estate.[64]

4. Statute-barred debts

21–24 Personal representatives have a duty to rely on all proper defences to a claim being made by a creditor and they commit a breach of duty (or *devastavit*) if they pay a debt which need not be paid.[65] To this general rule there is a single well-established exception: personal representatives may plead the Limitation Acts as a defence, but they are not under any duty to do so if the Acts have only barred the claimant's remedy and not extinguished his claim. Thus, if they think fit, personal representatives may pay a statute-barred debt of the deceased.[66] But this exception is anomalous and will not be extended.[67]

(a) *Debt already declared statute-barred*

21–25 If the court has already declared the debt to be statute-barred, the personal representatives have a duty to rely on the defence of res judicata and they must not pay the debt.[68]

(b) *Order for administration*

21–26 If the court makes an order for the administration of the estate, any creditor or beneficiary is entitled to raise the defence of limitation against a creditor who comes in under the order to prove his debt, notwithstanding the refusal of the personal representatives to raise this defence.[69]

[63] A personal representative may, as a condition of giving an assent, require security for the discharge of a liability: Administration of Estates Act 1925 s.36(10).
[64] *Simmons v Bolland* (1817) 3 Mer. 547; *Fletcher v Stevenson* (1844) 3 Hare 360; *Dobson v Carpenter* (1850) 12 Beav. 370; *Hickling v Boyer* (1851) 3 Mac. & G. 635; *Dean v Allen* (1855) 20 Beav. 1.
[65] *Re Rownson* (1885) 29 Ch.D. 358, 363–364; *Midgley v Midgley* [1893] 3 Ch.282, 289, 299 and 304. For their statutory powers in relation to debts (including power to pay or allow any debt or claim on any evidence that they think sufficient) see Trustee Act 1925 s.15 and above, para.20–15.
[66] *Norton v Frecker* (1737) 1 Atk. 524, 526; *Stahlschmidt v Lett* (1853) 1 Sm. & G. 415; *Hill v Walker* (1858) 4 K. & J. 166; *Midgley v Midgley*, above, at 289, 297, 304. See Limitation Act 1980 ss.5, 8 and 20 (debt not extinguished) and cf. s.17 (title to land extinguished).
[67] *Re Rownson*, above, at 363–365; *Midgley v Midgley* [1893] 3 Ch.282, 289, 299 and 304, above, at (this anomalous exception "is to be confined within the limits of its own anomaly").
[68] *Midgley v Midgley*, above.
[69] *Shewn v Vanderhorst* (1831) 1 Russ. & M. 347 (residuary legatee raised defence of limitation); *Moodie v Bannister* (1859) 4 Drew. 432; *Fuller v Redman* (No.2) (1859) 26 Beav. 614

But, exceptionally, creditors and beneficiaries are not permitted to raise this defence against a creditor who was himself the claimant in the administration proceedings. The personal representatives did not raise this defence against the time-barred claimant-creditor, and another creditor or beneficiary, who has the benefit of the administration order, cannot be permitted to raise it.[70]

(c) *Insolvent Estate*

If the deceased's estate is insolvent, only debts provable in bankruptcy may be claimed and a statute-barred debt is not provable in bankruptcy.[71] **21–27**

If a claimant sues for his debt and one of the personal representatives pleads limitation in his defence, but the other personal representative does not, the court acts on the defence as being more for the advantage of the estate.[72] Whether one personal representative may pay a statute-barred debt of the deceased if the other personal representative objects has never been decided[73]; perhaps one executor may do so under the rule that executors have joint and several authority.[74]

5. Interest on debts

If a debt of the deceased carries interest, it is payable by the personal representatives as part of the sum due from the estate. If a debt does not carry interest but the court directs an account of the deceased's debts to be taken, then, unless the court orders otherwise, interest is allowed on the debt at the rate payable on judgment debts from the date of the judgment directing the account. But if the estate is insolvent, the bankruptcy rules as to interest on debts are applicable.[75] **21–28**

II. SOLVENT ESTATES[76]

The deceased's estate is solvent if the assets are sufficient to pay all his funeral, testamentary and administration expenses, debts and liabilities.[77] In that event these expenses, debts and liabilities are payable in full and any balance of the deceased's estate is distributable to the beneficiaries **21–29**

(creditor raised defence of limitation). But the court does not raise this defence on behalf of an absent beneficiary, *Alson v Trollope* (1866) L.R. 2 Eq. 205.

70 *Briggs v Wilson* (1835) 5 De G.M. & G. 12, 21; *Fuller v Redman* (No.2) (1859) 26 Beav. 614, 617–619.

71 Administration of Insolvent Estates of Deceased Persons Order 1986 (SI 1986/1999); *Ex p. Dewdney and Ex p. Seaman* (1809) 15 Ves. 479. *Ex p. Roffey* (1815) 19 Ves. 468.

72 *Midgley v Midgley* [1893] 3 Ch.282 at 298 and 302.

73 *Midgley v Midgley* [1893] 3 Ch.282 at 297 and 301–302.

74 *Midgley v Midgley* [1893] 3 Ch.282 at 297: see above, para.20–54.

75 See below, para.21–83.

76 See generally *Hawkins on the Construction of Wills*, 5th edn (London: Sweet & Maxwell, 2000), Chap.23.

77 *Re Leng* [1895] 1 Ch.652, 658: see below, para.21–68.

entitled under his will or on intestacy. It is, therefore, in each beneficiary's interest to claim that the burden should not fall on assets to which he is entitled. This means that rules are needed to regulate the burden of the expenses, debts and liabilities and these rules as to incidence regulate "competition" between the beneficiaries.

21–30 Creditors are not concerned with the rules regulating the burden of the deceased's expenses, debts and liabilities: a creditor is not even bound by them and may obtain payment out of any assets regardless of these rules.[78] If a creditor is paid out of an asset which is not, under these rules, liable to bear the burden of his debt, the matter can be adjusted between the beneficiaries in the personal representatives' final accounts and, if need be, the doctrine of marshalling[79] provides a remedy for the disappointed beneficiary.

All the rules as to incidence now to be considered have one common feature: they may be varied by a contrary intention on the part of the deceased. It is, however, necessary to consider the expression of such a contrary intention separately in relation to each of the incidence rules.

A. THE STATUTORY ORDER OF APPLICATION OF ASSETS

21–31 Section 34(3) of the Administration of Estates Act 1925 provides that, where the deceased's estate is solvent, his real and personal estate shall, subject to any provisions contained in his will, be applicable towards the discharge of the funeral, testamentary and administration expenses, debts and liabilities payable thereout in the order mentioned in Pt II of the First Schedule to the Act. Special rules are applicable to debts charged on the deceased's property and to the incidence of inheritance tax: these special rules are considered later.[80]

The statutory order of application of assets set out in Pt II of the First Schedule applies in the case of deaths after 1925[81] and is as follows:

> "1 Property of the deceased undisposed of by will, subject to the retention thereout of a fund sufficient to meet any pecuniary legacies.[82]
>
> 2. Property of the deceased not specifically devised or bequeathed but included (either by a specific or general description) in a residuary gift, subject to the retention out of such property of a fund sufficient to meet any pecuniary legacies, so far as not provided for as aforesaid.[83]
>
> 3. Property of the deceased specifically appropriated or devised or

[78] *Re Tong* [1931] 1 Ch.202, 212; Administration of Estates Act 1925 s.35(3).

[79] See below, paras 21–66 et seq.

[80] See below, paras 21–44 et seq. and 21–55 et seq.

[81] Administration of Estates Act 1925 s.54.

[82] For the incidence of general pecuniary legacies, see below, paras 21–87 et seq.

[83] For the incidence of general pecuniary legacies, see below, paras 21–87 et seq.

bequeathed (either by a specific or general description) for the payment of debts.

4. Property of the deceased charged with, or devised or bequeathed (either by specific or general description) subject to a charge for the payment of debts.
5. The fund, if any, retained to meet pecuniary legacies.
6. Property specifically devised or bequeathed, rateably according to value.
7. Property appointed by will under a general power, including the statutory power to dispose of entailed interests, rateably according to value.
8. The following provisions shall also apply—
   (a) The order of application may be varied by the will of the deceased.
   (b)"

In this statutory order no distinction is made between realty and personalty. The Schedule refers repeatedly to "property," which is defined in the Administration of Estates Act 1925 as including any interest in real or personal property.[84] All the real and personal property falling within a particular paragraph is therefore liable rateably for the expenses, debts and liabilities.[85] **21–32**

Take an example of the operation of the statutory order. T gives his freehold house, Blackacre, to A; his shares in JKL Ltd to B; legacies of £20,000 to C and £8,000 to D (which legacies T directs to be paid out of his residuary personal estate); his residuary real estate to E; and his residuary personal estate to F. **21–33**

T dies in 2008 and all the beneficiaries survive him. None of T's property is undisposed of by his will so paragraph 1 of the statutory order is not applicable. The first step to take is to set aside out of the residuary personal estate a fund to satisfy the general pecuniary legacies of £20,000 and £8,000.[86] T's estate is applicable towards the discharge of expenses, debts and liabilities in the following order:

(i) Both T's residuary real estate (given to E) and his residuary personal estate (given to F) fall within paragraph 2. This property is primarily liable for expenses, debts and liabilities and it must be exhausted before any other property is touched. The residuary real estate and residuary personal estate bear this burden rateably in proportion to their respective values. Thus, if the residuary real estate is valued at £300,000 and the residuary personal estate (after setting aside £28,000 to pay the pecuniary legacies) is valued at £100,000, the residuary real estate bears three-quarters,

[84] Administration of Estates Act 1925 s.55(1)(xvii).

[85] *Re Harland-Peck* [1941] Ch.182, 187–189; *Re Anstead* [1943] Ch.161 (the headnote is wrong).

[86] *Re Anstead*, above, (unlike the example in the text, the will did not contain a direction to pay legacies out of residuary personalty); *Re Wilson* [1967] Ch.53, 70. For the classification of legacies and devises, see above, paras 9–07 et seq.

and the residuary personal estate one-quarter, of the burden of the expenses, debts and liabilities.

(ii) None of T's property falls within paragraphs 3 or 4, so the pecuniary legacy fund is liable next under paragraph 5. If (say) one-half of the (£28,000) pecuniary legacy fund is needed to meet expenses, debts and liabilities, then each pecuniary legacy abates proportionally: in that event, C and D each receive only one-half of their respective legacies.

(iii) Both Blackacre (realty specifically devised to A) and T's shares in JKL Ltd (personalty specifically bequeathed to B) fall within paragraph 6 and bear expenses, debts and liabilities rateably according to their respective values. Thus if Blackacre is valued at £400,000 and the JKL shares at £200,000, Blackacre bears two-thirds, and the JKL shares one-third, of the burden of any expenses, debts and liabilities falling on paragraph 6 property.

In this example T has not by his will varied the statutory order or given priority to a particular pecuniary legacy. T might, for instance, have directed that the legacy to C should be payable in priority to the legacy to D: in that event D's legacy would abate before C's legacy.[87]

Paragraph 1—property undisposed of by will

(a) *Property not effectively disposed of by will falls within this paragraph*

21–34 Paragraph 1 is not confined to property which the deceased does not attempt to dispose of by will, but includes property of which he attempts, unsuccessfully, to dispose: e.g. because of a lapse.[88]

(b) *Variation of the statutory order*

21–35 If the testator varies the statutory order, property falling within para.1 is not primarily liable. There should be relatively little difficulty where the testator has expressly provided that the statutory order should be varied, but the problem is to decide, as a question of construction, whether the testator has impliedly varied the order. Most of the decided cases deal with lapsed shares of residue and they fall into two groups. The distinction is, however, rather a fine one.[89]

(i) In one group the testator varies the statutory order *by directing expenses and debts to be paid out of residue as a whole*, thereby charging residue as a whole with their payment.[90]

[87] But C would not have been entitled to interest on his legacy in priority to the legacy to D, in the absence of express direction to this effect; *Re Wyles* [1938] Ch.313.

[88] *Re Lamb* [1929] 1 Ch.723: see also *Re Tong* [1931] 1 Ch.202; *Re Worthington* [1933] Ch.771; *Re Sanger* [1939] Ch.238. For the doctrine of lapse (and the exceptions to it), see above paras 14–11 et seq.

[89] See Simonds J in *Re Sanger*, above, at 248–249.

[90] *Re Harland-Peck* [1941] Ch.182; *Re Petty* [1929] 1 Ch.726; *Re Kempthorne* [1930] 1 Ch.268; *Re Berrey's* W.T. [1959] 1 W.L.R. 30; *Re Atkinson* [1930] 1 Ch.47 and *Re Martin* [1955] Ch.698.

(ii) In the other group the testator directs expenses and debts to be paid *but does not specify the property out of which they are to be paid.* This is construed as a direction to pay them in due course of administration pursuant to the statutory order.[91]

Paragraph 2—property included in a residuary gift

Paragraph 2 is worded so that property falls within it if it is not specifically devised or bequeathed but is included (either by a specific or general description) in a residuary gift.[92] **21–36**

Paragraphs 3 and 4—property specifically appropriated and property charged

(a) *Property falling within paragraphs 3 and 4*

A testator often appropriates his residuary estate for the payment of debts, or charges his residuary estate with the payment of debts. Paragraphs 3 and 4 do not, however, apply to property included in a residuary gift, because such property falls within the earlier paragraph 2.[93] **21–37**

(b) *Variation of the statutory order*

If a will appropriates, or charges, property for, or with, the payment of expenses and debts, it is necessary to decide (i) whether the will varies the statutory order so as to make that property primarily liable for expenses and debts, or (ii) whether that property merely falls within paragraphs 3 or 4. As Upjohn J said in *Re Meldrum*[94] it is "essentially a matter of construction of the will in each case whether the provisions of the schedule apply, or whether they have been varied by the terms of the will."[95] **21–38**

Paragraph 5—the pecuniary legacy fund

The expression "pecuniary legacy" is widely defined in s.55(1)(ix) of the Administration of Estates Act 1925 and "includes an annuity, a general legacy, a demonstrative legacy so far as it is not discharged out of the designated property, and any other general direction by a testator for the payment of money, including all death duties free from which any devise, bequest, or payment is made to take effect."[96] **21–39**

[91] *Re Lamb* [1929] 1 Ch.723; *Re Tong* [1931] 1 Ch.202; *Re Worthington* [1933] Ch.771; *Re Sanger* [1939] Ch.238.

[92] A general gift by the testator in his will of all his real estate, or of all his personal estate, may be a residuary gift within para.2, *Re Wilson* [1967] Ch.53.

[93] *Re Kempthorne* [1930] 1 Ch.268.

[94] *Re Meldrum* [1952] Ch.208.

[95] *Re Meldrum* [1952] Ch.208, 212. *Re Meldrum* is an example of a case where it was held that the statutory order had been varied, which may be contrasted with *Re Gordon* [1940] Ch.769 where the statutory order was held applicable; see also *Re Kempthorne* [1930] 1 Ch.268.

[96] See above, paras 9–06 et seq. for the distinction between a general legacy, a demonstrative legacy, and a specific legacy, or specific devise.

If part of the pecuniary legacy fund is needed to meet expenses and debts, all the pecuniary legacies abate rateably unless the testator has shown an intention that one or more pecuniary legacies are to have priority.

Paragraph 6—property specifically devised or bequeathed

21–40 Under paragraph 6 property specifically devised or bequeathed bears the burden of expenses and debts "rateably according to value." In applying paragraph 6 the relevant value is the value of each property at the testator's death. *Re John*[97] provides a classic illustration. T gave Blackacre (subject to a mortgage) to X and Whiteacre (subject to certain legacies given by T's will) to Y. Farwell J held that Blackacre and Whiteacre were liable to bear the burden of expenses and debts rateably according to the value of each property at the testator's death. In the case of Blackacre this was the probate value of T's equity of redemption, and in the case of Whiteacre the probate value of Whiteacre but without making any deduction for the legacies to be paid thereout.[98]

Paragraph 7—property appointed by will under a general power

21–41 Under s.27 of the Wills Act 1837 a general gift includes property over which the testator has a general power of appointment, unless the will shows a contrary intention.[99] Accordingly, such property passes under a residuary gift without any express appointment, unless the will shows a contrary intention. Alternatively, but with the same effect, the testator may make a gift of his residuary estate "including any property over which I have a general power of appointment."

21–42 It has been suggested that since 1925, if a residuary gift includes real or personal property over which the testator has a general power of appointment (either by virtue of s.27 or by express inclusion), the appointed property is liable for expenses and debts under paragraph 2, and not under paragraph 7, of the statutory order.[100] If this is so, it must be because the will has thereby varied the statutory order, as paragraph 2 applies only to property of the deceased.

Assets not included in the statutory order

21–43 Property which is subject to an option given by the testator's will has been held to fall outside the statutory order.[101] Again, property appointed by deed under a general power and property given by *donatio mortis causa* are

97 *Re John* [1933] Ch.370: see also *Re Cohen* [1960] Ch.179 (probate values and not later sale values).

98 Subject to the provisions of the will, the legatees take priority over Y and the legacies only abate if Whiteacre (after bearing its share of expenses and debts) is insufficient to pay them in full, *Re Saunders-Davies* (1887) 34 Ch.D. 482; *Re Bawden* [1894] 1 Ch.693.

99 See above, paras 11–33 et seq.

100 See *Hawkins on the Construction of Wills*, 5th edn (London: Sweet & Maxwell, 2000), p.388.

101 *Re Eve* [1956] Ch.479. For a more detailed discussion as to what happens where T has

liable for the deceased's debts in the last resort,[102] though neither is mentioned in the statutory order: there is no caselaw on the order of application of these assets inter se.

B. DEBTS CHARGED ON THE DECEASED'S PROPERTY

Under s.35 of the Administration of Estates Act 1925 a special rule applies to **21–44**
any debt charged on the deceased's property. A common instance is a mortgage debt due to a bank or building society and charged on the deceased's house. Under this rule, the property charged is primarily liable for the payment of the debt, unless the deceased has shown a contrary intention.

1. Property charged at death

(a) *Interest in property*

Section 35(1) applies to any interest in any property, whether real or **21–45**
personal[103]:

(i) if the deceased is possessed of or entitled to it at his death[104]; or
(ii) if by his will the deceased disposes of it under a general power of appointment (including the statutory power to dispose of entailed interests).[105]

Usually the property charged is an interest in land, but s.35(1) also applies to pure personalty—for example, to the deceased's shares which under the articles of association are subject to an equitable charge for money owing to the company by the deceased at his death.[106]

(b) *Charged with the payment of money at death*

The section applies to any charge "whether by way of legal mortgage, **21–46**
equitable charge or otherwise (including a lien for unpaid purchase money)." [107] It is not confined to charges created by act of parties[108] but

given X an option to purchase property comprised in T's estate, at a stated price, see paras 21–43 and 21–44 of the 12th edition of this book.

[102] See above, paras 21–07 et seq.

[103] Administration of Estates Act 1925 s.55(1)(xvii).

[104] *Re Coxen* [1948] 2 All E.R. 492 (motor car ordered by, but no particular car appropriated to, deceased: s.35 not applicable to unpaid price as deceased not entitled at death).

[105] See above, para.21–06. On a death before 1926 the Acts did not apply to entails, *Re Anthony* [1893] 3 Ch.398.

[106] *Re Turner* [1938] Ch.593: see also *Re Coxen*, above, at 496.

[107] *Re Birmingham* [1959] Ch.523.

[108] *Pembrooke v Friend* (1860) 1 J. & H. 132 (equitable mortgage by deposit of title deeds). It is no longer possible to create an equitable mortgage by deposit of title deeds, unless there is a valid contract to create a mortgage complying with s.2 of the Law of Property (Miscellaneous Provisions) Act 1984: see *United Bank of Kuwait Plc v Sahib* [1997] Ch.107.

extends to charges created by statute, such as the charge imposed by a court on the property of a judgment debtor.[109]

2. Incidence of the charge under section 35

21–47 Assuming that the deceased has not shown a contrary intention then "as between the different persons claiming through the deceased" the charged property is made primarily liable for the payment of the charge. The section regulates the incidence of the charge as between the different beneficiaries claiming through the deceased.[110]

3. Section 35 confined to regulating incidence between beneficiaries

21–48 Section 35 is concerned only with regulating the incidence of the charge as between the different beneficiaries.

(a) *Chargee's rights remain the same*

21–49 Section 35(3) makes it clear that the rights of the chargee (i.e. the person entitled to the charge) are not in any way affected. If the deceased was personally liable to the chargee for the debt, the chargee may obtain payment out of the deceased's other assets. If he does so, the doctrine of marshalling applies, so that the debt falls ultimately on the charged property.[111] A beneficiary entitled to the charged property under the deceased's will or on intestacy does not become personally liable to the chargee for the debt,[112] but if the beneficiary fails to make the payments due under the charge, the chargee is likely to enforce his remedies—such as the power of sale—against the property.

(b) *Debt not falling on property charged with it*

21–50 If the charged property of the deceased is not primarily liable for the debt, s.35 is relevant only so far as the debt cannot be discharged by the person, or from the property primarily liable.[113]

4. Contrary intention

21–51 The deceased's contrary or other intention (excluding or modifying the operation of s.35(1)) must be signified by will, deed or other document. In practice, if a testator wishes to give particular property free from charges, it is desirable for him to show his intention clearly in his will.[114]

[109] Charging Orders Act 1979 ss.1–3: see *Re Anthony* [1892] 1 Ch.450 (charge created by Judgments Act 1838 s.13).
[110] Including the Crown taking property as bona vacantia on an intestacy, Administration of Estates Act 1925 ss.46(1)(vi) and 57(1).
[111] See below, paras 21–66 et seq.
[112] *Syer v Gladstone* (1885) 30 Ch.D. 614 (the headnote is misleading).
[113] *Re Ritson* [1899] 1 Ch.128.
[114] *Re Ross, Petterson v Ross* [2014] W.T.L.R. 321.

(a) *Direction in will for payment from personal or residuary estate*

Under s.35(2) a general direction by a testator for the payment of debts out of his general personal estate, or his residuary estate, or his residuary real estate, is not enough to exclude the operation of s.35(1). There must, in addition, be words which, expressly or by necessary implication, refer to the charge. For example, by his will T makes a specific devise of Whiteacre to X, and at T's death Whiteacre is charged with a mortgage debt due from T. Whiteacre will be relieved of the primary burden of the mortgage debt if by his will T directs payment out of residue of all his debts, "including the mortgage debt charged on Whiteacre" *or* "including all my mortgage debts." Similarly Whiteacre will be relieved of this burden if by his will T directs payment out of residue of all his debts "except mortgage debts, if any, charged on Blackacre": these words by necessary implication show T's intention that the mortgage debt on Whiteacre is to be paid out of residue.[115] **21–52**

(b) *Direction in will for payment from special fund*

On the other hand a direction by T for the payment of his debts out of a special fund (not being his general personal estate, residuary real and personal estate, or residuary real estate) is sufficient to show his intention that any debt charged on Whiteacre is to be paid out of the special fund; in this case there need be no express or implied reference to the charge on Whiteacre. Thus, if T directs payment of his debts out of his Barclays Bank account, or out of the proceeds of sale of his property, Blackacre, this shows his intention that any debt charged on Whiteacre is to be paid out of this account or out of these proceeds.[116] **21–53**

If, however, the special fund is inadequate to pay off the whole of the debt charged on Whiteacre, Whiteacre remains primarily liable under s.35(1) for the payment of the unsatisfied balance.[117]

(c) *Document other than deceased's will*

In order to show a contrary intention (excluding or modifying the operation of s.35(1)) in a non-testamentary document, the deceased should indicate clearly (e.g. by a letter to his solicitors) how he intends the burden of the charge to be borne as between the beneficiaries after his death.[118] **21–54**

[115] *Re Valpy* [1906] 1 Ch.531. See also *Re Fleck* (1888) 37 Ch.D. 677 ("trade debts" to be paid from residuary personalty included trade debt secured by equitable mortgage); *Re Nevill* (1889) 59 L.J.Ch.511. cf. *Re Beirnstein* [1925] Ch.12 (direction to pay sums secured on mortgage does not apply to unpaid purchase money secured by vendor's lien).

[116] *Re Fegan* [1928] Ch.45.

[117] *Re Fegan* [1928] Ch.45 and see *Re Birch* [1909] 1 Ch.787.

[118] *Re Birmingham* [1959] Ch.523; *Re Wakefield* [1943] 2 All E.R. 29. Contrast *Re Ross, Ross v Perrin-Hughes* [2005] W.T.L.R. 191. The cases can all be reconciled, but the distinction between them is fine. Where the documentary evidence is not clear, much will depend on the degree to which inferences are drawn. It is suggested that the decision in *Ross* is correct and to be welcomed. The earlier decisions—*Wakefield* in particular—appear to be indirectly linked to the literal approach to the construction of wills (see Chap.10).

C. INCIDENCE OF INHERITANCE TAX

21–55 Rules are needed to determine the incidence of inheritance tax payable by personal representatives in respect of the deceased's death. There are two basic rules:

(1) Inheritance tax on the deceased's free real and personal estate[119] in the United Kingdom is a testamentary and administration expense[120] and is payable in accordance with the statutory order of application of assets.
(2) Inheritance tax on any other property falls on that property and must be borne by the beneficiary who takes it.[121]

Both these rules apply subject to any contrary intention shown by the deceased in his will. It is convenient to refer to such a contrary direction as a "free of inheritance tax" provision.

1. Inheritance tax as a testamentary expense

21–56 Inheritance tax payable by personal representatives is a testamentary and administration expense if it is payable in respect of the deceased's death on his free real and personal estate in the United Kingdom, i.e. on "the value of property in the United Kingdom which (a) vests in the deceased's personal representatives, and (b) was not immediately before the death comprised in a settlement."[122] Thus, if T makes specific gifts to his son of his freehold house in London and of his BP shares, any inheritance tax payable in respect of his death on the value of these assets is a testamentary expense and is payable in accordance with the statutory order of application of assets, unless there is a contrary direction in the will. As these gifts are specific, the house and the shares fall within paragraph 6 of the statutory order and are only liable for expenses and debts after property in paragraphs 1 to 5 has been exhausted.

21–57 Certain items of property are conditionally exempted from inheritance tax on death. For instance, pictures, books, works of art, scientific collections or other things which appear to the Treasury to be of national, scientific, historic or artistic interest are exempted from inheritance tax if an undertaking is given to keep them in the United Kingdom and to take steps for their preservation and for securing reasonable access to the public.[123] If these undertakings are broken, or if the object is disposed of, a charge to inheritance tax arises.[124] This inheritance tax is not, however, a testamentary expense: it is borne by the persons who would be interested

[119] "free estate" is explained below, see below para.21–56.
[120] Inheritance Tax Act 1984 s.211(1).
[121] Inheritance Tax Act 1984 s.211(3).
[122] Inheritance Tax Act 1984 s.211(1).
[123] Inheritance Tax Act 1984 ss.30–31, as amended by Finance Act 1985 Sch.26.
[124] Inheritance Tax Act 1984 ss.32 and 33: certain disposals do not make tax chargeable, ss.32(4) and (5).

in the proceeds of sale of the objects,[125] or who disposed of the objects.[126] Similar provisions apply to land which in the opinion of the Treasury is of outstanding scenic or historic or scientific interest, and to buildings for the preservation of which special steps should in the opinion of the Treasury be taken by reason of their outstanding historic or architectural interest.[127]

2. Inheritance tax borne by the beneficiary

Inheritance tax which is payable in respect of the deceased's death on any property other than the deceased's free real and personal estate in the United Kingdom falls on that property and must be borne by the beneficiary who takes it. This rule is contained in s.211(3) of the Inheritance Tax Act 1984, which also applies to all property movable or immovable outside the United Kingdom. It also applies to property which does not vest in the deceased's personal representatives, such as property given by *donatio mortis causa*[128] or statutory nomination,[129] and the deceased's severable share of property held jointly (which vests by survivorship in the other joint tenant). In each case, under the second rule, the personal representatives are entitled to claim repayment of any inheritance tax they have paid, from the person in whom the property is vested. In practice, in the case of property outside the United Kingdom, the personal representatives may experience difficulty in obtaining repayment.[130] **21–58**

3. Incidence of inheritance tax on a pecuniary legacy

(a) *Property from which immediate pecuniary legacy is payable*

The incidence of inheritance tax on an immediate pecuniary legacy depends on the nature of the property from which it is payable. This is determined by the provisions of T's will, or by the general rules as to the incidence of pecuniary legacies.[131] If under the provisions of T's will, or these general rules, the pecuniary legacy is payable out of T's free real and personal estate in the United Kingdom, any inheritance tax is a testamentary expense. On the other hand, so far as the pecuniary legacy is payable out of T's property outside the United Kingdom, the pecuniary legacy bears its own inheritance tax. **21–59**

[125] Inheritance Tax Act 1984 s.207(1) (breach of undertaking).
[126] Inheritance Tax Act 1984 s.207(2) (disposal).
[127] Inheritance Tax Act 1984 ss.31–33, as amended by Finance Act 1985 Sch.26.
[128] *Re Hudson* [1911] 1 Ch.206 (estate duty on a *d.m.c.* is not a testamentary expense): the bare legal title to the subject matter of a *donatio mortis causa* may vest in the personal representatives but the equitable interest vests in the donee, see above, para.6–62.
[129] *Re Walley* [1972] 1 W.L.R. 257 (estate duty on a statutory nomination not a testamentary expense).
[130] Section 211(3) also applies to any land (whether freehold or leasehold) which was settled land at the death of the deceased, even if, on his death, it ceases to be settled. Subject to minor exceptions, it ceased to be possible to create any new Settled Land Act settlements after 1995: Trusts of Land and Appointment of Trustees Act 1996 s.2(1).
[131] See below, Chap.22.

(b) *Deferred pecuniary legacy*

21–60 The position is different in the case of a deferred pecuniary legacy given by T's will. If T gives property on trust for P for life, and after P's death on trust to pay a pecuniary legacy to Q and subject thereto for R absolutely, Q and R must bear the inheritance tax payable on the property in respect of P's death rateably according to the respective values of Q's legacy and R's residue.[132]

4. Incidence of inheritance tax on an option

21–61 If T gives X an option to purchase from T's personal representatives at a stated price particular property in the United Kingdom comprised in T's estate, the inheritance tax is payable as a testamentary expense in accordance with the statutory order of application of assets, subject, of course, to any contrary direction in his will.

5. "Free of inheritance tax" provisions

(a) *The need for variation*

21–62 A testator may vary these incidence rules by his will as he chooses.[133] Of course, if the testator wishes to relieve one beneficiary of the burden of the tax which he would otherwise be liable to bear, the testator needs to consider which other beneficiary is to bear the burden of that tax.[134]

(b) *Construction*

21–63 The Inheritance Tax Act 1984 provides that so far as any provision in any document, whenever executed, refers (in whatever terms) to estate duty, death duties or capital transfer tax, it shall have effect, so far as may be, as if it also referred to inheritance tax chargeable on death.[135]

21–64 The construction of a "free of inheritance tax" provision always depends on the precise words of the particular provision, which must be read in the context of the will as a whole.[136] The existing case law on "free

[132] See *Berry v Gaukroger* [1903] 2 Ch.116. Probably Q's legacy does not bear inheritance tax payable in respect of T's death even though it falls on the property, see *Re McNeill* [1958] Ch.259 and *Re Maryon-Wilson's* W.T. [1968] Ch.268.

[133] Administration of Estates Act 1925 s.34(3) and Sch.1, Pt II, para.8(a) (as to testamentary expenses); Inheritance Tax Act 1984 ss.211(2) and (3).

[134] But an exempt gift of a share of residue (such as to a spouse or to a charity) can never bear inheritance tax attributable to a non-exempt share of residue, Inheritance Tax Act 1984 s.41.

[135] Inheritance Act 1984 Sch.6, para.1 and Finance Act 1986 s.100(1).

[136] See *Scarfe v Matthews* [2012] W.T.L.R. 1579. There is a note on this case in All E.R. Rev. 2012 at p.451 where the editor of this book suggests that the approach taken by the trial judge to the interpretation of the will as a whole was completely correct. But the problem arose because of poor (probably negligent) drafting and would have been more simply cured by rectification. The draftsmen should have suggested this.

of duty" (i.e. free of estate duty) provisions does, however, give some guidance to the likely construction of "free of inheritance tax" provisions. On the basis of this case law the court will probably adopt the following approach:

(i) The court will presume that a "free of inheritance tax" provision is intended by the testator to apply only to tax payable in respect of his own death and not to tax payable in respect of any other event, such as the subsequent death of a beneficiary who takes a life interest under the testator's will.[137]

(ii) A direction in a will to pay "testamentary expenses" out of residue will apply to inheritance tax only so far as it is a testamentary expense, and will not apply to inheritance tax payable on property outside the United Kingdom.[138] On the other hand, a direction in a will to pay "all inheritance tax" out of residue will include tax payable on property outside the United Kingdom[139] in respect of the dispositions made by the will.[140]

6. Incidence of inheritance tax where residue is partly exempt

The problem of the incidence of inheritance tax where part of the residue is exempt from the tax was discussed in Chapter 16.[141] **21–65**

D. MARSHALLING AS BETWEEN BENEFICIARIES

1. Need for marshalling

A creditor of the deceased may obtain payment out of any of the assets, regardless of the rules as to the incidence of the deceased's expenses and debts as between the beneficiaries entitled under his will or intestacy or any variation of these rules by the deceased.[142] If a creditor is paid out of an asset which, as between the beneficiaries, is not liable to bear the burden of his debt, the doctrine of marshalling provides a remedy for the disappointed beneficiary. The doctrine ensures that the incidence rules, and not the choice of a creditor or of the personal representatives, finally prevail as between the beneficiaries.[143] **21–66**

137 *Re Shepherd* [1949] Ch.117; *Re Embleton's W.T.* [1965] 1 W.L.R. 840.
138 *Re Owers* [1941] Ch.17.
139 *Re Pimm* [1904] 2 Ch.345; *Re Neeld* (No.2) [1965] 1 W.L.R. 73, 76.
140 *Re Walley* [1972] 1 W.L.R. 257 (on construction of will, estate duty direction extended to statutory nomination but not to inter vivos gifts).
141 See above paras 16–29 et seq.
142 See above, para.21–30.
143 *Aldrich v Cooper* (1803) 8 Ves. 382, 396; *Re Cohen* [1960] Ch.179, 190; *Re Ross, Petterson v Ross* [2014] W.T.L.R. 321. See also Administration of Estates Act 1925 s.2(3).

2. Effect of marshalling

21–67 Under the doctrine of marshalling equity adjusts the remaining assets so as to compensate B, the disappointed beneficiary. Suppose that the creditor has obtained payment out of Blackacre, which was specifically devised to B and which therefore falls within paragraph 6 of the statutory order of application of assets. If the deceased did not vary the statutory order by his will, any property falling within paragraphs 1 to 5 of the statutory order is liable for expenses and debts before Blackacre. So B is entitled to compensation out of any property falling within paragraphs 1 to 5.[144] Moreover, if other property was specifically devised or bequeathed by the deceased in his will, B is entitled to insist that it must contribute rateably to the payment of the debt.[145] Compensation is assessed so as to make good to the disappointed beneficiary what he has lost.[146]

III. INSOLVENT ESTATES

21–68 The deceased's estate is insolvent if the assets, when realised, will be insufficient to meet in full all his funeral, testamentary and administration expenses, debts and liabilities.[147] Solvency or insolvency is a question of fact.[148] If there is doubt as to the solvency of the deceased's estate, the prudent course is for the personal representatives to administer the estate in accordance with the rules applicable to an insolvent estate and make no distribution to the beneficiaries, until it becomes certain that the estate is solvent.

If the deceased's estate is insolvent but is not being administered in bankruptcy,[149] certain provisions of the law of bankruptcy are applicable in the administration of the deceased's estate. These provisions are specified in the Administration of Insolvent Estates of Deceased Persons Order 1986[150] and, unlike the incidence rules applicable in the case of a solvent estate, cannot be varied by a contrary intention on the part of the deceased.[151] The provisions regulate "competition" between the creditors as to which of them shall be paid.

21–69 Under the Administration of Insolvent Estates of Deceased Persons Order 1986:

[144] *Re Matthews'* W.T. [1961] 1 W.L.R. 1415, 1419: see also *Re Wilson* [1967] Ch.53, 72.
[145] *Tombs v Roch* (1846) 2 Coll. 490; *Gervis v Gervis* (1847) 14 Sim. 654.
[146] *Re Broadwood* [1911] 1 Ch.277.
[147] Insolvency Act 1986 s.421(4); see *Re Leng* [1895] 1 Ch.652, 658.
[148] *Re Pink* [1927] 1 Ch.237, 241–242: see also *Re Smith* (1883) 22 Ch.D. 586, 592 (the court may direct an inquiry whether the estate is insolvent) and *George Lee & Sons (Builders) Ltd v Olink* [1972] 1 W.L.R. 214 (inquiry ordered).
[149] The deceased may have been adjudicated bankrupt before his death, in which case the estate continues to be administered in bankruptcy.
[150] SI 1986/1999, made under the Insolvency Act 1986 s.421, and as amended by SI 2002/1309.
[151] *Re Rothermere* [1943] 1 All E.R. 307; *Turner v Cox* (1853) 8 Moo.P.C. 288.

(i) The reasonable funeral, testamentary, and administration expenses have priority over preferential debts.[152]

(ii) The bankruptcy rules apply to the administration of the estate "with respect to the respective rights of secured and unsecured creditors, to debts and liabilities provable, to the valuation of future and contingent liabilities and to the priorities of debts and other payments."[153]

Thus some, but by no means all, of the bankruptcy rules are applicable to the administration of the deceased's insolvent estate by personal representatives.

The administration of a deceased's insolvent estate may be carried out in three different ways:– **21–70**

(i) by the personal representatives out of court (this is the usual method);

(ii) under the directions of the court in an administration claim[154]; or

(iii) in bankruptcy, after an insolvency administration order has been made by the bankruptcy court for the administration in bankruptcy of the deceased's estate.

Under the Insolvency Act 1986, an insolvency administration order may be made upon the petition of the personal representatives or of a creditor whose debt would have been sufficient to support a bankruptcy petition against the deceased if still alive.[155] If such an order is made, the Official Receiver acts as receiver of the deceased's estate[156] until the appointment of a trustee in bankruptcy,[157] in whom the deceased's estate vests on his appointment.[158] The trustee carries out the administration in bankruptcy of the deceased's estate. But the same rules as to payment of funeral, testamentary and administration expenses and debts apply, irrespective of the way in which the administration of the deceased's insolvent estate is carried out.[159]

[152] See below, paras 21–79 et seq.

[153] Administration of Insolvent Estates of Deceased Persons Order 1986 (SI 1986/1999) Art.4(1).

[154] See below, paras 24–22 et seq. The court in which proceedings for administration have been commenced may, if satisfied the estate is insolvent, transfer proceedings to the bankruptcy court, Insolvency Act 1986 s.271, as modified by the Order (SI 1986/1999), para.3 and Sch.1. References to this Act "as modified" mean as modified by this Order.

[155] ss.264, 267, 269, and 271–273, as modified; the "bankruptcy level" is currently £5,000, s.267(4) and SI 2015/922; for other persons who may petition see s.264(1)(c) and (d).

[156] ss.287–289 and 291, as modified.

[157] ss.292–297, as modified: the Official Receiver may become the trustee.

[158] s.306.

[159] ss.305, 328–329 and 386–387 and Sch.6, as modified. Exceptionally s.347(1) (right of landlord to distrain for only six months' rent accrued due before the date of the insolvency administration order) applies in an administration in bankruptcy of the deceased's estate, but not otherwise, *Re Fryman's Estate* (1888) 38 Ch.D. 468; *Re Wells* [1929] 2 Ch.269.

A. ASSETS, EXPENSES AND DEBTS

1. What are assets?

21–71 The question as to the property which constitutes assets for the payment of the deceased's debts and liabilities was considered at the beginning of this chapter.[160] The special rules of bankruptcy—which in certain circumstances add the property of third persons to a bankrupt's assets for the benefit of his creditors—apply only if an insolvency administration order has been made by the bankruptcy court for the administration in bankruptcy of the deceased's estate: these special rules cover, for instance, transactions entered into by the deceased at an undervalue,[161] preferences by the deceased,[162] and extortionate credit transactions between the deceased and a creditor.[163]

Section 421A of the Insolvency Act 1986[164] allows his trustee in bankruptcy to apply to the court for an order requiring the bankrupt deceased's surviving joint tenant to pay to the trustee an amount not exceeding the amount which would restore the position to what it would have been if the deceased had been adjudged bankrupt immediately before his death. In other words, it gives the court a discretion to award to the creditors an amount up to the value of the deceased's interest. The court's discretion will generally by exercised in favour of the creditors.[165]

2. Funeral, testamentary and administration expenses

21–72 These expenses (so far as they are reasonable) take priority over the deceased's preferential debts.[166] In all probability the deceased's funeral expenses[167] retain their long-established priority over the testamentary and administration expenses.[168]

3. Debts and liabilities

21–73 The bankruptcy rules apply with respect to the debts and liabilities provable in the administration of the deceased's insolvent estate:

[160] See above, paras 21–01 et seq. On an administration of the deceased's estate in bankruptcy, such clothing, bedding, furniture, household equipment and provisions as are necessary for satisfying the basic domestic needs of the deceased's family are excluded from the deceased's estate, Insolvency Act 1986 s.283(2), as modified; see also ss.308–309. As to the deceased's dwelling-house see ss.313 and 336–337.

[161] ss.339 and 341–342, as modified.

[162] ss.340–342, as modified.

[163] s.343, as modified.

[164] As inserted by the Insolvency Act 2000 s.12(1), modifying the effect of the decision of the Court of Appeal in *Re Palmer* [1994] Ch.316.

[165] s.421A(3).

[166] See below, paras 21–81 et seq.

[167] See above, paras 21–09 et seq.

[168] *R. v Wade* (1818) 5 Price 621, 627; *Re Walter* [1929] 1 Ch.647 (funeral expenses of bankrupt).

(a) *Debts and liabilities provable at their value*

All debts and liabilities of the deceased, present or future, certain or contingent, to which the deceased was subject at the date of his death, are provable against his insolvent estate.[169] If a debt or liability of the deceased does not bear a certain value, by reason of its being subject to any contingency or for any other reason, its value must be estimated.[170] **21–74**

(b) *Set-off*

Where there have been mutual dealings between the deceased and another person, an account must be taken and the sum due from the one party must be set off against that due from the other, and only the balance of the account is to be claimed.[171] **21–75**

(c) *Interest on debts*

If a debt bears interest, arrears of interest are provable as part of the debt for any period up to the date of the insolvency administration order.[172] **21–76**

B. ORDER OF PRIORITY OF DEBTS

The order of priority of debts in the administration of a deceased's insolvent estate is governed by the bankruptcy rules.[173] **21–77**

1. Debts of secured creditors

A secured creditor holds security for his debt (whether a mortgage, charge, lien or other security) over property of the deceased.[174] A typical instance is a bank or building society holding a mortgage on the deceased's house. Under the bankruptcy rules the rights of a secured creditor are as follows: **21–78**

(i) He may rely on his security and not prove for his debt.[175] This is a safe course if his security is adequate.

[169] Insolvency Act 1986 s.382 (as modified by SI 1986/1999). Debts are to be quantified, as well as identified, as at the date of death, *Lockston v Wood* [2015] EWHC 2962 (Ch).
[170] Insolvency Act 1986 s.322(3): any person dissatisfied with the estimate may apply to the court, which may assess its value, s.303.
[171] Insolvency Act 1986 s.323; *Watkins v Lindsay & Co* (1898) 67 L.J.Q.B. 362; *Re D.H. Curtis (Builders) Ltd* [1978] Ch.162.
[172] Insolvency Act 1986 s.322(2), as modified. This reference to the date of the insolvency administration order is a drafting error: it should refer to the date of death of the deceased debtor, so as to be consistent with ss.328(4) and 329(2), as modified, which provide for interest since the date of death, see below, para.21–83.
[173] Administration of Estates of Deceased Persons Order 1986 (SI 1986/1999) Arts 3 and 4.
[174] Insolvency Act 1986 s.383(2): a lien on documents is disregarded unless the documents are held as giving a title to property, s.383(4).
[175] Insolvency Act 1986 s.285(4).

(ii) He may realise his security and prove for the balance of his debt.[176] This is a possible course if his security is inadequate.

(iii) He may set a value on his security and prove for the balance of his debt as an unsecured creditor.[177] This is a possible course if his security is inadequate, but he values it at his own risk. If he values it too low, the personal representatives (or trustee in bankruptcy) will exercise their right to redeem the security at his value.[178] If he values it too high, he will prove for too small a balance.[179]

(iv) He may surrender his security and prove for the whole debt.[180] This course is not advisable if his security has any value.

21–79 In so far as a secured creditor obtains the payment of his debt by realising his security, he enjoys priority over the deceased's funeral, testamentary and administration expenses and unsecured creditors. On the other hand, in so far as a secured creditor proves for his debt, he is in the same position, and entitled to the same priority, as an unsecured creditor.

The deceased's reasonable funeral, testamentary and administration expenses take priority over the debts of unsecured creditors. The latter are payable according to the following order of priority, under which four classes of debts exist, i.e. specially preferred, preferential, ordinary and deferred debts.

2. Specially preferred debts

21–80 The first class is specially preferred debts. These are:

(i) *money or property belonging to any friendly society*, which was in the possession of the deceased as an officer of the society[181]:

(ii) *proper expenses incurred by the trustee under a deed of arrangement* which has subsequently been avoided by the bankruptcy of the debtor,[182] or incurred as expenses of the administration of a voluntary arrangement under the Insolvency Act 1986.[183]

These specially preferred debts[184] must be met out of the deceased's insolvent estate before any of his other debts are paid.[185]

176 Insolvency Act 1986 s.322(1); Insolvency Rules 1986 (SI 1986/1925) rr.6.109 and 6.119.

177 Insolvency Rules 1986 rr.6.96 and 6.98. The creditor has a limited power to alter his valuation, r.6.115; *Re Becher* [1944] Ch.78.

178 Insolvency Rules 1986 r.6.117: alternatively they may insist on sale, r.6.118.

179 *Re Hopkins* (1881) 18 Ch.D. 370.

180 Insolvency Rules 1986 r.6.109(2).

181 Friendly Societies Act 1974 s.59.

182 Deeds of Arrangement Act 1914 s.21; see *Re Geen* [1917] 1 K.B. 183. The Deeds of Arrangement Act 1914 was repealed as from 1 October 2015 by the Deregulation Act 2015 Sch.6, para.1(1).

183 Insolvency Act 1986 ss.264(1)(c) and 276.

184 See Regimental Debts Act 1893 s.2 (preferential debts of persons dying while subject to service law); Ley (1971) 35 Conv.(N.S.) 420: see also Insolvency Act s.348(4).

185 Insolvency Act 1986 s.328(6).

3. Preferential debts

The preferential debts are next payable, ranking equally between themselves, so that if there are insufficient assets to pay them all in full they must all abate proportionately.[186] The preferential debts are listed in Sch.6 to the Insolvency Act 1986, as subsequently amended. The Schedule originally contained six categories of preferential debts,[187] but, in 2003, the first three categories—debts due to the Inland Revenue, to Customs and Excise and for Social Security Contributions—were all repealed, and, at later stage, another three categories were added. As a result, there are now, again, six categories, though their numbering is odd. They begin with category 4. **21–81**

The six categories of preferential debts are now as follows:

(i) *Category 4: Contributions to occupational pension schemes.*[188]
(ii) *Category 5: Remuneration of employees.*[189]
(iii) *Category 6: Levies on coal and steel production.*[190]
(iv) *Category 6A: Debts owed to the Financial Services Compensation Scheme.*
(v) *Category 7: Deposits covered by the Financial Services Compensation Scheme.*[191]
(vi) *Category 8: Other specified deposits.*[192]

4. Ordinary debts

Next in order of priority come the ordinary debts, i.e. all other debts except the deferred debts (considered below). **21–82**

All the ordinary debts rank equally between themselves and if they cannot be paid in full they must all abate proportionately.[193] A creditor does not obtain any priority over the other creditors by obtaining judgment for his debt against the personal representatives.[194]

5. Interest on preferential and ordinary debts since death

Next in order of priority, interest is payable on all the preferential and ordinary debts in respect of the periods during which they have been **21–83**

[186] Insolvency Act 1986 s.328 (1), (1A) and (1B).
[187] Before 1 January 1987, there were even more categories, including local rates and taxes.
[188] Being a sum to which Pension Schemes Act 1993 Sch.4 applies (imposing 4 or 12 months' time limits).
[189] This includes any amount owed by the deceased to an employee or former employee by way of remuneration in respect of the period of four months before his death, but not exceeding £800 (this being the limit currently prescribed by order by the Secretary of State, SI 1986/1996, art.4).
[190] Being levies, and surcharges for delay, referred to in Arts 49 and 50 of the E.C.S.C. Treaty.
[191] Added by the Financial Services (Banking Reform) Act 2013 s.13.
[192] Added by the Banks and Building Societies (Depositor Preference and Priorities) Order 2014, SI 2014/3486 art.11. These are designated "secondary preferential debts": Insolvency Act 1986 s.386(1B). They rank after all other preferential debts which are now designated "ordinary preferential debts": Insolvency Act 1986 ss.386(1A) and 328(1B).
[193] Insolvency Act 1986 s.328(3).
[194] *Pritchard v Westminster Bank Ltd* [1969] 1 W.L.R. 547.

outstanding since the death of the deceased. Interest on these debts ranks equally, irrespective of the priority accorded to the debts themselves.[195] The rate of interest payable on a debt is whichever is the greater of (i) the rate specified in s.17 of the Judgments Act 1838[196] at the death (currently 8 per cent),[197] and (ii) the rate applicable to that debt apart from the bankruptcy.[198]

6. Deferred debts

21–84 Deferred debts come last in the order of priority. They include debts owed in respect of credit provided by a person who was the spouse or civil partner of the deceased at the latter's death.[199]

C. FAILURE TO OBSERVE THE ORDER OF PRIORITY OF DEBTS

1. Liability for payment of inferior debt

21–85 A personal representative is under a duty to administer a deceased's insolvent estate in accordance with the statutory rules as to the payment of debts.[200] He is therefore liable for a breach of this duty (constituting a *devastavit*) if he fails to observe the order of priority of debts. Thus the personal representative incurs liability if he applies the deceased's assets in paying an inferior debt (e.g. a deferred debt) which he ought not to have paid, and leaves unpaid a superior debt (e.g. a preferential or ordinary debt) which he ought to have paid because he had notice of it. His payment of the inferior debt constitutes an admission by him that he has assets sufficient to satisfy all debts of which he then has notice and which have priority over the inferior debt: if the deceased's assets are not sufficient, the personal representative is personally liable to pay all such debts.[201] But the personal representative does not incur liability if, acting in good faith and without undue haste, he pays an inferior debt without notice of a superior debt.[202] A personal representative is generally under a duty to pay all debts of the same class *pari passu*.[203]

195 Insolvency Act 1986 s.328(4), as modified.
196 As amended.
197 Judgment Debts (Rate of Interest) Order 1993 (SI 1993/564).
198 Insolvency Act 1986 s.328(5), as modified.
199 Insolvency Act 1986 s.329, as modified.
200 Administration of Estates Act 1925 s.25 as amended by Administration of Estates Act 1971 s.9; Insolvency Act 1986 s.421; Administration of Insolvent Estates of Deceased Persons Order 1986 (SI 1986/1999).
201 2 Bl.Comm. 511: see *Britton v Batthurst* (1683) 3 Lev. 113; *Rock v Layton* (1700) 1 Ld.Raym. 589.
202 *Harman v Harman* (1686) 2 Show. 492; *Re Fludyer* [1898] 2 Ch.562 ("Since the case of *Harman v Harman* it has been considered settled law that an executor who pays creditors without notice of the existence of a creditor of higher degree is not liable to account for the sums so paid at the instance of that creditor"). Contrast the position of a personal representative who distributes to *beneficiaries* without notice of an unpaid debt of the deceased, above, paras 21–15 et seq.
203 *Pari passu* is a Latin expression meaning "on an equal footing" or "proportionately to their respective claims".

2. Personal representative having no reason to believe estate insolvent

Under s.10(2) of the Administration of Estates Act 1971 a personal representative who, in good faith and at a time when he has no reason to believe that the deceased's estate is insolvent, pays the debt of any creditor (including himself, unless he took letters of administration in his capacity as creditor) is not liable to account to creditors of the same class as the paid creditor if it subsequently appears that the estate is insolvent. This does not protect the personal representative against creditors of a superior class, to whom the personal representative is liable to account if he had notice of them.[204] Section 10(2) was introduced to enable a personal representative to pay tradesmen's bills at an early stage in the administration.[205] But it does not provide any protection to a personal representative if he has any reason to believe that the deceased's estate is insolvent because, for instance, a particular asset is of dubious value or a particular liability is of dubious extent.[206] **21–86**

IV. INCIDENCE OF GENERAL LEGACIES

The rules which govern the incidence of general legacies (including general annuities)[207] cannot be stated with any certainty.[208] Obviously rules are needed in order to determine: **21–87**

(a) which assets are applicable for the payment of general legacies; and
(b) the order in which such assets are to be applied for this purpose.

The rules in force on the death of a testator before 1926 were clear and well-settled, though perhaps in need of reform. Unfortunately, it is not certain to what extent the Administration of Estates Act 1925 has altered them. The primary responsibility for the present uncertainty rests with the draftsman of the Act but the judicial decisions since 1925 are themselves in a state of confusion.[209] To avoid possible litigation, any draftsman of a will needs to consider inserting an express provision as to the incidence of general legacies.

Where the testator dies after 1925,[210] s.33 of the Administration of Estates Act 1925 needs to be considered in relation to the administration of assets **21–88**

204 cf. Law Com. No.31, para.8, especially fn.16.
205 Law Com. No.31, para.8.
206 For the court's power to relieve a personal representative from liability see Trustee Act 1925 ss.61, 68(1), 68(17) and 69(1), and see below, para.24–21.
207 For annuities, see Chap.9.
208 See generally E. C. Ryder [1956] C.L.J. 80; *Theobald on Wills*, 17th edn (London: Sweet & Maxwell, 2010), 34–008 et seq.
209 *Re Taylor's Estate* [1969] 2 Ch.245, 253.
210 For the rules before 1925, see the 12th edition of this book paras 22–02—22–06.

on a partial intestacy, as well as s.34(3), which refers to the statutory order of application of assets set out in Pt II of the First Schedule.

1. Effect of section 33

21–89 The effect on the incidence of general legacies of s.33 of the Act is material only if the testator dies partially intestate.[211]

(a) *Section 33(2) makes undisposed-of property primarily liable*

21–90 If a testator dies after 1925 partially intestate, and s.33(2) applies in respect of the property undisposed of by his will, then under s.33(2) the net money arising from the sale of that property and the testator's ready money (if undisposed of by his will) are first to be applied in payment of the testator's expenses, debts and liabilities, and next a pecuniary legacy fund is to be set aside out of the residue of that money. Section 33(2), where it applies, altered the old rules as to the incidence of general legacies by throwing their burden primarily on the undisposed-of property, whether it is realty or personalty or both.[212]

(b) *When is section 33(2) applicable?*

21–91 Although there is some uncertainty as to when s.33(2) applies,[213] it clearly applies in the following two situations:

(i) T dies wholly intestate as to one or more assets of his estate: each such asset (if not already money) is held upon trust with the power to sell it given by s.33(1),[214] and s.33(2) applies to the net money arising from the sale and to any of T's undisposed-of ready money.[215]
(ii) T dies wholly intestate as to a share in his residuary estate (e.g. because of lapse): such share is held upon trust with the power to sell it given by s.33(1). Again s.33(2) applies to the net money arising from any sale.[216]

2. Effect of section 34(3) and the statutory order

21–92 The effect on the incidence of general legacies of s.34(3) and the statutory order of application of assets needs to be considered in several different situations:

211 s.33(1), as amended by the Trusts of Land and Appointment of Trustees Act 1996 s.33(7) makes it clear that s.33 takes effect subject to the provisions in the testator's will.
212 *Re Worthington* [1933] Ch.771; followed in *Re Berrey's* W.T. [1959] 1 W.L.R. 30.
213 See 12th edition of this book at para.22–12.
214 cf. *Re McKee* [1931] 2 Ch.145, 159, 160 and 165–166; *Re Plowman* [1943] Ch.269.
215 *Re Martin* [1955] Ch.698 (intestacy as to realty so that ss.33(1) and (2) applicable: but legacies held payable out of realty under para.1).
216 *Re Berrey's W.T.* [1959] 1 W.L.R. 30 (gift of residue by T to A, B, C and D equally; B predeceased T, causing B's share to lapse and go as on T's intestacy: held s.33(1) and (2) applied to B's share, and general legacies were payable primarily out of B's share).

(i) If the testator dies partially intestate and s.33(2) applies, but the legacies cannot be paid in full out of the pecuniary legacy fund set aside out of the undisposed-of property falling within s.33(2)—this undisposed-of property is first applied in payment of the testator's expenses, debts and liabilities;
(ii) If the testator dies partially intestate but s.33(2) does not apply; and
(iii) If the testator dies fully testate—in this case s.33 never applies.

Section 34(3) of the Administration of Estates Act 1925 provides that the testator's real and personal estate shall, subject to any provisions contained in his will, be applicable towards the discharge of "the funeral, testamentary and administration expenses, debts and liabilities payable thereout" in the statutory order mentioned in Pt II of the First Schedule. Under that statutory order the testator's undisposed-of property "subject to the retention thereout of a fund sufficient to meet any pecuniary legacies" is primarily liable under paragraph 1; and the testator's property included in a residuary gift "subject to the retention out of such property of a fund sufficient to meet any pecuniary legacies, so far as not provided for as aforesaid" is next liable under paragraph 2. As has been noted already, no distinction is made between realty and personalty in the statutory order, and all the realty and personalty falling within any particular paragraph is liable rateably for the testator's expenses, debts and liabilities.[217]

Under paragraphs 1 and 2 the order of resort is different from that speci- **21–93**
fied in s.33(2)—under both paragraphs 1 and 2 the pecuniary legacy fund is set aside *first*, and the *balance* of the undisposed-of property, or property included in a residuary gift, is liable for expenses, debts and liabilities.[218] The different order of resort specified in s.33(2) is probably due to a drafting error. Unfortunately different orders of resort may well produce different practical results: for instance, as regards the incidence of inheritance tax on the legatees if the undisposed-of property is not sufficient to pay all the expenses, debts and liabilities and legacies in full, and resort has to be made to property of a different nature included in a residuary gift.

The effect on the incidence of general legacies of s.34(3) and the statutory order depends on their proper construction. Unfortunately, the position is far from clear.[219]

3. Express provision in a will as to incidence of legacies

Accordingly the draftsman of a will should insert an express provision **21–94**
as to the incidence of general legacies and thereby exclude whatever rules would otherwise apply. A testator often gives his residuary real

[217] See above, para.21–32.
[218] *Re Anstead* [1943] Ch.161 (the headnote is wrong); *Re Wilson* [1967] Ch.53, 70.
[219] Contrast the approach taken in *Re Thompson* [1936] Ch676; *Re Anstead* [1943] Ch.161; *Re Beaumont's Will Trusts* [1950] Ch.462 and *Re Taylor's Estate* [1969] 2 Ch.245 with that taken in *Re Midgley* [1955] Ch.576; *Re Gillett's Will Trusts* [1950] Ch.102 and *Re Martin* [1955] Ch.698. For a more detailed discussion of the problem, and a fuller account of the caselaw, see the 12th edition of this book paras 22–15—22–22.

and personal estate to trustees upon trust or trust for sale and directs that out of the proceeds of such sale and his ready money they are to pay his funeral, testamentary and administration expenses and debts, and the general legacies given by his will or any codicil thereto. Such a direction ensures that, if some beneficial interest in his residuary estate fails, the general legacies are payable out of the whole residuary estate.[220]

[220] cf. Form 8 of the Statutory Will Forms 1925 (prescribed under Law of Property Act 1925 s.179 and which may be incorporated in a will); Form 8 makes the legacies payable primarily out of personalty.

Chapter 22

INCOME AND INTEREST

This chapter covers the rules governing the income or interest carried by gifts by will. By his will the testator may make a gift of property (i) to a person beneficially or (ii) to trustees upon trust for persons in succession (e.g. upon trust for A for life and subject thereto for B absolutely). In each case the question arises as to the income or interest which the gift carries. But in the case of the trust for persons in succession, a second question also arises: what constitutes income to be paid to the life tenant and what constitutes capital of the trust? The answer to this second question forms part of the law of trusts and is not discussed in this book.[1] **22–01**

A. SPECIFIC LEGACIES AND DEVISES

1. Immediate specific gifts

A specific legacy or specific devise which takes effect immediately carries with it all the income or profits accruing from its subject-matter after the testator's death. For instance, under a specific legacy of company shares the legatee is entitled to the dividends after the testator's death.[2] Similarly, under a specific devise of Blackacre which is subject to a tenancy at the testator's death, the devisee is entitled to the rent after the testator's death. **22–02**

[1] The former rule in *Allhusen v Whittell* (1867) L.R. 4 Eq. 295, which related to administration, was considered in para.23–27—23–30 of the 12th edition of this book. For the duty to convert under the former rule in *Howe v Earl of Dartmouth* (1802) 7 Ves. 137 and the former rule in *Re Earl of Chesterfield's Trusts* (1883) 24 Ch.D. 643, see Hanbury and Martin, *Modern Equity*, 20th edn (London: Sweet & Maxwell, 2015), paras 20–002–20–010. Before 2013, these rules were almost always excluded by express provision in the will or trust instrument. The Trusts (Capital and Income) Act 2013 s.1 dissapplies all these rules in relation to "new trusts" i.e. those created or arising on or after 1 October 2013 (SI 2013/676).

[2] *Re West* [1909] 2 Ch.180 (specific legacy of company shares carried dividends from death of testatrix); *Re Marten* [1901] 1 Ch.370: see also *Chester v Urwick* (1856) 23 Beav. 420 (specific legacy of one or other stocks at discretion of executors: held legatee entitled to dividends from testator's death) and cf. *Re Collins'* W.T. [1971] 1 W.L.R. 37, 42–43.

(a) *Apportionment of income*

22–03 In order to ascertain the amount of income accruing after the testator's death, it might, where a trust was created or where it arose before October 2013, have been necessary to apportion income under section 2 of the Apportionment Act 1870. This section provides that:

> "All rents, annuities, dividends, and other periodical payments in the nature of income shall, like interest on money lent, be considered as accruing from day to day, and shall be apportionable in respect of time accordingly."

The 1870 Act 1 did not apply to the profits accruing from the testator's own business of which he was the proprietor,[3] or from a share in a private partnership.[4] In these cases the profits were treated as having accrued entirely on the final day of the period for which they were declared.[5]

And, even in the cases where the Act would have applied, the testator might have—and usually would have—excluded its operation by words expressly so stating, or requiring that conclusion by necessary implication.[6]

Furthermore, s.1 of The Trusts (Capital and Income) Act 2013 dissapplies s.2 of the 1870 Act in relation to "new trusts", i.e. those created or arising or after 1 October 2013 and states[7] that "Any entitlement to income under a new trust is to income as it arises . . .".

(b) *Liabilities*

22–04 A legatee or devisee taking under an immediate specific legacy or devise must bear the liabilities incident to the subject-matter of the gift after the testator's death.[8] Suppose that the testator, T, owned a house which he had let to a tenant under a lease containing a covenant by T to keep the exterior of the demised premises in repair, and that T made a specific devise of the house to his nephew. In this case, the specific devisee must bear the expense of repairing in accordance with this covenant after T's death.[9] There are, however, two limits to the burden which the devisee must bear:

[3] *Re Cox's Trusts* (1878) 9 Ch.D. 159.

[4] *Jones v Ogle* (1872) 8 Ch.App.192; *Re Lynch-White* [1937] 3 All E.R. 551.

[5] *Ibbotson v Elam* (1866) L.R. 1 Eq. 188; *Browne v Collins* (1871) 12 Eq. 586; *Re Robbins* [1941] Ch.434.

[6] Apportionment Act 1870 s.7: see *Re Lysaght* [1898] 1 Ch.115; *Re Meredith* (1898) 78 L.T. 492: cf. *Re Edwards* [1918] 1 Ch.142; *Re Joel's* W.T. [1967] Ch.14. For possible reform, see Law Reform Committee's 23rd Report, *The Powers and Duties of Trustees*, Cmnd.8733 (1982) and Law Com. C.P. 175 (2004), *Capital and Income in Trusts: Classification and Apportionment* (recommends replacing provisions of Apportionment Act 1870 in relation to trusts with discretion to apportion when just and expedient, unless contrary intention shown in terms of trust).

[7] s.1(1).

[8] The outgoings must be apportioned if income is apportioned, *Re Joel's* W.T. [1967] Ch.14, 30–31. As to expenses incurred by the personal representatives in the upkeep and preservation of the subject-matter of a specific devise or specific legacy, see above, para.9–17.

[9] *Re Day's W.T.* [1962] 1 W.L.R. 1419; *Mansel v Norton* (1883) 22 Ch.D. 769. As to the liabilities

(i) If T had entered into a binding contract to have certain building work done at the house, the devisee is entitled to have this work carried out for his benefit after T's death at the expense of T's estate.[10]

(ii) If the covenant in the lease relates to something which was to be done by T (the landlord) preparatory to the complete establishment of the relation of landlord and tenant, then the burden of the covenant falls on T's estate and not on the devisee.[11]

Of course, if Blackacre is subject to a mortgage debt at T's death, s.35 of the Administration of Estates Act 1925 applies and Blackacre is primarily liable for the payment of the mortgage debt, unless T has shown a contrary intention.[12]

2. Contingent or deferred specific gifts

A specific legacy or specific devise may be contingent (e.g. "to X if he attains the age of 30 years"), or deferred to a future date which must come sooner or later (e.g. "to X after the death of my wife A"), or both contingent and deferred (e.g. "to X, after the death of my wife A, if he attains the age of 30 years"). **22–05**

Section 175(1) of the Law of Property Act 1925 provides that contingent or deferred specific gifts carry the intermediate income except insofar as such income is otherwise disposed of by the will.

Section 175 mentions a contingent or deferred specific devise or bequest,[13] and a specific devise to trustees upon trust for persons whose interests are contingent or deferred,[14] but the section does not mention a specific bequest to trustees upon trust for persons whose interests are contingent or executory. Such a specific bequest to trustees probably falls within the earlier reference to "a contingent or future specific. . .bequest."[15] **22–06**

Where it applies, s.175 makes a contingent or deferred specific gift of property carry the intermediate income of that property, but subject to the rule that the income can only be accumulated and added to the capital for as long as the statutory rule against accumulations permits.[16] Section 175

to be borne by a specific legatee of a leasehold property see *Theobald on Wills*, 17th edn (London: Sweet & Maxwell, 2010), para.34–032.

[10] *Re Rushbrooks's W.T.* [1948] Ch.421: cf. *Re Day's W.T.*, above.

[11] e.g. a covenant to repair where the object of the covenant was to ensure that the premises were put initially into a condition fit for the occupation of the tenant: see *Re Day's W.T.*, above; *Re Hughes* [1913] 2 Ch.491; *Re Smyth* [1965] I.R. 595.

[12] See above, paras 21–48 et seq.

[13] "future" in the section means deferred, *Re McGeorge* [1963] Ch.544, 550–552.

[14] "executory" in the section also appears to mean deferred, *Re McGeorge* [1963] Ch.544, 550–552.

[15] See P. V. Baker (1963) 79 L.Q.R. 184, 186. For the rules applicable to wills coming into operation before 1926 see *Hawkins on the Construction of Wills*, 5th edn (London: Sweet & Maxwell, 2000), pp.148–149.

[16] *Re McGeorge*, above. Where an instrument was made before 6 April 2010 there were statutory restrictions upon powers of accumulation, see the Law of Property Act 1925 s.164 as amended by the Perpetuities and Accumulations Act 1964 s.13. The restrictions still apply to a will made before 6 April 2010, even though the testator dies after that date. Where a will is

does not, of course, apply where the intermediate income is otherwise expressly disposed of.[17]

Section 175 probably accords with the likely intentions of a testator who makes a contingent specific gift, but the same cannot be said of the deferred specific gift.

22–07 Where there is a beneficiary living who is contingently entitled, s.31 of the Trustee Act 1925 often governs the destination of the intermediate income carried by the specific gift. The personal representatives have power during the infancy of the beneficiary to apply the whole or part of the income for his maintenance, education or benefit (accumulating any surplus income), and after the beneficiary has attained his majority the personal representatives must pay the whole income to him until he attains a vested interest, or dies, or his interest fails.[18] Section 31 applies so far as a contrary intention is not expressed in the will.[19] The section is not applicable to intermediate income carried by a deferred specific gift.[20]

B. GENERAL LEGACIES[21]

1. Interest runs from time for payment

22–08 The basic principle is that a general legacy carries interest from the time at which it is payable[22] and it is simple, not compound, interest. The justification for this rule is that the interest payable compensates the legatee for any delay in paying him his legacy.

The rule is not confined to a general legacy of a sum of money but applies, for instance, to a general legacy of company shares.[23]

2. Time for payment

22–09 The time for payment of a legacy (a) may be fixed by the testator and, if not, (b) has to be fixed by rules of law.

(a) *Time fixed by the testator*

22–10 If a testator directs a legacy to be paid "immediately after my death," the legacy carries interest from the date of the testator's death because the

made on or after 6 April 2010 the income may be accumulated for the whole of the perpetuity period of 125 years.

[17] *Re Hatfield* [1958] Ch.469.

[18] Trustee Act 1925 ss.31(1) and (2) and 68(17), as amended by Family Law Reform Act 1969 ss.1(3) and (4), Sch.1, Pt I and Sch.3, para.5(1). See generally Hanbury and Martin, *Modern Equity*, 20th edn (London: Sweet & Maxwell, 2015), paras 21–022 et seq.

[19] s.69(2); *Re Turner's* W.T. [1937] Ch.15.

[20] *Re McGeorge*, above.

[21] These rules also apply to demonstrative legacies.

[22] The rate of interest set by the court is in CPR 40 PD. 15; it is the basic rate on funds in court unless the court orders otherwise. The rate has been 4% since 1 February 2002.

[23] *Re Hall* [1951] 1 All E.R. 1073.

testator has fixed this date as the time for payment.[24] Similarly, a legacy directed to be paid to X at the age of 21 years bears interest from X's 21st birthday, whether the legacy is vested or contingent.[25] Again, a legacy directed to be paid on the death of a tenant for life carries interest from the death of the tenant for life.

(b) *Time fixed by rules of law*

If no time for payment is mentioned in the will, the time for payment is fixed by rules of law: **22–11**

(i) Immediate general legacy. The normal rule is that an immediate legacy is payable one year after the testator's death, i.e. at the end of the executor's year. This rule has been adopted for the sake of convenience[26] and is applicable even though the testator's estate does not produce any income.[27] **22–12**

The same rule applies to a general legacy upon trust for A for life and subject thereto for B absolutely.[28]

A legacy which is vested but is liable to be divested in a certain event (e.g. given to a child X, with a gift over to Y in the event of X dying under the age of 21) also carries interest from the end of the executor's year.[29]

(ii) Contingent or deferred general legacy. A general legacy which is contingent or deferred (or both) carries interest from the time at which it becomes payable. Such a general legacy is not mentioned in section 175 of the Law of Property Act 1925 and accordingly does not carry intermediate income under that section,[30] unlike a contingent or deferred specific gift. It follows that a general legacy to an unborn child carries interest only from the birth of the child,[31] and a general legacy to X if he attains the age of 18 years carries interest only from X's 18th birthday.[32] Again, a general legacy given to a person appointed executor and conditional on his accepting the office carries interest only from the time he accepts the office.[33] **22–13**

[24] *Re Riddell* [1936] W.N. 252; *Re Pollock* [1943] Ch.338; cf. *Webster v Hale* (1803) 8 Ves. 410 (legacy to be paid "as soon as possible": held no date fixed for payment, and interest payable from one year after testator's death). For the effect of Administration of Estates Act 1925 s.44, see below, para.23–02.

[25] *Heath v Perry* (1744) 3 Atk. 101; *Crickett v Dolby* (1795) 3 Ves. 10; *Tyrrell v Tyrrell* (1798) 4 Ves. 1; *Lord v Lord* (1867) L.R. 2 Ch.782; *Holmes v Crispe* (1849) 18 L.J.Ch. 439. But if X attains 21 years before T's death the legacy is payable one year after T's death, *Re Palfreeman* [1914] 1 Ch.877.

[26] *Wood v Penoyre* (1807) 13 Ves. 325a, 333–334.

[27] *Pearson v Pearson* (1802) 1 Sch. & Lef. 10; *Re Blachford* (1884) 27 Ch.D. 676); *Walford v Walford* [1912] A.C. 658.

[28] *Re Whittaker* (1882) 21 Ch.D. 657.

[29] *Taylor v Johnson* (1728) 2 P.Wms. 504.

[30] *Re Raine* [1929] 1 Ch.716.

[31] *Rawlins v Rawlins* (1796) 2 Cox. 425.

[32] *Re George* (1877) 5 Ch.D. 837; *Re Dickson* (1885) 29 Ch.D. 331; *Re Inman* [1893] 3 Ch.518.

[33] *Angermann v Ford* (1861) 29 Beav. 349; *Re Gardner* (1893) 67 L.T. 552. As to accepting office, see *Lewis v Matthews* (1869) L.R. 8. Eq. 277.

22–14 **(iii) Legacy directed to be severed.** A legacy which the testator directs to be severed from his general estate may carry interest for a beneficiary from the end of the executor's year, even though his beneficial interest in the legacy is contingent or deferred. Whether it does so depends on the purpose for which severance is directed. Thus a general legacy given to trustees upon trust to invest and hold the legacy, and the investments representing it, upon trust for X if he attains the age of 18 years is treated under the general rule as payable by the executor to the trustees at the end of the executor's year, and the legacy carries interest from the end of the executor's year. The same result follows if T by his will directs that the legacy be severed (or set apart) by his executor from his general estate and held for the benefit of X if he attains the age of 18 years.[34] But if by his will T directs that the legacy be set apart merely for convenience of administration (e.g. so as to enable the rest of his estate to be distributed) and not for some purpose connected with the legacy, or if without any such direction the executor in fact sets the legacy apart, the legacy carries interest for X only from his 18th birthday, and meanwhile the interest accruing from the fund which has been set apart falls into T's residuary estate.[35]

3. Interest runs from death under four exceptional rules

22–15 There are four exceptional rules under which a general legacy will, in the absence of a contrary expression, carry interest from the date of the testator's death.

(a) *Satisfaction of a debt*

22–16 A legacy to a creditor of the testator, which operates as a satisfaction of his debt, carries interest from the testator's death and not from the end of the executor's year.[36] This rule is not applicable if the testator fixed a time later than his death for payment of the legacy.[37]

(b) *Legacy charged only on realty*

22–17 A legacy which is charged only on realty carries interest from the date of the testator's death if the legacy is vested.[38] Again, this rule is not applicable if the testator fixed a later time for payment of the legacy. The rule does not apply to a legacy directed to be paid out of the proceeds of sale of

[34] *Re Medlock* (1886) 55 L.J.Ch. 738; *Johnston v O'Neill* (1879) 3 L.R.Ir. 476 ("the rule that the interest follows the capital prevails and the legatee gets his legacy with its interim accretions"); *Re Couturier* [1907] 1 Ch.470; *Re Pollock* [1943] Ch.338.

[35] *Festing v Allen* (1844) 5 Hare 573; *Re Judkin's Trusts* (1884) 25 Ch.D. 743; *Re Inman* [1893] 3 Ch.518.

[36] *Clark v Sewell* (1744) 3 Atk. 96, 98–99; *Re Rattenberry* [1906] 1 Ch.667: for satisfaction of a debt by a legacy see above, paras 13–02 et seq.

[37] *Adams v Lavender* (1824) M'Cl. & Y. 41.

[38] *Maxwell v Wettenhall* (1722) 2 P.Wms. 26; *Shirt v Westby* (1808) 16 Ves. 393: the rule does not apply if a legacy is charged on realty in aid of the personalty, *Freeman v Simpson* (1833) 6 Sim 75.

realty devised upon trust for sale—in that case, the legacy has been held to carry interest from one year after the testator's death, when the sale might reasonably have been effected.[39]

(c) *Testator's infant child*

22–18 If a testator gives a legacy to his infant child, or to an infant to whom he stands in loco parentis, the legacy carries interest from the date of the testator's death in order to provide maintenance for the child.[40] The rule is not applicable if the testator has by his will made some other provision for the child's maintenance.[41] Moreover, the rule applies only where the legacy is given directly to the child, and it is not applicable if the legacy is given to trustees upon trust for the child.[42]

The rule applies even though the legacy to the child is not payable until the child attains full age, or is contingent upon his attaining full age or previously marrying.[43] But the rule does not apply if the specified contingency has no reference to the child's infancy.[44]

The rate of interest carried is 5 per cent per annum if the income available is sufficient.[45] The interest may be applied for the child's maintenance, either under the statutory power of maintenance[46] or pursuant to an order of the court. Any surplus interest not applied for the child's maintenance is accumulated and added to the capital of the legacy.[47]

(d) *Intention to provide for maintenance of infant*

22–19 If a testator gives a legacy to an infant and shows in his will an intention to provide for the infant's maintenance,[48] the legacy carries interest from the date of the testator's death,[49] unless the testator has by his will made some other provision for the infant's maintenance.[50] Under this rule the

39 *Turner v Buck* (1874) L.R. 18 Eq. 301; cf. *Re Waters* (1889) 42 Ch.D. 517.

40 *Re Bowlby* [1904] 2 Ch.685; *Wilson v Maddison* (1843) 2 Y. & C.C.C. 372; *Harvey v Harvey* (1722) 2 P.Wms. 21; *Heath v Perry* (1744) 3 Atk. 101, 102; *Wynch v Wynch* (1788) 1 Cox 433.

41 *Hearle v Greenbank* (1749) 3 Atk. 695, 716; *Donovan v Needham* (1846) 9 Beav. 164; *Re George* (1877) 5 Ch.D. 837. If a share of residue is also given to the child contingently on attaining 21, the statutory power of maintenance (now in Trustee Act 1925, s.31) out of the income of this share of residue does not exclude this exceptional rule, *Re Moody* [1895] 1 Ch.101: sed quaere and cf. *Re Abrahams* [1911] 1 Ch.108, 114.

42 *Re Pollock* [1943] Ch.338.

43 *Re Bowlby* [1904] 2 Ch.685.

44 *Re Abrahams* [1911] 1 Ch.108: see also *Re Jones* [1932] 1 Ch.642 and the exceptional rule considered in (4) below.

45 Trustee Act 1925 s.31(3) (5 per cent. "subject to any rules of court to the contrary").

46 Trustee Act 1925 ss.31 and 68(1)(17), as amended by Family Law Reform Act 1969 s.1(3) and (4), Sch.1 Pt I and Sch.3, para.5(1).

47 *ibid*; see *Re Bowlby*, above.

48 Or education, *Re Selby-Walker* [1949] 2 All E.R. 178.

49 *Re Churchill* [1909] 2 Ch.431; *Re Stokes* [1928] Ch.716.

50 *Re West* [1913] 2 Ch.345.

legatee need not be the child or quasi-child of the testator, but the legatee must be an infant.[51]

This rule, unlike the previous one, applies to a legacy which is contingent upon an event having no reference to the legatee's infancy.[52]

4. Express direction as to payment of interest

22–20 It is preferable for the draftsman of a will to insert an express direction as to the date from which a general legacy to an infant is to carry interest, rather than leave these technical rules to apply.

C. RESIDUARY GIFTS

1. Immediate residuary gifts

22–21 A residuary bequest of personalty or residuary devise of realty[53] which takes effect immediately carries with it all the income or profits accruing from its subject- matter after the testator's death.

In examining the effects of contingent or deferred residuary gifts, it is necessary to consider residuary bequests and residuary devises separately, because s.175 of the Law of Property Act 1925 does not apply to residuary bequests.

2. Contingent or deferred residuary bequests

(a) *Contingent residuary bequests*

22–22 A residuary bequest of personalty which is contingent (but not otherwise deferred) carries intermediate income with it, provided the intermediate income is not otherwise disposed of by the will.[54] Thus, whilst the contingent event on which vesting depends remains undecided, any intermediate income not otherwise disposed of is either:

(i) dealt with in accordance with s.31 of the Trustee Act 1925 if there is a beneficiary living who is contingently entitled;[55] *or*
(ii) accumulated and added to capital.[56]

[51] *Raven v Waite* (1818) 1 Sw. 553.
[52] *Re Jones* [1932] 1 Ch.642 (the headnote is wrong).
[53] Rents accruing before death form part of the testator's personal estate, *Constable v Constable* (1879) 11 Ch.D. 681.
[54] *Green v Ekins* (1742) 2 Atk. 473; *Trevanion v Vivian* (1752) 2 Ves.Sen. 430 (gift of residuary personalty to A if he attains 21: held gift carried intermediate income which must be accumulated); *Bective v Hodgson* (1864) 10 H.L.C. 656.
[55] See above, para.22–07.
[56] For the statutory restrictions upon powers of accumulation which apply to wills made before 6 April 2010, see above fn.16. Where the restrictions apply, the intermediate income may be accumulated only for so long as the statutory rule permits—*Re Geering* [1964] Ch.136, 144.

(b) *Deferred residuary bequests*

By contrast, a residuary bequest of personalty which is deferred to a future date which must come sooner or later does not carry with it intermediate income arising between the testator's death and that date; if this intermediate income is not disposed of by the will, it goes as on the testator's intestacy. The rule applies to any deferred residuary bequest, whether it is vested[57] (e.g. a gift "to X after A's death"), vested subject to divesting[58] (e.g. a gift "to X after A's death, but if X dies before A to X's children equally"), or contingent[59] (e.g. "to X after A's death if X attains 30 years of age"). As Cross J put it in *Re Geering*,[60] "The very fact that a testator defers a gift to a future date is itself prima facie an indication that he does not intend the legatee to have the income of residue accruing before that date." **22–23**

3. Contingent or deferred residuary devises

Section 175 of the Law of Property Act 1925 (which applies to wills coming into operation after 1925)[61] provides that: **22–24**

> "a contingent residuary devise of freehold land, and a residuary devise of freehold land to trustees upon trust for persons whose interests are contingent or executory shall, subject to the statutory provisions relating to accumulations,[62] carry the intermediate income of that property from the death of the testator, except so far as such income, or any part thereof, may be otherwise expressly disposed of."

(a) *Contingent residuary devises*

A residuary devise of realty which is contingent (but not otherwise deferred) falls within s.175, whether made directly to the devisee or to trustees upon trust for a beneficiary whose interest is contingent. Thus a contingent residuary devise, like a contingent residuary bequest, carries intermediate income unless the income is otherwise expressly disposed of by the will. **22–25**

(b) *Deferred residuary devises*

Section 175 does not mention a deferred residuary devise but it does apply to a residuary devise to trustees upon trust for persons whose interests are "executory," and this appears to mean deferred.[63] **22–26**

[57] *Berry v Geen* [1938] A.C. 575; *Re Oliver* [1947] 2 All E.R. 162, 166.
[58] *Re Gillett's* W.T. [1950] Ch.102: cf. *Re Nash's* W.T. [1965] 1 W.L.R. 221.
[59] *Re Geering* [1964] Ch.136, not following *Re Drakeley's Estate* (1854) 19 Beav. 395 and *Re Lindo* (1888) 59 L.T. 462.
[60] *ibid* at 145. See also *Beard v Shadler* [2011] W.T.L.R. 1147.
[61] For the rules applicable to wills coming into operation before 1926 see *Hawkins on the Construction of Wills*, 5th edn (London: Sweet & Maxwell, 2000), pp.148–149.
[62] For the statutory restrictions upon powers of accumulation, which apply to wills made before 6 April 2010, see above fn.16.
[63] *Re McGeorge* [1963] Ch.544, 550–552.

There is a strong case for amending s.175 to make it accord with the likely intentions of a testator. It would also be helpful if the section codified the rules, stating in clear language which types of gift do, and which do not, carry intermediate income.[64]

[64] P. V. Baker, (1963) 79 L.Q.R. 184, 186–187.

CHAPTER 23

DISTRIBUTION OF THE ESTATE

In its narrower sense, the process of administration of the deceased's estate is complete when the personal representatives have realised the estate and paid, or made provision for the payment of, the expenses, debts, and liabilities of the deceased, and any inheritance tax payable in respect of his death. In its wider sense, administration embraces the culmination of this process—the distribution of the estate by the personal representatives to the persons entitled under the deceased's will or on intestacy.[1] These persons may be beneficially entitled to the distributed assets, or they may hold the distributed assets as trustees. **23–01**

A. DISTRIBUTION TO THE PERSONS ENTITLED

1. Time for distribution

Section 44 of the Administration of Estates Act 1925 provides that a personal representative is not bound to distribute the deceased's estate before the expiration of one year from the death.[2] By contrast, a personal representative has a duty to pay the deceased's debts with due diligence, which may require that payment should be made before the expiration of one year from the death.[3] **23–02**

Accordingly, a personal representative cannot be compelled to pay a legacy before the expiration of one year from the death, even though the testator directed the legacy to be paid within (say) six months after his death.[4] This rule may produce hardship if the legatee (e.g. the deceased's widow) is in immediate need of money. The court has power to make an interim order in favour of an applicant under the Inheritance (Provision

[1] See *Harvell v Foster* [1954] 2 Q.B. 367.

[2] Administration of Estates Act 1925 s.44 is expressed to be "subject to the foregoing provisions of this Act": this may refer to ss.36(10) and 43(2) of the Act, for which see below, para.23–46.

[3] See above, paras 21–12 et seq.

[4] See *Pearson v Pearson* (1802) 1 Sch. & Lef. 10, 12; *Brooke v Lewis* (1822) 6 Madd. 358. But the legacy carries interest from the time for payment fixed by the testator in his will, above, para.22–06.

for Family and Dependants) Act 1975 if the applicant is in immediate need of financial assistance.[5]

23–03 A personal representative is free to pay a legacy, or to distribute the residuary estate, before the expiration of the executor's year if he chooses[6]: and s.43(1) of the Administration of Estates Act 1925 empowers a personal representative to permit a person entitled to land to take possession of it (or receive the rents payable by tenants)[7] prior to an assent or transfer in his favour, without prejudicing the right of the personal representative to resume possession or to transfer the land.

On the other hand, a personal representative is not bound to distribute the deceased's estate at the expiration of one year from the death, for it may take longer to complete the administration.

2. Ascertaining the persons entitled

23–04 Personal representatives are under a duty to distribute to the persons properly entitled under the deceased's will or on intestacy.[8] If doubt arises as to the proper construction of the will, the personal representatives may apply to the court for this to be determined.[9] Again, it may be advisable to ask the court to conduct an inquiry to ascertain the beneficiaries.

(a) *Advertising for claims*

23–05 Under s.27 of the Trustee Act 1925[10] personal representatives may give notice of their intention to distribute and require any person interested to send in particulars of his claim to the personal representatives within a stated time, not being less than two months.[11] If the personal representatives satisfy these requirements, they may distribute to the persons entitled having regard only to the claims—whether formal or not—of which the personal representatives then have notice. In that event, the personal representatives are not, in respect of the distributed assets, "liable to any person of whose claim the personal representatives have not had notice at the time of distribution."[12]

23–06 There seems little reason to doubt that s.27 protects personal representatives against the claims of unknown beneficiaries, as well as against the claims of unknown creditors.[13]

[5] See above, paras 8–105 et seq.

[6] *Pearson v Pearson*, above; *Angerstein v Martin* (1823) 1 Turn. & R. 232, 241; *Re Palmer* [1916] 2 Ch.391, 398 and 401.

[7] Administration of Estates Act 1925 s.55(1)(xii).

[8] *Re Diplock* [1948] Ch.465, 503: *Re Hayes'* W.T. [1971] 1 W.L.R. 758, 765.

[9] See below paras 24–28 and 24–29.

[10] As amended by Law of Property (Amendment) Act 1926 ss.7 and 8(2) and Sch.1.

[11] See above, paras 21–15 et seq.

[12] Trustee Act 1925 s.27(2). *Re Aldhous* [1955] 1 W.L.R. 459: *Newton v Sherry* (1876) 1 C.P.D. 246; *Re Letherbrow* [1935] W.N. 34 and 48; *Re Ward* [1971] 1 W.L.R. 1376.

[13] See Law Reform Committee's 19th Report (*Interpretation of Wills*), Cmnd.5301 (1973), paras 51 and 65(8), which recommended s.27 should be amended to put this "beyond argument."

Section 27 does not prejudice the remedy of an unpaid beneficiary against a recipient of the deceased's assets. This is considered later.[14]

(b) *Leave of the court to distribute*

The court may make a "*Benjamin* Order" giving the personal representatives leave to distribute on a particular footing set out in the order, e.g. on the footing that a missing beneficiary under the testator's will predeceased the testator,[15] or that a son who died in the lifetime of the testatrix left no child who survived her.[16] The particular footing set out in the order is, of course, based on probable inferences from the proved facts, but the order does not constitute a positive declaration of rights[17] and, accordingly, it does not prevent any missing beneficiary (if he subsequently appears) from pursuing his remedy against a recipient of the deceased's assets.[18] Sometimes a *Benjamin* Order is made after an inquiry by the court has proved inconclusive,[19] but such an order may be made without any prior inquiry by the court if suitable advertisements for a missing beneficiary produce no claims,[20] or even without any advertisements if the inference from the proved facts is irresistible.[21] **23–07**

A *Benjamin* Order protects personal representatives, who distribute on the footing set out in the order. Unlike s.27 of the Trustee Act 1925, the protection is not conditional on the personal representatives having complied with statutory requirements as to advertising and making searches.[22] Before making a *Benjamin* Order the court itself decides what further advertisements—if any—ought to be made. Such an order is also advantageous to the known beneficiaries, or the next-of-kin, as the share of the missing beneficiary becomes distributable amongst them, subject to the (usually remote) possibility of the missing beneficiary appearing and recovering his share from them. **23–08**

[14] See below, paras 24–36 et seq.

[15] *Re Benjamin* [1902] 1 Ch.723 (P disappeared in September 1892; P's father died in June 1893 and by his will gave P a share of residue; despite inquiries and advertisements nothing heard of P: order that trustees be at liberty to distribute upon the footing P did not survive his father): see also *Re Taylor's Estate* [1969] 2 Ch.245; *Re Lowe's* W.T. [1973] 1 W.L.R. 882, 887; *Re Green's* W.T. [1985] 3 All E.R. 455.

[16] *Re Beattie*, unreported, see Mosse (1936) 81 L.J.News. 163.

[17] *Hansell v Spink* [1943] Ch.396, 399; *Re Green's W.T.*, above, at 462 ("The true view is that a *Re Benjamin* order does not vary or destroy beneficial interests. It merely enables trust property to be distributed in accordance with the practical probabilities ").

[18] See below, paras 24–36 et seq.

[19] As in *Re Benjamin*, above, (Master unable to certify whether P alive or dead, or, if dead, when he died); *Re Lowe's W.T.*, above.

[20] As in *Re Beattie*, above, (advertisements to ascertain if deceased son left any child); *Re Taylor's Estate*, above.

[21] As in *Re Green's W.T.*, above, (by her will T, who died in 1976, gave her estate to her son B; B had been a gunner in a bomber which went missing in a raid on Berlin in 1943; nothing ever heard of the bomber or its crew: irresistible inference crew perished, though T believed when she died that B was still alive).

[22] See above, paras 21–15 et seq.

(c) *Missing beneficiary insurance*

23–09 An alternative to a *Benjamin* Order is for the personal representatives to take out missing beneficiary insurance. In *Re Evans*[23] it was held that the premium was a proper and allowable expense of administration even though the policy was taken out to facilitate a distribution in favour of the personal representative. It was suggested[24] that personal representatives —particularly of small estates—should not be discouraged from seeking practical solutions to difficult administration problems without the expense of resort to the court.[25]

(d) *Adoption*

23–10 The duty of personal representatives to distribute to the persons properly entitled is modified by statute in cases where an adoption could affect entitlement. A personal representative is not under a duty to enquire whether any adoption has been effected or revoked before he distributes any property, even though that fact could affect entitlement to the property.[26] The personal representative is not liable if he distributes the property without regard to that fact if he has not received notice of it before the distribution; this protection of the personal representatives does not prejudice the remedy of the true beneficiary against a recipient of the deceased's assets.[27]

3. Beneficiary owes money to the estate

23–11 Suppose that B—as a beneficiary under T's will or intestacy—is entitled to money from T's estate; and B also owes money to T's estate. In this situation B is not permitted to take any money out of the estate until he has made good the money which he owes to it.[28] Accordingly, T's personal representatives have the right to apply any money due to B as a beneficiary in satisfaction of any money due from B to the estate.[29]

(a) *Money payable to B*

23–12 This right of "retainer" can be exercised by T's personal representatives only if B is entitled to a sum of money from T's estate. It cannot be exercised

[23] *Re Evans* [1999] 2 All E.R. 777.

[24] By Richard McCombe QC, sitting as a Deputy Judge of the High Court.

[25] Missing beneficiary insurance may be both cheaper and more effective than a *Benjamin* Order.

[26] Adoption and Children Act 2002 s.72(1): see also Legitimacy Act 1976 s.7(1)—no duty to enquire whether any person is illegitimate or has been adopted by one of his natural parents, and could be legitimated (or if deceased be treated as legitimated).

[27] Adoption and Children Act 2002 s.72(2) and (3); Legitimacy Act 1976 ss.7(2) and (3). For the remedy against a recipient see below, paras 24–36 et seq.

[28] *Re Rhodesia Goldfields Ltd* [1909] 1 Ch.239, 247 ("the rule is of general application that where a fund is being distributed, a party cannot take anything out of the fund until he has made good what he owes to the fund"). See generally B. S. Ker (1954) 18 Conv.(N.S.) 176.

[29] *Re Melton* [1918] 1 Ch.37: *Turner v Turner* [1911] 1 Ch.716.

if B is entitled to a specific legacy of something other than money, such as government stock.[30]

(b) *Money payable by B*

23–13 The other requirement is that B owes money[31] to T's estate. If the debt owed by B is payable by instalments, the personal representatives may retain any instalments already due, but they are not entitled to retain future instalments not yet due out of a legacy presently payable.[32] This requirement is also not satisfied if the debt due to T's estate is owed by B and another person jointly.[33]

The right of retainer is exercisable against the beneficiary B in respect of money which B owes to T's estate, but not in respect of money which anyone else owes to T's estate. It follows that if T by his will makes a gift to his children living at his death, and provides that the children of any deceased child shall take "such share as their parent would have taken if living", T's personal representatives cannot retain a debt due to T's estate from a deceased child out of the share payable to that child's children.[34]

(c) *Effect of limitation or bankruptcy*

23–14 If T's personal representatives could have recovered from B all the money due from him to T's estate, this right of retainer merely saves them the bother of obtaining and enforcing judgment against B. But the right of retainer is also exercisable:

(i) where the debt due from B was statute-barred at T's death[35]; or
(ii) where B goes bankrupt after he has become entitled as a beneficiary under T's will or intestacy to money from T's estate.[36] But if T's personal representatives prove in B's bankruptcy for the money due from B, they cannot then exercise the right of retainer.[37] Moreover, if B was an undischarged bankrupt when he became entitled as a beneficiary, T's personal representatives

[30] *Re Savage* [1918] 2 Ch.146 (specific legacy of colonial stock: rule not applicable—"you must have money payable against money payable"); *Re Taylor* [1894] 1 Ch.671 (specific legacy of profits of business to B: held executors had right to retain profits as against debt due from B to T's estate): cf. *Re Eiser's* W.T. [1937] 1 All E.R. 244 (executors need not retain income payable under discretionary trust).

[31] It suffices if B is liable in damages to T's estate, *Re Jewell's Settlement* [1919] 2 Ch.161, 173–177 (damages equal to surrender value of lapsed insurance policy).

[32] *Re Abrahams* [1908] 2 Ch.69.

[33] *Turner v Turner* [1911] 1 Ch.716 (debt due to T's estate from two partners jointly: held executors not entitled to retain legacy given to one partner); *Re Pennington and Owen Ltd* [1925] Ch.825.

[34] *Re Binns* [1929] 1 Ch.677; but it is different in the case of an advancement to T's deceased child because an advancement is a payment on account of that child's share, at 682–685; and see *Re Bruce* [1908] 2 Ch.682.

[35] *Courtenay v Williams* (1844) 3 Hare 539, affirmed (1846) 15 L.J.Ch.204 (debt still exists though remedy by claim barred); *Re Akerman* [1891] 3 Ch.212.

[36] *Re Watson* [1896] 1 Ch.925; *Re Melton* [1918] 1 Ch.37; *Re Lennard* [1934] Ch.235.

[37] *Stammers v Elliott* (1868) 3 Ch.App. 195.

may prove in B's bankruptcy, but they cannot exercise the right of retainer because there was never a time when there were cross-obligations to pay in full.[38]

4. Beneficiary an infant

23–15 As a general rule, a minor (i.e. a person who is under 18 years of age)[39] cannot give a valid receipt for money or securities to which he is entitled as a beneficiary under a will[40] or on intestacy, and neither can his parents,[41] guardian,[42] or adult spouse on his behalf.

(a) *Receipt by married infant for income*

23–16 Under s.21 of the Law of Property Act 1925 a married infant[43] has power to give valid receipts for all income—including accumulated income, but not capital—to which the infant is entitled.[44]

(b) *Provision in will*

23–17 The testator may by his will authorise payment of a legacy or share of residue to an infant beneficiary at a fixed age or on marriage, or direct that the receipt of an infant beneficiary who has attained a fixed age or married shall be a good discharge.[45] Another common provision is to authorise payment to the parents or guardians of an infant beneficiary. Under such provisions personal representatives have a discretion (which they may surrender to the court) to decide whether in all the circumstances payment would be for the infant's benefit.[46]

(c) *Appointment of trustees*

23–18 Instead of making a gift by will direct to an infant, a testator may (and often does) make the gift to one or more trustees upon trust for the infant[47]; in

[38] *Cherry v Boultbee* (1839) 4 My. & Cr. 442 ("there never was a time at which the same person was entitled to receive the legacy and liable to pay the entire debt"); *Re Hodgson* (1878) 9 Ch.D. 673.

[39] Family Law Reform Act 1969 ss.1(1) and (2). See *Re Hellmann's Will* (1866) L.R. 2 Eq. 363 (legacy may be paid when infant comes of age according to the law of his domicile or the law of the testator's domicile, whichever first happens) and *Re Schnapper* [1928] Ch.420; and see Dicey, Morris & Collins, *The Conflict of Laws*, 15th edn (London: Sweet & Maxwell, 2012), paras 27–023 et seq.

[40] *Harvell v Foster* [1954] 2 Q.B. 367, 377, 383.

[41] *Dagley v Tolferry* (1715) 1 P.Wms. 285 (£100 legacy to B, an infant, paid to B's father: executor held liable to pay legacy again to B's trustee in bankruptcy); *Rotheram v Fanshaw* (1748) 3 Atk. 628, 629.

[42] *Re Cresswell* (1881) 45 L.T. 468.

[43] i.e. an infant who is over the age of 16 but under the age of 18.

[44] See Trustee Act 1925 s.31(2)(i).

[45] *Re Somech* [1957] Ch.165.

[46] *Re Somech* [1957] Ch.165.

[47] In practice, a personal representative may also be a trustee and/or may be appointed testamentary guardian of the testator's infant children: see specimen will paras 9–01 et seq.

that case the receipt of the trustees is a good discharge to the personal representatives.[48]

Under s.42(1) of the Administration of Estates Act 1925 the personal representatives have power to appoint a trust corporation, or two or more individuals not exceeding four (whether or not including one or more of the personal representatives) to be the trustee or trustees of the property for the infant, provided that the infant is absolutely entitled under the will or on intestacy to a devise, or a legacy, or to the residue of the estate or any share therein. If, pursuant to s.42(1), personal representatives duly appoint trustees and vest the infant's property in them, the personal representatives, as such, are discharged from all further liability in respect of that property.[49] Henceforth each of the personal representatives is liable, as a trustee, only if he has been appointed one of the trustees of the infant's property.

(d) *Maintenance and advancement*

Personal representatives may make payments of income or capital for the benefit of an infant pursuant to any express power contained in the testator's will, the statutory powers of maintenance and advancement,[50] or any order made by the court.[51] **23–19**

(e) *Payment into court*

Personal representatives may pay money or securities to which an infant is entitled into court; the receipt or certificate of the proper officer is a sufficient discharge to the personal representatives.[52] But since 1925 payment into court is seldom necessary because personal representatives now have a wide power of appropriation under s.41 of the Administration of Estates Act 1925. **23–20**

B. APPROPRIATION

A personal representative has a wide power of appropriation under s.41 of the Administration of Estates Act 1925. The section applies whenever the deceased died.[53] If a personal representative exercises this power, two main consequences follow: **23–21**

[48] *Cooper v Thornton* (1790) 3 Bro.C.C. 96 (legacy of £100 given to X to be divided between himself and his family: held X took the legacy as trustee and payment to X discharged the executor).

[49] Administration of Estates Act 1925 s.42(1); see *Harvell v Foster* [1954] 2 Q.B. 367, 384 and below, para.23–56.

[50] Trustee Act 1925 ss.31, 32, and 68(1)(17) (s.31 as amended by Family Law Reform Act 1969 s.1(3) and (4), Sch.1, Pt 1 and Sch.3 para.5(1)); Administration of Estates Act 1925 s.47(1)(ii).

[51] See generally *Snell's Equity*, 33rd edn (London: Sweet & Maxwell, 2015), paras 28–036 et seq.

[52] Trustee Act 1925 ss.63 and 68(1)(17).

[53] Administration of Estates Act 1925 s.41(9).

(i) henceforth the beneficiary's interest is in the appropriated assets: if they increase in value, he gets the benefit; if they diminish in value, he bears the loss[54]; and

(ii) the appropriation clears the other assets for distribution to the other beneficiaries.

1. Statutory power of appropriation

23–22 Section 41 applies whether the deceased died testate or intestate.[55] The personal representative may appropriate any part of the deceased's real or personal estate,[56] in its actual condition at the time of appropriation, in or towards satisfaction of any legacy or any other interest or share in the deceased's property, whether settled or not. An appropriation must not, however, affect prejudicially any specific devise or bequest.[57]

(a) *When consent required*

23–23 Whether the personal representative needs the consent of any person to the appropriation depends on which of the following three alternatives is applicable:

23–24 (i) If the appropriation is made for the benefit of a person absolutely and beneficially entitled in possession, the consent of that person is required.[58] If the beneficiary is an infant, the consent may be given on his behalf by his parents, guardian, or by the court.[59]

23–25 (ii) An appropriation may be made in or towards satisfaction of a settled legacy, share or interest, i.e. any legacy, share or interest to which a person is not absolutely entitled in possession at the date of appropriation.[60] This includes, for example, a contingent or deferred legacy.

If the appropriation is made in respect of any settled legacy, share or interest, the consent of either the trustee thereof, if any (not being the

[54] *Ballard v Marsden* (1880) 14 Ch.D. 374, 376; *Re Richardson* [1896] 1 Ch.512; *Re Marquess of Abergavenny's Estate Act Trusts* [1981] 1 W.L.R. 843, 846.

[55] s.41(9).

[56] Including property over which a testator exercises a general power of appointment, including the statutory power to dispose of entailed interests, s.41(9).

[57] s.41(1), proviso (i).

[58] s.41(1), proviso (ii). At common law executors may appropriate to one of themselves, *Re Richardson* [1896] 1 Ch.512, and an administrator may appropriate to himself, *Barclay v Owen* (1889) 60 L.T. 220.

[59] ss.41(1), proviso (ii) and (1A) and 55(1)(iv); if the beneficiary lacks capacity see s.41(1), provisos (ii) and (iv) as amended by Mental Capacity Act 2005. An infant surviving spouse or civil partner may require, or consent to, the appropriation of the matrimonial home comprised in an intestate's residuary estate, see Intestates' Estates Act 1952 Sch.2, para.6(2); if the surviving spouse or civil partner lacks capacity, see para.6(1).

[60] s.41(8). This includes an annuity; s.41(9) authorises the setting apart of a fund to answer an annuity by means of the income of that fund or otherwise–presumably an appropriation under s.41 with the annuitant's consent clears the other assets for distribution to the other beneficiaries: cf. the effect of an appropriation not made under s.41, above, para.9–21.

personal representative), or the person who may for the time being be entitled to the income, is required.[61] Again, the consent of an infant may be given on his behalf.[62]

(iii) No consent to the appropriation is required if, independently of the personal representative, there is no trustee of a settled legacy, share or interest, and no person of full age and capacity entitled to the income thereof. But in this case the appropriation must be of an investment authorised by law or by the deceased's will,[63] whereas under heads (i) and (ii) above this is not necessary.[64] **23–26**

(b) *Protection of non-consenting persons*

In making the appropriation, the personal representative must have regard to the rights of any person not yet born, or who cannot be found or ascertained, and of any other person whose consent is not required (e.g. a person entitled in remainder to a settled legacy).[65] An appropriation duly made binds all the persons interested in the deceased's property whose consent is not required.[66] **23–27**

(c) *Valuation*

An appropriation is made at the value of the appropriated assets as at the date of the appropriation, and not as at the deceased's death.[67] **23–28**

For the purpose of appropriation the personal representative may ascertain and fix the value of the respective parts of the deceased's estate (and of the deceased's liabilities) as he may think fit, and for this purpose the personal representative must employ a duly qualified valuer where this is necessary.[68]

2. Express power in will

Section 41 does not prejudice any other power of appropriation conferred by law[69] or by the deceased's will.[70] **23–29**

[61] s.41(1), proviso (ii).
[62] See above, fn.59.
[63] s.41(1), proviso (v).
[64] s.41(1), proviso (ii) and s.41(2); but if the beneficiary lacks capacity see s.41(1), proviso (iv).
[65] s.41(5).
[66] s.41(4). For the protection of a purchaser of land from a person to whom it has been appropriated see ss.41(7) and (8) and 55(1)(xix).
[67] *Re Charteris* [1917] 2 Ch.379, 386; *Re Collins* [1975] 1 W.L.R. 309 ("a rule of administration too well established to require further discussion").
[68] s.41(3): cf. *Re Bythway* (1911) 104 L.T. 411 (executrix not entitled to appropriate to herself unquoted company shares at her own valuation); *Kane v Radley-Kane* [1999] Ch.274.
[69] See Law of Property Act 1925 ss.28(3) and (4) (power to partition land held in undivided shares) and Administration of Estates Act 1925 s.39(1); Trustee Act 1925 s.15(b) (power to sever and apportion blended trust funds or property): as to the common law power of appropriation, see *Re Lepine* [1892] 1 Ch.210; *Re Beverley* [1901] 1 Ch.681.
[70] See the Statutory Will Forms 1925, Form 6.

3. The self-dealing rule

23–30 In *Kane v Radley-Kane*[71] K died intestate leaving a widow and three sons by a previous marriage. The widow, who was entitled to a statutory legacy of £125,000,[72] obtained letters of administration to the estate and she then obtained a valuation of some shares which K owned in a private company. The shares were valued at £50,000. The net value of K's other assets was a little over £40,000 and the widow therefore appropriated the shares to herself. Less than three years after K's death, the widow sold the shares for a little over £1,000,000. It was held that, in appropriating the shares to herself, the widow was effecting a transaction in which her duty and interest were in conflict. This was a breach of the self-dealing rule—the rule that a purchase by a trustee[73] of trust property is voidable at the option of a beneficiary. Her stepsons were, therefore, entitled to avoid the transaction. If a personal representative wishes to appropriate property to himself, in satisfaction of a pecuniary legacy, he should either obtain the sanction of the court or the consent of the other beneficiaries or potential beneficiaries.

C. ASSENTS

1. Right of beneficiary during administration

(a) *No equitable interest in unadministered assets*

23–31 As a general rule, a beneficiary under a will or on intestacy has no legal or equitable proprietary interest in the unadministered assets of the deceased's estate.[74] Whatever property comes to a personal representative by virtue of his office comes to him "in full ownership without distinction between legal and equitable interests. The whole property [is] his."[75] The personal representative holds this property for the purpose of carrying out the administration of the deceased's estate. Of course, equity imposes on him fiduciary duties (sometimes called "trusts"), e.g. to get in the estate, to preserve the assets, to deal properly with them, and to apply them in due course of administration for the benefit of creditors and beneficiaries.[76]

[71] *Kane v Radley-Kane* [1999] Ch.274.

[72] See Chap.2.

[73] For the self-dealing rule, see Hanbury and Martin, *Modern Equity*, 20th edn (London: Sweet & Maxwell, 2015), paras 22–008 et seq.—the rule was applied in this case by analogy.

[74] *Commissioner of Stamp Duties (Queensland) v Livingston* [1965] A.C. 694 (gift of share of all real and residuary personal estate: the judgment of the P.C. analyses the case law); *Lord Sudeley v Att.-Gen.* [1897] A.C. 11 (gift of share of residuary real and personal estate); *Dr. Barnardo's Homes National Incorporated Association v Commissioners for Special Purposes of the Income Tax Acts* [1921] 2 A.C. 1 (gift of residuary estate); *Eastbourne Mutual B.S. v Hastings Corporation* [1965] 1 W.L.R. 861 (interest as sole next-of-kin on intestacy).

[75] *Commissioner of Stamp Duties (Queensland) v Livingston*, above, at p.707.

[76] *ibid* at p.707: see also *Re Hayes'* W.T. [1971] 1 W.L.R. 758, 764–765 and *Raymond Saul & Co v Holden* [2009] Ch.313.

But equity does not treat the unadministered assets as if they constituted a trust fund held upon trust for the beneficiaries.

(b) *Beneficiary has a chose in action to ensure due administration*

The true status of a beneficiary under a will or on intestacy is that he has a chose in action to have the deceased's estate properly administered.[77] He may, for instance, bring a claim to have the estate administered by the court, or for some other less sweeping remedy.[78] His remedies are considered in Chapter 25. **23–32**

This chose in action is transmissible by the beneficiary. In *Re Leigh's Will Trusts*[79] T made a specific gift to B of "all shares which I hold and any other interest which I may have" in S Ltd. T had never had any shares or other interest in S Ltd., but, at the date both of her will and of her death, she was the sole administratrix and sole beneficiary of the unadministered estate of her husband, who had died intestate. His estate included some shares in, and a debt due from, S Ltd. Buckley J held that the specific gift to B was effective.

The obligations of the executors in administering the estate can be varied by a direction given by all the relevant legatees and such variations are frequently effected in order to save tax.[80] In *Crowden v Aldridge*[81] there was a dispute as to whether memoranda to benefit the deceased's housekeeper, which had been signed by all the legatees, were effective to vary the devolution of the estate. The memoranda stated that the signatories were "prepared to enter into a deed to formalise this gift". Some of the beneficiaries, having signed the memoranda, refused to execute the deed. It was held that the variation by the memoranda was effective because, although the exact juridical analysis of the transaction was obscure,[82] it operated in the same way as a unanimous direction to trustees by all the relevant beneficiaries under a trust. The case appears to decide that "beneficiaries under an unadministered estate have a much wider power to make informal gifts than other persons have."[83] **23–33**

(c) *Specific gift by will*

It has been said that a beneficiary entitled under a specific bequest or devise takes an equitable interest in the subject-matter of the gift at the **23–34**

[77] *ibid* at p.717. But see also *Crowden v Aldridge*, [1993] 1 W.L.R. 433, discussed below, in para.23–33.

[78] A pecuniary or residuary legatee (or a creditor) may follow and recover assets improperly abstracted from the estate, but he does so on behalf of the estate, so that the assets are restored to the estate for use in due course of administration; the remedy "asserts the estate's right of property, not the property right of creditor or legatee," *Commissioner of Stamp Duties (Queensland) v Livingston* at pp.713–714. For this remedy see below, para.24–47.

[79] *Re Leigh's Will Trusts* [1970] Ch.277: see P.V.B. (1970) 86 L.Q.R. 20.

[80] See above, paras 16–45 et seq.

[81] *Crowden v Aldridge* [1993] 1 W.L.R. 433.

[82] *Crowden v Aldridge* [1993] 1 W.L.R. 433, 439.

[83] See criticism by J.G.Ross Martyn in [1994] Conv. 446. The variation was not made by deed and the person in whose favour it was made (the housekeeper) had supplied no consideration.

death of the testator,[84] although the legal estate vests in the personal representative, who may, of course, resort to the property for payment of the deceased's expenses, debts and liabilities. But this exception appears to be of doubtful validity as it is not consistent with the principle stated in paragraph 23–31, above.

2. Assent in respect of pure personalty

(a) *Subject-matter of assent*

23–35 At common law an executor[85] (and probably an administrator with will annexed)[86] may assent in respect of any gift of pure personalty by will, whether the gift is specific, general, or residuary. It is said that an administrator cannot assent in respect of pure personalty which passes on intestacy, though there appears to be no authority for this.[87]

(b) *Form of assent*

23–36 At common law an assent is not required to be—and in practice seldom is—made in writing. It may be made expressly (e.g. by a few informal words spoken by the executor),[88] or it may be implied from the conduct of the executor. Whether there has been an assent is generally a question of fact.[89]

(c) *Effect of assent*

23–37 An assent indicates that the executor does not require certain property for administration purposes and that the property may pass under the testator's will. The assent in effect activates the gift of the property by the testator's will.[90] If the property is given by the will to the executor himself, either beneficially or as trustee, after he has assented to the gift the property is vested in him as beneficiary or trustee (as the case may be), and not as personal representative.

23–38 In the case of a specific legacy—but not of a general legacy or of a residuary bequest—three other consequences follow from an assent:

[84] *I.R.C. v Hawley* [1928] 1 K.B. 578, 583; *Re Neeld* [1962] Ch.643, 687–688 and 691: see also *Williams v Holland* [1965] 1 W.L.R. 739, 743–744; *Re K* [1986] Ch.180, 188.

[85] An assent by one executor binds the other executors, even where the bequest is to himself, *Townson v Tickell* (1819) 3 B. & Ald. 31, 40; see above, paras 20–54 et seq.

[86] See Williams, *Law Relating to Assents* (London: Butterworth & Co, 1947), p.96 citing *Gundry v Brown* (1678) Rep. temp. Finch 370.

[87] See Williams, *Law Relating to Assents* (London: Butterworth & Co, 1947), pp.4 and 122–123; cf. Garner (1964) 28 Conv.(N.S.) 298 and 300–301.

[88] *Doe d. Sturges v Tatchell* (1832) 3 B. & Ad. 675; *Barnard v Pumfrett* (1841) 5 My. & Cr. 63, 70.

[89] *I.R.C. v Smith* [1930] 1 K.B. 713 (an outstanding mortgage does not necessarily prevent inference of an assent to a residuary gift): an assent to a gift of a life interest operates as an assent to the gift in remainder (and vice versa), *Stevenson v Mayor of Liverpool* (1874) L.R. 10 Q.B. 81. See also *Attenborough v Solomon* [1913] A.C. 76; *Wise v Whitburn* [1924] 1 Ch.460 and Williams, *Law Relating to Assents* (London: Butterworth & Co, 1947), pp.102 et seq.

[90] *Attenborough v Solomon* [1913] A.C. 76, per Lord Haldane at p.82.

(i) The legatee may bring a claim at common law to recover possession of the subject-matter of the legacy from the executor[91] or a third party.[92] A beneficiary cannot enforce his claim to a general legacy,[93] or a share of residue, or his rights on intestacy,[94] by a claim at common law. But even in the case of a specific legacy, the *legal* title to the subject-matter may not be capable of assignment by an assent. For instance, company shares are only transferable in the manner provided by the articles of the company,[95] i.e. by entering the name of the transferee in the register of members of the company.[96] After an executor has assented to a specific legacy of company shares, he holds the shares as trustee for the legatee until the legal title is duly transferred to the legatee;[97]

(ii) The legatee becomes entitled to the income or profits accruing from its subject-matter since the testator's death;[98]

(iii) The costs of transferring its subject-matter to the legatee must be borne by the legatee,[99] unless the testator directs that the costs of transferring the subject-matter of a specific legacy shall be paid out of his residuary estate.[100]

3. Assent in respect of land

Section 36(1) of the Administration of Estates Act 1925 confers power on a personal representative to "assent to the vesting, in any person who (whether by devise, bequest, devolution, appropriation or otherwise) may be entitled thereto, either beneficially or as a trustee or personal representative, of any estate or interest" in land, whether freehold or leasehold.[101] **23–39**

This statutory power to assent in respect of land may be exercised by any personal representative,[102] because the reference to an assent in

[91] *Doe d. Lord Saye and Sele v Guy* (1802) 3 East. 120; *Re Culverhouse* [1896] 2 Ch.251; *Re West* [1909] 2 Ch.180, 185.

[92] *Stevenson v Mayor of Liverpool* (1874) L.R. 10 Q.B. 81; *Re West* [1909] 2 Ch.180; *Re Clough-Taylor* [2003] W.T.L.R. 15.

[93] *Deeks v Strutt* (1794) 5 T.R. 690.

[94] *Jones v Tanner* (1827) 7 B. & C. 542.

[95] Companies Act 2006 s.544.

[96] See also Companies Act 2006 ss.770(1) and 773.

[97] *Re Grosvenor* [1916] 2 Ch.375, 378.

[98] *Re West* [1909] 2 Ch.180: see also *I.R.C. v Hawley* [1928] 1 K.B. 578 and cf. *Dr Barnardo's Homes National Incorporated Association v Commissioners for Special Purposes of the Income Tax Acts* [1921] 2 A.C. 1, 8, 11 (an assent to a residuary bequest does not relate back to death).

[99] *Re Grosvenor* [1916] 2 Ch.375 (assent to specific legacies of company shares: held costs of transfer to be borne by legatees); *Re Sivewright* [1922] W.N. 338: *Re Leech* [1923] 1 Ch.161. As to specific gifts of foreign assets see *Re Fitzpatrick* [1952] Ch.86 and authorities cited.

[100] Such a direction may extend to expenses incurred by the personal representative in the upkeep and preservation of the subject-matter of a specific legacy, see above, para.9–17.

[101] Administration of Estates Act 1925 s.55(1)(xix). An assent has to be registered if it relates to a freehold estate or a leasehold estate with more than seven years to run: Land Registration Act 2002 s.4.

[102] ibid s.55(1)(xi) provides that "personal representative" means the executor, original or by representation, or administrator for the time being of the deceased. All the personal representatives (still living) to whom a grant has been made in respect of the land must concur in an assent, ss.2(2) and 24, and see above, para.20–56.

favour of a person entitled by "devolution" covers the case of a beneficiary entitled under the intestacy rules. Again, an assent may be made in favour of a personal representative of a beneficiary who is entitled under the deceased's will or intestacy but who dies before distribution, or (alternatively) who predeceased the deceased but nevertheless takes under the deceased's will under an exception to the doctrine of lapse.[103] The reference to a person "otherwise" entitled apparently authorises an assent in favour of a purchaser, at any rate if the assent carries out a contract for sale made by the deceased in his lifetime.[104] It remains uncertain whether s.36(1) authorises an assent in favour of a purchaser from a beneficiary.[105]

(a) *Subject-matter of assent*

23–40 The statutory power to assent applies to any estate or interest in freehold or leasehold land "to which the testator or intestate was entitled and which devolved upon the personal representative."[106] The land devolving upon a personal representative includes land appointed by the deceased in his will under a general power of appointment, but not land which is conveyed to the personal representative after the death of the deceased, because the land did not devolve upon the personal representative.[107] In this case the personal representative should convey the land to the person entitled by deed.

(b) *Form of assent*

23–41 An assent to the vesting of an equitable interest in land is not required to be made in writing and may be made orally, or impliedly by his conduct.[108] Section 36(4) provides that:

> "An assent to the vesting of a legal estate shall be in writing, signed by the personal representative, and shall name the person in whose favour it is given and shall operate to vest in that person the legal estate to which it relates; and an assent not in writing or not in favour of a named person shall not be effectual to pass a legal estate."[109]

[103] See above, paras 14–21 et seq.

[104] *G.H.R. Co Ltd v I.R.C.* [1943] K.B. 303.

[105] See Williams, *Law Relating to Assents* (London: Butterworth & Co, 1947), pp.13 et seq.

[106] Administration of Estates Act 1925 s.36(1).

[107] *Re Stirrup's Contract* [1961] 1 W.L.R. 449 (assent under seal took effect as conveyance): but see Elphinstone (1961) 25 Conv.(N.S.) 490.

[108] *Re Edwards' W.T.* [1982] Ch.30, 40 (W owned Blackacre and died intestate, leaving H solely entitled; H obtained letters of administration and occupied Blackacre for 20 years until H died; no assent in writing by H in his own favour: held H had assented by his conduct to vesting of equitable interest in himself, so that it passed to H's executors).

[109] An assent has to be in a prescribed form: Land Registration Act 1925 s.41(4); Land Registration Rules 1925 r.170 and Sch.1, as amended by the Land Registration Rules 1996 and 1999. It is exempted from the requirement that a conveyance of a legal estate in land has to be by deed (Law of Property Act 1925 s.52). It is exempt from charge to stamp duty land tax: Finance Act 2003 Sch.3 para.3A.

In *Re King's Will Trusts*[110] Pennycuick J held that the same rule applies to an assent by a personal representative in favour of himself as it does to an assent in favour of another person. In that case T appointed A and B to be executors and trustees and made a specific devise of Blackacre to them upon trust. A and B obtained probate, A died, and B appointed X to be a trustee of the will. B then died, and B's executor, C, became executor by representation of T. X appointed Y to be a trustee of the will, and X then died. None of them—A, B or C—ever made any written assent to the vesting of the legal estate in Blackacre. Pennycuick J held that the legal estate in Blackacre was still vested in C as executor by representation of T, and he rejected the argument that, prior to the appointment of X, the legal estate had become vested in B in his capacity as trustee. **23–42**

Pennycuick J's construction of s.36(4) has been criticised on the ground that a legal estate does not "pass" if a personal representative merely assents in his own favour, so as to alter the capacity in which he holds the legal estate; accordingly it is argued that such an assent need not be in writing, but can be made orally or impliedly by conduct.[111] But Pennycuick J's construction seems to accord both with the wording and the object of s.36(4),[112] as a signed written assent by a personal representative in his own favour (whether beneficially, or as a trustee, or as a personal representative of another deceased) provides documentary evidence of the title to the legal estate.

The person in whose favour an assent (or conveyance) of a legal estate is made by a personal representative may (and should for his own protection) require that notice of it be written on, or endorsed on, or permanently annexed to, the probate or letters of administration at the cost of the deceased's estate; he may also require that the probate or letters of administration be produced to prove that this has been done.[113] This provision protects him against the possibility that the personal representative may execute another assent or conveyance in respect of the same property, before the first one is registered at H.M. Land Registry.[114]

(c) *Effect of assent*

An assent in respect of land is a form of conveyance.[115] Section 36(4) provides that an assent to the vesting of a legal estate in land shall operate to **23–43**

[110] *Re King's Will Trusts* [1964] Ch.542: see *Re Edward's W.T.*, above, at 33 and 40; *Beebe v Mason* (1980) 254 E.G. 987.

[111] For criticisms see Garner (1964) 28 Conv.(N.S.) 298; R. R. A. Walker (1964) 80 L.Q.R. 328. See also J. Farrand, *Contract and Conveyance*, 2nd edn (London: Sweet & Maxwell, 1973), pp.111 et seq. analysing the previous meagre case law. *Re King's Will Trusts* was *not* followed in the Irish case of *Mohan v Roche* [1991] 1 I.R. 560, which is noted by J.A. Dowling in [1992] Conv. 383.

[112] Ryder (1976) 29 C.L.P. 60 and 63.

[113] Administration of Estates Act 1925 s.36(5).

[114] Administration of Estates Act 1925 ss.36(6) and (7): see above, para.20–32. The question whether a personal representative can cease to hold property in that capacity and start to hold it in the capacity of trustee *without any assent or conveyance in his own favour* was considered in paras 24–60 et seq of the 12th edition of this book.

[115] See Law of Property Act 1925 s.52. The statutory covenants for title may be implied in an

vest the legal estate in the person named in whose favour it is given.[116] On the other hand, an assent in respect of pure personalty activates the gift of the property by the testator's will, so that the property passes under the will and not under the assent.

Section 36 regulates the effect of an assent in respect of land as follows:

(i) An assent relates back to the death of the deceased unless a contrary intention appears;[117]

(ii) Section 36(7) provides that an assent or conveyance by a personal representative in respect of a legal estate is, in favour of a purchaser for money or money's worth,[118] "sufficient evidence that the person in whose favour the assent or conveyance is given or made is the person entitled to have the legal estate conveyed to him and upon the proper trusts, if any." The purchaser is protected in this way unless notice of a previous assent or conveyance affecting that legal estate has been placed on or annexed to the probate or administration.

23–44 Probably the costs of an assent to the vesting of freehold or leasehold land in a specific devisee or legatee are payable as a testamentary expense, and do not have to be borne by the devisee or legatee.[119]

(d) *Protection of personal representative*

23–45 A personal representative has power to give an assent subject to any legal estate or charge by way of legal mortgage,[120] e.g. an assent in respect of the deceased's house subject to a mortgage or charge securing the deceased's debt to a lending institution.[121] As a condition of giving an assent or making a conveyance, a personal representative may require security for the discharge of any duties, debt, or liability to which the property is subject.[122] An instance is unpaid inheritance tax, payable in respect of the testator's death, to which his freehold house is subject under a direction in the will.[123] In order to protect himself the personal representative needs to insist on proper security being given for the discharge of this tax before he assents to the vesting of the house in the person entitled.[124] But an assent

assent, Administration of Estates Act 1925 s.36(3) and Law of Property Act 1925 s.76(1)(F) and Sch.2, Pt VI.

[116] See also s.36(2), which also applies to an assent to the vesting of an equitable interest.

[117] See also s.36(2), which also applies to an assent to the vesting of an equitable interest.

[118] Administration of Estates Act 1925 s.36(11): see above, para 20–29 fn. 91.

[119] Williams, *Law Relating to Assents* (London: Butterworth & Co, 1947), p.44. The costs involved in registering the beneficiary as the proprietor of the property at H.M. Land Registry should be borne by the beneficiary, unless the will provides otherwise. See Towns [1998] Conv. 380.

[120] Administration of Estates Act 1925 s.36(10): *Williams v Holland* [1965] 1 W.L.R. 739, 743–744.

[121] See Administration of Estates Act 1925 s.35 which is discussed above, paras 21–44 et seq.

[122] Administration of Estates Act 1925 s.36(10).

[123] See above, paras.21–55 et seq.

[124] cf. *Re Rosenthal* [1972] 1 W.L.R. 1273 (specific devise of house to S; house transferred to S

or conveyance by the personal representative does not, except in favour of a purchaser of a legal estate for money or money's worth, prejudice the right of the personal representative to be indemnified out of the property against any such duties, debt or liability.[125]

(e) *Compelling the personal representative to assent*

The personal representative is not entitled to postpone the giving of an assent merely by reason of the subsistence of any such duties, debt or liability if reasonable arrangements have been made for discharging them.[126] **23–46**

Under s.43(2) any person who, as against the personal representative, claims possession of land which devolved on the personal representative, or an assent or conveyance in respect of it, or to be registered as proprietor of it under the Land Registration Act 1925, may apply to the court for directions, and the court may make such vesting or other order as may be deemed proper. But such a person is not entitled to require the personal representative to execute an assent in his favour before the end of the executor's year.[127] Moreover, even after the executor's year has ended, the personal representative may still be justified in refusing to execute an assent, e.g. he may need to sell the property in order to apply the proceeds of sale in payment of the deceased's expenses, debts and liabilities,[128] or there may be doubt as to the construction of the gift of the property by the deceased's will.[129]

D. PERSONAL REPRESENTATIVE OR TRUSTEE?

1. Personal representative holds office for life

After a grant of representation has been made to him, a person holds the office of personal representative for the whole of his life,[130] unless the grant was of limited duration,[131] or he is subsequently removed from office.[132] Even though a personal representative has fully administered **23–47**

without any security for discharge of unpaid estate duty on it; S sold the house, went to live abroad, and failed to pay duty: held trustees not entitled to recoup duty falling on house out of residue, but must bear it themselves).

[125] Or, except in favour of a purchaser of a legal estate for money or money's worth, the right of the personal representative to recover the property, *ibid* ss.36(9) and (11): for the right to follow the property see s.38 and below, para.24–47. For the definition of purchaser see s.55(1) (xviii): see also *Re Lander* [1951] Ch.546, 551–552.

[126] Administration of Estates Act 1925 s.36(10).

[127] *Re Neeld* [1962] Ch.643, 688; cf. Administration of Estates Act 1925 s.44 which is expressed to be "subject to the foregoing provisions of this Act."

[128] See *Williams v Holland* [1965] 1 W.L.R. 739.

[129] *Re Neeld*, above, at 688–689.

[130] *Attenborough v Solomon* [1913] A.C. 76, 83; *Harvell v Foster* [1954] 2 Q.B. 367, 383.

[131] e.g. a grant of letters of administration (with the will annexed) for the use and benefit of a minor, who was appointed executor: the grant terminates when the minor attains 18 years of age or dies.

[132] See above, paras 19–44 et seq.

the deceased's estate, he retains the capacity to represent the estate in any future legal proceedings,[133] or to recover any assets which fall into the deceased's estate on the subsequent death of a testator, whose gift by will to the deceased takes effect under an exception to the doctrine of lapse.[134]

A personal representative continues to hold office as such, even though he no longer holds any property in that capacity.

2. Distinctions between personal representative and trustee

23–48 Broadly speaking, the function of a personal representative is to wind up a deceased's estate, whereas the function of a trustee is to hold property on trust. In spite of this basic difference in function, the office of personal representative resembles that of a trustee in many respects. The fiduciary duties of a personal representative are sometimes called "trusts."[135] The provisions of the Trustee Act 1925 and the Trustee Act 2000 apply to a personal representative where the context admits.[136] Moreover, as the Court of Appeal pointed out in *Harvell v Foster*:[137]

> "Part IV of the [Administration of Estates Act 1925], being the part devoted to the devolution of the estates of persons dying intestate and headed 'Distribution of Residuary Estate' is expressed throughout in terms of trusts."

In the case of a partial intestacy, s.49 of the Administration of Estates Act 1925 even provides that the personal representative "shall, subject to his rights and powers for the purposes of administration, be a trustee" for the persons entitled under the intestacy rules.

But the rules applicable to personal representatives do differ, sometimes significantly, from the rules applicable to trustees. These differences may make it essential to decide whether persons, who were both personal representatives and trustees, were at the relevant time holding the property in question in their capacity of personal representatives or of trustees. The following are instances where the rules differ:

(a) *Several authority of executors*

23–49 Joint executors, and perhaps joint administrators, have joint *and several* authority (subject to important exceptions), whereas trustees must always act jointly.[138]

[133] *Harvell v Foster*, above.

[134] See above, paras 14–21 et seq.

[135] *Commissioner of Stamp Duties (Queensland) v Livingston* [1965] A.C. 694, 707: see above, para.23–31.

[136] Trustee Act 1925 ss.68(1)(17) and 69(1); Trustee Act 2000 s.35.

[137] *Harnell v Foster* [1954] 2 Q.B. 367, 380.

[138] Trustees must act jointly *unless* the trust instrument provides otherwise, see above, para.20–58.

(b) *Receipt of sole personal representative*

A sole personal representative, acting as such, may give a valid receipt for, or direct the application of, the proceeds of sale of land.[139] A sole trustee may not do so, unless the sole trustee is a trust corporation.[140] **23–50**

(c) *Personal representative's duty is to the estate*

A trustee "has a duty to hold the balance evenly between the beneficiaries to whom the property belongs and for whom the trustee holds it."[141] On the other hand, a personal representative's duty during the administration of the deceased's estate is to consider the interest of the estate as a whole.[142] **23–51**

(d) *Death of sole representative*

If a sole (or last surviving) personal representative dies without having fully administered the deceased's estate, and there is no chain of representation through proving executors, a grant of administration *de bonis non* is made in respect of the deceased's unadministered estate, so as to enable the administration of the estate to be completed.[143] But if at his death the deceased held property as a sole (or last surviving) trustee, the property devolves on the trustee's personal representatives.[144] **23–52**

(e) *Limitation period applicable*

In general, the period of limitation in respect of any claim to the personal estate of a deceased,[145] or in respect of a claim to recover any land of a deceased,[146] whether under a will or intestacy, is twelve years, whereas the period of limitation for a claim by a beneficiary to recover trust property—or in respect of any breach of trust—is six years.[147] **23–53**

[139] Law of Property Act 1925 s.27(2) as amended by Law of Property (Amendment) Act 1926.
[140] Law of Property Act 1925 s.27(2) as amended by Law of Property (Amendment) Act 1926; Trustee Act 1925 s.14.
[141] *Re Hayes' W.T.* [1971] 1 W.L.R. 758, 764.
[142] *Re Hayes' W.T.* [1971] 1 W.L.R. 758. See also *Re Charteris* [1917] 2 Ch.379.
[143] See above, paras 18–36 et seq.
[144] See above, paras 20–02 et seq.
[145] Limitation Act 1980 s.22 (but the period of limitation for a claim to recover arrears of interest on a legacy is six years): no limit applies in case of fraud or property retained or converted to his own use by the personal representative, ss.21(1) and (2). For limitation see below, paras 24–13 et seq.
[146] Limitation Act 1980 ss.15(1) and (6) and Sch.1, para.2.
[147] Limitation Act 1980 s.21(3): but no limit applies in case of fraud, or of property retained or converted to his own use by the trustee, ss.21(1) and (2); an *executor de son tort* who converts property to his own use is, for this purpose, a constructive trustee and no limitation period applies to an action for the recovery of the property from him, *James v Williams* [2000] Ch.1.

(f) *Tax*

23–54 There are differences in the tax treatment of personal representatives and trustees—particularly in relation to the capital gains tax annual exempt amount. Personal representatives are entitled to a full annual exempt amount[148] for the tax year of the deceased's death and the two subsequent tax years,[149] whereas trustees are entitled to only half this amount for the duration of the trust.[150] Gains made by bare trustees count not as their gains but as gains made by the beneficiaries on whose behalf they hold the property.[151] *Cochrane's Executors v I.R.C.*[152] suggests that where there is a doubt as to whether disposals have been made by personal representatives acting as personal representatives, or acting as bare trustees, it will be held that the disposals have been made by them as personal representatives.

3. Transition from personal representative to trustee

23–55 Three different situations need consideration.

(a) *Personal representative not a trustee under the will*

23–56 In general, a personal representative does not become a trustee of property which T by a gift in his will (whether specific, general or residuary) gives to B absolutely, without creating any trust for B by his will. In that case it is the duty of the personal representative (acting as such) to distribute the property to B.[153]

If B, to whom T makes a direct gift by his will, is an infant, so that immediate distribution is impossible, it is the duty of the personal representative (acting as such) to retain the property in trust for B and to transfer it to B once he attains full age.[154]

Again, in general, a personal representative does not become a trustee of property which T by a gift in his will gives to other persons X and Y upon trust. In that case it is the duty of the personal representative (acting as such) to distribute the property to X and Y. The claim of the beneficiaries under the trust is against X and Y.[155]

148 £11,100 for the tax year 2015–16.

149 Taxation of Chargeable Gains Act 1992 s.3(7).

150 Taxation of Chargeable Gains Act 1992 s.3(8) and Sch.1.

151 Taxation of Chargeable Gains Act 1992 s.60.

152 *Cochrane's Executors v I.R.C.* (1974) 49 T.C. 299 (a Scottish case).

153 See *Re Richardson* [1920] 1 Ch.423 (gift of residuary estate to B); *Re Mackay* [1906] 1 Ch.25; *Re Barker* [1892] 2 Ch.491 (postponed legacy): and cf. *Re Oliver* [1927] 2 Ch.323. But an executor who has assented to a specific legacy of company shares holds the shares as trustee for the legatee until the legal title is duly transferred to the legatee, *Re Grosvenor* [1916] 2 Ch.375.

154 *Harvell v Foster* [1954] 2 Q.B. 367. See also *Re Davis* [1891] 3 Ch.119; *Re Mackay*, above.

155 *Re Oliver* [1927] 2 Ch.323, 330–331. For the effect of an assent to a specific legacy of company shares see above, fn.153.

(b) *Personal representative a trustee under the will*

A personal representative becomes a trustee of property under T's will because: 23–57

(i) a trust of the property is created by the will (often the trust is for beneficiaries taking successive interests in the property under the will)[156]; and

(ii) the personal representative is appointed to be a trustee of the property by the will or (alternatively) no effective appointment of any other trustee of the property is made by the will.[157]

When a personal representative assents in his own favour as trustee, he changes his capacity from personal representative to trustee.[158] The same principle applies where T by his will makes a specific gift of property on trust,[159] or a gift of a general legacy on trust.[160] As it is not certain whether a personal representative may start to hold property in the capacity of trustee without an assent or conveyance in his own favour, he should execute one.[161]

156 *Phillipo v Munnings* (1837) 2 My. & Cr. 309 (£400 legacy held on trust); *Re Swain* [1891] 3 Ch.233 (residue held on trust); *Re Timmis* [1902] 1 Ch.176; *Re Oliver* [1927] 2 Ch.323 (£2,000 legacy held on trust). See also *Re Claremont* [1923] 2 K.B. 718 (trust to sell residuary personalty and apply proceeds for benefit of T's two nieces): Law of Property Act 1925 s.34(3) as amended by T.L.A.T.A. 1996, (gift of land to tenants in common operates as gift to personal representatives, in trust for the persons interested).

157 *Re Cockburn's W.T.* [1957] Ch.438.

158 *Attenborough v Solomon* [1913] A.C. 76: see above, paras 20–58 and 23–36.

159 *Wise v Whitburn* [1924] 1 Ch.460 ("the effect of the assent was to strip the executors of their title as executors and to clothe them with a title as trustees"); *Dix v Burford* (1854) 19 Beav. 409.

160 *Phillipo v Munnings* (1837) 2 My. & Cr. 309: see also *Clegg v Rowland* (1866) L.R. 3 Eq. 368, 372–373; *O'Reilly v Walsh* (1872) 6 I.R.Eq. 555, 7 I.R.Eq. 167.

161 See Ryder (1976) 29 C.L.P. 60; Stebbings [1984] Conv. 423; *Re Cockburn's Will Trusts* [1957] Ch.438; *Re Ponder* [1921] 2 Ch.59; *Re Yeburgh* [1928] W.N. 208; *Eaton v Daines* [1894] W.N. 32; *Re Pitt* (1928) 44 T.L.R. 371; *Attenborough v Solomon* [1913] A.C. 76, 82–83; *Re Trollope's W.T.* [1927] 1 Ch.596; *Re King's W.T.* [1964] Ch.542; *Harvell v Foster* [1954] 2 Q.B. 367; *Toates v Toates* [1926] 2 K.B. 30; *Re Wilks* [1935] Ch.645.

Chapter 24

REMEDIES

A. LIABILITY OF PERSONAL REPRESENTATIVE

1. *Devastavit*

If a personal representative commits any breach of the duties of his office, causing a loss of assets, he is said to commit a *devastavit*, i.e. a wasting of the assets of the deceased's estate. A personal representative is personally liable to the deceased's creditors and beneficiaries for any loss caused by his *devastavit*. **24–01**

(a) *Nature of a devastavit*

Occasionally the duties of the office of personal representatives are termed "trusts"[1] and a breach of those duties is referred to as a "breach of trust."[2] The will of the testator may contain a gift of his residuary estate to his executors "upon trust" to carry out one or more of those duties, e.g. to pay the testator's expenses and debts. But it is sometimes important to distinguish between a *devastavit* and a breach of any trust created by the testator's will. For instance, a personal representative, by virtue of his office, has a duty to pay the deceased's debts with due diligence, having regard to the assets in his hands which are properly applicable for that purpose. This duty may be modified by the testator's will as against the beneficiaries, but not as against the creditors.[3] If the personal representative commits a breach of this duty, he is liable to the creditors for any loss suffered by them as a result of his *devastavit*, irrespective of his liability under any trust or power contained in the testator's will. **24–02**

The following are (non-exhaustive) instances of breaches by a personal representative of the duties of his office, which, if they cause loss to the deceased's creditors or beneficiaries, render the personal representative personally liable for a *devastavit*: **24–03**

[1] *Commissioner of Stamp Duties (Queensland) v Livingston* [1965] A.C. 694, 707.
[2] *Re Marsden* (1884) 26 Ch.D. 783.
[3] *Re Tankard* [1942] Ch.69, 72, 74: see above, paras 21–12 et seq.

(i) any breach by a personal representative of his duty to collect and get in the deceased's estate with reasonable diligence[4];
(ii) any breach of his duty to take reasonable care in preserving the deceased's estate[5];
(iii) any breach of his duty to deal properly with the assets of the deceased's estate, e.g. improperly converting the assets to his own use[6];
(iv) any breach of his duty to pay the debts of the deceased with due diligence[7];
(v) any breach of his duty to protect the estate against unenforceable claims, e.g. paying a debt which he need not pay[8];
(vi) any breach of his duty to administer the deceased's estate, if it is insolvent, in accordance with the statutory rules as to the payment of debts[9]; and
(vii) any breach of his duty to distribute the estate to the persons properly entitled under the deceased's will or intestacy.[10]

(b) *The Trustee Act 2000*

24–04 The Trustee Act 2000[11] introduces a statutory duty of care[12] which applies to trustees and to personal representatives.[13]

The statutory duty of care applies in the circumstances set out in the First Schedule to the Act and requires the trustee/personal representative to exercise such care and skill as is reasonable, having regard in particular to (a) any special knowledge or experience he has or holds himself out as having and (b) if he acts in the course of a business or profession, any special knowledge or experience it is reasonable to expect such a person to have. This new duty—which is not considered to be a statutory codification of the duty at common law[14]—can be excluded or modified.[15]

(c) *Devolution of personal representative's liability for a devastavit*

24–05 If a personal representative commits a *devastavit*—and dies—his liability for the *devastavit* devolves on his personal representative, to the extent of his available assets.[16]

[4] *Hayward v Kinsey* (1701) 12 Mod.Rep. 568, 573: see above, paras 20–12 et seq.
[5] See above, paras 20–18 et seq.
[6] *Marsden v Regan* [1954] 1 W.L.R. 423 (executrix gave away the deceased's furniture: held *a devastavit*).
[7] See above, paras 21–12 et seq.
[8] *Re Rownson* (1885) 29 Ch.D. 358, 363–364; *Midgley v Midgley* [1893] 3 Ch.282, 284, 299 and 304: for payment of statute-barred debts see above, paras 21–24 et seq.
[9] See above, paras 21–85 et seq.
[10] *Hilliard v Fulford* (1876) 4 Ch.D. 389: see above, paras 23–04 et seq.
[11] Which came into force on 1 February 2001; (SI 2001/49).
[12] Trustee Act 2000 s.1.
[13] Trustee Act 2000 s.35.
[14] See *Speight v Gaunt* (1883) 9 App. Cas. 1 for duty at common law.
[15] Sch.1, para.7.
[16] Administration of Estates Act 1925 s.29: s.29 also applies to an *executor de son tort* who commits a *devastavit*: see below, paras 24–51 et seq.

(d) *Effect of acquiescence in a devastavit*

If a creditor or beneficiary acquiesced in a *devastavit*, the personal representative is not, in general, liable to him. The same principle applies if a person acquiesced in a breach of trust.[17] The onus of proving acquiescence in the *devastavit* lies on the personal representative,[18] who must show that the creditor or beneficiary acquiesced in the *devastavit* with full knowledge of all the facts.[19] There is, however, no hard and fast rule that he must also have had knowledge of the legal consequences of those facts.[20] **24–06**

Acquiescence by one creditor or beneficiary does not affect the rights of any other person who has not acquiesced. If the personal representative is liable for his *devastavit* to any other person, then, under s.62 of the Trustee Act 1925,[21] the court may, in its discretion, impound all or any part of the interest of a beneficiary who has instigated, requested,[22] or consented in writing to the breach of duty by the personal representative,[23] by way of indemnity to the personal representative. The court does not impound the interest of a beneficiary under this section unless the beneficiary knew the facts which rendered what he was instigating, requesting, or consenting to in writing, a breach of duty by the personal representative, though the beneficiary need not know that those facts amounted in law to a breach of duty.[24]

2. Liability to account

A personal representative has a statutory duty to exhibit on oath a full inventory of the estate, and render an account of the administration of the estate, when required to do so by the court.[25] He must also keep clear and accurate accounts and permit the interested parties to inspect them free of charge.[26] By this means they may ascertain how the personal representative has carried out the administration. **24–07**

In equity, the liability of the personal representative to account does not merely provide the interested parties with information as to how the

[17] *Fletcher v Collis* [1905] 2 Ch.24: see generally Hanbury and Martin, *Modern Equity*, 20th edn (London: Sweet & Maxwell, 2015), paras 24–029 et seq.
[18] *Re Marsden* (1884) 26 Ch.D. 783, 790.
[19] *Re Marsden* (1884) 26 Ch.D. 783, 790
[20] *Holder v Holder* [1968] Ch.353, approving *Re Pauling's S.T. (No.1)* [1962] 1 W.L.R. 86, 108 (affirmed [1964] Ch303); *Re Freeston's Charity* [1978] 1 W.L.R. 741, 754–755.
[21] As amended by Married Women (Restraint upon Anticipation) Act 1949 s.1(4) and Sch.2.
[22] *Griffith v Hughes* [1892] 3 Ch.105 (the instigation or request may be oral).
[23] Trustee Act 1925 s.62 applies to a breach of the duties incident to the office of a personal representative, as well as to a breach of trust s.68(1)(17). Apart from s.62, equity has jurisdiction to impound the interest of a beneficiary who instigated a breach of trust, to the extent to which he benefited by the breach, *Raby v Ridehalgh* (1855) 7 De G.M. & G. 104.
[24] *Re Somerset* [1894] 1 Ch.231, 270 and 274.
[25] Administration of Estates Act 1925 s.25, as amended by Administration of Estates Act 1971 s.9: for applications for an inventory and an account see above, para.20–16.
[26] *Freeman v Fairlie* (1812) 3 Mer. 29, 43–44; *Ottley v Gilby* (1845) 8 Beav. 602 (legatee entitled to inspect, but not to a copy of the accounts at the expense of the estate); *Re Bosworth* (1889) 58 L.J.Ch.432.

personal representative has carried out the administration; it also provides a means of remedying many breaches of duty by a personal representative in the conduct of the administration. A personal representative may be ordered by the court to account in an administration claim or (alternatively) in a claim for specific relief.[27] A personal representative generally has to account for (a) his receipts and (b) his payments.

(a) *Accounting for receipts*

24–08 Under the form of order to account which is usually made against a personal representative—called an order for "a common account"—the personal representative must bring in an account showing the assets of the deceased's estate which he or his agent actually received. An executor, who owes a debt to the deceased's estate, is treated as having paid the debt to himself as executor, and he must therefore account for the amount of the debt as an asset of the estate which he received.[28] An administrator, who owes a debt to the deceased's estate, must account in the same way.[29]

Sometimes a personal representative is ordered by the court to account upon the footing of wilful default, i.e. to account, not only for assets which he or his agent actually received, but also for assets which he would have received but for his own wilful default. In this context wilful default means a breach of duty by the personal representative which caused a loss of assets.[30] The breach of duty may constitute a *devastavit*[31] or a breach of trust.[32] Wilful default does not require conscious wrongdoing by the personal representative.[33]

24–09 The personal representative may be ordered to account upon the footing of wilful default in respect of the whole estate or (alternatively) in respect of a particular asset or transaction. In *Re Tebbs*[34] the executors of T's will sold T's land to a company pursuant to an option to purchase conferred on the company by the will. The sale was made four years after T's death at the probate value of the land, instead of at its (higher) current market value as required by the option. This was a breach of trust by the executors. A residuary beneficiary sought an order against the executors for an account to be taken upon the footing of wilful default in respect of T's whole estate. The court ordered an account upon the footing of wilful default in respect

[27] See below, paras 24–22 et seq.

[28] *Ingle v Richards (No.2)* (1860) 28 Beav. 366; *Re Bourne* [1906] 1 Ch.697; *Jenkins v Jenkins* [1928] 2 K.B. 501; *Commissioner of Stamp Duties v Bone* [1977] A.C. 511, 518.

[29] Administration of Estates Act 1925 s.21A (added by Limitation Amendment Act 1980 s.10): s.21A also applies to an executor by representation.

[30] *Iliffe v Trafford* [2002] W.T.L.R. 507.

[31] *Re Stevens* [1898] 1 Ch.162.

[32] *Re Tebbs* [1976] 1 W.L.R. 924: see also *Re Wrightson* [1908] 1 Ch.789, 799–800 (active breach of trust: no "roving inquiry" ordered to ascertain other breaches); *Bartlett v Barclays Bank Trust Co Ltd (No.2)* [1980] Ch.515, 546 (wilful default means a "passive" as distinct from an "active" breach of trust): but surely an "active" breach, as much as a "passive" breach, may give rise to a reasonable prima facie inference that other breaches have occurred.

[33] *Bartlett v Barclays Bank Trust Co Ltd (No.2)*, above: see J. E. Stannard [1979] Conv. 345; cf. J. A. Andrews (1981) 1 Legal Studies 303, 310–311 and 322.

[34] *Re Tebbs* [1976] 1 W.L.R. 924.

of this land, but ordered a common account in respect of the rest of T's estate. The court had jurisdiction to make an order for an account upon the footing of wilful default in respect of T's whole estate,[35] but Slade J said that the test to apply was to ask, "is the past conduct of the trustees such as to give rise to a reasonable prima facie inference that other breaches of trust[36] not yet known to the claimant or the court have occurred?"[37] The evidence before the court did not give rise to such a prima facie inference.

(b) *Accounting for payments*

The personal representative must discharge himself as regards the assets he received by showing that he dealt with them in due course of administration. For instance, he may show that he applied the assets in paying expenses and debts of the deceased which were properly payable by him, or that he distributed the assets pursuant to an order of the court. He can also discharge himself by showing that the assets were lost in some way for which he was not responsible.[38] But if the personal representative has made a wrongful application of the assets, this is disallowed when the court takes the account of his payments.[39] **24–10**

3. Liability for co-representative

Under s.30(1) of the Trustee Act 1925, a personal representative was chargeable only for money and securities received by him notwithstanding his signing any receipt for the sake of conformity, and was answerable and accountable only for his own acts, receipts, neglects, or defaults, and not for those of any other personal representative "unless the same happens through his own wilful default."[40] Although this provision has been repealed by the Trustee Act 2000,[41] it has always been the case in equity that a trustee is not vicariously liable for the acts of his co-trustees, but only for his own defaults[42]; and the same rule appears to apply to personal representatives.[43] **24–11**

The rule in equity is that an executor, X, is not vicariously liable for his co-executor, Y, if Y commits a *devastavit* or a breach of trust.[44] Nevertheless, **24–12**

35 *Sleight v Lawson* (1857) 3 K. & J. 292; *Re Youngs* (1885) 30 Ch.D. 421, 431–432.

36 Or *devastavits*: the test appears equally applicable whether the breaches of duty constitute breaches of trust or *devastavits*.

37 *Re Tebbs* [1976] 1 W.L.R. 924 at p.930. cf. *Re Wrightson*, above, and *Bartlett v Barclays Bank Trust Co Ltd.* [1980] Ch.515, above.

38 *Job v Job* (1877) 6 Ch.D. 562; see above, paras 20–18 et seq. As to loss of assets in the hands of an agent see above, paras 20–65 et seq.

39 *Re Stevens* [1898] 1 Ch.162, 169–170 and 172; *Re Stuart* (1896) 74 L.T. 546, 547.

40 s.30(1) applied to a personal representative, ss.68(1)(17) and 69(1).

41 Trustee Act 2000 Sch.2, para.24.

42 See *Townley v Sherborne* (1633) J Bridg 35 at 36–37, and see *Snell's Equity*, 33rd edn (London: Sweet & Maxwell, 2015), para.30–004.

43 *Re Brier* (1884) 26 Ch.D. 238, 243: cf. *Re Munton* [1927] 1 Ch.262, 274–275. As to the effect of an express indemnity clause see *Mucklow v Fuller* (1821) Jacob 198.

44 *Hargthorpe v Milforth* (1594) Cro.Eliz. 318; *Styles v Guy* (1849) 1 Mac. & G. 422, 429 *(devastavit); Williams v Nixon* (1840) 2 Beav. 472.

X is fully liable for his own *devastavit* or breach of trust. The following are instances of X's liability:

(i) X is liable for his own breach of "the duty of all executors to watch over, and, if necessary, to correct the conduct of each other."[45] Thus, in *Styles v Guy*,[46] X was held liable for a *devastavit* because he failed to compel his co-executor Y to pay a debt which was due from Y to the testator T; six years after T's death Y became bankrupt and the debt was lost;

(ii) X is liable for his own breach of the duty of executors to deal properly, and in the ordinary course of business, with the assets of the deceased's estate. To quote Lord Cottenham in *Terrell v Matthews*,[47] "If money be required for the payment of debts or legacies, one executor is safe in joining in the sale of stock or other property, and permitting another executor to receive the proceeds for that purpose; but if he joins in such sales when the money is not required, and he had not reasonable grounds for believing that it was so required, he is liable for the money so received by his co-executor."[48]

These rules of equity relating to the liability of an executor are also applicable to the liability of an administrator for his co-administrator.[49]

4. Defence of limitation

(a) *Claim by creditor*

24–13 A personal representative may plead the defence of limitation to a claim by any person in respect of a cause of action which accrued during the lifetime of the deceased, in just the same way as the deceased might have done if he were still alive.[50] Time continues to run against the claimant during the interval between the death and the grant of representation to the deceased's estate.[51] Moreover, time still continues to run if the claimant becomes the executor or administrator of his debtor.[52]

45 *Styles v Guy*, above, at 433.

46 *Styles v Guy* (1849) 1 Mac. & G. 422; see also *Booth v Booth* (1838) 1 Beav. 125 (liable as stood by, knowing co-trustee was committing a breach of trust); *Williams v Nixon* (1840) 2 Beav. 472; *Candler v Tillett* (1855) 22 Beav. 257.

47 *Terrell v Matthews* (1841) 1 Mac. & G. 433n., 434–435.

48 See also *Chambers v Minchin* (1802) 7 Ves. 186; *Shipbrook v Hinchinbrook* (1810) 16 Ves. 477; *Underwood v Stevens* (1816) 1 Mer. 712. *Re Gasquoine* [1894] 1 Ch.470: cf. *Lowe v Shields* [1902] 1 I.R. 320 and *Clough v Bond* (1838) 2 My. & Cr. 490.

49 *Lees v Sanderson* (1830) 4 Sim. 28; *Clough v Bond*, above, at 496–498.

50 In general, a personal representative may, if he thinks fit, pay a statute-barred debt of the deceased, see above, paras 21–24 et seq.

51 *Rhodes v Smethurst* (1838) 4 M. & W. 42, (1840) 6 M. & W. 351; *Boatwright v Boatwright* (1873) 17 Eq. 71.

52 *Bowring-Hanbury's Trustee v Bowring-Hanbury* [1943] Ch.104.

(i) Charge by will for payment of debt. Where T owes a simple contract debt to C, and T by his will charges a particular asset of his estate with the payment of this debt, C's claim against T's personal representative, if founded on the simple contract debt, is barred after six years from the date on which his cause of action accrued.[53] On the other hand, C's claim to enforce the charge (whether on real or personal property) is barred only after 12 years from the date when his right to receive the money accrued.[54] **24–14**

Since 1925 no distinction is made between realty and personalty in relation to liability for T's debts[55]; so, if T gives all his real and personal estate to his executors for the payment of his debts, this direction probably creates no charge capable of giving simple contract creditors the benefit of a 12 year period of limitation.[56] The result is probably the same if T creates an express trust for the benefit of his creditors.[57] **24–15**

(ii) *Devastavit*. If a personal representative commits a *devastavit* by distributing assets without providing for payment of a debt, the creditor's claim against the personal representative personally for the *devastavit* is barred after six years from the date of distribution.[58] The same period of limitation applies where the creditor claims an account against the personal representative so as to remedy his *devastavit*.[59] **24–16**

(b) *Claim by beneficiary*

(i) Pure personalty. Section 22 of the Limitation Act 1980 provides that, subject to ss.21(1)[60] and (2): **24–17**

"(a) no action in respect of any claim to the personal estate[61] of a deceased person or to any share or interest in any such estate (whether under a will or on intestacy) shall be brought after the expiration of twelve years from the date on which the right to receive the share or interest accrued," and

"(b) no action to recover arrears of interest in respect of any legacy, or damages in respect of such arrears, shall be brought after

[53] Limitation Act 1980 s.5; *Barnes v Glenton* [1899] 1 Q.B. 885. A claim founded on a specialty debt (i.e. a debt contracted by deed) is barred after 12 years, ibid s.8.

[54] ibid s.20(1).

[55] See above, para.21–32. For the pre-1925 position see *Scott v Jones* (1838) 4 Cl. & F. 382; *Freake v Cranefeldt* (1838) 3 My & Cr. 499. cf. a pre-1926 direction to pay debts out of realty, *Re Stephens* (1889) 43 Ch.D. 39; *Re Balls* [1909] 1 Ch.791; *Re Raggi* [1913] 2 Ch.206.

[56] See generally Williams, Mortimer and Sunnucks, *Executors, Administrators and Probate*, 20th edn (London: Sweet & Maxwell, 2015), paras 66–08 and 66–09.

[57] See *Scott v Jones*, above, at 397–398: but cf. Williams, Mortimer and Sunnucks, *Executors, Administrators and Probate*, 20th edn (London: Sweet & Maxwell, 2015), para.66–09.

[58] Limitation Act 1980 s.2: *Re Gale* (1883) 22 Ch.D. 820; *Lacons v Warmoll* [1907] 2 K.B. 350; *Re Blow* [1914] 1 Ch.233.

[59] Limitation Act 1980 s.23: see *Re Blow*, above; *Re Lewis* [1939] Ch.232: the defence of limitation must be raised before the court directs the account to be taken, *Re Williams* [1916] 2 Ch.38.

[60] *Re Loftus* [2006] 1 W.L.R. 591.

[61] Personal estate excluding the deceased's leaseholds, Limitation Act 1980 s.38(1).

the expiration of six years from the date on which the interest became due."

The Court of Appeal has expressed the view that the limitation period runs not from the end of the executor's year but from the time when the personal representative is first in a position to distribute the residuary estate, i.e. when he has paid the costs, funeral and testamentary and administration expenses, debts and other liabilities properly payable, and provided for the payment of any pecuniary legacies.[62] In the case of a residuary legatee under a will, or a beneficiary entitled on intestacy, if an asset falls into the deceased's estate many years after his death, the 12 years' limitation period in respect of that asset runs from the date on which it came into the personal representative's hands.[63]

24–18 **(ii) Land.** A claim by a beneficiary to recover any land is barred after the expiration of 12 years from the date on which his right of action accrued.[64]

24–19 **(iii) No limitation period applicable.** Under s.21(1) of the Limitation Act 1980[65] no period of limitation applies to a claim by a beneficiary:

(a) in respect of any fraud,[66] or fraudulent breach of trust, or fraudulent breach of the duties incident to the office of a personal representative, to which the personal representative was a party or privy; or
(b) to recover from the personal representative property or the proceeds thereof in his possession, or previously received by him and converted to his use.[67]

If either of these exceptions is applicable, the equitable doctrine of *laches*[68] may be available as a defence for the personal representative.[69]

[62] *Re Loftus* [2006] 1 W.L.R. 591, disagreeing with Lawrence Collins J. See also *Evans v Westcombe* [1999] 2 All E.R. 777. The Court of Appeal also decided that an application to remove a personal representative was subject to the same rule.
[63] *Re Johnson* (1884) 29 Ch.D. 964 (next-of-kin entitled on intestacy held not barred in respect of reversionary interest which fell into deceased's estate within limitation period before action); *Adams v Barry* (1845) 2 Coll. 285 (residuary legatee).
[64] Limitation Act 1980 s.15(1): see ibid. s.15(6) and Sch.1, para.2. For this purpose land includes any legal estate or equitable interest in land: ibid. s.38(1); see also s.18(1). But there is no adverse possession among beneficial co-owners, Limitation Act 1980 Sch.1, para.9; *Earnshaw v Hartley* [2000] Ch.155.
[65] For definition of "trust" and "trustee" see Limitation Act 1980 s.38(1) and Trustee Act 1925 s.68(1)(17).
[66] *Re Sale Hotel and Botanical Gardens Co Ltd* (1897) 77 L.T. 681 (moral fraud not required), reversed on another point, (1898) 78 L.T. 368: cf. *Collings v Wade* [1896] 1 Ir.R. 340 (fraud must amount to dishonesty).
[67] *Re Howlett* [1949] Ch.768; *James v Williams* [2000] Ch.1 (*executor de son tort* held on the facts to be a constructive trustee, so no limitation period applied) c.f. *Paragon Finance Plc v D B Thakerar & Co* [1999] 1 All E.R. 400 (not cited in *James v Williams*); *Re Loftus* [2007] 1 W.L.R. 591. See also *Earnshaw v Hartley* [2000] Ch.155 (no adverse possession among beneficial co-owners).
[68] Limitation Act 1980 s.36(2); for *laches* see *Lindsay Petroleum Oil Co v Hurd* (1874) L.R. 5 P.C. 221, 239–240.
[69] *Re Loftus* [2006] 1 W.L.R. 591 (defence failed on the facts.)

(c) *Extension of limitation period*

The disability of the claimant,[70] or fraud, concealment, or mistake[71] may extend or postpone the period of limitation. Again, if a personal representative acknowledges[72] the claim of a creditor to recover any debt or other liquidated money claim, or the claim of a beneficiary to the deceased's personal estate or any share or interest therein, the claimant's right of action is deemed to have accrued on the date of the acknowledgment.[73] In order to be effective, an acknowledgment must be made in signed writing by the personal representative (or his agent) to the claimant (or his agent).[74] Similarly, if a personal representative (or his agent) makes any payment to the claimant (or his agent) in respect of such a claim, the claimant's right of action is deemed to have accrued on the date of the payment.[75] An acknowledgment of, or payment in respect of, any claim to the deceased's personal estate or any share or interest therein by one of several personal representatives is binding on the deceased's estate.[76] Any acknowledgment, or payment, makes the relevant period of limitation start to run afresh but cannot revive any right of action already barred by limitation.[77] **24–20**

5. Power of court to grant relief from liability

Under s.61 of the Trustee Act 1925,[78] the court has power, in its discretion,[79] to relieve a personal representative either wholly or partly from personal liability for any breach of trust,[80] or any breach of the duties incident to the office of a personal representative, if it appears to the court that the personal representative: **24–21**

(i) "has acted honestly and reasonably," and

[70] Limitation Act 1980 ss.28, 38 (infancy or unsoundness of mind).

[71] Limitation Act 1980 s.32. For a recent example of a case where limitation period was extended because of undiscovered mistake, see *Fea v Roberts* [2006] W.T.L.R. 255 (executor paid wrong beneficiary).

[72] The personal representative must acknowledge an existing liability, *Re Flynn (No.2)* [1969] 2 Ch.403; *Bowring-Hanbury's Trustee v Bowring-Hanbury* [1943] Ch.104. For an acknowledgment in a will see *Howard v Hennessey* [1947] Ir.R. 337.

[73] Limitation Act 1980 ss.29(5) and 38(9). As to an acknowledgment of the title of the person entitled to a right of action to recover land, see ibid ss.29 and 31(1).

[74] ibid s.30: see *Bowring-Hanbury's Trustee v Bowring-Hanbury*, above.

[75] ibid ss.29(5), 30(2) and 38(9): as to payment of part of the interest due, see s.29(6).

[76] ibid s.31(8). As to an acknowledgment of, or payment in respect of, a debt by one of several personal representatives, see ss.31(6), (7) and (9): *Re Macdonald* [1897] 2 Ch.181 (on effect of Lord Tenterden's Act 1828 s.1, now repealed).

[77] ibid s.29(7).

[78] For definition of "trust" and "trustee" see Trustee Act 1925 s.68(1) (17): see *Re Kay* [1897] 2 Ch.518; *Marsden v Regan* [1954] 1 W.L.R. 423.

[79] *Marsden v Regan*, above, at 437. The fact that a person acts on the strength of legal advice is not an automatic "passport to relief" under s.61, but it affords strong evidence that he has acted honestly and reasonably and ought fairly to be excused.

[80] *Re Rosenthal* [1972] 1 W.L.R. 1273 (s.61 does not apply to breach of trust merely contemplated by trustees).

(ii) "ought fairly[81] to be excused for the breach and for omitting to obtain the directions of the court in the matter in which he committed such breach."

The onus of proving that he acted honestly and reasonably rests on the personal representative.[82] If this first requirement is made out, the court considers whether the personal representative ought fairly to be excused, looking at all the circumstances of the particular case.[83] One material circumstance is whether the personal representative is a trust company,[84] or a professional person,[85] undertaking the office in return for remuneration; if so, the court is less likely to grant relief to such a personal representative than to one who acts gratuitously.[86]

Each case depends on its own particular circumstances.[87]

B. ADMINISTRATION PROCEEDINGS

1. Nature of administration proceedings

24–22 Administration proceedings include:

(1) Claims for the administration of the whole or some part of the deceased's estate by the court;
(2) Claims for specific relief, such as the determination of a particular question arising in the administration of the deceased's estate.

There is no rigid dividing line between claims for administration and claims for specific relief. In a claim for administration the court may order specific relief instead: and the claimant in a claim for specific relief usually applies, in addition, for an order for the administration of the deceased's estate if and so far as this is necessary.

Administration proceedings are often non-contentious, in the sense that

[81] *Marsden v Regan*, above, at p.434 ("in fairness to the executor and to other people who may be affected").
[82] *Re Stuart* [1897] 2 Ch.583.
[83] *National Trustees Co of Australasia Ltd v General Finance Co of Australasia Ltd* [1905] A.C. 373, 381.
[84] *National Trustees Co of Australasia Ltd v General Finance Co of Australasia Ltd* [1905] A.C. 373, 381 (trust company made wrong distribution, on its solicitors' bad advice: P.C. refused relief); *Re Pauling's S.T.* [1964] Ch.303, esp. at pp.338–339.
[85] *Re Windsor Steam Coal Co* (1901) *Ltd* [1929] 1 Ch.151, 164–165.
[86] In *Re Evans* [1999] 2 All E.R. 777, the administratrix was granted relief to the extent that the claim could not be satisfied out of assets which remained in her hands.
[87] See *Re Kay* [1897] 2 Ch.518 (executor paid income to widow after creditor had begun proceedings to recover moneys owed to him by deceased, estate insolvent, executor refused relief); *Re Lord de Clifford's Estate* [1900] 2 Ch.707 (executors paid sums for administration purposes to their solicitors, who became bankrupt); *Re Roberts* (1897) 76 L.T. 479 (executor failed to get in debt due to testator's estate); *Re Grindey* [1898] 2 Ch.593; *Marsden v Regan* [1954] 1 W.L.R. 423. For a survey of the cases see L. A. Sheridan (1955) 19 Conv. (N.S.) 420.

they are commenced so as to obtain the guidance of the court on difficulties arising in the administration of the estate. A personal representative is always entitled to seek the guidance of the court in matters of difficulty.

2. Claims for administration

(a) *Jurisdiction over administration*

In the High Court a claim for the administration of the estate of a deceased person is assigned to the Chancery Division.[88] Such a claim must be begun by claim form issued out of Chancery Chambers[89]or one of the Chancery district registries.[90] **24–23**

The following also have jurisdiction over the administration of a deceased's estate:

(i) the county court, if the estate does not exceed £350,000 in amount or value[91];
(ii) the Public Trustee, if the estate is solvent, its gross capital value is less than £1,000, and the persons beneficially entitled are persons of small means[92]; and
(iii) the bankruptcy court, if the deceased died insolvent.[93]

This consideration of administration proceedings is concerned with proceedings in the Chancery Division.

(b) *Parties to an administration claim*

An administration claim may be commenced by the personal representatives, by a creditor of the deceased[94] (suing either on his own behalf,[95] or **24–24**

[88] Senior Courts Act 1981 s.61 and Sch.1, para.1.
[89] The offices of the Chancery Division at the Royal Courts of Justice, Strand, London.
[90] Birmingham, Bristol, Caernarfon, Cardiff, Leeds, Liverpool, Manchester, Mold, Newcastle-upon-Tyne and Preston: C.P.R. 57.3(a) and 57.1(2)(b)(i) and (ii).
[91] County Courts Act 1984 ss.23 and 147: County Courts Jurisdiction Order 2014 (SI 2014/503). Where the county court does have jurisdiction, the claim form can only be issued out of a county court in a place where there is also a Chancery district registry. Probate claims are rarely commenced or heard in the county court.
[92] Public Trustee Act 1906 ss.2(4) and 3(1); *Re Devereux* [1911] 2 Ch.545 (gross capital value at date of application to Public Trustee). As to transfer from the court to the Public Trustee, see Public Trustee Act 1906 s.3(5). For the powers of the Public Trustee see Public Trustee Rules 1912 (S.R. & O. 1912 No. 348) rr.14–15.
[93] Above, paras 21–69 et seq.: see *Re Bradley* [1956] Ch.615. No petition can be presented to the bankruptcy court after proceedings for administration have been commenced in another court, but that court may transfer the proceedings to the bankruptcy court if satisfied that the estate is insolvent, Insolvency Act 1986 s.271 as modified by Administration of Insolvent Estates of Deceased Persons Order 1986 (SI 1986/1999).
[94] *Re Hargreaves* (1890) 44 Ch.D. 236. A business creditor of a personal representative, entitled by subrogation to payment out of the deceased's assets, may obtain an administration order, *Re Shorey* (1898) 79 L.T. 349.
[95] *Re James* [1911] 2 Ch.348.

on behalf of himself and all other creditors), or by any beneficiary interested in the deceased's estate under his will or on intestacy.[96]

No order for the administration of the deceased's estate can be made until a personal representative has obtained a grant of representation to the estate,[97] and the personal representative (or each of them, if more than one) must be made a party to the claim. Any number of claimants or defendants may be joined as parties.[98] An order for administration cannot be made against an *executor de son tort*,[99] although he may be compelled to account for the assets of which he has taken possession.[100]

If no grant of representation has been made, a creditor[101] or beneficiary[102] may apply to the court for the appointment of a receiver of the deceased's estate (and, if necessary, a manager of his business), so as to preserve the assets until a grant of representation is made. But if a probate claim has already begun, it is usually preferable to apply for the appointment of an administrator pending its determination, who has the wider rights and powers of a general administrator, other than the right of distributing the residue of the estate after payment of the deceased's debts and expenses.[103]

(c) *Order for administration*

24–25 If the court makes an order for general administration, the personal representatives must not exercise their powers without first obtaining the sanction of the court.[104] An order for administration (but not the mere commencement of an administration claim) also stops time running under the Limitation Act against the claims of creditors of the deceased.[105]

The court is not bound to make an order for administration unless, in the opinion of the court, the questions at issue between the parties cannot properly be determined otherwise than under such an order. If the court does make an order for administration, and orders the whole administration to be carried out under the direction of the court, the costs incurred are likely to be considerable.[106]

Instead of ordering the whole administration to be carried out under the direction of the court, the court may make a limited order.[107]

[96] *Peacock v Colling* (1885) 54 L.J.Ch.743 (a beneficiary contingently entitled may bring administration claim): cf. *Clowes v Hilliard* (1876) 4 Ch.D. 413.
[97] *Rowsell v Morris* (1873) L.R. 17 Eq. 20; *Re Sutcliffe* [1942] Ch.453. A creditor may obtain an order for administration against an administrator *pendente lite, Re Toleman* [1897] 1 Ch.866.
[98] C.P.R. 19.1.
[99] *Rowsell v Morris*, above, (order for administration cannot be made against personal representative of *executor de son tort*): cf. *Re Lovett* (1876) 3 Ch.D. 198.
[100] *Coote v Whittington* (1873) L.R. 16 Eq. 534: see below, paras 24–51 et seq.
[101] *Re Sutcliffe* [1942] Ch.453.
[102] *Re Oakes* [1917] 1 Ch.230.
[103] See above, paras 18–48 et seq.
[104] See above, para.20–61.
[105] *Re Greaves* (1881) 18 Ch.D. 551.
[106] See Law Reform Committee's, 23rd Report, *The Powers and Duties of Trustees*, Cmnd.8733 (1982), p.56 ("an extremely clumsy, costly and time consuming procedure and in practice it is only in wholly exceptional cases that its use can be recommended").
[107] For example, the court may order such particular accounts or inquiries as are needed,

3. Appointment of a judicial trustee

On the application of a personal representative or beneficiary, the Chancery Division may, in its discretion, appoint a person to be a judicial trustee to complete the administration of the deceased's estate.[108] A judicial trustee may be appointed to act alone, or jointly with any other person, and, if sufficient cause is shown, in place of the existing personal representatives.[109] The appointment of a judicial trustee provides "a middle course"[110] in cases where the administration of the estate by the personal representatives out of court has broken down,[111] and it is not desired to put the estate to the expense of the whole administration being carried out under the direction of the court. A judicial trustee, as an officer of the court, "acts in close concert with the court and under conditions enabling the court to supervise his transactions,"[112] but, unlike the position of a personal representative after an order for general administration has been made, a judicial trustee may exercise his powers without first obtaining the sanction of the court.[113] 24–26

4. Appointment of a substitute for, or removal of, a personal representative

The Chancery Division also has power in its discretion: 24–27

(i) to appoint a substituted personal representative in place of all or any of the existing personal representatives of the deceased; or
(ii) if there are two or more existing personal representatives, to terminate the appointment of one or more (but not all) of them.[114]

The power is exercisable on an application relating to the deceased's estate by a personal representative of the deceased or a beneficiary under the deceased's will or on his intestacy.[115] This provides an alternative course

or otherwise determine the particular questions which arise in the administration. Or if the claimant—being a creditor or a beneficiary—alleges that no accounts, or insufficient accounts, have been furnished by the personal representatives, the court may order that proceedings in the claim be stayed for a specified period, and that in the meantime the personal representatives shall furnish the claimant with proper accounts.

108 Judicial Trustees Act 1896 ss.1 and 2 (as amended by Administration of Justice Act 1982 s.57); Judicial Trustee Rules 1983 (SI 1983/370).

109 Judicial Trustees Act 1896 ss.1 and 2 (as amended by Administration of Justice Act 1982 s.57); Judicial Trustee Rules 1983 (SI 1983/370); *Re Ratcliff* [1898] 2 Ch.352, 355–356. A judicial trustee cannot be appointed in respect of only part of the estate vested in executors, *Re Wells* [1968] 1 W.L.R. 44.

110 *Re Ridsdel* [1947] Ch.597, 605.

111 *Carvel Foundation v Carvel* [2007] 4 All E.R. 81.

112 *Carvel Foundation v Carvel* [2007] 4 All E.R. 81. See Judicial Trustees Act 1896 ss.1(3) and (4).

113 *Re Ridsdel* [1947] Ch.597.

114 Administration of Justice Act 1985 ss.50(1) and (2): see above, paras 17–07 et seq.

115 Administration of Justice Act 1985 ss.50(1) and (5). The section can operate where a named executor has *not* yet obtained probate, *Goodman v Goodman* [2014] Ch.186.

to the appointment of a judicial trustee[116] in cases where an exercise of the power is appropriate in order to secure the proper administration of the deceased's estate out of court.[117]

5. Claims for specific relief

24–28 Instead of bringing a claim for the administration of the deceased's estate by the court, a personal representative, creditor, or beneficiary may bring a claim for specific relief, i.e. for the determination of any question, or for any relief, which could be determined, or granted, in an administration claim.[118] Such a claim for specific relief should be begun by a Pt 8 claim form.[119] The personal representative (or each of them, if more than one) must be made a party.[120] Often the personal representative is the claimant, seeking the guidance of the court in particular matters of difficulty which arise in the course of the administration of the deceased's estate out of court. In such a claim the personal representative has a clear duty to lay before the court all the relevant facts which are within his knowledge.[121]

24–29 The following are examples[122] of the specific relief which may be sought in such a claim:

(i) The determination of any question arising in the administration of the deceased's estate;
(ii) The determination of any question as to the composition of any class of beneficiaries;
(iii) The determination of any question as to the rights or interest of a person claiming to be a creditor or entitled under the deceased's will or on intestacy, e.g. the question whether a specific gift has been adeemed, or from what date a particular general legacy carries interest;
(iv) An order requiring a personal representative to furnish and, if necessary, verify accounts;[123]
(v) An order directing a personal representative to do, or not to do, a particular act, e.g. directing whether he should carry on the deceased's business,[124] or whether he should take, or

[116] On an application under s.50 the court may appoint a judicial trustee, ibid. s.50(4), and on an application for a judicial trustee the court may exercise its powers under s.50, Judicial Trustees Act 1896 s.1(7) as amended by s.50(6).

[117] For recent cases on s.50 see *Re Steel, Angus v Emmott* [2010] W.T.L.R. 531; *Dobson v Heyman* [2010] W.T.L.R. 1151 and *Kershaw v Micklethwaite* [2011] W.T.L.R. 413.

[118] C.P.R. 64.2. The court's jurisdiction to construe a will, or control the administration of a deceased's estate, cannot be ousted by the terms of the will, *Re Wynn* [1952] Ch.271.

[119] C.P.R. 64.3.

[120] C.P.R. 64.4.

[121] *Re Herwin* [1953] Ch.701, 708–709 and 714–715.

[122] See Practice Direction to Pt 64 for further examples.

[123] A legatee is entitled to inspect the accounts at the expense of the estate, but he must normally pay any expenses incurred in furnishing him with a copy, *Ottley v Gilby* (1845) 8 Beav. 602; *Re Bosworth* (1889) 58 L.J.Ch.432: cf. *Re Skinner* [1904] 1 Ch.289 (executors' gross neglect to account).

[124] See above, paras 20–34 et seq.

defend, legal proceedings on behalf of the estate.[125] If, without the direction of the court, a personal representative takes, or defends, legal proceedings, he is not allowed his costs out of the estate unless the costs were properly incurred for the benefit of the estate.[126]

6. Costs in administration proceedings

A personal representative is generally entitled to the costs of administration proceedings (in so far as they are not recovered from, or paid by, any other person) out of the estate as a matter of course.[127] The court may only order otherwise on the ground that the personal representative has acted unreasonably, or has in substance acted for his own benefit rather than for the benefit of the estate. The costs of all other parties to administration proceedings are in the discretion of the court.[128] **24–30**

In the case of a Pt 8 claim for specific relief (e.g. to determine the proper construction of the testator's will), the costs of all parties[129] are normally allowed out of the estate where there is some difficulty which justifies the application to the court.[130]

C. DEFENCES OF PERSONAL REPRESENTATIVE TO CREDITOR'S CLAIM

Instead of commencing administration proceedings, a creditor of the deceased may bring a claim against the personal representative to recover a debt due from the deceased.[131] In general, the personal representative may plead any defence to the claim which would have been open to the deceased, and in addition the personal representative may plead certain special defences: **24–31**

1. Administration complete *(plene administravit)*

This defence is to the effect that the personal representative has fully administered all the assets of the deceased which have come to his hands. If the claimant creditor joins issue on this plea, the burden of proof lies on **24–32**

[125] For the practice where the proposed legal proceedings are against a beneficiary see *Re Mortiz* [1960] Ch.251; *Re Eaton* [1964] 1 W.L.R. 1269; and where the proposed defence is against an adverse claim to the entire estate, *Re Dallaway* [1982] 1 W.L.R. 756; *Re Evans* [1986] 1 W.L.R. 101.

[126] *Re Beddoe* [1893] 1 Ch.547; *Stott v Milne* (1884) 25 Ch.D. 710.

[127] C.P.R. 48.4(2).

[128] Senior Courts Act 1981 s.51(1).

[129] The costs of the personal representative on the indemnity basis (C.P.R.48.4(3)), and of other parties on the standard basis.

[130] *Re Buckton* [1907] 2 Ch.406: *D'Abo v Paget (No.2)* [2000] W.T.L.R. 863; cf. *Re Halston* [1912] 1 Ch.435 (adverse litigation).

[131] For causes of action against the deceased which survive against his estate, see above, paras 20–07 et seq.

him to show that the personal representative still has, or ought to have, assets in his hands.[132]

If the personal representative's defence of *plene administravit* succeeds, the claimant (assuming that he is otherwise successful in the claim) may obtain judgment only against future assets, i.e. against assets of the deceased coming to the personal representative's hands after the date of the judgment.[133] So far as the personal representative's defence of *plene administravit* fails, the claimant (on the same assumption) may obtain judgment against the personal representative as such for a sum equal to the amount of the unadministered assets proved against him, but as to any balance only against future assets.[134]

2. Administration complete except *(plene administravit praeter)*

24–33 This defence is to the effect that the personal representative has fully administered all the assets of the deceased which have come to his hands, except assets of a stated amount which he admits are still in his hands. If this defence succeeds, the claimant (on the same assumption) may obtain judgment against the personal representative as such for a sum equal to the amount of the assets admitted, but as to any balance only against future assets.

3. Existence of debts having priority over the claimant's debt[135] and no assets *ultra*

24–34 If this defence succeeds, the claimant may only obtain judgment against future assets.

24–35 If a personal representative fails to plead these special defences, and the claimant obtains judgment against him, the personal representative thereby conclusively admits that at the date of judgment he had sufficient assets to satisfy the claim.[136] Accordingly, if the claimant levies execution but the judgment is not satisfied, a presumption arises that the personal representative has committed a *devastavit* in the interval between judgment and execution.[137] The personal representative is personally liable to the claimant for this *devastavit* unless the personal representative is able to rebut this presumption in some way, e.g. by proving that during this interval he handed over the assets to a receiver appointed by the court.[138]

[132] *Giles v Dyson* (1815) 1 Stark. 32; *Reeves v Ward* (1835) 2 Bing.N.C. 235.

[133] Called a judgment of assets *quando acciderint* or *in futuro*: for leave to issue execution on such a judgment see R.S.C., Ord.46, r.2(1)(c) in Sch.1 to CPR.

[134] *Jackson v Bowley* (1841) Car. & M. 97.

[135] For the order of priority of debts see above, paras 21–77 et seq.

[136] *Batchelar v Evans* [1939] Ch.1007; *Marsden v Regan* [1954] 1 W.L.R. 423 (personal representative does not thereby admit that he had sufficient assets to satisfy judgment for costs to be taxed); *Midland Bank Trust Co v Green (No.2)* [1979] 1 W.L.R. 460; *I.R.C. v Stannard* [1984] 1 W.L.R. 1039, 1041.

[137] *Leonard v Simpson* (1835) 2 Bing.N.C. 176.

[138] *Batchelar v Evans*, above: cf. *Marsden v Regan*, above, (presumption not rebutted, but relief from liability granted under Trustee Act 1925 s.61).

D. LIABILITY OF RECIPIENT OF ASSETS

1. Two equitable remedies

It is essential to distinguish between two different equitable remedies: **24–36**

(1) First, there is the equitable right to claim a refund from a person to whom the deceased's assets have been wrongly paid by the personal representative. This remedy is available against the recipient of the assets and he is not excused from repayment because he has spent the assets wrongly paid to him. But, as in the case of any personal claim, this remedy is only fully effective if the defendant is solvent;

(2) Secondly, there is the equitable right to trace and recover property from its holder, whether or not he was the recipient from the personal representative. If the property has become mixed with other property, the appropriate remedy may be a declaration of charge on the mixed fund. The equitable right to trace, being a proprietary claim, remains effective despite the insolvency of the holder of the property. But the right to trace is lost if the property ceases to be identifiable, and there is no right to trace against a bona fide purchaser of the property for value without notice.

Each of these remedies may be available in a case where the deceased's **24–37** assets have been wrongly distributed by the personal representative. The first remedy (claiming a refund) was created by the Court of Chancery in the seventeenth-century as it gradually wrested from the ecclesiastical courts jurisdiction over the administration of the estates of deceased persons.[139] This first remedy is certainly applicable in the administration of estates, though it may not be applicable in the execution of trusts.[140] The second remedy (tracing) is a more general remedy, which is not confined to the administration of estates, and only certain rules, which are particularly applicable to tracing as a remedy in the administration of estates, are considered here.[141]

A word of warning is needed on terminology. Even though these two remedies are markedly different, each of them is sometimes referred to as the remedy of "following the assets" and on occasion this phrase appears to be used in a sense embracing both these remedies at once.[142]

[139] per Lord Simonds in *Ministry of Health v Simpson* [1951] A.C. 251, 266: see also *Re Diplock* [1948] Ch.465, 489.

[140] *Ministry of Health v Simpson* [1951] A.C. 251 at 265–266: see also *Butler v Broadhead* [1975] Ch.97.

[141] See below, para.24–47. For the remedy of tracing generally see Hanbury and Martin, *Modern Equity*, 20th edn (London: Sweet & Maxwell, 2015), Chap.26, and L. D. Smith, *The Law of Tracing* (Oxford: Oxford University Press, 1997).

[142] The right to "follow" the assets is referred to in Administration of Estates Act 1925 s.38(1); Trustee Act 1925 ss.26(2) and 27(2); Legitimacy Act 1976 s.7(3); and Adoption and Children Act 2002 s.72(3). L. D. Smith, *The Law of Tracing* (Oxford: Oxford University Press, 1997)., p.4 uses "tracing" to identify an asset which has been substituted for another asset, "following"

2. Right of creditor, legatee or next-of-kin to claim refund

24–38 If T's personal representative wrongly pays assets to Y, instead of to X who—whether as creditor, legatee, or next-of-kin of T—is properly entitled to them, X has an equitable right to claim a refund from Y of such an amount as X cannot recover from the personal representative. This claim against Y does not carry interest.[143]

(a) *Basis of liability*

24–39 As Lord Simonds put it in *Ministry of Health v Simpson*,[144] this remedy was developed "by the Court of Chancery in the administration of assets of a deceased person to avoid the evil of allowing one man to retain money legally payable to another." It is immaterial whether the money is legally payable to X as an unpaid or underpaid creditor, legatee or next-of-kin of T. The evil to be avoided, and the remedy applicable, is the same. The defendant Y "has no great reason to complain that he is called upon to replace what he has received against his right."[145]

If X is T's creditor, X is entitled to payment out of any of T's assets regardless of the rules regulating the burden of T's debts as between the beneficiaries, and therefore X may generally claim a refund from any of the beneficiaries. But, as the creditor's remedy is equitable, the court may order the beneficiaries to refund upon such terms (e.g. as to the order of refunding) as the court deems it equitable to impose, so as to regulate the burden of the debt as between them.[146]

24–40 The leading authority on this remedy is the decision of the House of Lords in *Ministry of Health v Simpson*. In 1936 Caleb Diplock died intestate as to his residuary estate. He left a will by which he purported to dispose of his residuary estate by directing his executors to apply it for such "charitable or benevolent" objects in England as they might in their

to cover the situation where an asset has passed from one person to another, and "claiming" as the process which ensues when either (or both) of the other processes has been completed. This terminology was adopted by the House of Lords in *Foskett v McKeown* [2001] 1 A.C. 102, but care has to be taken in relation to the terminology used in earlier cases.

[143] *Re Diplock* [1948] Ch.465, 506–507. Interest may be recoverable under the equitable right to trace, ibid at 557–558.

[144] *Ministry of Health v Simpson* [1951] A.C. 251, 268. As to a creditor's claim, Lord Davey said in *Harrison v Kirk* [1904] A.C. 1, 7, "the Court of Chancery, in order to do justice and to avoid the evil of allowing one man to retain what is really and legally applicable to the payment of another man, devised a remedy by which, where the estate had been distributed either out of court or in court without regard to the rights of a creditor, it has allowed the creditor to recover back what has been paid to the beneficiaries or the next-of-kin who derive title from the deceased testator or intestate."

[145] *David v Frowd* (1833) 1 My. & K. 200, 211.

[146] *National Assurance Co v Scott* [1909] 1 I.R. 325 (creditor held entitled to refund from residuary legatees and, if need be, from pecuniary legatees). But if D's estate was administered by the court, and the creditor failed to prove for his debt, the creditor may only recover from each beneficiary the sum he was properly liable to bear, *Gillespie v Alexander* (1827) 3 Russ. 130 and 138; *Greig v Somerville* (1830) 1 R. & M. 338; *Davies v Nicolson* (1858) 2 De G. & J. 693, 702; *Todd v Studholme* (1857) 3 K. & J. 324, 336–337.

absolute discretion select. The executors, acting in good faith, distributed over £200,000 from the residuary estate among 139 charities before the next-of-kin challenged the validity of the residuary gift, which was held by the House of Lords to be void for uncertainty.[147] The next-of-kin exhausted their primary remedy against the executors in respect of the wrongful distribution of the estate,[148] and claimed to recover the balance from the wrongly paid charities. The claim against the charities was made under two alternative heads, namely (i) under the equitable right to claim a refund and (ii) under the equitable right to trace. In *Re Diplock*[149] the Court of Appeal held that both these remedies were applicable. An appeal by one charity (a hospital) against its liability under head (i) was unanimously rejected by the House of Lords in *Ministry of Health v Simpson*. The House of Lords held that, as the next-of-kin had exhausted their primary remedy against the executors, the next-of-kin were entitled to claim a refund from the hospital in respect of the money wrongly distributed to it by the executors. The hospital had spent this money on erecting new buildings, so that the next-of-kin had lost their right to trace, but the hospital was nevertheless under a personal liability to refund.[150] Although the action at common law for money had and received was then confined to mistakes of fact,[151] it was held that the claim in equity existed whether the mistake was one of fact or, as in this case, one of law.

(b) *Two requirements*

The equitable right to claim a refund is applicable if two requirements are satisfied: **24–41**

(i) Wrongful Payment by Personal Representative. The first requirement is that the personal representative must have wrongly paid assets of the deceased's estate to Y. This requirement is satisfied if the personal representative distributed assets to Y, who had no title at all and was a stranger to the estate.[152] **24–42**

In order to determine whether Y received more assets than he was properly entitled to receive, it may be necessary to ascertain the extent of the available assets at the time of the distribution to Y.[153]

Y's liability to refund does not depend upon his knowledge, or assumed

[147] *Chichester Diocesan Fund and Board of Finance v Simpson* [1944] A.C. 341: see above, paras 10–78 et seq. It is suggested that, were a gift of this sort to appear in a will today, it should be construed as a valid charitable gift; see above, paras 10–79 and 10–80.

[148] The executors paid £15,000 under a compromise approved by the court.

[149] *Re Diplock* [1948] Ch.465 (reviewing the case law).

[150] *Ministry of Health v Simpson* [1951] A.C. 251, 276. The claim is for the principal sum only without interest. A finding of constructive trusteeship would have resulted in liability to pay interest.

[151] The action now lies for recovery of money paid by mistake of law: *Kleinwort Benson Ltd v Lincoln City Council* [1999] 2 A.C. 349.

[152] *Re Diplock* [1948] Ch.465, 502: see *Re Lowe's W.T.* [1973] 1 W.L.R. 882, 887 (wrong payment to Crown).

[153] *Fenwick v Clarke* (1862) 4 De G.F. & J. 240 (accidental loss of other assets when bank

knowledge, that he is not properly entitled. In *Ministry of Health v Simpson* the hospital received and spent the money in good faith, believing that it was properly entitled, but was nevertheless held liable to refund the money.[154]

24–43 **(ii) Any remedy against personal representative exhausted.** The second requirement is that X must exhaust his primary remedy (if any) against the personal representative in respect of his wrongful payment to Y. This second requirement certainly has to be satisfied if X claims as T's legatee or next-of-kin[155] and probably the same rule applies if X claims as T's creditor.[156]

X's claim against Y for a refund is limited to the amount which X cannot recover from the personal representative.[157] If X cannot recover anything from the personal representative, he may claim a refund from Y of the whole amount which was wrongly paid to Y. This situation arises, for instance:

(i) if the personal representative is liable to X for a *devastavit* but is wholly without assets; *or*
(ii) if the personal representative is protected from liability to X because the personal representative acted under an order of the court in paying Y, e.g. under a *Benjamin* Order giving the personal representative leave to distribute on the footing that X, a missing beneficiary, predeceased T.

(c) *Defences*

24–44 X's claim against Y for a refund is liable to be defeated by the defence of limitation. If X claims as a legatee or next-of-kin entitled to T's pure personalty, s.22 of the Limitation Act 1980 is applicable and the period of limitation is 12 years from the date when X's right to receive his share or interest accrued.[158] Thus the same period of limitation applies to X's claim against Y for a refund as applies to X's claim against the personal representative.[159] If X claims as a creditor of T, X

unexpectedly failed); *Re Winslow* (1890) 45 Ch.D. 249. *Peterson v Peterson* (1866) L.R. 3 Eq. 111; *Re Lepine* [1892] 1 Ch.210.

154 *Ministry of Health v Simpson* [1951] A.C. 251 at 276. The action will not lie against a bona fide purchaser without notice (as opposed to a volunteer such as the hospital).

155 *Orr v Kaines* (1750) 2 Ves.Sen. 194 (X an underpaid legatee); *Re Diplock* [1948] Ch.465, 503–505; *Ministry of Health v Simpson* [1951] A.C. 251, 267–268.

156 *Hodges v Waddington* (1684) 2 Vent. 360; *Hunter v Young* (1879) 4 Ex.D. 256.

157 *Re Diplock*, above, at 503–505 (X may issue a claim form against Y for a refund before exhausting his remedy against the personal representative). See Goff and Jones, *The Law of Restitution* 7th edn (London: Sweet & Maxwell, 2007), para.30–002 for criticism of the limitation, which benefits the recipient at the expense of the personal representatives.

158 *Re Diplock* [1948] Ch.465, 507–516; affirmed *Ministry of Health v Simpson* [1951] A.C. 251, 276–277: for s.22, see above, para.24–17.

159 *Re Diplock*, above, at 514; *Ministry of Health v Simpson*, above, at p.277.

must bring his claim within six years from the accrual of his cause of action.[160]

Again, if X acquiesces in the distribution to Y by the personal representative and thereby releases X's claim in respect of the assets paid to Y, X cannot thereafter claim a refund from Y.[161]

Although the House of Lords in *Ministry of Health v Simpson* appeared not to recognise the defence of change of position—which involves an innocent recipient of property showing that he has so changed his position that it would be inequitable in all the circumstances to require him to make restitution in full or in part—the House of Lords in *Lipkin Gorman v Karpnale Ltd*[162] has accepted the defence. Their Lordships considered that this would encourage a more consistent approach to tracing at common law and in equity; and the recognition of the defence should also allow the personal action to develop in a fairer way. It must be emphasised that mere expenditure of the money sought to be recovered will not automatically amount to a change of position "because the expenditure might in any event have been incurred in the ordinary course of things."[163] **24–45**

3. Right of personal representative to claim refund

In general, a personal representative could not previously exercise the equitable right to claim a refund from Y, a beneficiary to whom he distributed the deceased's assets, except in limited circumstances.[164] This was because the common law action for money had and received used to be confined to mistakes of fact; it now applies to money paid under a mistake of law.[165] This means that the personal representative can now recover, whether his mistake is classified as a mistake of fact or law.[166] A personal representative has always been entitled to claim a refund from Y if a debt, of which the personal representative had no notice at the time of the distribution, was afterwards discovered and the personal representative was **24–46**

[160] Limitation Act 1980 s.5: if X claims a specialty debt, the period is 12 years, ibid s.8.

[161] *Blake v Gale* (1886) 32 Ch.D. 571: see *Ridgway v Newstead* (1861) 3 De G.F. & J. 474 (legatee's position altered) and cf. *Re Eustace* [1912] 1 Ch.561 (mere delay).

[162] *Lipkin Gorman v Karpnale Ltd* [1991] 2 A.C. 548.

[163] Lord Goff in *Lipkin Gorman v Karpnale Ltd* [1991] 2 A.C. 548 at 580. See also *Philip Collins Ltd v Davis* [2000] 3 All E.R. 808, 827 (Jonathan Parker J) for four non-exhaustive principles applicable to the defence.

[164] *Orr v Kaines* (1750) 2 Ves.Sen. 194; *Hodges v Waddington* (1679) 2 Cas. in Ch.9.

[165] *Kleinwort Benson Ltd v Lincoln City Council* [1999] 2 A.C. 349.

[166] Previously, the personal representative had to make good the sum overpaid from his own pocket so that the other beneficiaries were paid in full. See *Hilliard v Fulford* (1876) 4 Ch.D. 389, 394 (the personal representatives "who have made the error will have to pay for it"): see Goff and Jones, *The Law of Restitution*, 7th edn (London: Sweet & Maxwell, 2007), Chaps 4 and 5. The personal representative was always entitled to deduct the sum overpaid from any other sum falling due to Y from the personal representative, (*Livesey v Livesey* (1827) 3 Russ. 287 (overpayments of annuity deductible from future payments of annuity); *Dibbs v Goren* (1849) 11 Beav. 483; *Re Musgrave* [1916] 2 Ch.417.) unless in the particular circumstances this would have been inequitable. See *Re Horne* [1905] 1 Ch.76: cf. *Re Musgrave*, above, at 425 and *Re Ainsworth* [1915] 2 Ch.96, 104–106.

obliged to pay it.[167] The personal representative is not, however, entitled to a refund from Y if the personal representative had notice of the debt at the time of distribution.[168]

4. Right to trace

24–47 Legatees, devisees and next-of-kin are all entitled to exercise the equitable right to trace and recover property from the holder of it, other than a bona fide purchaser for value without notice or any person deriving title under him.[169] An unsatisfied creditor of the deceased is also entitled to exercise the equitable right to trace for the purpose of obtaining payment,[170] except against such a purchaser or any person deriving title under him.[171] The Administration of Estates Act 1925[172] provides that an assent or conveyance by a personal representative in respect of any property does not prejudice the equitable right of any person to trace the property in this way.

X may exercise his equitable right to trace, even though he has not exhausted his remedy (if any) against the personal representative in respect of his wrongful payment to Y. But in so far as X has already recovered from the personal representative, he loses his equitable right to trace.[173]

E. EXECUTOR DE SON TORT

24–48 The term *executor de son tort* (or executor in his own wrong)[174] is applied to a person who is not an executor or administrator but who nevertheless acts in some way as if he were an executor. Such a person is called an *executor* (and not an administrator) *de son tort* even if the deceased left no will.

A person appointed executor by the testator in his will can establish his title only by means of a grant of probate.[175] If such a person acts in some

[167] *Nelthrop v Hill* (1669) 1 Cas. in Ch.135, 136; *German v Lady Colston* (1678) 2 Rep. Ch.137: for the effect of advertising for claims, see above, paras 21–16 et seq. A personal representative may also be entitled to claim a refund from Y if he distributed to Y under a court order: *Newman v Barton* (1690) 2 Vern. 205; *Noell v Robinson* (1686) 2 Ventr. 358.

[168] *Jervis v Wolferstan* (1874) L.R. 18 Eq. 18, 25.

[169] *Re Diplock* [1948] Ch.465. The consideration need not be adequate: *Lipkin Gorman v Karpnale Ltd* [1991] 2 A.C. 548.

[170] *Salih v Atchi* [1961] A.C. 778, 793; *Davies v Nicolson* (1858) 2 De G. & J. 693.

[171] *Dilkes v Broadmead* (1860) 2 De G.F. & J. 566 (marriage consideration); *Spackman v Timbrell* (1837) 8 Sim. 253; *Salih v Atchi*, above, at 793—though the creditor "cannot follow the property against the purchaser, he can follow the purchase price in the hands of the [beneficiary]," or rely on his equitable right to claim a refund from the beneficiary: see also Administration of Estates Act 1925 s.32(2).

[172] Administration of Estates Act 1925 ss.38(1), (3) and 55(1)(xviii): see also s.36(9) and (11).

[173] *Re Diplock* [1948] Ch.465, 556–557.

[174] Administration of Estates Act 1925 s.28.

[175] See above, paras 18–15 et seq.

way as executor without any grant of probate, he is treated by the court as an *executor de son tort* (and not as an executor) because he cannot establish his title as executor.[176] On the other hand, once probate has been granted, this establishes his title as executor as from the testator's death. Logically he ought then to be regarded as an executor—and not as an *executor de son tort*—as from the testator's death.[177]

1. Acts creating liability as *executor de son tort*

(a) *Intermeddling*

If a person intermeddles with any of the deceased's assets in England or Wales[178] as if he were an executor, this makes him liable as *executor de son tort*. The rule applies to intermeddling with the deceased's realty[179] as well as his personalty. Examples include carrying on the deceased's business,[180] selling his goods,[181] and receiving payment of debts due to him.[182] Again, the act of transferring title to foreign personal representatives constitutes an intermeddling with the deceased's English estate.[183] In *I.R.C. v Stype Investments (Jersey) Ltd*[184] at C's death a Jersey company held English land on trust for C in fee simple, with the benefit of a contract for the sale of the land to P for £20 million. After C's death the company completed the sale and directed P to pay the price to its Jersey bank account. In a claim by the Inland Revenue Commissioners claiming capital transfer tax, the Court of Appeal held that the company was an *executor de son tort* because it had diverted £20 million, part of C's English assets, to Jersey out of the reach of C's personal representatives when constituted in England.[185] **24–49**

(b) *As if he were an executor*

To become liable as *executor de son tort* a person must intermeddle as if he were an executor. If he intermeddles out of humanity or necessity, this does not make him an *executor de son tort*.[186] **24–50**

[176] *Att.-Gen. v The New York Breweries Co Ltd* [1898] 1 Q.B. 205, affirmed [1899] A.C. 62.
[177] *Sykes v Sykes* (1870) L.R. 5 C.P. 113 (the headnote is misleading): cf. *Webster v Webster* (1804) 10 Ves. 93.
[178] *Beavan v Lord Hastings* (1856) 2 K. & J. 724 (intestate's brother obtained representation in Belgium but did not intermeddle with English assets: not *executor de son tort*).
[179] Administration of Estates Act 1925 s.28.
[180] *Padget v Priest* (1787) 2 T.R. 97; *Hooper v Summersett* (1810) Wightw. 16.
[181] *Read's Case* (1604) 5 Co. Rep, 33b; *Nulty v Fagan* (1888) 22 L.R. Ir. 604.
[182] *Sharland v Milldon* (1846) 5 Hare 469.
[183] *New York Breweries Co Ltd v Att.-Gen.* [1899] A.C. 62.
[184] *I.R.C. v Stype Investments (Jersey) Ltd* [1982] Ch.456.
[185] See Inheritance Tax Act 1984 ss.199(4) and 200(4).
[186] This is not expressed in Administration of Estates Act 1925 s.28 but is probably still the law: *Camden v Fletcher* (1838) 4 M&W. 378; *Harrison v Rowley* (1798) 4 Ves 212, 216; *Peters v Leeder* (1878) 47 L.J.Q.B. 573. In *Pollard v Jackson*, (1994) 67 P. & C.R. 327 the Court of Appeal held that a tenant who continued to occupy property after his landlord's death was *not* an *executor de son tort*.

2. Liability of *executor de son tort*

(a) *Liability to creditors and beneficiaries*

24–51 In general an *executor de son tort* is liable to creditors and beneficiaries of the deceased as if he were the lawful executor.[187] But under s.28 of the Administration of Estates Act 1925 he is only liable "to the extent of the real and personal estate received or coming to his hands".[188] Unlike a personal representative, an *executor de son tort* is not under any duty to collect and get in the deceased's assets.[189]

24–52 Under s.28, in determining the extent of the liability of an *executor de son tort*, two deductions are to be made from the assets for which he is liable. These two deductions are as follows:

(i) Any debt for valuable consideration and without fraud due to the *executor de son tort* from the deceased at death. Thus an *executor de son tort* may apparently "retain" for his own debt as against another creditor, even though the other creditor is of a higher degree[190] and even though the *executor de son tort* has reason to believe that the deceased's estate is insolvent. In this respect, surprisingly, an *executor de son tort* is treated more favourably than a personal representative.[191]

(ii) Any payment made by the *executor de son tort* which might properly be made by a personal representative. An *executor de son tort* may therefore deduct payments made by him in discharge of the deceased's funeral expenses and debts in due course of administration of the deceased's estate.[192]

The liability of an *executor de son tort* to a creditor or beneficiary ceases if, before they bring a claim against him, he delivers or accounts for all the assets received by him to the lawful personal representative of the deceased.[193] By this means an *executor de son tort* may purge his wrongdoing in receiving the assets.

An *executor de son tort* may be cited by a creditor or beneficiary to take

[187] Unlike an executor, in the absence of liability by estoppel, an *executor de son tort* is not personally liable to the lessor for breach of covenant in respect of the deceased's leaseholds of which he has taken possession, because the leases are not vested in him, *Mayor, Aldermen and Burgesses of Stratford-upon-Avon v Parker* [1914] 2 K.B. 562.

[188] Or, if he effected the release of any debt or liability due to the deceased's estate, to the extent of the debt or liability released.

[189] For duty of a personal representative see Administration of Estates Act 1925 s.25 as amended by Administration of Estates Act 1971 s.9; above, paras 20–12 et seq.

[190] See above, paras 21–77 et seq.

[191] See above, paras 21–85 et seq. Before 1926 an *executor de son tort* was not permitted to retain for his own debt, *Curtis v Vernon* (1790) 3 T.R. 587.

[192] *Oxenham v Clapp* (1831) 2 B. & Ad. 309.

[193] Again this is not expressed in Administration of Estates Act 1925 s.28 but is probably still the law; *Anon.* (1702) 1 Salk. 313; *Padget v Priest* (1787) 2 T.R. 97; *Curtis v Vernon* (1790) 3 T.R. 587, 2 H.Bl. 18; *Hill v Curtis* (1865) L.R. 1 Eq. 90.

probate if he has been duly appointed as executor[194] but he cannot be compelled to take a grant of letters of administration.[195]

(b) *Liability for inheritance tax*

An *executor de son tort* is liable for the inheritance tax attributable to the value of any property with which he intermeddles. He is treated as a person in whom such property is vested and in that capacity he is personally liable for inheritance tax chargeable in respect of the death of the deceased.[196] He is not liable for tax beyond the extent of such property.[197] **24–53**

(c) *Liability to the personal representatives*

An *executor de son tort* is liable to the lawful personal representatives under the general law (e.g. in tort[198] or quasi-contract) for his acts of interference with the deceased's assets.[199] The *executor de son tort* may, however, mitigate the damages awarded against him by showing that he has made payments in due course of administration of the deceased's estate: the lawful personal representatives would have been bound to make these payments and to this extent the deceased's estate has suffered no loss.[200] **24–54**

194 See above, para.17–26.

195 See above, para.17–51.

196 Inheritance Tax Act 1984 ss.199(4) and 200(1) and (4): see *I.R.C. v Stype Investments (Jersey) Ltd* [1982] Ch.456, 466; *I.R.C. v Stannard* [1984] 1 W.L.R. 1039. An *executor de son tort* may also be liable for inheritance tax on a chargeable transfer made by an inter vivos disposition of the deceased, ss.199(1) and (4). If owing to the wide definition of "personal representatives" in s.272 an *executor de son tort* is also liable as a personal representative under s.200(1), then probably under s.204(1) no liability arises for assets which he might have received but for his own neglect or default, because he is under no duty to get in assets.

197 Inheritance Tax Act 1984 s.204(3).

198 *Whitehall v Squire* (1703) Carth. 103 (conversion of deceased's horse); *Fyson v Chambers* (1842) 9 M. & W. 460 (conversion of deceased's household goods).

199 See *I.R.C. v Stype Investments (Jersey) Ltd*, above, at 476–477; *Official Solcitor v Stype Investments (Jersey) Ltd* [1983] 1 W.L.R. 214.

200 *Whitehall v Squire*, above; *Padget v Priest* (1787) 2 T.R. 97, 100; *Mountford v Gibson* (1804) 4 East. 411, 450 and 454. If an *executor de son tort* pays a creditor of the deceased in due course of administration, the creditor is not liable to the lawful personal representatives if the creditor reasonably believed that the *executor de son tort* was the lawful personal representative, *Thomson v Harding* (1853) 2 E. & B. 630, and cf. *Mountford v Gibson* (1804) 4 East 441.

INDEX

This index has been prepared using Sweet and Maxwell's Legal Taxonomy. Main index entries conform to keywords provided by the Legal Taxonomy except where references to specific documents or non-standard terms (denoted by quotation marks) have been included. These keywords provide a means of identifying similar concepts in other Sweet & Maxwell publications and online services to which keywords from the Legal Taxonomy have been applied. Readers may find some minor differences between terms used in the text and those which appear in the index. Suggestions to: sweetandmaxwell.taxonomy@thomson.com

(All references are to paragraph number)